Encyclopedia of Television News

Encyclopedia of Television News

Edited by Michael D. Murray

Oryx Press
1999

The rare Arabian Oryx is believed to have inspired the myth of the unicorn. This desert antelope became virtually extinct in the early 1960s. At that time, several groups of international conservationists arranged to have nine animals sent to the Phoenix Zoo to be the nucleus of a captive breeding herd. Today, the Oryx population is over 1,000, and over 500 have been returned to the Middle East.

© 1999 by The Oryx Press
4041 North Central at Indian School Road
Phoenix, Arizona 85012-3397

Published simultaneously in Canada
Printed and bound in the United States of America

∞ The paper used in this publication meets the minimum requirements of American National Standard for Information Science—Permanence of Paper for Printed Library Materials, ANSI Z39.48, 1984.

Library of Congress Cataloging-in-Publication Data

Encyclopedia of television news / Michael D. Murray, editor.
    p. cm.
    Includes bibliographical references and index.
    ISBN 1-57356-108-8 (alk. paper)
    1. Television reporting of news—United States—Encyclopedias.
I. Murray, Michael D.
PN4888.T4E53   1999
070.1'95—dc21   98-36705
                                                      CIP

CONTENTS

CONTRIBUTORS

Alan B. Albarran, Ph.D.
Center for Communication Arts
Southern Methodist University
Dallas, TX 75275

Sherry L. Alexander, Ph.D.
Communication Department
Loyola University
New Orleans, LA 70118

Craig Allen, Ph D.
Walter Cronkite School of Journalism
Arizona State University
Tempe, AZ 85287

Jerry L. Allen, Ph.D.
Office of the Graduate School Dean
University of New Haven
West Haven, CT 06516

Edd Applegate, Ed.D.
College of Mass Communication
Middle Tennessee State University
Murfreesboro, TN 37132

Carol A. Atkinson, Ph.D.
Department of Communication
Central Missouri State University
Warrensburg, MO 64093

Albert Auster
Department of Communication
Fordham University
Bronx, NY 10458-5151

Mary E. Beadle, Ph.D.
Department of Communication
John Carroll University
University Heights, OH 44118

Maurine H. Beasley, Ph.D.
College of Journalism
University of Maryland
College Park, MD 20742

Mark Binkley, Ph.D.
Broadcast Meteorology Department
Mississippi State University
Mississippi State, MS 39762

Connie Book, Ph.D
Department of Communication
North Carolina State University
Raleigh, NC 27695-8104

Bonnie Brennen, Ph.D.
School of Mass Communication
Virginia Commonwealth University
Richmond, VA 23284-2034

Dom Caristi, Ph.D.
Department of Telecommunication
Ball State University
Muncie, IN 47306

Ginger Rudeseal Carter, Ph.D.
Journalism Department
Georgia State College
Milledgeville, GA 31061

Lloyd Chiasson Jr., Ph.D.
Department of Communication
Nicholls State University
Thibodaux, LA 70301

Lovette Chinwah
Department of Communication
Central State University
Wilberforce, OH 45384

Mark Conrad, J.D.
School of Business
Fordham University
New York, NY 10021

Don H. Corrigan
Department of Journalism
Webster University
St. Louis, MO 63119

Dan B. Curtis, Ph.D.
Department of Mass Communication
Central Missouri State University
Warrensburg, MO 64093

Grant Curtis
Department of Mass Communication
Central Missouri State University
Warrensburg, MO 64093

William R. Davie, Ph.D.
Department of Communication
University of Southwestern Louisiana
Lafaytte, LA 70504

Karen Lane DeRosa
Political Communication Center
University of Oklahoma
Norman, OK 73019

Pamela K. Doyle, Ph.D.
College of Communication
University of Alabama
Tuscaloosa, AL 35487

Gary R. Edgerton, Ph.D.
Communication Department
Old Dominion University
Norfolk, VA 23529

Matthew C. Ehrlich, Ph.D.
Department of Journalism
University of Illinois
Urbana, IL 61801

Sandra L. Ellis, Ph.D.
Department of Journalism
University of Wisconsin
River Falls, WI 54022

Stuart L. Esrock, Ph.D.
Department of Communication
University of Louisville
Louisville, KY 40292

Bruce J. Evensen, Ph.D.
Department of Communication
DePaul University
Chicago, IL 60614-3298

Ronald T. Farrar, Ph.D.
College of Journalism
University of South Carolina
Columbia, SC 29208

Joe S. Foote, Ph.D.
College of Mass Communication
Southern Illinois University
Carbondale, IL 62901

Marjorie Fox
Electronic Media Division
University of Cincinnati
Cincinnati, OH 45221-0003

Ronald Garay
Manship School of Mass Communication
Louisiana State University
Baton Rouge, LA 70803

Jeanne Marie Garon
Department of Communication
Loyola University
New Orleans, LA 70118

Donald G. Godfrey, Ph.D.
Walter Cronkite School of Journalism
Arizona State University
Tempe, AZ 85287-1305

Victoria Goff, Ph.D.
Department of Communication
University of Wisconsin
Green Bay, WI 54311

Joye C. Gordon
Department of Mass Communication
Nicholls State University
Thibodaux, LA 70310

Agnes Hooper Gottlieb, Ph.D.
Department of Communication
Seton Hall University
South Orange, NJ 07079-2687

David M. Guerra
Radio-Television-Film Department
University of Arkansas–Little Rock
Little Rock, AR 77204

Roger Hadley, Ph.D.
Sarkeys Telecommunication Center
Oklahoma Baptist University
Shawnee, OK 72801-2590

LuEtt Hanson, Ph.D.
School of Journalism
Kent State University
Kent, OH 44242

Margot Hardenbergh, Ph.D.
Lowell Thomas Communications Center
Marist College
Poughkeepsie, NY 12601-1387

Jack Hodgson
School of Journalism
Oklahoma State University
Stillwater, OK 74078-0195

Patricia Holmes, Ph.D.
Department of Communication
University of Southwestern Louisiana
Lafayette, LA 70504-3650

Gloria G. Horning
School of Journalism
Florida A & M
Talahassee, FL 32307

Suzanne Huffman, Ph.D.
Center for Communication Arts
Southern Methodist University
Dallas, TX 75275-0113

William E. Huntzicker, Ph.D.
School of Journalism
University of Minnesota
Minneapolis, MN 55414

Danette E. Ifert, Ph.D.
Department of Communication
West Virginia Wesleyan University
Buckannon, WV 26201

Ann D. Jabro, Ph.D.
School of Communications
Robert Morris College
Coraopolis, PA 15108-1189

Dwight Jensen
School of Journalism
Marshall University
Huntington, WV 25755

Donald Jung, Ph.D.
Department of Communication
University of Missouri–St. Louis
St. Louis, MO 63121

Lynda Lee Kaid, Ph.D.
Political Communication Center
University of Oklahoma
Norman, OK 73019

Douglas J. Kocher, Ph.D.
Department of Communication
Valparaiso University
Valparaiso, IN 46383-6493

Yasue Kuwahara, Ph.D.
Communication Department
Northern Kentucky University
Highland Heights, KY 41099

Kevin C. Lee, Ed.D.
Department of Communication
West Virginia Weslyan University
Buckhannon, WV 26201

Elizabeth J. Leebron, Ph.D.
Department of Broadcasting
Temple University
Philadelphia, PA 19122

Charles Lewis, Ph.D.
Mass Communications Department
Mankato State University
Mankato, MN 99164

Val E. Limburg
Murrow School of Communication
Washington State University
Pullman, WA 99164

Gregory C. Lisby, Ph.D.
Department of Communication
Georgia State University
Atlanta, GA 30303

Fran R. Matera, Ph.D.
Walter Cronkite School of Journalism
Arizona State University
Tempe, AZ 85287

Peter Mayeux
Broadcasting Department
University of Nebraska
Lincoln, NE 68588-0131

Jeffrey M. McCall, Ph.D.
Department of Communication
DePauw University
Greencastle, IN 46135

Thomas L. McPhail, Ph.D.
Office of Vice Chancellor–Academic Affairs
University of Missouri–St. Louis
St. Louis, MO 63121

Milan D. Meeske, Ph.D.
School of Communication
University of Central Florida
Orlando, FL 32816-1344

Derek Moore
School of Public Health
University of Minnesota
Minneapolis, MN 55414

Roy L. Moore, J.D., Ph.D.
College of Communication
University of Kentucky
Lexington, KY 50506-0042

Claus Mueller, Ph.D.
Graduate Program in Social Research
Hunter College
New York, NY 10021

Lawrence J. Mullen, Ph.D.
Greenspun School of Communication
University of Nevada-Las Vegas
Las Vegas, NV 89154-5007

Ellen E. Murray
Olin School of Business
Washington University
St. Louis, MO 63121

Joan O'Mara, Ph.D.
Hillyer College
University of Hartford
West Hartford, CT 06117

Linda M. Perry, Ph.D.
Department of Communication
Purdue University
West Lafayette, IN 47906

Daniel W. Pfaff, Ph.D.
School of Communications
Pennsylvania State University
University Park, PA 16802

Steven Phipps, Ph.D.
Department of Communication
University of Missouri–St. Louis
St. Louis, MO 63121

Paul Alfred Pratte, Ph.D.
Department of Communication
Brigham Young University
Provo, UT 84602

Cindy Price
College of Mass Communication
Southern Illinois University
Carbondale, IL 62901

James E. Reppert
Mass Communication Department
Southern Arkansas University
Magnolia, AR 71753-5000

Ford Risley, Ph.D.
College of Communications
Pennsylvania State University
University Park, PA 16802

Elizabeth Ryan
School of Journalism
University of Kentucky
Lexington, KY 40506

Susan Plumb Salas
Department of Communication
Pepperdine University
Malibu, CA 90263

Kathryn J. Sasina
Annenberg School of Communication
University of Southern California
Los Angeles, CA 90089

Richard J. Schaefer, Ph.D.
Department of Communication
University of New Mexico
Albuquerque, NM 87131-1171

Alan Schroeder
School of Journalism
Northeastern University
Boston, MA 02115

Philip Seib, J.D.
Center for Communication Arts
Southern Methodist University
Dallas, TX 75275-0113

Edward H. Sewell Jr., Ph.D.
Communication Studies Department
Virginia Tech University
Blacksburg, VA 24061-0311

Donald C. Shields, Ph.D.
Department of Communication
University of Missouri–St. Louis
St. Louis, MO 63124

B. William Silcock
School of Journalism
University of Missouri
Columbia, MO 65201

Kim A. Smith, Ph.D.
Journalism & Mass Communication
Iowa State University
Ames, IA 50011

Michael R. Smith
Journalism Studies
Taylor University
Fort Wayne, IN 46989

Tommy V. Smith, Ph.D.
Department of Journalism
University of Southern Mississippi
Hattiesburg, MS 39406

Julia A. Spiker, Ph.D.
Political Communication Center
University of Oklahoma
Norman, OK 73019

Sreenath Sreenivasan
School of Journalism
Columbia University
New York, NY 10027

Burton St. John
Department of Communication
University of Missouri–St. Louis
St. Louis, MO 63121

John C. Tedesco
Department of Communication
University of Oklahoma
Norman, OK 73071

Lee Thornton
College of Journalism
University of Maryland
College Park, MD 20742

Doug Underwood
Department of Mass Communication
Central Missouri State University
Warrensburg, MO 64093

James Upshaw
School of Journalism
University of Oregon
Eugene, OR 97403-1275

Max Utsler, Ph.D.
William A. White School of Journalism
University of Kansas
Lawrence, KS 66045

Patsy G. Watkins, Ph.D.
Journalism Department
University of Arkansas
Fayetteville, AR 72701

Jan Whitt, Ph.D.
School of Journalism
University of Colorado
Boulder, CO 80309

Betty Houchin Winfield, Ph.D.
School of Journalism
University of Missouri
Columbia, MO 65205

Lena Liqing Zhang, Ph.D.
Communication Department
Eastern Connecticut State University
Willimantic, CT 06226

Dhyana Ziegler, Ph.D.
College of Communications
University of Tennessee
Knoxville, TN 37996

FOREWORD

It was 1:39 p.m., Eastern Time, when the UPI wire moved Merriman Smith's report that President Kennedy had been wounded, perhaps fatally, by an assassin's bullet. A minute later, Walter Cronkite was on the CBS television network, audio only, beating his competition with the devastating news. So began almost four days of marathon coverage by all media, but it was television more than any other medium that brought the tragedy home. Television that weekend—November 22-25, 1963—bound the nation, all peoples, together. As Eric Sevareid said, we had found our common hearth.

The power of television news. It unmasked Joseph McCarthy. The "See It Now" documentary produced by Edward R. Murrow and Fred W. Friendly and the Army-McCarthy hearings on ABC showed the opportunist senator from Wisconsin for what he was. Television showed the Vietnam War for what it was, a disaster. Television played a major role in the civil rights struggle of the 1960s. It showed school children cursed because of their color and dogs set on people demonstrating peacefully for justice. We saw human beings walk on the moon. We saw and felt all this. Reuven Frank, former president of NBC News, was right when he emphasized how the power of television was not really in the transmission of information but rather the transmission of experience.

Television news transformed politics. Because it brought viewers the national conventions, party managers turned the conventions into orchestrated events equivalent to political commercials. No longer were nominations determined by a speaker's rhetoric or delegates' votes but largely by state primaries conducted weeks, even months earlier. Winners and losers are declared in television debates, and politicians, mindful of the evening news, provide the sound bites that producers like but which, because of hype, provide more headlines than light.

Such power demands responsibility. TV journalism has been fortunate in the men and women like Edward R. Murrow, Pauline Frederick, Walter Cronkite, and Ann Compton who, early on, set standards for responsible reporting. In this day when competition and the pursuit of ratings too often lead to irresponsibility in news programming—more crime and celebrity reporting, less reporting from Washington and overseas—those standards for reporting what is material to our society are more relevant than ever.

Biographies of television correspondents, editors, and producers challenged with this responsibility appear in the *Encyclopedia of Television News* edited by Michael D. Murray of the University of Missouri—St. Louis. The work is all-encompassing. It covers not only those engaged in television news but also subjects like the Fairness Doctrine, news consultants, checkbook journalism, and the introduction of videotape. I was at CBS when the switch was made from film to tape, and I recall how liberated we felt because news footage no longer had to be developed but could be rushed onto the air. Color, too, had been added. Now the blood of our wounded in Vietnam was red.

In covering the whole range of broadcast journalism—issues, programs, personalities—the scope of this work is, I believe, unparalleled. The inquiring reader will find here a vast storehouse of biography and history.

Edward Bliss, Jr.
Editor Emeritus, The CBS Evening News
Professor Emeritus, American University

PREFACE

Television news has had an explosive impact on our lives. In its short history, it has come to assume a dominant position in information dissemination. A 1996 survey by Times-Mirror indicates that the American people prefer television to print and other elements of the mass media as a source of news by a margin of 65 percent. In a follow-up report in 1997, Times-Mirror showed that almost one-quarter of the U.S. population receives their news exclusively from television, an increase of more than 10 percent in a little over a decade. A study released in 1998, conducted by Project for Excellence in Journalism and the Medill News Service Washington Bureau, reported that network newscasts are becoming more like their prime-time newsmagazine counterparts in terms of the types of stories they report and also the approach they employ. The study, discussed in the May, 1998 issue of The Communicator, a publication of the Radio-Television News Directors Association, concluded that the biggest shift in the network news was movement toward scandal reporting and more of a people-oriented manner of presentation. Many studies have shown the growing importance of television news—by virtue of its dominance over other sources—and researchers have begun to explain how television news assists viewers' identification with issues even as the medium is further evolving. Because of the increased prominence of television news, there is a need to enhance understanding of the field for both the general public and for aspiring broadcast journalists.

The first half-century of television news reporting has provided a credible beginning for this form of journalism, but the medium has a long way to go in enlarging and improving news-gathering efforts and specialization. With 20 bureaus and nearly three dozen correspondents outside of the United States, for example, Cable News Network (CNN) seems an impressive venture—until it is compared with the well-established competing newspaper services and traditional press associations. Even with the critical challenges international press organizations have recently faced, they continue to far surpass television and cable news-gathering operations. There are a number of historic technological, economical, and even philosophical reasons for this. Most broadcast networks first evolved as entertainment centers, then developed their news departments. Additionally, many television stations were owned by newspapers and suffered from a "second-class" status when it came to information gathering. By the time television news became a profitable aspect of the television business, the parameters of professional behavior and overall performance expectations were established. Many of the unique characteristics of the medium and of those individuals populating network news are explored in the various entries in this work.

The *Encyclopedia of Television News* includes 309 entries on the people who built broadcast journalism, the programs for which they are best known, and the concepts and issues evolving from their efforts. Most of the pioneers in television news started in radio. Many others, such as Walter Cronkite and David Brinkley, have roots in print journalism. Nevertheless, some of the most prominent early figures in the field, including Edward R. Murrow, began in broadcasting. Each of the entries on individuals provides basic biographical information and a selective overview of major contributions. Additionally, entries focusing on issues, themes, or programs refer to significant participants; thus, many individuals who do not have separate entries are acknowledged for their roles in programs or other spheres of activity.

On the contemporary scene, emphasis is placed on the major network magazines and documentary series—in greater depth than is usually explored elsewhere. Topical entries have been chosen from a wide variety of sources and from all aspects of television news. They are meant to illustrate key issues and serve as links for the reader who wants to explore new territory. Some major television series are analyzed in detail, partly because they have become landmarks, but also to help the general reader better understand the editorial process associated with their development.

The *Encyclopedia of Television News* is an ambitious collaborative venture; the authors come from a wide range of academic backgrounds, and their contributions tap a variety of source material. The roster of names and the institutions they represent reflects their excellence and expertise. Most are faculty in college or university departments of journalism, mass media, and communication studies. Authorities from schools of business, medicine, and law are also represented. Over 100 researchers—scholars and broadcasters, working in the fields of journalism history, biography, broadcast regulation, and programming—have come together to clarify and discuss this still-developing industry. Many are national leaders in the study of topical areas of television news or public affairs programs. Some have written entries for television programs with which they were associated; others offer insights into individuals based on having conducted interviews, explored archives, or corresponded with their subjects. Some have worked in television newsrooms at the local level; others have held major network assignments. Entries sometimes reflect personal perspectives on issues with which the au-

thor has firsthand knowledge. Because of their standing—and the continuing, expanding influence of television news—authors were encouraged to offer historical insight into controversies faced by the individuals who were the pioneers of the profession, as well as to provide the standard historical coverage to be expected in a work of this scope. "Further Readings" are noted at the end of each entry for the researcher seeking more information. It is important for the reader to note that most of the information contained in the book was collected in the two-year period ending December, 1997; the information was current as of that date. In some cases, significant related events occuring since then have been updated.

As a result of contributors' efforts, a more comprehensive understanding of the field will emerge and provide some distinct signposts for the future. The items are arranged in alphabetical order to provide as comprehensive a list of items as the exigencies of space and time allow. Some of the entries are as short as a few hundred words and are, in effect, expanded program definitions or descriptions of events; others are 1,500 words or more and introduce more detail, and, in some cases, theoretical aspects of the subject. Television is a team effort, and we have attempted to discuss important team members. As a result, most of the major aspects of the field and many of the minor ones are addressed.

It is important to acknowledge, however, that just as in the broader public context, the work of the most visible individual contributors to television news tends to be most easily recognized by peers. In fairness, this work reflects this broad industry-wide bias. Those individuals appearing in front of the camera are unique in that they are singularly promoted by their employers—the major networks—in order to attract a large audience. So it is with this work. It is also important to recognize that some network programs have undergone dozens of personnel changes, making it difficult to ensure that all important contributors are fully covered.

In some instances it is the original, the best known, or even the most recent broadcaster receiving the most credit. An effort was made to include some who work behind the scenes, especially some

key managers who offered important historic innovations and also some individuals who show
promise in the field of television news. This listing
is not exhaustive. Many of the television professionals have labored long and hard in local broadcast news; these contributions are no less significant—only less visible. It is significant to note that
nearly all national figures started at the local level.

This project has also reinforced what those of
us who have researched broadcast news from its
earliest beginnings already know—with rare exceptions, the knowledge of the field has been
poorly preserved. Researching and writing for this
project reinforced just how sporadic the collection,
documentation, and maintenance of video materials
of television have become. Over recent years, control of individual stations, and even of entire networks, has changed hands many times. With each
change, information often has been lost or has
strayed, sometimes due to cuts in archival departments. There are, of course, some dramatic national institutional exceptions, including the
Broadcast Pioneers Library; the Museum of
Broadcast Communications in Chicago; the Museum of Television and Radio, with locations in
both New York and Los Angeles; the Newseum;
and, the Smithsonian Institution.

Some state historical libraries and academic
institutions, such as those in California, Wisconsin,
and Missouri, have also developed important holdings, and the public has begun to recognize the
value of historic preservation. Also, important
sources have evolved around themes or particular
program collections. The Peabody Collection at the
University of Georgia offers potent insights into
some of the most significant programming of the
early television era. The Vanderbilt News Archive
in Nashville, Tennessee offers some specialized
public affairs material of great value. The collection at the University of California–Los Angeles
provides program scripts and related documents, as
does the library of the Academy of Television Arts
and Sciences, also in Los Angeles. A number of
university libraries have recently begun to target the
broadcasting area for future development. The
Mugar Collection at Boston University has, for example, acquired some important material, and
many schools with key alumni in the field have

also been successful in collecting relevant material. Contributors to this work made good use of
those collections.

My goal is to provide a beginning, a tool useful to students of the television, journalism, and
broadcast fields; television journalists; and the general public—anyone interested in information
gathering for television, its achievements, and its
many challenges. This reference work will make
the field of television journalism better understood
and draw attention to some of those broadcasters
who have done, or are doing, excellent work. Television news is still in the early stages of development. The field as a whole remains at a critical
juncture in which additional resources are sorely
needed. There are no definitive answers to many of
the major issues and challenges we face. The *Encyclopedia of Television News*, by bringing disparate
information together, offers a better understanding
of how the field functions and also provides en-
couragement for those seeking to address issues of
the future.

In acknowledging the many people who have
helped in the production of this book, I must express thanks to my undergraduate institution, St.
Louis University, and to my first employer, CBS
News. I am also indebted to a number of local stations, especially NBC affiliates WAVE-TV in Louisville and KSDK-TV in St. Louis, where I found
professional homes. Jerry Allen, Edward C. Lam-
bert, G. Joseph Wolfe, Keith Sanders, Paul Nelson,
and my graduate adviser at the University of Missouri–Columbia, John Kline, has each left an indelible mark. I also thank my first full-time academic tutor, Edward Sewell, and the communication faculty at Virginia Tech University. The administration of the University of Louisville permitted me to develop a new academic program while I
balanced weekends working on a public affairs
program for the market leader in Kentucky. Of
course my home base, the University of Missouri–
St. Louis, has been a constant source of inspiration
and has permitted me similar liberties in taking on
assignments for the first Pulitzer-owned television
station. For the insights of a distinguished faculty
and their students' assistance, as well as library
facilities and information specialists (often working under some challenging circumstances), I am
grateful to the entire University of Missouri system.

A number of fellowships and grant opportunities encouraged this work. Financial support from the National Endowment for the Humanities and the University of California–San Diego; the Weld Fellowship at Stanford University; a Freedom Forum Fellowship from Columbia University; the John Adams Fellowship from the University of London; and the Goldsmith Research Award from Harvard all assisted in this effort. Scholars and administrators from those institutions, especially Marvin Kalb, Everette Dennis, Gary McDowell, and Michael Schudson, from both the beginning and end of this journey, are gratefully acknowledged, as are Laura Wade and a number of careful editors at The Oryx Press, especially Debra Traylor and Elizabeth Welsh. A special thank you goes to the administration of the University of Missouri–St. Louis, including Blanche Touhill, Jack Nelson, Doug Wartzok, Tom McPhail, and Martin Sage.

Colleagues who offered significant counsel and a great deal of editorial support on this project deserve my most hearty thanks; these include: Craig Allen, Arizona State University; Jerry Allen, University of New Haven; Shirley Biagi, California State University–Sacramento; Barbara Cloud, University of Nevada–Las Vegas; Stuart Esrock, University of Louisville; Bruce Evensen, DePaul University; Joe Foote, Southern Illinois University–Carbondale; Marjorie Fox, University of Cincinnati; Don Godfrey, Arizona State University; Val Limburg, Washington State University; Roy Moore, University of Kentucky; Steve Phipps, University of Missouri–St. Louis; Alf Pratte, Brigham Young University; Bill Silcock, University of Missouri–Columbia; Kim Smith, Iowa State University; Jim Upshaw, University of Oregon; Betty Winfield, University of Missouri–Columbia; and Dhyana Ziegler, University of Tennessee.

To all contributors who suffered through extensive rewrites, lengthy e-mail queries, and the many fact-checking exercises a reference work of this scale requires, I am very grateful and respectful of efforts to produce an important and useful book. Most of all, I wish to pay tribute to a very understanding wife. She has stuck by me through many challenging assignments in both broadcasting and academe. Carol Murray is *ex officio* editor of my work, so it is appropriate to bestow upon her "Executive Producer." To my daughters, Ellen Elizabeth and Katherine Ann—the ladies who form the genesis of my personal advisory board—I am also very grateful.

Michael Murray, St. Louis, Missouri

A

ABC News

The American Broadcasting Company (ABC) struggled against the Columbia Broadcasting System (CBS) and the National Broadcasting Company (NBC) in its early years as a network—not only in news, but also in programming. ABC began as a radio network in 1943. Ten years later, it merged with United Paramount Theatres, and Leonard Goldenson became company president. Although ABC was able to develop a loyal following among young viewers during the 1960s, with popular programming, its news programs suffered. Frank Pierce's appointment as ABC's president in 1974 proved important for the network. ABC began to attain a stronger share of the entertainment program market, leading a host of shows, and eventually landing ABC atop the network race. Under Pierce, ABC became the highest rated network in prime time. In addition to its success in prime time, ABC Sports was revolutionizing programming under the direction of Roone Arledge. ABC News continued to lag, however.

Not until 1970, with the recruitment of Harry Reasoner from CBS, was ABC able to make strides in its news division. Reasoner's defection, followed by Frank Pierce's coup in hiring Barbara Walters away from NBC in 1976, started the ball rolling for ABC News. In 1977, based on his success in revolutionizing sports programming at ABC, Roone Arledge was promoted to president of ABC News.

Almost immediately following this appointment, ABC News aquired the reputation of a company building one of broadcasting's premier news organizations.

Arledge's innovative creations in sports, such as *ABC's Wide World of Sports* and *Monday Night Football*, translated well to news with the introduction of hugely successful programs like *World News Tonight with Peter Jennings*, *Nightline*, *This Week with David Brinkley*, *20/20*, *Prime Time Live*, and *Turning Point*. These programs have routinely ranked among the highest shows of their kind in critical acclaim. ABC News programs have featured some of the most respected broadcast journalists in the nation, including David Brinkley, Ann Compton, Sam Donaldson, Diane Sawyer, Cokie Roberts, Peter Jennings, Ted Koppel, Barbara Walters, and Hugh Downs.

World News Tonight was introduced in 1978. Peter Jennings assumed the anchor position in 1983. In just five years, it ranked number one among America's nightly news broadcasts. Jennings, with nearly 30 years of broadcast reporting experience from the United States, the Middle East, and Europe, provides incisive leadership in domestic and foreign news coverage. Regular segments of "Person of the Week," "American Agenda," and "Your Money, Your Choice" round out the international news and investigative reporting segments that have anchored *World News Tonight* for more than 15 years.

In addition to the success of Peter Jennings and *World News Tonight*, ABC offers the nightly news program *Nightline*. Anchored by Ted Koppel, *Nightline* runs opposite *The Tonight Show with Jay Leno* and the *Late Show with David Letterman* in most major American media markets, demonstrating ABC's commitment to news. *Nightline*, which premiered in 1980 following the success of the late-night news broadcasts "The Iran Crisis: America Held Hostage," offers in-depth news and live television interviews concerning major news events of the day. The standard format features Koppel in the studio interviewing experts with differing perspectives on current events.

The strongest program for the ABC News team is *20/20*. This Wednesday and Friday evening weekly broadcast has remained among the highest rated prime-time television shows for almost 20 years. The hour-long newsmagazine, which features co-hosts Hugh Downs and Barbara Walters, has received nearly 300 of journalism's most prestigious awards, and *20/20* is most noted for its investigative features and exclusive personality profiles. Sam Donaldson and Diane Sawyer joined as co-anchors in 1998.

This Week with David Brinkley, which premiered in 1981 with acclaimed 50-year broadcast news veteran host David Brinkley, was the highest-rated program in its category. This hour-long Sunday morning news program, renamed *This Week* following Brinkley's retirement in 1996, features a roundtable discussion among Sam Donaldson, George Will, and Cokie Roberts. *This Week* is the recipient of several journalism awards in recognition of its steadfast commitment to examination of the Washington political landscape.

Among the other regularly scheduled ABC News programs were *Prime Time Live*, with Diane Sawyer and Sam Donaldson; *Turning Point*, with rotating anchors Diane Sawyer, Forrest Sawyer, and Barbara Walters; *World News Saturday/Sunday*, with anchor Carole Simpson; and *World News This Morning*, a 90-minute early morning broadcast, and *World News Now*, both hosted by Thalia Assuras. *World News Now* is ABC's response to CNN, presenting all the world's top stories every half hour from 2:00 to 6:00 A.M.

In addition to its regularly scheduled news programming, ABC features special news re-ports—*Peter Jennings Reporting*, *National Town Meeting*, *Viewpoint*, and *Answering Children's Questions*. These special reports offer viewers in-depth analysis of some of the day's most compelling news. For example, *National Town Meeting* which aired in 1991, featured Mikhail Gorbachev and Boris Yeltsin answering questions from American citizens. *Viewpoint* offers criticism and analysis of media coverage of news events.

ABC News also produces home video versions of its newsmagazine programs and segments, and its interactive division produces laserdiscs, CD-ROMs, and educational software. ABC News employs more than 1,000 individuals worldwide, including more than 100 news correspondents. Domestic news bureaus are located in 11 American cities, including New York, Los Angeles, Chicago, and Dallas. International news bureaus are located in more than 25 cities, including London, Johannesburg, Beijing, Bangkok, Panama City, and Delhi. Through a powerful combination of regularly scheduled news programming and special news features, ABC has maintained its distinction as a preeminent news organization, and is now considered a leader in newsgathering and reporting.

See also Roone Arledge, David Brinkley, Barbara Walters.   *John C. Tedesco*

Further Reading

Goldenson, Leonard H., and Marvin J. Wolf. *Beating the Odds: The Untold Story behind the Rise of ABC*. New York: Charles Scribner's Sons, 1991.

Quinlan, Sterling. *Inside ABC: American Broadcasting Company's Rise to Power*. New York: Hasting House, 1979.

Williams, Huntington. *Beyond Control: ABC and the Fate of the Networks*. New York: Atheneum, 1989.

Elie Abel

Elie Abel was born on October 17, 1920, in Montreal, Quebec, Canada. He was educated at McGill University in Montreal and at Columbia University in New York. He served overseas with the Royal Canadian Air Force during World War II. Elie Abel achieved status in television news as a State Department correspondent, London bureau chief, and diplomatic correspondent, all for NBC News.

Abel started his career working at various Canadian newspapers in 1945 before joining the *New York Times*. He left the *New York Times* in 1959 to become the chief of the Washington bureau of the *Detroit News*. Recruited in 1961 to cover the State Department for NBC, Abel distinguished himself as a diplomatic correspondent and chief of the network's London bureau. He received a George Foster Peabody Award and an Overseas Press Club Award for government decision-making processes and interpretation of international news.

Leaving broadcasting in 1970, Abel joined Columbia University as dean of the Graduate School of Journalism, becoming its Godfrey Lowell Cabot Professor. At that time, he also chaired the jurors for the duPont-Columbia Awards, overseeing the award process. He left Columbia to become the Harry and Norman Chandler Professor of Communication at Stanford University, his current position, and also held a fellowship at the Kennedy School at Harvard. Abel authored a number of books, including a collaboration with W. Averell Harriman on American involvement in Vietnam. *See also* duPont-Columbia University Awards.   *Michael D. Murray*

Further Reading

Abel, Elie. *Leaking: Who Does It? Who Benefits? At What Cost?* New York: Priority Press, 1987.
Abel, Elie. *The Missile Crisis.* New York: Bantam, 1966.
Abel, Elie, ed. *What's News: The Media in American Society.* San Francisco: Institute for Contemporary Studies, 1981.

Advertising and TV News

For better or worse, television news in the United States is a commercially supported program format. Television executives reinforce the view that interesting, innovative television programming attracts viewers and creates synergy with audiences that advertisers desire. And while that has always been true for entertainment programming, the same can also be said of television news. Increasingly, news must be commercially viable to attract viewers, and hence advertising support, so that it continues to be profitable for a station or network.

Financial journalists such as Adam Smith maintained that as long as the news media relies on corporate sponsorship, there will always be at least some questions as to how news can be reported objectively. Despite an occasional publicized incident, most television executives downplay the potential of such bias. Station management attempts to maintain a strong separation between the news and sales departments to forestall problems. While stations sometimes air stories detrimental to clients, advertiser threats seldom result in changes in media purchases. In a related vein, MSNBC covers software giant Microsoft in the same way they cover the activities of any other business, even though the firm is a full partner with NBC in the television venture.

While the relationship of television news to advertising rarely manifests itself by corrupting the integrity of journalism, it does more often reveal itself in other forms. Most notably, all television news operations face the very real pressure of attracting viewers in large numbers in order to generate advertising dollars. By the same token, a news organization cannot be journalistically vigorous unless it is financially strong. Hempel says television news professionals sometimes do not like to admit there is a demand for revenue, but they understand the reality that they are commercial artists.

Hence, to be assured that the news product can be sold, it has to be acceptable and likable to audiences—particularly in the highly competitive news environment. To meet these criteria, Hempel says television news has undergone numerous presentational changes over the years including the use of more complex and inviting set designs, increased emphasis on visuals in stories, higher quality graphics and production values, and customized newscast openings. Stations increasingly use complex technology to bring breaking stories to the air before their competition does so. On-air personnel are researched for likability and coached on presentation, dress, and makeup. Stations also spend enormous amounts of money to promote on-air personnel and newscasts to attract viewers in desirable demographic categories.

The escalating competition for viewers and advertising dollars has meant changes in the types of stories that television news covers. Tabloid-style stories that appeal to the mass audience—like Liz Taylor's health and the divorce of Diana, the princess of Wales—are prominent in newscasts. Critics charge that local television news stations have become a haven for video coverage of crime and violence instead of for stories about local politics and government, education, religion, or social issues. Critics also complain that local television newscasts provide a nightly overdose of overblown, sensationalized video, in pursuit of higher ratings. While some news directors say they are trying to steer away from the most exploitive types of coverage, they also admit that gratuitous video does attract an audience.

With the pressure for commercial acceptance, the very nature of television news may be changing. Critics fear that as television news becomes driven by the primacy of ratings, it may transform itself into a form of entertainment in which information gets swept away in favor of emotion. ABC News's Roone Arledge has frequently taken the position that part of the alteration lies in the changing nature of events around the globe. According to the long-time network executive, America has moved from an age of news to an age of entertainment because the end of the cold war removed much of the life-or-death tension and the public's attention shifted from substantive information to celebrity gossip.

As television news operations seek more advertising revenue, they are resorting to a variety of strategies to attract loyal viewers. Participatory talk shows are increasing on cable networks and on some local stations. Some stations are implementing "public" or "civic journalism," taking viewer polls or sponsoring community issue forums. These tools are used to determine what issues viewers want addressed, and stations adjust their coverage accordingly. Ultimately, the battle to attract viewers forces a redefinition of news if stations adhere to viewers' wishes.

Most television news executives still feel a responsibility to strive for a balance. Network sources have always noted that the American public does not have much interest in foreign news so it is not covered in detail on their nightly newscast. Still these sources say that does not absolve networks of the responsibility to air foreign news to give the audience information it needs, beyond what it wants. So, while television news continues to alter its form and content to meet the needs of advertising sponsors, its executives continue to face the challenge of maintaining objectivity and journalistic integrity in a commercialized environment.
Stuart L. Esrock

Further Reading:

Kiska, T. "Local TV News Shows Hooked on Violence." *The Detroit News On-line*, 16 February 1997. Available: <http://www.detnews.com/1997/metro/9702/ 16/02160089.htm>.

Zoglin, R. "The News Wars." *Time*, 21 October 1996, 58–64.

AFTRA

The American Federation of Television and Radio Artists (AFTRA) is a national union of professional performers and broadcasters comprising 36 locals with over 75,000 members. It developed as a by-product of broadcast popularity. During the 1920s, NBC and CBS were established, the first transcontinental radio broadcast was aired, and the first network radio drama was presented. By 1937, the nation's ears were tuned to the radio, and the number of broadcast professionals grew rapidly—without a labor contract in place to protect wages and working conditions. On both east and west coasts, radio employees organized and joined forces to create the Radio Artists Guild (RAG). It soon became apparent to RAG that affiliation with a national labor body would strengthen the effort to guarantee better working conditions for all. George Heller, a Broadway actor, was the key organizer lobbying for a radio contract. The Actors' Equity Association division known as Radio Equity was led by Heller.

Within two months, Radio Equity grew to a membership of over 400, and a separately chartered organization was deemed necessary. Equity, the Screen Actors Guild, and the American Guild of Musical Artists agreed to underwrite the charter for a new organization. On August 16, 1937, Actors' Equity Association relinquished jurisdiction, and the American Federation of Radio Artists (AFRA) was formed, with headquarters in New York. Eddie Cantor was elected AFRA's first national president, and Emily Holt became its first national executive secretary. AFRA board members included, among others, Edward Arnold, Phil Baker, Jack Benny, Edgar Bergen, John Boles, Bing Crosby, Eddie Cantor, Martin Gabel, George Heller, Frank Chapman, Ted De Corsica, Warren Hull, Paul Stewart, and Rudy Vallee. Local organizations of AFRA (locals) were formed in Los Angeles, New York, Chicago, Cincinnati, San Francisco, and Detroit. By the end of 1937, AFRA boasted 2,000 members. Its first convention was held in St. Louis in November of 1938.

AFRA's co-founders crafted a federation of autonomous locals, one in each center (defined as four or more stations), whose executive secretary, serving as chief administrator and negotiator, would bargain for contracts geared to each center's staff and freelance artists. The New York office was established to negotiate and protect the contracts of artists working at the networks. The federation was governed by its members, with policy making and management vested in a national board of directors. The board was elected by the membership, and AFRA policy was formed by elected local delegates participating and voting at yearly conventions.

AFRA's first major contract, The Minimum Sustaining Agreement for Network Radio, was won on July 19, 1938. In January of 1939, AFRA reached an agreement with 170 advertisers on the National Code of Fair Practice for Commercial Broadcasting and won union shop and union scale status. The Code of Fair Practice for Transcriptions and Recordings for Radio Broadcast Purposes was added in May of 1941. This code covered the making of and the use of programs and advertisements at alternative times in the broadcast schedule.

The advent of television transformed home entertainment, and many of the top radio shows became programs for television. One of the most popular types of early television programming was the variety show, and with it came a whole new category of performers. At the same time, television news captured the scene with vivid footage. The Television Authority (TvA) was established in December 1949 to represent all performers on television through a television union. The national board was composed of 10 ranking members from the Actors' Equity Association, Chorus Equity Association, AFRA, Artists (AGVA), and the Los Angeles-based Screen Actors Guild (SAG) and Screen Extras Guild (SEG), as each shared a vested interest in the emerging field of television.

AFRA leaders soon realized the newly formed TvA was trying to organize the many members of AFRA and that both unions would be better served by a merger. On September 20, 1952, TvA and AFRA merged to form AFTRA, and George Heller was elected as its national executive secretary. That same year, AFTRA's national constitution went into effect, with board members and convention delegates elected on the basis of proportional representation. AFTRA's membership totaled 8,500. Headed by Heller, AFTRA negotiated with the networks in 1954 for the first pension plan ever established for any television broadcast performers' union. The next year, 1955, Heller died at age 49 of cancer. He was succeeded by Alex McKee who secured the first agreement calling for additional payments for rebroadcast of television programs. In 1956, AFTRA's Welfare Plan was inaugurated.

In 1959, Virginia Payne became AFTRA's national president and the first woman to hold a top elected post in any performers' union. In 1960, AFTRA and SAG conducted the first joint negotiations for television commercials and resumed past discussions of merger. David L. Cole, a noted labor mediator, was commissioned by the two unions to prepare a feasibility study. The SAG merger committee rejected the Cole proposal, as well as AFTRA's suggested modifications.

The first Network News contract was created in 1967. Newscasters previously were categorized under "announcers." In 1968, the "news broadcasters" category was officially created in AFTRA with Roy Neal serving as the first news representative on the AFTRA National Board. In 1974, William F. Buckley challenged AFTRA's union shop agreements as they affected news broadcasters, but the U.S. Supreme Court declined to review the case. Bill Hillman, in 1979, was the first news broadcaster to be elected president of AFTRA. The National News Unit was created by AFTRA in 1981 to improve service to news correspondents. On July 16, 1987, AFTRA celebrated its 50th anniversary by holding the national convention in St.

Louis, the site of its first official meeting on November 14, 1938. *See also* William F. Buckley, Jr..

Susan Plumb Salas

Further Reading
Barnouw, Erik. *The Golden Web*. New York: Oxford University Press, 1968.
Harvey, Rita Morley. *Those Wonderful, Terrible Years*. Carbondale and Edwardsville: Southern Illinois University Press, 1996.
Lichty, Lawrence W., and Malachi Topping. *American Broadcasting: A Source Book on the History of Radio and Television*. New York: Hastings House, 1975.

Agnew Anti-Press Campaign

Speaking in Des Moines, Iowa, on November 13, 1969, one year after his election as Richard Nixon's vice president, Spiro T. Agnew delivered a blistering attack on the country's network television news programs. He criticized them as hostile, unpatriotic purveyors of negativism. He characterized network news executives as belonging to an unelected elite, out of touch with mainstream Americans who, he said, supported administration policy for gradual reduction of U.S. forces in the Vietnam War, rather than immediate withdrawal. He blamed the liberal-slanted media for deepening divisions in American society and for making it harder to end the war.

The cause of Agnew's annoyance was "instant analysis" by television commentators following President Nixon's televised address on November 3, 1969. Their speculation about the president's motives distorted reality, Agnew asserted, and amounted to subversion of the public trust the networks were pledged to honor in exchange for broadcast licenses. With that speech and several more authored by Patrick J. Buchanan, Agnew mobilized anti-media sentiment among those he called the "silent majority." A forceful speaker whose speeches were widely quoted, Agnew lambasted several media outlets, including the *New York Times*, the *Washington Post*, *Time* magazine, *Newsweek* magazine, ABC, CBS, and NBC, heaping particular scorn on those headquartered in the

east. He labeled them as being so suffused with anti-administration bias as to be enemies of democracy, in need of closer governmental supervision to get back in touch.

Encouraged by the generally positive public response to these attacks, the Nixon administration took a number of additional anti-media actions between 1970 and 1974. These included stiffer broadcast licensing requirements; higher fines for infringements of Federal Communications Commission rules; and subpoenas of telephone records of newspapers, media groups, and syndicated columnists considered unfriendly to the Nixon White House. The existence of a list of administration enemies (some of whom became subjects of federal tax audits), which reached 550 individuals and included media people, was disclosed in 1973. In these and a variety of other ways, the administration sent the message that it would force the media to become less critical.

Intimidation worked for a time. The networks discontinued immediate analysis of presidential speeches. But public confidence in the administration diminished in late 1973 when Agnew was fined $10,000, placed on probation, and forced to resign after pleading no contest to tax evasion. He had been under federal investigation for alleged improprieties as Baltimore County executive and Maryland governor prior to being elected vice president. In 1974, President Nixon, too, resigned to avoid impeachment proceedings growing out of the Watergate investigation.

Many in broadcasting argued that Agnew's anti-media campaign reinforced their contention that federal fairness requirements notwithstanding, courts should grant broadcasters the same First Amendment autonomy enjoyed by the print media to question and criticize the government. *See also* Pat Buchanan. *Daniel W. Pfaff*

Further Reading
Keogh, James. *President Nixon and the Press*. New York: Funk & Wagnalls, 1972.
Lashner, Marilyn A. *The Chilling Effect in TV News*. New York: Praeger, 1984.
Porter, William E. *Assault on the Media: The Nixon Years*. Ann Arbor: University of Michigan Press, 1976.

Roger Ailes

Roger Ailes, an early architect of television talk shows and a media strategist for the Republican Party, became the chief executive in charge of Fox News in 1996. He was born on May 15, 1940, in Warren, Ohio. Much of his childhood was spent in hospitals due to a chronic illness.

Ailes began broadcasting on the campus radio station at Ohio University as a co-host of an early morning show, *The Yawn Patrol*. After graduation, he declined an offer to work as a disc jockey in Columbus, Ohio, in order to work at KYW-TV in Cleveland. He became the assistant director of the *Mike Douglas Show* and was promoted to executive producer at the age of 25. Under Ailes's supervision, it became America's most-watched syndicated TV talk show. A conversation with one particular guest on the show in 1967 changed his life—presidential candidate Richard Nixon criticized television as a "gimmick," but Ailes argued that no candidate could be elected without knowing how to use it. Nixon recruited him to join his 1968 campaign, and the next year he started a production and consulting firm in New York. One of his first clients was the Republican National Committee.

Ailes also worked for Republican presidential candidates Ronald Reagan and George Bush. He is credited with having written the then 73-year-old Reagan's disarming reply to critics of his age during the presidential debate with Walter Mondale, "I am not going to exploit for political purposes my opponent's youth and inexperience," and also George Bush's retort to Dan Rather's live televised inquiry on Iran-Contra, "How would you like it if I judged your career by those seven minutes when you walked off the set in New York?" Ailes's aggressive tactics won him the dubious title, "the dark prince of negative advertising." He retired from political consulting in 1992.

In 1993, Ailes became president of CNBC, the cable network owned by NBC, and began a second cable network, *America's Talking*, in 1994. Known for his personal touch in coaching candidates and performers with videotape and graphics, Ailes took advantage of a public move to the right and brought the conservative views of Rush Limbaugh to television for Multimedia Entertainment. He also served as creative consultant for several television talk show hosts including Dee Dee Myers, Tom Snyder, and Geraldo Rivera. When NBC announced it was replacing *America's Talking* with MSNBC, a joint cable venture of NBC and the Microsoft Corporation, Ailes left the cable network and went to work for Rupert Murdoch's News Corporation. The new chairman and CEO of Fox News promised that the network's coverage would be "viewer friendly," in contrast to that seen on other networks. *See also* Rush Limbaugh.   *William R. Davie*

Further Reading

McGinn, Daniel. "The Roger Ailes Makeover," *Newsweek*. 31 October 1994, 45.
Miller, Stuart. "Roger Ailes hits TV with a Rush," *Variety*. 21 June 1993.
Ross, Chuck. "Ailes Sets Out to Lead Fox into News Business." *Advertising Age*. 1 July 1996.

Christiane Amanpour

Courtesy Cable News Network, Inc.
© 1996. Photo by Andrew Eccles

Christiane Amanpour made her reputation as a combat reporter for Cable News Network (CNN) in conflicts in the Persian Gulf, Somalia, Haiti, and Bosnia. She is recognized for her aggressiveness and humanistic reporting in her live dispatches from war-torn fronts and for bringing the Balkan conflict to the world's attention. Born in London in 1958, Amanpour, the eldest of four daughters, grew up in a privileged, wealthy household in Teheran, where she raced Arabian horses and swam competitively. She describes herself in those years as being a tomboy, who had "the world's best childhood." Her family, which was politically well connected, enjoyed a friendly relationship with Shah Reza Pahlavi. During the Islamic revolution of 1979, however, they lost all but their lives in a flight from Iran. These experiences crystallized Amanpour's career goal to become a foreign correspondent—if she was going to be affected by events, she wanted to be part of them.

Amanpour studied at Holy Cross Convent school in Buckinghamshire, England. She graduated summa cum laude in 1983 from the University of Rhode Island with a degree in journalism. She joined CNN in 1983 as assistant for the network's international news desk. By 1989, she had moved up to the CNN correspondent position in Germany, arriving just in time to cover the democratic revolution erupting across central and eastern Europe, then dashing off to Romania to cover events there. Amanpour became well known to American television-viewing audiences through her live-from-the-front reporting of the Persian Gulf War and Operation Desert Storm. But it was her early coverage of the Balkan conflict that cemented her reputation as a journalist with exceptional news instincts who could humanize a conflict.

Some have found her relentless reporting exasperating, including President Bill Clinton, to whom she directed a challenging question during a 1994 CNN-sponsored global town forum. Speaking from Sarajevo on the issue of American involvement in Bosnia, Amanpour tried to pin down the president's reply concerning his policy. Her professional objectivity has been questioned by some, who see her impassioned reports and direct identification of the Bosnian Serbs as the aggressors in the Balkan conflict as examples of biased journalism. Amanpour's response has been that she only reports what she sees; in her opinion, objectivity means giving a hearing to all sides, but not treating all sides equally.

Amanpour has won the highest awards in journalism for her Bosnian reporting, including, in 1994 the George Foster Peabody Award, the George Polk Memorial Award, the Alfred I. duPont-Columbia University Silver Baton, and the Pulitzer Prize. In the spring of 1996, Amanpour

signed a rare cooperative short-term contract with both CNN and CBS News that enables her to make five appearances on CBS's *60 Minutes* over the course of a year. Amanpour has a reputation for being as direct and unadorned in her professional appearance as in her reporting. She married U.S. State Department spokesperson James Rubin near Rome, Italy on August 8, 1998. *See also* CNN (Cable News Network).   *Patsy G. Watkins*

Further Reading

Bennetts, Leslie. "Woman O' War." *Vanity Fair.* September 1996. 146–150; 167–168.
Nordland, Rod, and Kendall Hamilton. "One Star, Two Nets: CNN and CBS Will Share the Daring Amanpour." *Newsweek*, 8 July 1996, 60.
Ricchiardi, Sherry. "Giving Great War." *American Journalism Review*, September 1996, 30–31.
Robins, J. Max. "Christian Soldiers Onward," *TV Guide,* 4 October 1997, 26–29.

Archives for Television News

Historical research of television news is growing in importance, both professionally and academically, as an increasing number of archivists and collectors have restored and exchanged broadcast materials. Television and film producers have taken advantage of opportunities presented with these archives, using the recorded image in modern documentaries, newsmagazines, and news programming. These resources provide a previously unavailable visual, and by virtue of related support material, historical context. Scholarly research of video and audio archives has progressed at a slower rate. Many archivists still echo the cries of the former curator of the Milo Ryan CBS Phono Archive, Milo Ryan, when he noted available materials and asked: "Where are the scholars?"

The number of television news archives is growing. Many of these began with the transition in news technology when stations went from film to electronic news-gathering techniques. At that time, station personnel found themselves with film they felt had historic value. Some of this ended up in local archives or with historical societies around the nation, but unfortunately much of it was also destroyed or lost. Professor Marvin Bensman of the University of Memphis, a noted authority, points out on the Web page of his own collection that broadcast archives serve three primary missions: to store; to exhibit, distribute, transcribe, catalogue, and sell; and to restore and preserve materials.

The reluctance of scholars to use the broadcast archives across the nation has some historical rationale—the materials are seen as untrustworthy by traditional historians. This skepticism is not without reason. The non-media historian is suspicious of broadcast sources because traditionalists often lack knowledge of the electronic media process; distortion of facts has occurred within the media, on occasion, for the sake of dramatic effect and profit. The evaluation of any recorded broadcast requires the researcher to employ a wide range of techniques extending beyond the traditional skills of historiography.

This skepticism toward primary electronic media source materials should not negate their historical value, but it does present a challenge to the investigator who uses the program as a primary resource. Those who research programs—particularly news programs—as primary sources must look to the program source itself, as one would with any primary source. The researcher must also seek to understand program development, documenting the details from production notes and other available material. The researcher needs to develop technical skills to deal with evidence as well as understanding the medium. As information passes through the various stages, each step in the process must be analyzed in terms of the value of the information as evidence and the effect the process has had overall. The challenge to the professional researcher is to maintain the integrity of the evidence and make the ethical decisions that would protect historical fact as opposed to sacrificing fact for the sake of economics or dramatization.

A number of major national news archives with a television component now exist. They include: The Museum of Television and Radio, Beverly Hills, California; the Library of Congress—Motion Picture, Broadcasting and Recorded Sound Division, Washington, D.C.; National Archives—Motion Picture Sound and Video Branch, Washington, D.C.; The George Foster Peabody Collection—University of Georgia, Athens, Georgia; Museum of Broadcast Communication, Chicago Illinois; Public Affairs Video Archives—C-SPAN, Purdue University, West Lafayette, Indiana; The Museum of Broadcasting, New York, New York; Vanderbilt Television News Archive, Nashville, Tennessee; Newseum, Freedom Forum, Arlington, Virginia; and Mass Communication History Collection—State Historical Society of Wisconsin, Madison, Wisconsin. *See also* Vanderbilt Television News Archive.

Donald G. Godfrey

Further Reading

Godfrey, Donald G. *Reruns on File: Guide to Electronic Media Archives*. Hillsdale, New Jersey: Lawrence Erlbaum Associates Publishers, 1992.

Prelinger, Richard & Celeste R. Hoffnar. *Footage 89: North American Film and Video Sources*. New York: Prelinger Associates, 1989.

Roone Arledge

© 1990, ABC, Inc.

Roone Pinckney Arledge, Jr. was born on July 8, 1931, and began his broadcasting career after receiving a bachelor of arts degree from Columbia University's School of International Affairs in 1952. After a brief stint with the Dumont television network, Arledge joined NBC in 1955 and eventually received his first Emmy in 1959 as a producer of a Saturday morning children's program. In 1960, Arledge moved to ABC and televised sports, where he quickly advanced from producer to vice president (1963) and then president (1968) of ABC sports. As head of sports broadcasting at ABC, Arledge was credited with numerous technical and programming advancements, including the creation of *Wide World of Sports*, *The American Sportsman*, *Monday Night Football*, and *The Super Stars*. He also created or fine-tuned the use of slow motion, instant replay, handheld and isolation cameras, sophisticated graphics, underwater video, split screens, and field microphones.

During ABC's presentation of the 1972 Olympics at Munich (one of 10 Arledge executive-produced), 11 Israeli athletes were held hostage and eventually murdered by Palestinian terrorists. Arledge's orchestration of coverage by Jim McKay, Peter Jennings, and Howard Cosell changed forever the way television covered breaking news; after Munich, viewers were no longer satisfied with waiting to receive coverage of important events. In 1977, ABC appointed Arledge president of its consistently weak news division. He held that position in conjunction with the presidency of ABC Sports until 1986, when he became exclusively president of ABC News. As president of ABC News, Arledge has made the network a news leader. Likewise, he has transformed the manner in which news is reported, packaged, and presented.

Coming from a sports background, Arledge had to overcome initial hostility to his ascension as president of ABC News; however, he quickly gained respect as a man dedicated to the success of the news division. He lured talent away from rival networks, particularly CBS; implemented high-tech graphics; pioneered the use of the split-screen interview; added showmanship to the newscasts; and expanded the network's news coverage. He also created *20/20*, *Nightline*, *This Week with David Brinkley*, and *PrimeTime Live*. Over the years, Arledge has received dozens of Emmys for his news and sports coverage. He has won the University of Missouri Honor Medal for distinguished service to journalism in 1977, and the George Foster Peabody Award three times. He was elected into the Television Academy Arts and Sciences Hall of Fame and the U.S. Olympic Hall of Fame in 1990, and the National Association of Broadcasters Hall of Fame in 1994. *See also* ABC News.

Grant Curtis

Further Reading
Quinlan, Sterling. *Inside ABC*. New York: Hastings House, 1979.
Roberts, R. "Roone Arledge and the Rise of Televised Sports." *USA Today*, January, 1992, 89–92.
Rushin, S. "1954–1994 How We Got Here." *Sports Illustrated*, (16 August 1994, 35–66.

Army-McCarthy Hearings

The Army-McCarthy hearings is an informal title given to a series of hearings conducted by the U.S. Senate in 1954. These hearings were significant both for their political drama and for their role in ending what became known as "McCarthyism." The Army-McCarthy hearings also were among the first of many such congressional proceedings that, in later years, attracted millions of American television viewers. The roots of McCarthyism lay in post-World War II fears that communism was creeping into numerous American institutions, particularly the government. This fear was compounded in 1949, when the Soviet Union successfully exploded its first nuclear device, and in June 1950, when American soldiers were dispatched to battle the troops of communist North Korea. Moreover, the conviction in 1950 of U.S. State Department official Alger Hiss, who had engaged in espionage for the Soviet Union, led to anxiety over the possibility that the government had been infiltrated by nests of communist spies.

Into this cauldron of anti-communist intrigue stepped U.S. Senator Joseph (Joe) R. McCarthy, Republican from Wisconsin. Senator McCarthy chose anti-communism as a cause he would champion after exploring several other issues that he felt would promote his political career. The senator's first foray as an anti-communist crusader occurred in February 1950 during a Lincoln Day speech in Wheeling, West Virginia. It was there, and at subsequent political gatherings, that McCarthy waved sheets of paper on which he claimed were names of government employees who were known communist sympathizers. The purported names were never publicly revealed.

Such accusations, fueled by existing suspicions and international unrest, focused attention on McCarthy. His reputation was further enhanced by the attention he received from the American press. Confidential information about communist affiliations that McCarthy claimed to have received from paid staff assistants, as well as from unpaid informants, provided a constant stream of unsubstantiated grist for the reporting mill. Senator McCarthy's prominence grew even more in January 1953 when Republican leaders designated him to chair the U.S. Senate's Government Operations Committee. This allowed McCarthy to appoint himself chair of the committee's Permanent Subcommittee on Investigations, a subcommittee whose chief role under McCarthy would be to examine communist infiltration of the U.S. government.

Senator McCarthy's chief committee investigators were Roy Cohn and G. David Schine. They were responsible for uncovering information that McCarthy used when asking government employees about questionable activities construed by the senator as communist-related. The basis for the senator's claims often was little more than rumor, but his bullying methods of interrogation and the reluctance of his Senate colleagues to control him made any challenge to McCarthy's accusations exceedingly risky. Senator McCarthy's tactics, and the assumptions under which he operated, finally were questioned by noted CBS reporter Edward R. Murrow. Murrow and producer Fred Friendly devoted Murrow's March 9, 1954, *See It Now* television program to a critical appraisal of Senator McCarthy's work. CBS allowed Senator McCarthy network television time on April 6, 1954, to respond to the program's uncomplimentary portrait. Less than three weeks later, the momentous Army-McCarthy hearings were set to begin.

The basis for convening the Army-McCarthy hearings was twofold. Senator McCarthy's subcommittee earlier had investigated allegations that certain members of the military stationed at Fort Monmouth, New Jersey, were affiliated with the Communist Party. While these investigations were in progress, the U.S. Army drafted Senator McCarthy's assistant G. David Schine. Schine's colleague, Roy Cohn, reportedly attempted to cajole the Army into either discharging Schine or assigning him to special duty as a McCarthy investigator. When the Army refused, Cohn persuaded Senator McCarthy that Schine was being held hos-

tage by the Army in reprisal to Senator McCarthy's Fort Monmouth investigation. The actions of both McCarthy and the Army in the Schine matter, as well as the Army's alleged complicity in a conspiracy to protect communists within ranks, became the subjects of the Army-McCarthy hearings.

The public phase of the Army-McCarthy hearings began on April 22, 1954, and continued with one major interruption until June 17, 1954. Senator McCarthy, being one of the subjects of the inquiry, momentarily relinquished his subcommittee chairmanship to Senator Karl Mundt, a Republican from South Dakota. For some 36 days, the Permanent Subcommittee on Investigations heard testimony from high-ranking Army personnel, including Secretary of the Army Robert Stevens. The hearings were the first of their kind to be carried live to a nationwide television audience. The ABC and Dumont networks broadcast the hearings from gavel to gavel. NBC carried the first two days of the hearings but chose to carry only filmed highlights of the hearings thereafter, and CBS carried only filmed highlights of the hearings throughout their duration. The opening day television audience for the Army-McCarthy hearings peaked at nearly 30 million viewers. In all, television coverage of the inquiry consumed a total of approximately 187 hours.

Little substance came from the hearings, although there did emerge the heroic personality of U.S. Army counsel Joseph Welch, whose oratorical remonstrance to Senator McCarthy—"Have you no sense of decency, sir, at long last?"—seemed to plant the wedge that anti-McCarthy forces had been looking for to help bring an end to the senator's tirades. Joseph McCarthy's personality, fully exposed under the glaring eye of television, proved an even greater liability to his political future. The senator's favorable ratings in public opinion polls plunged following the conclusion of the Army-McCarthy hearings. McCarthy's colleagues, many of whom were repulsed by his conduct and questionable investigatory tactics, voted 67–22 on December 2, 1954, to censure him. He quickly became *persona non grata* to Senate colleagues and reporters alike. On May 2, 1957, Joseph McCarthy died of an alcohol-related liver ailment. ***See also*** Edward R. Murrow. *Ronald Garay*

Further Reading

Fried, Richard M. *Nightmare in Red: The McCarthy Era in Perspective.* New York: Oxford University Press, 1990.

Garay, Ronald. *Congressional Television: A Legislative History.* Westport, CT: Greenwood Press, 1984.

U.S. Senate, Special Subcommittee on Investigations for the Committee on Government Operations. *Charges and Countercharges Involving: Secretary of the Army Robert T. Stevens, John G. Adams, H. Struve Hensel and Senator Joe McCarthy, Roy M. Cohn, and Francis P. Carr.* Report 2507, 83rd Congress, 2d Session, 1954.

Peter Arnett

Courtesy Cable News Network, Inc.
© 1993. Photo by George Bennett

In his autobiography, *Live from the Battlefield* in 1994, veteran war correspondent Peter Arnett said he follows two simple rules: report only what he sees firsthand and "never...do anything dangerous for fun." Arnett has followed these rules while covering every major war and insurrection in the last 35 years, from the rebellion in Laos in 1960 to the Vietnam War from 1962 to 1975, to the U.S. bombing of Baghdad in 1991, to Bosnia in 1994. His exploits have earned him a reputation among his colleagues as "soldier's reporter" and a "correspondent's correspondent."

Arnett was born on November 13, 1934, in Riverton, New Zealand. After apprenticeships at newspapers in New Zealand and Australia, Arnett boarded a tramp steamer bound for London in 1957. He disembarked in Thailand, where he worked as reporter for the English-language newspaper, the *Bangkok World*, for three years. In 1961, Arnett became a stringer for the Associated Press (AP) in Southeast Asia. Moving to South Vietnam as a correspondent for the AP in 1962, he covered the war until the fall of Saigon in 1975. His enterprise and accuracy earned him a reputation as a fearless correspondent. But his reporting of military defeats drew the ire of officials in South Vietnam and Washington, including President Lyndon Johnson. Arnett was awarded a Pulitzer Prize in 1966 for his series of stories in 1965 about the U.S. Information Service staging a fake battle involving South Vietnamese troops.

For the balance of the 1970s, Arnett served as a roving correspondent in the United States for the AP. In 1981, he left AP to become a television correspondent for Ted Turner's fledgling Cable News Network (CNN). After briefly covering the White House for CNN, Arnett again turned to battlefronts in El Salvador, Lebanon, Afghanistan, Grenada, and Angola.

His emergence as a TV reporter surprised many of his colleagues. "He's a short little guy with a flat nose. All of us wondered how he could function in American TV," Horst Faas, a photographer who worked with Arnett in Vietnam, told the *New York Times*. But the high-tech capabilities of modern TV news coverage proved a format well suited for Arnett's strength as a reporter—accurately covering breaking news events in distant places under difficult and sometimes dangerous circumstances.

In January 1991, Arnett, along with colleagues John Holliman and Bernard Shaw, covered the U.S. bombing of Baghdad live for CNN at the start of the Persian Gulf War. Arnett managed to stay in Baghdad, after other western correspondents left or were ejected by the Iraqi government, by hiding behind a locked door in his hotel room and not taking shelter during air raids. For a month and a half, he reported to the world what was happening in Baghdad through his regular CNN broadcasts, including an exclusive interview with Saddam Hussein.

On June 7, 1998 Arnett was correspondent for a CNN report for a magazine program, *NewsStand: CNN and Time,* alleging that sarin nerve gas was used by U.S. military forces on American defectors in Laos in 1970. Arnett also co-authored an article for *Time* magazine entitled "Did the U.S. Drop Nerve Gas?" The allegations that nerve gas was used and also that the mission's purpose was to kill American defectors in that story, referred to as "Tailwind," were disputed by a number of military sources. CNN conducted a follow-up investigation into their story and subsequently, both the network and *Time* magazine retracted and apologized for their reports. Arnett received a reprimand from the network. The process by which the CNN story was constructed was carefully examined by the national news media, particularly the American newspaper press, and also came under fire. *See also* CNN (Cable News Network). *Kim A. Smith*

Further Reading

Arnett, Peter. *Live from the Battlefield.* New York: Simon and Schuster, 1994.

Hohenberg, John. *The Pulitzer Prize Story II, 1959–1980.* New York, Columbia University Press, 1980.

Isaacson, Walter. "Tailwind: An Apology," *Time,* 13 July, 1998, 6.

Prochnan, William. "If There's A War, He's There," *New York Times Magazine,* 3 March, 1991, 30–34.

Thomas, Evan and Vistica, Gregory L., "What's the Truth About Tailwind?" *Newsweek,* 22 June 1998, 32.

Dr. Robert Arnot

Dr. Robert "Bob" Arnot has been the chief medical correspondent for both CBS and NBC News, as well as a best-selling author of several health and fitness books. He has covered such stories as the medical aspects of the Persian Gulf War and starvation in Rwanda, where he contracted cholera.

Dr. Arnot was born in 1948. He graduated from Dartmouth College in 1972 with a bachelor of medical science degree. In 1974, he obtained his M.D. from McGill University in Montreal. He was an emergency room physician from 1976 to 1984. From 1977 to 1980, he was the physician to the United States Ski Team and at the Winter Olympics in Lake Placid. In 1980, Arnot became the national medical director for the National Emergency Service, a capacity in which he was responsible for education and quality enhancement for more than 2,500 doctors in 116 hospitals across the country.

Arnot was hired as a medical reporter for CBS News in 1982 as part of the trend of networks to hire medical experts as health correspondents. He began reporting for *CBS This Morning* in 1987. In 1993, he was named the health and medical correspondent for *The CBS Evening News* and later assumed the same position at NBC, reporting for *Dateline NBC.* His books include *Dr. Bob Arnot's Guide to Turning Back the Clock.* *See also* Dateline NBC. *Derek Moore*

Further Reading

Aumente, Jerome. "A Medical Breakthrough." *American Journalism Review*, December, 1995, 27–32.

Williams, Scott. "Rwanda Brings Grief to Medical Reporter. *St. Louis Post-Dispatch*, 26 August, 1994, 10F.

B

Sherlee Barish

Sherlee Barish started the first executive placement firm for broadcast news positions in 1960. For more than 30 years, until her death at age 69 in 1996, she was among the most important talent brokers in the television news industry. First, as broadcast news' most prominent professional headhunter, Barish placed on-air talent, news directors, general managers and other executives at local television stations around the country. Barish's fee for the service, paid by the employer, generally was 20 percent of the new hire's annual salary.

Born in 1927, Barish was educated in the South. A graduate of Florida State College for Women, she acted with the Norton Gallery Theatre Group in the 1940s before securing her first broadcasting position in 1950 as a receptionist, earning $35 a week at a radio station. Then, she worked in television syndication before opening Broadcast Personnel Agency in 1960. Barish switched gears after about a dozen years and became a talent agent. She had been reluctant at first to work as an agent because it meant taking money from friends, but when the business slowed, Barish found it necessary to create her personnel management talent agency, Sherlee Barish & Associates, specializing in television news talent.

She became an important agent for on-air talent. In a 1977 page-one profile of Barish in the *Wall Street Journal,* an anonymous executive made disparaging remarks about the nature of the talent agency trade but conceded that Barish performed her job well. Barish herself said that part of her position was to smooth the feathers of disgruntled prima donnas. She operated her business mostly by telephone, first from an office in New York City, then later in Milford, Pennsylvania, before finally relocating to Sarasota, Florida, in 1992.

Barish described in the *Wall Street Journal* how she spent her workday maintaining contacts with news people and television executives, then passed her evenings viewing the more than 1,000 demo videotapes sent to her annually. Barish said it was her job to find what the television stations were looking for: "...a twenty-five-year old with ten years of experience." After her death, a fellowship to help young television reporters improve their skills was established in her memory by the Radio-Television News Directors Foundation, part of an organization that Barish had been active in throughout her career.

Agnes Hooper Gottlieb

Further Reading
Cooney, John E. "For a TV Newsman, The Key to Success Can Be a Phone Call." *Wall Street Journal.* 15 February 1977, 1.

Hickey, Neil. "She Knows Where the Bodies Are." *TV Guide*, 1 February 1975, 20–22.

Prato, Lou. "Remembering Sherlee." *The Communicator*, June 1996, 19.

"Sherlee Barish." Obituary. *The Palm Beach Post*, 5 May 1996, 1B.

Roberta Baskin

Head of the investigative unit of the CBS News program *48 Hours*, Roberta Baskin has an extensive background in investigative reporting. Born on January 16, 1952, in New York, she served as director of consumer affairs for the city of Syracuse before beginning her broadcast career. She served as a consumer reporter for WMAQ-TV in Chicago and later was investigative reporter for WLS-TV, also in Chicago. She held the same position at WJLA-TV in Washington, D.C., and went on to become chief investigative correspondent for the syndicated program *Now It Can Be Told.*

Baskin joined CBS News in April 1992 as a Washington correspondent, then moved to *Street Stories* in July of that same year. She reported bus accidents staged by the Department of Insurance in New Jersey to demonstrate how fraudulent claims could be made and also uncovered product reliability problems, such as faulty automobile seat belt design. Using industry files, she demonstrated that center-button seat belt buckles released when subjected to severe jolts. Baskin and the father of a teenager killed in a vehicle equipped with such buckles demonstrated for viewers how the seat belts can fail. They tested the belts in the car that had been in the fatal collision, showing how the accident may have taken place. Automobile industry spokepersons reacted by placing an advertisement in the *New York Times*, which responded to this.

Baskin has received every major award for broadcast journalism excellence, including 11 Emmy Awards, an Investigative Reporters and Editors Award, and the Edward R. Murrow Award. Her husband, James Trengrove, is a senior producer for the *NewsHour with Jim Lehrer.*

Michael D. Murray

Further Reading
"CBS Buckles Down over Seat Belts." *Washington Journalism Review*, January/February 1993, 13.
Lissit, Robert. "Gotcha!" *American Journalism Review,* March 1995, 17–21.
Murray, Michael D. *The Political Performers: CBS Broadcasts in the Public Interest.* Westport, CT: Praeger Publishers, 1994.

Burton Benjamin

Burton Benjamin is known in television journalism as a documentary producer, a CBS News vice president, and author of *Fair Play*, chronicling CBS's handling of a controversial program on General William C. Westmoreland. Born on October 9, 1917, in Cleveland Ohio, Benjamin earned a bachelor of arts degree from the University of Michigan. He worked for United Press and the Newspaper Enterprise Association in the 1940s. He served in the Coast Guard during World War II.

Benjamin became a television writer in 1955 and later executive producer of a number of major CBS News series including *The Twentieth Century* and *You Are There*. He was senior executive producer of the *CBS Evening News* from 1968 to 1975, and again from 1981 until his retirement in 1985. His many distinguished awards include eight Emmys, including one for producing *Solzhenitsyn* in 1974. He also received a Peabody, two Ohio State University Awards, and the American Bar Association's Silver Gavel Award. Benjamin also taught at Manhattanville College in New York, served as a trustee for the Scarborough School, Scarborough, New York, and upon retirement from CBS, became senior fellow at Columbia University's Freedom Forum Media Studies Center. He died in 1988 at the age of 70 at his home in Scarborough. *See also* CBS News.

Donald Jung

Further Reading
Benjamin, Burton. *Fair Play: CBS, General Westmoreland, and How a Television Documentary Went Wrong.* New York: Harper and Row, 1988.
Corry, John. "Weighing the Facts in Westmoreland vs. CBS." *New York Times*, 4 September 1983, B19.
"Westmoreland Takes on CBS." *Newsweek*, 22 October 1984, 60–64.

Jules Bergman

Jules Bergman covered the science and space beat for ABC from 1955 until his death in 1987. Whether covering the first space mission or the first heart transplant, Bergman combined research and on-the-scene reporting to bring a clear picture to television viewers. He said his goal was to make the complicated simple for the viewer.

Born in New York City on March 21, 1929, Jules Verne Bergman (named after science-fiction writer Jules Verne, reportedly a tenth cousin) attended City College of New York, Indiana University, and Columbia University. Bergman was a medical student when his father died; young Jules quit school so his brother could finish, saying they both would not otherwise make it. His love of science and medicine never diminished. Bergman's career as a journalist began with a stint as a copy boy and news desk assistant at CBS in New York City in 1947. He went from CBS to *Time* magazine, then joined WFDR Radio in New York as news director. Bergman joined the ABC radio/television network in 1953, moving from junior reporter to senior reporter in two years. In 1960, Bergman received a prestigious Sloan-Rockefeller Advanced Science Writing Fellowship at Columbia University, where he specialized in space reporting. After he returned, Bergman was named ABC science editor.

While covering Project Mercury, Bergman became known for "method reporting." While some journalists simply reported on the tests the astronauts were undergoing, Bergman participated. During astronaut selection, Bergman took the same NASA qualification tests; during Mercury flights, Bergman would allow himself to be strapped into a harness similar to the one used by the astronaut. Bergman was also tenacious in his reporting. He told *Newsweek* in 1962 that covering the space beat was a high-pressure job, claiming that he felt more stress when on the air than the guy in the capsule. At the time of his death in 1987, Bergman had covered all 54 manned space flights in the United States; of these, the Apollo 13 explosion was said to be his most exciting space story.

Jules Bergman also loved to fly, and his experience as a pilot led to two books on aviation, *Ninety Seconds to Space: The F-15 Story* (Doubleday 1960) and *Anyone Can Fly* (Doubleday 1964); Bergman also produced an Emmy-nominated program on airplane safety, "Crashes: The Illusion of Safety," in 1975. During

his career, Bergman covered the first flight of almost every new U.S. military and commercial aircraft, as well as major airline disasters in the world. Bergman also covered major medical news, including the surgeon general's report on smoking, and the radiation-emitting accident at Three Mile Island. In the 1970s, Bergman turned to the production of documentaries for ABC News. "Fire," a 1975 program, won an Emmy Award; others included "Earthquake" in 1972; "What About Tomorrow?" a six-part series in 1973, and "Asbestos: The Way to Dusty Death" in 1979. Jules Bergman was found dead of natural causes in his New York City apartment on Febuary 12, 1987. *See also* Space Coverage.   *Ginger Rudeseal Carter*

Further Reading
"Jules Bergman." Obituary, *Chicago Tribune*, 14 February 1987, C-14.
"The Interpreters and The Golden Throats." *Newsweek*. 8 October 1962, 101.

Tom Bettag

Tom Bettag was born in Evansville, Indiana, in 1944, earned a bachelor of arts in history from the University of Notre Dame in 1966, and a master of science from the Columbia University Graduate School of Journalism in 1967. After graduating from Columbia, he spent a year as an assistant to Fred Friendly, a former CBS News president who was then teaching at the university and hosting programs for the Public Broadcasting Service. Bettag followed in his mentor's footsteps and, in the process, made a number of key contributions to the field of television news, not the least of which is his work with Ted Koppel on *Nightline*.

Bettag has built a reputation as a solid producer who goes out of his way to make the jobs of his reporters and anchors easier. Within the news business, he is also known for his ability to inspire the team around him and to keep a low profile in a very high-pressure job. His first position at CBS News was as an assignment editor in Washington, D.C., in 1969. In 1977, he spent a sabbatical year in Japan as a Fulbright scholar. Over a 20-year span, he held various posts at CBS, including senior broadcast producer for the *CBS Evening*

News and producer for both *60 Minutes* and *CBS Sunday Morning*. He also played key roles in the network's political coverage and the 1980 and 1984 presidential campaigns.

In the years before he joined CBS News, Bettag worked as a news writer for WNEW-TV in New York City and reported for the *Grand Rapids Press* and the *Saginaw News* in Michigan.

Tom Bettag's work is viewed in households across the country. As executive producer of *Nightline* on ABC, Bettag has been in charge of one of the most important programs in network history since 1991. Working closely with anchor Ted Koppel, he has made *Nightline* an authoritative source of hard-hitting and in-depth news. Bettag arrived at ABC after working as executive producer of the *CBS Evening News with Dan Rather* from 1986 to 1991. At the time, *Nightline* was over 10 years old but on shaky footing. ABC News president Roone Arledge tapped the mild-mannered producer to bring in an outsider's perspective to the program. Bettag proceeded to make big changes, including a new focus on investigative reporting; town-meeting broadcasts on special issues often broadcast from university locales; and short documentaries focusing on special topics. As a result, *Nightline* is now a must-see for anyone interested in serious television news.

Among Bettag's many awards are over a dozen Emmys, two Peabodys, six Alfred I. duPont-Columbia University Silver Batons, and three Overseas Press Club Awards. *See also* CBS News. *Sreenath Sreenivasan*

Further Reading

Gunther, Marc. "Koppel takes High Road to Late-Night Success." St. Louis Post-Dispatch, 6 December 1993, D6.
Johnson, Peter. "Bettag: Secret Weapon at *Nightline*." *USA Today*, November 1995, C-3.
Koppel, Ted, and Kyle Gibson. *Nightline*: *History in the Making of Television*. New York: Times Books, 1996.

Jim Bittermann

Jim Bittermann has worked as a network correspondent in Europe for 20 years for three major network news operations, one of the longest tenures of any postwar television correspondent. Bittermann has covered most of the major stories in Europe including wars, presidential campaigns, and natural disasters, but is best known for his witty and perceptive features that have portrayed European life to American television viewers. Since 1996, Bittermann has been a CNN correspondent in Paris and a contributor to National Public Radio (NPR). In 1997, he was the lead CNN correspondent in the hours immediately after the death of Diana, Princess of Wales, when CNN had some of its largest audiences ever.

Bittermann began his network career in 1978 as an NBC correspondent assigned to Rome, then Paris. There he received a National News Emmy for his coverage of the 1988 Sudan famine. From 1990 to 1996, he was a Paris-based correspondent for ABC. Before joining the networks, Bittermann was a correspondent for the Canadian Broadcasting Corporation's *News Magazine* and a television reporter in Cleveland, Pittsburgh, and Milwaukee. He also was a staff aide on two Democratic presidential campaigns and a newspaper reporter in Waukegan, Illinois.

Bittermann was born in 1947 and is a 1969 graduate of Southern Illinois University in Carbondale. His wife, Pat Thompson, is an independent producer and program maker who was a longtime producer for both ABC and NBC News in Paris. Early in their careers, Bittermann and Thompson worked as a correspondent/producer team covering stories throughout Europe. *See also* CNN (Cable News Network). *Joe S. Foote*

Further Reading

Bittermann, Jim. "The Best of Times." In *Live from the Trenches: The Changing Role of Television Correspondents,* edited by Joe S. Foote, Carbondale, IL: Southern Illinois Press, 1998.
Smyth, Jeff. "As Network News Cuts Back, Technology Offers Other Opportunities." *St. Louis Journalism Review*, May 1996, 13.

Blacklisting

Witch-hunts for communists officially began on October 20, 1947, when a subcommittee of the House Un-American Activities Committee (HUAC) of the U.S. Congress investigated charges that Communist Party members had infiltrated the movie industry and were using films to disseminate propaganda. The HUAC hearings lead to the conviction of 10 Hollywood writers, producers, and directors who refused to answer the committee's questions about their alleged Communist Party affiliation. These "unfriendly" witnesses—Alvah Bessie, Herbert Biberman, Lester Cole, Edward Dmytryk, Ring Lardner Jr., John Howard Lawson, Albert Maltz, Samuel Ornitz, Adrian Scott, and Dalton Trumbo—became known as the Hollywood 10. They served prison sentences for contempt and were blacklisted (designated unhirable) by motion picture executives, who feared that if they took no action, the government would take control and censor the industry.

The political climate of the motion picture industry changed with the HUAC hearings. When individuals were asked to testify, either in public or secretly, they were required not only to admit to their own questionable or subversive activities but also to provide the names of colleagues whose behavior may have been suspect. Those who did not testify were blacklisted and could no longer find work. The HUAC hearings set the red-baiting style and tone for Senator Joseph McCarthy's hunt for communist infiltration of the U.S. government, and institutionalized a movement against dissent.

The House and Senate committees investigating the alleged infiltration of communists in the movie industry also scrutinized television, and formalized blacklisting began with the June 1950 publication of *Red Channels, the Report of Communist Influence in Radio and Television*. Issued by American Business Consultants, who published *Counterattack, the Newsletter of Facts on Communism*, the special report listed 151 prominent individuals the editors claimed had past or present ties to "communist causes." Organizations were deemed subversive based on the judgment of the United States Attorney General, HUAC, and other sources.

Actors Jose Ferrer, Judy Holliday, Henry Morgan, and Edward G. Robinson; commentators William Shirer and Howard K. Smith; musicians Leonard Bernstein, Burl Ives, and Lena Horne; and writers Lillian Hellman, Arthur Miller, and Dorothy Parker were just a few of those included in the pamphlet. Although the editors of *Red Channels* did not claim that everyone listed was a communist, they believed that each person included had done something questionable and should be required to prove his or her anti-communism. To clarify its position, *Red Channels* appropriated a quote from *Broadcasting Magazine*: "Where there's red smoke there's usually Communist fire."

Soon known as "the bible of Madison Avenue," network executives, radio-television packagers and sponsors, as well as advertising agencies relied on *Red Channels* and accepted *Counterattack's* standards. Vincent Hartnett, who wrote the introduction to *Red Channels*, offered background checks and kept updated mimeographed lists of blacklisted individuals, titled *Confidential Notebook*, that he sold for $5 a copy. Launching his own "talent consultant" business, AWARE Inc., Hartnett charged his clients about $20 for each thorough background check.

Despite efforts by the American Civil Liberties Union and others to protect free speech, and although, by 1952, political screening was almost universally practiced in the television and film industry, an elaborate blacklisting machinery was in order. Conservative and right-wing groups, including the American Legion and the Veterans Action Committee of Syracuse Supermarkets, run by Laurence Johnson, compiled their own lists. Many people, previously not listed in *Red Channels*, now found that they were "in trouble."

Newspaper columnists, including Walter Winchell and Westbrook Pegler, encouraged the blacklisting frenzy as they vied to expose "commies" and "pinkos." Actors, commentators, directors, producers, singers, and writers who had been listed in *Red Channels*, cited in *Counterattack*, or otherwise charged with communist sympathies soon found it virtually impossible to get work without prior clearance. Clearance involved a lengthy and difficult process of convincing those responsible for an individual's blacklisting that the person had been wrongly listed. Persons charged were required to clear themselves in such a way as to reassure employers that they would not run into difficulty if they hired those individuals. It was imperative that a worker who wished to be cleared provide evidence that he or she was not a communist or communist sympathizer, and in many cases, the person had to show that he or she was "actively" anti-communist.

For a fee, "public relations experts" assisted with the clearance process. They arranged an FBI interview in which the blacklisted individual answered questions and declared his or her patriotism. The clearance expert helped determine where the client was blacklisted and who outside the television industry was damaging their reputation. The process often involved multiple confessions during emotional meetings, after which, if successful, the individual was then considered employable. Some blacklisted writers attempted to sell their scripts under false names. Yet, even when they succeeded, they often paid most of their earnings to "fronts" who represented themselves as the authors.

Television and motion picture blacklistings shattered thousands of lives and destroyed hundreds of careers. For more than 10 years, many writers, singers, producers, directors, commentators, actors, and radio and television journalists faced prison terms and were denied the right to earn a living. Broadcaster John Henry Faulk's libel suit against AWARE, Hartnett, and Johnson, helped end blacklisting. In 1957 Faulk was fired by WCBS after he was accused of being a communist. Following a lengthy court battle, in 1962 Faulk was awarded more than $1 million in damages. Although on appeal the award was reduced to $550,000 the judgment exposed the blacklisting system and began to vindicate those individuals who had been blacklisted by the industry. *See also* Army-McCarthy Hearings.

Bonnie Brennen

Further Reading

Belfrage, Cedric. *The American Inquisition 1945–1960*. Indianapolis: Bobbs-Merrill, 1973.
Caute, David. *The Great Fear: The Anti-Communist Purge under Truman and Eisenhower*. New York: Simon & Schuster, 1978.
Cogley, John. *Report on Blacklisting: Radio-Television*. New York: Fund for the Republic, 1956.
Fariello, Griffin. *Red Scare, Memories of the American Inquisition: An Oral History*. New York: Norton, 1995.
Faulk, John Henry. *Fear on Trial*. New York. Simon & Schuster, 1964.
Miller, Merle. *The Judges and the Judged*. Garden City, NY: Doubleday, 1952.

Edward Bliss Jr.

Photo courtesy of Edward Bliss Jr.

Edward Bliss Jr. was a leading writer and editor for two of television's most highly respected figures, Edward R. Murrow and Walter Cronkite. He also edited the anthology of Murrow's broadcasts and wrote widely on his unique contributions in the field of broadcast news. As a writer, Bliss offered insights into some of the historic programs and personalities with whom he had direct involvement. Later, he had a distinguished career in education as the founder of the broadcast journalism program at American University in Washington, D.C.

Bliss was born on July 30, 1912, in Fuzhou, China, where his parents worked as missionaries. He was raised in Massachusetts where he attended the Northfield–Mount Hermon School and edited the school newspaper. He intended to become a physician like his father but discovered that he did not take to the necessary subjects. He received a bachelor of art degree from Yale University in 1935. After college, he sought a newspaper job and found one in Bucyrus, Ohio, the county seat for Crawford County, where he was able to master a wide variety of skills under the tutelage of Rowland R. Peters, who had been a reporter for the *Chicago Tribune*. He stayed at the small-town newspaper a year, then moved to Columbus, where he was on the staff of the Scripps-Howard paper for seven years. In 1943 he departed for New York and CBS Radio.

Bliss started as a writer and, after three years was promoted to editor. He was recruited in October 1955 to write, edit, and produce radio programs for Murrow, a position he held for five years. He became known as Murrow's "hard news" writer, distinct from Murrow's "think pieces." Bliss was never involved with the lighter side of Murrow's work, such as the celebrity interview program, *Person to Person*. At one time, Bliss considered making on-air contributions himself, and he began with a short segment for the *News of America* program, but did not feel comfortable in that role. When Murrow left to direct the U.S. Information Agency, Bliss joined Fred Friendly briefly as a producer then became assistant to Richard Salant, the CBS News president.

Salant graduated from Harvard University in 1935; Bliss finished Yale that same year, and the two often joked about their backgrounds. Bliss's duties consisted of fact checking, responding to various requests for information regarding news, and special events coverage. He was once assigned to produce a half-hour editorial-documentary for CBS president Frank Stanton on the topic of the "Rayburn Rule," an effort by Speaker Sam Rayburn to keep television cameras out of the House of Representatives. Entitled "For Our Own Open House," it aired in 1962. The program was canceled by William S. Paley because of unhappiness on the part of some affiliates, particularly in the south, where CBS coverage of the civil rights movement had begun to create tension. With his strong ties to Murrow, Bliss was sometimes called upon to comment on issues related to broadcast performance and public interest concerns.

Shortly after joining the Kennedy administration, Murrow died. His widow, Janet Brewster Murrow, asked Bliss to edit the work of her late husband. The result was *In Search of Light: The Broadcasts of Edward R. Murrow*. This book contains many of the historic broadcasts from the popular *This Is London* and *Hear It Now* radio series.

Over a half century, Bliss has written on many of the historic figures with whom he worked, but especially Murrow. He has lectured on Murrow's influence on the profession and his disappointment with the way broadcasters were becoming responsive to advertiser concerns. Bliss viewed Murrow as a trailblazer and setter of high standards for broadcast news.

When CBS News in 1963 decided to initiate the first regular half-hour evening newscast with Walter Cronkite, Bliss was selected as editor. He was involved in all of the major stories of that era, including the assassination of John F. Kennedy. Bliss left CBS to start the broadcast journalism program at American University in February 1968 and was able to get the school to allow his students to prepare and air three newscasts a day on the university's FM station. They also did a magazine show on Sunday. Former students include Bob Edwards of National Public Radio, Deborah Potter of the Cable News Network, and ABC-TV's chief congressional correspondent Jackie Judd. Also, in addition to having written a best-selling broadcasting textbook with CBS veteran John Patterson, *Writing News for Broadcast*, Bliss has written a wide variety of articles for both the popular and trade press, including *Television Quarterly* and *Communicator,* on the importance of writing well.

Bliss wrote the first comprehensive history of broadcast journalism, *Now the News*. He also served as a judge for National Emmy Awards and the annual competition of the Walter Cronkite Scholarship for the National Academy of Television Arts and Sciences' Midwestern Chapter. He retired from teaching in June 1977. Bliss received the Paul White Award from the Radio-Television News Directors Association on October 2, 1993, in Miami Beach. *See also* CBS News, Walter Cronkite.   *Ellen E. Murray*

Further Reading

Bliss, Edward, Jr. "Battle Hymns and Autumn Wonders." *Washington Journalism Review*, February 1985, 43–45.

Bliss, Edward, Jr. *In Search of Light: The Broadcasts of Edward R. Murrow.* New York: Alfred A. Knopf, 1967.

Bliss, Edward, Jr. *Now the News: The Story of Broadcast Journalism.* New York: Columbia University Press, 1991.

Wolf Blitzer

Courtesy Cable News Network, Inc.
© 1994, Photo by George Bennett

Wolf Blitzer is one of Cable News Network's first correspondents to achieve national prominence without the benefit of any network broadcast experience. He became familiar to millions of Americans during the Persian Gulf War. Blitzer was born in 1948 in Augsburg, Germany, and raised in Buffalo, New York. In 1970, he received a bachelor of arts degree in history from the State University of New York at Buffalo and, in 1972, a master's degree in international journalism from the School of Advanced International Studies at Johns Hopkins University. After graduating, Blitzer went to work for the Reuters News Service in Tel Aviv, Israel, and later for the *Jerusalem Post* as the Washington correspondent.

In 1982, Blitzer made guest appearances on CNN and other networks as an expert on the Middle East, and in May 1990, he became a full-time correspondent for CNN at the Pentagon. In August 1991, Blitzer was sent to Moscow to report on the failed coup attempt and then spent nearly a month there reporting on the Soviet military. He became immersed in Soviet affairs and was one of the first western reporters invited into the KGB headquarters to see their intelligence operations. In a 10-part series for CNN, he reported on the transition of power between Mikhail Gorbachev and Boris Yeltsin and on the state of the Soviet military.

Blitzer began covering the Pentagon two months before war broke out between Iraq and Kuwait. He gave as many as 12 live reports a day during the conflict. CNN received a Golden Cable ACE Award in 1991 for its Gulf War coverage. In November 1992, Blitzer was named CNN's senior White House correspondent. Blitzer was honored in 1994 by the *American Journalism Review* with a "Best in the Business Award," for his reports on the White House. In 1996, Blitzer won an Emmy for his coverage of the Oklahoma City bombing.

Blitzer has also written two books—*Between Washington and Jerusalem: A Reporter's Notebook* (1985), based on his observations of U.S.-Israeli relations, and *Territory of Lies* about the Jonathan Pollard spy case. It was selected by the *New York Times Book Review* as one of the most notable books of 1989. In addition, Blitzer has hosted *Inside Politics Weekend* and currently hosts CNN's *Late Edition. See also* Cable News Network, Persian Gulf War.   *William R. Davie*

Further Reading

Blitzer, Wolf. *Between Washington and Jerusalem: A Reporter's Notebook.* New York: Oxford University Press, 1985.

Blitzer, Wolf. *Territory of Lies: The Exclusive Story of Jonathan Jay Pollard, The American Who Spied on His Country for Israel and How He Was Betrayed.* New York: Harper, 1989.

"Stalking the Pentagon," *New York* 11 February 1991.

Michael Bloomberg

Michael Bloomberg is a leader in the field of business information. His company, Bloomberg Financial Markets, provides a number of information services, including Bloomberg Information Television. He was born in 1942 and raised in Medford, Massachusetts. He earned an undergraduate degree from Johns Hopkins University and a masters of business administration from Harvard in 1966. Following graduate school, Bloomberg held several positions, including a clerk in the trading room, a bond trader, then a partner, before joining the investment firm Salomon Brothers. He began there as a trading clerk and eventually became the head of equity trading. He was regularly promoted and eventually named head of equity trading. Disagreements with the board of directors of Salomon Brothers over what he regarded as excesses in hiring practices, accounting practices, and executive perks led to his ouster in 1981.

With his $10 million severance package, Bloomberg started his own company. He recognized the financial community needed better information services, and in 1982 began selling computer terminals, both specialized networks and financial information providers that enable traders and stockbrokers to quickly check prices and manage financial data. By 1997, over 75,000 Bloomberg terminals were in use, generating over $1 billion in revenue. Bloomberg's company publishes *Bloomberg Magazine* (a supplement to U.S. newspapers), owns Bloomberg Information Radio, and produces Bloomberg Information TV and several weekly syndicated radio news programs. Bloomberg Business News is syndicated on radio, and Bloomberg Business Television is cablecast by satellite 24 hours a day.   *Alan B. Albarran*

Further Reading
Bloomberg, Michael. *Bloomberg on Bloomberg.* New York: John Wiley, 1997.
"The World of News According to Bloomberg." *Broadcasting & Cable,* 16 August 1996, 57.

Ken Bode

A nationally prominent broadcast journalist and political analyst, Ken Bode has managed to have both an academic and a professional career at the same time. He has been a correspondent, political analyst, and moderator for CNN and PBS and has served as the director of the Center for Contemporary Media at DePauw University. Bode received his undergraduate degree from the University of South Dakota in 1961 and his masters from the University of North Carolina in 1963. After earning a doctorate in political science from the University of North Carolina in 1966, Bode taught at

Michigan State University from 1965 to 1968 and at the State University of New York in Binghamton in 1968 and 1969. From June 1969 to April 1970 he was Research Director for the National Democratic Party and served in 1970 as a legislative assistant to a fellow South Dakotan, Senator George McGovern.

Bode was born in Chicago, Illinois, on March 30, 1939. He began his journalism career in 1975 as a political editor for the *New Republic.* In 1979, he was hired as a political correspondent for NBC News, and for 10 years appeared on the *Today Show* with "Bode's Journal," a regular feature. He reported for *Nightly News,* appeared on *Meet the Press,* and was a floor reporter at the national political conventions in the 1980s. During this period, Bode maintained his ties with academia with postdoctoral fellowships at Princeton and Yale.

Bode's work as a political correspondent involved traveling up to 200 days a year, and this prompted his decision in 1988 not to renew his contract with NBC News. He wanted to get completely out of the network news routine, and he decided to return to university life, joining DePauw University. However, his absence from network news was short lived. Three months after his arrival to DePauw University in Greencastle, Indiana, CNN hired him to do monthly reports from his midwestern base. Bode joined CNN's documentary unit and won awards for "S&L: The Full Story" (1990) and "Return to Wounded Knee" (1991) and contributed to the political series, *Democracy in America,* with "The Public Mind of George Bush" (1992) and "Bill Clinton of Arkansas" (1992).

In 1994, Bode succeeded Paul Duke in 1994 as the moderator of the PBS political talk program *Washington Week in Review,* enlivening its format by introducing videotaped segments, satellite interviews, and roundtable discussions. He insisted on placing more women on the program and took pride in the show's agenda, steering clear of sensational topics. Bode freelances and reviews for a wide variety of publications including the *Journal of Politics,* the *New York Times,* the *Washington Post, Columbia Journalism Review, Political Science Quarterly,* and the *Washington Monthly.* In

1997, he was selected as the new dean of the Medill School of Journalism at Northwestern University.   *William R. Davie*

Further Reading

Bode, Ken. "Getting on Daddy Track." *Parents,* October 1990, 239, 244.

Bode, Ken. "Political Booknotes." *Washington Monthly*, November 1994, 55.

Kurtz, Howard. *Hot Air*. New York: Random House, 1996.

Ed Bradley

Ed Bradley is a member of an elite group of CBS News professionals who have mastered a variety of duties and who have been honored on many occasions for their abilities. He has worked as a CBS White House correspondent, an anchor for the *CBS Sunday Night News*, a principal correspondent for the *CBS Reports* documentary series, and is currently co-editor and correspondent for *60 Minutes*.

Born on June 22, 1941, Bradley is a former sixth-grade mathematics teacher, who earned a bachelor of science degree in education in 1962 from Cheyney State College in Pennsylvania. From 1963 until 1967, he worked as a reporter at WDAS Radio in Philadelphia, then joined WCBS Radio in New York, a position he held until 1971. He moved to CBS as a stringer for the Paris bureau and a year later was assigned first as a network stringer, to Saigon. Bradley became a CBS correspondent in April 1973 and was wounded while on assignment in Cambodia. He was working at the CBS Washington bureau in 1974 when he volunteered to return to the Far East to cover the fall of the Vietnamese and Cambodian capitals to the communists. He was one of the last American correspondents evacuated when the Khmer Rouge captured Phnom Penh in 1975. He subsequently received a George Polk Memorial Award and a duPont-Columbia citation.

In 1976, soon after his return to the United States in 1976, Bradley was assigned as one of three CBS White House correspondents. In the same year, he was named to succeed Morton Dean as anchor of the *CBS Sunday Night News* show. Bradley handled the White House duties until he became principal correspondent for *CBS Reports* in 1978. He received a number of awards for his *CBS Reports* documentary, "The Boat People." Telecast on January 19, 1979, viewers saw Bradley plunge into the South China Sea off Malaysia to rescue a boatload of Vietnamese refugees. The "Boat People" program received a commendation at the International Festival of the British Academy of Film and Television Arts, and it earned Bradley an Emmy, an Alfred I. duPont–Columbia University Award, and the Overseas Press Club's Edward R. Murrow Award.

Many believe Bradley's most distinguished work for *CBS Reports* was the 1979 program "Blacks in America: With All Deliberate Speed," a two-hour examination of progress made by African Americans since 1954, when the U.S. Supreme Court outlawed discrimination in public schools. Widely covered by the press, this program generated discussion and debate and earned Bradley his second Emmy and duPont-Columbia awards.

When Dan Rather left *60 Minutes* to become the anchor for the *CBS Evening News* in 1981, Bradley was named as his successor. During his first year at *60 Minutes,* he logged about 100,000 miles while traveling on assignment, visited more then 45 cities, and conducted numerous interviews while investigating leads. Bradley's reports on *60 Minutes* have earned him several awards. Three of his *60 Minutes* segments have won Emmy Awards: "Lena," a profile of Lena Horne in which the two strolled hand-in-hand through Central Park, "In the Belly of the Beast," an interview with convicted murderer and author Jack Henry Abbott; and "Schizophrenia," a 1985 report on the puzzling brain disorder that leaves many of its victims out of touch with reality. *See also 60 Minutes.*

Patricia Holmes

Further Reading

Brady, James. "In Step with Ed Bradley." *Parade Magazine*, 24 March 1996, 22.

Campbell, Richard. *60 Minutes and the News: A Mythology for Middle America*. Urbana: University of Illinois Press, 1991.

Johnson, Peter. "No. 1 Show Keeps Ticking after 25 Years." *USA Today*, 12 November 1993, 1.

Rita Braver

Rita Braver joined the Washington bureau of CBS News as a clerk on the news desk in 1972. Since that time, she has had a variety of assignments including chief White House correspondent, responsible for coverage of the Clinton administration, a position she landed when Susan Spencer left to do "Eye on America" segments for the *CBS Evening News*, in September of 1993.

Braver was born in Washington, D.C., on April 12, 1948. She graduated from the University of Wisconsin–Madison in 1970 and began broadcasting at the CBS affiliate station in New Orleans, WWL-TV, that same year. At CBS, she has been a program producer and editor, as well as a reporter. She served as a CBS News law correspondent, covering the Justice Department, the Supreme Court, and, the Federal Bureau of Investigation. She led the CBS network's coverage of the Iran-Contra investigation and Washington, D.C., mayor Marion Barry stories, and broke stories on the Jonathan Pollard spy case and the Walker family spy ring. In a 1986 story about investigative reporting, Braver was credited with always being first on the trail of important stories.

As chief White House correspondent, Braver covered the 1996 presidential race, traveling extensively in order to cover President Clinton's trips to Asia, Australia, Europe, Mexico, and the Middle East. She and her husband, prominent attorney Robert Barnett, live in the nation's capital. When her assignment to the White House beat was announced, Braver's husband said he would no longer do legal work for President Clinton.

Michael D. Murray

Further Reading

"Bylines." *American Journalism Review,* September 1993, 12.

Matusow, Barbara. "NBC's Intrepid Investgators: Brian Ross and Ira Silverman." *Washington Journalism Review,* June 1986, 22.

David Brinkley

For more than 50 years, David Brinkley has delivered news and political information to millions of Americans. A native of Wilmington, North Caro-

Courtesy ABC, Inc.

lina, Brinkley started writing while a high school student, for his hometown newspaper, the *Wilmington Morning Star*. He attended Vanderbilt University, then worked for United Press International after his World War II service.

Born on July 10, 1920, Brinkley began his broadcasting career in 1943 as a White House correspondent for NBC News. In 1956, Brinkley was teamed with Chet Huntley to cover the presidential nominating conventions. As a result of the excellent ratings because of their work, NBC developed *The Huntley-Brinkley Report*. This news program ushered in the modern era of television news reporting, in which the production alternated between two co-anchors, Huntley in New York City and Brinkley in Washington, D.C. Their show was hugely successful, as indicated by a 1965 consumer research survey. Huntley and Brinkley had become more recognizable than Cary Grant, James Stewart, and the Beatles. *The Huntley-Brinkley Report* aired for nearly 15 years and was one of the longest running news programs in television history.

Brinkley covered every U.S. president since Franklin Roosevelt and every presidential party convention since 1956. Huntley retired in 1970 and died in 1974 of cancer. Brinkley shared anchor chores briefly with John Chancellor and Frank McGee. He did the nightly commentary, then returned as coanchor in 1976. In 1981, Brinkley joined ABC News as the anchor of the Sunday morning program *This Week with David Brinkley,* which became the leading Sunday morning news program—due to its inventiveness, dynamic format, and popular anchor. In 1988, the *Washington Journalism Review* named *This Week with David Brinkley* the "Best Weekend Network Television Talk Show," and in 1988, the program won the George Foster Peabody Award.

Throughout his career, Brinkley has interviewed many of the world's prominent political leaders. Two notable Brinkley reports are: "Ronald Reagan: A Farewell Interview," which captured Reagan's reflections on his presidency; and the 1994 story of the impact of World War II on small-town America for ABC's *Prime Time Live*, which won Brinkley his third Peabody Award. Brinkley has won 10 Emmy Awards, the 1995 Museum of Television and Radio Lifetime Achievement Award, and the Radio-Television News Directors Association's Paul White Award for distinguished service.

In addition to broadcasting, Brinkley is the author of a best-selling book, *Washington Goes to War.* In his autobiography, entitled *David Brinkley: A Memoir,* published in 1995, Brinkley shares stories of his career and life experiences. In 1996, Brinkley retired from *This Week,* ending his full-time broadcast career on election day. His most recent book, *Everyone Is Entitled to My Opinion,* gives readers an inside perspective and is full of his characteristic wit. ***See also*** ABC News, Chet Huntley. *John C. Tedesco*

Further Reading

Brinkley, David. *David Brinkley: A Memoir.* New York: Alfred A. Knopf, 1995.

Brinkley, David, *Everyone is Entitled to My Opinion.* New York: Alfred A. Knopf, 1996.

Brinkley, Joel. "Son Knows Best: There Sure Is a Story Here." *New York Times,* 5 February 1997, B-7.

Murray, Michael. "Creating a Tradition in Broadcast News: A Conversation with David Brinkley." *Journalism History,* Winter 1995, 164–169.

Tom Brokaw

History will, no doubt, credit Tom Brokaw with having helped usher American television viewers into the multimedia age. Brokaw's popularity and savvy have given him long tenure as anchor of

Courtesy NBC News

NBC *Nightly News* and stature as that network's most prominent human asset. Brokaw was born on February 6, 1940, in Webster, South Dakota. He grew up in the Mount Rushmores state, a circumstance to which some attribute his empathy with heartland audiences. While in high school, he worked in radio and was assigned to local election-night coverage in 1956, when Dwight Eisenhower became president. In 1962, after graduation from the University of South Dakota, he stepped into a local news job in Omaha, Nebraska.

His intelligence and ease on the air—despite a slight speech impediment—rapidly drew attention. By 1965, he was anchoring the news in Atlanta, Georgia, and the following year NBC hired him, at 26, to anchor in Los Angeles. Although fun-loving, Brokaw became a studious reporter of world affairs and politics, including internal network politics. In 1973 he became an NBC White House correspondent during the Watergate period, attaining by his early thirties the highest-profile television reporting job. Three years later, he was named one of the anchors of the NBC *Nightly News.* By the following year, Brokaw reigned alone over the flagship newscast.

During the 1980s and 1990s, as information sources proliferated, television news audiences shrank. Brokaw's NBC *Nightly News* increasingly dueled with Peter Jennings's ABC *World News Tonight* for dominance, while CBS struggled. For promotional reasons, and because technology made it feasible, anchors increasingly went to where world events were happening. Brokaw has reported from combat zones including Lebanon, Kuwait, and Somalia, and was alone in anchoring from the Berlin Wall as it fell. Brokaw has interviewed world leaders; led major political coverage; co-anchored *Now*, a short-lived magazine; played roles in a series of special reports on China and on U.S. crime; and has won numerous awards.

By the mid-1990s, Brokaw was appearing on programs produced jointly on cable TV and on the Internet by MSNBC, thus increasing his visibility to audiences and helping NBC move into "new media." He was named the most trustworthy anchor in a *TV Guide* poll in 1996, the year of his 30th anniversary with NBC. Brokaw playfully told an interviewer that when he leaves television someday, he might go West, grow a ponytail, and get a tattoo and a motorcycle. *See also* NBC News.   *James Upshaw*

Further Reading

Adalian, Josef. "Peacock Man Won't Strut His Stuff." *New York Post,* 25 April 1996, 97.
Goldberg, Robert, and Gerald Jay Goldberg. *Anchors: Brokaw, Jennings, Rather and the Evening News.* Birch Lane Press, 1990.
Huff, Richard. "Well-Anchored: Tom Brokaw Celebrates 30 Years with NBC." *New York Daily News,* 28 April 1996, 7.

Pat Buchanan

Pat Buchanan, a political conservative, has served as a standard-bearer among the new school of "activist" journalists. His experience, spanning four decades, includes working for newspapers and writing syndicated columns and books, as well as appearing on television's *After Hours, Crossfire,* and *The McLaughlin Group.* Patrick Joseph Buchanan was born in Washington, D.C., on November 2, 1938, and was raised in Chevy Chase, Maryland. In 1961, he graduated cum laude from Georgetown University, Washington, D.C., and he earned a master's degree in journalism from Columbia University in New York in 1962. On May 8, 1971, Buchanan married Shelley Ann Scarney, then a receptionist in the Nixon White House. His

sister, Bay Buchanan, served as Treasurer of the U.S. during the Reagan administration.

Buchanan's conservative activism began with his support for presidential candidate Barry Goldwater in 1964 while serving as an editorial writer for the *St. Louis Globe-Democrat.* Later, Buchanan set aside his career to serve as an executive assistant for Richard Nixon's campaign for the presidency. During his association with Nixon, Buchanan served as a speech writer for Spiro Agnew, targeting the role of media intrusion into politics. Buchanan targeted the concentration of power in three major networks reflecting similar views and policies. He expanded his position in a book entitled *The New Majority* published in 1973. Buchanan's political activism heightened with his appointment in 1985 to the post of director of communication for president Ronald Reagan. His political activism peaked with his bid to win the Republican presidential nomination in the 1996 primary campaign. He currently hosts *Crossfire* on CNN. *See also Crossfire,* Agnew Anti-Press Campaign.   *Donald C. Shields*

Further Reading

Alter, Jonathan. "The Beltway Populist." *Newsweek* 4 May, 1996, 24–27.
Buchanan, Patrick J. *The Great Betrayal: How American Sovereignty and Social Justice Are Being Sacrificed to the Gods of the Global Economy.* Boston: Little Brown, 1998.
Stebgal, Richard. "The Making of Buchanan." *Time,* 26 February 1996, 32–34.
Willis, Garry. "The Golden Blade." *New York Times Review of Books,* 13 February 1992, 22–26.

William F. Buckley Jr.

Conservative magazine editor and television personality William F. Buckley Jr. was born in New York City on November 24, 1925. In 1943, Buckley entered the University of Mexico, but left after a semester to join the U.S. Army during World War II. He was discharged in 1946. He then attended Yale University from 1946 to 1950, where he studied economics, history, and political science.

Buckley received his bachelor's degree in 1950 and remained at the university as an instructor. A year later, in 1951, he wrote *God and Man at Yale: The Superstitions of Academic Freedom*, a book attacking anti-Christian, pro-liberal ideas taught by some of the faculty members at Yale. Buckley left Yale and worked as an agent for the Central Intelligence Agency. In 1952 he became an associate editor of the *American Mercury*. He resigned, and for the next several years worked as a free-lance writer. He and his brother-in-law, L. Brent Bozell, wrote *McCarthy and His Enemies* in 1954, a defense of Senator Joseph R. McCarthy. A year later, Buckley raised almost $300,000 and launched the conservative magazine, the *National Review*. Primarily a journal of political essays, it became the most important American right publication.

Buckley also continued to write books. In 1959, he wrote *Up from Liberalism*. In the 1960s, he helped initiate several conservative activities, including Young Americans for Freedom, and a year later, he helped form the New York Conservative Party. In 1962, he began writing a syndicated newspaper column. The weekly television program *Firing Line*, which featured a debate on a sociological or political issue, first aired in 1966, on WOR-TV in New York. Five years later the Public Broadcasting System purchased the show, and Buckley became a national television celebrity. He has hosted numerous *Firing Line* specials. Buckley has supported a number of political figures including Barry Goldwater, Richard Nixon, and Ronald Reagan. He was appointed by President Nixon, in 1969, to the advisory board of the U.S. Information Agency. However, he resigned in 1972 when he disagreed with the Nixon administration's policies toward the agency. In 1974, in the aftermath of the Watergate scandal, he and his brother, Senator James L. Buckley, called for President Nixon's resignation.

In 1986, Buckley wrote *Right Reason,* which examined Mexico, Poland, and Spain, as well as certain figures such as Karl Marx, Pope Paul VI, and Henry Kissinger. Buckley retired from editing the *National Review* in the early 1990s, but continues to tape *Firing Line* and to write books and his newspaper column. *See also* AFTRA.

Edd Applegate

Further Reading

Buckley, William F. *Happy Days Were Here Again: Reflection of a Libertarian Journalist.* New York: Random House, 1993.
Buckley, William F. *Nearer, My God: An Autobiography of Faith.* New York: Doubleday, 1997.

Ken Burns

Courtesy Lisa Berg/General Motors

Ken Burns has been one of public television's most celebrated and prolific producers for the past decade. He has created 13 major Public Broadcasting System (PBS) specials, addressing a wide range of topics from American history—*The Brooklyn Bridge* (1982), *The Shakers: Hands to Work, Hearts to God* (1985), *The Statue of Liberty* (1985), *Huey Long* (1986), *Thomas Hart Benton* (1989), *The Congress* (1989), *The Civil War* (1990), *Empire of the Air: The Men Who Made Radio* (1992), *Baseball* (1994), *The West* (1996), *Thomas Jefferson* (1997), *Lewis and Clark: The Journey of the Corps of Discovery* (1997), and *Frank Lloyd Wright* (1998)—which have all won various awards and recognition from both professional and scholarly organizations.

Kenneth L. Burns was born in Brooklyn, New York, on July 29, 1953, and grew up in Ann Arbor, Michigan. He is a 1975 graduate of Hampshire College in Amherst, Massachusetts, where he studied under still photographers Jerome Liebling and Elaine Mayes and received a degree in film studies and design. Upon graduation, he and two of his college friends started Florentine Films. They struggled for a number of years doing free-lance assignments, finishing a few short documentaries before beginning work in 1977 on a film based on David McCullough's book, *The Great Bridge* (1972). Four years later, they completed *The Brooklyn Bridge*, winning several honors, including an Academy Award nomination, and ushering Burns into the ambit of public television.

In 1979, while editing *The Brooklyn Bridge,* Burns moved Florentine Films to Walpole, New Hampshire, surviving on as little as "$2,500 one year, in order to stay independent." So much about Burns's career defies conventionality. He operates his own independent company in a small New England village more than four hours north of New York City, hardly a crossroads in the highly competitive and often insular world of corporate-funded, PBS-sponsored productions. His televison career is a popular and critical success story in an era when the historical documentary generally holds little interest for most Americans. His 13 PBS specials are strikingly out of step with the visual pyrotechnics and frenetic pacing of most reality-based television programming, relying instead on techniques that are decades old.

Beginning with the program *The Brooklyn Bridge* and continuing through *Frank Lloyd Wright*, Burns employs readings from personal papers, diaries, and letters; interpretive commentaries from onscreen experts (usually historians); "rephotographing" techniques (examining photographs, paintings, drawings, daguerreotypes, and other artifacts with a movie camera); and musical sound tracks featuring period compositions and folk music. The effect of this collage is to create the illusion that the viewer is being transported back in time, literally finding an emotional connection with the people and events of America's past.

Ken Burns's body of work casts an image of America that is built on consensus and is celebratory in nature, highlighting the nation's ideals and achievements.

Burns is a moralist. Taken as a whole, his films stand as morality tales, drawing upon epic events, landmarks, and institutions of historical significance. He is best known for his 11-hour documentary series, *The Civil War*, which attracted 40 million viewers in September 1990, making

Burns a household name. Much of the success of this series can be equated to the extent with which Burns made this 130-year-old conflict immediate and comprehensible to a contemporary audience. He adopted a similar strategy with *Baseball*, concerning himself as much with social history as the game.

Likewise, Burns refers to his explorations into the nation's racial and ethnic heritage as the "connecting thread" in his films. For example, he evokes John Adams's description of Thomas Jefferson as a "man [who] distilled Enlightenment thinking. Yet he owned more than 200 human beings and never saw fit in his lifetime to free them." With each of his productions, Burns has seized the attention of major segments of the American viewing public because of the subjects he chooses and the way he presents them.

Burns is executive producer on two additional projects for PBS. His 12-hour history *Jazz* is scheduled to premiere in the fall of 2000. He also has an agreement with General Motors overseeing a series entitled *American Lives*, where documentarians produce biographies of important historical figures. His involvement with *American Lives* ensures that Burns will be a fixture at PBS into the next century.   *Gary R. Edgerton*

Further Reading

Edgerton, Gary. "Ken Burns's America: Style, Authorship, and Cultural Memory." *Journal of Popular Film and Television* 21.2 (1993): 50–62.

Edgerton, Gary. "Ken Burns's American Dream—Histories-for-TV from Walpole, New Hampshire." *Television Quarterly* XXVII.I (1994): 56–64.

Edgerton, Gary. "Ken Burns's Rebirth of a Nation: Television, Narrative, and Popular History." *Film & History* 22.4 (1992): 118–133.

Chris Bury

Chris Bury was born on December 10, 1953. He is a 1975 political science graduate of Southern Illinois University at Carbondale.

Bury has held various reporting positions, including co-host and principal reporter for *EXTRA* in 1981, an award-winning television magazine program at KTVI-TV in St. Louis.

Bury joined ABC News in 1982 as a general assignment correspondent in Chicago. In 1983 and 1984 he reported on the Democratic and Republican national political conventions, the vice presidential campaign of George Bush, and the controversial presidential campaign of Gary Hart. During the 1992 presidential election, Bury served as the *World News Tonight* correspondent covering the Clinton campaign.

Bury has been a correspondent for ABC News *Nightline* since 1993. Based in Washington, D.C., Bury covers the major events of the Clinton administration, including the Whitewater investigation and questionable campaign financing. He has reported on many major international and domestic stories—the current American military policy in Haiti, the ongoing political battle over health care reform, and the 1993 siege of the Branch Davidian compound in Waco, Texas.

He received the Alfred I. duPont-Columbia Journalism School Award for Outstanding Television Reporting for "Children in Crisis," an ABC *World News Tonight* series on children in poverty.

Cindy Price

Further Reading

Bury, Chris. "Behind the Scenes with the Political Correspondent." In *Live from the Trenches: The Changing Role of Television Correspondents,* edited by Joe S. Foote. Carbondale, IL: Southern Illinois University Press, 1998.

Smyth, Jeff. "As Network News Cuts Back, Technology Offers Other Opportunities." *St. Louis Journalism Review*, May 1996, 13.

Bush Confrontation with Rather

One of the most famous moments in television news occurred on the *CBS Evening News* on January 25, 1988, when an interview with then vice president George Bush by the network anchor Dan Rather turned into a tense and lively encounter. It became a defining moment of the 1988 presidential campaign. The interview began routinely; one of many profiles CBS News was doing for the 1988 presidential primaries. The format for the "campaign profile" was an interview with the candidate, background information, and profiles edited for airing on the *CBS Evening News*. A few weeks earlier, CBS had approached the Bush campaign about doing a profile. Skeptical about the treatment he might receive, Bush insisted that the interview be live. CBS reluctantly agreed and prepared background material focusing on Bush's role in the Iran-Contra affair.

Early in the evening newscast on January 25 (just two weeks before the 1988 Iowa caucuses), Rather began the segment about Bush with a few opening remarks and then turned viewers' attention to a 5-minute report on Bush's role in the Iran-Contra affair. The piece was extremely critical of the vice president's role and his ties to Oliver North, and it put Bush on the defensive for the live interview that followed. In the interview, Bush immediately took the offensive, accusing CBS of inviting him under false pretext to discuss Iran-Contra instead of being profiled as a presidential candidate. Nine minutes of an intense encounter between Bush and Rather was witnessed by television news viewers.

Rather repeatedly implied that Bush was "covering up" his involvement in Iran-Contra. Bush countered that there was "nothing new" to be uncovered and that he had already been absolved of any wrongdoing, insisting that the agreed-upon purpose of the interview was to talk about his position on such policy issues as education. Rather's hostility came across often as his questions turned to commentary and his frustration led to comments such as, "you've made us hypocrites in the face of the world." A particularly significant moment came when Bush, insisting that he be judged on his whole record—not just Iran-Contra—likened his situation to Rather's own professional experience by asking Rather how he would like to have his whole career judged on the basis of an incident in which he had angrily walked off the set, leaving six minutes of blank air time, when CBS proposed shortening the evening news for a tennis match.

The intensity of this encounter between Bush and Rather cannot be overestimated. As a segment of network evening news, it was extraordinary on several counts. Not only was the atmosphere between them tense, but the structure of the segment itself was unusual, providing in the documentary and interview almost 15 minutes of uninterrupted airtime. The flow of the conversation was unusual, violating viewers' expected norms of polite respect, as Bush and Rather often interrupted each other (57 times in the nine-minute interview). Observers differ over the impact of the encounter on the 1988 campaign. Polls immediately after the event and research studies both indicated that the encounter had boosted Bush's image, perhaps lessening the perception that he was unwilling to explain his position and respond to criticism. *Time* magazine called it one of the 10 most significant events of the 1988 campaign. Others felt it left both men tarnished and as less sympathetic figures. *See also* Dan Rather.   *Lynda Lee Kaid*

Further Reading

Alter, Jonathon, and Howard Fineman. "The Great TV Shout-Out." *Newsweek*, 8 February 1988, 19–23.

CBS Evening News, January 25, 1988. Copies of the nine-minute exchange between Bush and Rather are available from C-SPAN, c/o Purdue University Video Archives.

Sloan, David, et al. *The Media in America*. Scottsdale, AZ: Publishing Horizons, 1993.

C

C-SPAN

Cable-Satellite Public Affairs Network (C-SPAN) is nonprofit public-service programming produced by the cable television industry. Its mission is to provide live, gavel-to-gavel coverage of the proceedings of the U.S. House of Representatives and the U.S. Senate, as well as other forums where public policy is discussed. Coverage is provided without commentary or analysis. Another aspect of the C-SPAN mission is to provide unfiltered two-way communication—from public officials and other decision makers to viewers, without distorting points of view, and from viewers, through a call-in program, to decision makers and journalists. C-SPAN receives no government funding, but is financed by the cable systems that offer the network. C-SPAN's board of directors, which is comprised of executives from cable companies, establishes policy but is not involved in editorial decision making.

The cable industry created C-SPAN in 1977 specifically to cover the U.S. House of Representatives. When the House turned on its cameras, on March 19, 1979, a C-SPAN staff of four made coverage available to 3.5 million cable homes. In 1980, C-SPAN covered its first presidential election and began a nationwide viewer call-in program. By 1982, C-SPAN's schedule expanded to 24 hours a day, seven days a week, with three live call-ins each day, and in 1986 when televised proceedings began in the Senate, C-SPAN2 was created. In 1991, C-SPAN and C-SPAN2 began

closed captioning. C-SPAN offered more than 1,200 hours of presidential election coverage in 1993. By 1996, C-SPAN had a staff of 180, with programming available to nearly 60 million households.

C-SPAN and C-SPAN2 also cover select international events. As early as 1983, the network carried proceedings of the Canadian House of Commons. Regular coverage of the British House of Commons began November 21, 1989. C-SPAN expanded international coverage in 1990, airing sessions of the Polish National Legislature, the Israeli Knesset, and the Hungarian Parliament, as well as programming from the Persian Gulf, Japan, and Germany.

Public affairs events come in a wide range of formats, including speeches, news conferences, forums, and hearings, and editors are responsible for keeping track of these events. One editor, for example, follows events on Capitol Hill, while another monitors events elsewhere in Washington. Editors find out about events through notices and invitations. They spend several hours each day seeking out events and monitoring changes in scheduling. By mid-afternoon, editors have developed lists of the next day's events, and they meet to determine which ones C-SPAN will cover. Editorial decisions are based on four basic conditions: events should be of a public affairs nature; subjects should be issues of national importance; selections should be balanced between the different sides of an issue; and speakers should be closely related to the topics under discussion. The broadcast is relayed by satellite to cable companies worldwide. Each event that airs is recorded and stored at the Public Affairs Video Archives (PAVA) at Purdue University. *Linda M. Perry*

Further Reading
Auletta, Ken. *Three Blind Mice*. New York: Random House, 1991.
Foote, Joe S. *Television Access and Political Power*. New York: Praeger, 1990.
Head, Sydney W., and Christopher H. Sterling. *Broadcasting in America*. Boston: Houghton Mifflin, 1982.

Camel News Caravan

In 1948, NBC began to broadcast the *Camel Newsreel Theatre*, anchored by newsman John Cameron Swayze. The name of the program was soon changed to *Camel News Caravan*. Swayze was noted for three sayings he used commonly on the program: "A good, good evening to you," "...hopscotching the globe," and "I'm glad we could be together." The program was sponsored by Camel cigarettes.

Swayze was known for his prodigious memory. Monday through Friday, while the program was on the air, he arrived at the NBC News studios on 106th Street in New York at about 3 P.M., wrote his own script, and read it three or four times in the privacy of the announcer's booth. Swayze did not use cue cards (and the TelePrompter had not been invented), but he was able to maintain eye contact and relate the news, usually following his script closely from memory.

The *Camel News Caravan* did not do as well as NBC hoped, particularly as viewer sophistication increased in that early era. The competing CBS news program, *Douglas Edwards with the News*, had higher ratings. Bill McAndrews, the president of NBC News, visited Huntington, West Virginia, when he heard that the NBC affiliate there, WSAZ, had a highly rated news program. During his three-day visit, McAndrews noted that the WSAZ newscast had two anchors—one in Huntington and one in Charleston, West Virginia. He returned to New York and, after some considerable negotiation, took the *Camel News Caravan*

off the air and replaced it with *The Huntley-Brinkley Report*, which featured one news anchor in New York City and the other in Washington, D.C. That was in the fall of 1956.

The demise of the *Camel News Caravan* signified two important changes in the NBC News policy—the network stopped associating the name of a sponsor with a newscast, and from then on, all newscasters were required to be working reporters (Swayze had been at one time, but not while he was at NBC). *See also* John Cameron Swayze.

Dwight Jensen

Further Reading
Barnouw, Erik. *Tube of Plenty: The Evolution of American Television*. New York: Oxford University Press, 1990.
Frank, Reuven. *Out of Thin Air: The Brief Wonderful Life of Network News*. New York: Simon & Schuster, 1991.
Matusow, Barbara. *The Evening Stars: The Making of the Network News Anchor*. Boston: Houghton-Mifflin, 1983.

Cameras in the Courtroom

The controversy regarding allowing cameras in courtrooms has been around for more than 70 years. However, recent developments allowing the use of cameras in 48 state courts and the introduction of cameras into federal courts necessitate a fresh look at the use of courtroom cameras (film and still cameras), as well as radio and television equipment.

Canon 35 (later named Canon 3A(7)), the American Bar Association's (ABA) 1937 ruling prohibiting courtroom cameras, stood for nearly 50 years. Recently, however, some revisionists brought to light some curious aspects of the ban. For instance, it had been generally accepted that the behavior of cameramen inside the courtroom at the 1935 trial of Bruno Hauptmann, for the kidnapping and murder of the Lindbergh baby, caused the ABA to pass the ban. However, critics Richard Kielbowitz and Susanna Barber have pointed out that other factors contributed to the circus-like atmosphere of the Hauptmann trial, not the use of courtroom cameras.

The ban was in effect for more than 50 years, with only one significant revision—television was specifically added to the prohibition in 1952. By 1965, all state bar associations except Colorado and Texas had adopted camera bans. In *Estes v. Texas*, 1965, the U.S. Supreme Court, by a vote of 5–4, overturned the conviction of Billie Sol Estes for swindling, based on the denial of due process. A pretrial hearing had been televised live, and although live broadcasting was forbidden during the trial itself, silent cameras operated intermittently, and excerpts of the trial were shown on nightly newscasts. In *Estes*, Justice Tom Clark wrote that television might improperly influence jurors, impair witness testimony, distract judges, and burden defendants. However, Justice Potter Stewart wrote the dissent on First Amendment grounds.

Courtroom cameras in Florida led to a second landmark Supreme Court decision, *Chandler v. Florida* in 1980. Television stations had successfully petitioned the state to allow cameras in the courtroom. The defendants in *Chandler* appealed their burglary convictions on the grounds that the camera coverage, despite their protests against using cameras, had denied them due process. Chief Justice Warren Burger delivered the 8–0 opinion of the Court, which upheld the convictions and stated that the mere presence of cameras did not violate fair trial rights. Justice Burger said although "(D)angers lurk in this as in most experiments," unless television coverage under all conditions were prohibited by the Constitution, states must be free to experiment with courtroom cameras.

Today, cameras are generally allowed unless there are exceptional circumstances. Moreover, almost all criminal convictions have been upheld despite some defendants' claims, as in *Chandler,* of denial of due process because of the presence of cameras. Some research has been conducted, albeit mostly under experimental conditions, to test apparent effects of courtroom cameras. Empirical evidence gathered to date generally fails to support speculation that cameras interfere in any way with the judicial process.

As of 1997, 48 states (all but Mississippi and South Dakota, and also the District of Columbia) permit some type of coverage, on an experimental or permanent basis. Thirty-seven states allow some coverage of both trial and appellate courts, eight allow coverage of appellate courts only, and three allow coverage of trial courts only. All states that allow cameras have adopted guidelines covering exemptions for certain types of cases, such as those involving juveniles or sex crimes, as well as testimony of certain witnesses. In about half of the states, jurors may not be shown on camera. Other guidelines include requiring advance notice and consent of parties before coverage is permitted; limiting the number of and placement of cameras; prohibiting audio pickup of bench conferences; pool coverage by the media; banning any distracting sound or light; and requiring equipment and personnel to remain stationary.

Cameras had been specifically banned in federal courts since the 1946 adoption of Rule 53 of the Federal Rules of Criminal Procedure. In 1972, the Judicial Conference, a policy-making group of judges, incorporated the ABA Code of Judicial Conduct Canon 3A(7). However, in 1990, the Judicial Conference revised Canon 3A(7) to allow for a three-year experiment with cameras in civil courts. The Judicial Conference in 1996 gave each of the 13 federal appellate circuits the right to decide whether to permit cameras in the courtrooms. As of 1997, two U.S. Courts of Appeal, in New York and San Francisco, had approved camera coverage, and five circuit courts—Boston, New Orleans, Chicago, Denver, and Atlanta—had banned cameras. About a dozen of the 94 federal district (trial) courts permitted camera coverage of some trials.

A significant step was taken in the development of camera coverage when the courtroom television cable network signed on in 1991. By the end of the company's fifth year of operation, Court TV reached more than 23 million viewers, about one-fourth of televison households in the country, and had covered more than 400 trials. Court television had also released condensed coverage of cases on video and had announced plans to supply audio coverage of some trials over the Internet, as well as plans to develop regional courtroom coverage channels. Highly publicized trials that were covered gavel to gavel included the police brutality trial involving Rodney King, the Menendez brothers case, and the criminal trial against O.J. Simpson. In the Simpson case, more than 2,000 hours of live coverage aired on cable television, and an estimated 150 million viewers in the U.S. watched live coverage of the verdict on the three major television networks, as well as on cable.

With all but two states allowing some form of camera coverage, the introduction of cameras into federal courts, and the advent of Court TV, cameras are becoming a fixture in American courtrooms.

Sherry L. Alexander

Further Readings

Alexander, S.L. "The Impact of California v Simpson on Cameras in the Courtroom." *Judicature*, January-February 1996, 169–172.

Barber, Susanna. *News Cameras in the Courtroom: A Free Press–Fair Trial Debate*. Norwood, NJ: Ablex Publishing, 1987.

Dick Cavett

Comedian, author, actor, and talk-show host Dick Cavett first gained national attention for his late-night program, the *Dick Cavett Show*, which aired from 1969 to 1974 on ABC. He was born on November 19, 1936, in Gibbon, Nebraska, and educated at Yale University. His popular late-night program distinguished itself from its competitors, NBC's *The Tonight Show* with Johnny Carson and CBS's *Merv Griffin Show*, by Cavett's ability to combine intelligent humor with guests who often debated serious current social and political issues.

Such diverse guests as architect Buckminster Fuller, poet Allen Ginsberg, comedian Groucho Marx, actress Patricia Neal, and musician John Lennon were common on the *Dick Cavett Show*. One show included director Tyrone Guthrie, writer Norman Mailer, and philosopher Paul Weiss exchanging views on life, death, boxing, and the theater. Another program featured a debate about the Vietnam War between anti-war activist/singer Joan Baez and pro-war Louis Nizer.

Though the *Dick Cavett Show* was eventually canceled because of low ratings, the Emmy-winning program was praised by critics. According to television critic Richard Schickel, the *Dick Cavett Show* was literate, receptive to cultural trends, and willing to accept guests who could not rate an appearance on other shows. Schickel also credited Cavett for resisting praise he received as television's lone intellectual. Cavett told a *New York Times* reporter in the early 1980s that he spent half his life denying he is an intellectual and "can easily prove it."

Cavett did not set out to become a talk-show host. After graduating from Yale in 1958 with a degree in drama, he moved to New York City to pursue an acting career, but he had little success. In 1960, while working as a copy boy for *Time* magazine, Cavett submitted two pages of jokes to *Tonight Show* host Jack Paar, who hired him as a writer. He continued to write for *The Tonight Show* when Johnny Carson took over that program in 1962.

Cavett made his stand-up comedy debut at the Bitter End in Greenwich Village in 1964 and continued to hone his act on the night club circuit at such places as the Improvisation in Greenwich, Mr. Kelly's in Chicago, and "the hungry I" in San Francisco. These appearances led to frequent guest spots on *The Tonight Show*, the *Ed Sullivan Show*, *What's My Line*, and the *Kraft Music Hall*. Based on his growing popularity, in 1967 ABC hired Cavett to host a morning talk show (short-lived but Emmy-winning), followed by his late-night show in 1969.

After the *Dick Cavett Show* was canceled, Cavett appeared in summer prime-time specials for CBS, universally panned by critics. Since then, he has pursued a multi-faceted career, including writing two best-selling books with Christopher Porterfield, hosting a talk show on public television from 1977 to 1983, acting in several Broadway plays, narrating Home Box Office's *Magic Moments*, and doing voiceovers for numerous commercials.

Kim A. Smith

Further Reading

Cavett, Dick, and Christopher Porterfield. *Cavett.* New York: Harcourt, Brace and Jovanovich, 1974.

Cavett, Dick and Christopher Porterfield. *Eye on Cavett.* New York: Arbor House, 1983.

CBS News

As the history of broadcast journalism is written, one network stands out above all others. CBS News set the standard for the best and the brightest television newsmen and newswomen. CBS Radio was founded in 1928 by William S. Paley who purchased Philadelphia radio station WCAU after having been a major program sponsor. Paley set the stage for the development of the radio news division, which was first known as the Special Events Department. Since CBS's chief competition at the time was NBC—which aired most of the entertainment programming—Paley decided to invest in public affairs and news programming. His radio network was represented by Boake Carter, best described as the "quintessential commentator." Larry LeSueur of the United Press (UP) was brought in to advise as a newsman in an attempt to improve that status—the same Larry LeSueur who would later become one of "The Murrow Boys," the group of newsmen pulled together by Edward R. Murrow in 1940 for CBS News. LeSueur's involvement marked the real beginning of the highly regarded news operation at CBS. UP subsequently turned out other members of the notable CBS News team.

Two bona fide newsmen from print journalism (which at that time was almost all there was), Ed Klauber of the *New York Times* and Paul White of UP, were hired by Paley to run the Special Events Department in an effort to bring prestige to the radio network. They joined CBS in 1930 and started the *CBS World News*. During that era, other noted radio journalists heard on CBS included the famous voice of H.V. Kaltenborn broadcasting from Europe, Lowell Thomas, Elmer Davis, and Robert Trout, who began his long tenure with CBS in the late 1920s as an announcer.

News stringers—usually working for newspapers or the wire services—were common to the networks in the 1930s, reporting the events from Europe leading up to World War II. One of those was William L. Shirer, a foreign correspondent based primarily in Berlin, who at various times reported for two newspapers as well as two press services. Shirer received a job offer in 1937 from Edward R. Murrow, who was serving CBS in London. That began one of the closest professional relationships the men would ever have, though it eventually ended in a stormy climax in 1947.

Murrow had been hired by CBS in 1935 as director of talks and education, then later as European director. With Shirer reporting from Berlin and Murrow in London, Hitler's march on eastern Europe was well covered by CBS—at least when Shirer could get on the air, since German radio had an exclusive arrangement with NBC. It was at this time that the CBS News team actually began. In order to adequately cover the developing world war, Murrow began hiring a staff of journalists.

The gathering storm in Europe brought to CBS some of the greatest news correspondents ever assembled by a network. Many of them would become known as "The Murrow Boys." Among these renowned journalists were Eric Sevareid, often called "the dean of commentators"; Howard K. Smith, who authored and traveled on *The Last Train from Berlin*; Charles Collingwood, a "dandy" dresser with considerable poise in his delivery; Richard C. Hottelet, who provided the first news report of the Battle of the Bulge; Winston Burdett, for many years the CBS Rome correspondent; and Bill Downs, along with LeSueur and Shirer.

Following World War II, the CBS News team grew and spread out to bureaus all around the world. With the advent of network television in the late 1940s, these newsmen had to adjust their work to fit the camera. Many succeeded, though some had difficulty. By the early 1950s, the first CBS television news program in prime time began broadcasting. At the anchor desk was Douglas Edwards, who had joined CBS Radio in 1943. On television, *Douglas Edwards with the News*, directed by Don Hewitt (now executive producer of *60 Minutes*), attracted more than 14 million viewers. The show continued until 1962 when Walter Cronkite took over and made the *CBS Evening News with Walter Cronkite* the most watched network evening newscast. Cronkite—dubbed "the most trusted man in America"—retired from CBS in March 1981.

The controversy in the wake of Cronkite leaving the anchor chair became a public event. CBS newsmen Roger Mudd and Dan Rather vied for the coveted seat. Rather won, and Mudd was then hired by NBC.

Over the years, the CBS News presidents have had significant influence on both the philosophy and the direction of their divisions. Sig Mickelson was the first of only a select few who held that prestigious post. He brought Walter Cronkite to CBS viewers and also established the anchorman concept in presidential elections. He was succeeded by Richard Salant who would hold the presidency two different times, from 1961 to 1964 and again from 1966 to 1979.

In 1976, Salant would establish—for the first time in a single document—the CBS News Standards, making it mandatory for all CBS news personnel to read and to follow them. Fred Friendly, once Murrow's producer, served the two interim years before resigning in protest over CBS's decision not to cover, gavel to gavel, the Vietnam War hearings. Bill Leonard followed Salant in 1979, followed by those who would serve as CBS presidents during the tumultuous 1980s: Van Gordon Sauter, Howard Stringer, and David Burke.

The 1980s saw the vaunted CBS News operation fall on hard times. The era of mergers and buyouts hit CBS with a fury. The network was also impacted by the "new kid on the block," Cable News Network (CNN) and its formidable CEO, Ted Turner, who wanted to acquire CBS. The serious effort at a takeover by Turner pushed CBS chairman Tom Wyman to call on Larry Tisch, the Loews empire builder (with a portfolio valued at nearly 14 billion dollars), for help. During this time, many in CBS News became deeply concerned over its future. CBS, weakened by Turner's buyout attempt, provided the window Tisch needed to buy up enough CBS stock to take control of the company and implement his bottom-line approach to management.

CBS News's leadership was coming to an end. Over the next few years, the news operation would experience less and less funding, the departure of some news personnel, and, some would say, a dismantling of its news division. There would be a change in news philosophy, espoused by news chief Van Gordon Sauter, from hard news reporting to a softer approach. Meanwhile, CNN would succeed in reaching profitability, gaining

international respect, and becoming an increasingly active competitor. In a failed attempt to rescue CBS News, six top news people—led by Don Hewitt and including Dan Rather, Mike Wallace, Diane Sawyer, Bill Moyers, and Morley Safer—offered to buy the news division. The *CBS Evening News* had already fallen to third place in the ratings and would be hard-pressed to gain back its first-place status.

Much of the turmoil had ended by the 1990s, but the other networks, including NBC (which had been purchased by General Electric in 1985) and ABC (taken over by Capital Cities in 1985), continued ahead of CBS in the prime time evening news ratings.

The history of CBS News has been one of golden years with the highest level of respectability, followed by seriously troubled times. Though a stabilizing effect has taken place in the late 1990s, the network is no match for the Murrow and Cronkite eras. CBS News still carries status among electronic journalists of having once been the undisputed leader in the field. *See also* Walter Cronkite.   *David M. Guerra*

Further Reading

Auletta, Ken. *Three Blind Mice: How the TV Networks Lost Their Way*. New York: Random House, 1992.

Bliss, Edward, Jr. *Now the News: The Story of Broadcast Journalism*. New York: Columbia University Press, 1991.

Leonard, William. *In the Storm of the Eye: A Lifetime at CBS*. New York: G. P. Putnam, 1987.

McClellan, Steve. *Andrew Heyward: CBS News' Mr. Fixit*. Broadcasting and Cable. 15 January 1996, 120.

Metz, Robert. *Reflections in a Bloodshot Eye*. New York: Signet, 1975.

CBS News Guidelines

Of the major U.S. television news networks, only CBS alone has historically made its manual of news standards and practices publicly available. In 1976, the network's guidelines were compiled into a 64-page, loose-leaf book. These highly detailed *CBS News Standards* were subjected to only 17 minor revisions until 1991. CBS continues to issue the book to all its news workers and has made it available to the public.

In the 1930s, Ed Klauber and Paul White imposed the standards of objective and interpretive print journalism on the network's distinguished radio journalists: H.V. Kaltenborn, Elmer Davis, Robert Trout, and John Daly. But long-standing CBS employees also attribute much of the interest in news guidelines to the chair of the CBS board, William Paley. Paley took a keen interest in news, which led to the network's hiring of news deputies Klauber, White, and Edward R. Murrow. Paley continued his interest and involvement in the news areas from CBS's inception in 1928 through World War II, particularly whenever CBS practices came under fire.

From the 1930s through the rise of television, Klauber and White wrote and distributed individual internal policy memos whenever difficult journalistic issues arose. Sometimes the policy issues were presented for public consumption, as in 1943 when White suggested that the listener should be left with no impression as to which side the broadcast analyst favors in the case of controversial issues. Such memos, and the newsroom discussions that accompanied them, fostered a common law of CBS News policies that shaped procedures through the 1950s.

At that time, CBS's geographic reach and employee ranks had become so large that word of mouth could no longer be relied on to communicate corporate policy. The regularly scheduled meetings of CBS network managers also had become fountainheads for written policies. The managers dealt with any problems that arose, including journalistic controversies. Over time, managers embraced the idea of creating a book of CBS News policies to show both news workers and the public, what CBS considered to be good news practice. During the 1960s and early 1970s, the network's news practices had also come under sharp attack by conservatives in Congress, the Nixon administration, and portions of the general public. Creating written guidelines enabled CBS to articulate its standards to critics, as well as corporate stockholders.

In 1970, CBS News president Richard Salant asked CBS News administrative vice president David Klinger to begin drawing together the news memos and guidelines that had been written since the network's inception. Salant later wrote that he distributed the completed book to news workers and the public in 1976 so that network personnel would know what was expected and also in order that "the public could measure performance versus policy." The *CBS News Standards* book drew an unequivocal line between the techniques used in its entertainment shows and those used in its news and public affairs programming. The standards went beyond the problems of recording, editing, and offering context for news reports to dealing with conflicts of interest and acceptance of gifts from sources. It also included personnel standards for CBS News workers, as well as practices related to advertisers' influence and requests for news materials by parties outside the news division.

Management efforts to create such a detailed set of news guidelines irritated many CBS journalists. They found the guidelines, which often were cited in the network's internal news investigations, to be too detailed, rigid, and bureaucratic to serve as a useful tool. Yet in the late 1970s and early 1980s, the *CBS News Standards* became a model for other written news guidelines. When Richard Salant retired from CBS and joined NBC News, he created a similar set of detailed guidelines that NBC News gave to its journalists. *See also* Richard Salant.   *Richard J. Schaefer*

Further Reading
CBS. *CBS News Standards.* New York: CBS News, 1976–1990.
Schaefer, Richard J. "The Development of the CBS News Guidelines During the Salant Years." *Journal of Broadcasting & Electronic Media* Vol. 42, No. 1, Winter 1998, 1–20.

CBS Reports

CBS Reports was a documentary program series inaugurated on October 27, 1959, in the aftermath of the quiz show scandals. Executive producer Fred Friendly (Edward R. Murrow's colleague on the *See It Now* series) once suggested that the program was an attempt by CBS to undo the damage caused by the quiz show scandals and the resulting investigations. Friendly, who was executive producer for the new program later became the president of CBS News.

CBS Reports continued as a regular series for seven years, producing 146 hour-long investigative documentaries, including *Harvest of Shame, Murder and the Right to Bear Arms, Biography of a Bookie Joint, Ku Klux Klan: The Invisible Empire, The Selling of the Pentagon,* and *Who Speaks for Birmingham?* Some shows caused controversy; many achieved critical acclaim. Friendly later reported that the costs of the program ran between $80,000 and $100,000 an episode and that the advertising spots were continually sold out. In spite of its critical and commercial success, there was pressure to replace it with the more lucrative entertainment programming. "When television is good," said Newton Minow in his "vast wasteland" speech, "nothing is better." In that well-known speech in which he castigated broadcast performers from his position of chairman of the FCC, he cited *CBS Reports* as one of television's great achievements—nothing better. *See also* Fred Friendly, Edward R. Murrow.   *Donald G. Godfrey*

Further Reading

Barnouw, Erik. *Tube of Plenty.* New York: Oxford University Press, 1990.
Friendly, Fred W. *Due to Circumstances Beyond Our Control.* New York: Random House, 1967.
Hickey, Neil. "Can CBS News Make a Comeback," *Columbia Journalism Review,* January/February 1998, 28–35.

John Chancellor

Born in Chicago on July 14, 1927, John Chancellor had neither Walter Cronkite's ratings nor Eric Sevareid's reputation, but during five decades at NBC, plain-spoken and professorial Chancellor helped to develop key aspects of television news, including the role of floor reporter at national political conventions. In a dozen years as anchor of the nightly news and over a decade more as the show's commentator, Chancellor won the respect and admiration of colleagues and viewers alike by never seeing himself as more important than the story he was covering.

Chancellor's spare writing style and professional manner were developed during a long apprenticeship at the *Chicago Daily News* and the *Chicago Sun-Times,* where he went from a 14-year-old ad runner to a rewrite man, a feature writer, and finally, a street-smart reporter. Chancellor "drifted" into the field of broadcasting in 1950, after being laid off from the *Chicago Sun-Times* along with 70 others in an economy move. He took a job at Chicago's fledgling NBC station, WNBQ, with the notion he would stay only a short time, until he picked up another newspaper job. At the time, established newspaper and radio reporters would have little to do with television news.

Chancellor's account of a gun battle between police and a murder suspect got him a job at the network. His reports from the 1952 Republican Party convention were the first of 20 national nominating conventions he would cover. National acclaim and local threats followed his coverage of the school integration crisis in Little Rock, Arkansas. Returning to the city years later, Chancellor observed that that week-long standoff between national guardsmen and black students trying to enter Central High School in Little Rock, in 1957, showed television's potential to cover and amplify critical topics.

As NBC's senior correspondent, Chancellor reported on the Algerian War in 1958 and on the Moscow trial of downed U-2 pilot Francis Gary Powers in 1960. He was a panelist on the Kennedy-Nixon televised debates of 1960, and in a memorable bit of ad-libbing, talked to the American people for more than an hour while NBC awaited John F. Kennedy's victory speech in Hyannis Port, Massachusetts. In 1961, Chancellor replaced Dave Garroway as host of *Today*—an unhappy assignment in which he refused to do commercials or submit himself to the show's softer format. After 14 months he gave it up. The next year he became NBC's national affairs correspondent, covering the European Common Market and the White House. One of his most famous moments was the night he was ejected from the raucous 1964 Republican National Convention in San Francisco for blocking an aisle. As guards led him away, he told viewers, "I've been promised bail, ladies and gentlemen, by my office." As he disappeared from view he could be heard signing off, "This is John Chancellor, somewhere in custody."

In 1966, a reluctant Chancellor became, at President Lyndon Johnson's insistence, the director of *Voice of America*, the news arm of the U.S.

Information Agency. Chancellor was credited with giving credibility to the organization by never putting out a story he knew to be false. Returning to NBC in 1967, Chancellor covered the Six Day War in the Middle East and was a roving correspondent for three years on the *Huntley-Brinkley Report*. In 1970, he joined Frank McGee and David Brinkley as the third host on the network's nightly news. A year later, he became the program's only anchor, continuing in this capacity until Brinkley rejoined him for three years beginning in 1976. Between 1979 and 1982, Chancellor again was anchoring alone, but succeeded in departing from rigidly formatted newscasts to have interviews with American presidents and foreign leaders.

By April of 1982, Chancellor wanted to become a commentator on *NBC's Nightly News*. After 2,860 programs as the anchor, he was ready to turn over the job to others. As always, he had a definite idea about the kind of commentator he wanted to be, stressing the need for the audience to know his views on certain topics. Chancellor long fought some of the self-promoting tendencies of the broadcast news business. In 1987, he identified the importance of source attribution as a key challenge to the industry. He also deplored the tendency toward invasion of privacy and exploration of grief in a search for ratings. He recommended a moratorium of putting overly emotional people on the air. Chancellor thought the 1990s preoccupation with punditry would eventually alienate viewers. He also argued that broadcast journalism had a responsibility to provide society with "an early warning system" of events that influence the lives of citizens.

Before leaving *NBC Nightly News* in 1993, Chancellor decried the merger mania that had taken over the national television networks. He felt it placed broadcast journalism in the hands of corporate executives, with limited news background, who mistakenly thought that all newsmen were interchangeable. To a great extent, Chancellor had presided over television's transformation to the American marketplace, but in his final commentary, feared the isolation of Americans brought about by technology, especially television and computers.

Chancellor wrote, narrated, and hosted specials and television documentaries after leaving *Nightly News*. He had surgery for stomach cancer in 1994 and appeared to be recovering when the disease reappeared in 1996. When he died two days short of his 69th birthday, appreciations in print and over the air acknowledged the passing of a consummate professional, whose respect for broadcast journalism earned him the admiration of his peers and his audience. ***See also*** NBC News.

Bruce J. Evensen

Further Reading

Burke, Tom. "I'd Like to Think I've Got a Certain Job Security." *TV Guide,* 22 June 1974, 20–24.

Carden, John, "A Conversation with John Chancellor," *Television Quarterly*, Vol.10, No. 3, Spring 1973, 24–29.

Chancellor, John. *Peril and Promise: A Commentary on America*. New York: Harper & Row, 1990.

Chancellor, John, and Walter R. Mears. *The New News Business: A Guide to Writing and Reporting*. New York: Harper Collins, 1995.

Robert Chandler

Born on September 25, 1928, Robert Chandler had a distinguishing career as a CBS News executive from 1963 to 1985. Perhaps his greatest contribution to the history of television news was a simple suggestion he made to *60 Minutes* executive producer Don Hewitt in 1968. Hewitt wanted a more personalized style of news journalism as opposed to the conventional stiff, network style presentation but still wanted a program that focused on tough interviews, a watchdog for the American people. Chandler, vice president of CBS News at the time, suggested to Hewitt that perhaps the show should have two hosts and used Mike Wallace and Harry Reasoner as examples. Even though the program created constant challenges to Chandler during his career at CBS News, *60 Minutes* became the network's hallmark program.

Chandler graduated from City College of New York and began his journalism career as a reporter for *Variety*, covering radio and television. He got his first job at CBS in 1963 as the head of Information Services, and for the next 20 years he served in multiple roles for the news divsion. In 1982, he took an active role in attempting to legally define a level of protection for notes and videotapes acquired by CBS's journalists. A judge had ordered Mike Wallace to turn over his notes on a investigative piece about the fast food industry. The judge felt that even though the notes and raw footage had not aired, he needed the material to clarify evidence presented in the case. Chandler fought the network's decision to hand over the materials, arguing that it would open journalists to "fishing expeditions" by the judiciary. Chandler warned network executives that if they continued to cooperate with the investigation, the independence and integrity of a free press would be seriously threatened.

In the early 1980s, Chandler, who at the time handled CBS's convention and political coverage, was called to testify before Congress about election coverage and early predictions. Chandler maintained a firm line with Congress for continuing to report early election returns and taking exit polls. He developed a network election night coverage policy to consider each state's returns one at a time and a final call announcing the winner of the presidential race only when a candidate reached 270 electoral votes. Chandler's policy remains intact at CBS.

When financial challenges in 1985 pushed CBS to offer early retirement to employees who had provided more than two decades of service, Chandler accepted the offer. At the time, he was serving as senior vice president of administration. Soon after retiring from CBS, he was named the managing editor of NBC's short-lived newsmagazine *1986*. Retired from NBC, Chandler has dedicated his work efforts to producing independent documentaries, several of which have aired on PBS. *See also* 60 Minutes. *Connie Book*

Further Reading

Chandler, Robert. "Putting the CBS News Budget into Perspective." *Broadcasting,* 13 April 1987, 32.

Hewitt, Don. *60 Minutes.* New York: Random House, 1985.

Madsen, Axel. *60 Minutes: The Power and Politics of America's Most Popular TV News Show.* New York: Dodd, Mead & Co., 1984.

Sylvia Chase

A charter member of the correspondent team on ABC News *20/20*, Sylvia Chase appeared on that newsmagazine's first broadcast in June of 1978. Chase first joined ABC News in September 1977. She co-anchored the *ABC News Weekend Report* and also served as a general assignment correspondent. Previously, at CBS News (1971–1977), she anchored *CBS Newsbreak* and hosted CBS News broadcast *Magazine*. Chase joined CBS News in 1971 as a general assignment reporter and later worked as a reporter/producer. She was named a CBS News correspondent in 1974. Prior to joining CBS News, Chase worked for KNX Radio News in Los Angeles. She also held various positions in the California State Legislature and managed several political campaigns. She anchored the news in San Francisco from 1985 to 1990, then rejoined ABC News as correspondent for *Prime Time Live* in October of 1990. Born in North Field, Minnesota, she earned a bachelor's degree in English at the University of California, Los Angeles in 1961.

During a recent season, Chase reported on an organization dedicated to reforming drug-addicted musicians; examined a diet pill newly approved by the FDA which has been linked to incurable lung disease; reported on cutting-edge techniques being used in plastic surgery; and profiled champion ice skater Rudy Galindo. Chase also reported on scandalous conditions of neglect in Medicaid-supported nursing homes caring for severely disabled children.

During the 1994–95 season, Chase investigated mistakes made in hospitals, revealing that as many as 100,000 preventable deaths occur each year in U.S. hospitals. She has also reported on the murders of gay men in Texas, sexual abuse of women prisoners, and the upsurge in triplet births, and she has examined the issue of Alzheimer's disease from the perspective of a patient afflicted with the condition. Chase also uncovered how shoppers are overcharged at supermarkets with scanners; reported on the diabetes epidemic among Zuni Indians in New Mexico; and interviewed the survivor and a grand jury member in the Texas "condom rape" case. Chase also reported on the North Korean spy responsible for the 1987 bombing of a KAL plane.

Chase has also broken ground on a number of investigative news fronts, including a report on a private psychiatric hospital chain revealing a pattern of insurance gouging and false arrest and patient kidnaping in a Texas facility. Allegations of brutality and racism were revealed in an investigation of the sheriffs' departments in California and Mississippi. Chase also reported that Florida health authorities disagree with the conclusions of the Centers for Disease Control (CDC) concerning how dental patient Kimberly Bergalis contracted AIDS. Guidelines for sterilization of dental equipment were stiffened by both the CDC and the American Dental Association in the wake of the Chase investigation. *See also 20/20*

Joye C. Gordon

Futher Reading:

Dullea, Georgia. "The Women in Television : a Changing Image, A Growing Impact." *New York Times,* 28 September 1974, 18.

Gelfman, Judith. *Women in Television News.* New York: Columbia University Press, 1976.

William, Henry. "You Can Go Home Again." *Channels*, September 1987, 41–63.

Checkbook Journalism

Checkbook journalism, the controversial practice of paying sources for their information, has become common practice in news gathering. It has grown as the standards for what gets published and what does not have changed under the mounting competitive pressure to attract more viewers. Paying for information was first viewed as a significant problem in print journalism. Both newspapers and magazines concluded that the pressure to compete for readers made it expedient to pay for stories and pictures. Selected print publications still engage in checkbook journalism, but recent concerns have focused on television, where there has been a tendency to blur the distinction between news *per se* and news programming.

One example has been the practice by networks of buying the personal reminiscences of political figures. These so-called "electronic memoirs" have usually consisted of on-air interviews on various newsmagazine shows. Several ethical questions arise as a result. One question relates relates to the bidding wars that have developed when former presidents or other noteworthy citizens negotiate to sell their reminiscences. Another is the fine line between personal recollections and hard news exclusives. CBS, which purchased a number of memoirs in the mid-1970s, initially argued that it was an acceptable practice to buy memoirs since public figures spent a lot of time preparing them and they often appear in the form of excerpts in major publications.

A variation of electronic memoirs occurs when officials have been employed by networks to develop personal accounts and to appear in news specials. Former president Gerald Ford was paid $1.5 million to prepare his memoirs and consult with NBC on current political developments. Ford retained control over the content of his memoirs and eliminated the first 30 days of his presidency, during which time he had pardoned former President Nixon.

The practice of buying amateur videos of news events is another instance of checkbook journalism. Stations seek out private individuals who have video of a news event and pay them cash to show it. The film shot in conjunction with the assassination of John F. Kennedy is an example of the potential value of such material. More recently, video of law enforcement officers beating motorist Rodney King is another prime example. News executives who use amateur videos on-air often justify doing so by saying that this type of material allows them to show an event when they might not otherwise have a visual record. This, they say, enhances the public's right to know.

Video news releases represent another form of checkbook journalism. News is created and is distributed through video release or electronic news conferences. Stations do not pay for the material, but accept and air it in hopes of attracting viewers and increasing advertising revenues. Video news releases are often slick, picture-rich items designed to catch the eye. The public usually has no knowledge that the items were selected for their expedience. Politicians have begun to use a variation of video news releases by buying time on a satellite and offering to do interviews with local anchors. The ethical problem is that often the candidates, not the station, pay for the interview. Politicians also buy infomercials—full-length programs in which they present their views. Both infomercials and satellite interviews include a brief disclaimer indicating that the candidate paid for the content, but viewers may miss or ignore the information.

Tabloid television shows have also been prominent users of checkbook journalism, and there is active bidding for information from people who are involved in current news. People associated with tragic or unusual events are often the sources for such paid information items, although the fact that the material was purchased is seldom disclosed. Television executives also pay great amounts of money for the rights to special event programming. Bidding wars ensue for the rights to the Olympics, the World Series, and a variety of other sporting events. Billions of dollars are spent for the exclusive rights to these events, which networks hope will boost the network's image, increase ratings, attract advertisers, and allow heavy promotion of prime-time programs. The concern with televising such events is not the exorbitant sums of money, but the practice of purchasing exclusive rights to cover something that is supposed to be a major news event. The public must view the network that has the exclusive rights, never knowing if another network might cover the event better.

The final area where television employs checkbook journalism is in buying the rights to real-life dramas. Almost any big news story with a tragic or unusual aspect will end up as a television movie. Real-life stories may be fictionalized or developed from court transcripts, but buying the rights provides the best method of developing a made-for-TVmovie. Local television stations often capitalize on network stories by tying local segments to the topic. The concern is that when actors from these movies are shown in newscasts with the people they portray, the line between news and entertainment becomes unclear.

Although the concept of checkbook journalism was first applied to print news reporting, television so frequently blurs the line between journalism and entertainment that such techniques as video press releases and "exclusive" stories raise little concern when the ethics of the practice are questioned. Much television programming, such as sports programs and special events, is news; however, the content is often thought of as entertainment. Since television stations and networks compete with one another for ratings and advertisers, ethical concerns take a backseat to pragmatic decisions. The problem with paying sources is that the media are being manipulated and that a measure of control is lost. Unfortunately at times, it seems, television programmers are willing to give up this control. *Milan D. Meeske*

Further Reading

Sanders, Steve. "To Pay or Not to Pay: A Case of Checkbook Journalism." *Mass Comm Review,* 1995, 23–28.
Warren, George. "Big News, Little Cameras." *Washington Journalism Review,* December 1990, 37–39.

"Checkers" Speech

In the middle of his 1952 campaign for the vice presidency, Richard Nixon was charged with being the beneficiary of $18,000 from wealthy Californians to defray his political expenses when he was a Senator. On September 18, 1952, the *New York Post* broke the story with the headline "Secret Nixon Fund." Other newspapers picked up the story and demanded an explanation. The *New York Herald Tribune* called for Nixon's withdrawal from the Republican ticket. Some party leaders urged Nixon to resign. Meanwhile, presidential candidate Dwight Eisenhower refused to take a stand for or against Nixon. Instead, Eisenhower felt that Nixon should appear on television and publicly disclose the facts about the fund.

On September 23, 1952, Richard Nixon was scheduled to speak to a national radio and television audience that included a network of 64 NBC television stations, 194 CBS Radio stations, and the 560 stations of the Mutual Broadcasting System radio network. In 1952, about 40 percent of the U.S. homes had television sets and 80 percent had radios. The 30-minute telecast was scheduled to air immediately following the popular *Milton Berle Show.* A live audience was not present that

Tuesday night at the NBC studio in Hollywood, California, but the largest television audience up to that time witnessed what was to be called the "Checkers" speech. Richard Nixon was seated behind a library table before the cameras, with his wife Pat seated nearby; his political career was at stake.

The "Checkers" speech can be easily divided into three sections. In the first section, Nixon denied unethical conduct in having the fund. He denied that the money was from contributors who received special favors. In the second section, Nixon switched to an emotional autobiographical account of working in a grocery store as a youngster, working his way through college, his marriage to Pat, practicing law, serving in World War II, and running for Congress. The title of the speech "Checkers" was drawn from the emotional allusion Nixon made about the gift of a little cocker spaniel dog to his children. His daughter, Trisha, named it Checkers. "And you know, the kids love the dog and I just want to say this right now, that regardless of what they say about it, we're gonna keep it," he said.

Nixon added to the drama by pointing out that his family was one of modest circumstances: "My mother and dad had five boys and we all worked in the store. Pat doesn't have a mink coat, but she does have a respectable Republican cloth coat." Nixon further evoked emotion by reading excerpts of a letter from a 19-year-old housewife of a U.S. Marine in Korea. She sent a check for $10 to help in Nixon's campaign. "It's one that I will never cash," Nixon said. Some sources point out that this letter from the soldier's wife, which is represented as an expression of confidence written after the fund's disclosure, was actually received and used by Nixon much earlier in the campaign.

In section three of Nixon's speech, he abruptly changed to counterattacking the ethical qualifications of the Democrats. Nixon suggested investigating the financial integrity of the Democratic ticket—Adlai Stevenson and John Sparkman. He attacked the Truman administration for fostering communism, Korea, and corruption. He vowed to fight future smear attempts and those who oppose him.

The "Checkers" speech was overwhelmingly well received by the public, with more than 2 million letters and telegrams flooding the Republican National Headquarters within a week. In fact, in terms of public response, "Checkers" stands as a phenomenal success —Nixon and his family appeared on national television, and he extricated himself from the scandal with a performance that assured his place on the ticket. Other critics targeted the numerous emotional appeals Nixon made, without ever admitting to poor judgment. The "Checkers" speech was the first time television played a major part in a presidential campaign, and it contributed to the remarkable comeback of Richard Nixon. He proved himself a master of the new medium.   *Roger Hadley*

Further Reading

Baus, Herbert M., and William B. Ross. *Politics Battle Plan.* New York: Macmillian Company, 1968, 157.

Bendiner, Robert. "How Much Has TV Changed Campaigning," *New York Times Magazine,* 2 November 1952, 13.

"The Defense of Checkers." *Commonwealth,* 10 October 1952, 3.

Connie Chung

Connie Chung (Constance Yu-Hwa Chung) is a well-known female broadcast journalist. Born on August 20, 1946, in Washington, D.C., she was a news anchor for two major networks, CBS and NBC, and is currently at ABC News. She is regarded as one of the hardest-working journalists in the business. Born into a Chinese diplomat family in 1946 in the United States, Chung grew up in Washington, D.C., fostering her interest in politics. After a summer internship with New York congressman Republican Seymour Halpern, she changed her major from biology and graduated in 1969 from the University of Maryland with a bachelor of science degree in journalism.

Chung started her television career at WTTG in Washington, D.C., in 1969, where she began as a secretary in the news department, advancing to newswriter, and then to on-air reporter. She joined CBS News in 1971. Her contributions in the 1970s with CBS included coverage of George McGovern's presidential campaign and of President Richard Nixon's trip to the Middle East and the Soviet Union. She covered major political stories with determination and gained a reputation for quality reporting. In 1976, Chung's career changed when she moved to Los Angeles to anchor local newscasts for KNXT. There she became a dominant anchor figure, credited with raising the station's ranking from third to second place. In time, she became one of the best compensated local news anchors in the country, and in 1983, she moved to NBC. She anchored *NBC News at Sunrise* and occasionally hosted *Today*. She later co-anchored, with Roger Mudd, the NBC's magazine program *American Almanac*. She covered political conventions and solo anchored prime-time specials. She played a key role in NBC's reporting from China in 1987. Raising the ratings for NBC's morning news further enhanced her stature.

After a network "star war" in 1989, Connie Chung left NBC to rejoin CBS, anchoring *Saturday Night with Connie Chung* in 1989, *Face to Face with Connie Chung* in 1990, and *Eye to Eye with Connie Chung* in 1992. She started co-anchoring *CBS Evening News* with Dan Rather in 1993. Her newsmagazine *Saturday Night with Connie Chung* at times took a different approach, with performers playing the roles of real people, in an attempt to provide in-depth understanding of the story. Dubbed an infotainment-type program, it generated criticism for re-creation of events. On May 20, 1995, CBS announced that they would remove Chung as co-anchor of the "*CBS Evening News*." She resigned shortly afterwards and in November of 1997 joined ABC.

Chung has gained wide recognition as a broadcast journalist from various organizations, including an honorary degree from Norwich University. She won five Emmy Awards for consistently outstanding performance. She received a George Foster Peabody Award in 1980 for *Terra: Our World*, a series of educational programs on environmental issues. She is married to Maury Povich, a veteran television anchor and host of *A Current Affair*.   *Lena Liqing Zhang*

Further Readings:
Hickey, M. C. "This Is Her Life." *Ladies' Home Journal,* October 1993, 64–68.
Malone, M. *Connie Chung: Broadcast Journalist.* Springfield, N. J.: Enslow Publishers, 1992.

Morey, J. N., and W. Dunn. *Famous Asian Americans.* New York: Cobblehill Books, 1992.

Civil Rights Coverage

Television news has received mixed reviews regarding its contributions to civil rights in the United States. Blacks, women, and other minorities have been underrepresented in news organizations even into the 1990s, and news content has often reflected the lack of minority perspectives. Critics include the news media as the sources of negative stereotypes of blacks and other minorities in contemporary American society. And, even though television news played an important role in the Civil Rights movement of the 1960s, very few journalists could claim to have taken leadership roles while maintaining the need to stay objective and aloof.

Nowhere was this more true than in the South during the days of desegregation. Hodding Carter suggested that the southern press as a whole responded very poorly to the rising call for civil rights legislation. In their book *Race and the News Media*, Paul Fisher and Ralph Lowenstein wrote that some journalists even promoted "states' rights" to continue segregation, while defending the myth of white superiority. African American history generally has little to say about the contributions of television news to the Civil Rights movement. Taylor Branch asserts that in 1957, Martin Luther King Jr. was only the second black person ever to appear on NBC's *Meet the Press.* The first to appear was National Association for the Advancement of Colored People leader Roy Wilkins in 1956. In his first appearance on *Meet the Press*, King defended the sit-ins taking place in the South. In July of 1962, King declined an invitation from *Meet the Press* founder Lawrence Spivak to discuss the growing Civil Rights movement, opting instead to remain in an Albany, Georgia, jail in protest of unconstitutional segregation laws.

Segregated transportation and public facilities—buses, water fountains, rest rooms, seating, service—were the law throughout the South in 1958, when Joseph Brechner established WLOF-

TV Channel 9 in Orlando, Florida. Churches and businesses were mostly segregated. Most blacks in the area lived in ghettos referred to as "quarters." WLOF-TV (which became WFTV when the call letters were changed in 1963) led the southern news organizations as an early and outspoken advocate for civil rights.

WLOF-TV also took a leading role on the political front in helping its community shake off the remnants of slavery that lingered due to rigorously enforced Jim Crow laws. Brechner helped Orlando Mayor Robert Carr start orderly desegregation by becoming a leader on the Mayor's Interracial Advisory Committee, which appealed to black and white businessmen, as well as all leaders, for peaceful desegregation. Brechner also asked business leaders to hire blacks and to increase on-the-job training for black employees. WLOF-TV had already trained and hired blacks as technicians and station news personnel.

In 1960, the year the lunch-counter sit-in movement began in Greensboro, North Carolina, Brechner took over the daily operations of the station and began editorializing for action to avoid problems in race relations. Under Brechner's guidance, the WLOF-TV news department covered the Civil Rights movement in 1961 and 1962, before it became national news in 1963. Brechner and Ray Ruester, the news director and on-air commentator, backed up the news coverage with award-winning and sometimes controversial commentary—editorials, discussion shows, and documentaries.

In 1961, ABC produced the documentary "Walk in my Shoes," which chronicled social problems in America from the perspective of African-Americans. On September 19, 1961, WLOF-TV was one of more than a hundred stations across the nation to carry the documentary, but the only affiliate in Florida to do so. Stations in many parts of the South did not air the program. A WLOF-TV editorial a week later called the program "an honest, tough-talking, graphic study of a minority group in America as seen through their own eyes" and noted that the program's sponsor, Bell & Howell, had been threatened with boycotts. Then, in 1963, as WFTV, the station supported the nonviolent tactics of civil disobedience. The editorials even took on the Ku Klux Klan, which had threatened to blow up the station's transmission tower.

In 1963, the urgency of the Civil Rights movement was brought to the nation's consciousness with images on network news of police abuse on passive demonstrators. The Southern Christian Leadership Conference started its Birmingham campaign in April of 1963, with a series of sit-ins and marches. On May 2, 1963, hundreds of children joined the demonstrations, resulting in the arrests of 959 people. On May 3, Birmingham police used dogs and high-pressure water hoses on the demonstrators. Graphic photographs and television footage resulted in national and international outrage. This incident, more than any event to date, according to David Garrow in *Eyes on the Prize*, "made Americans more profoundly aware of the obstacles and opposition facing the southern black freedom struggle."

After the incident, Martin Luther King Jr. assured his followers that they were no longer alone because the struggle had made it onto NBC's *Huntley-Brinkley Report*. After that, the national media increased coverage, and as they did, the Civil Rights movement gained momentum. Localized demonstrations grew, and a national march on the nation's capital was planned for the end of summer. That August, ABC news produced a five-part series, "Crucial Summer: The 1963 Civil Rights Crisis." In station promotions, WFTV urged viewers to watch the series "to understand better the issues involved in the Civil Rights march which climaxes this crucial summer." All three networks, led by CBS, provided at least some live coverage of the March on Washington. CBS also filmed parts of the voting registration movement in Greenwood, Mississippi. From 1960 to 1968, WFTV produced at least 87 television editorials about civil rights. The Federal Communications Commission found WFTV a model of fairness in its portrayal of civil rights and other community issues. The editorials continued until the FCC approved a licensing-dispute settlement in 1969 at which time the owner agreed to lease its facilities to other applicants. ***See also*** Minority Groups, Race Relations Coverage.

Linda M. Perry

Further Reading

Branch, Taylor. *Parting the Waters: America in the King Years 1954–63*. New York: Simon & Schuster, 1988.

Fisher, Paul, and Ralph Lowenstein. *Race and the News Media*. New York: Praeger, 1967.

Perry, Linda M., "A TV Pioneer's Crusade for Civil Rights in the Segregated South: WFTV, Orlando, Florida." In *Television in America: Local Station History from Across the Nation*, edited by Michael D. Murray and Donald G. Godfrey, 128–154. Ames: Iowa State University Press, 1997.

Michele Clark

Michele Clark was born on December 8, 1941, in Gary, Indiana. She studied at Grinnell College in Iowa and Roosevelt University in Chicago, where she grew up. She worked as a writer at WBBM-TV in Chicago and graduated from the minority journalism program at Columbia University in 1970, a program developed by Fred Friendly, then at the Ford Foundation. Clark was the first student admitted to that program, which was developed in response to the death of Martin Luther King Jr., and the Kerner Commission Report, which indicted the press for its failure to address minority issues, including hiring.

After graduation from the Columbia program, Clark returned to Chicago to work as a general assignment reporter at WBBM-TV but within six months, returned to New York and began working at CBS News. During the 1972 political primaries, she reported from New Hampshire, Wisconsin, and California. Clark was the first black woman to cover a national political convention as a network correspondent, a fact that Walter Cronkite announced to viewers during the Democratic National Convention in July. She was also substitute anchor for the CBS *Morning News*. Clark died in an airplane crash in a residential area of Chicago at the age of 29 on December 8, 1972.

After her death, the Radio-Television News Directors Foundation established the Michele Clark Fellowship, first awarded in 1979, to outstanding young people with an interest in studying broadcast journalism. For a brief period, 1973–1974, the summer minority journalism program at Columbia University also bore Michele Clark's name.

Michael D. Murray

Further Reading

"Fellowship Encourages Other Young Journalists." *Communicator*, September 1995, 94.

Leydig, Kimberly, and Sue O'Brien. "A Reporter's Short, Sensational Career," *Communicator*, September 1995, 91–94.

"Michele Clark, CBS News Correspondent." Obituary *Washington Post*, 10 December 1972, B4.

CNN (Cable News Network)

Robert Edward (Ted) Turner launched the Cable News Network (CNN) on June 1, 1980, pioneering the concept of 24-hour television news, emphasizing live reporting of events. By introducing live television from around the world, Turner could claim improved international understanding. Until Turner's 24-hour news network went on the air, the idea seemed unrealistic. He had a questionable news track record on his own cable-distributed national superstation, WTBS, his upstart superstation only carried news, and start-up resources were limited.

Turner hired Maurice Wolfe (Reese) Schonfeld in 1978 to help. Schonfeld had been a producer for UPI Movietone News and manager for UPI Television News where he led efforts to provide news to independent stations in competition with the three major networks. Schonfeld knew how to operate on a tight budget, and he claimed that the networks and AT&T conspired to prevent independent news operations from using telephone lines to transmit news reports in a crisis. Schonfeld thought that the networks were limited by their entertainment priorities and their 22-minute daily news programs. Schonfeld tutored Turner in the news business and some basic news concepts, such as preventing advertisers' interference with on-air talent selection.

Initially, several events seemed to conspire to keep CNN off the air, including a false report that Turner had died in a boating accident and a factual report that the satellite designed to transmit CNN's signal had disappeared. Turner announced his plans for creating CNN just after receiving news that *Satcom III,* the privately owned RCA satellite that was to carry CNN's signal, had suddenly and inexplicably gone blank after its launch into space. Trouble continued up to the last minute. While Turner dedicated the station to world peace in a live broadcast and ceremony, producers argued over how to introduce their first broadcast. When the time came, the anchors simply began reading the news.

Turner bet his entire fortune and all the credit he could muster on CNN. He succeeded with a lower budget than the networks because of the Atlanta location (instead of New York), nonunion workers, and a staff dedicated to news. Although some staff people thought Turner's judgment was questionable, they also found him inspirational and did more work for him, for less pay, than their counterparts at the networks. Some young staff learned the business as they went, and sometimes they made mistakes. With an emphasis on live coverage, some warned that the network would cover a lot of two-alarm fires that turned out to be small stories, but Turner's staff responded that viewers would not know the outcome unless they watched to the end.

Critics underestimated the impact of a news channel with live remotes around the world. Turner's friend, President Jimmy Carter, treated the new network on a par with other major networks accommodating CNN's live needs and providing equal access to the newcomer. Other events helped CNN. In its first year, CNN covered the MGM Grand hotel fire in Las Vegas, the eruption of Mount St. Helens volcano, and the national Republican and Democratic conventions. Iranian revolutionaries had taken Americans hostage in the U.S. embassy in Tehran in November 1979, creating an ongoing story that CNN's staff was eager to cover. However, with live television coverage, international terrorists found an immediate audience for hostage taking and other dramas. When the Persian Gulf War began in early 1991, CNN's reporters were the only ones allowed to remain in Baghdad, even while American planes bombed the city. Some network affiliates took CNN feeds along with—or instead of—their own. The Gulf War finally made CNN competitive, and subsequent events increased its popularity. Live cover-

age narrated by talk-show host Larry King made an international event of the police chase of O.J. Simpson's Bronco after the murder of the former football player's wife. Subsequent coverage of Simpson's trials drew an audience craving for live coverage.

Dependent upon advertisers and subscription fees from cable systems, Turner found himself to be an advocate for paid cable television. Turner soon had to diversify in order to compete with the networks. CNN's *Headline News* began on December 31, 1981, providing news summaries and updates every half hour. The major networks have followed CNN's example by increasing live event coverage and frequent news updates. Other television news organizations also followed CNN's example. *Court TV* specialized in criminal and civil trials on television. NBC News created CNBC, specializing in business news, and later joined with the Microsoft Corporation to create MSNBC, challenging CNN on both television and the Internet.

Time Warner acquired Turner Broadcasting Company with its CNN subsidiaries in 1995, with Time Warner chairman Gerald M. Levin promising to give the 24-hour news network a central role in what has become the world's largest entertainment company. At the time of the merger, CNN had 2,500 editorial employees in 30 bureaus around the world. Time, Inc. publishes 24 magazines, and CNN soon began carrying programs based on some of them, including *CNN-SI* with *Sports Illustrated* and *CNN-Time's* weekly "Impact" magazine program. Executives began exploring ways editorial efforts could bridge print and broadcast media. *Fortune* and *Money* magazines contributed to CNN *Financial News (CNNfn)*, competing with CNBC for the small business-oriented audience.

In June 1998, CNN introduced an hour-long newsmagazine, *NewsStand*. The joint venture with Time Inc.-owned magazines helped CNN formalize ties with three of the nation's leading special interest publications: *Time*, *Fortune*, and *Entertainment Weekly*. The production partnership began with separate publication support each of the three evenings it initially aired—Sundays, Wednesdays, and Thursdays—with a goal of daily programming by the following year. The brainchild of CNN president Rick Kaplan, it started with an established team of hosts and contributors including Jeff Greenfield, Bernard Shaw, Willow Bay, Stephen Frazier, and Judd Rose. The opening segment of the series, airing Sunday, June 7, 1998, reported on the use of lethal nerve gas in a mission to Laos by U.S. Army Commandos sent to kill American defectors during the Vietnam War. That report for *NewsStand*, prepared jointly by CNN and *Time*, estimated that up to 20 American defectors were killed, along with as many as 80 other people, in the secret raid of September 1970 called "Operation Tailwind." Less than a month after the airing of that segment of *NewsStand,* CNN retracted the nerve gas report. The network hired attorney Floyd Abrams to investigate the story, and he discovered that CNN's research could not support the story conclusions. *See also* Ted Turner

William E. Huntzicker

Further Reading

Goldberg, Robert, and Gerald Jay Goldberg. *Citizen Turner: The Wild Rise of an American Tycoon .* New York: Harcourt Brace and Company, 1995.
Petrozello, Donna. "CNN Gets Into Long Form," *Broadcasting & Cable,* 1 June 1998, 35.
Smith, Perry M. *How CNN Fought the War: A View from the Inside.* New York: Birch Lane Press, 1991.
Whittemore, Hank. *CNN: The Inside Story: How a Band of Mavericks Changed the Face of Television News.* Boston: Little, Brown and Company, 1990.

Barbara Cochran

In April of 1997, Barbara Cochran was named president of the Radio-Television New Directors Association (RTNDA) and the Radio-Television News Directors Foundation (RTNDF). She heads the largest national organization designed specifically to address the needs of broadcast news executives. Among her goals as president are: protection against challenges to electronic journalism on First Amendment grounds and helping the public to understand standards of journalism.

Photo courtesy Radio-Television News Directors Association

Cochran was born on June 16, 1945 in Akron, Ohio. She graduated from Swarthmore College and holds a master's degree from the Columbia University School of Journalism. She began working as a journalist at the *Washington Star* newspaper and in 1979 took a position at National Public Radio (NPR). In the early 1980s, she headed the news division of NPR and helped create the radio news program *Morning Edition.* From there she became an NBC political editor in 1983 and eventually the executive producer of *Meet the Press* in 1985. Cochran moved to CBS in 1989, where she was in charge of the CBS News coverage in Washington, D.C., and from July of 1995 to 1997, was an executive producer for politics at CBS News. Cochran is now working fulltime with the RTNDA.

She is married to ABC News chief congressional correspondent John Cochran. *See also* RTNDA.   *Michael D. Murray*

Further Reading

Albiniak, Paige. "Covering the Journalism Waterfront." *Broadcasting & Cable,* 3 August 1998, 60.
"Cochran Named RTNDA President. *Communicator,* May 1997, 8.
Jessell, Harry L. "Cochran Takes Over at RTNDA." *Broadcasting & Cable*, 24 March 1997, 18.
Trigoboff, Dan. "Cochran Presses Her Case." *Broadcasting & Cable*, 15 September 1997, 50–53.

John Cochran

John Cochran was born on March 15, 1939, in Montgomery, Alabama. He graduated from the University of Alabama, and in 1967, received a master's degree from the University of Iowa. He started his career as a journalist working part-time in radio while still in college, and after graduating, he joined WSOC-TV in Charlotte, North Carolina, as a reporter and anchor. He then became a reporter for WRC-TV in Washington, D.C., and in 1972, started working for NBC. Cochran reported on the Vietnam War as a free-lance correspondent in 1966 and was responsible for covering the Christmas bombing of Hanoi in 1972—the first journalist to report that action. Other major stories of the era, including the Watergate scandal and resignation of Richard Nixon, were covered from his prominent post as a Capitol Hill correspondent.

Cochran held positions at NBC as a chief diplomatic correspondent in 1987 and 1988 and as a chief European correspondent, while headquartered in London from 1978 to 1987. He spent two decades as a senior correspondent, covering the White House, Capitol Hill, and the Pentagon, for *NBC Nightly News.* He has received two Emmy Awards: one for reporting in Poland in 1981; the other for his anchoring during the overthrow of the Communist regime in Romania in 1989. In 1994, Cochran moved to ABC and covered the Washington scene for ABC News.

Cochran currently reports for the *World News Tonight, Nightline,* and *ABC News Specials.* He is married to Barbara Cochran, former political editor at NBC News in Washington, D.C., and current president of the Radio-Television News Directors Association.   *Michael D. Murray*

Further Reading

Braestrup, Peter. "Vietnam, in Retrospect." *Media Critic,* Fall 1995, 32–44.
Goldberg, Robert, and Gerald Jay Goldberg. *Anchors.* New York: Birch Lane Press, 1990.
Rowe, Chip. "Bylines: Other Washington Faces." *American Journalism Review,* March 1994, 10.

Charles Collingwood

Collingwood was born in Three Rivers, Michigan, on June 4, 1917. He received his bachelor of arts (cum laude) degree in pre-law from Cornell in May 1939 and was awarded a Rhodes scholarship. He began his studies at Oxford the following fall and was also hired part-time as a local correspondent for United Press. He left Oxford in 1940 to pursue a full-time career in journalism.

Collingwood began his career as a reporter for United Press in London in 1939–1941 covering the war in Europe. With great news sense and a natural radio voice, he built his reputation as a radio war correspondent with on-the-spot coverage of the North African campaign. In 1941, at the age of 23, he was hired as the youngest of "Murrow's boys," an elite group of war correspondents hired by Edward R. Murrow of CBS to provide overseas coverage of World War II. As a radio reporter, Collinwood covered the war in North Africa and Europe until 1946. Known as an "ace" correspondent, he often scooped his newspaper colleagues with his radio reports about the war. He was able to convey to the U.S. audience the first indications that the Allies were meeting resistance in the North African campaign.

On his return to the U.S. in 1946, Collingwood became the first CBS correspondent to cover the United Nations. He has served as a White House correspondent, the chief of the CBS London bureau, and a chief foreign correspondent for CBS News. He covered the war in Vietnam, President's Nixon's visit to China, the Arab-Israeli War, and the Soviet occupation of Prague. Collingwood was the first American correspondent admitted into North Vietnam, and, in 1973, he co-anchored the broadcast of Princess Anne's wedding in London. Closer to home, he hosted *Person to Person* (succeeding his friend Murrow) and a famous 1962 special, "A Tour of the White House" with Mrs. Kennedy. He also was a reporter for *CBS Reports* and *Chronicle.* He covered the 1948 Republican National Convention, and in 1954, he co-hosted, with Dorothy Doan, *The Good Morning Show,* CBS's answer to NBC's highly successful *Today* program.

Collingwood received a Peabody Award in 1943 for outstanding reporting of the news. Other journalism honors included awards from the National Headliners Club and the Overseas Press Club. In 1975 he was appointed by Queen Elizabeth as a commander in the Order of the British Empire in recognition of his contributions to British-American friendship. He also was a chevalier of the French Legion of Honor. Collingwood retired from CBS News in 1982 and served as special correspondent until his death on October 3, 1985. The occasion of Collingwood's funeral is mentioned in a number of the books about CBS as being the symbolic event signaling the end of the Murrow era at that network. *See also* CBS Reports.

Mary E. Beadle

Further Reading

Bliss, Edward Jr. *Now the News: The Story of Broadcast Journalism.* New York: Columbia University Press, 1991.
Gates, Gary Paul. *Air Time: The Inside Story of CBS News.* New York: Harper and Row, 1978.
Leonard, Bill. *In the Storm of the Eye: A Lifetime at CBS.* New York: Putnam, 1987.

Ann Compton

Ann Compton has led the way for female broadcast journalists breaking into coverage of presidential politics, an area of journalism that was once the exclusive domain of male reporters. She was born on January 19, 1947 in Chicago, Illinois. After graduating from Hollins College in 1969, Compton began her television news career in Roanoke, Virginia, where she was a reporter, an anchor, and a state house correspondent for WDBJ-TV. She was hired by ABC in 1973 and covered the White House in the 1970s and Congress in the 1980s. Compton served as a panelist during the 1988 and 1992 presidential debates. When she became ABC's chief White House correspondent in 1996, Compton was the first woman to be named to a full-time position covering the White House.

Compton has expressed concern that advances in communications technology used by correspondents who cover Congress may actually be distancing reporters from face-to-face reporting on Capitol Hill. Improved technical facilities installed in the 1980s made it possible for reporters to monitor Congress without actually being present in the same room. Additionally, newer, more media-savvy members of Congress began scheduling more and more press conferences in front of groups of reporters reducing the time reporters were spending in one-on-one conversations with the lawmakers. Compton believes reliance on these technological improvements may have a negative effect on Capitol Hill reporting.

Compton became embroiled in a controversy that was the topic of debate in media organizations across the nation. She was one of many famous journalists earning money by speaking to trade associations, charities, corporations, and academic institutions from the 1970s into the 1990s. In 1994, ABC tightened the rules concerning speaking fees earned by on-air talent. Richard Wald, senior vice president of news, said the move was designed to protect the network from conflict-of-interest accusations. Compton joined a number of well-known members of the ABC news team, including David Brinkley, Sam Donaldson, Chris Wallace, Brit Hume, and many others, issuing a letter of objection to that policy change.

Compton has covered five U.S. presidents and is a founding member of the Gannett Foundation Media Center's National Advisory Committee. She received an Exceptional Merit Media Award

(EMMA), from the National Women's Political Caucus in 1987 for the radio series *Women in Politics*. *See also* Women in Television News.

Sandra L. Ellis

Further Reading

Beasley, Maurine H., and S. Gibbons. *Taking Their Place: A Documentary History of Women in Journalism*. Washington, D.C: University Press of America, 1993.

Matusow, Barbara. *The Evening Stars*. Boston: Houghton-Mifflin, 1983.

Shepard, A. "Take the Money and Run." *American Journalism Review,* June 1995, 18–25.

Consultants

News consultants (or "news doctors") are most easily defined as research companies that specialize in helping local stations improve news and program ratings. Consultants provide research data to help electronic media management in the decision-making process. Theoretically, the research helps take the risk out of decision making. Historically, news consultants were primarily interested in news programming and audience development. Today they are constantly researching the marketplace, assessing and reassessing the audience and potential audience of a particular station.

There are three major consultants: Frank Magid and Associates; McHugh & Hoffman, Inc.; and Audience Research and Development (AR&D). These firms have been in business since the 1960s and 1970s and are among the largest full-service research firms. They all started as "news consultants" but have diversified as the industry has grown. Today some firms specialize in producer training. These include Reimer and Associates, the Broadcast Image Group, and Feedback Unlimited. Don Fitzpatrick and Associates also deals in talent and management placement consultation. The firms have become as diverse as the need for information about the audience. Today consultants not only provide services for the local stations, but also for program producers, developers, syndicators, networks, and growing national systems. They are not a United States phenomenon, but work around the globe.

The involvement of a consultant within a news program has not come without controversy.

The traditional newsperson decries the consultant's lack of news judgment because it is believed that news consultants have taken the industry away from traditional news values and toward a marketplace definition of news. In other words, the traditional components of news have changed from audience, timeliness, proximity, unusualness, conflict, and impact on the consumer to tabloid, marketplace values of prominence, and conflict alone. The emphasis is no longer on what the audience "needs to know," but on what the audience "wants" to know.

Cultural critics abroad have claimed that news consultants are further "Americanizing" the foreign news systems and social values of other audiences around the globe. This Americanizing of international programming has come from both imported American programming and consultants working abroad. This activity has led some countries to enact legislation mandating national material and limiting American content in domestic programming.

On the other hand, the news consultants have also been criticized for "boiler plating" their research—doing the same research in every U.S. community. The results, according to some critics, is that all stations begin to look alike. The consultants also produce a lot of fear within the newsroom as the research is largely proprietary and can be personal when it involves the careers of the on-air personnel. The reason, however, that the research is so closely guarded is that it is produced primarily to give the station a competitive edge. Therefore, a leak of the results to competing stations could dull that edge. The research information comes with a high price, and stations are not anxious to have this information become public.

The layout and design of a news consultant's research report is not unlike that of any other behavioral science report. Indeed, the consultants are applying the scientific techniques of social and behavioral research as they pertain to the broadcast program situation. The methodology is not complex, and one can access similar information in many research and university settings. The news consultant's research, however, is localized, targeted and specialized for the station and its marketplace. The reports assess attitudes and opinions toward a specific program in a given market. They are survey reports which tabulate both statistical information and open-ended questions. The questions of the survey revolve around the basic statement of the research problem. The organization of the report and the questionnaire generally follow the basic outline of the questions. Despite criticism, the news consultants continue to play an important role in audience research and development. They have made a difference in local, national, and international operations. *See also* Frank Magid.   *Donald G. Godfrey*

Further Reading

Barton, Andy. "Ten Years After." *Communicator*, February 1995, 11–12.
Stone, Vernon A. "TV News Work Force Grows, Declines Continue in Radio." *Communicator*, May 1993, 26–27.

Alistair Cooke

Photo by Jeff Overs © BBC

Alistair Cooke was born on November 20, 1908, in Manchester, England, and was educated at Cambridge and Harvard universities. He reported on American affairs for British newspapers: *Times* (London) and the *Manchester Guardian*. He began doing film criticism for radio in America and became a naturalized citizen in 1941. From 1952 to 1960, Cooke hosted the acclaimed television series *Omnibus*. During the American Bicentennial, his documentary television series *America: A Personal History*, produced by the British Broadcast-

ing Corporation (BBC), was telecast in the United States and later published in book form.

The *America* project compressed 500 years of history into 650 minutes of film. Two researchers and three film crews traveled more than 10,000 miles for the series—from Maine to Hawaii, with some filming taking place in England, Spain and France. The series utilized a collage of images, representing historic America through period prints, engravings, documents, and photos, alternated with narration by Cooke on location. The creative use of narrative and photographic elements added to the project. To heighten viewer interest, Cooke offered parallels between the past and present. Viewers were able to experience contemporary history through Cooke's own remembrances and his personal reaction to catastrophic events such as the bombings at Pearl Harbor and the Vietnam War protests.

The series was not without criticism, however. Some priorities were questioned, since the contributions of the Pilgrims were set aside while a great deal of attention was paid to the explorations of Coronado. On the other hand, more than a dozen television critics commended Cooke for his work as the author and narrator of *America*. In addition, the National Academy of Television Arts and Sciences bestowed four Emmy Awards on the program, the only television series to be awarded Emmys for both entertainment and documentary. Cooke was credited for his explanation of historic events and also his observations on unique features of America.

In addition to the *America* documentary series, Cooke hosted *Masterpiece Theatre* for the Public Broadcasting System (PBS). He has authored a dozen books, including three volumes of radio talks based on his BBC program *Letters from America*, which celebrated a half-century on the air—it the longest running one-man series in broadcasting history. He was a recipient of both the Benjamin Franklin Award of the Royal Society and a Peabody Award. Cooke was also made an honorary Knight of the British Empire in 1973 for his contributions to Anglo-American mutual understanding.   *Ellen E. Murray*

Further Reading

Cooke, Alistair. *Alistair Cooke's America.* New York: Alfred A. Knopf, 1974.

Cooke, Alistair. *America Observed.* New York: Alfred A. Knopf, 1988.

Cooke, Alistair. *Fun & Games with Alistair Cooke.* London: Pavilion Books, 1994.

Bob Costas

Photo courtesy of Bob Costas

From guest appearances on *Saturday Night Live* to interviews with politicians, Bob Costas effortlessly shifts between program formats, always eloquent and witty. Known for his work with NBC Sports, Costas has won 10 Emmy Awards. But it is his non-sports work that has elevated and made Costas unique.

Costas was born in the borough of Queens in New York City on March 22, 1952. He was raised on Long Island, spending a sizeable portion of his childhood listening to baseball broadcasts from around the country and learning what he calls the storytelling and mystique of radio. Costas quickly realized his dream of a broadcast career, landing his first professional radio job while still a 21-year-old student at Syracuse University. Only a year later, Costas won a basketball play-by-play position with KMOX Radio in St. Louis, partly on the strength of an audition tape, adjusted to make him sound more mature.

After a series of assignments announcing regional coverage of professional football and bas-

ketball, Costas quickly moved to network television. NBC Sports hired him in 1980, and since then he has covered every major U.S. sport. He has done play-by-play, in-studio hosting, and anchoring coverage of Super Bowls, World Series, and NBA Championships.

In recent years, Costas has moved away from sports announcing. He has been a substitute host on NBC's *Today* and has also served as a contributor to *Dateline* and to MSNBC's *Internight.* Talk-show host Charlie Rose labels Costas as good a pure broadcaster as he has ever seen, because he understands the medium.

Costas's versatility was best displayed on the Emmy-winning *Later with Bob Costas,* aired from 1988 to 1994. When NBC talk-show host David Letterman recommended him for a general interview format show because of his intelligence and personable manner, Costas had to be talked into the job. Despite his reticence and a time slot after midnight, *Later* quickly developed an almost cult-like following. The show was critically acclaimed because of Costas's interview style and a diverse guest list of news makers and celebrities that included everyone from Paul McCartney to Elie Wiesel and Barry Goldwater.

The most prestigious assignment of Costas's career has been hosting Olympic broadcasts. In 1992, and again in 1996, Costas served as the anchor for NBC's two-week-long coverage of the Olympics. Beyond dispensing information, Costas saw his anchor role as capturing the drama of the Olympics and bringing perspective to enhance viewers' enjoyment and understanding.

Costas's youthful appearance belies his professional stature and accomplishments. He is often interviewed about the cultural and business implications of sports and has appeared on *Nightline* and National Public Radio. He has been mentioned as a potential commissioner of major league baseball and is scheduled to again host NBC coverage of the Olympics in 2000 and 2002. Costas lives in St. Louis with his wife and two children. ***See also*** Sports Coverage. *Stuart L. Esrock*

Further Reading

Carter, Bill. "Raising the Quip Toss to an Olympic Sport."*New York Times,* 22 July 1992, C1, C10.

Halberstam, David. "Little Big: Bob Costas on Jocks, Jerks and the Best Job in the World." *Men's Journal,* September 1993, 114–122.

Parker, M. "The Man Who Really Knows the Score." *Newsweek,* 22 July 1996, 51.

Katie Couric

Courtesy NBC News/*Today*

When NBC's morning program *Today* needed a new star in the spring of 1991, Katie Couric was hired to fill one of television's most conspicuous jobs. She offered a sunny, candid personality that was an instant hit with audiences.

Couric was born on January 7, 1957, in Washington, D.C., and was raised in Arlington, Virginia. She graduated with honors from the University of Virginia. In 1979, she became an assignment-desk assistant for ABC News in Washington, D.C., where she impressed senior journalists. In 1980, Couric moved to a desk job at CNN. Filling in once as an anchor, executives felt she looked and sounded too young, but she kept working as a CNN associate producer and reporter and as a local reporter in Miami and Washington, D.C. She joined NBC in 1989, assigned to cover the Pentagon and soon was shifted to the *Today* show.

Couric quickly proved equal to her *Today* partner, veteran Bryant Gumbel, through repartee and a gritty journalistic spirit. She functioned as a Pentagon correspondent for *Today* during the Gulf War and interviewed General Norman Schwarzkopf at the close of that conflict. President Bush strayed near her at the White House and was subjected to a tough impromptu interview. She grilled 1996 presidential candidate Bob Dole so intensely that his wife Elizabeth, appearing on other shows, reportedly snubbed *Today*. Couric has been a recipient of the Sigma Delta Chi and National Headliners Club Awards. She was married to the late Jay Monahan, an attorney and network legal analyst. ***See also*** *Today.* *James Upshaw*

Further Reading
Bumiller, Elisabeth. "What You Don't Know about Katie Couric." *Good Housekeeping,* August 1996, 72.
Rader, Dotson. "We Mustn't Let All the Bad News Eclipse the Good." *Parade Magazine,* 17 December 1995, 4.
Zurawik, David. "*Today* Returns to 'Girl Next Door' Host." *Orlando Sentinel Tribune,* 8 April 1991, D1.

Christine Craft

A local news anchor in the 1970s and 1980s, Christine Craft achieved fame in 1983 for alleging fraud and sex discrimination after a Kansas City television station took her off the air. Craft's allegations served as a *cause célèbre* for many television journalists who feared that beauty and cosmetic factors were interfering with the news process. Eventually, Craft rose as a symbol for concerns about gender equality in the media. Craft was able to effectively make her case and initially won support, but in the end, she was defeated in a lawsuit filed against Metromedia, the owner of the Kansas City station. The final result of the case was an affirmation of the existing television news "star system" and a legal precedent for broadcasters' use of audience rating and news consultants' research in the hiring and firing of on-air personnel.

Craft was born in 1945 in San Marino, California, and received a bachelor of arts degree in education in 1968 from the University of California–Santa Barbara. She worked briefly for CBS Sports before taking a job as a news anchor at KEYT in Santa Barbara in 1979. Her move to Kansas City, to assume a similar position at Metromedia's KMBC, came two years later. Her on-air debut was accompanied by several complaints from viewers, some about her appearance.

These comments were followed by "make over" sessions in which Craft was advised on wardrobe and cosmetics by the Dallas-based news consulting firm, Audience Research & Development (AR&D). In August 1981, eight months after her first Kansas City broadcast and two months after an AR&D research report had shown a low "Q score" (a measure of an anchor's popularity), Craft was demoted to a weekend position. Craft resigned form KMBC and two years later sued the broadcast company for fraud and sex discrimination.

Craft's first trial in July of 1983 received national publicity, much of it based on Craft's allegation that she had been demoted because she was "not pretty enough and not deferential to men." The jury ruled in favor of Craft—a decision that would have allowed her to collect a half-million dollars in damages—but it was later overturned. The final ruling was based on a nearly identical case in Rhode Island, in which a federal court had upheld the firing of a similarly aggrieved news anchor because of viewer response. The judge had written, "consultant's reports and ratings routinely serve as the basis for personnel changes." The Craft case ended in 1986 when the Supreme Court denied a final petition. After this, Craft worked for a small television station in Sacramento before writing a book about her experiences, entering law school, and then becoming a radio talk-show host. In public appearances she has given stern warnings to anyone intent on following in her footsteps in television. "It is a field without a soul," she maintains. *See also* Women in Television News.

Craig Allen

Further Reading

Craft, Christine. *An Anchorwoman's Story.* Santa Barbara, CA: Capra, 1986.
Craft v. Metromedia, Inc., 766 F. 2d 1205 (8th Cir. 1985); 106 Sup.Ct. 1285.
Gielow, L.S. "Sex Discrimination in Newscasting." *Michigan Law Review,* 1985, 443–74.

Catherine Crier

Catherine Crier, a native Texan, has pursued an unconventional path to a career in television news. That path has taken her from trial lawyer, to Republican politician, to civil judge, and to television news personality. She says the role of a lawyer and judge is not very different from that of a journalist—both involve hitting the streets, interviewing witnesses, evaluating evidence, writing reports, and presenting a clear and concise story.

Catherine Jean Crier was born in Dallas, Texas, on November 11, 1954. She received a bachelor of arts degree from the University of Texas at Austin in 1975. She received her doctor of law degree from Southern Methodist University in Dallas in 1977, at the age of 22.

After law school, Crier worked as an assistant district attorney for Dallas County and later as a civil litigation attorney with a private law firm in Dallas. In 1984, when she was 29, she ran on the Republican ticket for judge of the state civil court and won, becoming the youngest person in Texas history to be elected a judge. She presided over the 162nd District Court in Dallas County, Texas, from 1985 until 1989, when she resigned to pursue a television career.

It was at a Christmas party in Dallas in 1988 when Crier was spotted by a talent agent named Jack Hubbard. This led to her being hired by Cable News Network (CNN) in 1989 to co-anchor CNN's early-evening newscast *The World Today* with Bernard Shaw. In 1991, she added a live morning talk program, *Crier & Company,* to her duties at CNN. Her work at CNN led to an offer from ABC, and in 1993, she joined *20/20* newsmagazine as a correspondent in 1993. At ABC, Crier also created and hosted the prime-time special "America's War on Drugs—Searching for Solutions."

Crier left ABC in late 1996 to join the Fox News Channel and to host a live, nightly, one-hour interview program, *The Crier Report,* featuring newsmakers of the day. In 1997, Crier was criticized for anchoring a bogus "Special Report" during the Super Bowl on Fox. The "news bulletin" she read concerned a Blues Brothers' prison break and was in fact the network's introduction to their half-time entertainment program featuring the Blues Brothers. This incident resulted in a clarification of the need to separate news from entertainment programming on the part of many broadcasters.

Suzanne Huffman

Further Reading

Fensch, Thomas, ed. *Television News Anchors.*
   Jefferson, NC: McFarland & Company, Inc.,
   Publishers, 1993.
Kamp, David. "The Crier Game." *Gentlemens
   Quarterly,* Spring 1993, 298–303.
Park, Jeannie. "Here Comes the Judge—Catherine
   Crier Now Presides at the News Desk." *People
   Weekly,* 6 November 1989, 59–60.

Walter Cronkite

CBS Photo Archive

No broadcaster epitomizes the development of
American television news more than Walter
Cronkite, the longtime anchor of the *CBS Evening
News.* Voted "The Most Trusted Man in America"
in 1973, Cronkite has been viewed as the dean of
broadcast journalists. Years after his retirement in
1981, he remained active in the field of television.
In his career, Cronkite worked for newspapers,
wire services, radio and television, and in documentary film.

Walter Leland Cronkite Jr. was born in St.
Joseph, Missouri, on November 4, 1916. An article
in *American Boy* magazine about a foreign correspondent intrigued the young man, so young
Walter tried out the field of journalism at San
Jacinto High School in Houston, Texas, where he
worked on the student newspaper and yearbook.
After high school, Cronkite became the campus
correspondent for the *Houston* Post while a student at the University of Texas in Austin. He also
worked part-time for a Houston radio station,

KNOW, but eventually Cronkite left that job, and
college, for a full-time job with the *Post,* a position
he held for one year. In his television documentary, "Cronkite Remembers," he recalls that he
applied for a position as a staff announcer at
KNOW but was not hired because the station manager said he would "never make it as a radio announcer."

According to his official CBS biography,
Cronkite worked in radio as a sports announcer at
Kansas City's KCMO radio after he left the *Post.*
In those days, Cronkite—at the controls back at
the studio—"faked" the play by play for the local
football broadcasts. He would announce the scores
while playing tapes of high school bands and describing the attire of local residents. In 1937,
Cronkite left radio to join United Press (UP) and
became a World War II correspondent, covering
several battles, including the invasion of
Normandy in June of 1944 and the Battle of the
Bulge. After the war, he was the chief UP correspondent at the Nuremberg war crime trials. He
then became the UP's Moscow bureau chief.

Cronkite stayed with United Press until 1948,
briefly returning to radio after the war's end. For
the next two years, Cronkite was the Washington
correspondent for a group of 10 midwestern radio
stations. Cronkite joined CBS News in 1950 following a call from Edward R. Murrow. CBS had
acquired a television station in Washington, D.C.,
and Cronkite was assigned to the bureau to do a
television show. It was his first foray into television. Cronkite said the early days of television
news consisted of "pictorial radio news," and he
tried to make the newscasts newsy and legitimate.
Within a year, he was appearing on nationally
broadcast public affairs programs like *Man of the
Week* and *It's News to Me.* In February of 1953,
Cronkite narrated the first documentary in the series *You Are There.* He was also the host of CBS's
first morning news show.

The 1948 political conventions were covered
briefly by a handful of television stations, but
when television began its national gavel-to-gavel
coverage of political conventions in 1952, Walter
Cronkite was in the anchor seat. He wrote often
regarding television's potential influence on politics, views which were later realized. In the late

1950s, with the launch of Sputnik and the beginning of the space race, Cronkite became CBS's lead space reporter for NASA Projects Mercury, Gemini, and Apollo. When astronaut Neil Armstrong stepped off the Eagle onto the face of the moon, Cronkite was at the anchor desk, wiping away tears of joy and excitement.

On April 16, 1962, Cronkite was named anchor of the *CBS Evening News*, then a 15-minute show. Sixteen months later on September 2, 1963, Cronkite presided over the first half-hour network broadcast of television's evening news. Cronkite, then deeply involved with reporting on the space program, said some feared this appointment would interfere with his coverage of Project Mercury. He saw to it that his roles as broadcaster and reporter were in synch. Cronkite's first show with a half-hour format began with an interview with President John F. Kennedy. Only two months later, Cronkite led Americans through the aftermath of the assassination and the funeral of President Kennedy. Cronkite is remembered for his emotional reaction to the death of the president—another occasion that moved the broadcaster to tears.

Cronkite's reporting also took him to the site of his third war, Vietnam. At the end of a special report on the Tet offensive, Cronkite uttered the words that, according to some, brought about an end to the presidency of Lyndon B. Johnson. Cronkite called for an end to the Vietnam conflict. In an editorial comment in January 1968, something he rarely did, Cronkite said, "It is increasingly clear to this reporter that the only rational way out will be to negotiate—not as visitors, but as an honorable people who lived up to their pledge to defend democracy, and did the best they could." White House press secretary Bill Moyers later indicated that Johnson expressed the view that if he had lost Cronkite, then he felt he had lost America.

On March 6, 1981, after 19 years, Cronkite retired as the anchor of the *CBS Evening News* and became a special correspondent. *Time* magazine wrote, "After Friday, there won't be anybody to say with insistent confidence, 'and that's the way it is.'" His production company, Cronkite/ Ward, started in the mid-nineties. His retired anchor status ended in October 1998 with the an-

nouncement that he would lead CNN's coverage of John Glenn's return to space. ***See also*** CBS News.

Ginger Rudeseal Carter

Further Reading
Cronkite, Walter. *A Reporter Remembers.* New York: Simon and Schuster, 1997.
Gates, Gary Paul. *Air Time.* New York: Harper & Row, 1978.
James, Doug. *Walter Cronkite: His Life and Times.* Brentwood, TN: JM Press, 1991.
Murray, Michael D. *The Political Performers.* New York: Praeger, 1994.
Slater, Robert. *This . . . Is CBS.* Englewood Cliffs, N.J.: Prentice Hall, 1988.

Crossfire

Crossfire is a nightly, half-hour-long, public affairs television program devoted to the discussion of current political issues. Guests on *Crossfire* typically include past and present White House staffers, diplomats, cabinet officials, congressional representatives, senators, business leaders, labor organizers, and other newsmakers. These guests participate either from the program's Washington, D.C., studio or by satellite link from other cities. The basic format of *Crossfire* includes two hosts, one each selected to represent conservative and liberal viewpoints and two guests, one each representing conservative and liberal perspectives on the issues under discussion. The four participants explain and defend their own views while attempting to refute the views of others on the topics being addressed. Typical topics discussed on *Crossfire* include the role of women in America, minimum wage laws, political scandals, legalization of drugs, U.S. foreign policy, media coverage, and domestic political campaigns.

Crossfire first aired in 1982 as a local radio program in the Washington, D.C., area. Patrick Buchanan, a newspaper columnist, familiar to many for his outspoken views and attempts to attain the Republican nomination for the presidency, was one of the two original hosts of the program and represented the conservative point of view. Tom Braden, a newspaper columnist and former CIA operative, was the program's other original host and usually embodied a more liberal viewpoint than Buchanan. The program was obtained by Ted Turner's Cable News Network (CNN) and is currently broadcast live every weeknight from Washington, D.C. *Crossfire* is one of CNN's most popular programs, as evidenced by its high ratings. Patrick Buchanan and Tom Braden remained as hosts of the program from its inception as a radio show through its change to a television format and acquisition by CNN.

John Sununu, former chief of staff under President George Bush, took Buchanan's place on the conservative end of the ideological spectrum when Buchanan left to campaign for the Republican Party's presidential nomination in 1992. After withdrawing from the presidential contest, Buchanan rejoined the program. Following Pat Buchanan's return, he and Sununu began to alternate hosting duties as representatives of the conservative perspective. When Buchanan left the program again to pursue his political interests, he was replaced by conservative newspaper columnist and television personality Robert Novak, who appears on another public affairs program, *Evans & Novak*.

Tom Braden was with the program until 1989, when his position was taken over by Michael Kinsley. Kinsley previously had edited and written for the *New Republic* magazine where he was known for his insightful commentary and analysis of both liberal and conservative positions. He remained with *Crossfire* until the end of 1995. The mantle of the left was next given to Geraldine Ferraro, former New York congressional representative and 1984 Democratic Party vice presidential nominee, and to Bill Press, former chair of the California State Democratic Party. Both joined the program in the middle of 1996. *Crossfire* currently uses an alternating hosts format—wherein one of the more liberal hosts, Geraldine Ferraro or Bill Press, appears with one of the more conservative hosts, John Sununu or Robert Novak, on any given evening.

Crossfire, like many similar public affairs discussion programs on television, has been criticized by a number of newspaper and magazine columnists for a decidedly right-wing bias. While the conservative commentators on *Crossfire* believe and advocate conservative views, the liberal commentators more often represent centrist views rather than extreme liberal perspectives. As a result, some have argued that *Crossfire* and similar programs exclude genuinely liberal political viewpoints from public discourse.

Crossfire's popularity with viewers has led CNN to create a new weekend offering called *Crossfire Sunday*. This program focuses on a single topic each week. *Crossfire Sunday* currently features Bob Beckel, a former Democratic campaign official, representing liberal views, and Lynne Cheney, author and former chair of the National Endowment for the Humanities, representing a conservative ideological stance for the program. *See also* Pat Buchanan.

Danette E. Ifert

Further Reading

Bennett, W. Lance. *News: The Politics of Illusion.* New York: Longman, 1996.

Hitchens, Christopher. "Out of the Crossfire." *The Nation,* 4 March 1996, 8.

Kurtz, Howard. "Caught in the Crossfire." *American Journalism Review,* January/February 1996, 40–46.

D

Dateline NBC

Dateline NBC, produced by NBC News, is an hour-long, prime-time newsmagazine program, which premiered in March of 1992. The multi-evening weekly telecasts include investigative features and newsmaker profiles. The program has aired live, in-depth stories of breaking news, including the TWA Flight 800 crash, the Unabomber investigation, the Oklahoma City bombing, Los Angeles earthquakes, and other important stories, on a more frequent basis than most newsmagazines. The program has broken news with stories concerning the abuse of women, the Marine Corps hazing, in-depth reports on medical ethics in right-to-die cases, and an investigation into the child welfare system.

Jane Pauley and Stone Phillips are the primary anchors. In 1997, *Dateline NBC* was honored with several awards for journalism excellence, including a silver baton from the Alfred T. duPont-Columbia University Awards. While *Dateline* was once castigated for coverage of a truck safety test, resulting in an explosion that had been planted by the staff, the series has, more recently, also garnered considerable praise, receiving eight Emmy Awards, seven National Headliner Awards, the Silver Gavel from the American Bar Association, and the Edward R. Murrow Award (the highest programming recognition of the Radio-Television News Directors Association).

Dateline received more awards in the 1995–1996 season than any other network newsmagazine, and in 1997, the program was honored with Edward R. Murrow Awards in five diffferent categories: feature reporting, investigative reporting, new series, spot news, and sports reporting. Winning topics included investigative stories:"Airline Security," offering viewers results of a three-month-long examination of how airport security personnel are screened, trained, and monitored; plus "A Mother's Love," an account of a severely dyslexic student and his mother. The student became one of the youngest students ever to enter Yale's law school. Another story focused on a smear campaign against the reporter Valerie Helmbreck.

Dateline reporters honored with Murrow awards included anchor Jane Pauley, Victoria Corderi, Chris Hansen, Keith Morrison, and Dennis Murphy. Coverage of the death and funerals of both Diana, Princess of Wales, and Mother Teresa of Calcutta, received praise from around the globe for *Dateline* and NBC as did medical reports by Dr. Bob Arnot. For the first time since 1988, *Dateline* dominated over ABC's *Monday Night Football* in ratings for the week, beginning September 1, 1997. *Dateline NBC* is currently seen internationally on NBC Europe and NBC Asia, reaching more than 79 million households in 59 countries. The international version of *Dateline NBC*, created exclusively for pan-European audiences, features reports from NBC correspondents world-wide. *See also* Dr. Robert Arnot.

Gloria G. Horning

Further Reading
Donlon, Brian, and James R. Healey. "NBC Looks at What Went Wrong; Staff Reprimands May Follow." *USA Today,* 10 February 1993, 3D.
McClellan, Steve. "Family Feud." *Broadcasting & Cable*, 5 May 1997, 26.
Rice, Lynette. "Are You Ready for Some 'Date-line'?" *Broadcasting & Cable,* 15 September 1997, 29.

Peter Davis

Peter Davis has written and produced some of the most renowned and provocative documentaries aired on television in the United States. He has described his documentary work as adversarial, opposed to powerful institutions that rarely have to justify themselves or their policies to the public. Davis's place in broadcast history was assured through his efforts as writer-producer of the 1971 *CBS Reports* documentary entitled "The Selling of the Pentagon."

Davis was born in Los Angeles in 1937 and graduated manga cum laude from Harvard in 1957. He worked at the *New York Times*, was drafted into the army in 1959, and upon completion of military service, helped produce documentaries for Sextant Productions and NBC. After joining CBS News in 1965, Davis served as writer and associate producer under Martin Carr on the award-winning documentary "Hunger in America" in 1968. He also wrote and produced the *CBS Reports* documentaries "Heritage of Slavery" (1968) and "The Battle of East St. Louis" (1968).

At the time he started writing and producing "The Selling of the Pentagon" in 1970, the 33-year-old Harvard graduate had the ideal military training for the task, having served for two years as an army public relations officer. "The Selling of the Pentagon" exposed the U.S. military's extensive self-serving public relations efforts at a time when many Americans were questioning the militarist tendencies of U.S. foreign policy, especially in Vietnam. Conservatives criticized the program's theme and production techniques, embroiling the network in controversy. After rebroadcasting the documentary along with follow-up programs in which various spokespeople were permitted to air their views, CBS successfully defied a congressional subpoena requiring it to provide outtakes from the documentary.

Since leaving CBS News in 1972, Davis has worked as a free-lance writer and independent documentary producer. In 1975, his theatrically distributed documentary *Hearts and Minds* won an Academy Award. The film used classic still photo and illustration compilation techniques to portray the tragic outcome of the Vietnam Wars for the French, Americans, and Vietnamese. In addition to *Hearts and Minds,* Davis produced the critically acclaimed *Middletown* series, which aired on PBS in 1982. The six-part series used unobtrusive direct cinema techniques, in which no narration is employed, to document life in a typical American town, Muncie, Indiana. Davis also co-produced the HBO production *The Best Hotel on Skid Row* and more recently collaborated with his son, Nick, on *Jack*, a biographical work on John F. Kennedy that aired on CBS in 1993.

Peter Davis lives in Maine and continues producing documentaries, writing for national magazines, and writing books, including *Hometown, Where Is Nicaragua?* and *If You Came This Way.*

Richard J. Schaefer

Further Reading
House, Proceedings Against Frank Stanton and Columbia Broadcasting System, Inc., July 13, 1971. 92nd Cong., 1st sess. 1971. Report No. 92–349.
Schaefer, Richard J. "Deconstructing Military Propaganda: CBS's 'The Selling of the Pentagon.'" *Studies in Communication,* 1995, Vol. 5 69–100.
Willis, Alliene H. "An Analysis of the Controversy Surrounding 'The Selling of the Pentagon,'" Ph.D. diss., Emory University, 1987.

Democratic National Convention, 1968, Chicago

The Vietnam War divided the American people—and the news media were viewed as a major element of the story, responsible for reporting on both the war and its effects. Many Americans objected to President Lyndon Johnson's increase in the U.S. military presence in Vietnam from thousands to more than half a million troops, and antiwar marches and demonstrations, teach-ins, and draft-card burnings occurred throughout the country. All were reported on television. In 1968, when antiwar Senator Eugene McCarthy received 42 percent of the Democratic vote in the New Hampshire primary, opponents of Lyndon Johnson's candidacy saw hope. Robert F. Kennedy entered the race, as well, and Johnson withdrew his name in late March. Then, in June, Robert Kennedy was assassinated—just two months after Martin Luther King's murder. Newspaper columnist Walter Lippmann predicted the Democrats would nominate Hubert Humphrey, thus making a dream come true for Republicans. When the Democrats convened in Chicago at the end of summer, tempers were short and prospects for live television coverage exacerbated the already volatile antiwar atmosphere.

Antiwar, anti-Johnson demonstrators began to congregate in Chicago two weeks before the convention. There were reports that Mayor Richard Daley gave his police a "shoot to kill" order. Six thousand National Guards and 7,500 regular Army troops came to to back up the Chicago police. Into this powder keg stepped the convention delegates. Chicago exploded and network television covered it.

The first confrontation between police and demonstrators occurred in a dark Chicago park. Reporters got to the scene, and many of the beatings continued under the lights of the cameras. Police attempted to stop the filming. Many correspondents were struck by law enforcement officers—some while on the floor of the Democratic National Convention. Walter Cronkite called the police "thugs" on the air, Jim Burnes of ABC said, "The police have gone mad," and some likened the Chicago police to the Gestapo.

More that 100 civilians and 83 police officers were injured, and 653 people were jailed. No one was killed. Idaho journalist Perry Swisher wrote that all the people injured were hurt in the line of duty—police obeying orders, journalists covering the melee, and young people fighting for their rights.

The day after the convention, CBS let Mayor Daley tell his side of the story unchallenged. Daley later demanded time on the other networks, which refused. Following the riots, a few organizations canceled conventions scheduled for Chicago. The Democratic Party did not hold another convention in Chicago until 1996. A study of the convention, the Kerner Report, later described what had happened as "a police riot."   *Dwight Jensen*

Further Reading

Gitlin, Todd. *The Whole World Is Watching.* Berkeley, University of California Press, 1980.

Small, William. *To Kill a Messenger: Television News and the Real World.* New York: Hastings House, 1970.

Turner, Kathleen J. *Lyndon Johnson's Dual War: Vietnam and the Press.* Chicago: University of Chicago, 1985.

David B. Dick

Photo courtesy of David B. Dick

David B. Dick was born on February 18, 1930, in Cincinnati, Ohio, and was raised in Bourbon County, Kentucky. He received both a bachelor's and a master's degree from the University of Kentucky. Dick began his career in 1959 as a writer for WHAS AM-FM and WHAS-TV in Louisville, where he became a reporter. In 1966, he left for CBS News, where he worked as a correspondent based in Washington, D.C. He was assigned to the network's Southeast bureau in Atlanta in 1970. This was followed by a year as chief of the Latin

American bureau in Venezuela. The remaining years of his career were spent in Dallas with the Southwest bureau.

During his 19 years at CBS, Dick covered the three presidential campaigns of Alabama governor George Wallace, and he received an Emmy in 1972 for coverage of the attempt on Wallace's life. Dick reported on the fighting in El Salvador, Nicaragua, and Beirut, and on Argentina's invasion of the Falklands. Assignments included international and domestic disasters and stories about ordinary people who seldom make headlines.

In 1985, he retired from CBS and joined the faculty at the University of Kentucky, where he served as director of the Journalism School, and retired as a professor in 1996. During 1988–1990, he published a weekly newspaper, the *Bourbon Times,* which won more than 25 Kentucky Press Association Awards during his tenure. Dick continues as a syndicated columnist for *Kentucky Living,* the largest circulation magazine in Kentucky.

Roy L. Moore

Further Reading

Dick, David. *Follow the Storm.* Paris, KY: Plum Lick Publishing, 1993.
Dick, David. *Peace at the Center.* Paris, KY: Plum Lick Publishing, 1994.
Dick, David. *The Quiet Kentuckians.* Paris, KY: Plum Lick Publishing, 1996.
Dick, David *The View from Plumb Lick.* Paris, KY: Plum Lick Publishing, 1993.

Nancy Dickerson

Nancy Dickerson Whitehead was an aggressive reporter who paved the way for future generations of women in the field of television news. She was the first female correspondent for CBS, the first woman to report from the floor of a political convention, and the first woman to have a daily network news program. Nancy Dickerson Whitehead was born in 1929 in Wauwatosa, Wisconsin; received a bachelor of science degree in education from the University of Wisconsin in 1948; and taught in a Milwaukee public school for three years.

After moving to Washington, D.C., in 1951, Dickerson worked as a staff assistant to the Senate Committee on Foreign Relations doing research and editorial assignments. By working with the Senate committee, she became knowledgeable about political issues and came to know many congressional figures. This led her to CBS in 1954, where she became the producer of *The Leading Question* and the associate producer of the news-interview program *Face the Nation.* This created the chance for Dickerson to begin a career as a reporter in which she had opportunities to conduct personal interviews with historic figures such as Presidents Kennedy, Johnson, and Nixon.

In 1971, Dickerson represented the Public Broadcasting System for *A Conversation with President Nixon,* which was seen on all networks. She was the recipient of numerous honorary degrees and journalism awards including the Pioneer Award from the New England Women's Press Association, the Peabody Award, and the Silver Gavel. She published her memoir, *Among Those Present,* in 1976. She died on October 18, 1997, in Manhattan, from complications after suffering a stroke.

Susan Plumb Salas

Further Reading

Dickerson, Nancy. *Among Those Present.* New York: Random House, 1976.
Matusow, Barbara. *The Evening Stars.* Boston: Houghton Mifflin, 1983.

Documentary Television

The television documentary format was adopted from the early anthropological film documents of Robert Flaherty, the work of still photographers, and newsreel efforts such as *The March of Time* film series. Most broadcast historians trace the first television documentary work to the series *See It Now,* created by Edward R. Murrow, Fred W. Friendly, and their colleagues at CBS. *See It Now* was a program that Murrow and Friendly adapted from the *Hear It Now* CBS Radio show. *See It Now* started on November 18, 1951. This series established the standards attributed to an effective TV documentary: visuals of important contemporary events or people, effective writing, and an engaging on-screen narrator or reporter.

See It Now demonstrated that the documentary is often most effective when it takes on controversial subjects, tragedies, or crises. *See It Now*'s most effective stories included a series on civil liberties, Murrow's criticism of Senator Joseph McCarthy, an intense review of the link between cigarette smoking and cancer, and a report on J. Robert Oppenheimer and the development of nuclear technology. Within its first six months, *See It Now* moved to prime time, where it remained until its demise on July 5, 1955.

In 1953, ABC took its first plunge into documentaries by airing *The Big Picture*, a series of films created by the Army Pictorial Center. The stories focused on the army from several different angles: military history, famous generals, and great battles. Despite the fact that professional actors were sometimes used and that most of the footage came from the army's archives and training footage, the program stayed on the air through September of 1959.

In 1957, CBS introduced *The 20th Century*, hosted by Walter Cronkite. This program devoted its coverage to current news makers in politics, medicine, and the arts. When the show celebrated its 10th anniversary, it changed its title to *The 21st Century* and shifted its focus to advances in technology, the arts, and lifestyles. It was canceled right after the new year in 1970. Throughout the 1950s and 1960s, *CBS Reports* also appeared irregularly, but provided highly-acclaimed accounts concerning the lives of migrant farm workers, and the Nuremberg trials, coupled with extensive interviews with John F. Kennedy, Carl Sandburg, and Charles DeGaulle.

Then, in February of 1971, CBS broadcast "The Selling of the Pentagon," which dealt with the military's extensive use of public information techniques to promote the Cold War and U.S. military and political intervention overseas. The program also revealed blatant deception of the press by staging troop activity in ways that would create a positive impression of American military intervention in Vietnam. Complaints about the program from the military brought subsequent investigations from both the Federal Communications Commission and the U.S. House of Representatives. Ultimately, CBS faced no adverse action

from either government entity, although Dr. Frank Stanton was threatened with a contempt citation for failure to provide outtakes of the program. The network also aired two follow-ups of that documentary, allowing the military to voice its concerns about the construction of the program.

Throughout the 1950s, NBC intermittently broadcast news documentaries, but did not establish a regular presence until it unveiled *White Paper* in 1960. In the 1970s, NBC's documentaries usually came under the title *NBC Reports*. It was during this time that the network developed an impressive array of stories on the Army spying on American citizens, chemical and biological weapons, and retrospectives on the Vietnam War. One 1972 program in particular, "Pensions: The Broken Promise," was so controversial that it touched off a "Fairness Doctrine" complaint and follow-up governmental investigations that lead to the Pension Reform Act of 1974. By 1976, NBC took the unprecedented approach of canceling an entire evening of prime-time programming to air a three-hour report on foreign-policy issues.

PBS advanced one of the more ground-breaking or direct cinema-style documentaries in 1972. The series, *An American Family*, covered six months in the life of the William C. Loud family of Santa Barbara, California. The 12-hour series featured filmmaker Craig Gilbert's *cinema-verité* style, approaching the subject with minimum intrusion and emphasising the Loud's daily lives. The series revealed a divorce and the repercussions of some challenging events, including an automobile accident. Pat Loud, the mother, later wrote a book about the experience.

As news divisions faced increasingly tighter budgets in the 1980s, the use of the television documentary began to wane. Further eroding the format was the ramification of CBS's 1982 "The Uncounted Enemy: A Vietnam Deception." In this report, CBS maintained that former U.S. Army General William Westmoreland deliberately deceived the American public by conspiring to alter estimates of Viet Cong and North Vietnamese troop strengths. Westmoreland filed a $120 million libel lawsuit, claiming defamation. In the midst of a trial that cost both parties more than $19 million in legal costs, they settled with CBS issuing a statement that Westmoreland had faithfully executed his duties. CBS admitted errors in judgment but continued to maintain that the story was essentially accurate. Veteran CBS executive, Burton Benjamin, did a formal study of the program, outlining the errors and publishing the results.

By the middle 1990s, the profile of the television documentary was further subsumed by the advent and popularity of television newsmagazines with documentary elements such as *60 Minutes*, *20/20,* and *Dateline.* Today, the PBS *Frontline* series best adheres to a *cinema-verité* approach to the format with limited narration, extended format, and hour-long stories on important topics such as facilitated communications for the autistic, the growing use of Prozac, and profiles on 1996 presidential contenders Bill Clinton and Bob Dole. PBS also gained considerable attention and praise in the documentary area by airing the works of Ken Burns, including his classic *Civil War* documentary television series.   *Burton St. John*

Further Reading

Bluem, A. William. *Documentary in American Television,* New York: Hastings House, 1965.
Hammond, Charles Montgomery. *The Image Decade: Television Documentary, 1965–1975.* New York: Hastings House, 1981.
Murray, Michael D. *The Political Performers: CBS Broadcasts in the Public Interest.* Westport, CT: Praeger Publishers, 1994.

Phil Donahue

Phil Donahue, regarded as the father of talk-show hosts, was born in Cleveland, Ohio, in 1935. In 1957, he received a bachelor's degree in business administration from Notre Dame University. Working first as a replacement announcer, he found reading news briefs, station breaks, and commercials to be boring. He was determined to become a broadcast journalist. After pursuing various positions, in 1959, he was hired by WHIO-AM-TV in Dayton, Ohio, to do morning newscasts. Soon he was working as a street reporter for the station's news broadcasts, obtaining interviews with Jimmy Hoffa and Billie Sol Estes. Both of these programs were later broadcast on the *CBS Evening News.* In 1963, he took over *Conversation Piece*, a 90-minute daily radio phone-in talk program.

In 1967, he became the host of *The Phil Donahue Show*, a morning interview program on Dayton, Ohio's WLWD-TV. The show pioneered as an educational, informative talk show. The program's real innovation was the degree of audience participation. Realizing that the audience asked good questions during commercials, Donahue one day jumped out of his chair and went into the audience. In 1974, the show moved to the studios of WGN-TV in Chicago, and its name was shortened to *Donahue.* By 1979, the program was syndicated to over 200 stations.

Among those whom Donahue interviewed over the years are Madalyn Murray O'Hair, Billie Jean King, Albert Speer, Susan Brownmiller, David Duke, Ayn Rand, Nelson Mandela, and Ralph Nader. Donahue insisted on controversial topics and has broken many TV taboos. Early programs included the display of an anatomically correct boy doll and broadcasts from the Ohio State Penitentiary for a week of programs on the criminal justice system. His program was the first to feature an openly gay man. Among topics Donahue discussed with his audience and his guests are homosexuality and the Church, the insensitivity of the funeral industry, premarital sex, natural childbirth, unwed motherhood, textbook censorship, faith healing, breast augmentation, and sterilization.

In 1996, Donahue concluded 29 years on the air. In preparing his final show, he sifted through 7,000 hours of on-air memories. The creator of the talk program as we know it today, facing competition from younger and brasher hosts, had seen his ratings drop steadily. But his program offered serious topics as well as titillating ones. People sometimes overlook the many important serious topics he addressed as seen in interviews with Peter Arnett, Jesse Jackson, and personalities involved in serious issues, such as the Iran-hostage scandal. For 29 years, Donahue was consistently informative, entertaining, perceptive, and insightful. He is the recipient of 20 Emmy Awards. Donahue is married to Marlo Thomas.   *Joan O'Mara*

Further Reading

Carbaugh, D. *Talking America: Cultural Discourses on Donahue.* Norwood, N.J.: Ablex, 1988.

Donahue, Phil. *Donahue, My Own Story.* New York: Simon & Schuster, 1979.

Unger, Arthur. "Donahue vs. 'The Elitists.'" *Television Quarterly,* 1991, 31–43.

Sam Donaldson

©1996 ABC, Inc. Photo by Terry Ashe

Sam Donaldson, a 30-year veteran of ABC News, while being stereotyped by some as being the perennial shouter at presidents, has achieved much distinction for covering such major national and international stories as the Vietnam War, the Iranian hostage crisis, Watergate, the Persian Gulf War, and every presidential campaign since 1964. Born in El Paso, Texas, in 1934, Donaldson received his bachelor's degree from Texas Western College and did graduate work at the University of Southern California. While in college, Donaldson worked as a disc jockey at local radio stations and as an announcer on local television. He still contends that "the real freedom and romance of broadcasting is to be found in radio."

After a two-and-a-half-year stint in the U.S. Army as an ROTC-commissioned second lieutenant, Donaldson began his broadcast career in 1959 at a CBS affiliate KRLD-TV, in Dallas. A year later, he joined WTOP-TV in Washington, D.C., and in 1961, succeeded Roger Mudd as the weekend news anchor. He gained a reputation for being a fair, but very direct reporter and interviewer. He also produced and moderated a weekly interview program before joining ABC News in 1967 as a Capitol Hill correspondent. Donaldson served as ABC's chief White House correspondent from 1977 until 1989, and as the anchor of *World News Sunday* for 10 years, from 1979 to 1989. He became a regular member of the panel of *This Week with David Brinkley* two months after its premiere, on November 15, 1981. Since David Brinkley's retirement, Donaldson co-anchors *This Week* with Cokie Roberts. Donaldson co-anchored *Prime Time Live* with Diane Sawyer until fall 1998 when that program became part of *20/20.*

Known for his ability to ask tough questions, Donaldson's style has at times led some viewers to label him "rude," but he is generally perceived to be one of the most objective and hardworking journalists in television. He was among a large number of ABC News staff to question a change in policy regarding fees for public speaking engagements. Donaldson has been honored for professional achievements on many occasions, receiving three Emmy Awards and a George Foster Peabody Award for his reporting. The *Washington Journalism Review* named him the "Best Television White House Correspondent in the Business" in 1985, and the "Best Television Correspondent in the Business" in 1986, 1987, 1988, and 1989. He also received the Edward R. Murrow Award from Washington State University in 1998.

Donaldson, whose 1987 autobiography, *Hold on, Mr. President*, was an international best-seller, lives in McLean, Virginia, with his wife, Jan Smith Donaldson, who is also a television news reporter.

Jerry L. Allen

Further Reading

Donaldson, Sam. *Hold on, Mr. President.* New York: Ballantine, 1987.

Fitzwater, Marlin. *Call the Briefing! Reagan and Bush, Sam and Helen: A Decade with Presidents and Press.* New York: Times Books, 1995.

Matusow, Barbara. *The Evening Stars: The Making of the Network News Anchor.* Boston: Houghton Mifflin, 1983.

Shepard, Alicia. "Talk is Expensive." *American Journalism Review,* May 1994, 20–27.

Bob Dotson

Robert Charles "Bob" Dotson is known for his well-written, insightful stories about the common threads of life in the United States. He estimates that he has traveled over 3 million miles and to all 50 states. He was born in 1946 in St. Louis, Missouri. He graduated from the University of Kansas and completed a master of science degree at Syracuse University. He credits his first boss, Fred Shook (later he became a journalism professor), for teaching him to write well. Professor Shook also encouraged Dotson to complete *In Pursuit of the American Dream*, published in 1985, which expands on many of his early broadcast stories from across America.

© 1997, ABC, Inc.

Dotson started his career as a reporter at WKYC-TV and began filing reports for the *Today* program in 1978. As a correspondent for *NBC Nightly News with Tom Brokaw* and *Dateline*, Dotson has been honored often for his work. He is the recipient of an Emmy Award, a duPont-Columbia Award, a Clarion Award from Women in Communications, and the Robert F. Kennedy Award. He also introduced a segment, "Assignment America," focusing on the fabric of the country.

Michael D. Murray

Further Reading

Dotson, Bob. *In Pursuit of the American Dream.* New York: Antheneum, 1985.
Pennington, Gail. "Former Hometowner Visits St. Louis for Travel Show." *St. Louis Post-Dispatch*, 5 September 1996, G6.

Hugh Downs

The man that the *Guinness Book of World Records* cites as holding the record for the greatest number of hours on network television, over 10,000, initially resented the medium for diverting revenue from radio. He was born in February 1921, in Akron, Ohio. After studying at Bluffton College in Ohio for a year, Hugh Downs, at the age of 18, began his broadcasting career in Lima, Ohio. While searching for a job, Downs walked into a local radio station, delivered an impromptu audition that the station manager deemed "very bad," and departed with an on-air job paying $12.50 a week.

In 1940, Downs moved to Detroit's WWJ-AM radio station where he was an announcer and newscaster until he entered the infantry during World War II. After a brief military tour, he moved to Chicago and joined WMAQ radio in 1943, a move that would eventually launch his television career. There were fewer than 400 television sets in Chicago at the time when Downs made his 1945 inaugural broadcast—a 15-minute newscast for NBC's WBKV-TV. During the next nine years, Downs continued as an announcer for *Kukla, Fran and Ollie*, a children's show, and a soap opera, *Hawkins Falls*.

Downs moved to New York in 1954, where he co-hosted NBC's *The Home Show,* and from 1956 until 1957 was the announcer for *Caesar's Hour.* When *The Home Show* ended in 1957, Downs began his relationship with *The Tonight Show* as the program's announcer and guest host. Additionally, Downs filled in at the *Today* show, until becoming the host in 1962. He was also the host of *Concentration*, a game show, from 1958 to 1968. In 1972, Downs took a leave of absence from television. He taught, wrote two books, and served as the president of the National Space Agency. During this time he also won an Emmy for *Over Easy*, a PBS series on aging. Downs has received Emmy Awards for "Live from Lincoln Center: Yo-Yo Ma in Concert" and for a broadcast interview exploring manic depression. Though retired, Downs wanted to return to television and do a multi-subject hour-long program. In 1978, he was able to do so, with ABC's *20/20*. Roone Arledge, president of ABC News, asked Downs to take over as host of the show after its poor debut. He helped turn the program around and, along with co-host Barbara Walters, has made it the second longest-running newsmagazine on television.

In 1990, Downs was honored as the International Radio and Television Society's Broadcaster of the Year. In addition to his duties at *20/20*, Downs provides commentaries for ABC Radio's *Perspectives* and is a lecturer on, among other subjects, gerontology (for which he received a postgraduate degree). Downs chairs the Research and Education Committee for the Geriatrics Advisory Council of the Mount Sinai Medical Center.

Grant Curtis

Further Reading

Johnson, S. "Seeing TV with *20/20* Vision: Hugh Downs Once Thought the Medium Was a Fad." *Chicago Tribune,* 15 May 1995, 1C.
Lacy, M., "Downs' Style Still Fresh, Strong*," Austin American-Statesman,* 7 May 1995, 10.

duPont-Columbia University Awards

Since 1942 the duPont-Columbia University Awards have been bestowed upon what is considered the best in broadcast journalism. Radio and television programming produced by independents, cablecasters, public broadcasters and commercial entities in small, medium, and major local markets and national markets all compete for the distinguished honor of an Alfred I. duPont-Columbia University Award. The most prestigious award, the Gold Baton, is bestowed on the program or series exemplifying excellence. Silver Batons are also presented. All winners receive a special silver sculpture designed by the American architect Louis Kahn.

Jessie Ball duPont established the Alfred I. duPont Awards Foundation Trust in 1942 to honor the memory of her husband who died in 1935. These were established first in the area of radio and expanded to include television in 1951. The Awards ceremony was first televised by PBS in 1978 and the annual duPont Forum on issues of broadcast policy and practice is distributed via the PBS Adult Learning Satellite Service.

For a period of time, beginning in the late 1960s, an Alfred I. duPont-Columbia University Survey of Broadcast Journalism also chronicled the state of broadcast journalism by tracking broadcast coverage of important news stories. Those studies compiled demographic information about broadcast journalists and electronic newsrooms, as well as popular perceptions of the field of broadcast news and the newscasters themselves. Today, the work of many major figures in broadcast news is recognized nationally as the best in the business by being selected for duPont-Columbia Awards. In addition, a large number of network news leaders also participate in the annual duPont-Columbia conferences. The annual Forum and Awards ceremony takes place in January. The ceremony is held at Columbia University in New York City.

Ann D. Jabro

Further Reading

Barnouw, Erik. *Tube of Plenty: The Evolution of American Television* New York: Oxford University Press, 1990.
Barrett, Marvin, ed. *The Alfred I. duPont-Columbia University Survey of Broadcast Journalism 1968-1969.* New York: Grosset & Dunlap Inc., 1969.

E

Douglas Edwards

Douglas Edwards was the anchorman for television's first regularly scheduled network news broadcast. His unassuming demeanor, the quality which both landed and later cost him his job, defined the function of the "anchor" before the term was coined. Born in Ada, Oklahoma, on July 14, 1917, Edwards got his first taste of broadcasting at the age of 15, when he landed a part-time radio job in Troy, Alabama, and worked at the station for three years. He continued in radio throughout college, attending the University of Alabama and the University of Georgia. After working briefly as a staff announcer at WAGF in Dothan, Alabama, he joined WSB Radio in Atlanta, Georgia, as an announcer and news reporter. In 1938, he moved to Detroit and and worked at WXYZ for two years. He returned to Atlanta and WSB in 1940 as an assistant news director before accepting an announcing position with CBS Radio in New York.

Edwards was not enthusiastic about returning to announcing after establishing himself in news, and within six weeks, he became a back-up newscaster for Mel Allen and John Daly. When Daly was sent overseas in 1943 during World War II, Edwards took over his position. In 1945, he was assigned to the CBS London bureau, then headed by Edward R. Murrow. After the war, Edwards stayed on in Europe to head the Paris bureau and helped CBS prepare coverage of the Nuremberg war crimes trials.

On his return to New York, he was interviewed on CBS's experimental television news show, a 15-minute program that aired every Thursday, and was soon narrating the news on the program. When networks made a commitment to move into television journalism with their decision to cover the 1948 political convention in Philadelphia, Edwards was CBS's main commentator. He and his team of producers gained critical acclaim despite many logistical problems. Buoyed by the success of its convention coverage, CBS decided to strengthen programming with a regular nightly newscast, and Edwards was the network's first choice to host the program. He was considered "a natural." *CBS TV News*, a 15-minute program, aired five nights a week; was broadcast to New York City, Boston, Philadelphia, and Washington; and gained Edwards audience recognition. In 1951, coaxial cable came into use, enabling the broadcast to reach the West Coast, and Edwards began the telecast with what would become his customary greeting: "Good evening, everyone, from coast to coast."

Within six years, Edwards's name recognition made the program popular. He won a Peabody Award in 1956 for his coverage of the sinking of the Andrea Doria. In 1962, however, he was replaced by Walter Cronkite. The network executives decided the newscast needed someone more assertive. The same qualities for which Edwards was promoted were ones which got him demoted—his unassuming manner, nonthreatening voice, general amiability, and technically sound, but unimaginative newswriting. He retired in 1988, after spending 40 years anchoring a daily television newscast without interruption. He died on October 13, 1990, in Sarasota, Florida.   *Gregory C. Lisby*

Further Reading
Gates, Gary Paul. *Air Time.* New York: Harper & Row, 1978.
Matusow, Barbara. *The Evening Stars.* Boston: Houghton Mifflin Co., 1983.
Schoenbrun, David. *On and Off the Air.* New York: E.P. Dutton, 1989.

Electronic Newsgathering (ENG)

When video cameras and videotape were first introduced into television newsrooms, the system was called Electronic Newsgathering (ENG) to distinguish it from film technology and equipment. ENG technology became standardized by the mid-1980s. Smaller in size than earlier formats, the ENG format uses a smaller videotape that moves from one open-faced reel to the other, housed inside a plastic casing. The quality of new tape formats has a richness and depth that film cannot imitate.

Four elements distinguish ENG from other video formats. First, the tape moves over the recording heads at a slant, unlike the older Quad videotape technology. Second, the equipment is much more portable. Videotape recorders used in the field were much smaller than the film cameras. In the early days of ENG, the equipment was carried on the shoulder, but today ENG equipment is often less than 10 pounds, with a camera small enough to put into a briefcase.

A third characteristic of ENG is its editing capabilities. In the early days of ENG, field tapes were brought back to the station for editing, using a set of helical record playback machines linked by an edit-controller. Electronic editing increased the speed with which stories could be shot and edited. The fourth element of ENG is the mobility of the equipment—from microwave transmitters to satellite dishes and remote ENG trucks. The system can be mounted into a van, and personnel can edit the story on location seconds after it is shot and transmit it by satellite back to the station, having it ready for a newscast minutes away. This new status has enhanced the editing process itself and due to the innovative use of satellite technology, also the speed with which the edited images can be transmitted.

The speed with which one can produce a story utilizing ENG could not be emulated in the days of news film. Film had to be processed before editing. New technology provides for quick editing of a story, and as time permits, audio and video can be added to enhance the overall impression of the piece, providing clarity and depth. The portability of the equipment has brought cameras, via helicopters, to remote locations. The transportability of the technology allows stations to extend their coverage area, providing greater breadth and depth. ENG also allows stations to broadcast live from the scene of major events. Videographers can record events up to, and during, a newscast for immediate feed into the program via satellite. While these applications are exciting, they raise questions regarding journalistic responsibility, especially in those instances in which breaking news coverage invites intrusion into the event being reported.
                    Elizabeth J. Leebron

Further Reading
Cohler, David Keith. *Broadcast Journalism: A Guide for the Presentation of Radio and Television News.* Englewood Cliffs, NJ: Prentice-Hall, 1985.
Orlik, Peter B. *The Electronic Media.* Boston, MA: Allyn and Bacon, 1992.
Yoakam, Richard D., and Charles F. Cremer. *ENG: Television News and the New Technology.* New York: Random House, 1985.

Linda Ellerbee

Linda Ellerbee calls herself a survivor who has survived layoffs, cancellations, and breast cancer. Through it all, she has remained a dedicated journalist, bringing important issues to the forefront. Ellerbee was born on August 15, 1944, in Bryan, Texas. In her book *And So It Goes: Adventures in Television*, Ellerbee said she enrolled in Vanderbilt University and that her only journalistic experience at the time was as a cartoonist on a magazine. By 1969, she had dropped out of school, married, had two children, divorced, and had moved to Chicago, San Francisco, and finally, Alaska.

In Alaska, she worked as a speech writer and was affiliated with KJNO Radio. She was homesick, and sent job inquiries to stations across the country. The Associated Press (AP) in Dallas hired her, and she moved back to Texas with her children. Ellerbee was fired from AP for writing what she calls "The Letter." She had used the AP's word processing system to write a chatty, and defamatory, letter to a friend in Alaska. It was saved in the computer and the next day, accidentally moved on the AP wire to four states. She subsequently was fired. Ellerbee moved to KHOU-TV in Houston, Texas and, from there, to WCBS-TV in New York City.

In 1975, she was hired by NBC News. First she was a field reporter in Washington, D.C., assigned to cover the U.S. House of Representatives, where, Ellerbee told a reporter for *People* magazine, she grew to dislike politics. She also tried out, unsuccessfully, for a slot opposite Tom Brokaw on the *Today* show. In 1978, she was paired with Lloyd Dobyns on *NBC News Weekend*. She then moved, in 1982, to *NBC News Overnight*, where Ellerbee drew acclaim for her commentary. By 1985, Ellerbee had published her first book and also had been released from her contract with NBC. She moved to ABC in 1986, where she anchored *Our World* and produced a weekly segment for *Good Morning America*. In 1988, she covered the political conventions for CNN.

Ellerbee formed the production company Lucky Duck with Rolf Tessam. Writing in her book *Move On: Adventures in the Real World*, Ellerbee wrote about how the company almost failed; and how a television commercial she did for a coffee company, by accentuating a move away from news, exacerbated her problems. However, through a series of successful programs for PBS, ABC, Lifetime, and Nickelodeon, the company survived and has become successful. One Nickelodeon special won a CableAce Award, and her *Nick News W/5* received a duPont-Columbia Award. During the early 1990s, Ellerbee was diagnosed with breast cancer. Her ordeal was captured in an award-winning ABC special. *The Other Epidemic: What Every Woman Needs to Know About Breast* Cancer was produced by Lucky Duck and aired in 1993.

Ginger Rudeseal Carter

Further Reading

Ellerbee, Linda. *And So It Goes: Adventures in Television.* New York: Berkley Books, 1986.
Ellerbee, Linda. *Move On: Adventures in the Real World.* New York: G.P. Putnam's Sons, 1991.
Goodman, Mark. "Life Force: Linda Ellerbee Beat Breast Cancer with Calculated Ferocity." *People,* 20 September 1993, 59–60.

Emmy Awards

Boycotts, controversy, rule fluctuation, favoritism, the "kiss of death," the war, political activism—the word associations are endless when it comes to the awards ceremony to acknowledge television's "best"—the Emmy Awards. Over time, the Emmy has matured to symbolize television's truly outstanding work, as judged by its industry peers. It is considered the measuring stick of television's artistic mission, entertainment, and public information potential. The award's name was to have been "Ikes," a shortened version of "iconoscope tube." However, as "Ike" was associated with a past war hero and president, it was abandoned. The Society of Television Engineers' president, Harry Lubcke, named the award "Emmy"—a variation of "Immy," which was the nickname used for the "image orthicon camera tube."

Emmys are credited with salvaging careers and making careers, especially on the entertainment side of the business. The awards are also known for encouraging programming trends and new directions, breathing new life into canceled series, and stimulating viewers to "tune-in" and view the newly proclaimed award winners. Networks tally score cards of program nominations and wins, in hopes of breaking achievement records. The competition has become especially ferocious since cable joined the competition 10 years ago. Since 1986, cable nominations and awards have increased six fold, and the last decade has seen significant inroads by newer networks such as Fox, which hosted the ceremony for the first time.

The coveted statuette was designed by film engineer Louis McManus and depicts a winged woman holding an electron. The winged woman was McManus' wife, Dorothy. This artifact symbolizes the ultimate accomplishment; it is what writers, directors, producers, editors, camerapersons, production artists, sound technicians, local and national station executives, animation artists, talent agents, deal makers, and others (in and out of the field) frequently use to measure excellent work and gauge success.

The Emmy Awards were the brain child of Syd Cassyd, a journalist and production person. In 1946, he founded and served as the first chairman of the Academy of Television Arts and Sciences. The organization was devoted to promoting the cultural, educational, and research aims of television. Cassyd's vision of the academy was mostly academic—a professional forum where ideas would be discussed, exchanged, and debated, with position papers offered for public scrutiny. Edgar Bergen, the renowned ventriloquist, was elected as the academy's first president in 1947. In 1948, the organization was formally incorporated as a nonprofit entity.

Just months after its founding, the first of many ongoing conflicts erupted. For a program to win one of the first Emmys bestowed in 1948, it had to be produced in Los Angeles. This rule excluded programs produced in New York and other major production centers. Ed Sullivan, a Broadway newspaper columnist and radio and television performer, responded to Hollywood's Emmy restrictions by creating alternative awards called "Michaels" in 1950. He rallied New York's television elite to support his effort, which eventually led to the formation of an east coast chapter of the academy.

While the "Michaels" were somewhat short-lived, the dissension between Hollywood and New York only deepened until, in 1957, a separate organization, the National Academy of Television Arts and Sciences, with Sullivan as its first president, was formed. From 1955 to 1971, the New York and Hollywood ceremonies were simulcast. As television matured, distribution outlets increased, and each ceremony's locale became synonymous with specific skills and programming genres. The battle between the East and West escalated. Other disputes regarding judging, program length, program focus, news versus entertainment awards, and creative versus technical awards have altered how the ceremony is presented annually.

In 1976, a major dispute regarding the judging of entries between the Hollywood and New York chapters provoked the splitting of the academy into two entities. The National Academy of Television Arts and Sciences (NATAS), headquartered in New York, is responsible for news and documentary, daytime, sports, international, and local Emmy Awards ceremonies. The Academy of Television Arts and Sciences (ATAS), with headquarters in Hollywood, awards the prime-time programs the Emmy distinction. Both organizations offer internships, have speakers' bureaus, sponsor newsmakers' luncheons, and are involved in a number of other activities.

Both NATAS and ATAS have been accused of trying to satisfy the demands of everyone in the broadcast industry—the critics, the public, and their members. These efforts to appease everyone are often criticized. Emmy category titles, as well as the rules governing competition, have changed on occasion, as well as in response to criticism after the awards are made. In an attempt to showcase the industry's responsible programming, the newly created President's Award, designed to honor a special, movie, or series that best explores social or educational issues, was unveiled during a 1996 meeting between television executives and President Bill Clinton. There has been discussion of a possible reunion between the East and West coast organizations, but nothing substantive has developed to date. Despite the conflict surrounding the Emmys, winning an Emmy remains the ultimate for any person in the industry.

Ann D. Jabro

Further Reading

Barnouw, Erik. *Tube of Plenty: The Evolution of American Television.* New York: Oxford University Press, 1990.
Bash, Alan. "Emmy up for Grabs." *USA Today,* 13 June 1996, D3.
O'Neil, Thomas. *The Emmys Star Wars, Showdowns, and the Supreme Test of TV's Best.* New York: Penguin Books, 1992.

Ethical Issues

Each day as reporters, editors, and producers make decisions regarding what news to report, they rely on the expectations and values of business and political professionals, their audience, and themselves. These expectations and values guide choices in determining what is "right" or "wrong," "proper" or "improper," and "good" or "bad," and in determining the recognized patterns of moral reasoning. These patterns of choices are called ethics. When stories are considered for airing, professional standards of propriety are a part of the process. Often, the personal values used by a reporter or editor may differ from those of viewers. If a story wanders into a legal area, a trained journalist will usually recognize it. Such is not the case in ethics.

Inattention to the values, norms, or expectations of others can lead a reporter to become the object of criticism. The problem is best explained by referring to some actual ethical issues that have plagued broadcast journalists. These issues can be categorized as six major ethical concerns.

Deception. In 1997, a North Carolina court found ABC News guilty of deception when two reporters lied about their employment histories in order to get jobs, enabling them to set up hidden cameras to videotape what they called unsanitary food-handling practices in what became *Food Lion Inc. v. Capital Cities/ABC Inc.* While journalistic muckraking practices to reveal violations of law have been commonplace since the early 1900s, there usually had not been concern about surreptitious, or deceptive practices. Here the ethical question was, "Should 'harmless' deception be used to uncover dangerous violations of the law?" The dilemma was whether the value of needing to disclose information was more important than lack of deception. Jury members decided on the legal aspects of the case. Other observers pondered the ethical concerns.

Invasion of privacy. Reporters represent the public in their inquiry of what is going on in the world. Hoards of reporters and photographers seek out information and take pictures of prominent figures. It is said that the loss of privacy is part of the price of fame. But what if circumstances of fate have brought individuals unwanted attention? At the 1996 Summer Olympics in Atlanta, law enforcement officials were anxious to find the perpetrator of a bombing. A security guard was questioned. This information was brought to press atten-

tion. Some press reports strongly hinted that the security guard was the FBI's lead suspect, although he had not been formally charged or even arrested. This person's privacy was gone. Later, he brought a suit against the *Atlanta Constitution* and NBC News, which was settled out of court in his favor.

For the press, it was a matter of choosing the public's right to know against one man's right to privacy. Some ethicists might argue that concern for the individual and a sense of compassion should be the ethical measure. To a journalist, however, the right to disclose information ranks higher.

Confidentiality. Does the press itself have rights of privacy to keep certain information secret? Should it have privileges beyond those of ordinary citizens? If the information is not shielded from law enforcement or the public, confidential sources may not disclose vital information which may be damaging to them. Some states have created "whistle blowing" laws for this purpose. Citizens should never be afraid of disclosing abuses, but what if it jeopardizes their livelihood? But, what if a reporter fabricates a story, just to make a point, refusing to disclose a nonexistent source? Here there is little question as to proper ethical behavior. Deception should never be covered by a claim of confidentiality. Such scenarios help create a climate of public mistrust of the press.

Depictions of violence. The omnipresence of video cameras makes possible the capturing on videotape of rare events. Often these videos are sold by amateur videographers to local television stations. If the event was spectacular enough, network news may pick them up. Such multi-source information may include unpleasant scenes— people being swept away by flood waters, industrial mishaps, or recreational accidents. In earlier times, depiction of dead or bloodied bodies was taboo. Now it is commonplace. On one occasion, reporters showed a person setting himself on fire. They waited to get video of the flaming body before attempting to put out the fire. To what extent are reporters obliged to the idea of getting an exciting story at the risk of suffering? These are not merely rhetorical questions, but serious ethical judgments.

Fairness. Most reporters work under the ethics of fairness, balance, and objectivity. If there is damning information about a party, even though this is the focus of a noteworthy story, it should be balanced with that party's perspective. Indeed, broadcasters were once obligated by the Federal Communications Commision "Fairness Doctrine," upheld by the U.S. Supreme Court, that if a report showed one side of a controversial issue, it must balance it with the other side of the issue. That doctrine no longer exists.

Access. Government activities must be accessible to the electorate. The federal government has the Freedom of Information Act, and many states have open meeting acts, or open records acts allowing accessibility of information to the public, including the press. But what happens when records or meetings contain sensitive or private information? Can broadcasters be trusted not to air information that would cause disruptions, embarrassment, or invasion of privacy? In some instances, there may be protective laws that exempt access. But in many cases, the decision is left to the discretion of the reporter. When a videographer follows police into the home of a suspect and captures private settings, should such video be aired? Perhaps the answer hinges on whether the station is likely to get sued or whether the person is arrested and charged with a crime. The issue is one of "getting the story" versus respect for human dignity. Reporters may be daunted by the question of when the need for a story overrides personal welfare. Such is the plight of ethical issues in television news.

Journalists continue to be faced with challenging ethical issues: consideration of the values of their news viewers, problems of deception and invasion of privacy, handling of confidentiality in uncovering details of a story, how to portray violence—even when factual, gaining access to necessary information, and a constant self-examination of whether there has been fairness and balance in presenting the story. Other considerations, such as the business demands to appeal to a large, thus profitable, audience, also pose dilemmas for journalists in how to best cover stories. As long as the television newsperson deals with the judgments involving his or her individual values, there will be differences of opinion as to how well the public is being served by news stories on television.

Val E. Limburg

Further Reading

Limburg, Val E. *Electronic Media Ethics.* Boston: Focal Press, 1994.

Matelski, Marilyn J. *TV News Ethics.* Boston: Focal Press, 1991.

News Media and the Law. Arlington, VA: quarterly publication of the Reporters Committee for Freedom of the Press.

Eyewitness News

Eyewitness News was the proprietary trade name for a particular style of television newscast developed by some local television stations in the 1960s and 1970s. It was very significant because it humanized the news and diverged from the more strict and traditional "man-on-camera" newscast seen at the network level. While a large number of local television stations used the name "Eyewitness News" for only a relatively short period, its techniques redefined the newscast for local television stations and by the 1980s, had begun to change the face of network news.

Eyewitness News had five key provisions: emphasis on visual elements and "action" video, sometimes in the form of "live" reports, which made pictures more important than words; weather and sports segments, with an emphasis on the weather; a male and female co-anchor arrangement, and an on-air reporting team comprised a "family"; the involvement of reporters in the stories they covered and the application of a narrative "storytelling" approach; and the projection of the personalities of the newscasters to the viewers. Although familiar to viewers of the modern television newscast, these different provisions represented bold, and often radical, departures in television news at the time they first appeared.

Eyewitness News began to emerge as an alternative to network news in 1963 at Westinghouse's Cleveland station, KYW, when its news director, Al Primo, placed a heavy emphasis on the use of film and videotape and instituted almost total reliance on visual aspects of the newscast. Prior to this, viewers usually watched as the news anchor read all of the news out loud while looking into a studio camera. The first of hundreds of television stations to emulate Eyewitness News was Cleveland's

WJW, which was also the first station to enlist a news consultant. The consulting firm McHugh & Hoffman and also the firm Frank N. Magid Associates would eventually spread the Eyewitness News concept to more than 200 local television stations across the country. In 1965, Eyewitness News further advanced when KYW moved from Cleveland to Philadelphia, and Primo, still the news director, formed the first on-camera reporting team. This step deviated from the tradition that allowed only the news anchors to be seen on camera. Major developments in the Eyewitness News format occurred at two additional TV stations—WLS in Chicago and WABC in New York, both owned by the ABC network. Under ABC executive Richard O'Leary, WLS adopted one of the first co-anchor arrangements and then had the two anchors, Fahey Flynn and Joel Daly, converse on the air about the stories they were reporting. The WLS innovation, proclaimed as "happy talk," became an emblem of the Eyewitness News technique, and the two anchors, Flynn and Daly, became quite popular. Then at WABC, which had hired Primo as its news director in 1968, they started using on-camera field reporters. Because the originators of Eyewitness News had sought to challenge the networks, they were the first to hire large numbers of women and minorities. On WABC's Eyewitness News, Rose Ann Scamardela became New York's first female main anchor. Also at WABC, minority reporters, including Geraldo Rivera, Melba Tolliver, Gloria Rojas, and Gil Noble, were widely identified with Eyewitness News. This helped to open the doors for other minority and women reporters.

One of the last elements to develop in the Eyewitness News technique was the requirement for "action" video. As perceived by viewers, a weakness in Eyewitness News had been its extremely slow and methodical pace, a matter corrected in the 1970s when a faster-paced newscast called "Action News" challenged Eyewitness News in Philadelphia. The result in Philadelphia was a synthesis of Action News and Eyewitness News, which placed rigid time restrictions on interview segments, known as "sound bites," as well as on the field reports. Also, because of this synthesis, the trade name "Eyewitness News" declined. What began as

Eyewitness News eventually became known simply as the "people's newscast" or "people's news," with a strong emphasis on human interest stories and feature reports with a personal orientation.

It was called people's news because it targeted the "mass" audience and did so with great effectiveness. It was not uncommon in the 1970s for stations such as KYW, WLS, and WABC to command half of the local audiences. A migration of this mass audience from the more traditional network-styled newscasts to Eyewitness News was especially visible in New York City, where in July of 1972, a long-standing rival newscast on NBC's flagship station WNBC was left with a zero rating.

Another aspect in the development of Eyewitness News was the intense criticism it received, particularly from those in network news. In the 1970s, at the peak of his acclaim, CBS anchor Walter Cronkite deplored what he considered the sensational content of Eyewitness News. Another CBS figure, Eric Sevareid, went public with similar complaints. A main area of concern, not just in the 1970s, but in the years that followed, was the role of the news consultants in spreading from coast-to-coast what seemed to be an Eyewitness News "magic formula." By the mid-1990s, this concern had not disappeared.

Nevertheless, the 1990s gave Eyewitness News new energy and additional meaning, and virtually all local television stations and the networks in the United States had adopted the techniques of Eyewitness News. Many of its promoters looked abroad for new markets. American-style Eyewitness News programs were introduced in Great Britain, Germany, numerous Eastern European countries, and several Latin America countries. ***See also*** Al Primo. *Craig Allen*

Further Reading

Barrett, Marvin. *Moments of Truth?* New York: Crowell, 1975.

Czerniejewski, Halina J., and Charles Long. "Local Television News in 31 Flavors." *The Quill,* May 1994, 21–28.

Dominick, Joseph R., Alan Wurtzel, and Guy Lometti. "Television Journalism vs. Show Business: A Content Analysis of Eyewitness News." *Journalism Quarterly,* 1975, 213–18.

F

Face the Nation

CBS began airing *Face the Nation* on November 7, 1954, from Washington D.C. Patterned after NBC's *Meet the Press*, a permanent correspondent and guest journalists questioned a newsmaker about current issues. One minor variation used on *Face the Nation* was that both guests and journalists faced directly into hidden cameras when they asked or answered questions. Also, panelists did not need to be recognized by the moderator before they asked questions.

The competition between the programs, however, was not based on camera angles or questions. It was based on the ability to spot the right guests and get to them first. *Face the Nation*'s staff's aggressive manner went so far as to stow away a staff member aboard an incoming ocean liner to get the first chance at approaching a visiting statesman. George Herman was the original moderator, with Sylvia Westerman and Mary O. Yates as producers. In 1956, Stuart Novins became the moderator. CBS did not have national sponsorship, having turned down some sponsors because of objectionable commercial content.

In 1957, Nikita Khrushchev accepted an invitation to appear on *Face the Nation*. Daniel Schorr and Stuart Novins interviewed him in Moscow. Schorr had been assigned to the Moscow bureau for at least 18 months prior and had developed a rapport with Khrushchev. The CBS crew shot 5,400 feet of film. The program aired on June 2, 1957, at 3:30 on a Sunday afternoon and caused a sensation. President Eisenhower called it a "unique performance" and intimated that CBS carried the program in order to improve its ratings. Edward R. Murrow called the president's remarks "ill-chosen" and "uninformed." Some congressmen were outraged, but most credited the network for its journalistic initiative. Lyndon Johnson, then the majority leader of the Senate, called for regular broadcasts of this kind, and CBS did arrange some additional interviews with international leaders, including Nehru of India.

Ted Ayers, the producer of *Face the Nation,* believed that there were no indiscreet questions, only indiscreet answers. As if to prove his point, Ayers's first guest was the controversial Senator Joseph McCarthy. Another of Ayer's early coups was scheduling a union chief just prior to the guest's appearance before the Select Senate Committee Investigating Labor Racketeering. On air, and not under oath, he admitted extensive borrowing from his organization's funds, but later in Washington before the senate committee, he invoked the Fifth Amendment.

Currently, *Face the Nation* is moderated by Bob Schieffer, the anchor since May of 1991. Schieffer also serves as the CBS News chief Washington correspondent. In April of 1997, Gloria Borger, political columnist for *U.S. News and World Report* joined Schieffer as a panelist. *See also* CBS News. *Mary E. Beadle*

Further Reading

Gates, Gary Paul. *Air Time: The Inside Story of CBS News.* New York: Harper & Row, 1978.

Matusow, Barbara. *The Evening Stars.* Boston: Houghton Mifflin Co., 1983.

Fairness Doctrine

For nearly 40 years, from 1949 to 1987, the Fairness Doctrine required broadcasters to air a diversity of views on public issues. When it was repealed in 1987, the Fairness Doctrine was one of the most widely debated policies in broadcast regulation history. The Federal Communications Commission (FCC) adopted the policy in 1949 when it issued the report *In the Matter on Editorializing by Broadcast Licensees.* The report repeated a former FCC policy which denied broadcasters the right to air editorials or in any way be on-air advocates of public issues. The Fairness Doctrine required broadcasters to devote a reasonable percentage of air time to discussions of important public issues and to present contrasting views on those issues. The requirement was defined in a series of FCC rulings in particular cases. One such ruling involving Times-Mirror Broadcasting Company, in 1962, defined the FCC's personal attack obligation.

In carrying out its mission, under the Radio Act of 1927 (which created the foundation of present telecommunication law) and the Communications Act of 1934, to regulate broadcasters in the public interest, convenience, or necessity, the FCC determined whether license renewal would be in the public interest. It arbitrated disputes between stations and individuals, and those decisions could be appealed in the courts. Congress gave statutory recognition to the Fairness Doctrine in 1959, when it amended the Communications Act to create exemptions from Section 312, the equal opportunities provision. The amendment specified that compliance with Section 312 would not relieve broadcasters of the obligation to provide "discussion of conflicting views on issues of public importance."

The U.S. Supreme Court upheld the constitutionality of the Fairness Doctrine in 1969 in *Red Lion Broadcasting v. FCC.* The FCC had declared that Red Lion Broadcasting had aired a personal attack and must offer the offended person reply time, whether or not he paid for it. The Court upheld the requirement for a right of reply to persons whose character had been attacked on the air during discussions of controversial public issues. The Court reasoned that the FCC had acted within its statutory authority, and the personal attack rule implemented congressional policy that broadcast licensees serve the public interest; the rule was not an abridgement of freedom of the press because the First Amendment can be applied differently to the broadcast media, and the public spectrum is a scarce public resource that can be regulated for more effective use in the public interest; the people, as a whole, retain First Amendment rights in broadcasting, and it is the right of the public to receive information for self-governance, which is paramount over the First Amendment rights of broadcasters.

The debate over the Fairness Doctrine and its applications continued. In 1971, the FCC initiated an inquiry into the doctrine and its efficacy. The FCC said that the doctrine's goal to foster "uninhibited, robust, wide-open" debate on public issues was clear. Rather, the issue was whether "fairness" policies actually promoted that goal or if alternatives would be more effective. The inquiry resulted in the 1974 Fairness Report in which the FCC reaffirmed its approach to Fairness Doctrine enforcement.

Ten years later, in an era of deregulation, the FCC instituted another inquiry in light of significant changes in the media marketplace and new developments in First Amendment jurisprudence and communication law. The U.S. Supreme Court, in 1984, stated in *FCC v. League of Women Voters* that it would reconsider the constitutional basis of the Fairness Doctrine if the FCC demonstrated that it had the effect of reducing free speech over the airwaves. Justice William Brennan, writing for the Court, noted that restrictions on the broadcast media had been upheld only when the restrictions were "narrowly tailored to further a substantial government interest, such as ensuring adequate and balanced coverage of public issues." This inquiry culminated in the 1985 Fairness Report, in which the FCC concluded that the Fairness Doctrine no longer served the public interest, because it was no longer an appropriate means to further the interest in assuring access to diverse points of view. The FCC found that the doctrine actually inhibited the presentation of controversial issues, especially unorthodox opinions, and imposed unnecessary costs on broadcasters and the government. The FCC deferred to Congress for an appropriate course of action. Congress, in 1986, directed the FCC to consider alternative means of administering and enforcing the Fairness Doctrine.

Meanwhile, in September 1986, the U.S. Court of Appeals for the District of Columbia Circuit had determined that the Fairness Doctrine was not mandated by the Communications Act. In 1987, the same Court of Appeals remanded a Fairness Doctrine complaint for further consideration of the doctrine's constitutionality. The FCC concluded in *Syracuse Peace Council v. Television Station WTVH* that it could no longer enforce the Fairness Doctrine on constitutional grounds and voted to abolish it. The courts have upheld the ruling.

In compliance with Congress's directive to consider Fairness Doctrine alternatives, the FCC reported in August 1987, that no alternative other than elimination of the doctrine in its entirety would better serve First Amendment principles and the public interest objective. Congressional efforts to codify the Fairness Doctrine so far have been defeated. The FCC has retained a few related policies, including the personal attack and political editorials rules. Broadcasters still must provide reply time for personal attacks aired during discussions of public issues and opportunities for political candidates to respond to editorials attacking them or supporting their opponents.

Linda M. Perry

Further Reading

In the Matter of Inquiry into Section 73.1910 of the Commission's Rules and Regulations Concerning Alternatives to the General Fairness Doctrine Obligations of Broadcast Licensees, FCC 87-264, 63 R.R. 2d 488 (1987).

Red Lion Broadcasting Co., Inc., et al. v. FCC, 395 U.S. 367 (June 9, 1969).

Syracuse Peace Council v. Television Station WTVH, 2, FCCR 5043 (1987) and *Syracuse Peace*

Council v. FCC, 867 F. 2d 654 (D.C. Cir. 1989), and 493 U.S. 1019 (1990).

FCC (Federal Communications Commission)

The Federal Communications Commission (FCC), the independent federal agency established by the Communications Act of 1934 to regulate interstate and international electronic communication, wired and wireless, has five members (reduced from seven in 1983), one of whom serves as the chair. Members are appointed by the president of the United States and approved by the Senate. The term of office for commissioners is five years, and they may serve multiple terms. No more than three commissioners from one political party may serve simultaneously.

The FCC was preceded by the Federal Radio Commission (FRC), established in 1927. When the Communications Act was passed, it replaced the FRC with the FCC. Despite opposition from broadcasters who did not want government to play a role in broadcasting, President Franklin Delano Roosevelt signed the bill creating the FCC on July 1, 1934. One significant difference between the FCC and its predecessor is that the radio commission was established as a temporary agency, intended to distribute licenses, then cease to exist, turning over its remaining duties to the Commerce Department. When Congress established the FCC, it recognized that the agency would play a role long after the initial licenses were distributed. The FCC does not regulate the frequencies on which government operates transmitters, although FCC policy may impact government communications.

As an independent agency, the "checks and balances" on the FCC are not the same as for an administrative agency (such as the Food and Drug Administration), which answers directly to the president. While the president selects the chair and the commissioners, who must be approved by the Senate, he does not have the authority to remove commissioners during their terms. The FCC is much more beholden to Congress, which controls not only appropriations, but also its existence. Since 1981, the FCC is no longer a permanent agency, but instead must be reauthorized by Congress every two years. Congress also has the authority to amend the Communications Act. Such amendment could result in changes in the FCC's duties or structure. The passage of the Telecommunications Act of 1996 included a number of tasks that Congress required the FCC to accomplish, along with the dates for action.

Although the FCC has only five commissioners, there are hundreds of staff members in dozens of different departments, including offices across the country. The FCC is divided administratively into a number of offices and bureaus. Of greatest interest to broadcasters is the Mass Media bureau, which processes license applications and renewals, among other duties. Each of these offices and bureaus is further subdivided into divisions. In the case of the Mass Media bureau, the four divisions are for audio services, video services, policy and rules, and enforcement.

In its attempt to carry out the wishes of Congress as expressed in the Communications Act, the FCC creates rules. Proposals for new rules come from a variety of sources. If the FCC plans a new rule, it first issues a Notice of Proposed Rule Making, a formal notice that the FCC is considering a rule and providing for a required length of time that the commission must allow for public comments. After sufficient comment and discussion, new rules are adopted in FCC Reports and Orders and are published in the *Federal Register*.

The FCC does not actively monitor the broadcasts of stations. It relies on information provided to it by the broadcasters themselves and their audiences. Determinations about whether a station deserves to have its license renewed are based on documents filed by the station, any public comments the commission receives, or challenges to the renewal by interested parties.

The commission is able to enforce regulations primarily through the threat of action. The majority of license renewals are granted with no disciplinary action. Should the commission find rules violations, however, its actions can range from a letter of admonition to fines of up to $250,000, a short-term renewal of the license, or even the revocation of a license. It is the threat of this action which keeps broadcasters in compliance.

The FCC has the ultimate authority to revoke a station's license or deny its renewal, although action is rarely taken. In more than 50 years, the FCC has taken such actions only 147 times—fewer than an average of three per year out of thousands of license renewals. More than one-third of these revocations or nonrenewals were due to misrepresentations to the commission. Although very infrequently taking action, the FCC has acted severely in cases where licensees have intentionally lied.

Of all the powers given to the FCC, the Communications Act specifically states that the commission may not censor the content of broadcasts. According to Section 326, "Nothing in the Act shall be understood or construed to give this Commission the power of censorship over the radio communications or signals transmitted by any radio station." In spite of this, FCC reprimands and fines of stations broadcasting indecent material at inappropriate times have been upheld by the U.S. Supreme Court. The FCC acknowledges its obligation to stay out of content decisions in most areas. The commission has declined to base license decisions on the proposed format of a radio station and does not stipulate the amount of time stations should devote to public service announcements.

The FCC has a dual role. While it makes the rules and regulations to carry out the Communications Act, it also serves as a judicial body, hearing appeals of its decisions. In this role, the FCC serves as the equivalent of a federal district court. FCC decisions which are upheld in appeal can then be challenged by appealing directly to the Federal Court of Appeals for the D.C. Circuit. The majority of commissioners over the years have been lawyers rather than engineers. Fewer than half the commissioners have served their full terms.   *Dom Caristi*

Further Reading

Foote, Joe S. *The Networks, the Presidency, and the "Loyal Opposition."* Westport, CT: Praeger, 1990.
Hilliard, Robert. *The Federal Communications Commission: A Primer.* Boston: Focal Press, 1991.
In United States Office of the Federal Register. "Chapter I: Federal Communications Commission." *Code of Federal Regulations, Title 47.* Washington, D.C.: U.S. Government Printing Office, 1997.

48 Hours

On September 12, 1996, the New York-based *48 Hours* news program marked its ninth season with "Incredible Journeys: A Decade of *48 Hours*." The program was a tribute to the accomplishments of *48 Hours* in which Dan Rather covered a variety of topics, including the U.S. war on drugs; a 17-year-old murder case; and a successful young man who once lived on the streets of New York. The selection of topics for the tribute is typical of those covered during the years the program has been on the air. The show has won critical acclaim for its innovative, in-depth, as-it-happens style and has won 16 Emmys, a George Foster Peabody Award, and an Ohio State Award, among others.

The mission of the CBS newsmagazine has been to follow the stories of ordinary people in extraordinary circumstances. Using *cinema-verité* techniques seldom offered on American television, *48 Hours* has made popular use of hand-held cameras. The technique gives each broadcast a sense of immediacy. The innovative camera work of the *48 Hours* crews has even been imitated on some prime-time dramatic shows. *48 Hours* airs Thursdays evenings and exposes viewers to major social issues: crime, homelessness, AIDS, and the changing American family. *48 Hours* journalists have covered the fall of the Berlin Wall, the devastation of Hurricane Andrew, a Los Angeles earthquake, and the crash and investigation of TWA Flight 800.

The long-term success of *60 Minutes* encouraged the creation of *48 Hours*, and on January 19, 1988, CBS introduced the program with anchor Dan Rather. *48 Hours* gave CBS News its third hour of prime-time programming, along with *60 Minutes* and *West 57th Street*. Early correspondents included Bernard Goldberg, Phil Jones, Harold Dow, Erin Moriarty, Richard Schlesinger, and Susan Spencer.

Still anchored by Rather, the program continues to feature correspondents Dow, Moriarty, Schlesinger, and Spencer, and has added Roberta Baskin and Bill Lagattuta. Other national and foreign correspondents also contribute. Each week they cover a particular topic, with as many aspects as possible during a 48-hour period. Viewers follow correspondents as they develop stories over the two-day period. In its early days, *48 Hours* featured everything from a community hospital to a college basketball tournament. The first three programs dealt with Miami's drug image, holiday congestion at Denver's airport, and the work of the staff at Dallas's Parkland Memorial Hospital.

Today, the program often focuses on social controversies. Topics range from the serious, such as drugs and war, to the light, such as shopping trends and celebrities. Contributors have included Doug Tunnell, Victoria Corderi, James Hattori, Betsy Aaron, Edie Magnus, and Peter Van Sant. Under the leadership of Susan Zirinsky and William M. Brady, *48 Hours* shifted format somewhat, making way for multiple topics with variety and better coverage of breaking news. *See also* Dan Rather. *Jan Whitt*

Further Reading

Auletta, Ken. *Three Blind Mice.* New York: Random House, 1996.
"48 Hours on Crack Street," *CBS News Special* (September 2, 1986).
Murray, Michael. *The Political Performers: CBS Broadcasts in the Public Interest.* New York: Praeger, 1994.

Ed Fouhy

© 1995 Focused Images. Photo courtesy of Ed Fouhy

Edward M. Fouhy was born in Boston on November 30, 1934. Prior to assuming his role as executive director of the Center for Civic Journalism, Fouhy spent over 20 years with CBS. His best-remembered CBS work was as the Washington producer of the *Evening News with Walter Cronkite,* from January 1969 to June 1974. Fouhy's other roles for CBS included Washington bureau chief, from 1978 to 1980 and News vice president from 1980 to 1981. During the Vietnam War, Fouhy was CBS's Saigon bureau chief. At ABC he was vice president of News as well as Washington bureau chief. Fouhy was executive producer for NBC News's prime-time newsmagazines. Before entering broadcasting, he was a wire service reporter.

Not only is Edward Fouhy the recipient of prestigious awards, including the Drew Pearson Award and five Emmys, but he has fulfilled roles for several agencies and commissions. In 1988 he was appointed executive producer of the presidential debates by the Commission on Presidential Debates. He conducted workshops on civic journalism for the U.S. Information Agency during the international "Civitas @ Prague '95" conference. He is a member of the Trans-Atlantic Dialogue on Broadcasting. Fouhy currently serves as executive director of the Pew States Policy News Initiative. Fouhy has been an adjunct professor in the School of Foreign Service at Georgetown University. His articles on journalism-related subjects have appeared in a variety of publications.

Steven Phipps

Further Reading

Boyer, Peter J. *Who Killed CBS?* New York: Random House, 1988.
Gates, Gary Paul. *Air Time: The Inside Story of CBS News.* New York: Harper & Row, 1978.

Fred Francis

Fred Francis, a long-time NBC television correspondent, became familiar to many Americans through reports from the Pentagon during the 1990 Persian Gulf War. Noted for his insider journalism, with contacts inside the intelligence community, he saw to it that the books glimpsed daily on the shelves behind him were shuffled between newscasts, intriguing viewers.

Born on February 24, 1945, in Boston, Francis opened the network's first Miami bureau in 1975. He later covered war in El Salvador and Nicaragua and turmoil in Castro's Cuba. He reported the U. S. hostage crisis in Iran, fighting in Northern Ireland, and missile proliferation in Third World countries. At the Pentagon, Francis broke stories on the downing of an Iranian airliner and secret Israeli-South African military links. He drew on highly placed sources, including General Colin Powell, then head of the Joint Chiefs of Staff, to correctly predict Iraq's defeat in the Gulf War.

Francis's war coverage won him prominence and almost made him anchor of a newsmagazine show. He was reportedly slotted for such a program when the network switched gears in an effort to recover from a 1993 deceptive-practices scandal. Francis reported stories for a revamped program and also for *Dateline NBC.* He was later named senior correspondent for investigative reporting and special events. Francis has won a duPont award and a national Emmy.

James Upshaw

Further Reading

Fong-Torres, Ben. "The New Faces of TV War: A Primer on the People behind the Gulf Reporting." *The San Francisco Chronicle,* 5 February 1991, B3.
Johnson, Peter, "NBC's" Fred Francis is up to His Old Tricks Again," *USA Today,* 22 August 1991, 3D.
Kurtz, Howard. "SEX! MAYHEM! NOW! In the Newsmagazine Derby, NBC's Star-Driven Vehicle Puts a Sheen on Sensationalism," *The Washington Post,* 14 March 1994, D1.

Reuven Frank

One of network television's most highly regarded senior executives, Reuven Frank spent over a quarter of a century at NBC News. He created and produced *The Huntley-Brinkley Report* and five distinguished documentaries. He also structured and produced live coverage of every political convention from 1956 to 1972 and served two stints as the network's news president.

Born in Montreal, Quebec, Canada, on December 7, 1920, Frank attended the University of

Toronto and the City College of New York. He graduated from the Columbia University Graduate School of Journalism and served with the U.S. Army for four years. In 1950, he joined NBC News as a writer, after serving on the staff of the *Newark (N.J.) Evening News*. In 1956, Frank created, and then produced *The Huntley-Brinkley Report*. Initially the program floundered, both in the ratings and in advertiser support. But it eventually obtained full sponsorship by Texaco and began to dominate the network ratings. The anchors, Chet Huntley and David Brinkley, became icons of the early age of television news. They were promoted heavily by the network, and Frank was hailed as the individual who created television news' most successful anchor team.

Frank left *The Huntley-Brinkley Report* in 1962 to make documentaries, including "The Tunnel," which won three Emmy Awards and was named television program of the year by the National Academy of Television Arts and Sciences. "The Tunnel," airing December 10, 1962, focused on refugees escaping the Iron Curtain from East Berlin. The opportunity to film an escape was presented early, when the Berlin Wall was built. This allowed television viewers an insider's look at the construction of an escape route beneath the Wall, and because of its theme—the quest for freedom—the program was praised for both journalistic and artistic merit. It now stands as a historical document of the era.

Frank returned to NBC in May 1963 and became president of the news division, deciding that the updated dual anchor concept at NBC, with Tom Brokaw and Roger Mudd, was not working. On the crest of an election year, Frank opted for Brokaw as the single anchor, in part because of Brokaw's ability to ad-lib. Brokaw took over during the summer of 1983, and while the network struggled considerably, languishing in third-place initially, the ratings eventually picked up and the show led the field of nightly news broadcasts.

Later, Frank served as consulting producer of an IBM-funded series on public television about increased standards in the global marketplace and as a senior fellow at The Freedom Forum, Columbia University. He has written about the evolution of television news, having experienced its development first hand. Frank has also spoken out against declining news standards and authored a popular account of his life in network television, *Out of Thin Air*. **See also** NBC News.

Michael D. Murray

Further Reading

Bluem, A. William. *Documentary in American Television.* New York: Hastings House, 1969.
Frank, Reuven. *Out of Thin Air.* New York: Simon & Schuster, 1991.
Frank, Reuven, "Television News: Chasing Scripts, Not Stories," *Broadcasting & Cable,* 8 March 1993, 12.

Pauline Frederick

A trailblazing woman in broadcast news, Pauline Frederick had a career that spanned 40 years. She became known as the dean of national newswomen, primarily on the basis of her work as a United Nations correspondent. Frederick was born in Gallitzin, Pennsylvania, on February 13, 1908. After graduating from American University and receiving a master's degree in international law, she was hired by the *Washington Star*.

She moved to NBC Radio in the 1930s, broadcasting interviews and working as an assistant to commentator H.R. Baukhage. On a journalist's trip in 1945, she broadcast from China. Leaving NBC to become a correspondent for the North American Newspaper Alliance, she covered the Nuremberg trials in Germany, freelancing for ABC Radio. Facing the sentiment against women broadcasters on the grounds their voices lacked authority, she was unable for some time to get a permanent job with a network.

Her break came in 1948, when she joined ABC to cover the United Nations (UN) after she had proven herself able to establish her expertise, even over more experienced male colleagues. That same year, ABC assigned her to report the first televised Democratic National Convention. She subsequently broadcast news reports simultaneously over ABC radio and television. In 1953, she was hired by NBC and covered the United Nations until 1974, when the network's mandatory retirement policy forced her departure. Her reports on international crises, including the Middle East, the Cuban missile crisis, and the Vietnam War, linked her so strongly in the public mind with the United Nations that when Dag Hammarskjold, the secretary-general, was killed in an airplane crash, she received sympathy notes. Within a year after her retirement, she returned to the air as an analyst for National Public Radio. A tireless advocate of the United Nations as a forum for international peace, Frederick was critical of the U.S role in the Vietnam War.

Known for her balanced, concise reports, Frederick won praise for her ability to remain calm under pressure. Playing down her role as a pioneering woman in a male-dominated field, she made a point of not accepting favors. Frederick was the first woman to serve as the president of the UN Correspondents Association. As the moderator of the 1976 debate between candidates Jimmy Carter and Gerald Ford, she also scored another first for a woman journalist.

In addition to receiving 23 honorary doctorates, she was the first women to win both the prestigious Alfred I. duPont and George Foster Peabody Awards for distinguished broadcasting. Frederick was married to Charles Robbins, former president of the Atomic Industrial Forum. She died of a heart attack on May 9, 1990, at the age of 84 in a nursing home in Lake Forest, Illinois.

Maurine H. Beasley

Further Reading

The personal papers of Pauline Frederick are in the Sophia Smith collection, Smith College, Northampton, MA.

Hosley, David H., and Gayle K. Yamada. *HARD NEWS: Women in Broadcast Journalism.* New York: Greenwood Press, 1987, 62–66.

Sanders, Marlene, and Marcia Rock. *Waiting for PRIME TIME: The Women of Television News.* Urbana: University of Illinois Press, 1988, 8–11.

Fred Freed

One of America's leading documentary television producers, Fred Freed was born on August 25, 1920, and raised in Portland, Oregon. He graduated with a history degree from Princeton University and was accepted into Harvard and Yale law schools but enlisted in the U.S. Navy instead. Af-

ter concluding his military service in 1946, he worked as a researcher at *Esquire* magazine, then became a writer for Bill Leonard's radio series, *This is New York.* He went to work for NBC in 1956, then the following year, switched to CBS, spending four years at that network before returning to NBC in 1961 to produce Dave Garroway's first *Today* program.

Freed became the executive producer of *NBC White Paper*. This series extended the tradition begun at CBS with the *See It Now* series. The *NBC White Paper* series began under the supervison of Irving Gitlin. At the very outset, social problems such as civil rights were targeted for attention. In addition, profiles of foreign governments, investigations and observations on U.S. foreign policy, and various economic interests abroad became legitimate subjects.

Freed provided the creative impulse and impetus for *White Paper* projects from 1961 to 1972. There was an extensive financial commitment on the part of NBC News for the series, with limited return on the investment. But still, NBC took the opportunity to illuminate key political and social issues for the American public as well as important current events. For example, Freed's work on "The Death of Stalin," "The Rise of Khushchev," programs on the John F. Kennedy assassination, "Summer '67: What We Learned," and the "Vietnam Hindsight" programs were by-products of being active at a time when these crucial news events were taking place. Probing reports on pollution, the relationship between cigarettes and cancer, the right to bear arms, the plight of the urban poor, and the changing work environment for blue collar workers were all produced under Freed's watchful eye.

Freed gained a special reputation for investigations which focused especially on organized crime and public health. He won his first two Emmy Awards in 1964 for programs about Cuba: "Bay of Pigs" and "The Missile Crisis." Freed also won praise for the series *The Ordeal of the American City,* sponsored by AT&T, and he received two Peabodys and six Emmys. He died in 1974, at the age of 53, at his home in New York City.

Michael D. Murray

Further Reading

Barnouw, Erik. *Tube of Plenty.* New York: Oxford University Press, 1990.

Freed, Fred. "NBC Producer of Documentaries, Dead." *New York Times,* 1 April 1974, 34.

Yellen, David. *SPECIAL: Fred Freed and the Television Documentary.* New York: MacMillan, 1972.

Fred W. Friendly

Fred Friendly was born in New York City in 1915 and spent much of his younger life in Providence, Rhode Island. There he began his career in broadcasting in 1937 as a local radio producer-reporter, shortly before serving in World War II as a military newspaper correspondent in the Information and Education section of the China-Burma-India Theater.

Friendly's first real claim to fame came in 1947 when he explained his idea for an album of recorded history of the years 1933 to 1945. He intended to collaborate with Edward R. Murrow, who had achieved fame broadcasting shortwave reports from London during World War II. Murrow narrated scripts written by Friendly. The result was the album *I Can Hear it Now*, released in 1949, which achieved impressive sales. This was to be the beginning of several successful efforts of the "Murrow-Friendly partnership," as it became known. The next year, they produced Volume Two. Shortly thereafter, Friendly produced *The Quick and the Dead*, a four-part NBC radio documentary about the birth of the atomic bomb. By now, CBS management was attracted to the idea of a permanent Murrow-Friendly partnership.

The first regular series of the pair was *Hear it Now*, a weekly one-hour news-documentary series produced about the time of the volatile Korean War, the threat of Chinese communism, and the introduction into America of the medium of television. After one year, the radio series was replaced with a television series, *See it Now*, one of the first television documentaries, and one that earned both Murrow and Friendly the respect of being part of a new breed, "broadcast journalists," able to deal with news and public affairs in both radio and television.

The partnership was to last until the end of the decade. It was a formidable combination, and during their work together, they explored, in 1953, the dismissal of Milo Radulovich, who was stripped of his commission in the U.S. Navy because of an alleged connection of a family member to Communism. This and similar charges of Communist alliances were being made by a junior U.S. senator from Wisconsin, Joseph R. McCarthy. In the minds of Friendly and Murrow, the charges were unfair and bypassed the American justice system. In 1954, the two decided to air a *See it Now* program on McCarthy by revealing his own words that were instilling fear in the hearts of the common man in America. It took courage, for it was likely the pair would be branded Communist, a disgrace during that era of history. Murrow and Friendly both decided to strike on the side of courage and justice. McCarthy's subsequent attempts to disgrace them went unbelieved by viewers who had seen and heard the senator's own words.

Friendly continued to work with Murrow throughout that fateful decade of the 1950s. Toward the end of their partnership, they produced a *CBS Reports* program, "Harvest of Shame," documenting the plight of migrant farm workers in the United States. The program aired in 1960, and left an impact that both Friendly and Murrow intended—federal legislation was initiated to protect such workers. The broadcast followed the migrant laborers to their jobs and showed the subhuman living, working, and traveling conditions many endured on a daily basis, reflecting the callous view of some growers that it was far better for the laborers to have some limited income through periodic work rather than to be unemployed throughout the year. The children of the migrants were shown living in unsupervised squalor, and their lack of educational opportunities was also addressed in the program.

From 1959 until 1964, Friendly was executive producer of *CBS Reports*, extending past the time when Murrow left to become director of the U.S. Information Agency in 1961. In 1964, Friendly became the president of CBS News. After two years in that position, he again displayed his courage in a quarrel over the airing of the Senate Foreign Relations Committee hearings on Vietnam. The network television head, John A. Schneider, had decided to have the network carry reruns of *I Love Lucy* and *The Real McCoys* in place of hearings that proved to be vital information for the United States and its citizens. Friendly pleaded and tried to work with CBS CEO William Paley and CBS Chief Frank Stanton. But the decision had been made, primarily for monetary reasons, since the carrying of Congressional hearings was sustaining programming at the time—not commercially supported. Friendly, already known for his temper, resigned in a fit of anger. He reported in his letter of resignation that when he saw the reruns rather than the important news coverage he wished his news division to carry, he wanted to report: "Due to circumstances beyond our control, the broadcast originally intended for this time will not be seen." News judgments had been superseded by business decisions, a perspective that was not acceptable to Friendly. He subsequently wrote in detail of the experience in his book *Due to Circumstances Beyond our Control.*

After CBS, Friendly was appointed to a named professorship, becoming the Edward R. Murrow Professor at the Columbia School of Journalism, where he served for three decades. He was also active as the Ford Foundation Advisor on Communication, where he etched out "News and the Law" seminars. The seminars, held at various venues around the country, used a Socratic method of posing ethical dilemmas to those in journalism, law, and communication education. Friendly was fond of quoting to practicing journalists the Socratic notion that "An unexamined life is not worth living." He continued to shift his focus to training journalists and future journalists to think about the difference they can make, both mutually and separately in their communities, in matters of public affairs coverage, international affairs, civil rights, and equal justice.

Friendly died of a stroke at his home in New York on March 3, 1998. He was 82.

Val E. Limburg

Further Reading

Friendly, Fred W. *Due to Circumstances Beyond Our Control....* New York: Alfred Knopf, 1967.
Konner, Joan. "Fred Friendly, 1915–1998," *Columbia Journalism Review,* May/June 1998, 6.

Murray Fromson

Murray Fromson's career in journalism has spanned three decades, covering the Korean and Vietnam wars and three presidential campaigns. Born in New York in 1929, Fromson was inspired by journalists at an early age. However, it was in 1950, in Los Angeles, when his journalistic career took off. Working as a sports reporter for the *Los Angeles Mirror*, he was drafted by the army and was sent to the Korean War. During his tour of duty, Fromson reported for *Stars and Stripes* and interned with the Associated Press (AP) in Tokyo. At the end of the war, he became the youngest AP foreign correspondent and opened the first postwar AP Korean bureau.

Fromson was CBS senior correspondent in Asia, then in Moscow, during détente, reporting on the U.S.-Soviet arms control talks. At home, he covered the Nixon, Johnson, and Goldwater presidential campaigns; civil rights; the Apollo space program; and the anti-Vietnam War movement. Fromson left broadcasting in 1978 to act as deputy campaign manager for Governor Edmund G. Brown Jr., but returned to broadcasting in 1980 to produce and moderate the PBS series *California Week in Review.* In the late 1980s, he did commentary on KABC radio.

Currently, Fromson is the director of the School of Journalism and the director of the Center for International Journalism at the University of Southern California. He was cited in two Overseas Press Awards for his reporting of the fall of Saigon. He is a member of many professional organizations, including the Inter-American Press Association, the Reporters Committee for Freedom of the Press, and the First Amendment Coalition of California.   *Susan Plumb Salas*

Further Reading

Paper, Lewis. *Empire: William S. Paley and the Making of CBS.* New York: St. Martin's Press, 1987.
Slater, Robert. *This Is CBS.* Englewood, Cliffs, NJ: Prentice Hall, 1988.

Frontline

Frontline is the leading U.S. television documentary series. Public television officials wanted to create a series that would fill a void by the commercial networks, which largely had abandoned documentaries. The creation of *Frontline* followed several failed attempts to develop a documentary series. In 1981, the Corporation for Public Broadcasting allocated $5 million for the new series, the largest program develpment grant it had ever awarded. Public television officials turned to David Fanning at WGBH-TV in Boston to serve as the executive producer. Because of his personal interest in South Africa, Fanning's first project concerned African churches.

By the time of the *Frontline* opportunity, Fanning already had produced the award-winning documentary program *World* from 1977 to 1982. Fanning helped form the Documentary Consortium, consisting of public television stations WGBH, WNET-TV in New York, KCTS-TV in Seattle, WTVS-TV in Detroit, and WPBT-TV in Miami. The consortium provided funding for *Frontline* and helped ensure that public stations would buy the program and air it in a regular time slot. At the same time, the consortium served as a supervisory board to protect *Frontline's* editorial independence and shield it from interference from both inside and outside the PBS system.

Fanning and senior producer Michael Kirk helped design a series that would differ significantly from past network documentary programs. They wanted to tell compelling human-interest tales rather than have weighty discussions of abstract issues. They wanted individual filmmakers to "author" individual programs, rather than have a set group of network-style correspondents report them. And they wanted to attract an audience. With that in mind, they hired NBC anchor Jessica Savitch to host the new program (but only after unsuccessfully courting Charles Kuralt and Bill Moyers).

Frontline premiered on January 17, 1983, with "The Unauthorized History of the NFL." It outlined allegations of connections between gambling and professional football and the laxity of the NFL in cracking down on gambling. Critics attacked the program, with the National News Council charging it with unfair and distorted reporting in speculating about the cause of death of an NFL team owner. Michael Kirk would later say *Frontline* was not as successful with its earliest investigative efforts as it later would be. Programs were being rushed on the air before confusing points in the scripts could be cleared up and certain allegations could be fully corroborated. In addition, a new host had to be hired after Savitch died in a car accident in October of 1983. Judy Woodruff of PBS's *MacNeil/Lehrer NewsHour* was selected.

Eventually, *Frontline* would evolve into a highly respected series, demonstrating that good television and good journalism were not mutually incompatible. At a time when the networks had largely abandoned documentaries, *Frontline* attracted up to 10 million viewers each week with hour-long public affairs programs uninterrupted by commercials. By the end of 1996, the series had produced more than 300 programs, and it had won 22 Emmy Awards, three Peabody Awards, and 11 duPont-Columbia Awards. The programs have been written and reported by journalists including Bill Moyers, William Greider, Seymour Hersh, and Peter Boyer.

Frontline has not been above tackling sensational issues. It achieved some of its highest ratings in 1987, with "Death of a Porn Queen." The program told of a teenager who ran away from home and became entangled in the pornography industry. She turned to drugs and finally committed suicide. The original title of the documentary was "Death of an American Girl," but the title was changed for *Frontline*, which was one indication of David Fanning's showman's instincts. The program was less about sex and violence than it was about a troubled teenager and the way she was exploited.

Other notable *Frontline* programs similarly have taken dramatic issues and presented in-depth stories about individuals or communities caught up in those issues. Examples include 1989's "Children of the Night," about a group of young runaways in California; 1991's "Who Killed Adam Mann," concerning a five-year-old boy beaten to death by his parents; and 1994's "Romeo and Juliet in Sarajevo," about a Serbian man and Muslim woman who fell in love and tried, unsuccessfully, to escape the violence in Bosnia.

The series also has covered domestic politics, race, the environment, and international affairs. Examples include "The Choice," which provided in-depth biographies of the candidates in the 1988, 1992, and 1996 presidential races; 1990's "Seven Days in Bensonhurst," on the death of a young African American in a white neighborhood; 1993's "In Our Children's Food," on pesticide use and regulation; and multi-part reports on apartheid, U.S. policy in Central America, and the Persian Gulf War.

Finally, *Frontline* has been noted for focusing early attention on major news stories. In 1986's "Who's Running This War?" it examined Oliver North and the Nicaraguan contras eight months before the Iran-contra scandal broke. And in 1991's "The Election Held Hostage," *Frontline* was one of the first to investigate a possible deal between representatives of Ronald Reagan and Iranians holding Americans hostage during the 1980 presidential campaign.

Frontline has not been without controversy, even after its somewhat rocky beginning. Some independent documentary producers have criticized the series for monopolizing scarce funds within the public television system, and some conservatives have criticized the series for having a liberal bias. Nevertheless, *Frontline* has continued to reap praise for being one of the few places left on American television where the public affairs documentary survives and flourishes.

Matthew C. Ehrlich

Further Reading

Corry, John. "Public Broadcasting Pieties." *Media Critic,* Fall 1995, 22–27.

Hall, Jane. "The Long, Hard Look: A Producer's Passion for 'Rattling Good Stories' Helps *Frontline* Win Awards—and Preserve a Dying Genre." *Los Angeles Times,* 13 October 1991, Calender Section, 6.

Unger, Arthur. "Frontline's David Fanning: Upholding the Documentary Tradition." *Television Quarterly,* vol. 25, no. 3, 1991, 27–41.

Betty Furness

Betty Furness was a commercial performer in the 1950s who became a leading consumer advocate in the 1970s. She was born on January 3, 1916, in New York City and grew up on Park Avenue. She began her career as a screen actress in 1932, appearing in 35 movies. She ended her movie career in 1937 and appeared in summer stock and road companies in plays such as *My Sister Eileen* and *Doughgirls.* In 1948, she moved to television, appearing on a 15-minute Dumont network program. She became the television spokesperson for Westinghouse appliances in 1949, appearing in that company's commercials, which were featured for 11 years on the drama *Studio One* and at political conventions in 1952, 1956, and 1960.

Although credited with a famous television *faux pas*, Furness never struggled to open a refrigerator door, though her substitute, on one occasion, did. She did, however, once struggle with trying to remove an "easy to remove" vacuum cleaner hose, which caused concern to Furness and the Westinghouse executives, but not to her fans, who wrote letters of support. Another indication of her celebrity status occurred during the 1952 Republican National Convention when an editorial cartoon asked "Who's winning...? Taft? Ike? or Betty Furness?"

In 1961, Furness became active in public affairs programming, worked for CBS Radio, and hosted a number of local New York television shows for WNTA-TV and WABC-TV. Furness was nominated for Emmy Awards in 1963. In 1964, she entered public service, working with VISTA and Head Start. In 1967, she was appointed, by President Lyndon Johnson to be a special assistant for consumer affairs. She was instrumental in passing several pieces of legislation including: "truth in lending," requiring flame retardant fabrics for children's clothing and bedding; prohibition of the issuance of unsolicited credit cards; and changes in the inspection of meat sold in the United States. In 1970, she was appointed by Governor Nelson Rockefeller to head the New York State's Consumer Protection Board and served for one year. In 1973, Mayor John Lindsay appointed her Commissioner of the New York City Department of Consumer Affairs, where she remained until 1974. Then she joined WNBC-TV in New York as a consumer reporter and contributor to network programs such as *Today*. In 1976, she became a temporary co-host of *Today* when Barbara Walters left for ABC.

Her work on WNBC-TV contributed to the station's winning a Peabody Award and an Emmy Award for Outstanding Informational Programming. Furness won two Emmys for reporting consumer news. Her special series "Adoptions" won her and producer Rita Satz seven major broadcasting awards in 1981, including the Sigma Delta Chi Award for Public Service in Television Journalism. She has received four honorary degrees and has served as president and on the Board of Governors of the New York Chapter of the National Academy of Television Arts and Sciences (NATAS). In recognition of her contributions to television, NATAS inducted her into the Silver Circle in 1992. In 1967 Furness married her third husband, CBS executive Leslie Midgely. She died on April 2, 1994 in New York City.   *Mary E. Beadle*

Further Reading

Hilliard, Robert L., and Michael C. Keith. *The Broadcast Century*. Boston: Focal Press, 1992.

O'Dell, Cary, and Betty Furness. *Women Pioneers in Television*. Jefferson, NC: McFarland & Company, 1997.

G

Jamie Gangel

Reporter Jamie Gangel scored a reporting coup in November 1993, when she took viewers on the first-ever tour of the Central Intelligence Agency (CIA) for NBC's *Today* show and NBC *Nightly News*. She was also the first reporter to do an in-depth interview with President George Bush after he left office. Gangel was born and raised in New York City. She earned a bachelor of science degree from Georgetown University's School of Foreign Service in 1977 and studied international economics at Harvard University, and started working in broadcasting in 1978 at two jobs—assignment editor for WJLA-TV and a stringer for all-news radio station WTOP in Washington, D.C. When the *Washington Star* folded, Gangel's coverage of the event earned her the Associated Press Award for best spot news. In 1982, she moved to Miami and WPLG-TV, where she was a general assignment reporter and substitute anchor.

She returned to Washington, D.C., in 1984 and to NBC to do general-assignment and political reporting from the State Department and White House. After Democrats nominated Walter Mondale for president in 1984 and Mondale chose Geraldine Ferraro to be the first woman to run for vice president as candidate for a major party, Gangel covered Ferraro's campaign. She also covered stories in Latin and Central America and in Africa, and she served as part of the Pentagon pool of reporters covering the Persian Gulf War. In Feb-ruary of 1992, NBC News named her national correspondent for *Today,* where she remains covering a variety of issues.   *Elizabeth Ryan*

Further Reading

Hosley, David, and Gayle Yamada. *Women in Broadcast News*. New York: Greenwood Press, 1987.

Johnson, Peter. "Jamie Gangel Doesn't Put Off What She Can Do on *Today.*" *USA Today,* 16 November 1993, D3.

Dave Garroway

Dave Garroway was host of the first network morning news program, *Today,* on NBC from 1952 to 1961. Born in Schenectady, New York, in 1913, Garroway attended high school and college in St. Louis, Missouri, graduating in 1935 from Washington University. After a brief stint at the Harvard Business School, Garroway and a friend developed a publication of 800 mispronounced words, *You Don't Say!....Or Do You?*

A supervisor of NBC guest relations helped him secure an entry-level job as an NBC page in 1937. He tried the company's announcers' program, but finished next to last, so Garroway became the "special-events" person at KDKA, NBC's affiliate in Pittsburgh. His next job at NBC's WMAQ radio in Chicago was interrupted by service in the Navy, but he returned in 1946 to host a two-hour jazz program, where he perfected innovations with language. *Garroway at Large* first aired in April 1949 on NBC's WNBQ-TV in Chicago, and there, in bow tie, tweed jacket, and horn-rimmed glasses, Garroway moved smoothly between singers, orchestras, and an occasional guest comedian. Shortly after the show's cancellation in 1951, Garroway learned that NBC was creating a program to air from New York's Rockefeller Center weekday mornings from 7 A.M. to 9 A.M. He quickly made his interest known, and after considering stars like Fred Allen and Bob Hope, NBC decided Garroway was right for the job.

Today did not have a smooth beginning. It was criticized for its "command-post" appearance with a bank of clocks, rows of telephones, loudspeakers, short-wave radio consoles, and technical problems. Garroway created order out of the chaos, but *Today* lost money until joined by a magician and a monkey. The magician was Matthew J. Culligan, an advertising specialist who believed that if Garroway pitched products the audience used in the morning, the products would sell. Madison Avenue bought Culligan's reasoning, and the red ink began to disappear. J. Fred Muggs was the monkey—actually a dressed-up chimpanzee. He rambled around, fooling with Garroway and mugging in the plate-glass window at onlookers. Garroway was later joined by conventional colleagues Frank Blair, Jack Lescoulie, Betsy Palmer, and one particular *"Today* girl," Barbara Walters.

In 1961, Garroway, wanting to spend more time with his children, decided to leave *Today* and signed off with "Peace" for the last time. In 1962, he anchored program segments for National Educational Television, and in 1969, he hosted a late-morning program in Boston, yet he never enjoyed the success he had with *Today*. On July 21, 1982, after undergoing heart surgery at the age of 69, Dave Garroway committed suicide. He was a television pioneer who made the average person feel important.

William R. Davie

Further Reading

Barnouw, Erik. *Tube of Plenty.* New York: Oxford University Press, 1990.
Bliss, Edward, Jr. *Now the News: The Story of Broadcast Journalism.* New York: Columbia University Press, 1991.

"Peace, Old Tiger." *Time,* 28 December 1962.
"Professor Garroway of 21-inch U." *Time,* 28 December 1962.

Michael Gartner

Michael Gartner is one of a handful of newspersons who prospered in both print and broadcast. Gartner has been a reporter, an editor, a columnist, and also president of the American Society of Newspaper Editors. From 1988 to 1993, he served as a vice president of NBC News. He was born on October 25, 1936, in Des Moines, Iowa. A third-generation newsperson, his father Carl David Gartner worked for the *Des Moines Register* for 50 years. After receiving a bachelor of arts degree in 1960 from Carleton College in Minnesota, Gartner was employed by the *Wall Street Journal* for 14 years, rising to front page editor and columnist. He also received a law degree from New York University and although not practicing law, became skilled in First Amendent issues.

In 1974, Gartner left the *Wall Street Journal* to return to Iowa as the executive editor of the *Des Moines Register*. After engaging in a take-over attempt which failed, the paper was purchased by Gannett in 1986. Gartner then became one the founders of Midway Newspapers, a small group of newspapers, including the *Iowa Daily Tribune*. Making an estimated $3 to 4 million from the sale, Gartner was chosen to manage Gannett's *Louisville Courier-Journal* in 1987. Known for his cost-cutting abilities, as well as news-gathering and writing skills, Gartner was named to succeed Lawrence Grossman as president of NBC News in July of 1988. At the time, NBC News lagged in the ratings behind the network's entertainment division. During his tenure, Gartner helped to reverse news division losses of $100 million to profits of $15 million annually. He also created an overnight news program and expanded *Today*.

During his tenure in television, Gartner became somewhat controversial. In his first months on the job he reduced the NBC News budget from $300 million to $245 million, noting that the budget was still higher than those of many major organizations, including the *New York Times*. He also dismissed 110 employees. In 1989, Gartner refused to meet the salary demands of correspondent Connie Chung, who then accepted a multimillion dollar offer from CBS. NBC lost several other experienced reporters during this period, including Jack Reynolds, Steve Delaney, Richard Valeriani, and Chris Wallace. Gartner also received criticism for NBC's failure to come up with a competitive newsmagazine. But his greatest criticism followed NBC's confession about the news division's involvement in a staged truck explosion. Although praised for his candor in quickly apologizing for the deception, Gartner later resigned from NBC and returned to newspaper work.

Gartner remains the editor and part-owner of the *Iowa Tribune*. He writes columns for the *Wall Street Journal* and *USA Today*, where he once served as a consultant.   *Paul Alfred Pratte*

Further Reading
Alter, Jonathan. "On the Ropes at NBS News." *Newsweek*, 8 March 1993, 49.

Flander, Judy. "Michael Gartner and NBC News." *Washington Journalism Review*, October 1989, 22–27.

Radolf, Andrew. "ASNE Responds to Gartner." *Editor & Publisher*, 12 December 1987, 14, 47.

Bill Geist

Born on May 10, 1947, in Champaign, Illinois, Bill Geist graduated from his hometown school, the University of Illinois, in 1968. He also completed a master of arts degree in journalism from the University of Missouri in 1972, and worked as a reporter and columnist at the *Chicago Tribune*, before joining the *New York Times* in 1980 and writing the "About New York" column.

In 1987, Geist became a CBS News correspondent, contributing regular, often satirical reports on life in America for *CBS News Sunday Morning*, as well as *48 Hours* and *CBS Evening News, Sunday Edition*. He was recruited by *On the Road* correspondent Charles Kuralt, and he credits Kuralt for having sustained interest at *Sunday Morning* in underappreciated stories. Geist's report on the 66th anniversary of America's famous highway, Route 66, earned him an Emmy Award

in 1992. His books include *Little League Confidential* (an account of his experience coaching his children's little league baseball teams), *Monster Trucks and Hair in a Can*, *The Zucchini Plague and Other Tales of Suburbia and City Slickers,* and *The Big Five-Oh!* He continues to write regularly for a number of publications, including the *New York Times*, *The New Yorker,* and *TV Guide*.
          Michael D. Murray

Further Reading
Geist, Bill. *The Big Five-Oh!* New York: William Morrow & Co., 1997.

Geist, Bill. *Little League Confidential.* New York: Macmillan, 1992.

Geist, Bill. "Tribute: Charles Kuralt." *TV Guide,* 30 August 1997, 6–7.

Mal Goode

Mal Goode was a pioneer in broadcast news, the first African American to be hired as a correspondent by one of the nation's networks. Goode's life and work served as an inspiration to a generation of black broadcast journalists.

The grandson of slaves and the son of a steelworker, Goode was born in White Plains, Virginia, in 1908. He worked in a steel mill in order to put himself through the University of Pittsburgh, graduating in 1931. He did not enter the field of journalism until 1948, when he took a job at the *Pittsburgh Courier* in the circulation department, eventually becoming a reporter. His broadcast career began at WHOD radio in Pittsburgh in 1950.

Baseball great Jackie Robinson lobbied ABC to open the door to black reporters, and the network responded by hiring Goode in 1962. He was 54 years old. Goode became frustrated by low-level assignments and infrequent on-air appearances. His break came during the Cuban Missile Crisis of October 1962. At the height of that story, he was on the air frequently from the United Nations. Goode covered national political conventions, the Poor People's March, and the assassination of Martin Luther King, Jr. He worked for ABC for two decades, was adviser for another 15 years, and died in 1995, at the age of 87.
          Lee Thornton

Further Reading

Dates, Jannette L., and William Barlow. *Split Image: African Americans in the Mass Media.* Washington, D.C.: Howard University Press, 1990.

Noble, Gil. *Black is the Color of My TV Tube.* Secaucus, NJ: Lyle Stuart, 1981.

Fred Graham

As the law correspondent for CBS News who became the first anchor of *Court TV,* Fred Graham covered some of the most notable trials and activities of the U.S. Supreme Court, the Justice Department, and the FBI. Born in Little Rock, Arkansas, on October 6, 1931, Graham moved to Nashville as a teenager. After graduating from Yale University in 1953, he served in the Marine Corps. He received his law degree from Vanderbilt University and attended Oxford University on a Fulbright scholarship. After practicing law in Nashville, he moved to Washington, D.C., to work for the Senate Judiciary Committee, and then the U.S. Labor Department.

In 1965, Graham became a Supreme Court correspondent for the *New York Times,* and in 1972, he became a legal affairs correspondent for CBS. He covered the Watergate hearings, receiving a Peabody Award for his work. In 1987, Graham was laid off from CBS during the network's wave of cutbacks. He returned to Nashville to anchor WKRN-TV. Admitting that he was not very good at anchoring, he left to write a book about his network experiences, *Happy Talk—Confessions of a TV Newsman.* He was approached by Court TV, a cable network devoted to the legal system. Graham joined *Court TV* in 1990 and has served as its chief anchor and managing editor.

Mark Conrad

Further Reading

Graham, Fred. *Happy Talk—Confessions of a TV Newsman.* New York: W.W. Norton, 1990.

"A New Day in Court—Graham Back as Chief Anchor for Cable Channel." *Chicago Tribune,* 12 December 1991, Zone C15.

"The Trials of Fred Graham." *Washington Times,* 18 May 1992, D1.

The Great Debates

The series of four televised debates between presidential candidates Richard Nixon and John F. Kennedy during the 1960 election was a watershed event, marking the first time two presidential candidates appeared in such a televised format. Each of the debates was watched by an audience estimated at about 70 million viewers, the largest broadcast audience in American political history. More significantly, the debates permanently changed the face of politics, cementing a relationship to television that has weakened the power of political parties and hastened the use of campaign media advisers.

By 1960, television had come to 90 percent of American homes. To encourage interest in debates, the three television networks offered free time for the four debates, and both parties accepted the offer. Congress suspended the "equal time" rule, so that air time would not have to be given to the 14 minor party candidates. No one knew how much effect a political debate would have. But after election day, in which Kennedy won the popular vote by only 113,000 votes of the 68.8 million cast, there was little question that the debates, most notably the first one (held on September 26, 1960), influenced the public's perception of the candidates. The outcome would set a standard for future candidates on how to orchestrate such events.

The four appearances actually were more like joint press conferences than classic "debate" confrontations. In a traditional debate, opponents talk to each other; in this debate, it was the candidate who spoke to the audience who turned out to be the winner. The first debate occurred at the studios of Chicago's CBS station WBBM-TV and was hosted by Howard K. Smith and produced by Don Hewitt. The focus was to be domestic policy, but the issues were subsumed by the images of Nixon and Kennedy. Before the debate, representatives of both candidates negotiated rules, lighting, camera angles, types of chairs, and even the color of the paint of the set. Although Nixon was considered by many to be an expert debater, his advisers were worried about how he might appear on camera. They were concerned because he had suffered a knee injury shortly before the debate and had lost weight and not fully recovered. Nixon's facial appearance also looked dour because of his pale skin. In what would become a major error, Nixon declined the services of a makeup artist.

Kennedy's staff had fewer concerns. He was tanned from campaigning in California and had rested on the day of the debate, while Nixon had campaigned earlier in the day. By the time the candidates arrived at WBBM, Nixon, wearing a gray suit, looked tired. Kennedy wore a dark suit, which complemented his features. An aide, noticing Nixon's five-o'clock shadow, went to a drugstore and bought a container of Lazy Shave to cover the candidate's stubble. As viewers would later see, it did not help.

What the candidates said would be overshadowed by their appearances. Nixon spoke well, but looked haggard. Kennedy maintained steady eye contact with the camera; when he did not, he appeared to be listening intently, but calmly, to Nixon. Nixon followed a traditional debate style. When speaking, he looked at Kennedy. When not speaking, he looked around the studio. The debate featured a number of candidate "reaction shots." Kennedy had 11 such shots, taking 118 seconds; Nixon had 9, totalling 85 seconds. Nixon's aides criticized the type and timing of shots of him as unflattering—either they were too "tight" or they showed him favoring his sore knee. What also affected Nixon's appearance were the hot camera lights, including spotlights his advisers recommended to help his appearance, but by the end of the debate, Nixon seemed to be sweating profusely.

The Cold War and the fight against communism was the focal point of the debates. Even though the first debate was devoted to domestic policy, Kennedy tried to include a discussion of the Cold War and economic issues. The first debate featured a question from NBC's Sander Vanocur about a remark President Eisenhower had made regarding the importance of Nixon's role as vice president. The question called for specific ideas Nixon had provided the administration during Eisenhower's presidency. Nixon's advisers felt that question was unfair.

The second debate, held in Washington, D.C., and hosted by NBC's Frank McGee, focused on foreign policy. Attitudes toward Cuba and the U-2 incident (when a U.S. spy plane was shot down by the Soviets, forcing the cancellation of a summit meeting between Soviet Prime Minister Khrushchev and President Eisenhower) were considered. Also, a dispute over two small islands, Kimoy and Matsu, between communist China and Formosa, was discussed. In the last two debates, more questions arose about China policy, labor unions, nuclear testing, and education. In the latter three debates, Nixon wore darker suits, stood in front of more appealing backgrounds, and had regained his normal weight. He looked more confident and appealing than in the opening debate, in part because he used the services of a theatrical makeup artist.

But it was the first debate that would have the most impact. Although it would not be known or fully appreciated right away, it appeared that Kennedy was a confident challenger. His crowds grew, and he started to attract independent and undecided voters; public opinion surveys consistently reported that a majority of viewers felt the debates influenced their decision. In a Roper poll, 72 percent of those who were influenced by the debates voted for Kennedy. Even though Nixon was more poised in later debates, as he learned afterwards, the first impression on television had devastating consequences. Interestingly, those who had listened to the debates on the radio thought Nixon won the first debate.   *Mark Conrad*

Further Reading

Ambrose, Stephen. *Nixon—The Education of a Politician.* New York: Simon and Schuster, 1987, 570–83, 592–94.

White, Theodore H. *The Making of the President 1960.* New York: Atheneum, 1961, 279–95.

"As It Happened: The First Kennedy-Nixon Debate" (A&E Video 1990); and "The Making of the Great Debate" (A&E Video 1985).

Jeff Greenfield

Political and media analyst for ABC News for many years, Jeff Greenfield joined CNN in 1998. He is author of numerous books and articles on American campaign politics. He received three Emmys for work on *Nightline* and South Africa specials, and one for a prime time special on Ross Perot. He was born in New York City in 1943. His father was a lawyer, and his mother an educator. He graduated with honors from the University of Wisconsin, receiving a bachelor of arts degree in 1964, and from Yale, 1967 earning his bachelor of law degree in 1967. Greenfield entered politics as a legislative aide to the late Senator Robert F. Kennedy from 1967 to 1968. He was an assistant to New York Mayor John Lindsay from 1968 to 1970. In the 1970s, Greenfield worked for the consulting firm Garth Associates and wrote or coauthored seven books. He appeared as an analyst on PBS' *Firing Line* with William F. Buckley and *We Interrupt This Week.*

Greenfield was CBS' media critic for coverage of the 1980 political conventions and presidential campaign. Joining ABC in 1983, Greenfield covered political primaries, conventions, debates, election night tallies, and inaugural festivities. He provided analysis for *World News Tonight* and appeared regularly on *Nightline* and as a frequent essayist on *World News Sunday.* Greenfield was twice named to *TV Guide's* "All Star" news team as best political reporter. The *Washington Journalism Review* named him "The Best in the Business" as a media critic in 1992. *The People's Choice* (1995), a political satire, is Greenfield's first novel. He is working on a a satire on big media. He lives in New York City and Salisbury, Connecticut.

Kevin C. Lee

Further Reading

Greenfield, Jeff. "An Abusive Press?" speech to Colorado Press Association, 20 February 1987. Reprinted in Shirley Biagi, *Media Impact.* Belmont, CA: Wadsworth, 1998, 8–9.

Greenfield, Jeff. "A Nation of Spectators," *Communicator,* August 1994, 13.

Greenfield, Jeff. *Television: The First Fifty Years.* New York: Abrams, 1977.

Lawrence K. Grossman

Lawrence K. Grossman is a television executive who criss-crossed the industry in many roles, including president of NBC News and of the Public Broadcasting Service (PBS). His audience-centered approach led to program development. He was born Lawrence Kugelmass in Brooklyn on June 21, 1931. His father died when he was an infant, and his mother Rose's second husband, Nathan Grossman, provided a new last name, although he retained the K from Kugelmass as a middle initial.

Grossman was the managing editor of the *Columbia Daily Spectator* while attending Columbia University. After graduating in 1952, he spent a year at Harvard Law School. *Look* magazine's promotions department hired him in 1953, but after three years there, he accepted an advertising position at CBS. Grossman switched to NBC in 1962 and became that network's advertising vice president. There he made contacts with Robert Kintner, the president of the network, and Grant Tinker, the vice president for programming. In 1966, Grossman resigned from NBC and formed his own consulting agency, Forum Communications, Inc. It challenged the license of station WPIX, claiming the station inadequately served the community by falsifying news and by practicing racial discrimination. After fighting for 10 years, Grossman's group received a $9 million settlement. He resigned as president of Forum Communications in 1976 and became the president and CEO of PBS.

PBS was in need of Grossman, who believed in programming for the widest audience. His administration, however, was criticized for its plan to centralize programming and for its lack of a strong liaison with local stations. Some critics claimed Grossman had forgotten the PBS goal—to fulfill programming needs not being met by commercial stations. However, he provided leadership and established important news programs—*Frontline* and *Inside Story*—and expanded the *MacNeil/ Lehrer Report* to the *Newshour.* When Grossman left in 1984, PBS had twice as many regular viewers as when he arrived.

Grossman replaced Reuven Frank as president of NBC News in 1984. He subsequently took NBC News to first place. In the mid-1980s, the dynasties that had once controlled networks were losing audience. When the profits fell, takeovers began, and in 1986, General Electric bought NBC. This immediately impacted NBC News, which cut its staff by 400. Grossman resisted deeper cuts and resigned in 1988. In 1989, he was named to the Frank Stanton Chair on the First Amendment at Harvard, and he served as Senior Fellow with the Freedom Forum. In 1991, he became president of Brookside Productions & Horizons Cable, televising events from different locales. Grossman also wrote two books: *Somehow It Works*, dealing with the 1964 presidential election, and *The Electronic Republic*, predicting an evolutionary direct democratic system of government based on use of the Internet.   *William R. Davie*

Further Reading

Grossman, Lawrence K. *The Electronic Republic.* Viking/Penguin and 20th Century Fund, 1996.

Grossman, Lawrence K. *Somehow It Works, A Candid Portrait of the 1964 Presidential Election.* New York: Doubleday, 1965.

Mink, Eric. "Larry Grossman's Program for NBC News." *Washington Journalism Review*, May 1985, 55–61.

Bryant Gumbel

Bryant Gumbel is one of the first African American broadcasters who excelled nationally as a sportscaster, newscaster, and interviewer during his tenure of over 20 years at the NBC network. He was born in New Orleans in 1948 and grew up in Chicago. He graduated from Bates College in Lewiston, Maine, in 1970, with a liberal arts degree and one year later became a staff writer for *Black Sports*. He was promoted to editor-in-chief, and his work caught the attention of a programming director at KNBC in Los Angeles, who hired him in October of 1972 as a weekend sportscaster. Gumbel is fond of saying that he had never been west of the Mississippi before his work in television. He became a weekday sportscaster at KNBC within a year and moved up to the position of sports director in 1976. His activities as a sportscaster at KNBC were not limited to just local stations. He began with NBC in the fall of 1975 and within the next seven years became the host of virtually every one of that network's sports programs.

Gumbel began appearing on *Today* in September 1980, with his sports reports three times a week. He became the host of *Today* when he replaced Tom Brokaw on January 4, 1982 and remained in that position until January 3, 1997. During his record-setting 15-year tenure on the show, it was estimated that he appeared on 7,500 hours of live broadcast, interviewed 12,000 people, and asked 160,000 questions. He did broadcasts from all regions of the world, including Moscow, Saudi Arabia (during the Persian Gulf War), Ho Chi Minh City (on the tenth anniversary of the fall of Saigon), the Vatican, and sub-Saharan Africa.

Gumbel also was seen often during prime time. He hosted the NBC coverage of the 1988 Summer Olympics from Seoul, South Korea; broadcast the Super Bowl and the World Series; hosted *Main Street* (a news series for teenagers); hosted and produced *The R.A.C.E.* (a special program on racial issues); and co-anchored, with Tom Brokaw, the 1992 national election coverage.

Former President George Bush called Gumbel "one of the best, fairest, and toughest interviewers." Gumbel is also known for several skirmishes that include his conflict with the late-night talk show host David Letterman, and a letter critical of *Today* weatherman Willard Scott. Gumbel's broadcasting skills have been recognized in the form of many awards, including a sports Emmy, a news Emmy, the Edward R. Murrow Award, and the Associated Press Best Broadcaster of the Year Award. He was twice named the Best Morning Television News Interviewer in *The Washington Journalism Review* Annual Readers Poll. After leaving *Today* and NBC, Gumbel signed a five-year contract with CBS in March of 1997 and briefly hosted the public affairs series *Public Eye*. He also hosted the prime-time Emmy Awards in 1997. *See also Today*.   *Yasue Kuwahara*

Further Reading

Auletta, Ken. *Three Blind Mice*. New York: Random House, 1991.

Goldberg, Robert, and Gerald Jay Goldberg. *Anchors*. New York: Birch Lane, 1990.

H

Happy News

Loosely defined, "happy news" generally refers to a trend aimed at developing a positive approach to broadcast news content and presentation. "Happy news" has a long tradition, dating back to the 1970s, when news consultants encouraged it at hundreds of local television stations. Despite its frequent excesses and name, "happy news" represented a serious dimension in television—in its various forms, it remained the main response to persistent demands by the American public that television journalists balance the bad news with good news.

Attempts to advance "happy news" in television extended from similar efforts by some early radio reporters, most notably network commentator Gabriel Heatter, who opened his newscast with the signature line, "Ah, there's good news tonight." Although much of Heatter's "good news" had serious undertones, particularly around the time of World War II, he helped leaven what had seemed to radio listeners, in his words, "a parade of doom and gloom." By demonstrating the appeal of a more optimistic agenda, Heatter inspired many others in radio, including Paul Harvey, and cleared the way for the assimilation of "happy news" in television.

Very early, "happy news" served as a dividing line between network and local television newscasts. In the 1950s and 1960s, network news figures such as Douglas Edwards, Walter Cronkite, Chet Huntley, and David Brinkley rejected the concept and cleaved to stark news presentation in step with the domestic discord and Cold War tensions of the times. On the local level, however, news producers were quick to embrace "happy news," for two reasons. First, local newscasters were more proximate to the viewing audience and did not feel the need to maintain a solemn, formal air. Second, local networks were the first to hire news consultants and apply their sophisticated audience research. The 60 to 70 percent of "average" viewers (those in the middle and lower socio-economic strata who were defined as the "mass audience") were emphatic that more relevant and uplifting news was needed in order to temper the networks' emphasis on the dark and obscure.

Largely because it was advocated by news consultants, a major passage in the evolution of "happy news" occurred in the 1970s when about 200 local television stations abandoned single news anchors, adopted co-anchors, and had them engage in "happy talk." The first occurence was at Chicago television station WLS in 1968, when station executive Richard O'Leary instructed anchors Fahey Flynn and Joel Daly to break from their scripts and personally react to some of the day's more dreary news. Chicago viewers flocked to the Flynn-Daly newscast, which became a dominant sensation in the television news community. The phrase "happy talk" was coined in 1970 by *Variety* reporter Morry Roth, who drew national attention to the spright dialogue of Flynn and Daly and the huge audiences they generated. "Happy talk" was further defined in the early 1970s by the team of Roger Grimsby and Bill Beutel at WABC in New York. By the mid-1970s, because of uniformly positive research and high ratings, news consultants had implemented "happy talk" at client stations all over the country.

"Happy talk," though, eventually confused the original issues of "happy news." In many locales "happy talk" got out of hand. Viewers sometimes saw slap-stick routines on the news set and frisbees flying in the studio. Some local television news anchors became lightning rods for critics, including leading figures from network news. In several public appearances in the 1970s, CBS anchor Walter Cronkite deplored Eyewitness News and the "happy" approach it always seemed to convey. By the early 1980s, however, "happy talk" had been reigned in and newer concerns developed for meeting the public's desire for an optimistic news perspective.

The largest of these concerns related to coverage of crime and violence. By the late 1980s, criticisms of television news centered on what seemed to be an endless agenda of homicides, hostage situations, and drive-by shootings. News consultants who had researched perceptions of crime and violence for many years reported conflicting findings. While average viewers continued to press for a good news-bad news balance, upwards of 70 percent insisted that reports of crime and violence must appear. This apparently was because of an exponential increase in urban crime in the 1960s and 1970s. Viewers did not want the worst news left out because they were directly affected by violence in their own neighborhoods, and they needed crime-related news as a surveillance device. Such views were widely expressed in lower-income, blue-collar families, television's core audience.

At the local level, where a need for "happy news" remained most acutely felt, anxieties about crime news ushered two new trends into the 1990s. The first was providing viewers a "news of hope," in which feature stories increasingly stressed crime-prevention measures, and specific reports emphasized such things as the number of survivors rather than the number of victims. The second trend, called "family sensitive news," restricted coverage of homicides and shootings and concen-

trated on this type of news on late-night newscasts, presumably when young children were not watching. These measures provided only half-way solutions. The "family sensitive" concept was criticized as a means of "censoring" news. A bigger issue, identified in research not just by news consultants but also by academic researchers, was a compulsion by editors and reporters to "ambulance chase" and focus on minor incidents without proper perspective.

It was as a reaction to these matters that debates over "happy news" continued. Critics and many in the journalistic community wound up divided on "happy news"; while insisting that it pandered to the public, most experts conceded that negative news, notably crime and violence, served the same function. Yet, over time, the public itself was less torn—it wanted balance. ***See also*** Consultants, Tabloid Television. *Craig Allen*

Further Reading

Deeb, Gary. "What You See is What 'News Doc' Prescribes." *Chicago Tribune,* 8 March 1978, 1–4.
Klein, Paul. "Happy Talk, Happy Profits." *New York,* 28 June 1971, 60–61.
Powers, Ron. *The Newscasters.* New York: St. Martin's Press, 1977.

Don Hewitt

Frank Micelotta for CBS News

Founder and executive producer of television's most successful newsmagazine program *60 Min-*

utes, Don Hewitt was born on December 14, 1922, in New York City and grew up in New Rochelle, New York. He dropped out of New York University to join the staff of the *New York Herald Tribune* at the age of 19. During World War II, Hewitt was a correspondent for the War Shipping Administration. After the war, he joined the Associated Press in Memphis, then returned to New York and the *Pelham Sun,* a suburban paper. He then became a night telephoto editor for Acme News Pictures, the photo arm of United Press, selecting photos and writing captions for newspapers around the country. He left Acme News Pictures to enter the fledgling television industry and in 1946, directed the first CBS evening news program, *Douglas Edwards and the News.*

He worked tirelessly to improve visual aspects of the evening news in that very primitive era of television and had become an executive producer when Walter Cronkite took over the program. Hewitt distinguished himself during network political convention coverage and was on hand to direct the first of the so-called Great Debates in1960, featuring presidential candidates John F. Kennedy and Richard M. Nixon. Eventually, news president Fred Friendly gave Hewitt his own documentary unit, and Hewitt took the opportunity to develop an alternative to the broadcast genre, which he believed was too long and impersonal. Hewitt's concept, to divide the public affairs hour in order to address the viewer's short attention span, won over CBS management, and *60 Minutes* took to the air in 1967, with Harry Reasoner and Mike Wallace sharing the on-air hosting duties.

The program struggled in a Tuesday evening time slot before it was moved to Sunday night. It became a major ratings success beginning in 1975, when it entered television's "Top Ten." The immediate result of this success story was that it reshaped the packaging of television news. Hewitt's underlying rule—to stress interesting individuals—was enhanced by investigative reports. Mike Wallace was recognized as television's masterful interviewer and interrogator. Ed Bradley, Lesley Stahl, and Steve Kroft emerged as major players in this ensemble of broadcasting's best and brightest. Andy Rooney, a former writer for Harry Reasoner, evolved into a fixture and a national icon.

Over the years, Hewitt's reputation for innovation and his ability to convey important information in a dynamic manner became recognized throughout the industry as he presented his views in speeches to professional groups. When CBS faced challenges from outside economic forces, Hewitt and his colleagues investigated purchasing the network to help maintain news standards.

Since its inception, *60 Minutes* has received every major award and has become the most imitated public affairs program in television history. Hewitt received the Paul White Award from the Radio Television News Directors Association in 1988. In April of 1992, Hewitt received the Goldsmith Award for Lifetime Achievement from the Kennedy School of Government, Harvard University. *See also 60 Minutes,* CBS News.

Michael D. Murray

Further Reading

Brady, James. "In Step with Don Hewitt." *Parade Magazine,* 8 February 1998, 26.
Campbell, Richard. *60 Minutes and the News.* Urbana: University of Illinois Press, 1991.
Hertsgaard, Mark. "The *60 Minutes* Man." *Rolling Stone,* 30 May 1991, 47–53.
Hewitt, Don. "Blame Me!" *Communicator,* February 1995, 38.

Andrew Heyward

Andrew Heyward is the current president of CBS News. A 1972 magna cum laude graduate of Harvard University, Heyward considered attending law school but instead joined the New York independent station, WNYW-TV, as a production assistant. He advanced quickly to producer, and then was hired by the CBS flagship station WCBS in New York. Within a year, he was news producer at WCBS. Advancing to executive producer of WCBS's evening newscast, he considered a position at ABC News, but instead was offered a job with CBS and accepted.

Heyward rose quickly from field producer to senior producer of the *CBS Evening News.* He developed *48 Hours* and produced *Eye to Eye with Connie Chung.* In 1994, he assumed the vice presidency of CBS News and was executive producer of the *CBS Evening News.* He took over the

CBS News presidency in January of 1996, the seventh person to hold that post in 15 years. He is credited with helping to restore morale and rebuild personnel resources at CBS News. Heyward negotiated a deal permitting CNN's Christiane Amanpour to report for CBS's *60 Minutes*, for example, and also hired NBC *Today* anchor Bryant Gumbel, with duties to include hosting a CBS newsmagazine.   *Michael D. Murray*

Further Reading

Auletta, Ken. *Thee Blind Mice: How the TV Networks Lost Their Way.* New York: Random House, 1991.

McClellan, Steve. "Andrew Heyward: CBS News' Mr. Fixit." *Broadcasting & Cable,* 15 January 1996, 120.

Zurawik, David, and Christina Stoehr."Saving CBS News." *American Journalism Review,* April 1997, 16–23.

John Hockenberry

Courtesy MSNBC

John Hockenberry, born in June 1956 in Dayton, Ohio, first gained fame as a general assignment reporter for National Public Radio (NPR). He studied at both the University of Chicago and the University of Oregon and started his broadcasting career at KLCC in Eugene, Oregon, in 1980. He joined NPR in Washington, D.C., in November of 1981. He broadcast for that network for nearly a decade, serving also as a national correspondent and a program host. Since that time, he has served

as a correspondent for both ABC News and NBC News, where he currently hosts *Edgewise* for MSNBC and serves as a correspondent for *Dateline NBC*.

A paraplegic since an auto accident in February of 1976 at the age of 19, his recent book, *Moving Violations: War Zones, Wheelchairs and Declarations of Independence*, describes a variety of his reporting experiences, including coverage of the funeral of the Ayatollah Khomeini. He was sent to Jerusalem to cover the Palestinian uprising against Israel in the final weeks of 1987 and also reported on the massive famine in October 1992 in Mogadishu, Somalia, for ABC News. He also covered the Persian Gulf War and was one of the first Western broadcasters to report from Northern Iraq and Southern Turkey refugee camps.

Though always attempting to avoid the expectation that he specialize in reporting on disabilities for fear that he might be typecast in that role, he has, on a few occasions, reported on disability-related issues, such as the inaccessibility of the New York subway system. He is credited for his careful research, thoughtful writing, and for the sensitivity and perspective he brings to these stories. He was honored early in his career for his report on a disabled person from Iowa City, Iowa, who was able to succeed in an on-the-air position in the radio broadcasting business in spite of having Tourette's syndrome. More recently, in September of 1997, he reported for *Dateline NBC* on the many challenges the 49 million disabled people currently face in America each day, including difficulty gaining access to a location for a job interview. In reporting for this particular story, Hockenberry reviewed the Americans with Disabilities Act of 1990 with viewers and explained changes which had taken place in the workplace. He offered analysis of challenges arising in complying with efforts for accommodation. The report also included detailed information on employment practices and fair housing.

Hockenberry has written for a wide variety of popular publications including the *New York Times*, the *Washington Post*, and the *Columbia Journalism Review*. His memoir received the American Library Association Notable Book

Award in 1996 and, prior to that, received two Champion Tuck Business Reporting Awards, a Benton Fellowship, and a Unity in Media Award. He has also been honored with two Peabody Awards. *Michael D. Murray*

Further Reading

Gunther, Marc. "The Cable Guy." *American Journalism Review,* January/February 1997, 42.
Hockenberry, John. *Moving Violations: War Zones, Wheelchairs and Declarations of Independence.* New York: Hyperion, 1995.

Richard C. Hottelet

Richard C. Hottelet was one of the handful of foreign correspondents hired by Edward R. Murrow. After the war, Hottelet, reporting from central Europe and then the United Nations, was to make his name synonymous with a style of news analysis that combined a beat reporter's ability to get the story with comprehensive knowledge of whatever events, country, or subject he was covering.

Hottelet was born in New York City in 1917. He attended Brooklyn College and received his bachelor of arts degree in 1937. After graduation, he continued his studies at the University of Berlin and joined United Press in 1938. After America's entry into World War II, Hottelet was jailed by the Gestapo along with a fellow journalist and was only released when an exchange was arranged for two German newsmen held by the Allies. In 1942, he joined the office of War Information in London, and then in 1944, he was hired by Edward R. Murrow for CBS News.

One of Hottelet's earliest assignments was to cover the Air Force during the D-Day invasion. Later on a trip in a B-26, he was forced to parachute to safety when his plane was shot down. He covered the First Army, accompanied Allied ground forces into Germany, and was one of the first reporters to broadcast from inside Nazi Germany, from the Nazi concentration camp at Dachau, and to report the U.S–Soviet armies linkup at the Elbe River. In July of 1945, he made a homecoming of sorts, when he entered Berlin with the Second Armored division and was the first reporter to broadcast from occupied Berlin.

After the war, Hottelet reported from Eastern Europe and was among the first to report from post-war Poland. In 1946, as relations between the United States and the Soviet Union deteriorated, he was forced to close the CBS Moscow bureau. In 1950 he opened the CBS Bonn bureau and served in that post until 1956. In those years, Hottelet is perhaps best remembered for heated exchanges with David Schoenbrun, the CBS Paris bureau chief, on the year-end CBS News series *Years of Crisis.*

In 1960, after a reporting stint from Latin America, he was appointed CBS UN correspondent, a position which he held for 20 years. In 1985, Hottelet retired from CBS. Hottelet's broadcasting career, however, was far from over. In 1993, at the age of 76, he began a series of broadcasts called *America and the World,* sponsored by the Council of Foreign Relations, for National Public Radio (NPR). Indeed, Hottelet still does occasional news analysis for NPR. *Albert Auster*

Further Reading

Cloud, Stanley, and Lynee Olsen. *The Murrow Boys: Pioneers on the Front Lines of Broadcast Journalism.* Boston: Houghton Mifflin, 1996.
Persico, Joseph E. *Edward R. Murrow: An American Original.* New York: Laurel, 1990.
Sperber, A.M. *Murrow: His Life and Times.* New York: Bantam, 1986.

Brit Hume

Photo courtesy of Brit Hume

Brit Hume became well known as an investigative journalist and chief White House correspondent for ABC News during the Bush administration. His work for ABC's *Close-Up* documentary film series in 1979 earned him television's first Academy Award nomination. Hume received an Emmy for White House coverage during the Persian Gulf War, and *American Journalism Review* named him "Best White House correspondent." He left ABC to join Fox in January 1997 as its chief correspondent and managing editor.

Alexander Britton Hume was born in Washington, D.C., in 1943. He got his start in journalism with the *Hartford Times* in 1965, shortly after earning his bachelor of arts degree at the University of Virginia. He moved up quickly at United Press International's (UPI) Connecticut and Washington, D.C., offices and at the Baltimore *Evening Sun*. Hume spent part of 1969 on a Washington Journalism Center fellowship investigating the United Mine Workers at the exhortation of Ralph Nader.

In 1970, Hume joined Jack Anderson's syndicated newspaper column's investigative team for "Washington Merry-Go-Round" while continuing work on a book outlining union corruption and hazardous working conditions characteristic of coal mining in the 1960s. In 1973, Hume became Washington editor of *MORE* magazine, a press criticism journal. Lacking an investigative journalist for *Close-Up*, ABC hired Hume as a consultant. Hume's second book, *Inside Story*, appeared in 1974. It featured accounts of his investigative work for Jack Anderson. Most prominently, he broke the ITT-Dita Beard story, detailing favorable company treatment for ITT by the Nixon administration in exchange for nearly half a million dollars for the 1972 Republican Convention.

For *Close-Up*, Hume co-authored and narrated several highly regarded specials in the late 1970s, including "Nobody's Children" and "Battleground Washington: The Politics of Pressure." He got his first live air time with ABC in 1976 as general correspondent, covering the U.S. House of Representatives in 1977 and the Senate in 1981. In January 1988, Hume began covering the George Bush White House. He continued that beat through Bill Clinton's first term. A noted on-air confrontation came during Clinton's presentation of Ruth Bader Ginsberg as a Supreme Court nominee, when Hume asked Clinton to comment on a series of abrupt staff changes. President Clinton said he had given up trying to "disabuse" the press of anything.

For ABC, Hume filed stories for *Nightline* and *This Week with David Brinkley*, and he anchored *The Weekend Report*. Joining Fox News, Hume is co-author of the syndicated *Washington Post* column "Computer Reporter." Hume is married to Kim Schiller, a former producer at ABC, and current deputy bureau chief for Fox News in Washington.

Kevin C. Lee

Further Reading

Hume, Brit. "My Fall Into Disabuse." *The American Spectator,* September 1993, 22–23.

Murphy, Mary. "Hume with a View." *TV Guide,* 30 August 1997, 36–40.

Ellen Hume

Ellen Hume has worn many hats. An Annenberg Senior Fellow in Washington, D.C., she serves as executive director of the Public Broadcasting Service's Democracy Project. She regularly appears as a commentator on the Cable News Network's *Reliable Sources* series and also participates in such national news and public affairs programs as the PBS shows *The NewsHour* with Jim Lehrer and *Washington Week in Review,* and the *CBS Evening News*. She is also heard on National Public Radio (NPR) and numerous commentary programs.

Born on April 24, 1947, in Chevy Chase, Maryland, Hume received her bachelor of arts degree with honors from Radcliffe College and has taught at Harvard University, where she served as executive director of the Joan Shorenstein Barone Center on the Press, Politics and Public Policy at the Kennedy School of Government. She also served as political writer and White House correspondent for the *Wall Street Journal* (metro), as national reporter for the *Los Angeles Times*, and as business reporter for the *Detroit Free Press*. Because of the diversity of her background and experience, Hume is frequently called upon to comment on press performance. She was one of the leading figures assessing coverage of international reporting on the occasion of the death of Britain's Princess Diana in a car crash on August 31, 1997.

Kathryn J. Sasina

Further Reading

Hume, Ellen. "Dumping Meese: Close Reagan Advisers Mount Drive to Force Attorney General Out." *The Wall Street Journal*, 27 April 1988, 1.
Hume, Ellen. *Tabloids, Talk Radio, and the Future of News*. Washington, D.C.: The Annenberg Program in Communications Policy Studies of Northwestern University, 1995.

Charlayne Hunter-Gault

Photo by Christopher Little for MacNeil/Lehrer Productions

Charlayne Hunter-Gault pursued her lifelong dream of being a journalist, working for almost 20 years with the Public Broadcasting Service (PBS), as national correspondent and substitute co-anchor for the PBS *NewsHour*. In 1997, she resigned from PBS to accompany her husband, Ron, to South Africa, where he had been appointed managing director of J.P. Morgan, South Africa. Her reports about the African continent continue for National Public Radio (NPR).

Hunter-Gault was born in Due West, South Carolina, on February 27, 1942. She was the first black woman admitted to the University of Georgia, where she faced angry mobs and vandalism of her property. Originally denied admission, she at-

tended Wayne State University in Detroit while the case went through the courts. Integration was ordered in 1961. After graduating from the University of Georgia in 1963, she accepted a job as a secretary with *The New Yorker* magazine and was promoted to a staff writer in 1964. In 1967, Hunter-Gault won a Russell Sage Fellowship to study social science at Washington University in St. Louis. Later that year, she joined NBC's WRC-TV in Washington, D.C., as an investigative reporter and anchorwoman. However, in 1968, she moved to the staff of the *New York Times* in order to run the Harlem bureau and to cover the urban black community.

Described as a reporter with an eye for detail, she brought an understanding of the problems of inner city blacks. Her involvement in the Civil Rights movement provided her contacts among black leaders, which added depth and credibility to her stories. In 1970, she managed to persuade the editors of the *New York Times* to change their policy and refer to African Americans as blacks rather than as Negroes. In 1978, she joined the *MacNeil/Lehrer Report* as the third correspondent and substitute anchor. In 1983, when the program expanded to one hour, she was named a national correspondent. Her stories focused on personal concerns rather than daily news.

Her many awards reflect her social concerns. She has won Emmys for on-the-spot reports from Grenada and for her profile of Elmo Zumwalt III, who contracted cancer from Agent Orange while serving during the Vietnam War, under his father. She has won three Publisher Awards from the *New York Times,* including one in 1970 for coverage of the life and death of a 12-year-old heroin addict. Other awards include the National Urban Coalition Award and the American Women in Radio and Television Award. In 1986, she won the prestigious Peabody Award for Excellence in Broadcast Journalism for "Apartheid's People," showing effects of separatism in South Africa.

She has also contributed to *Vogue*, *Ms.*, *Life*, *Essence*, and *Saturday Review* magazines. She often speaks on college campuses and serves on the boards of the Committee to Protect Journalists, the Center for Communication, and the Foundation for Child Development. She left her regular spot on the *The NewsHour with Jim Lehrer* in the summer of 1997 and is now a regular contributor to NPR.   *Mary E. Beadle*

Further Reading

Flander, Judy. "A 'Shero' for All Seasons." *Communicator,* October 1995, 13.

Hines, D.S. *Black Women in America*. Brooklyn, N.Y.: Carlson Publishing, 1993.

"Interview with Charlayne Hunter-Gault," Women in Journalism, Oral History Project 1983, National Press Club, 14th and F Street NW, Washington, D.C. 20045. 70 pages: Video.

Chet Huntley

Chet Huntley joined NBC News in 1955 and within a year, teamed up with David Brinkley to cover national political conventions. The team worked so well together that network executives replaced John Cameron Swayze's evening news broadcast with *The Huntley-Brinkley Report* on October 29, 1956, giving NBC News a more professional news image. The fifteen-minute newscast expanded to a half hour in 1963, and the team was together until Huntley's retirement on July 31, 1970. For much of nearly 15 years, the program led in the ratings and made Huntley and Brinkley familiar faces to more than 20 million viewers.

Born on December 10, 1911, in Cardwell, Montana, Chester Robert Huntley grew up in a succession of small Montana towns, including Logan, Big Timber, Whitehall, Bozeman, and Reedpoint. He nostalgically described his childhood and espoused the virtues of rural life in his book, *The Generous Years*. He attended Montana State College in Bozeman and the University of Washington in Seattle, where he began his broadcast career at a local radio station in 1934. For writing and broadcasting the news, he was paid $10 a month plus laundry service, and to make ends meet, he sometimes traded sponsor accounts for food.

He worked for KFI Radio in Los Angeles in 1937, CBS Radio in California in 1939, and ABC in 1951. Huntley sued a listener who called him a communist for criticizing Senator Joseph McCarthy's anticommunist charges. Huntley won a $10,000 judgment, which he never collected. An NBC talent search lured Huntley to NBC, where officials hoped that with his solemn demeanor and voice, he could compete with CBS's Edward R. Murrow. The Huntley-Brinkley team began the news with a distinctive theme (the second movement of Beethoven's Ninth Symphony) and sign-off: "Good night, David." "Good night, Chet." "And good night for NBC News."

In 1967, Huntley crossed the picket lines of striking American Federation of Television and Radio Artists, saying reporters should not be represented by the same unions as entertainers. His partner, Brinkley, honored the strike. Huntley became the spokesperson for network news reporters responding to attacks by Vice President Spiro Agnew in 1969. After Huntley retired from NBC in 1970, he started Big Sky, a ski resort northwest of Yellowstone Park, with funding from major corporations.

Huntley died of cancer on March 20, 1974, at Big Sky, Montana. *See also* David Brinkley.

William E. Huntzicker

Further Reading

Beaubien, Michael P., and John S. Wyeth Jr. *Views on the News: The Media and Public Opinion: The Chet Huntley Memorial Lectures*. New York: New York University Press, 1994.

Brinkley, David. *David Brinkley: 11 presidents, 4 wars, 22 political conventions, 1 moon landing, 3 assassinations, 2000 weeks of news and other stuff on television and 18 years of growing up in North Carolina*. New York: Alfred A. Knopf, 1995.

Huntley, Chet. *The Generous Years: Remembrances of a Frontier Boyhood*. New York: Random House, 1968.

I

Gwen Ifill

Already established as a respected reporter for the *Washington Post* and the *New York Times,* Ifill joined NBC News in the nation's capital on September 26, 1994. Ifill was raised in New York. A 1977 graduate of Simmons College in Boston, she began her journalism career at the *Boston Herald American* while still an undergraduate. From 1981 to 1984, she worked at the *Baltimore Evening Sun* as a general assignment reporter.

As a member of the *Washington Post* staff from 1984 to 1991, Ifill gained attention for her coverage of scandals involving the Housing and Urban Development Department. She joined the *New York Times* as a congressional correspondent in 1991 and covered the Bill Clinton 1992 presidential campaign. She was named White House correspondent when Clinton assumed the presidency, then switched to NBC News in Washington where she covers political issues for *Nightly News with Tom Brokaw*, *Today*, and *Meet the Press*. A 1995 survey of the most visible national network reporters by the Center for Media and Public Affairs (CMPA) rated Ifill among the top 50 reporters. She is also a frequent guest on the Public Broadcasting Service program *Washington Week in Review*.   *Michael D. Murray*

Further Reading

Fibich, Linda. "Under Siege." *American Journalism Review,* September 1995, 22.
Flander, Judy. "Tough but Graceful: NBC's Gwen Ifill." *The Communicator,* August 1996, 17–21.

Ifill, Gwen. "Seeing Beyond Politics." *Nieman Reports,* Fall 1997, 24.

Infotainment

Talk shows about transvestite priests. Reporters shooting *themselves* with stun guns. Five-word sound bites whipping by. Heavily promoted prime-time car-crash video. Murders relived in grainy slow motion. Celebrity trails elbowing national crises off the air. Television always was rooted in entertainment but it can be argued that in the late 20th century, the medium's more serious commitments to news and public affairs has dissolved into another concept—infotainment.

Society already has words for media fusions—teleplay, docudrama, infomercial. The increased influence of show-business values on news and information needed its own identifiable label. When the perfect term was found, its origins were as murky as UFO footage. Language columnist William Safire suggested "infotainment" may have been coined by Ron Eisenberg in the February issue of *1980 Phone Call* magazine. In any case, a database search of publications shows that the word appears rarely until the late 1980s and early 1990s. Then, quickly rising in popularity, it was used hundreds of times a year by the mass media to identify some of their own manifestations.

Like many words invented through splicing, "infotainment" has a chunky and vaguely comic lilt—a clue to its usual application. It is uttered most often by critics of television and by issue-oriented journalists within the medium. But if its purposal is monochromatic, its shading is diverse. Sometimes infotainment refers to talk shows and "tabloid" programs which routinely twist human concerns into spectacle, blending grave subjects with garish people and events. Sometimes infotainment means newscasts or newsmagazines that, in their overall content and style, reach mainly for visceral appeal. The term also is applied to individual news reports which deliver grains of useful information wrapped in sensational video.

Infotainment's explosion tends to mask a human history rich in such blended messages. Mixing information with provocative or diverting material is an ancient practice. In early oral cultures, much "news" was embedded in creative, often apocryphal stories. Monks toiled over handwritten chronicles with no access to fact checking or to significant readership. Most people simple passed information from mouth to ear. Later, Shakespeare, a classic (and classical) subversive, infused plays with political analysis, without sacrificing their power to distract and delight. Many fiction writers use journalism as a professional sideline while incorporating real events into their yarns. And broadcasting's founders knew that their medium, given the nature of its tools, was likely to sell more farce than facts, but could sell facts too.

But as the year 2000 nears, many news consumers have grown disaffected and restless and are flitting among a huge variety of programming choices. Many producers try infotainment as a way of holding onto audiences. Whirling graphics, anchor chit-chat, and news-selection formulas favor not intellectual, but visceral impact on viewers. Often arriving without context in bursts of vivid sounds and pictures, many television news stories stretch for emotional impact. They tend to lack an equal measure of social resonance—in fact, any meaning at all beyond the moment. "Live" technology proliferates across the country, tempting stations to squander air time on transient emergencies.

Critics fret that, like a fine old house in a neighborhood gone seedy, what remained of serious news and discourse on television has been cheapened by its surroundings. In his book *Amusing Ourselves to Death*, scholar Neil Postman says the modern problem is that television has made entertainment the format for the representation of experience, assuring viewers that even news should not be taken seriously. The banter called "happy talk" was invented for local television anchors in the 1960s. Once the gravity of newscasts had been disrupted, news consultants and promoters turned many anchors into near-clowns, an extreme example being when a San Francisco news team appeared on horseback in cowboy suits, riding to the metaphorical rescue of the uninformed, its six-guns spraying bulletins.

With its cheery populism, and even without gimmicks, local news in the 1970s looked radically different from the network news. But by the 1980s, networks were struggling to win back disaffected viewers or to recruit fresh ones, and so moved toward infotainment. Almost all news programs began sporting flashier visuals, ever-younger and prettier on-air personnel, and less complex reporting than in years past. Print journalism, desperate for advertising dollars as many newspapers failed, started to ape the visceral punch of television and reduce the depth of its reporting.

Infotainment was created, not by journalists, but by media managers and owners. Pushing advertisers' products to the greatest number of consumers was their central purpose. Television's friendly hosts and increasingly soft stories seemed to support this. Again, the concept predated them. One early case, largely unremarkable in its time, became fodder for decades of journalism seminars: Edward R. Murrow's association with not only the historic documentary program *See It Now,* but also with *Person to Person*, which featured Hollywood stars, having mass popularity.

In the 1980s, a television newsmagazine, CBS's *West 57th*, emphasized the glamor of its reporters in a fashion reminiscent of the old police drama *The Mod Squad,* and an NBC nod to history, *Yesterday, Today, and Tomorrow,* in the tradition of *You Are There*, depicted reality through reenactments. Many journalists found these programs to be unprofessional; critics mostly hated them; viewers shunned them; and the programs died. However, undaunted, some broadcast executives continued to treat news as "storytelling," excluding from coverage many of the dry but vital complexities of their times.

At its worst, an approach once employed by some exemplary television journalists was distorted by some unprincipled broadcasters. Some would carry the medium's essential nature to dangerous extremes. They would avoid journalism's tougher obligations, fill slack air time with showy trifles, and present oversimplified, drama-based, titillating portrayals of life—infotainment—as virtually the only "news" worth having. *See also* Tabloid Television. *James Upshaw*

Further Reading

Altheide, David L. *Creating Reality: How TV News Distorts Events.* Beverly Hills, CA: Sage Publications, 1976.

Campbell, Richard. *60 Minutes and the News: A Mythology for Middle America.* Urbana: University of Illinois Press, 1991.

Postman, Neil. *Amusing Ourselves to Death: Public Discourse in the Age of Show Business.* New York: Viking, 1985.

International Coverage

In spite of political pressures and the development of new distribution technologies, the last twenty years have not seen a significant increase of foreign program material on U.S. television. In the mid-1990s, only about 2 percent of news production shown originated outside the U.S., with dissemination restricted primarily to public television and programs aimed at specific ethnic groups. A less prominent notable exception has been CNN's *World Report,* with original news items produced in the Third World. A less prominent exception is educational broadcasters' use of foreign language television as material for language instruction.

There have been some initiatives to enhance the news flow from the Third World, such as establishment of the Inter Press Agency and numerous efforts sponsored by major U.S. foundations. Yet, those efforts did not result in an increase of Third World coverage by mainline networks. The frequently articulated critique still holds that, in general, U.S. television carries items about developing countries (rarely, if ever, produced there)

only if they concern catastrophes or stories involving U.S. interests and citizens, in particular specific economic or military reporting. Third World news per se has not become more important, in spite of coverage of the Persian Gulf War, the Bhopal disaster, widespread famines in Africa, or carnage in Bosnia. Emphasis on domestic issues and sensationalism has not dramatically changed.

New technologies like satellite broadcasting and multi-channel cable systems have facilitated greater coverage of developing countries with respect to culture, the arts, and the environment. Upscale cable programmers such as Discovery Communications, National Geographic Television, and the Travel Channel represent this trend. Cable channels designed for specific ethnic target audiences have also introduced original program material about and from developing countries. Most of the material programmed about the Third World appears to reflect the perspective of its mainly North American and European producers and directors. Except for ethnic and educational cable programmers, direct acquisition of productions made by developing countries is virtually unknown.

This does not reflect a bias against developing countries, but rather represents structural factors such as audience preference, production considerations, and noted parochialism. Similarly, coverage of U.S. or West European media no longer appears a priority among policy makers in developing countries because there has been a regional and local television reorientation. Privatization of media, decrease of foreign assistance, and the impotence of national bodies such as UNESCO to impact the "free flow of information," combined with the obvious commercial indifference to policy issues involved, makes the quest for comprehensive coverage moot.

Several other trends preclude an increase of television coverage from developing countries. Major U.S. networks have closed many news offices and have cut back on the number of their full-time foreign correspondents. As the Boell Foundation's Media Watch studies show, there has been increased use of stringers, reporting only those stories which can be sold.

There have been important developments, however, such as a shift in the 1990s to specialized cable networks, such as the International Channel, which carries foreign language productions, with an audience of 8 million and about 150 hours of material each week. Of the 90 hours originating in developing countries, including Eastern Europe, only 8 hours are programmed in English, with others, primarily Japanese, subtitled in English. Programs feature news, culture, variety shows, motion pictures, and sports. They are aimed at U.S. ethinic communities and the few business travelers and students commanding the language of the program. Reflecting the programming possibilities offered by multi-channel cable systems and reduced satellite feed and production costs, the International Channel also plans to offer channels exclusively dedicated to Chinese and Arabic programs.

Virtually no Latin American programs are carried on the International Channel, since several cable channels including Galavision and Univision carried on systems throughout the United States have been serving the Latin American communities. These programs reach 4.4 million hispanic cable television households in the U.S. CBS's Telenoticias, a 24-hour Spanish language news service, is produced in Miami by Latin Americans in Spanish and Portuguese. At the local level, foreign language programs and other productions from and about developing countries can be found on university channels, as well as on public access or leased programs. It is unlikely that these reach American opinion leaders, or even intend to influence them.

Apart from the rapid rise of ethnic television markets exposed to news feeds from developing countries, application of the Internet for the dissemination of Third World news is the most important change in information flow. Europeans and Americans, as well as most major Third World television news operators and governmental agencies are already on the Internet, and Asian countries are following. Cost reductions for electronic hardware and software, advanced data compression technologies, rapid expansion of computer access, development of high-speed modems, and other technological advances have created conditions for transmitting television news via the Internet, requiring lower up-front investment in facilities and satellite feeds. Radio-Television Hong Kong plans to transmit material on the Internet, for example, with the focus on news for the overseas Chinese. Accessible to Americans, program material is provided in both Chinese and English. The BBC claims its Web site is visited by up to 100,000 non-British individuals per day.

Critics of the one-way flow of information and television programming share the background assumption that greater television coverage of Third World affairs will somehow broaden the scope of coverage and expand the decison-making process beyond North America's boundaries, but the notion has never been tested. After all, the strategic knowledge policy makers need is not derived from foreign-language television programs but generated more through interpersonal and print communication. It is somewhat ironic that more incorporation of television news and production from and about the Third World into U.S. programming reflects market trends prompted by new technologies, rather than the policies adopted by national or international assemblies.

Claus Mueller

Further Reading

Dunow, Kenneth R. *European Media Markets: Commercial and Public Media in Fifteen Countries.* Washington, D.C.: National Association of Broadcasters, 1992.
O'Heffernan, Patrick. "Television and Crisis: Sobering Thoughts on Sound Bites Heard Round the World." *Television Quarterly,* Fall 1990, 9–14.
Petrozello, Donna. "CNN Remakes Itself." *Broadcasting & Cable,* 11 August 1997, 23–24.

International Crisis Reporting

Television news reporting, particularly live coverage, has affected not only how international crises are reported, but also how some of those crises have evolved. Policy makers increasingly recognize this. They know that television coverage influences the pace of world events and the tactics of those who shape such events. Private correspondence by diplomatic pouch has, in some cases, been replaced by messages sent to other governments indirectly via television. Advocates of openness applaud this, but the realities of diplomacy and crisis resolution do not always conform to the demands of television's perpetual deadline.

Television also can have a profound effect on public opinion. The drama inherent in covering of a breaking story can sometimes elevate a situation to a "crisis" level and spur the public to demand that the government do something. Adopting a wait-and-see approach, even if it is the wisest course, may become politically untenable. Meanwhile, television journalists' loss of the protective filter of time may mean that editorial judgments are made on the run, even though a crisis should mandate extraordinary journalistic responsibility.

The 1991 coup in the Soviet Union illustrates the techniques and effects of television-dominated crisis reporting. The first word that President George Bush received about the apparent ouster of Soviet President Mikhail Gorbachev came not from intelligence or diplomatic sources, but from CNN. When Bush decided to back Boris Yeltsin's opposition to the coup, he sent the message to the principals in the Soviet Union and to the rest of the world via CNN. The perpetrators of the coup had taken control of Soviet television, and so it did not cover the demonstrations Yeltsin led in Moscow's streets; however, CNN reports reached a large enough Soviet audience to help Yeltsin build support for his anti-coup effort.

As other television news services compete with CNN to reach worldwide audiences, competition may build to see who can be the first to report an incipient crisis. Crisis reporting demands respect for "real-time" ethical decision making; that is, without the benefit of reflection. Unfortunately, the old wire service rule of "get it first, but first get it right" is in danger of being sacrificed in pursuit of higher ratings.

Yet, crisis reporting can play a valuable role in making the public aware of human disasters. In 1984, television coverage of the famine in Ethiopia helped spur governmental and public relief efforts, and in the aftermath of the 1991 Persian Gulf War, television reports about the plight of Kurds fleeing

Saddam Hussein's Iraq helped push the Bush administration to intervene on the refugees' behalf. In these and similar cases, television's presence did some good—desperate people received help. The question arises, however, about whether decisions to deliver aid should be based on where cameras happen to be present. Government response to heart-wrenching television images is reaction, not policy. *See also* CNN (Cable News Network).

Philip Seib

Further Reading

Donovan, Robert J., and Ray Scherer. *Unsilent Revolution.* New York: Cambridge University Press, 1992.

Seib, Philip. *Headline Diplomacy: How News Coverage Affects Foreign Policy*, Westport, CT: Praeger, 1997.

Serfaty, Simon, ed. *The Media and Foreign Policy.* New York: St. Martin's Press, 1991.

International Radio and Television Society

The International Radio and Television Society (IRTS) is open to individuals enagaged in communication through radio, television, and cable. Its purpose is for the exchange of ideas in areas affecting their common interests and welfare. The IRTS, founded in 1952, currently has approximately 1,900 members and a professional staff of eight. The executive director of the administrative arm of the organization, the IRTS Foundation is Joyce Tudryn, who assumed office on June 1, 1994. Members are typically individuals interested in broadcasting and cable management, sales, or production. The society, with headquarters at 420 Lexington Avenue in New York City, seeks to educate members through seminars, luncheons, and its quarterly newsletter. It conducts a summer internship program for college students majoring in communications, as well as faculty and industry seminars to expose educators to key issues facing these industries.

IRTS was formed by the merger of the American Television society, Radio Executives Club, and the Radio and Television Executive Society. The society annually presents its Broadcaster of the Year Award, recognizing an outstanding media figure, and its IRTS Gold Medal, recognizing outstanding contributions to, or achievements in, broadcasting, broadcast advertising, or cable. It also recognizes faculty contributions with the Stephen H. Coltrin Award for Excellence in Communications Education and a Dr. Frank N. Stanton Fellow for outstanding contribution to electronic media education. IRTS publications include the *International Radio and Television Society Foundation—Roster Yearbook* and the quarterly newsletter *IRTS Foundation News.*   *Donald Jung*

Further Reading

"Tudryn Succeeds Labunski at IRTS." *Broadcasting & Cable,* 7 February 1994, 63.

Internet–Television News Applications

The unsuccessful 1991 Soviet coup which trapped Mikhail Gorbachev in his dacha and started Boris Yeltsin's rise to power also marked one of the first uses of the global Internet as a reporting medium. With wire service and access to foreign news temporarily cut off, some reporters within the former Soviet Union were able to issue reports about developments via the Internet. Until that time, the Internet was something few people in television news used or, for that matter, even knew much about. From its earliest beginnings in 1969 as a U.S. military agency's experiment in linking computers to exchange scientific data, to now, the Internet has become the most important new communication technology since cable, and one which has had a marked impact on television news during the decade of the 1990s.

By 1995, television viewers were hearing reporters reference Internet sources and seeing Internet addresses of local stations. Viewers with personal computers at home and work, connected by telephone or networked data lines to the Internet, were also able to access their favorite television news, delivered as text, through an Internet information service known as the World Wide Web, a 1990 multimedia development of the European Particle Physics Laboratory (or CERN). Large and small television news organizations were quick to realize the potential of having a presence on the Internet through the Web.

It was the advent of the World Wide Web, coupled with popular computer software access "browsers" such as Netscape, that offered possibilities for text delivery of news through this new medium. Delayed and real-time audio news made its first appearance with Internet radio in the early 1990s. By the mid-1990s, there were hundreds of Internet radio stations using audio streaming technology to deliver delayed and live "broadcasts" by the World Wide Web. These stations were particularly popular on college campuses. Along with these developments, the increasing demand for computer-assisted reporting (CAR) in broadcast newsrooms accelerated the importance of the Internet to newsgathering. CAR includes the use of Internet-based databases as background for stories, or even as the focus of a story.

Transmission of real-time video television news via the Internet posed much thornier bandwidth and other technological difficulties. As the 1990s drew to a close, however, interactive Internet-delivered programming via television broadcast signals and cable was becoming a reality, enabling World Wide Web access with only small control boxes on the television set, thus bypassing the need for a powerful PC as part of the video news delivery component structure. By 1997, WebTV, NetChannel, and WorldGate all prepared to launch new, simpler, and more inexpensive devices promising to solve the video bandwidth problems posed by telephone-line-delivered video Web news content.   *Douglas J. Kocher*

Further Reading

Hafner, Katie, and Matthew Lyon. *Where Wizards Stay Up Late: The Origins of the Internet.* New York: Simon and Schuster, 1996.

Houston, Brant. *Computer-Assisted Reporting: A Practical Guide.* New York: St. Martin's Press, 1996.

Krol, Ed. *The Whole Internet.* Sebastopol, CA: O'Reilly and Associates, Inc., 1994.

J

Walter Jacobson

Walter Jacobson has been a fixture in Chicago television, most notably in the years between 1973 and 1989 when he was the co-anchor and the commentator for WBBM-TV. After graduating from Grinnell College in 1959 and Columbia University's graduate school of journalism, Jacobson worked for the United Press International and the *Chicago American*. He joined WBBM in 1963 and then moved to WMAQ-TV, also in Chicago, in 1971. His big break came in 1973, when he and Bill Kurtis were hired by WBBM as co-anchors. They were the hard news alternative to a competitor's happy-talk format. It took six years to rise to the top of the ratings, but once there, they maintained their position for five years.

A popular feature of the news was Jacobson's nightly commentary, "Perspectives." One of Jacobson's "Perspectives" got WBBM into trouble. In 1981, he charged that Viceroy Cigarettes had an advertising strategy to attract young people. Brown and Williamson sued for libel and won. Seven years later, an appeals court set the judgment against CBS at $3 million.

Jacobson resigned from WBBM in 1993 and joined the newly revamped Chicago Fox station, WFLD. He is among a very small number of local broadcasters known nationally for their distinguished work. He still offers editorials, including taking occasional positions on broadcasting issues, as on August 4, 1998, when he questioned the ef-fectiveness of TV Marti, the federal government's televised anti-Castro propaganda effort. He has been recognized with numerous local Emmys, a Peabody, and a 1981 duPont-Columbia Award.

Marjorie Fox

Further Reading:
Associated Press. "Award Against Jacobson Upheld. Supreme Court Lets Stand $3 Million Libel Decision." *Chicago Tribune,* 5 April 1988, Sports Final-5.
Jacobs, Scott. *The Channel Two Chronicles.* Chicago: September 1978, 184.

Peter Jennings

© 1997 ABC, Inc. Photo by Gwendolyn Cates

Peter Jennings is one of the best-known of a number of Canadian-born broadcasters who have made important journalistic contributions to the mass media in the United States. Jennings was voted "best national TV anchor," "most trustworthy anchor," and "most professional news anchor" by his peers and trade publications in the 1980s. For example, *Broadcasting & Cable* reported in 1993 that 67 percent of local broadcast news executives around the country said he was the best network news anchor. His reputation helped elevate ABC News to a top position among the major networks after years in the bottom position behind CBS and NBC.

Born in Ontario, Canada, in 1939, Jennings was influenced by his father, a well-known broadcaster for the Canadian Broadcasting Company (CBC). Describing himself as "bone lazy," Jennings dropped out of school in the 10th grade and worked at a variety of jobs, including a position as host of a late-night radio show and for the Canadian equivalent of *American Bandstand*. After being noticed by ABC News reporter John Scali, Jennings went to work for his network as a reporter in Canada and later as a national correspondent in the United States. In 1965, at the age of 27, he became the youngest anchor ever on prime-time television. Jennings later conceded that his elevation to the anchor spot, competing with Walter Cronkite of CBS and Chet Huntley and David Brinkley of NBC, had been premature.

Jennings was transferred to the London bureau and other CBC bureaus in the Middle East, where he became well known for international reporting. In 1969, he became the first television correspondent to formally open a bureau for an American television network in the Arab world in Beirut. After more than two decades as an overseas correspondent, he was named by ABC News president, Roone Arledge, as anchor and senior editor of ABC's *World News Tonight* in August of 1983. He had become acquainted with Arledge during the 1972 Olympics, when Jennings was asked to handle non-sport assignments at the international events. When Arab commandos seized the Israeli compound, Jennings impressed viewers around the world with his detailed explanation.

In addition to his reputation for foreign coverage, Jennings also received professional acclaim for hosting television documentaries dealing with drugs and illiteracy, for his reporting of the Reagan-Gorbachev summits, and for his coverage of national political conventions. Jennings attributes his enthusiasm for the American political system, in part, to his background as a Canadian, which he says made him take the United States less for granted. He has received many awards as reporter and anchorperson for a leading network news program, including recognition from the *Washington Journalism Review* and *New York Magazine*. **See also** *World News Tonight*.

Paul Alfred Pratte

Further Reading

Atkins, Norman. "The ABC's of Peter Jennings." *Rolling Stone,* 4 May 1989, 60–67.

Monroe, Bill. "A Six Year Gallery of Journalistic Brilliants." *Washington Journalism Review,* March 1990, 26–35.

"State of the Art: TV & Radio News, An Interview with Peter Jennings." *Broadcasting & Cable,* 27 September 1993, 36–40.

Dr. Timothy Johnson

Dr. Timothy Johnson is best known as medical editor for ABC News and for apperances on such programs as *World News Tonight*, *Nightline*, *20/20*, and *Good Morning America*. He is also a prolific author and the editor of several books, including *The Harvard Medical School Health Letter Book*; *Your Good Health: How to Stay Well, and What To Do When You're Not;* and *Let's Talk: An Honest Conversation on Critical Issues,* with former U.S. Surgeon General C. Everett Koop.

Dr. Johnson grew up in Rockford, Illinois and graduated from Augustana College in Rock Island, Illinois. He holds a masters degree from the Harvard School of Public Health. After spending two years in the seminary, he entered Albany Medical College in New York. After his residency, he became director of Emergency and Ambulatory Services for Union Hospital outside Boston. During the early 1970s, Johnson began working part-time for WCYB, the ABC affiliate in Boston. In 1975, he started his association with ABC's *Good Morning America*. He became medical editor of ABC News in 1984.

In addition to being a television reporter and writer, Johnson is a Harvard University medical school lecturer and a clinical associate at Massachusetts General Hospital in Boston. He is also an associate minister at Community Covenant Church in Peabody, Massachusetts. He lives in the Boston area.   *Derek Moore*

Further Reading
Aumente, Jerome. "A Medical Breakthrough." *American Journalism Review*, December 1995, 27–32.
Pierce, Larry. "Protests Cause Media Doctor to Cancel Speech." *Christianity Today,* 8 March 1993, 58.

Ed Joyce

Born in 1932, Edward Joyce was just 24 years old when he arrived at CBS in 1955, he was and very much intrigued with the idea of becoming a television newsman. The news decade belonged to CBS, and Joyce learned from what most would call "masters" of the medium—Edward R. Murrow, Fred Friendly, Don Hewitt, and Walter Cronkite. He received his first management job in 1966 as a radio news director at WCBS radio, and by 1969, he was executive producer of special events coverage for the entire radio network. By 1977, he had become vice president for news for the five CBS-owned stations. He was put in charge of WBBM-TV in Chicago and KNXT-TV in Los Angeles, before becoming the general manager of the network's New York flagship station, WCBS-TV, in 1981.

Criticizing today's news as catering to viewers wants, versus needs, in his book *Prime Times, Bad Times*, Joyce remembers the old CBS News with fondness. Unfortunately, he was at the helm in late 1983, when forces within and beyond the newsroom caused the network to decline. Within the newsroom, Walter Cronkite had retired, and his successor, Dan Rather, did not have the support that Cronkite had garnered. At the same time, the news division was being pushed to turn a profit. For Joyce this meant watching as less money was being spent on quality documentaries and more money was being spent on visual amenities, feature stories, or human-interest stories that entertained, rather than informed the viewer.

Joyce also complained that money formerly used for gathering news was being paid to news anchors who sometimes seemed to function more like entertainers than journalists. When Joyce was named president of CBS News, he promised more documentaries (a dozen a year) and more investigative journalism. Joyce wanted to return to the old days of CBS News, when more resources were earmarked for in-depth reporting. Management did not share the same view, perhaps because documentaries did not involve the same profit potential as programs like *West 57th,* and Joyce was unable to deliver on his promise of more documentaries.

Joyce's thoughts on his tenure at CBS, first as executive vice president and then as president, were documented in his personal memoir, *Prime Times, Bad Times*. He wrote of some of the great lessons he learned while working in the news, how he became the president of CBS News, and what led to his firing a year later. The book is considered an insider's view of the turmoil that dethroned CBS News during the 1980s. Joyce retired in 1986 at the age of 55 and now spends his days managing his horse ranch in southern California.
                              Connie Book

Further Reading
Boyer, Peter. *Who Killed CBS?* New York: Random House, 1988.
Joyce, Ed. *Prime Times, Bad Times*. New York: Doubleday, 1988.
Sandler, A. "Changing Horses." *Variety*, 4 April 1994.

K

Bernard Kalb

Bernard Kalb's career as a diplomatic correspondent, anchor, and media critic has taken him around the globe for three news networks. From the 1960s to 1980s, Kalb and his brother Marvin made a lasting impact on network news as astute international reporters and distinguished writers. Kalb accompanied President Nixon during his opening trip to China in 1972, and President Reagan during his first summit with Mikhail Gorbachev in Geneva in 1985.

Kalb was born in New York City. He served as a foreign correspondent for the *New York Times* for 15 years before joining CBS in 1962 as the bureau chief for Southeast Asia and India. His documentary "Viet Cong" won an Overseas Press Club Award. From 1970 to 1972, he anchored the *CBS Morning News*. A close working knowledge of Secretary of State Henry Kissinger enabled Kalb and his brother to bring insiders' perspectives to their 1974 biography, *Kissinger*. In 1980, both Kalb brothers moved to NBC on the heels of Bill Small, who left CBS to become president of NBC News.

Kalb served the United States from 1984 to 1986 as assistant secretary of state for public affairs and state department spokesperson. He became a correspondent for the PBS four-part series *Global Rivals*, a chronicle of U.S.-Soviet relations. Kalb's journalism earned him fellowships with both the Council of Foreign Relations and the Freedom Forum Media Studies Center at Colum-

bia University. At CNN, Kalb is moderator of *Reliable Sources*, providing weekly coverage of news. He was also a media critic for CNN's *Campaign USA '96* coverage. *Kevin C. Lee*

Further Reading

Gates, Gary Paul. *Air Time: The Inside Story of CBS News*. New York: Harper & Row, 1978.
Leonard, Bill. *In the Storm of the Eye*. New York: G. P. Putnam's Sons, 1987.

Marvin Kalb

Photo by Martha Stewart

Marvin Kalb's career as a diplomatic correspondent spanned three decades and two networks. He made his mark on network news as an astute international reporter. A noted author on Soviet-American relations and fluent in Russian, Kalb is a seven-time recipient of the Overseas Press Club Award for his reporting. Recognition for his coverage of international issues also includes a duPont-Columbia Award and two Peabody Awards.

Kalb was born in New York City in 1930. He completed his bachelor's degree at City College in 1951, and with money from scholarships and fellowships, he earned a master of arts degree in Chinese and Russian history at Harvard in 1953. Following two years in the United States Army, Kalb moved to Moscow as a translator for the Anglo-American Joint Press Reading Service at the American Embassy. He traveled widely, researching a proposed doctoral dissertation at Harvard. This led him to write in 1958, his well-received book *Eastern Exposure*.

At the invitation of Edward R. Murrow, Kalb opted out of his doctoral studies to join CBS News. Working his way up from a midnight desk assignment, he was named Moscow correspondent in 1960. He reopened the Soviet bureau following a diplomatic tiff over the network's 1958 drama *The Plot to Kill Stalin* and in addition to broadcasts, wrote timely articles on American-Russian tensions for several leading publications.

Kalb wrote *Dragon in the Kremlin* and moved to Washington, D.C., in 1963 as CBS's chief diplomatic correspondent. Continuing to focus on Russia, he led a network team through rural villages along the Volga River for a January 1966 documentary. Praised by U.S. reviewers, the revealing "Volga" was criticized by Soviet officials. Kalb's book *The Volga: A Political Journey Through Russia*, based on his script for the production, appeared in 1967. At the height of the Vietnam War, Kalb collaborated with a former colleague, Elie Abel, on the comprehensive survey *Roots of Involvement: The U.S. in Asia, 1784–1971*, published in 1971. Two years later, Kalb's name appeared on President Nixon's "enemies list" along with four other reporters and 13 government officials. In an attempt to supress criticism, White House operatives had also tapped phone lines. In July of 1973, Kalb's Washington office was broken into twice. A close association with the secretary of state throughout their over-seas assignments allowed Kalb and his brother Bernard to bring their insiders' perspectives to the 1974 political biography *Kissinger*. Kalb followed it with another collaborative work in 1977, a novel entitled *In the National Interest*, with co-author Ted Koppel.

In 1980, after contemplating a run for the U.S. Senate in Maryland as a Democrat, Kalb switched networks, moving to NBC and serving as chief diplomatic correspondent and moderator of *Meet the Press*. His exposé on Castro's Cuba and "The Man Who Shot the Pope" report attracted critical acclaim. He was one of four questioners for the final Reagan-Mondale debate in 1984. Shortly before his retirement from NBC, Kalb received a duPont-Columbia Award for a report on "star wars" weaponry and a Peabody Award for a Vietnam War documentary.

Kalb was named the first director of Harvard's Shorenstein Barone Center for Press, Politics and Public Policy in 1987, and hosted PBS's *Candidates '88*. He is the author of *The Nixon Memo*, and co-author, with his brother, of *The Last Ambassador*. **See also** *Meet the Press.*

Kevin C. Lee

Further Reading

Jones, Alex S. "Marvin Kalb to Direct Center at Harvard Graduate School." *New York Times,* 23 March 1987, 13.

Kalb, Marvin. "Press-Politics and The Public Dialogue." *Political Communication Report,* 3 June 1992, 1.

Kalb, Marvin. *The Nixon Memo.* Chicago: University of Chicago Press, 1995.

Floyd Kalber

Floyd Kalber is a respected broadcast journalist, anchor, and correspondent. He established a local television newsroom in Omaha, Nebraska, during television's early years and has distinguished himself as a network political correspondent.

Kalber was born on December 23, 1924, in Omaha. He graduated from Benson High School in 1942 and served in the U.S. Army during World War II. After one semester as a journalism major at Creighton University in Omaha, the lure of his first job in broadcasting ended his college career.

At KGFW radio in Kearney, Nebraska, he learned announcing, production, and writing skills from 1946 to 1948. He worked as sports director at newly established WIRL in Peoria, Illinois, until a demonstration of television in New York City so struck him that he shifted his career to television news.

Kalber established the news department and served as news director and anchor at KMTV, which had just begun regular programming in his hometown, Omaha. The station's staff grew, and Kalber decided to move to a larger market. From 1960 to 1976, he was the popular evening news anchor on WMAQ-TV in Chicago. For eleven of those years, Kalber was also the NBC network correspondent in Chicago. He covered national political conventions from 1960 to 1972, and in 1968, covered Vietnam and Martin Luther King's assassination. He also anchored the Apollo 11 and 12 space flight coverage for the NBC Sunday News.

From 1976 to 1979 Kalber was the newscaster and anchor for NBC-TV's *Today* program. Explaining his departure, he has admitted, "It was not that I didn't like the work. It was getting up at three o'clock in the morning." Kalber was also an NBC network correspondent on many specials and documentaries from October 1979 to 1981. From 1981 to 1984, he retired to New Canaan, Connecticut. A broadcast manager at ABC-TV, Dennis Swanson, finally persuaded Kalber to return to Chicago and work for his former competitors at WLS-TV. In January 1984, Kalber began to co-anchor the weekday 6:00 P.M. WLS-TV *Eyewitness News*.

Kalber has received a number of awards including five Emmys, four of them for his work in Chicago and one for his contributions to NBC's *The Huntley-Brinkley Report*. He resides in the western suburbs of Chicago, Illinios. Kalber retired from WLS-TV in March 1998.

Peter E. Mayeux

Further Reading

Berens, Charlyne. "TV's been very, very good to him." *Alumni News,* Lincoln, NE: College of Journalism & Mass Communications, University of Nebraska–Lincoln, Spring 1995.
Trigoboff, Dan. "Kalber Signs Off." *Broadcasting & Cable,* 9 March 1998, 87.
(Untitled) 60-minute videotape interview of Floyd Kalber. Professor Larry Walklin, University of Nebraska–Lincoln, December, 1994.
Wintner, Barbara Snyder. "The Unflappable Floyd Kalber." *The Daily Herald,* Arlington: IL, 17 September 1992, B-1.

Peter Kalischer

Ebullient, gregarious, and always colorful, Peter Kalischer embodies the concept of the traditional hard-nosed reporter. Best known for his work as a CBS foreign correspondent, Kalischer covered Vietnam prior to the U.S. involvement. In 1963, he won an Overseas Press Club Award for best television reporting on the fall of Ngo Dinh Diem, the South Vietnamese president murdered in a military coup.

Kalischer was born in New York City. He toured the world reporting for United Press as a correspondent in Japan and Korea. In July of 1950, he covered the initial American battle in Korea near Osan, and when North Korean tanks cut off a detachment of Americans soldiers, he became the first newsman in the Korean conflict to be captured. In 1957 Kalischer joined CBS and served as a foreign correspondent in Japan, Korea, Vietnam, Bangladesh, and Israel. Along with Malcolm Browne of the Associated Press, Neil Sheehan of United Press International, and correspondent David Halberstam, Kalischer made headlines when he was attacked and beaten by Vietnamese police as he covered a Buddhist demonstration in Saigon in 1963. Some of Kalischer's best-known works can be found in numerous *CBS News Special Reports* about Vietnam from 1961 to 1966.

In 1966, CBS named Kalischer chief correspondent for western Europe, Poland, the Middle East, Greece, and Turkey. From 1966 to 1978, he served as a Paris correspondent for CBS. He became an associate professor in broadcasting at Loyola University in New Orleans and retired in 1982. Always competitive, he actively pursued two of his passions, tennis and chess, up to his death. He died in New Orleans in 1991 at the age of 76.

Lloyd Chiasson Jr.

Further Reading

Peter Kalischer Obituary. *New Orleans Times–Picayune,* 19 July 1991, B9.
"Vietnam Perspective: How We Can Win," *CBS News Special Report* (1965).

H.V. Kaltenborn

In 1939, when Hollywood filmmaker Frank Capra wanted to convince movie audiences that all of America was tuned in when Mr. Smith went to Washington, he chose broadcaster H.V. Kaltenborn to announce Jimmy Stewart's Senate filibuster. Cinema mimicked reality. In 1938, at the height of the Munich crisis, Kaltenborn made headlines by providing 20 days of unparalleled coverage (he slept on a cot in CBS's New York studios), delivering commentaries on Hitler's and Mussolini's plans for Europe. Ten years later, Harry Truman teased Kaltenborn about his certainty that Republican Thomas Dewey would win the 1948 presidential election. Truman's imitation of the high-pitched, clipped phrases of the Milwaukee-born broadcaster worked, for in the middle of the twentieth century, few voices were better known than that of H.V. Kaltenborn.

Kaltenborn combined news with analysis during his 35-year career in radio and television. Since his days at the *Milwaukee Journal* and the *Brooklyn Eagle,* Kaltenborn considered himself a "contemporary historian." He made history when he broadcast the first editorial opinion over the air on April 4, 1922. Twenty-four years later, when *Motion Picture Daily* readers voted him "best news analyst and commentator on the air," Kaltenborn underscored journalism's responsibility to inform opinion. Kaltenborn moved to NBC in 1940 and helped pioneer television news, but admitted a preference for radio. He lamented television's concentration on visuals that entertained more than informed.

A confirmed internationalist, Kaltenborn was attacked by the America First Committee in the 1930s, and in the 1950s, he was attacked by left wing radicals. His reports, often delivered without notes, evolved into several best-selling books. His popularity peaked in World War II, when more than one million people responded to a poll of theatergoers by asking for Kaltenborn's views during the first six months of fighting. Kaltenborn retired from NBC in September 1955, but returned to cover the presidential election of 1956 and the New York gubernatorial election of 1958. His on-air advocacy of Nelson Rockefeller instead of W. Averell Harriman met with the disapproval of the network officials who were dedicated to objectivity, and he was dropped from future programming. His death at the age of 86, on June 14, 1965 (barely two months after Edward R. Murrow), marked the end of an era in television news, which was in Kaltenborn's view, a time when newscasters had a duty to serve the public with information and opinion that attempted to make sense of a complex and interdependent world.

Bruce J. Evensen

Further Reading

Kaltenborn, Hans V. Personal papers at the State Historical Society of Wisconsin. Madison, Wisconsin. NBC Papers include many of his radio and television scripts, also at the Wisconsin State Historical Society.
Kaltenborn, Hans V. *Broadcast the Crisis.* New York: Random House, 1938.
Kaltenborn, Hans V. *Europe Now: A First Hand Report.* New York: Didier, 1945.
Kaltenborn, Hans V. *Fifty Fabulous Years.* New York: Putnam, 1950.
Kaltenborn, Hans V. *Kaltenborn Edits the War News.* New York: Dutton, 1942.

Kefauver Crime Hearings

Estes Kefauver was chairman of the U.S. Senate's Special Committee to Investigate Organized Crime in Interstate Commerce in 1951, when the hearings were televised. Television made Kefauver, the junior senator from Tennessee, one of the best-known political leaders in the country and front-runner for the 1952 Democratic presidential nomination. But paradoxically, television and the very existence of the crime committee made him unpopular with some party leaders. At a time when most convention delegates were uncommitted, he suffered a startling defeat to a more palatable Adlai Stevenson.

Although the high visibility of his activities and his popularity were enough to ensure Kefauver the vice presidential nomination in 1956, Stevenson and Kefauver were soundly defeated by Eisenhower and Nixon. Television confirmed Kefauver's faith in the worth of a politically educated public, yet that same public, indignant over his committee's discoveries, could not stay aroused long enough to insist upon corrective legislative measures. Kefauver believed in television's ability to publicize governmental hearings and inform the public about issues. Yet, as a result of the "circus-like atmosphere" that television helped create, only three of the committee's contempt citations were upheld on appeal.

The crime committee was in the right place, at the right time, and with the right topic, but the presence of the television cameras changed the tone of the proceedings. No one expected such effects. Four previously televised congressional hearings had not produced similar results. There were few television stations in 1951, and programming was still fairly unsophisticated. Fewer than 8 million television sets were in use in the fall of 1950, although researchers subsequently estimated that between 20 to 30 million people saw the telecasts of the hearings.

During the first months of the crime committee's hearings in 1950, Kefauver took most of the testimony himself. Television coverage was limited to newsreel shots or short takes on regular news programs. This changed when the committee arrived in New Orleans on January 25, 1951. There the committee acceded to the request of WDSU-TV to televise parts of the open hearings. This proved to be so popular that the station was pressed to carry the entire proceedings, instead of only a few hours. Detroit viewers reacted the same way two weeks later, as did St. Louis and San Francisco viewers as the hearings moved to those cities.

Within two months, the committee's reputation changed dramatically. "Sure-fire" entertainment programming, such as the *Howdy Doody Show*, had to be canceled when Kefauver's committee came to town. The print media, especially newsmagazines, began writing about the committee in "show biz" terms. It was referred to as "What's My Crime." The March 12, 1951 *Time* magazine cover story was about the committee's

work, and featured a cover drawing of Kefauver beside a many-tentacled, masked octopus representing organized crime. Not mentioned by the magazine was its planned sponsorship of the ABC broadcasts of the New York hearings. As a result of network involvement, the hearings in New York and Washington, D.C., were eventually broadcast over 15 days in 21 television markets in the East and Midwest. Thus, it is not difficult to understand the committee's aura of a virtuous knight battling evil.

Perhaps the best remembered testimony before the crime committee was from Frank Costello, who at first refused to appear if his face were televised. Rather than cite him for contempt, the committee compromised. Kefauver ordered the television cameras to be kept off Costello's face. The result was viewers hearing the calm testimony of a man claiming innocence and seeking exoneration, while at the same time seeing his nervous, fidgeting hands.

The public's infatuation with the televised hearings presented Kefauver with a dilemma. Network time cost money, and no matter how popular the hearings were, television stations lost money if they carried them without an advertising sponsor. As a result, advertisers were allowed to sponsor parts of the broadcasts by different stations. Advertising content quickly became so crass, in Kefauver's opinion, that on March 26, 1951, he banned all sponsorship of the hearings and directed that future televising costs be borne by the stations. "Governmental proceedings are not a fit subject to aid the sale of a commercial product," he told the National Association of Broadcasters on April 17, 1951.

Television coverage of the crime committee's hearings was a heavily discussed topic throughout the country when Kefauver stepped down as chairman on May 1. Newspapers gave the story 10 times as much space as they devoted to the Korean War. Movie theaters were forced to install television sets in an attempt to attract wayward moviegoers to return. The home audience for daytime radio shrank dramatically. The networks were ready for the hearings to end, because they found something much better—a tremendous audience for regular daytime television programming. The

U.S. Congress, on the other hand, was ready for the hearings to end, because of growing complaints that its probes were being used for "political purposes" and to give congressmen heightened appeal, with the hearings regarded as "a modern morality play." The House of Representatives subsequently banned the televising of committee hearings—a ban that remained in effect until 1979.

Gregory C. Lisby

Further Reading

Gorman, John. *Kefauver: A Political Biography.* New York: Oxford University Press, 1971.

Kefauver, Estes. *Crime in America.* Garden City, NY: Country Life Press, 1951.

Lisby, Gregory C. "Early Television on Public Watch: Kefauver and His Crime Investigation." *Journalism Quarterly,* vol. 12, No. 3, Summer 1985, 236–242.

Alexander Kendrick

Alexander Kendrick was one of the correspondents hired by Edward R. Murrow after World War II. Kendrick's reports from central and eastern Europe, especially from the CBS Vienna bureau during the early days of the cold war, were always incisive and displayed a rare wit. He was born in Philadelphia on July 6, 1910. After graduating from high school, he went to work for the *Philadelphia Inquirer*. He worked for the *Inquirer* for the next 17 years as a rewrite man, a reporter, a copywriter, a columnist, a literary editor, and a foreign correspondent—primarily in Russia and the Middle East. During 1939–1940, Kendrick was a Nieman Fellow at Harvard, and in 1942, he won the Sigma Delta Chi Best Editorial Writing Award.

During World War II, Kendrick covered the Soviet front and was with Soviet forces as they pushed into Poland. He reported one of the first eye-witness accounts of the death camps. In 1945, he joined the *Chicago Sun* and returned to Russia as a correspondent. In 1948, CBS News appointed him their Vienna correspondent, and in 1950, he returned to the United States and was briefly assigned to the staff of the CBS Washington affiliate. However, he returned to Vienna the next year. One reason for his return to Vienna was his being named as a communist in the book *Red Channels*.

Kendrick was probably listed because of his skepticism about the George Polk case. Kendrick believed that Polk, a CBS journalist who had been covering Salonika Bay in 1948, may have been killed by the Greek government rather than Greek communists.

In 1962, Kendrick, then assigned to CBS's London bureau, covered the meeting between John F. Kennedy and Nikita Khrushchev in Vienna. There he astonished his colleagues with his fluency in Russian by simultaneously translating Khrushchev's words. That same year, Kendrick was appointed head of the CBS London bureau, a position he held until 1965, when he was succeeded by Dan Rather. Returning to the United States in 1965, he covered the Civil Rights movement and then went to the Middle East to cover the Arab-Israeli War.

Kendrick, renowned for his story-telling ability, frequently appeared on the *CBS Evening News with Walter Cronkite*, reporting on the lighter side of the news. In addition, he had his own program, *Alexander Kendrick Reporting*, and he contributed to *The World This Week* and *The World Tonight* on CBS Radio. In 1969, Kendrick wrote the first biography of Edward R. Murrow and five years later, a book about American policy during the Vietnam War. Kendrick retired from CBS in 1976. Alexander Kendrick died in Philadelphia on May 20, 1991, at the age of 80. *See also* Edward R. Murrow.

Albert Auster

Further Reading

Cloud, Stanley, and Lynne Olson. *The Murrow Boys: Pioneers on the Front Lines of Broadcast Journalism.* Boston: Houghton-Mifflin, 1996.

Kendrick, Alexander. *Prime Time: The Life of Edward R. Murrow.* Boston: Little Brown, 1969.

Sperber, A.M. *Murrow: His Life and Times.* New York: Bantam, 1986.

Kennedy Assassination

A watershed in the history of broadcast journalism occurred during four tragic days—November 22–25, 1963. Starting with the news of President John F. Kennedy's assassination in Dallas during the early afternoon of November 22, the next few days saw unprecedented television coverage of events surrounding the murder. Americans and people worldwide viewed television news like never before. Nine out of ten Americans watched at times—along with millions by satellite in Europe, Asia, Australia, and Africa.

The three major networks provided nearly uninterrupted telecasts from the afternoon of Friday, November 22, to Monday, November 25. Included was the first "live" murder when Jack Ruby shot Lee Harvey Oswald. Networks carried no commercials during the four days, and many local stations followed the example. Live broadcasts were mixed with videotape in what was later said to be the finest television news, commentary, and tribute in history. Coverage was mostly calm and comprehensive, and it helped give a nation in shock a sense of security.

It was 12:30 P.M. on a sunny day in downtown Dallas when the president's motorcade turned a corner near the end of the parade route. Shots rang out, and the president's limousine and escorts suddenly accelerated, heading toward Parkland Hospital. At 12:34 P.M. United Press International (UPI) teletype began clattering out the first bulletin announcing the firing of shots. The New York UPI office broke into the transmission with the message, "Dallas, it's yours." This meant that other bureaus should refrain from transmitting so Dallas could foward material unimpeded. Minutes after the first transmission, UPI's Merriman Smith dictated "flash" announcements from Parkland Hospital that Kennedy had been wounded by an assassin's bullets, perhaps fatally. It noted the status of Texas Governor John B. Connally, who was also seated in the president's vehicle.

ABC's Don Gardiner broadcast the first UPI announcement a mere six minutes after the shooting. Walter Cronkite of CBS News broke into the network's soap opera *As the World Turns,* at 12:40 P.M. with information from the second UPI bulletin and told viewers, "First reports say the president was seriously wounded." By this time, a nationwide television audience was growing. For example, the New York City television audience leaped from 30 to 70 percent. At 1:32 P.M., the Associated Press (AP) quoted two priests who reported Kennedy's death. Three minutes later, UPI confirmed it. As Walter Cronkite conveyed the news to viewers, tears welled in his eyes.

The assassination eclipsed other news. Local stations canceled regular programming as networks began to supply material. UPI and AP used every available wire to provide outlets with news. Jacqueline Kennedy was shown accompanying the president's body from Parkland Hospital to Love Field for transport to Washington, D.C. Later, at Washington's Andrews Field, viewers watched the president's casket descend from Air Force One. A scene taken with a telescopic lens showed a close-up of Jacqueline Kennedy joining the casket. Viewers saw her suit and stockings still caked with blood. President Lyndon Johnson, who had taken the oath of office on the flight, descended and said in his first public statement, "I will do my best. That is all I can do. I ask your help—and God's." Between live coverage, networks ran tape of events that took place before the shooting, such as the Kennedys waving to crowds.

Reports of the arrest of a suspect, Lee Harvey Oswald, began to grow more detailed. Networks switched from Washington to Dallas, where police seemed eager to cooperate with news media, particularly television. Through Saturday, November 23, police provided material to reporters. Clues, such as the rifle found in the Texas Book Depository, were displayed. Oswald was exhibited. On Saturday night, Oswald was scheduled to be moved from the city jail to a county jail, but police rescheduled the transfer to Sunday noon to accommodate broadcasters, despite Justice Department requests for a secret night move.

On Sunday, November 24, television cameras focused on the Capitol rotunda, where the president's body rested. Other events were also being covered, such as the caisson departing from the White House going to the Capitol. At 12:21 P.M., eastern time, ABC and CBS covered the move, but NBC switched to live coverage of Oswald's transfer from Dallas police headquarters. Viewers saw Oswald, flanked by detectives, being escorted from the basement. Suddenly a man thrust through the crowd and fired a handgun at Oswald, who twisted and fell. The shot was clearly heard, and NBC's Tom Pettit shouted, "He's been shot! Lee Oswald has been shot!" In this chaos, viewers saw Oswald's assailant, Jack Ruby, overpowered and Oswald's body carried to the armored car.

NBC was the only network to carry the shooting live, but the other networks had access to videotape of the scene. Soon all three networks were repeating it. At the time of the murder, 40 percent of the nation's television sets were on. An hour later, that percentage had almost doubled. Viewers saw reports detailing Ruby's life and quickly learned of Oswald's death. Soon after, they viewed Jacqueline and Caroline Kennedy walking to the coffin in the Capitol rotunda. CBS research showed that 93 percent of the nation's homes watched coverage of the funeral and burial on Monday, November 25. Television cameras were stationed at all major intersections to show the procession move toward Arlington Cemetery. By Monday night the four-day telecast was over. The average American home had had a television set on for at least 13 consecutive hours. Many praised the role of television in covering the events, but some criticized coverage as being too theatrical, suggesting theatrics contributed to Oswald's shooting. The coverage showed the world the power of television news. *Charles Lewis*

Further Reading

Barnouw, Erik. *Tube of Plenty: The Evolution of American Television*, rev. ed. New York: Oxford University Press, 1990.

Emery, Michael, and Edwin Emery. *The Press and America: An Interpretive History of the Mass Media.* 8th ed. Englewood Cliffs, N.J.: Prentice Hall, 1996.

Sterling, Christopher, and John Kittross. *Stay Tuned: A Concise History of American Broadcasting.* 2nd ed. Belmont, CA: Wadsworth, 1990.

Kennedy Press Conferences

Five days after taking the oath of office as the 35th president of the United States, John F. Kennedy held the first of what would become a celebrated series of live, televised press conferences. The timing of this innovation could scarcely have been more propitious. The 1960 campaign debates between John F. Kennedy and Richard M. Nixon had attracted the largest audience in television history and established the democrat from Massachusetts as a major television personality to be reckoned with. Furthermore, by 1960, the conquest of America by television was nearly complete—with 87 percent of the nation's homes having sets.

Kennedy would conduct 64 regular press conferences during his presidency, one about every two weeks. Although other presidents met the news media more frequently, Kennedy was the first to use the televised press conference as a principal means of communicating with the American public. Astute observers of press relations were aware that Kennedy had once functioned in a reporter's role.

Initially Kennedy's advisers were reluctant to broadcast the press conferences live. According to Kennedy's press secretary, Pierre Salinger, the argument against live television press conferences was that in certain circumstances a verbal slip by a president could push the world closer to disaster. Reporters from the print press, who traditionally had dominated presidential news conferences until that time, also resisted the idea. One newspaper reporter accused Salinger of turning the presidential press conference into a sideshow. Others feared that the events would degenerate into propaganda tools with little legitimate news value.

Kennedy prepared intensely for the press conferences, just as he had for the 1960 debates. The president's staff would meet and agree on the 20 or 30 questions the correspondents were likely to ask and then brief him accordingly. On the eve of a news conference, Kennedy would study the voluminous briefing material that his staff had put together. The next morning, he continued his preparations by convening a breakfast meeting with top aides, trying out answers, suggesting alternative strategies, and offering some comic replies. These replies frequently convulsed those in attendance but, of course, could not be given in public. Later that day, Kennedy would go over to the auditorium at the State Department for the televised exchanges.

Television viewers and news reporters alike were struck by the president's quick, irrepressible wit. Asked by a female reporter how his administration was advancing the women's rights plank of the campaign platform, Kennedy shot back, "Well, I'm sure we haven't done enough. . ." Pressed for a comment on public perceptions that journalists at the news conferences were subjecting the president to "some abuse or a lack of respect," he turned it into an opportunity to mock treatment of politicians by the press. When a reporter cited a Republican National Committee resolution that termed the president "pretty much a failure," Kennedy responded quickly with, "I'm sure it was passed unanimously." In the laughter of the press corps, one heard the approval and admiration of a nation.

However entertaining, the press conferences also embraced substantive topics—Soviet-American relations, nuclear weapons, racial equality, education, trade concerns, labor relations, the space program, and most notably, the Cuban missile crisis. Citizens who watched the news conferences received a wide-ranging education on the issues of the day. Kennedy's talent for sparring with the press was so natural that some sources claimed that his successor completely misperceived the process. David Gergen once noted that Lyndon B. Johnson believed that the questions for Kennedy's appearances had been prepared and distributed to the press. Johnson asked George Reedy, his press secretary, when he was going to get a list of questions. Reedy had to inform his boss that Kennedy was just adept at press conferences.

The public, too, may have come to expect its chief executive to be adept at the press conference format, since audiences for the Kennedy television appearances were so remarkably large. An estimated 65 million people in 21.5 million homes across America saw Kennedy's inaugural press conference. A 1961 poll showed that 90 percent of those interviewed had watched one or more of the first three news conferences. This had the effect of drawing even more viewers to subsequent appearances. On average, the conferences drew an audience of around 18 million.

John F. Kennedy's final press conference took place on November 14, 1963—eight days before his assassination in Dallas. Careful attention to these press conferences provides a guide to Kennedy's views on policy issues and could serve, according to his former press secretary, Pierre Salinger, as substitute for the memoir he might have written. Salinger also recommended them as important keys to his personality, adding that they reveal as much about Kennedy the man as they do about his ideas and presidential philosophy. Kennedy's grasp of the infinite details of the business of government, his quickness of mind, his capacity for righteous indignation, and his ready humor are all clearly evident.

Alan Schroeder

Further Reading

Chase, Harold W., and Allen H. Lerman. eds. *Kennedy and the Press: The News Conferences.* New York: Crowell, 1965.

Kalb, Marvin, and Frederick Mayer. *Reviving the Presidential News Conference: Report of the Harvard Commission on the Presidential News Conference.* Cambridge: Joan Shorenstein Barone Center, 1988.

Salinger, Pierre. *With Kennedy.* Garden City, N.Y.: Doubleday, 1966.

Schlesinger, Arthur M. Jr. *A Thousand Days: John F. Kennedy in the White House.* Boston: Houghton Mifflin, 1965.

Vanocur, Sander, executive producer. "Television and the Presidency." Three-Part Video Series, The Freedom Forum, First Amendment Center at Vanderbilt University. 1994.

Arthur Kent

Courtesy Cable News Network, Inc.
© 1995 Photo by Andrew MacNaughton

Foreign correspondent Arthur Kent leaped to unintentional celebrity status with his coverage of the Persian Gulf War in 1991. Viewers watched in fascination as NBC's Kent reported from a hotel rooftop in Dhahran, Saudi Arabia, while missiles exploded in the background. Nicknamed the "Scud Stud" and also Desert Fox, Kent became one of the better-known media figures during the 43-day conflict. A newly formed Arthur Kent fan club quickly claimed 2,000 members.

Kent was born on December 27, 1953 in Medicine Hat, Alberta, Canada. He came from a journalism family. His father was a crusading editor at the *Calgary Herald* for 20 years. Two siblings also work in the broadcast industry. Kent got an early start in the business working for CJOH-TV while attending Carleton University in Ottawa. The Canadian Broadcasting Corporation (CBC) was so impressed with his work, it recruited him as soon as he finished college. At 21, Kent became the youngest correspondent in the network's history.

Kent left CBC in 1980, heading for Afghanistan to produce a documentary on that war-torn country and to free-lance as a correspondent. He traveled deep into the Afghan countryside carrying his own camera and accompanying *mujahedin*, rebels who were conducting guerrilla warfare against Soviet-backed Afghans. For several years, Kent reported for NBC and CBC and wrote for the weekly *London Observer*. In 1989, NBC offered Kent a full-time assignment as a foreign correspondent based in the Rome bureau. Kent reported stories throughout the world, winning two Emmys. One award was for his coverage of the Romanian revolution that led to the execution of dictator Nicolae Ceausescu; the other was for the 1989 NBC special "China in Crisis," focusing on the student rebellion in Beijing's Tiannamen Square.

After the Gulf War, relations between Kent and NBC soured. The correspondent, still working out of Rome, was assigned to NBC's new weekly newsmagazine *Dateline NBC*. Disagreements over editorial decisions and his contract led to a widely reported feud with *Dateline* producers in July 1992. By August, NBC had suspended Kent without pay, claiming he had refused an assignment to Zagreb, Croatia. Kent countered, saying the network was trying to force him out. Kent became the talk of the television news business when he picketed NBC at the entrance to its Rockefeller Center headquarters in New York and handed out leaflets

with his version of the contract dispute. After eight days, the network fired him. He sued NBC, and 18 months later (one month before the suit was scheduled to go to trial) Kent won a large undisclosed settlement from the network.

After leaving NBC, Kent returned to free-lancing until he was hired as a foreign correspondent for CNN. Kent is based in London and his first book, the autobiographical *Risk and Redemption: Surviving the Network News Wars*, was published in October 1996.   *Sandra L. Ellis*

Further Reading

Goldberg, Robert, and Gerald Jay Goldberg. *Anchors.* New York: Birch Lane Press, 1990.

Kent, Arthur, *Risk and Redemption: Surviving the Network News War.* Tortola, British Virgin Islands: Interstellar, 1997.

Rosen, M. "Kent's State—He's Gone." *People Weekly,* 7 September 1992, 83–84.

Kerner Commission

The media's failure to report racial issues was a key finding of the National Advisory Commission on Civil Disorders in 1968. The commission, appointed by President Johnson in the aftermath of riots in many American cities during the summer of 1967, was named after its chair, former Illinois Governor Otto Kerner, and charged with discovering why the riots happened and what could be done to prevent future outbreaks. After 20 days of formal hearings and fact-finding visits to 23 cities, the commission said riots were the result of racism and poverty. It called for a massive effort to combat those ills. The Kerner Report warned that America was becoming "two societies—one black, one white—separate and unequal."

The commission studied the reporting of urban riots, and it did a content analysis of network television and local coverage in 15 cities from three days before, to three days after the disturbances. The commission also did a print media survey. Investigators interviewed news personnel, public officials, and residents. The panel reached three conclusions. First, it said the media, overall, made an effort to give a balanced account of disorders. The second conclusion said that despite this, the "overall effect was an exaggeration of both mood and event." Occasional instances of exaggeration or distortion were noted. The commission urged news organizations to develop guidelines for coverage of disorders.

Finally, though the commission did not find serious fault with the reporting on disturbances, it did find that the media failed to report adequately on "underlying problems of race relations." It characterized this as its most important finding. The commission said the media failed to report routinely on blacks and thereby contributed to the black/white separation. It noted that newsrooms rarely employed blacks, with fewer than 5 percent of editorial positions held by blacks and less than one percent of supervisory positions held by minorities. The Kerner Report called on the media to hire blacks and to report on the difficulties of cities with passion and depth.

In the months and years immediately following the Kerner Report, the media engaged in self-examination and made some strides in hiring minorities in television news departments. But upon subsequent anniversaries of the report's release, critics noted there were still relatively few minorities in decision-making positions. And they noted that as television news became more competitive and market driven, in-depth stories about racial issues continued to be rare. The racial division in America was especially noted on the 25th anniversary of the Kerner Report. After the 1992 rioting in Los Angeles and with sharply differing reactions among blacks and whites to the verdict in the O.J. Simpson case, observers said the "two societies" warning of the Kerner Commission had come to pass.   *Marjorie Fox*

Further Reading

Dodson, Angela. "25 Years after Kerner." *The Quill,* April 1993.
The Kerner Report, 1968 Report of the National Advisory Commission on Civil Disorders. New York: Pantheon Books, 1988.
Sweeney, Louis. "Press Learns from Riot Coverage." *The Christian Science Monitor,* 11 June 1992, sec. media, p. 12.

Larry King

Courtesy Cable News Network, Inc.
© 1993. Photo by Andrew Eccles

Previously ignored by American politics, the talk show genre played an unprecedented role in the 1992 presidential campaign, with Larry King leading the revolution. As a principal of talk radio and CNN programming, King has been on the forefront of interactive news for a long time. King's first day on the air was May 1, 1957. Born on November 19, 1933, in Brooklyn, New York, Lawrence Harvey Zeiger, at age 23, became Larry King and was given the morning drive-time slot at a Miami radio station. Soon after, he was doing interviews from the front window of a Miami Beach restaurant.

By the late 1960s, King hosted a radio and a television show, called the Miami Dolphins' games, and wrote a column for the *Miami Herald*. Making poor decisions and living beyond his means, King was arrested in 1971 for stealing money given to him to give to the New Orleans district attorney's investigation into the assassination of President Kennedy. Although the charges against King eventually were dropped, he lost his jobs in radio, television, and print. By 1975, King returned to Miami radio in a nightly talk show. His first line in four years began with "As I was saying . . . " In 1978, the *Larry King Show* debuted on 28 stations across the country on the Mutual Broadcasting System. Within four years, the midnight to 5:30 A.M. show was carried on more than 250 stations across America.

In 1985, Ted Turner recruited King to do a prime-time show on television's first all-news network. *Larry King Live* is now consistently one of CNN's highest-rated programs. Seen in 170 million households in over 200 countries, it is the world's only live, international, call-in program. In his debut week on CNN, King interviewed Mario Cuomo and George Will. Recently, King interviewed Bill Clinton, Benjamin Netanyahu, Yassir Arafat, Shimon Peres, Louis Farrakan, Bob Dole, Al Gore, Marlon Brando, Barbra Streisand, and Ross Perot.

Perot announced his candidacy for the presidency on February 20, 1992, on *Larry King Live* and consequently mandated the appearance of Bill Clinton and the incumbent president, George Bush, on talk television. The 1992 campaign unfolded in the electronic town hall of talk television, with *Larry King Live* as the foundation. In his latest book, *On the Line: The New Road to the White House* (with Mark Stencel), King provides a chronology of the development of the talk campaign. For his election coverage in 1992, King received the ACE President's Award. King's other honors and awards include the George Foster Peabody Award, the Broadcaster of the Year Award from the International Radio and Television Society, and the ACE Award for Best Interview/Talk Show Host in 1986, 1987, 1988, and 1989.

The influence of King in the political dialogue did not end with the 1992 election. The Ross Perot–Al Gore NAFTA debate on *Larry King Live* was the most watched regularly scheduled cable program in history, with an 18.1 rating. In addition to his well-known radio and television programs, King also provides a two-and-a-half minute interview segment on the Mutual Broadcasting System and a weekly column for *USA Today*. Dubbed a master interviewer, King remains best known for his unique role in interactive television. His shows feature celebrity interviews, contemporary issue debates, and politics—all with the input of his audience. His credence is in the value of unfiltered talk and in the viewers, listeners, and callers who are partners is his career.   *Karen Lane DeRosa*

Further Reading

Cohen, Rich. "The King and I." *Rolling Stone,* 14 November 1996, 75–81, 127, 130.

King, Larry. *Tell It to the King.* New York: Putnam, 1988.

Rice, Lynette. "Live with Larry King." *Broadcasting & Cable,* 13 December 1993, 81–82.

Wilkinson, Alec. "The Mouthpiece and Handsome." *The New Yorker,* 28 March 1994, 53–56, 65–67.

Robert Kintner

Like many of his contemporaries, Robert Edmonds Kintner began his career in newspaper journalism. He was born in Stroudsburg, Pennsylvania, on September 12, 1909. After graduating from Swarthmore College, Kintner was hired as a business reporter by the now-defunct *New York Herald Tribune*. Prior to America's entry into World War II, he and Joseph Alsop (with whom he wrote a column for four years) wrote two books. In 1944, after being injured in an airplane crash while serving in the Army Air Corps, Kintner became a vice president with the fledgling American Broadcasting Company. Six years later, he was promoted to president—a position he occupied until 1956.

During his tenure at ABC, Kintner was associated with several events that made television news history. According to former NBC News president Reuven Frank, Kintner agreed to share ABC's television lines with NBC in June 1953. As a result, the two networks scooped rival CBS in coverage of Queen Elizabeth II's coronation. The telecast of recorded kinescopes of the British Broadcasting Corporation's live coverage of the event gave the struggling ABC network a boost.

The next year, ABC became the only television network to broadcast live coverage of the congressional hearing chaired by Senator Joseph R. McCarthy, who was spearheading efforts to weed out alleged communists in government. Kintner decided to carry the hearings live as a means of enabling his network to gain a foothold in daytime television, dominated by soap operas and game shows on NBC and CBS. That ploy brought ABC credibility and an audience.

In 1957, Kintner joined his former rival, NBC, as president, a position he held until 1965.

His reign at NBC was associated with a series of landmarks similar in importance to those he had at ABC. However, they did not come without controversy. He teamed Chet Huntley and David Brinkley for *The Huntley-Brinkley Report*, which dominated news ratings for years and established a model for network news. When President John F. Kennedy was assassinated on November 22, 1963, Kintner canceled all regular programming and commercials in favor of live 24-hour coverage of the funeral and surrounding events. As a result, the murder of Kennedy's alleged killer, Lee Harvey Oswald, was carried live on NBC. Kintner achieved recognition for live coverage of special events, and under his leadership, NBC attempted to carry special news stories longer than its primary competitor, CBS News.

Kintner is portrayed in Robert Redford's 1994 feature film *Quiz Show* as being involved in the scandals that rocked broadcasting in the 1950s. However, critics such as Reuven Frank and Daniel Schorr question whether Kintner actually participated in that alleged conspiracy. Over the years, Kintner won several awards, including the Keystone Award of the National Association of Radio and Television Broadcasters. He died in 1980. In 1996, Kintner was posthumously inducted into the Broadcasting and Cable Hall of Fame. *See also* ABC News, NBC News. *Roy L. Moore*

Further Reading

Frank, Reuven. "NBC's Crowning Touch: How We Beat CBS and Got the Scoop on the Coronation." *Washington Post,* 29 May 1988, C5.
Schorr, Daniel. "*Quiz Show* Rigged Again." *Christian Science Monitor,* 23 October 1994, 18.
Smith, J. Y. "Robert E. Kintner, Ex-Head of ABC and NBC Radio and TV Dies." *Washington Post,* 23 December 1980, C6.

Kitchen Debate

During a visit by Vice President Richard Nixon to the Soviet Union on July 24, 1959, a day-long series of arguments and accusations occurred between Richard Nixon and Soviet Premier Nikita Khrushchev and became known as "The Kitchen Debate." NBC and ABC taped and showed part of that exchange at an "American National Exhibi-

tion" in Moscow. The debate occurred during a day of meetings between Nixon and Khrushchev, first at the premier's office, then at the exhibition. It was marked by finger-shaking, arguments, and some laughs. The basic point of the debate was how to evaluate the exhibit of model homes, appliances, and technology from the United States. Khrushchev considered it bourgeois trivia; Nixon argued for the American worker's freedom to choose the best lifestyle.

The exhibition itself was a useful propaganda device—offering evidence of the superiority of the capitalist system with all new, convenient, labor-saving equipment. It featured appliances, cars, and computers. At the time of the exhibition's opening, which attracted large crowds of Moscovites, the technological rivalry between the two nations was fueled by the Soviets' launching the Sputnik spacecraft. The televised portion of the "debate" occurred at RCA's mock television studio. With cameras rolling, Khrushchev stated that his country would catch up and surpass America, while pointing his fingers at the camera. Nixon responded by admitting that the Soviets were ahead in space but that the U.S. was superior in color television. Khrushchev, with requisite bluster, rejected this comparison.

The rest of the five-hour debate occurred away from cameras. The two toured a model kitchen of the representative suburban American home. Nixon, sensing an opportunity to counter Khrushchev's allegations, noted merits of American homes and the ability of a steelworker to afford one. Khrushchev scoffed, noting that Russian homes last longer. The talk shifted to war and peace. Khrushchev became indignant, accusing Nixon of threats. By the end of the contretemps, both men were jabbing fingers. At another point, Khrushchev was spewing profanities.

A final round occurred during a lunch at Khrushchev's dacha. Nixon called that discussion about nuclear arms "the real debate," but, like the segment occurring in the kitchen, it was not recorded. Both Nixon and Khrushchev agreed that viewers in their countries should see the debate, but taking no chances, an Ampex executive smuggled the tape out of Russia the next day by wrapping it in an old shirt. When he arrived in

New York, the executive notified President Dwight Eisenhower that the tape was on its way to Washington. A copy of the 18-minute tape from the RCA studio was flown to Washington and shown to an audience estimated to be 72 million.

In a sense, the "Kitchen Debate" focused on what was at stake in the Cold War. It was an undiplomatic give and take between two leaders long accustomed to fighting in a political arena. It also brought some of this undiplomatic sparring to American homes. In one sense, both men were using their debating skills to play to their audiences. Nixon was about to face John F. Kennedy in the upcoming 1960 presidential election and looking "tough" against the communist leader Khrushchev could win him political points. The issue of containing communism would be a major one, and Nixon could claim that he stood up to Khrushchev—with cameras rolling.   *Mark Conrad*

Further Reading

Barnouw, Erik. *The Image Empire.* New York: Oxford University Press, 1970.

Nixon, Richard M. "Memo to President Bush: How to Use TV—and Keep from Being Abused by It." *TV Guide*, 14 January 1989, 16.

Ted Koppel

© 1997 Gregory Heisler/ABC, Inc.

Ted Koppel has used the stage of network news' late-night offering to establish himself as broadcast journalism's premiere interviewer. The success of ABC's *Nightline* program can be linked to the poise, judgment, and sense of fairness of its host. Koppel was named host when the program premiered in March 1980. It evolved from ABC's late-night specials hosted by Frank Reynolds, *The Iran Crisis: America Held Hostage,* covering the American hostages held in Iran. Koppel, as ABC's State Department correspondent at the time, received much air time during the specials and was the logical choice to fill in as host. Koppel became the permanent host of *Nightline* when Reynolds found doing both the evening news and the specials too taxing.

Koppel, a native of Lancashire, England, was born on February 8, 1940, and moved to the United States when he was a teenager. He holds degrees from Syracuse and Stanford universities. ABC hired him in 1963, and he became part of incoming ABC News president Elmer Lower's efforts to identify and groom talent that could lift ABC to respectability in news. Koppel was 23 years of age when he was hired at ABC to be a general assignment reporter. His previous professional experience was as an off-air writer and desk worker at a New York City radio news department. Koppel was ABC's chief diplomatic correspondent from 1971 to 1980. Prior to that, while Hong Kong bureau chief, he covered stories from the Pacific, including Australia and Vietnam. For two years, ending in 1977, he anchored *The ABC Saturday Night News*. When ABC News president Roone Arldege moved him out of that position, Koppel considered resigning.

Koppel's skillful work on *Nightline* brought him national attention, and he received acclaim from the critics for his direct, but fair, interviewing style. *Nightline* emerged from the Iran hostage specials to cover a wide range of issues, and Koppel demonstrated versatility with his insights on many subjects. The format of *Nightline* features an overview on an issue followed by Koppel leading a discussion among spokespersons. He provides participants, frequently from opposing sides, the opportunity to make their points. Koppel is quick to point out inconsistencies or challenge a guest to substantiate a point.

Koppel's *Nightline* has covered every significant issue since its premiere in 1980 and included as interviewees virtually every major news maker. Topics have included national elections, the

Whitewater investigations, the Unabomber case, and health care reform. Koppel is the co-author of two books, one written in 1996 about the development of *Nightline*.   *Jeffrey M. McCall*

Further Reading
Bliss, E. *Now the News: The Story of Broadcast Journalism.* New York: Columbia University Press, 1991.
Koppel, T., and K. Gibson. *Nightline: History in the Making and the Making of Television.* Westminister, MD: Times Books, 1996.
Weisberg, J. "King Koppel." *Vanity Fair,* January, 1994, 96–99.

Steve Kroft

Steve Kroft, the youngest current co-editor of *60 Minutes*, the CBS newsmagazine, is best known for his investigative reports and high-profile interviews. Sixteen years as a CBS correspondent have taken him to places where few American television reporters have gone. Several of Kroft's stories from abroad have broken new ground. He was the first American journalist to gain access to the site of the Chernobyl nuclear disaster. In 1992, his Persian Gulf War story about "friendly fire" won a Peabody Award.

Kroft, born in Kokomo, Indiana, on August 22, 1945, began his career overseas. He worked as a reporter and photographer in Vietnam for the U.S. Army after graduating from Syracuse University in 1967. He went on to receive a degree from the Columbia University Graduate School of Journalism in 1975. Prior to joining CBS in 1980, Kroft was a reporter in Miami, Jacksonville, and Syracuse. At CBS, he worked for the network's regional bureaus, before moving to London and then to the newsmagazine *West 57th*. Don Hewitt of *60 Minutes*, looking to infuse some young blood into his top-rated program, hired Kroft in 1989.

Some of Kroft's domestic news work has also gained attention. His exclusive interview in January 1992 with then-governor Bill Clinton and his wife, Hillary, was partly responsible for helping Clinton fight allegations of sexual infidelity. In addition to his Peabody Award, Kroft has won four

Emmys. His wife, Jennet Conant is a *Vanity Fair* contributing editor.   *Sreenath Sreenivasan*

Further Reading
Campbell, Richard. "Don Hewitt's Durable Hour; A Pioneering Newsmagazine Hits 25." *Columbia Journalism Review,* September 1993, 23–26.
Coffey, Frank. *60 Minutes: 25 Years of Television.* New York: General Publishing Group, 1993.

Irv Kupcinet

When Federal Communications Commission chairman Newton Minow described 1960s television as "a vast wasteland" he decidedly did not mean *At Random*, the late-night talk show seen on Saturdays in Chicago, hosted by *Chicago Sun-Times* columnist Irv Kupcinet. *Kup's Show*, as it came to be known, was a pioneer program, receiving a Peabody Award and 15 Emmys during a 27-year run that grew to include a 50-station national network.

Born in Chicago on July 31, 1912, Kup received his journalism degree from the University of North Dakota in 1934 and had planned a career in football after being drafted by the Philadelphia Eagles. But a shoulder injury ended his football career and led to sportswriting, and by 1943, he had a column in the *Chicago Daily Times* (which merged with the *Chicago Sun* in 1948 to become the *Chicago Sun-Times*). Kupcinet became a recognized face and voice in Chicago. For 24 years he broadcast Chicago Bears football games on radio. He even appeared in Otto Preminger's feature film *Anatomy of a Murder* in 1959.

Premiering on Chicago's WBBM in February of 1959, *At Random* was one of the few places a serious-minded audience could see Newton Minow discuss television's uncertain future or watch Mortimer Adler, the world's foremost Aristolean, exchange views with teamster Jimmy Hoffa. Kupcinet liked odd couplings and would keep watchers awake until the early morning hours, in unrehearsed discussions that ranged from three to four hours, until Kup decided it was finished. Kupcinet came by his guests naturally. His *Chicago Sun-Times* column enjoyed circulation in more than 100 newspapers and put him in touch with a wide-range of news makers. Chicagoans got into the habit of going to bed early and rising when the show came on.

Kup's Show annually sold more books than any other television program of that era. Authors, filmmakers, scientists, sports figures, politicians, industrialists, and labor leaders were drawn to this frank and full discussion. An August 1960 program, for instance, featured an extraordinary panel of journalists. Edward R. Murrow and Walter Cronkite were joined by columnists Walter Winchell and Drew Pearson, as well as others, for a consensus view that Nixon would beat Kennedy in the White House race. Other shows were spiced by Alfred Hitchcock's explanation that actors were "temperamental children" or Ronald Reagan's analysis of why he might become involved in the California governor's race. The Smothers Brothers explained their opposition to the Vietnam War. William Westmoreland told viewers the war was winnable. J. William Fulbright argued it was not.

The highly publicized murder in November 1963 of Kup's daughter, Karyn, placed him in the news and showed his grace under pressure. Kup by the 1980s had become one of Chicago's favorite sons. For the first time in municipal history, a bridge was named for a living American. Kup's wife, Essee, produced his program as it moved from CBS to NBC and ABC to PBS. Their son, Jerry, became a Hollywood director. Audiences in the 1990s could still read Kup's column. His three-times-a-week reports have been on WBBM since October of 1978. The several-minute summaries remind veteran late-night viewers of four decades earlier, when a cigar-smoking columnist strode with the strength of a former athlete onto a set each Saturday night with a camera dollying after him. Kup would take his seat at a table, put down the cigar, pick up a coffee cup, and introduce the program that welcomed conversation lasting longer than a generation.   *Bruce J. Evensen*

Further Reading
At Random program segments. Museum of Broadcast Communication, Chicago Peabody Collection, University of Georgia, 1960–1961.
"Salute to Kup's 50 years." *Chicago Sun-Times,* Special Editions. 17–18 January 1993, 33.

Bob Kur

Bob Kur has covered science, health, and politics and specialized in family issues and social trends in his more than 25 years. His reports have appeared frequently on *NBC Nightly News*. Working in broadcast news since 1971, Kur is a graduate of Ithaca College with a master's degree from Columbia University. Kur got his start researching, writing, and reporting for a news program produced by the Eastern Educational Network. In 1973, he was hired by NBC's Washington, D.C., affiliate WRC-TV. Kur's first political convention was in 1976, when he covered the Maryland and Washington, D.C., delegations for WRC and for the network. NBC hired Kur as a correspondent following the election, and he was based in Cleveland. A year later, he was transferred to Chicago News, and a year after that, he moved to Washington, D.C.

Kur had a number of important assignments, including seven years at the U.S. House of Representatives, presidential campaigns from 1979 through 1992, the State Department, and the Iran-Contra hearings in 1987. In 1981, breaking news sent Kur to Egypt, interrupting his vacation in the Middle East, when Anwar Sadat was assassinated. In 1982, Kur reported on Israel's invasion of Lebanon.

Kur has filled in as anchor on the *Today* show and *NBC News at Sunrise,* and he has also anchored weekend editions of *NBC Nightly News*. In April 1996, he became the news anchor for the *Today* show's weekend editions, working out of the Washington, D.C., news bureau.
Sandra L. Ellis

Further Reading
Goldberg, Robert, and Gerald Jay Goldberg. *Anchors.* New York: Birch Lane Press, 1990. <http://www.msnbc.com/Onair/nbc/nightlynews/default.asp>.

Charles Kuralt

CBS Photo Archive

Charles Kuralt was one of the most talented and important storytellers in American history. He just happened to do some of his best work on television. In a 37-year career at CBS News, he had one of the most recognizable faces and voices in the country. His work, especially his love for words and the way he wove them, set him apart. As the host of two landmark series, *On the Road* and *CBS Sunday Morning*, he set the highest standards.

Whether he was reporting from a tiny town in the Midwest or from a battlefield in Vietnam, Kuralt tried to tell stories that viewers could understand. For *On the Road*, which he began in 1967, he traveled around the country in a motor home, covering every state in the Union. His storytelling ability was sometimes compared to that of Mark Twain and John Steinbeck. *Time* magazine called him "the laureate of the common man." For 15 years, as host of *CBS Sunday Morning*, he brought to millions of Americans one of the most unique shows on television. His background in newspapers is obvious—he brought solid writing and reporting skills to his work.

Charles Kuralt was born on September 10, 1934, in Wilmington, North Carolina. He majored in history at the University of North Carolina in Chapel Hill and began his journalism career as a reporter and later, editor of the *Daily Tar Heel*. He joined the *Charlotte (NC) News* as a reporter and columnist in 1955, and two years later, at the age of 22, he joined CBS News as a writer. At the age of 24, he was the youngest person ever to become a CBS News correspondent. Kuralt worked for three years in Rio de Janeiro before moving to Los Angeles.

While best known for covering his own country, Kuralt has reported from around the world. Kuralt published seven books, including *A Life on the Road*, a best-selling, nonfiction work. Kuralt retired from the CBS network in May of 1994. In 1997, he was named host of the program *I Remember* on CBS Eye on People, a cable network. Among the many awards he won are 3 Peabody Awards, 13 Emmy Awards, and the duPont–Columbia Silver Baton. He received several of the highest annual honors in the business, including those of the National Press Club and the National Association of Broadcasters. In 1996, he was named to the National Academy of Television Arts and Sciences' Hall of Fame. He died at his home in New York City of complications from lupus on July 4, 1997. *Sreenath Sreenivasan*

Further Reading

Champlin, Charles. "Kuralt: Still a Roads Scholar." *Los Angeles Times,* 14 October 1988, C3.

Kuralt, Charles. *A Life on the Road*. New York: G.P. Putnam's Sons, 1990.

Kuralt, Charles. *On the Road with Charles Kuralt*. New York: G.P. Putnam's Sons, 1985.

Bill Kurtis

Photo by Will Crockett for Kurtis Productions, Ltd.

Bill Kurtis had a long career as an anchor for WBBM-TV, the CBS-owned station in Chicago, and a concurrent role as an award-winning documentary reporter and producer. Born in Pensacola, Florida, on September 21, 1940, Kurtis grew up in Kansas, and obtained a degree in journalism from the University of Kansas and a law degree from Washburn University. He had his first stint as an anchor for WBBM while still in his twenties, but did not do well in the ratings. He then spent three years as a CBS correspondent and was lured back to Chicago by WBBM in 1973. He and Walter Jacobson were paired as the hard-news alternative to happy talk. Part of their strength was an in-depth reporting team lead by Kurtis. It took time to rise to the top of the ratings, but once there, they maintained their position. Kurtis reported on the effects of Agent Orange in Vietnam, for which he received many major awards, including Emmys, and his documentary on American-Asian children in Vietnam received an Overseas Press Club Award.

In 1982, Kurtis joined Diane Sawyer on *The CBS Morning News*. After Sawyer left for *60 Min-utes*, Kurtis was paired with Phyllis George. The program did not do well, and Kurtis returned to WBBM in 1985. WBBM never regained the ratings it previously enjoyed, and the station's anchor team broke up in 1993, when Jacobson left for the Fox-owned station in Chicago. Kurtis left the anchor role entirely in 1996.

Much of Bill Kurtis' energy currently goes towards his company, Kurtis Productions, Ltd., which produces documentaries. A skilled photographer, Kurtis's 1983 collection, *Bill Kurtis on Assignment*, was published by Rand McNally.

Marjorie Fox

Further Reading

Boyer, Peter J. *Who Killed CBS? The Undoing of America's Number One News Network, 1988.* New York: St. Martin's Press, 1989.

Deeb, Gary. "Bill Kurtis: Everybody's Friend Moves On to New York and the Challenge of Befriending a Nation." *Chicago Sun-Times,* 28 February 1982, 28.

Jacobs, Scott. "The Channel Two Chronicles." *Chicago Magazine,* September 1978, 184.

L

Andrew Lack

Born on May 16, 1947, in New York City, Andrew Lack's producer's skill was nurtured at the Sorbonne in Paris and the School of Fine Arts at Boston University. At CBS News for 16 years, Lack launched *West 57th*, the Generation X version of the newsmagazine he produced for *60 Minutes*. Nearly a decade with *CBS Reports* helped him earn 16 Emmys. In the early 1990s, an era of frantic competition when fresh voices from Fox and the globally dominant CNN, strained to outshout traditional networks, Lack focused production talents at NBC.

Lack dusted off the bruised feathers of the once proud peacock still embarrassed from *Dateline's* unscientific "crash test" on exploding trucks. Turning turmoil into triumph, Lack expanded the newsmagazine to four nights, including direct competition with *60 Minutes*. With renewed self-respect, NBC rallied behind Lack's leadership. The showcase of news programs included an array of talent ranging from a reawakened *NBC Nightly News with Tom Brokaw* to Tim Russert who took over *Meet the Press*. Heavily cross-promoted, the female talent lineup included Jane Pauley co-anchoring *Dateline NBC*, plus Katie Couric who woke up large numbers of Americans each morning from Pauley's old home set at *Today*. Beyond nurturing talent, Lack harnessed technology to rebuild news, cross-breeding Internet technology with cable, hatching the new platform MSNBC on July 15, 1996.   *B. William Silcock*

Further Reading
"Lack is Back 'Til 2002." *Broadcasting & Cable,* 1 July 1996, 36.
Puglisi, Rob. "Talking News." *The Communicator,* December 1994, 13.

Matt Lauer

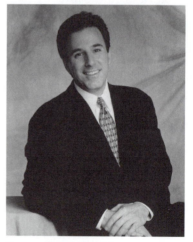

Courtesy NBC News/*Today*

Bryant Gumbel's successor as host of NBC's popular morning program *Today*, Matt Lauer has held a variety of broadcast news positions since January of 1994, including the job of providing news updates and special reports for that long-time leader in its time slot. Three years later, Lauer took over as host. He also served as co-anchor of *News 4/Live at Five with Sue Simmons* for WNBC-TV in New York and prior to that, hosted a live three-hour daily talk program for New York's WWOR-TV.

Lauer was born in New York, New York, on December 30, 1957, and spent his last two years of high school in Greenwich, Connecticut. He reported from that community, just 28 miles from New York, as part of the "Going Home" series on MSNBC in 1997. One of the most affluent communities in the nation, Greenwich was the focus of Lauer's report which zeroed in on teens and parental pressures to succeed, finding some difficulty in coping with their high expectations. Lauer visited four continents over five days in May 1998 as part of the "Where in the World is Matt Lauer?" *Today* theme.

Lauer's first broadcasting position was as producer for the noon news on WOWK-TV in Huntington, West Virginia, where he earned a slot as a reporter. He subsequently hosted *PM Magazine* assignments in Richmond, Providence, and New York, joining WNYW-TV in 1986. He moved to WCAU-TV in Philadelphia, then WNEV-TV in Boston. As the current host of *Today*, Lauer follows Dave Garroway, Hugh Downs, John Chancellor, Tom Brokaw, and Bryant Gumbel.

Michael D. Murray

Further Reading

"In Spiffy Stunt, 'Today's' Matt Lauer Will Broadcast from 5 Secret Sites." *St. Louis Post-Dispatch*, 26 April 1998, D4.

"Next on Today." *St. Louis Post-Dispatch,* 24 December 1996, 2A.

Powell, Joanna. "Mad About Matt." *Good Housekeeping,* May 1998, 124–27.

Jim Lehrer

Jim Lehrer co-anchored *The MacNeil-Lehrer NewsHour* on PBS for 20 years before rising in 1996 to executive editor and anchor of *The NewsHour With Jim Lehrer*. Lehrer also served, in 1992 and 1996, as moderator for the U.S. presidential debates. Lehrer and Robert MacNeil are partners in MacNeil/Lehrer Productions, coproducer of *The NewsHour*.

Jim Lehrer was born on May 19, 1934, in Wichita, Kansas. After graduating from the University of Missouri, Lehrer began his career in

Photo by Don Perdue

1959 in Dallas, where he was a reporter for the *Morning News* and *Times-Herald*. He became the *Times-Herald's* city editor in 1968 and moved into public broadcasting as executive director of public affairs and host and editor of the nightly news at KERA-TV, Dallas. As PBS public affairs coordinator in Washington, Lehrer teamed up with MacNeil in 1973 to cover the Watergate hearings, and he anchored coverage of Richard Nixon's impeachment inquiry.

Lehrer was a Washington correspondent for the half-hour *Robert MacNeil Report*, premiering in October 1975 on Thirteen, WNET, New York. Renamed *The MacNeil-Lehrer Report* in 1976, the program won more than 30 awards for journalistic excellence by the time *The MacNeil-Lehrer NewsHour* was launched in September 1983. *The MacNeil-Lehrer News Hour* drew criticism in 1995 when media/conglomerate TCI purchased two-thirds of the company. Lehrer has hosted two critically acclaimed MacNeil/Lehrer Productions specials: *The Heart of the Dragon*, a series on China, and *My Heart, Your Heart*. Lehrer has won Emmys, Peabody Awards, and the University of Missouri School of Journalism Medal of Honor. Lehrer has also written many plays and books, including *The Last Debate* (a satire about journalism), memoirs, and a novel that was made into a film.

Linda M. Perry

Further Reading

Cohen, Jeff, and Norman Solomon. "'MacNeil/Lehrer Newshour' at 20: Hold the Cheers." *Media Beat,* 27 September 1995.

"Jim Lehrer, Executive Editor and Anchor," Off Camera, Video, *The NewsHour with Jim Lehrer*, Public Broadcasting System.

Bill Leonard

William A. "Bill" Leonard attended Dartmouth College during the Depression years and became managing editor of the school newspaper, *The Dartmouth*. He graduated in 1937 and interviewed for a position at CBS News right out of college, but did not get hired on at the network until eight years later. Instead, he spent three years as a small town newspaper reporter, a couple of years at an advertising agency's research department in New York City, and four years in the U.S. Navy.

Leonard was hired by WCBS Radio to host the program *This is New York* on December 31, 1945. The show lasted 17 years, with Leonard as the host for 13. He became the toast of New York radio and moved to television, reporting for the *CBS Evening News*. His broadcast coverage of the underprivileged and reports on treatment of the mentally ill earned him the Albert Lasker Award for Medical Journalism in 1956. Three years later, he narrated the Emmy-award winning documentary "Harlem: A Self Portrait" and was invited to become a *CBS Reports* correspondent. Fred Friendly offered him a challenge to prepare a documentary on the notorious dictator Rafael Trujillo of the Dominican Republic. Leonard responded with a program for which he completed all aspects of production, reporting, and narrating and which won the Ed Stout Award for Outstanding Foreign Reporting.

Leonard was put in charge of the CBS News election unit in 1962, at a time when the national news organizations were beginning to coordinate coverage as part of the development of the News Election Service. He assumed the vice presidency of the network news operation two years later. He also served as CBS chief lobbyist in Washington, D.C.

Leonard initiated a wide variety of projects including *60 Minutes* and *CBS Sunday Morning*. A decade later, in April 1979, he was promoted to president of CBS News. He negotiated the change of the anchor position for the *CBS Evening News* from Walter Cronkite to Dan Rather and discussed his experience in news in a popular book, *In the Eye of the Storm: A Lifetime at CBS*. Leonard left his post as network president in 1982 and later served as director of the Alfred I. duPont–Columbia University Awards. He was one of the few senior television news executives to have functioned at the highest levels, in both network management and behind the microphone and received a Peabody Award for Lifetime Achievement. Leonard married "Kappy" Wallace, Mike Wallace's former wife, in May 1957. ABC chief correspondent Chris Wallace was a stepson. Leonard died of a stroke at age 78 on October 23, 1994, in Laurel, Maryland. *See also* CBS News, *60 Minutes*.

Michael D. Murray

Further Reading

Leonard, William. *In the Storm of the Eye: A Lifetime at CBS.* New York: G.P. Putnam, 1987.
Matusow, Barbara. *The Evening Stars: The Making of the Network News Anchor.* Boston: Houghton Mifflin, 1983.
"On the Record: An Interview with Bill Leonard." *Washington Journalism Review,* September/October 1978, 29–33.

Irving R. Levine

Photo courtesy of Irving R. Levine

Over a 45-year career with NBC News, Irving R. Levine became a familiar fixture among American television viewers, recognizable for his trademark bow tie and for his role as a pioneer of economics reporting on television. When Levine retired from

NBC as chief economics correspondent in 1995, he was the longest-serving correspondent at the network.

Born in Pawtucket, Rhode Island, Irving R. Levine's journalism career took him from writing newspaper obituaries in his native Rhode Island to covering some of the major international and business stories of the day. Levine joined NBC in 1950, reporting on the Korean War, first as a part-time stringer and then as a network correspondent. After Korea, Levine spent two years in New York before beginning a 15-year period in the European capitals of Moscow, Rome, and London. Among the stories Levine covered from Europe were the Berlin airlift, the Soviet invasion of Czechoslovakia, the Eisenhower-Khrushchev summit, and the Kennedy-Khrushchev Vienna summit.

Levine's 1971 reassignment to Washington, D.C., brought with it a newly created beat: economics, which no one, at least at first, either understood or appreciated. According to Levine, the beat was regarded as unproductive until August of 1971, when President Richard Nixon imposed wage and price controls, taking America off the gold standard. Then suddenly, the economy became a big story. The interest grew, and today networks address the need for relevant, informed information. Levine's lean, direct style set the standard for the evolving field of economic journalism.

In his role as NBC's chief economics correspondent, Levine accompanied presidents Ford, Carter, Reagan, Bush, and Clinton to the annual G7 Economic Summit meetings. He also traveled to China with Treasurer Secretary Michael Blumenthal to cover the start of the U.S.-China trade talks, made regular appearances on *Meet the Press,* and presented weekly commentaries on NBC's cable network, the Consumer News and Business Channel (CNBC). Levine describes his work as that of a translator who can offer insight for those outside his area of specialization.

In addition to his television work, Levine is the author of four books—*Main Street USSR, Travel Guide to Russia, The New Worker in Soviet Russia,* and *Main Street Italy*. At the end of his career as a reporter in 1995, Levine became the Dean of the School of International Studies at Lynn University in Boca Raton, Florida.

Alan Schroeder

Further Reading

Hovelson, Jack. "This is Irving R. Levine." *The Des Moines Register,* 17 October 1995, 1T.

Johnson, Peter. "Retirement Leaves Levine Fit to Not Be Bow-Tied." *USA Today,* 26 October 1995, 3D.

Lissit, Robert. "Not Just Another Pretty Face." *American Journalism Review,* July–August 1994, 44–47.

Library of American Broadcasting

The Library of American Broadcasting, formerly called the Broadcast Pioneers Library, contains a wide-ranging collection of both textual and nonprint materials relating to broadcast history, including resources pertaining to television news. Located at the University of Maryland, in addition to nearly 200 linear feet of clipping and vertical files, this combined library and archives includes approximately 3,000 books; 1,000 oral histories, interviews, and speeches; 4,000 pamphlets; 260 periodical titles; 25,000 photographs; 3,300 recordings; 1,300 scripts; 100 scrapbooks; and a collection of video and film materials. Many of the materials, including rare, first editions tracing the evolution of broadcasting, are not available elsewhere.

Originated in 1964 as part of the Broadcast Pioneers History Project, the library was conceived by William Hedges, former NBC executive and president of the National Association of Broadcasters (NAB), who oversaw the collection of some 13,000 items that have become the core of its holdings. As the Broadcast Pioneers Library, it opened in 1971 in the NAB building in downtown Washington, D.C. The library remained there until 1994, when it moved to the University of Maryland. Subsequently its name was changed to more accurately reflect its scope. It is housed in the university's Hornbake Library alongside the National Public Broadcasting Archives, making the two collections parallel resources for research into both commercial and noncommercial broadcasting.

The Broadcast Pioneers Education Fund, a board composed of 30 persons associated with broadcasting or related fields, governs the library. The board, which elects its own officers, provides administrative and financial support. An academic advisory board is being organized. Among key holdings related to television news are the Westinghouse News Collection, 1958–1982, consisting of 2,300 audiotape reels of raw feeds from the Westinghouse Washington bureau, with emphasis on coverage of the Vietnam War and Watergate; the papers of Sol Taishoff, founder of *Broadcasting* magazine; and the archives of the Television Information Office (1960–1989), set up to disseminate information on the television industry following the quiz show scandals.

Among other notable holdings are photos, slides, and negatives dating from the 1920s to the present offering a pictorial account of the evolution of U.S. broadcasting; the Radio Advertising Bureau Collection containing radio product commercials representing the scope of American industry in the 1950s and 1960s; Standard Program Library subscription discs supplementing radio programming in the 1940s and 1950s; and material from prominent broadcasters. These include the papers of Helen J. Sioussat, who arranged public affairs programming at CBS from 1937 to 1958; Edward M. Kirby, chief of radio for the War Department during World War II; and Edythe Meserand, first president of American Women in Radio and Television. The library seeks donations in all areas of broadcast history. It is open from 9 A.M. to 5 P.M., Monday to Friday. Reference service is offered for both the broadcasting industry and academia. *See also* Archives for Television News.

Maurine H. Beasley

Further Reading

Godfrey, Donald G. *Reruns on File: A Guide to Electronic Media Archives.* Hillsdale: N.J.: Lawrence Erlbaum, 1992.

Library of American Broadcasting Materials, Hornbake Library, University of Maryland, College Park, MD 20742-7011.

Rush Limbaugh

Rush Limbaugh's voice dominates the political talk programming that became so popular in the 1990s. His programs have become rallying points for the conservative faithful and are the foundation of a multimillion-dollar empire including everything from books to t-shirts.

Born in Cape Girardeau, Missouri, on January 12, 1951, Limbaugh became a radio devotee while in his teens. He worked as a disc jockey and at other jobs at first, with notable lack of success. In 1984, KFBK in Sacramento, California, hired Limbaugh as a talk-show host. He became a hit by raising controversial issues while avoiding the rudeness that was the trademark of some talk-show colleagues. Within a year, he nearly tripled his audience. In 1988, in partnership with syndicator Ed McLaughlin, Limbaugh moved to WABC. He developed a loyal following that he could easily mobilize. When a South Bend, Indiana station told Limbaugh it was dropping his program because of listener complaints, he denounced the move and urged fans to protest. The Indiana station was deluged with calls, and the show continued.

After Bill Clinton's election in 1992, Limbaugh emerged as one of the the most visible critics of the White House and the Democratic Congress. His audience continued to grow, reaching an estimated 20 million listeners a week. Because of his sharp attacks on the Democrats, he was credited with being a major factor in the election of a Republican Congress in 1994. Limbaugh's success is due largely to his ability to entertain, not just proselytize. He has said that his principal job is not to champion political causes, but to hold an audience. His syndicated half-hour television show developed a conservative, almost cult-like following. People would meet in groups and party settings to view his program. Conservative viewers especially enjoyed Limbaugh's frequent use of edited news video showing Bill and Hillary Clinton at public appearances, press conferences, and various other settings, with the freewheeling conservative introducing the Clintons' statements on issues of the day and then mocking their every word. But it turned out that he never seemed as comfortable on camera as he did behind a radio microphone, and he ended his television program in 1996.

A devoted admirer of Ronald Reagan, Limbaugh urged George Bush, in 1992, and Bob Dole, in 1996, to stick to "Reaganesque" themes. He performed a great service for the Clinton administration in 1993, when he endorsed the North American Free Trade Agreement (NAFTA) and attacked Ross Perot's anti-NAFTA crusade. As Republicans sought to plan their party's future in the aftermath of Clinton's 1996 re-election, Limbaugh maintained his status as an ideological beacon, the Newt Gingrich of the airwaves, trying to keep the party on a conservative course. *See also* Roger Ailes. *Philip Seib*

Further Reading

Kurtz, Howard. *Hot Air: All Talk, All the Time.* New York: Times Books, 1996.

Limbaugh, Rush. *The Way Things Ought To Be.* New York: Pocket, 1992.

Seib, Philip. *Rush Hour: Talk Radio, Politics, and the Rise of Rush Limbaugh.* Fort Worth: Summit Group, 1993.

David Lowe

Born in 1913 in New York City, David Lowe was raised in humble circumstances. Known as the producer for *CBS Reports* during the early 1960s, his credits include some of the network's most editorially-pointed and controversial documentaries—"Harvest of Shame," "Abortion and the Law," "Ku Klux Klan: The Invisible Empire," and "Who Speaks for Birmingham?"

Scholars point to Lowe as the person most responsible for "Harvest of Shame." Even before he was hired at CBS, Lowe had repeatedly appealed to Fred Friendly to do a migrant labor program. Friendly eventually acquiesced by assigning Lowe to the project in the fall of 1959. When he started at CBS, Lowe had few news or documentary credentials, although he had served briefly as the director of news for the short-lived DuMont Network, which folded in 1955.

When he joined *CBS Reports*, Lowe was known as a lawyer and fundraiser. He had also been an unsuccessful producer of Broadway plays

and, like Friendly, dabbled at producing quiz shows. Lowe was married to the well-known critic for the *New York World-Telegram,* Harriet Van Horne. Prior to that he had been married to entertainer Judy Holiday. Within a month after joining Friendly and *CBS Reports*, the charming and affable Lowe was able to get vegetable growers to talk about migrant labor. He spent much of 1960 following agricultural laborers, filming their story. At CBS, David Lowe's work unflinchingly addressed many of the most highly-charged social issues of the day. He died of a heart attack in 1965 at the age of 51. *See also CBS Reports.*

Richard J. Schaefer

Further Reading

Bluem, A. William. "David Lowe—In Memorium." *Television Quarterly,* 1965, Vol. 4, No. 4, 60–62.

Bluem, A. William. *Documentary in American Television.* New York: Hastings House, 1965.

Schaefer, Richard J. "Reconsidering 'Harvest of Shame'": The Limitations of a Broadcast Journalism Landmark." *Journalism History,* 1994, 121–32.

Elmer Lower

Photo by Dmitri Kessel

In a half century of journalism, Elmer Lower covered everything from three wars to the first moon walk and rescued one network news operation from virtual obscurity. Over the course of his career, the former ABC News president has been honored with two Emmys and distinguished service awards from a host of journalism organizations.

Lower was born on March 7, 1913, the son of a Kansas City alderman with a deep passion for politics. He graduated from the University of Missouri School of Journalism in 1933 and accepted his first professional assignment with the *Louisville Herald-Post*. Lower credits the $10-a-week Depression-era job with providing a foundation in "street reporting" that served him well. After a series of wire service positions from 1934 to 1942, Lower was employed as a photo-journalism specialist for the government when World War II escalated. During two years with the Office of War Information, Lower traveled to Cairo, Algiers, Naples, and London to distribute pictures. He then joined *Life* magazine and later completed a second term as a government information officer in post-war Germany.

Like many other journalists, Lower made the move to television as America settled into a post-war boom. From 1953 to 1963, Lower helped to shape the emerging medium, serving CBS as a Washington bureau chief and later NBC as a vice president and executive producer of political and space coverage.

In 1963, Lower accepted the daunting challenge to head up the news division of the lowest-rated network. During 11 years as ABC News president, Lower increased staff from 250 to 750; expanded nightly newscasts to 30 minutes; hired young talent like Peter Jennings, Ted Koppel, and Sam Donaldson; and helped boost ratings from almost invisible figures to respectable ones. Donaldson believes Lower may have saved the news operation from extinction because of his ability to produce quality news on tight budgets.

Before leaving his post at ABC, Lower also made an industry-wide mark. In 1964, he worked with competitors to form the cooperative News Election Service to tabulate votes in national elections. In 1968, Lower also changed coverage of the political conventions from "gavel-to-gavel" to a nightly 90-minute package. Other networks quickly emulated this format. In 1974, Lower moved to the ABC boardroom as a corporate vice president. He retired in 1978, and started a new career in academia as a teacher and journalism school administrator.

Among his post-retirement activities, Lower served as interim dean of the University of Missouri School of Journalism and completed a term as a director of the Public Broadcasting Service. He continues to speak around the world about television news and press freedom. *See also* ABC News. *Stuart L. Esrock*

Further Reading

Clavin, Tom. "Long Island Q & A: Elmer W. Lower—TV May Be Starting To Give Meaningful Campaign Coverage." *New York Times,* 8 March 1992, Section 12-2.
Otter, Jack. "A Journalist of Principle." *The East Hampton Star,* 30 July 1992, II-26.

Joan Lunden

The first official co-host for one of the most successful morning programs in television history, Joan Lunden showed how curiosity, civility, determination, and patience can pay off. Born in 1950 as Joan Blunden in Fair Oaks, California, and a graduate of American River College, Lunden sought employment in television at a time when the role of women was expanding, with news management recognizing the need to diversify on-air staff.

Lunden's first television position was at KCRA-TV in Sacramento as a news department trainee in 1973. She progressed to weatherperson, consumer reporter, producer, and anchor. In 1975, Lunden was hired as a reporter for WABC's *Eyewitness News* in New York. The coast-to-coast move prompted a name change from Blunden to Lunden to avoid media "blunders." In 1976, Lunden was promoted to weekend co-anchor, and in 1980 she replaced Sandy Hill on *Good Morning, America*.

Joan Lunden's presence on *Good Morning, America* altered how television management and the American public view women. She became one of the best-known working mothers in America. This prompted media coverage contributing to the development of another dimension of Joan Lunden's career with her husband, Michael Krauss as her collaborator. They launched a series of family-related projects, including child-rearing tips, which aired on ABC-TV's *Mother's Minutes* (also released as a book in 1986); a child-raising show, *Mother's Day,* aired on Lifetime Cable Channel; an instructional home video on newborns, *Your Newborn Baby—Everything You Need to Know* (also released as a book in 1988); and a nationally syndicated column, "Parent's Notes."

These projects gave her leverage when she renegotiated her contract with ABC's *Good Morning, America* in 1986. She left the table as the cohost of the program and with a substantial salary increase. Since Lunden was on *Good Morning, America* for almost 20 years, audiences shared many highs and lows of her life—the births of her three daughters, the pain of divorce in 1991, and her transformation to co-host. In 1990 Lunden wanted to shed weight and develop an exercise program, and with dieting and exercise came a video produced by Laura Morton, *Workout America,* and a 1996 book, *Joan Lunden's Healthy Cooking,* by Lunden and Morton. She has

also authored *Good Morning, I'm Joan Lunden* with Ardy Friedberg.

The entertainment division of ABC lost control of *Good Morning, America* in 1995 to the news division. In 1997, it was announced that Lunden would leave her morning role to develop prime-time specials for ABC. She expressed interest in executive producing, acting, and doing more writing. Another book is in progress, *Joan Lunden's Healthy Living,* with co-author Laura Morton.   *Ann D. Jabro*

Further Reading

Lunden, Joan, and Laura Morton. *Joan Lunden's Healthy Living: A Practical, Inspirational Guide to Creating Balance in Your Life.* New York: Crown Publishers, 1997.

Lunden, Joan, and Laura Morton. *Joan Lunden's Healthy Cooking.* Boston: Little Brown Company, 1996.

Lunden, Joan, and Ardy Friedberg. *Good Morning, I'm Joan Lunden.* New York: Putnam, 1986.

M

Catherine Mackin

Catherine "Cassie" Mackin was a highly regarded political reporter for NBC and ABC in the 1970s and early 1980s. According to Timothy Crouse, the author of *The Boys on the Bus*, Mackin was virtually alone in pointing to President Nixon's shortcomings during his campaign in 1972. Mackin was the first woman to be a television network floor correspondent during the presidential nominating conventions.

Mackin was born in 1940 in Baltimore and graduated from the University of Maryland in 1960. She started on the rewrite desk of the *Baltimore News-American* and then became a Washington correspondent for the Hearst newspapers. Mackin was Nieman Fellow at Harvard University in 1967–1968 and joined WRC-TV in Washington in 1969. In 1971, she became a correspondent for NBC and was widely recognized for her political reporting. She was a convention floor reporter and election night anchor in both 1972 and 1976. Mackin covered Congress and also anchored the *NBC Sunday Night News*.

Mackin switched to ABC News in 1977, the first in a series of big hires by Roone Arledge. He paid her a six-figure salary, in part, to attract others. Mackin reported for *ABC World News Tonight* and *20/20* and participated in discussions on *This Week with David Brinkley*. She died of cancer in 1982.

Marjorie Fox

Further Reading

Crouse, Timothy. *The Boys on the Bus.* New York: Random House, 1973.

Gunther, Marc. *The House that Roone Built.* Boston: Little Brown and Company, 1994.

"TV Correspondent Cassie Mackin Dies." *United Press International,* 20 November 1982.

Robert MacNeil

Photo by Don Perdue

Canadian native Robert MacNeil—"Robin" to friends and colleagues—is best known as co-anchor for two decades of PBS's *The MacNeil-Lehrer NewsHour*, the first hour-long U.S. evening newscast. This unique noncommercial program brought in-depth reporting, interviews, and analysis to television news. The *NewsHour* has endured as one of PBS's most popular shows, attracting a loyal nightly viewership of 5 million. It has also won many awards, including duPont-Columbia, Emmy, and Peabody Awards.

Born in Montreal in 1931, MacNeil was raised in Halifax, Nova Scotia. MacNeil entered the military but dropped out of naval training in 1950. After a number of radio jobs as an actor for the CBC and disc jockey for a Halifax station, he moved to New York in pursuit of an acting career. Having completed a bachelor of arts degree from Ottawa's Carleton University, MacNeil got his first television experience as host of the CBC's *Let's Go to the Museum,* a weekly 30-minute educational program. Still interested in theater, he moved to England. He eventually landed a job with Reuters News Service as a rewrite man and stringer for the CBC.

NBC News hired MacNeil as a London-based correspondent in 1960. Assigned to Havana in 1962, he reported the aftermath of the U.S. naval blockade, and as White House correspondent, MacNeil rode in President Kennedy's Dallas motorcade on November 22, 1963. The only journalist to jump from the news bus and follow police up a grassy knoll after the shooting, he contributed to NBC's coverage of the assassination from a phone he grabbed in Parkland Hospital. In May 1965, NBC asked him to anchor New York's WNBC newscast. Disillusioned with NBC, in 1967 MacNeil embarked on an eight-year adventure as a trans-Atlantic reporter for the BBC's documentary *Panorama.* During that time, he wrote and narrated *The Whole World Is Watching*, a documentary on the 1968 Democratic National Convention in Chicago. In 1973, MacNeil served as the senior PBS correspondent, where he hosted *Washington Week in Review* and *A Public Affair/Election '72* with Sander Vanocur. His first collaboration with Jim Lehrer was co-anchoring the Emmy-winning coverage of Senate Watergate hearings.

MacNeil became an executive editor and anchor of WNET New York's *Robert MacNeil Report* in October 1975. Joined by Lehrer in Washington by satellite, the program was distributed by PBS as *The MacNeil/Lehrer Report.* In 1983, it was christened *The MacNeil/Lehrer NewsHour.* The duo bought out Gannett's half-interest in the program in 1986, making it the only major news program owned by anchors. After MacNeil's October 23, 1995, departure, the show continues as *The NewsHour with Jim Lehrer.*

MacNeil's career includes notable interviews with Rose Kennedy and presidents Gerald Ford and Jimmy Carter. He wrote *The People Machine* in 1968, a critical exposé of television's influence on politics, and *Wordstruck* in 1973, companion to the PBS-BBC series *The Story of English.* In *The Right Place at the Right Time,* written in 1982, MacNeil recounts, among other memoirs, bumping into Lee Harvey Oswald while seeking a phone to call in the Kennedy assassination.

MacNeil has two works of fiction, *Burden of Desire,* written in 1992, and *The Voyage,* written in 1995. He plans to continue as a novelist. He is recipient of Broadcaster of the Year, Paul White, and Medal of Honor awards. *Kevin C. Lee*

Further Reading

Baker, John F. "Robert MacNeil: From Newsman to Novelist." *Publishers Weekly,* 16 October 1995, 38–39.
Kolbert, Elizabeth. "Robert MacNeil Gives a Thoughtful Goodbye." *New York Times,* 15 October 1995, 39.
Wackerman, Daniel. "The News and Other Stories: A Conversation with Robert MacNeil." *America,* 21 October 1995, 12–15.

Frank N. Magid

One of the most influential people in the development of local television news has never worked as a journalist. Yet, Frank N. Magid has done much as a news consultant to bring viewer-driven content to local and network news. In the process, he has been hailed as a visionary and disparaged as a news "doctor." There is no doubt, however, that his recommendations, which are based on viewer research, helped change the way broadcast newsrooms operate.

Magid was not the first to use the science of human behavior and market research to study broadcast audiences in consultation with local stations. That distinction belongs to Phil McHugh and Peter Hoffman, who formed McHugh and Hoffman in Birmingham, Michigan, in 1962. Their backgrounds were in advertising and market research. Both wondered why viewers preferred one program over another. Station managers and news directors began to seek help improving their market share or ratings in the late 1960s and early 1970s as local news began to account for more profit.

Frank Magid founded his successful Cedar Rapids, Iowa, market research company in 1957, after earning a degree from the University of Iowa. His first clients were with businesses wanting to know why people behaved as they did. He brought his research methods to television 10 years later, when he was asked to help WWL, New Orleans. A few years after, when Magid began consulting with WFIL-TV (now WPVI) in Philadelphia, its local news had a minuscule 6 rating. Within a year, the station held a commanding 29, and other general managers wanted to know Magid's secret.

The key was that the research was designed for each client, asking viewers which television reporters they liked and trusted. Other data included viewer age, gender, income, social class, and lifestyle. This demographic and subjective information was distilled into recommendations to help build and exploit strengths while correcting weaknesses. Magid's research recommending more video segments and shorter stories helped ABC's *Good Morning, America* achieve success. He also recommended using a beat system so reporters would develop expertise in subject areas.

Research found audiences preferred pleasant on-air personalities. Reporters who could not "connect" with viewers were a problem. Writing and reporting skills were no longer the only criteria by which television journalists were judged. Traditional staffers complained that serious topics, often difficult to present visually, were disappearing. The Radio Television News Directors Association investigated these charges and concluded that news consultants, and their recommendations, represented one of the greatest tools a news director could have.

Frank N. Magid Associates is headquartered in Marion, Iowa, primarily because Magid likes the lifestyle there. The company has grown to more than 350 employees and now has an office in London, England. In addition to hundreds of local television station projects, Magid has consulted with the major networks. *See also* Consultants.

Elizabeth Ryan

Further Reading

Allen, Craig. "Consultant's Debate." *RTNDA Communicator,* 1995, 106–110.
Powers, Ron. *The Newscasters,* New York: St. Martin's Press, 1977.
Whye, Mike. "When Frank Magid Speaks, His Clients Listen." *The Iowan,* Fall 1994, 58–69.

Gordon Manning

During the spring of 1985, Tom Brokaw, while in Nicaragua, approached two Soviet reporters. When they asked where Brokaw worked, he said NBC News. The two wondered if he knew Gordon Manning. "Of course," Brokaw replied. When the Soviets pressed him further, Brokaw assured him he knew the one and only Gordon Manning. The Soviet's response was, "Thank God there's only one." Manning's reputation as a one-of-a-kind ball of energy was known throughout the Soviet political regime. Thanks to the diligent efforts of Manning, NBC secured an exclusive sit-down interview with Mikhail Gorbachev on the eve of his 1987 Washington summit conference. Manning's efforts were recognized with a 1987 George Polk Award.

Born in 1918 in Massachusetts, Gordon Manning has been ruled by three critical questions: Who cares? Why do they care? and Why do they care now? These questions governed his news judgment. A Boston University graduate, Manning began at the United Press Association where the motto was, "a deadline every minute." This fast-paced environment was a good match with his energy level. World War II and the navy interrupted his career briefly, but in 1946, Manning moved to Washington, where he began with *Collier's.* Within a year, he was managing editor. When the magazine was about to fold, Manning left for *Newsweek* magazine. At *Newsweek,* Manning distinguished himself as a thinker, planner, and doer.

This brought Manning to the attention of CBS News president Fred Friendly. Friendly had missed the opportunity to cover the Alaskan earthquake of 1964. Swearing he would never endure that kind of embarrassment again, he decided he needed a man like Manning who initiated *Newsweek's* coverage. Soon after, Manning reentered the kind of news environment he so loved, where news happened everyday—all day. Manning soon distinguished himself by creating a half-hour, Saturday edition of the *CBS Evening News*. He became known for being able to look beyond the technological challenges to focus on content. When Friendly resigned as president over a program conflict, Manning was asked to step in, but he refused. After that, Manning never regained his ground with CBS executives and left in 1975.

Shortly after departing CBS, Manning arrived at NBC as executive producer of specials and political coverage. At NBC, Manning was excused from the day-to-day operations and spent his time developing important programs, such as a human rights documentary comparing the United States and the Soviet Union. His endeavor won a duPont-Columbia Award in 1977. Perhaps Manning's greatest accomplishments rest in his ability to gain access to major newsmakers. His persistence prompted Gorbachev to salute Manning as an "initiator." Retired now, Manning still serves as a consultant to NBC News, generating ideas for news coverage.

Connie Book

Further Reading

Gates, Gary Paul. *Air Time: The Inside Story of CBS News.* New York: Harper and Row, 1978.
Profiles. *The New Yorker,* 30 May 1988, 49–66.
Slater, Robert. *This is CBS: A Chronicle of 60 Years.* N.J.: Prentice Hall, 1988.

Cynthia McFadden

Cynthia McFadden's television career combines her knowledge of broadcasting and law. Prior to joining ABC as legal affairs correspondent in 1994, McFadden was an anchor and senior producer at the Courtroom Television Network. McFadden, who holds a law degree from Columbia University School of Law, has covered hundreds of legal events from around the country including the rape trial of William Kennedy Smith, the murder trial of Lyle and Erik Menendez, the trial of police officers charged with beating

Rodney King, the sanity hearing of Jeffrey Dahmer, and the hearings on the nomination of Clarence Thomas to the Supreme Court.

Perhaps the most publicized case covered by McFadden is that of O.J. Simpson. McFadden's reports aired on *World News Tonight; Good Morning, America; PrimeTime Live; Nightline; Day One*; and *20/20*. Her exclusive interview with defense attorney Johnnie Cochran and his wife, Dale, for *Day One* was the couple's first joint appearance after allegations of domestic abuse were made by Cochran's first wife. On *20/20*, McFadden was the first to talk to F. Lee Bailey after his cross-examination of Los Angeles Police detective Mark Fuhrman. She also interviewed dismissed juror Michael Knox for *Nightline*.

McFadden has produced and anchored special programming for Lifetime Television, PBS's *Frontline,* and Great Britain's Channel Four. She has been honored with numerous awards for programs she has produced, including the George Foster Peabody Award, the Ohio State Award, three Silver Gavels from the American Bar Association, and the Blue Ribbon of the American Film Festival.

Joye C. Gordon

Further Reading

Edwards, Ellen. "The Reporter's Trail by Fire; Cynthia McFadden Moved to ABC and Landed the Hottest Job." *The Washington Post,* 21 March 1995, B1.
Gliatto, Tom. "Change of Venue." *People Weekly,* 17 January 1994, 54.
Kalogeraki, George. "A Lady and Her Court." *Vanity Fair,* January 1994, 116.

Frank McGee

Frank McGee was one of the most respected and soft-spoken newsmen who ever appeared on the NBC network. McGee was the head of news at NBC affiliate WSAF-TV in Montgomery, Alabama, in the mid-1950s. Due to his coverage of racial strife there, he gained the attention of Julian Goodman at the network in New York. Goodman, who especially noted McGee's calm demeanor, even when reporting on turbulent events, hired him for NBC's Washington staff. In 1957, one of McGee's first assignments for the network was in

Little Rock, Arkansas, where he covered the integration of Central High School, a major story of that era of television news.

Born in Monroe, Louisiana, in 1922, McGee grew up in Oklahoma. In 1940, after high school, he enlisted in the U.S. Army. After World War II, McGee studied at the University of California at Berkeley, before transferring back to his home territory and the University of Oklahoma. While at the University of Oklahoma, he was employed at KGFF, a radio station in Shawnee. McGee's many diverse jobs at the small station included advertising sales and music librarian. From 1950 to 1955, he worked at WKY in Oklahoma City as a newscaster, before moving on to Montgomery.

In the early 1960s, McGee covered U.S. presidential conventions and elections along with the more day-to-day network assignments. From these events, McGee moved to an anchor position for several live Mercury space shots. In 1965, he was the anchorman for NBC during the Gemini space flight that included Major Edward H. White's historic "First American to Walk in Space" event. After covering Pope Paul VI's visit to New York in 1966, McGee received a George Foster Peabody Award. In 1967, building upon his experience in covering race relations from his Little Rock days, McGee spent a month in Vietnam collecting material for a one-hour documentary about race relations in the military, "Same Mud, Same Blood." The special was awarded a Brotherhood Award from the National Conference of Christians and Jews.

In the late 1960s, McGee became an anchorman of the NBC News program entitled *Monitor*. He also anchored the *Sixth Hour News* at WNBC-TV in New York. In 1970, McGee started as co-anchor of the *NBC Evening News* with both John Chancellor and David Brinkley, respectively. On October 12, 1971, McGee became the host of the *Today* show in New York. He remained as host of *Today* until shortly before his death on April 17, 1974.   *Tommy V. Smith*

Further Reading

Frank, Reuven. *Out of Thin Air: The Brief Wonderful Life of Network News*. New York: Simon & Schuster, 1991.

Matusow, Barbara. *The Evening Stars, The Making of the Network News Anchor*. Boston: Houghton Mifflin, 1983.

Powers, Ron. *The Newscasters: The News Business as Show Business*. New York: St. Martin Press, 1977.

Marcy McGinnis

Courtesy CBS News

Marcy McGinnis was promoted to CBS vice president of news coverage in a shake-up fueled by dissatisfaction over the network's late start in reporting 1997's major news event—the death of Princess Diana in a Paris automobile crash. McGinnis was chosen to replace Lane Venardos, who had masterminded CBS coverage of the Persian Gulf War and Tiananmen Square. At the time of her promotion to the CBS News number three position, McGinnis was London bureau chief.

McGinnis was born on April 9, 1950, in Long Branch, New Jersey. She graduated in 1970 from Marymount University in Arlington, Virginia, and joined CBS as an administrative assistant in the Special Events Unit. She worked her way through the ranks of the news division, first as an assistant producer from 1973 to 1976, then associate producer from 1976 to 1982, before being named producer in 1982. McGinnis produced events occurring in Europe, Asia, South America, Canada, and Mexico and helped cover the 1984 presidential campaign. Her political coverage continued in 1988 as the senior producer in charge of special events for CBS Newspath, a service supplying feeds to affiliates and international clients.

In March 1992, McGinnis was transferred to London as CBS News deputy bureau chief and director of CBS Newspath, Europe. Three years later, McGinnis was promoted to vice president, Europe, and London bureau chief. In this position, she supervised coverage of news events in London and directed network coverage in Europe, Africa, and the Middle East.   *Agnes Hooper Gottlieb*

Further Reading

Durocher, Debra D. "Shaking Up CBS." *American Journalism Review News Link Database,* 28 October–3 November 1997.
McClellan, Steve. "Venardos Replaced at CBS News." *Broadcasting & Cable,* 13 October 1997, 30.

John McLaughlin

John McLaughlin was born in Providence, Rhode Island, in 1927. He grew up in a devoutly Catholic, staunchly Democratic, second-generation Irish- American, upper-middle-class family. McLaughlin, much like the anti-communist hero of the 1950s dramatic television series *I Led Three Lives,* has been a priest and teacher, social critic and commentator, communications owner and talk-show personality—serially. He attended LaSalle Academy, Providence, Rhode Island, and began training for the priesthood at age 18 at Weston College, a Jesuit institution in Massachusetts. After teaching in Catholic high schools, he attended Columbia University in New York and earned his doctorate. While there he worked for *America,* a Jesuit weekly opinion journal, eventually becoming assistant editor.

On December 13, 1969, Father McLaughlin wrote a piece in *America* supporting Vice President Spiro Agnew's stinging attack on television news delivered in Des Moines, Iowa. Disagreements with *America's* editor led to McLaughlin's departure from *America* early in 1970. He moved to Rhode Island, changed his party affiliation, and ran as an anti-Vietnam Republican for the U.S. Senate, but garnered only 32 percent of the vote in the general election.

McLaughlin then began writing speeches for White House special assistant Ray Price. He officially joined President Nixon's speech-writing team on July 1, 1971. He soon began working as a fact finder and troubleshooter. Among his trouble-shooting duties were two secret missions to Vietnam, Laos, and Cambodia for the National Security Council. He brought back positive reports of limited civilian casualties and little ecologcal damage from U.S. bombing raids. During the 1972 campaign, Father McLaughlin made many speeches in support of the morality of the administration's military policy of Cambodian bombing raids and mining Haiphong harbor.

McLaughlin became a media celebrity soon after the release of the White House Watergate tapes. On May 8, 1974, McLaughlin, in a press conference, dismissed President Richard Nixon's use of profanity as "emotional drainage." Strife with the hierarchy of the Catholic Church ensued. McLaughlin decided to marry, and he petitioned for and received laicization by Pope Paul VI. McLaughlin and Ann Dore, the former director of communication for the 1972 Committee to Re-Elect the President, married on August 23, 1975, in a civil ceremony. The couple began McLaughlin and Company, a media relations and public affairs consulting company.

McLaughlin hosted a weekend radio talk program over Washington's WRC in the early 1980s. Then the conservative Edison Electric Institute funded the television pilot for *The McLaughlin Group* in 1982. The PBS talk program, seen weekly nationwide, favors the political right. The interaction of regulars and guests is lively, energetic, loud, and boisterous.   *Donald C. Shields*

Further Reading

Bethell, Tom. "Man in a Hurry." *National Review,* 31 December 1985, 110–12.
Lieberman, David. "Item 1: John McLaughlin is (a) TV's Most Powerful Pundit or (b) Its Biggest Blowhard." *TV Guide,* 4–10 May 1991, 14–16.
Remnick, David. "The McLaughlin Group." *Esquire,* May 1986, 76–80.

Marshall McLuhan

Herbert Marshall McLuhan, considered one of the foremost theorists on the subject of the mass media, including television and computer technology, used examples from television news to highlight his writing. Born in Edmonton, Canada, in 1911, he attended the University of Manitoba and taught at St. Louis University in the United States, while completing a doctoral dissertation at Cambridge University. His students included Father Walter Ong, S.J., distinguished author and former president of the Modern Language Association.

With Canada entering World War II, McLuhan was drafted and returned to serve overseas. Following the war in 1946, he joined the University of Toronto and remained there for the balance of his career. His final position was as the director for the Center for Culture and Technology, a position he held until just prior to his death in 1980.

In his early days at Toronto, McLuhan became friends with and was greatly influenced by Harold Adam Innis, who had studied communication. With McLuhan, Innis furthered the concept of the central role of communication technology in determining the social, as well as economic impact on new technologies. McLuhan spent a year at the University of Wisconsin in the early 1960s and began exploring media technology in greater depth, resulting in the publication of *Understanding Media* in 1964.

His early books, *The Mechanical Bride,* written in 1951, and in 1952, the *Gutenberg Galaxy,* attracted a limited audience, but *Understanding Media* quickly became influential across North America and in Europe. McLuhan, in his writings from that time, refused to use traditional research methods. He promoted the idea of technological determinism in which the media were primary determinants of culture—much more important than the messages they conveyed. He described each communication technology as a force for change based on the senses individuals had to perceive messages. McLuhan became the guru of pop culture and demonstrated that he understood the global effect of television decades before others understood him or his ideas.

During the 1970s, McLuhan became a celebrity. He was the subject of network documentaries, his writing appeared in the *New York Times*, he was interviewed by *Playboy,* and he made a cameo appearance in a Woody Allen film. Author Tom Wolfe took up McLuhan's concept of "the global village," and researchers at General Electric and Bell Labs began scientific investigations of "the medium is the message."

During his career, McLuhan went from being an obscure academic, to the most influential writer to have affected North American popular culture. He did this, in part, on his own, by producing a few major books, but most of his fame came from becoming a celebrity, annointed by the media itself.

Thomas L. McPhail

Further Reading

Innis, Harold Adam. *The Bias of Communication.* Toronto: University of Toronto Press, 1964.

McLuhan, Marshall. *Understanding Media: The Extensions of Man.* New York: McGraw-Hill Book Company, 1964.

McPhail, Thomas, and Brenda McPhail. *Communications: The Canadian Experience.* Toronto: Copp, Clark, Pittman, Ltd., 1990.

Michel McQueen

Michel McQueen had spent more than a decade in print journalism before becoming a broadcaster. McQueen covered state and local politics for the *Washington Post* and national politics and policy for the *Wall Street Journal*, where she was a White House correspondent. In 1992, she joined ABC News as correspondent for *Day One.* She contributed a wide range of reports to that newsmagazine show, including an exclusive interview with the Jackson family, an investigation into investments made by members of Congress, a report on children's racial attitudes, and a report on the international campaign to ban the use of land mines, for which she was awarded an Emmy.

McQueen has contributed to a number of other ABC programs, including an hour-long documentary on the Anita Hill–Clarence Thomas controversy for ABC's *Turning Point.* She also has reported on a broad spectrum of personalities and achievers, including Anthony Griffin, an African-

American civil rights attorney who took on the challenge of representing the Ku Klux Klan in a First Amendment case. She is a regular panelist on the PBS show *Washington Week in Review*, produced by WETA in Washington, D.C.

McQueen has earned numerous awards, including the 1992 Candace Award for Communications from The National Coalition of 100 Black Women and the 1995 Joan Barone Award for Excellence in Washington-based National Affairs/ Public Policy Broadcasting given by the Radio and Television Correspondents' Association. A native of Brooklyn, New York, McQueen graduated cum laude from Radcliffe College at Harvard University in 1980.   *Joye C. Gordon*

Lisa McRee

Lisa McRee is a native Texan who is the new co-host of ABC's *Good Morning, America*. McRee was born on November 9, 1961, in Fort Worth, Texas, and earned her undergraduate degree from the University of California at San Diego. McRee joined ABC and progressed steadily through the news ranks. She anchored at WFAA, ABC's affiliate in Dallas, from 1989 until December 1991. Then she went to work for *Lifetime Magazine*, a prime-time news and public affairs program produced by ABC News for the Lifetime Cable television network.

McRee was selected to report for the ABC newsmagazine, *Day One*, and she was one of the original anchors of *World News Now*, ABC's overnight news broadcast. She was anchoring at KABC in Los Angeles in 1997, when she was tapped to succeed Joan Lunden on *Good Morning, America*. Lunden had been on the program for many years and was extremely popular, so in announcing this key hire for the network, ABC News chairman Roone Arledge took special care to describe McRee as an experienced, serious journalist but also one with unmistakable warmth and a keen sense of humor.   *Suzanne Huffman*

Further Reading

Bark, Ed. "Co-Anchor Leaving Channel 8 for ABC." *Dallas Morning News,* 11 December 1991, 32A.

Perkins, Ken Parish. "Good Morning, Y'all." *Fort Worth Star-Telegram,* 2 July 1997, 1.

Matt Meagher

Courtesy *Inside Edition*

A leading investigative journalist, Matt Meagher was born on October 15, 1948 in Syracuse, New York. He received his bachelor of arts degree in history from Westfield State College in Westfield, Massachusetts, and a masters of science in journalism degree from Boston University. Meagher began his career by reporting and producing first at WBUR-FM, then WTSP-TV, in St. Petersburg, Florida. While at WTSP, Meagher produced several prime-time documentaries. He later headed investigative reporting at two St. Louis television stations, KTVI and KMOV, before filling the same role at WBZ-TV in Boston.

Meagher is currently the senior investigative reporter for the syndicated television newsmagazine series *Inside Edition*. The George Polk Award was given in 1996 to Matt Meagher as reporter and Tim Peek as producer of "Door to Door Insurance," an exposé by *Inside Edition* of exploitation of the poor by some insurance companies. This was the first time a syndicated newsmagazine had won the award.

Meagher's reports have also earned him eight Emmys, the Alfred I. duPont-Columbia Award, the Sigma Delta Chi, and National Headliner Awards. His investigation into the use of unsafe trucks by rental truck customers was called by Investigative Reporters and Editors (IRE) the best investigative report on network and syndicated television in 1996 and earned him an award by the New York City Chapter of the Sigma Delta Chi Deadline Club.   *Steven Phipps*

Further Reading

Bash, Alan. "Syndicated 'Inside Edition' Wins Major Journalism Award." *USA Today,* 11 March 1997, 3D.

"Honors for *Inside Edition.*" *Broadcasting & Cable,* 21 April 1997, 38.

Meet the Press

NBC's *Meet the Press* started on November 6, 1947, and is the oldest, continuously scheduled program on network television. *Meet the Press* was the original press conference of the air and set the pattern for other news interview programs that followed—a moderator and a select number of journalists ask questions of the guests, leading news figures, in an unrehearsed situation. The first broadcast originated in Washington, D.C., but was only seen in New York City. The first guest was James A. Farley, former postmaster general and past chairman of the Democratic National Committee.

The initial program discussed the meeting of the allied deputy foreign ministers in London to discuss German peace terms at the end of World War II. No audio, video, printed transcript, or photograph of the first program remains. By the third program, *Meet the Press* was being aired in Washington D.C. Originally seen on Thursday nights, it was moved to Sunday evenings, and eventually to Sunday mornings. Today, *Meet the Press* is still produced in Washington, D.C., but is broadcast on about 400 radio and television stations and in 29 countries through the American Forces Radio and Television Network, the Superchannel in Europe, and Asia NBC.

Meet the Press began in 1945 as a radio program on the Mutual Broadcasting System (MBS). It was developed by producers Martha Rountree and Lawrence E. Spivak as a promotion for his *American Mercury* magazine. Rountree served as

the moderator until November 1953. Spivak purchased Rountree's interest in the entire production that year, then sold his rights to NBC in 1955. He still remained with the program as producer, moderator, and permanent panelist until his retirement in 1975. After retirement, Spivak did return a few times as a special guest panelist. Spivak, a demanding interviewer, was a sensitive producer and reportedly told his guests not to appear on *Meet the Press* if they were concerned about being interviewed. Spivak died in 1993 at the age of 93. Rountree went on to ABC, where she produced and moderated *Press Conference.*

The early prominence of *Meet the Press* came from Spivak's ability to get the right newsmakers on the air and to ask them some key, tough questions. He would question a guest's previous public statements if they were contradictory. The intense questioning could be exhausting. John F. Kennedy once referred to the program as the "fifty-first state."

Another reason for the show's early success was the importance of the topics discussed. Americans got the first official word of the Russian atomic bomb from an inadvertent remark by General Walter Bedell Smith on a 1949 program. Thomas Dewey used the show in 1950 to eliminate himself from the presidential race and to offer support for General Dwight Eisenhower. John F. Kennedy made his debut on *Meet the Press* in 1951 as a young congressman. Spivak noted the need for fresh faces and the fact that Kennedy fit the bill. In 1972, Spivak interviewed, live via satellite, Philippine president Ferdinand Marcos, who had just established martial law in his country.

Meet the Press also presented dramatic television that influenced national and international events. Adlai Stevenson credited a 1952 appearance on the show as generating the momentum that led to his winning the Democratic presidential nomination. In 1955, Senator Walter George, chairman of the Senate Foreign Relations Committee, suggested that world tensions might be eased by a "meeting at the summit." President Eisenhower had already expressed his opposition to such a meeting, but George's suggestion received a favorable reaction abroad, and within seven days, Eisenhower reconsidered. Russian officials formally requested the talks that were finally convened in Geneva.

On another night, Senator Theodore Bilbo of Mississippi armed with pistol and accompanied by police and FBI, came through a line of 1,000 protestors. While on the air, he grew angry and proclaimed that he was a member of the Ku Klux Klan. His appearance on *Meet the Press* was replayed frequently on stations across the country over the next few days. Expulsion proceedings from the Senate were pending when Bilbo died not long afterward.

Whittaker Chambers, an ex-communist, appeared, and without benefit of congressional immunity, proclaimed Alger Hiss a communist. Hiss sued Chambers, who defended himself by producing the "pumpkin papers" that led to Hiss's conviction. Senator Jacob Javits, seeking the Republican senatorial nomination, went on the show when charges of past association with communists threatened his career. Javits reported that his appearance on *Meet the Press* did more for him than anything else.

The moderators for *Meet the Press* were:

- Martha Rountree (and occasionally, Lawrence Spivak)
  (6 November 1947–1 November 1953)
- Ned Brooks
  (22 November 1953–26 December 1965)
- Lawrence Spivak (1966–9 November 1975)
- Bill Monroe
  (16 November 1975–9 September 1984)
- Marvin Kalb and Roger Mudd
  (16 September 1984–2 June 1985)
- Marvin Kalb
  (19 June 1985–3 May 1987)
- Chris Wallace
  (10 May 1987–4 December 1988)
- Garrick Utley
  (29 January 1989–1 December 1991)
- Tim Russert
  (8 December 1991–)

Tim Russert, who had begun as a panelist in 1990, was designated the program's ninth moderator on December 8, 1991. On September 20, 1992, the program expanded to a full hour from its half-hour format of 45 years. Occasionally, when the topic needed the time, the show ran for 90 minutes. Although the program still follows the original format, Russert often interviews guests and has journalists respond to the interviews. In 1996, reorganization at the network placed *Meet the Press's* Web site under MSNBC, a news and financial cable network. Also in 1996, *Meet the Press* was the first network program to be broadcast in a high-definition television format. In November 1997, *Meet the Press* celebrated 50 years on the air. All the remaining kinescopes and videotapes of its interviews with world and national leaders are in the Library of Congress. A studio set that was used for 18 years is in the permanent archives of the Smithsonian Institution. *See also* Lawrence Spivak.   *Mary E. Beadle*

Further Reading

Ball, R., and NBC News. *Meet the Press: 50 Years of History in the Making.* New York: McGraw Hill, 1997.
"Durable Interrogator." *Time,* 6 November 1972, 71–72.
Rudolph, Ileane. "Bless This Press: *Meet the Press.*" *TV Guide,* 8 November 1997, 37–39.

James Metcalf

James Metcalf is one of the most difficult persons in television news to categorize. He was a news anchor, a humanist, and a poet. He was an innovator who successfully fused news and art. Metcalf was best known for *Sunday Journal*, a program about Louisiana, its people, and nature. He wrote and produced the program from 1973 until his death in 1977. In 1976 he won a Peabody Award for his *Sunday Journal* production about Holy Thursday in the town of Lacombe, Louisiana.

Metcalf was born on May 11, 1927, in Burburnett, Texas. After being raised in Eastland, Texas, he entered the Army Air Corps in 1942 and later participated in the invasion at Normandy. In 1950, Metcalf began his broadcasting career as a station announcer for KTLW radio in Texas City, Texas. He remained in Texas for the next 16 years, working for KABC radio and then as news broadcaster for WOIA-TV in San Antonio. In 1966, Metcalf worked as an anchor and newsman for

WWL-TV in New Orleans. By 1972, he was writing and producing *Jim Metcalf's Scrapbook*, a two- to three-minute segment within the broadcast combining news and aesthetics. By 1973, the success of *Scrapbook* led to *Sunday Journal*, a 30-minute combination of journalism, poetry, and music, which often successfully competed against network programming. From 1974 to 1979, four books of Metcalf's poems were published, pointing to the success of *Sunday Journal*—Metcalf's ability to write original poetry for a televised format was a significant element in the success of *Sunday Journal*, a precursor to CBS's *Sunday Morning*. He died on March 8, 1977, in New Orleans, Louisiana. *Lloyd Chiasson Jr.*

Further Reading

Metcalf, Jim. *Jim Metcalf's Journals*. New Orleans: Gretna, 1974.

James Metcalf Obituary. *New Orleans States-Item*, 9 March 1977, B-12.

Sig Mickelson

Photo courtesy of Sig Mickelson

Sig Mickelson was born on May 24, 1913, in Clinton, Minnesota. He received a bachelor of arts degree from Augustana College in Sioux Falls, South Dakota, in 1934, and a master's degree from the University of Minnesota in 1940. Shortly after graduating from Augustana, Mickelson embarked on his career in journalism, working as a part-time reporter for the *Argus Leader* and as a newscaster for radio station KSOO, both in Sioux Falls.

Mickelson joined the academic ranks, serving on journalism faculties at Louisiana State University, the University of Kansas, and the University of Minnesota. He returned to the newsroom in 1943, joining WCCO, the CBS-owned station in Minneapolis, first as news and public affairs director and then as production manager. In 1949, CBS moved Mickelson to New York City and named him the network's director of discussion. In 1951, he became CBS's director of news and public affairs, and in 1954, his position was elevated, first to that of chief executive of the network's combined news division, and soon thereafter to that of president of CBS News, a position Mickelson held for seven years.

One of Sig Mickelson's first moves as CBS news and public affairs director was to secure the talents of a then little-known reporter named Walter Cronkite to anchor CBS's coverage of the 1952 Republican and Democratic National Conventions, both of which were meeting in Chicago. Telecasts of the two conventions would be carried live for the first time over a coast-to-coast network of CBS television affiliates. Mickelson and producer Don Hewitt developed the concept of a news "anchor" especially for the role they envisioned for Cronkite. Many television historians now cite CBS's 1952 political convention coverage as America's first successful major-scale televised news event.

Coverage of political conventions also played a key role in Sig Mickelson's departure. When CBS was bested in the 1960 convention coverage ratings by the NBC reporting team of Chet Huntley and David Brinkley, Mickelson was replaced by Richard Salant as CBS News president in February 1961. Mickelson moved from CBS News to a position as vice president and member of the board of Time-Life Broadcast, Inc. and then on to similar positions with the Encyclopedia Britannica Educational Corporation. He returned to academe as a professor at Northwestern University's Medill School of Journalism and followed his three years at Medill with a three-year appointment as president of Radio Free Europe/Radio Liberty from 1975 to 1978.

Sig Mickelson moved once more to the classroom as a professor at San Diego State University from 1978 to 1990 and at Louisiana State University from 1991 to 1993. Mickelson continues to chair LSU's Manship School of Mass Communication's Board of Visitors and serves as distinguished professor of mass communication.

Ronald Garay

Further Reading
Halberstam, David. *The Powers That Be.* New York: Alfred A. Knopf, 1979.
Mickelson, Sig. *From Whistle Stop to Sound Bite.* New York: Praeger, 1989.
Slater, Robert. *This . . . Is CBS: A Chronicle of 60 Years.* Englewood Cliffs, NJ: Prentice Hall, 1988.

Minority Groups: Coverage and Representation

The broadcast industry has been very backward in coverage and representation of minority groups for much of its history. But broadcasters have responded slowly to the need for change. Some argue that the stimulus for this change has come less from conscience, and more due to regulation, court rulings, the recommendations of the Kerner Commission, and changing market conditions. Change has, nonetheless, arrived.

From its earliest days in the 1920s, radio did little to cover Blacks, Native Americans, Asians, Spanish Americans, and other minorities who could also lay claim to owning the airwaves. Few minority news voices were heard during the pre–World War II days. The major acknowledgment of minorities came from stereotypical entertainment figures such as the characters on *Amos n' Andy,* Jack Benny's assistant, Rochester, and the Lone Ranger's trusty Indian companion, Tonto. During television's first 40 years of existence, J. Fred McDonald points out that the depiction of Blacks was at best, ambivalent, and often included persistent stereotypes; there was a reluctance to develop, or star, black performers; and minorities were also excluded from production positions.

After ignoring the recommendations of the 1947 Hutchins Commission for the media to project a more representative picture of constituent groups in society, broadcasting was shocked into action by the Civil Rights movement of the 1960s. Stimulus came from Blacks demonstrating outside institutions not honoring their advances over national television and the riots of 1965, 1967, and 1968. The scathing report of the Kerner Commission not only pointed to long-ignored problems—housing, employment, and education—but to the press's neglect of positive television images and a failure to acknowledge the sense of hopelessness of living in the ghetto.

Broadcasters were nudged by a socially responsible Congress and federal court rulings to become more diverse in their programming and in employment practices. In 1966, the U.S. Supreme Court ordered the Federal Communications Commission (FCC) to recognize a citizens' group seeking to stop the license renewal of a Jackson, Mississippi, television station accused of racist policies in *Office of Communication, United Church of Christ v. FCC.* For a brief period, the government gave minorities special preference when applying for broadcast licenses. Race-conscious measures, geared to serve governmental objectives, were approved in *Metro Broadcasting v. FCC* in 1990. In 1995, however, affirmative action programs designed to give minorities preferential treatment were reversed. In a 5–4 decision, the high court changed the 1990 decision and ruled that minority preference programs administered by the FCC were overly broad.

Stimulated by favorable court rulings, as well as goals by professional organizations, and encouraged by the FCC and market forces, advances were also made on behalf of women. Connie Chung joined NBC News and was given some latitude in assignments addressing special concerns because of the status she had achieved and the audience she was attracting to that network and her programs. Charlayne Hunter-Gault, one of the two black students who integrated the University of Georgia in the early 1960s, became a key reporter and sometimes host for the *MacNeil-Lehrer NewsHour.* Carole Simpson achieved status as the weekend anchor for ABC News. Oprah Winfrey emerged as one of the nation's most influential broadcasters.

While fewer in number to women, other minority broadcasters made strides in the 1970s and 1980s. *Black Journal* and *Tony Brown's Journal* started on PBS. Two black males achieved status at the network's nationally televised programs. Ed Bradley, a former Philadelphia school teacher, became a correspondent at CBS's most highly regarded program, *60 Minutes.* Bryant Gumbel joined NBC's *Today,* then moved over to CBS with his own program. Prominent minority broadcasters Max Robinson and Bernard Shaw assumed national anchor slots.

William Wong, a columnist for the *Oakland Tribune,* pointed out that although television coverage of Asian Americans remains mostly "spotty and sensationalized," print coverage, while retaining some polar good-bad images, has become "increasingly nuanced, textured and more true to life." This is due in part to greater numbers of Asian American journalists, some of whom are bringing more informed coverage. This development is seen as a positive move and one that may offer additional television oppotunities. In addition, by the end of the 1980s, some network and chain operations were controlled by African American owners. At the same time, additional steps were being taken on the national level to monitor discrimination in broadcast employment and ownership.

By 1988, the number of minorities in broadcast news nearly doubled from the previous decade. While the numbers increased, image problems had not been totally resolved, since far too often Blacks were chosen only as a replacement for a minority professional who had been lost. The reality was, however, that by the 1980s, African Americans were creating their own forums to fill the gap in coverage of issues relating to their lives. By then, Black Entertainment Television was airing *BET News* with stories by, about, and decidedly for the Black audience.

Notwithstanding the improvement in coverage and the increase of minorities in broadcasting, some research still suggests a disturbing by-product of television news' reporting and editing process. Decisions by television journalists often ap-

pear to feed stereotypes, encouraging white hostility and the fear of African Americans. Television news, especially as it is presented at the local level, frequently presents a picture of Black society as violent and threatening toward Whites and causing problems for the law-abiding and tax-paying majority. This offers a recurring perceptual problem which continues to feed prejudice. Some observers believe that only constant efforts and monitoring within the media mainstream—especially television—will change this pattern of perception. These measures would help ensure that the future will be different for African American and other minorities. In addition, continuing strides regarding development and control of their own media images will, no doubt, provide similar positive effects. ***See also*** Civil Rights Coverage.

Paul Alfred Pratte

Further Reading

Dates, Jannette L., and William Barlow. *Split Image: African Americans in the Mass Media.* Washington: Howard University Press, 1990.

MacDonald, J. Fred. *Blacks and White TV: African Americans in Television Since 1948.* Chicago: Nelson-Hall Publishers, 1992.

Wilson, Clint C., and Felix Gutierrez. *Minorities and Media: Diversity and the End of Mass Communication.* Newbury Park: Sage Publications, 1985.

Newton Minow

Best known for his "vast wasteland" speech, Newton Minow served little more than two years as chair of the Federal Communications Commission (FCC). Minow was born in Milwaukee, Wisconsin, on January 17, 1926. He received his bachelor of science and law degrees from Northwestern University and served in the U.S. Army in the China-Burma-India Theatre in World War II. Minow was law clerk to Chief Justice Fred Vinson and assistant counsel to Illinois Governor Adlai Stevenson. He was appointed FCC chair on March 2, 1961, by President John F. Kennedy and left office to return to private law practice on June 1, 1963. Minow was an active chair, most notably for his involvement in advancing noncommercial television.

Just two months after his appointment, Minow spoke before the National Association of Broadcasters in Washington, D.C. Noting television's potential, Minow said that, with few exceptions, programming was not what it could be. He asserted that anyone watching a full day's television programming would "observe a vast wasteland." The speech contained an implied threat because Minow alerted station managers of their public service obligations and the need to demonstrate their commitment at license renewal time. He tied the station's service obligation to the cause of freedom for a new generation, thus linking his talk to themes presented in the John F. Kennedy presidential campaign.

Broadcasters' reaction to the speech was to call the new FCC chair arrogant and naive, but the public reaction was something else. It appeared as though Minow had touched a raw nerve, in part because he represented the John F. Kennedy theme of the "New Frontier" at an especially interesting and critical time period, during the first year of Kennedy's administration. The new FCC chair warned that successful license renewal applications would require news, public affairs, and local programming. The fact that Minow itemized a specific list of programs which he felt were worthwhile created the impression among broadcasters that he was attempting to impose his idea of good taste on the rest of America. He also offered his opinion on types of programs he viewed as contributing little to the national dialogue. These included violent gangster and western programs, as well as game shows and cartoons with excessive commercial interuptions. Broadcasters viewed this speech as unnecessary intrusion.

Minow eventually became recognized as a champion of educational television and organized the FCC's Educational Broadcasting branch in 1962. He made it possible for a New York City nonprofit group to obtain a license which might have otherwise gone to a commercial interest. When the station had been put up for sale, the nonprofit group was unable to offer more than the commercial bidders, and the FCC launched an investigation into noncommercial television in New York, freezing commercial license activity there. Fearing a long delay and loss of revenue, the owners sold the station to the nonprofit group. Also of note during Minow's chairmanship was the passage of a law requiring new television sets to be capable of receiving UHF television channels. The 1963 law increased the reach of UHF stations and helped advance that struggling system. *See also* Federal Communications Commission.

Dom Caristi

Further Reading

Barnouw, Erik. *The Image Empire.* New York: Oxford University Press, 1970.

Krasnow, Erwin, Lawrence Longley, and Herbert Terry. *The Politics of Broadcast Regulation.* New York: St. Martin's Press, 1982.

Minow, Newton M. *Abandoned in the Wasteland.* New York: Hill and Wang, 1995.

Andrea Mitchell

Courtesy NBC News

Andrea Mitchell has reported on important political events and people in Washington, D.C., for NBC News since the late 1970s. She earns praise from colleagues and the public for her analysis of domestic politics and interpretation of U.S. foreign relations. In November 1994, she became the first person named to serve in the newly created post of chief foreign affairs correspondent for NBC News. In this position, she provides analysis of international events and U.S. foreign policy initiatives. Mitchell is recognized for the high quality of her work and also for its quantity, as she is also one of the most visible and prolific news correspondents.

In 1994, Mitchell filed 181 stories, more than any other of the more than 100 evening news correspondents working in the nation.

Born in New York City in October 1946, Mitchell received her education and spent the early part of her career in Philadelphia. She graduated with a bachelor's degree from the University of Pennsylvania in 1967. Her first job was as a political reporter for KYW news radio in Philadelphia. She held this position for nine years, before moving to television, accepting a post as a political correspondent for Philadephia's KYW-TV in 1972. She remained with KYW-TV until 1976. The next year, Mitchell moved to Washington, D.C., where she worked as a correspondent for CBS affiliate WTOP-TV, reporting on Maryland politics, before she entered the national news arena by becoming a general assignment and energy correspondent for NBC.

During Mitchell's tenure as energy correspondent, perhaps her most noteworthy coverage was the 1979 accident at Pennsylvania's Three Mile Island nuclear facility and its aftermath,which increased her national visibility. As NBC White House correspondent from 1981 to 1988, she was responsible for political reports and analysis from the White House for both the *NBC Nightly News* and NBC's *Today* show. Mitchell frequently traveled with President Ronald Reagan on both domestic and foreign trips, including international summits with then Soviet leader Mikhail Gorbachev. Her major stories during her time as White House correspondent focused on arms control, budget battles, and the Iran-Contra affair.

Mitchell covered presidential races, reporting on the campaigns of Ronald Reagan and Bill Clinton. At the 1988 Republican National Convention, she was the first to announce that Indiana Senator Dan Quayle would be George Bush's running mate. In December 1988, Mitchell moved to Capitol Hill when she was selected to be NBC's chief congressional correspondent, where she reported on the savings and loan bailout, the Clarence Thomas hearings, and congressional budget hearings.

Mitchell has also served as a substitute anchor for *Meet the Press,* among other programs. She was panelist for the Commission on Presiden-

tial Debate's second debate between George Bush and Michael Dukakis in 1988. More recently, Mitchell participated in a 1994 interview of Serbian President Slobodan Milosevic for CNN's *Larry King Live.* She also appeared on the *Diane Rehm Show* on NPR and *Oprah* for a program devoted to television news. She has been the recipient of many awards, including the American Political Science Association Award for public affairs reporting and a 1977 Associated Press Broadcasting Award. Mitchell also serves as an overseer for the College of Arts and Sciences at her alma mater, the University of Pennsylvania, and works with Washington area Girl Scouts. *Danette E. Ifert*

Further Reading

"Covering the White House: A Center Dialogue." *The Center Magazine,* November/December 1985, 31–44.

Eastland, Terry. "Andrea's Abomination." *American Spectator,* January 1992, 57–9.

Goldberg, Robert, and Gerald Jay Goldberg. *Anchors.* New York: Birch Lane, 1990.

Russ Mitchell

Russ Mitchell was selected in 1997 to anchor *CBS News Saturday Morning,* first with Susan Molinari, who left the U.S. House of Representatives to accept that co-anchor position before leaving the program in June 1998 to return to other pursuits. Previously, Mitchell anchored the *CBS Sunday Night News* and served as a Washington-based correspondent providing coverage for Campaign '96. Mitchell became known in the mid-1990s through his work on *Eye to Eye with Connie Chung.* He reported on domestic topics such as a black West Point Cadet who was severely beaten and then discharged from the academy and a mother fighting the state over custody of her child. The child suffered from attention deficit disorder, and she could no longer handle him. Mitchell also reported on stories throughout the world including Russia, Chile, Indonesia, France, and Haiti.

He first joined CBS News in 1992 as anchor of the overnight program *Up to the Minute* and as a New York-based correspondent. Prior to that time, he was a weekend anchor and reporter at

CBS affiliate KMOV-TV in St. Louis. Mitchell's other anchoring and reporting jobs included KTVI-TV, St. Louis; WFAA-TV, Dallas; and KMBC-TV, Kansas City. Mitchell was born on March 25, 1960, in St. Louis, Missouri. He grew up in Webster Groves, Missouri, and began broadcasting at KOMU-TV while a student at the University of Missouri–Columbia, where he graduated in 1982.

His honors include two Emmys from the Midwest chapter of the National Academy of Television Arts and Sciences (NATAS), a Best UPI Reporter Award, and a 1995 National Association of Black Journalists News Award. He won an Emmy in 1997 for his coverage of the crash of TWA Flight 800. *Max Utsler*

Further Reading

Berger, Jerry. "Eye to Eye with Russ Mitchell." *St. Louis Post-Dispatch,* 25 April 1996, D1.
"CBS News Adds Saturday Morning." *Broadcasting & Cable,* 15 September 1997, 64.

Moon Landing

Covering the John F. Kennedy assassination and funeral may have established the importance of network television news in public life, but live broadcast coverage of the Apollo program and the July 20, 1969, moon landing meant television could take viewers to worlds the words of the print press could only approximate. In the view of some, Walter Cronkite's reporting of the eight-day, 750,000-mile mission made the 52-year-old CBS News anchor the preeminent newsman on the air and led to a decade-long dominance over the network's closest competitor, NBC News.

The Apollo 11 moon mission was the culmination of President John F. Kennedy's Cold War call to beat the Soviet Union to the moon. The $30 billion national effort (involving 20,000 industrial and university contractors, 400,000 workers, and 20 pioneering flights) was a made-to-order media event. Grammar schools stopped to take notice when Alan Shepard made his suborbital flight in 1961 and during John Glenn's three-orbit, four-hour flight in February 1962. The fiery launch pad deaths in January 1967 of the first Apollo crew only intensified national fears that the Russians would win the race the moon. When the Apollo 8 crew circled the moon on Christmas Eve, 1968, and read the creation story to a spellbound nationwide broadcast audience, it showed the central significance space and television played in stimulating the national agenda and imagination.

Charles Kuralt of CBS News observed that in July of 1969 Americans were moon mad. Witnessing man's landing and walking on the moon was a public media event, with large screens set up at Rockefeller Center and city squares throughout the nation, orchestrated to capture the historic moment. Worldwide, the people of planet earth held "moonathons" and anxiously awaited transmission of Neil Armstrong's first step on the moon. Armstrong would set up a black-and-white camera on the ladder of the lunar module to relay his famous first steps on the moon to earth. There was speculation everywhere about what he might say. The press had even reported on how viewers could photograph (with their personal cameras) the moment for posterity.

NBC News could claim that more people watched the lift-off of Apollo 11 on the morning of July 16 than CBS and ABC combined, but CBS News had, in Cronkite, the only major correspondent to cover every American-manned space launch for more than a decade and a person clearly identified with the space story. CBS's 31 hours of continuous coverage spanning the Apollo 11 moon landing and walk included expert analysis from Wally Schirra (the only astronaut to fly missions on Mercury, Gemini, and Apollo), as well as comments from Arthur C. Clarke, author of *2001: A Space Odyssey*, who years earlier had foreseen an American manned mission to the moon by the end of the 1960s. CBS spent the resources to outpace NBC coverage, and it showed. Full-scale models of the command and lunar modules, manned by CBS reporters and NASA advisers, duplicated the actions of the astronauts in a quarter-acre studio. A worldwide reporting team captured, by satellite, international analysis and reaction to the American triumph.

It was not only Cronkite's knowledge of the Apollo program but his enthusiasm for space travel that set CBS News coverage apart. He was six when he first flew in the open cockpit of a biplane and later reported on hot bombers and V-2 rockets while a wire service reporter in World War II. Often criticized for being a NASA booster, he admitted to "a boyish excitement" over "the great adventure of space." He went through simulators to get an astronaut's feel of flight and then begged CBS to expand its space coverage. Cronkite first reported the space race from the back of a station wagon a mile from the launch site. He fearfully held the window of a trailer when the buffeting of a Redstone rocket threatened to shatter it.

Twenty-five million Americans watched the Apollo 11 lift-off on network television, and tens of millions more in 33 countries across six continents watched. They saw a long range shot of Apollo on the launch pad and heard NBC's Chet Huntley read from a prepared script during the countdown to the launch, while David Brinkley and Frank McGee largely relied on the droning of Mission Control. Frank Reynolds and Jules Bergman at ABC News, while specialized in science reporting, were able to offer little better. CBS viewers, however, saw the network cut from Cronkite and Schirra to the simulators, and just after ignition, as the spacecraft cleared the launch tower. Cronkite repeatedly expressed his personal excitement during the launch and much later, in his memoir, *A Reporter's Life,* published in 1996, he discussed some of the criticism he had received at appearing just a little too involved and supportive of the event for a totally dispassionate and objective newsperson.

An estimated one billion people saw Apollo 11 land on the moon on the fourth day of the mission. Those who witnessed it on CBS News, however, saw it 40 seconds before anyone else. That was because the network's simulator showed the spacecraft landing on the moon according to its flight schedule. But Armstrong couldn't see the surface of the landing site and maneuvered his lunar module until he did. Audiences prematurely celebrated, not knowing that the spider-like spacecraft was still fifty feet above the lunar surface. Finally, fuel nearly gone, Armstrong reported the Eagle's landing as he and Cronkite, now both speechless, wiped away tears.

The six-and-a-half hour interval between the moon landing and man's setting foot on the moon

was a rest period for the astronauts but hardly that for the networks. The most ambitious programming ever gave worldwide reaction to the American achievement, complete with poetry readings, spiritual musings, and solemn civic spectacles celebrating "the most astonishing moment man has ever known." At 10:56:20 P.M. (EDT) on Sunday, July 20, the gray and ghostly form of astronaut Neil Armstrong floated the last few feet from lunar module to the moon itself. "That's one small step for man," he could be heard saying, "and one giant leap for mankind." Nineteen minutes later, Armstrong was joined by his co-pilot Edwin E. Aldrin, Jr. In the two hours and two minutes that followed, a second camera caught the astronauts planting an American flag in the lunar surface and collecting rock and soil samples from the Sea of Tranquility. A telephone call from President Richard Nixon congratulated the American team on making everyone on earth "truly one."

It had, of course, been the American television networks that brought the world closer by their extraordinary coverage of Apollo 11. The faultless lift-off from the lunar surface, the redocking with the command ship, and the picture-perfect splashdown on July 24, 950 miles southwest of Hawaii, were chronicled by Cronkite and his colleagues as a triumph of the human spirit. CBS News could now claim more Americans watched its space coverage than NBC and ABC combined. For the rest of his career, Cronkite would be asked about his plans to be the first journalist in space, a fitting follow-up to his broadcast performance on this story. On one occasion, then CBS News president Richard Salant said that Cronkite had earned that seat in space, "as long as it's in economy class." Cronkite's continuous seventeen-and-a-half hours of Apollo coverage set marks for endurance and joyous enthusiasm.

The 1960s had seen the assassination of one president and the ruining of another through the war in Vietnam. Civil strife tore at the nation's colleges, and race riots set fire to its cities. The 1970s would have their share of scandal and sad spectacle. But the moon landing seemed to suggest that a brighter future was still possible. That future would be captured and authenticated by television. The networks spent $11 million to cover the flight of Apollo 11, and when it was done, television news commanded a new place in American life. Communal experiences would now be mediated, with television simultaneously connecting communities within and across national boundaries as never before. *See also* Walter Cronkite.

Bruce J. Evensen

Further Reading
"Apollo 11: Moon Landing. First on the Moon," A documentary produced by the National Aeronautics and Space Administration (1969).
Armstrong, Neil, Michael Collins, Edwin E. Aldrin, Jr., Gene Farmer, and Jane Dora Hamblin. *First on the Moon.* Boston: Little, Brown, 1970.
Byrnes, Mark E. *Politics and Space: Image Making by NASA.* Westport: Praeger, 1994.
"Cronkite Remembers: The Space Program," A documentary written and hosted by Walter Cronkite, airing on the Arts and Entertainment Network (February 1997).
"Moon Landing," A CBS documentary airing in July 1989 commemorating the 20-year anniversary of network coverage of the Apollo 11 moon landing and *Moon Shot* and *Moon Walk*, NBC documentaries airing in July 1989 commemorating the 20-year anniversary of network coverage of the Apollo 11 moon landing.
Shepard, Alan, and Deke Slayton. *Moon Shot: The Inside Story of America's Race to the Moon.* Atlanta: Turner, 1994.

Edward Morgan

Edward P. Morgan was an incisive commentator on radio and television and a pioneer in news and news analysis for public television in the United States. He was equally at home in both the print and broadcast media. His forthrightness and analytical ability were widely praised and were recognized with Peabody, duPont-Columbia, Hillman, and George Polk Awards.

Born in Walla Walla, Washington, in 1910, Morgan was attracted to journalism by an uncle who was an editor at *Popular Mechanics* magazine. He started his career as an unpaid sports writer for the *Seattle Times* in 1932. For nine years, starting in 1934, he was a United Press correspondent, reporting from the West Coast, Hawaii, and Mexico. He reported for the *Chicago Daily News* during World War II and then became a foreign correspondent for *Collier's* magazine.

In 1951 he joined CBS, where he worked with Edward R. Murrow, becoming the network's director of radio and television news in 1954. From 1955 to 1975, he was a radio and then television news commentator for ABC, and from 1966 to 1975, he also wrote a column for the *Newsday* syndicate. ABC granted him a year's leave in 1967 to be the chief correspondent for the experimental Public Broadcasting Laboratory of National Educational Television, forerunner of the noncommercial Public Broadcasting Service (PBS).

Morgan did not hesitate to deliver stinging critiques when he saw the need for correctives, even in his own field of mass media. In his final radio commentary before going to the Public Broadcasting Laboratory, for example, he criticized use of contests by newspapers to attract and keep readers and the mediocrity of most television content, saying that sometimes commercials were superior to the programs they sponsored. A measure of the respect Morgan enjoyed was evident in the unfettered freedom he enjoyed as an ABC commentator. Neither the network nor his sponsor, the AFL-CIO, withdrew support even when he spoke disparagingly of broadcasting or about corruption in organized labor.

Morgan's professionalism was dramatically tested in 1956, when the luxury liners *Andrea Doria* and the *Stockholm* collided off Massachusetts. His only child, Linda, 14, was a passenger on the *Andrea Doria*. At first believing she had died, he did not reveal his intense personal concern to his listeners in many broadcasts during the 24 hours before he was informed that she had survived.

Morgan was a press panelist for one of the 1960 Nixon-Kennedy debates, and was teamed with Howard K. Smith for ABC television's coverage of the assassination of President Kennedy and for coverage of the 1964 elections. He died in McLean, Virginia, on January 27, 1993, at the age of 82.

Daniel W. Pfaff

Further Reading
Miall, Leonard. "Obituary: Edward Morgan." *The Independent,* 26 February 1993, 27.
Obituary. *New York Times,* 29 January 1993, A18.
Smith, Howard K. *Events Leading up to My Death.* New York: St. Martin's Press, 1996.

Erin Moriarty

Courtesy CBS News/*48 Hours*

Erin Moriarty grew up in Columbus, Ohio, and graduated cum laude from Ohio State University in 1974 with a bachelor's degree in behavioral sciences. She also earned a Juris Doctor degree from Ohio State University in 1977 and practiced law for two years. Moriarty moved into broadcast news in 1979, becoming the first *PM Magazine* host. She moved to Baltimore in 1980 to work as a consumer reporter for WJZ-TV, and in 1982, she was employed as a legal reporter at WJW-TV in Cleveland, Ohio.

In 1983, she moved to Chicago to begin working as the consumer reporter for the NBC's WMAQ-TV. In 1986, she became the consumer reporter for the *CBS Morning News*. In 1990, she moved briefly to the *CBS Evening News,* before being promoted to full-time correspondent for the prime-time magazine series *48 Hours*. Moriarty has won serval awards including the 1989 Outstanding Consumer Service Award and 11 national Emmys. *Pamela K. Doyle*

Further Reading

Rice, Lynette. "Network News Magazines: Competition Is King." *Broadcasting & Cable,* 4 November 1996, 29.
Zurawik, David, and Christina Stoehr. "Eclipsing the Nightly News." *American Journalism Review,* November 1994, 32–38.

Bill Moyers

Bill Moyers was born on June 5, 1934, in Hugo, Oklahoma, but he was raised in Marshall, Texas. While in high school, he worked as a reporter for Marshall's *News Messenger*. When he attended North Texas State University, now University of North Texas, he contributed to the student newspaper and worked in university information. Moyers was hired by Senator Lyndon B. Johnson in the summer of 1954, when Johnson was campaigning for reelection.

Moyers, instead of returning to North Texas State, transferred to the University of Texas at Austin. He majored in journalism and worked at KTBC-TV, which was owned by Lady Bird Johnson. Two years later he received his bachelor's degree in journalism, then he attended the University of Edinburgh. When he returned a year later, he attended the Southwestern Baptist Theological Seminary in Fort Worth, and he graduated in 1959. Moyers' interest in politics was rekindled several months later, and he spent months serving, first as Johnson's personal assistant, then special assistant, and finally his executive assistant. He helped coordinate Johnson's vice presidential campaign. When Johnson became vice president, Moyers resigned to become the associate director of public affairs for the Peace Corps.

When President Kennedy was assassinated, Moyers offered his services to President Johnson and subsequently became an adviser to the president on domestic affairs, the White House Chief of Staff, and the president's press secretary. In 1966, after he had grown disillusioned with Johnson's escalation of the war in Vietnam, Moyers resigned to return to journalism. Offered the publisher's position at *Newsday*, Moyers immediately recognized the influence and potential impact of his leadership at a large newspaper. Moyers strengthened the paper's Washington bureau. He hired Nicholas Thimmesch, Pete Hamill, Daniel P. Moynihan, and Saul Bellow. Moyers published news analyses, investigative articles, and feature stories.

When Harry Guggenheim sold the paper to the Times-Mirror Company, Moyers resigned and several weeks later traveled by bus across the

United States. His journey of some 13,000 miles was later recorded in his best-selling book, *Listening to America: A Traveler Rediscovers His Country*. The book was filled with visual descriptions of cities, towns, and individuals. Through conversations on various subjects—from the Kent State killings to the Vietnam War—Moyers captured the intense beliefs and the varied themes of American life.

In the 1970s, Moyers turned to broadcasting, first as a host of the public affairs program *This Week* for National Educational Television, then as the editor-in-chief of the *Bill Moyers' Journal*, which later became *Bill Moyers' Journal: International Report*. In addition, he contributed a "back-of-the-book" column to *Newsweek* for a year and anchored the Public Broadcasting Service program *USA: People and Politics*. Moyers' programs were intriguing. He interviewed writers, economists, historians, and other public figures; devoted shows to ideas and issues, including the Watergate scandal; and interviewed journalists and politicians from all over the world, primarily to gain perspectives on international issues.

In 1976, he was hired by CBS, where he served as editor and chief reporter of *CBS Reports* for three years. Moyers made numerous documentaries, including "The Fire Next Door," which examined arson in the Bronx, and "The Vanishing Family: Crisis in Black America," which examined the various cultural problems of African-American families. He focused specifically on the problem of black teenage pregnancy, a topic critics agreed few white men could examine objectively on a nationally televised forum without being accused of discrimination or racism. The program was commended for its attention to black fathers. Michael Novak called it one of the "bravest" documentaries ever made because it provided some gruesome and destructive statistics, but also addressed the issues of morals and family values, offering some hope.

Moyers returned to PBS in 1979, then went back to CBS two years later. He served as a commentator on the *CBS Evening News*. Concurrently, he produced documentaries for PBS, including the popular *Creativity* series. He left CBS in 1986,

when the news programs started to shift emphasis from hard news to entertainment. Moyers produced several lengthy popular series for PBS in the late 1980s and early 1990s, including "The Secret Government," which examined the Iran-Contra scandal; "A World of Ideas with Bill Moyers," which featured interviews with numerous philosophers; "Joseph Campbell and the Power of Myth"; and "Healing and the Mind." The content of these programs appears in books, and many are distributed in video format. For instance, *The Secret Government* and *Joseph Campbell and the Power of Myth* were published in 1988. *A World of Ideas: Conversations with Thoughtful Men and Women about American Life Today and the Ideas Shaping Our Future* was published in 1989 and contains 41 interviews from the series.

A year later, *Global Dumping Ground: The International Traffic in Hazardous Waste* was published. Like the report on PBS, this book made a strong case against the export of hazardous waste. However, as Moyers pointed out, exporting hazardous waste was a lucrative business and consequently difficult to stop. Furthermore, it was less expensive to ship toxic waste to another country than it was to dispose of it safely. In 1993, *Healing and the Mind* was published. Moyers interviewed health experts and examined health practices all over the world, both for the series and the book. His 1996 PBS series, *Genesis,* featured prominent authorities in several disciplines, discussing the *Bible.* The book *Genesis: A Living Conversation,* based on the series, was published the same year.

Edd Applegate

Further Reading

Bergreen, Lawrence. "The Moyers Style." *American Film,* February 1980, 53.

"Fifth Estater: A Class Act." *Broadcasting,* 19 November 1984, 95.

Katz, Jon. "Brooding, Pious and Popular: Bill Moyers is the Media's Pastor of Public Affairs." *St. Louis Post-Dispatch,* 25 March 1992, 78.

Novak, Michael. "The Content of Their Character." *National Review,* 28 February 1986, 47.

Ward, Geoffrey C. "Matters of Fact: Touring the Century with Bill Moyers." *American Heritage,* December 1983, 12–13.

MSNBC

NBC and Microsoft Corporation jointly announced MSNBC, a 24-hour television news service combined with an online site, on December 14, 1995. To help finalize the deal, Microsoft paid $220 million for half-ownership of *America's Talking*, an all-talk network subsidiary on NBC. In addition, each company pledged to devote another $200 million to MSNBC over the next five years. Microsoft Corporation's Bill Gates touted the effort as an unprecedented grouping of both television and online technology, designed to make the news more appealing. NBC pointed out that the viewer would be able to see a news story on *Dateline NBC*, then access related audio, video, and historical background from MSNBC Online.

Over the next six months, *America's Talking* studios in Fort Lee, New Jersey, were converted into an around-the-clock operation. On July 15, 1996, MSNBC began broadcasting to a potential 22 million households. Featured news accounts included the Olympics, virtual reality, Boris Yeltsin, and an extensive look at the American economy. Brian Williams moved from his White House correspondent's position to anchoring the prime-time *The News with Brian Williams*, and a host of other established NBC faces appeared—Tom Brokaw and Katie Couric among them. MSNBC Online included interactive versions of various subjects and also provided news menus that would allow the user to customize news, weather, and stock reports.

One of the more original programs offered was Jane Pauley's *Time and Again*. The program featured historical accounts, using NBC archival footage. For a story on the Vietnam War, the program featured 1966 footage of President Johnson addressing American soldiers in Vietnam.

Initial criticism of MSNBC focused on the online service. It was slow and sometimes unavailable. Some critics maintained that MSNBC Online failed to provide any relevant content concerning the TWA Flight 800 explosion, which happened just days after the service began. One user could only find two Flight 800 stories on the site, both dated, and one was a wire-service story. But within three days of the event, MSNBC was credited for the most comprehensive coverage of the story, which began 52 minutes after the crash and continued, with Brian Williams at the microphone, without commercial breaks until 1:30 A.M. Appointing Williams to that assignment was touted by NBC President Andrew Lack as proof that MSNBC would not be populated by "second stringers." By the November 1996 presidential election, the responsiveness of the online site had also improved. According to one reporter, the site had been bogged-down by net surfers through the early evening. But by 8:45 P.M. (EST), it was easily accessible and declaring Clinton the winner.

In April 1997, MSNBC studios moved from the Ft. Lee location to the former Jamesway Corporation Warehouse in Secaucus, New Jersey. The new studio—a 115,000-square-foot, fully digital facility—cost almost $65 million. The new facility housed television-related employees and also a contingent of Internet specialists, whereas a separate MSNBC Internet operation was housed at Microsoft's Redmond, Washington, headquarters. By the summer of 1997, MSNBC's stateside television audience penetration still hovered near the 22 million mark, but analysts predicted that it would increase to 35 million households by the year 2000. Expectations for a worldwide television reach were much rosier, with some experts forecasting 200 million homes through NBC special programming in Europe, Asia, and Latin America.

Burton St. John

Further Reading
Gunther, Marc. "The Cable Guy." *American Journalism Review,* January/February 1997, 43.
"MSNBC Blankets Big Story." *Broadcasting & Cable*, 22 July 1996, 35.
"Time Warner Picks MSNBC." *Broadcasting & Cable,* 23 September 1996, 12.

Roger Mudd

Roger Mudd, one of network television's leading Washington correspondents for more than 20 years, was known for his courtly style and tough interviewing methods. Highly respected for his intellectual depth and political expertise, he nonetheless was twice passed over for the top network anchor spot, first at CBS and later at NBC. He then went on to a new career in public and cable television.

Roger Mudd, host *History Alive* and *History Sunday*, the History Channel. Photo by Tess Steinkolk

Mudd was born in Washington, D.C., in 1928. After high school, he enlisted in the U.S. Army; World War II ended before he saw any fighting. He graduated from Washington and Lee University and went on to earn a master's degree in history from the University of North Carolina. He taught history at a preparatory school in Georgia for a year before landing his first journalism position at the *Richmond News Leader* in 1953. He later became a news editor at a Richmond radio station owned by the *Richmond News Leader,* and after this, he worked in radio and television in Washington. In 1961, he joined CBS News.

As a correspondent, Mudd gained a reputation as an astute observer of Capitol Hill, rising to become one of the network's leading reporters and eventually becoming a regular substitute for Walter Cronkite. He did exhaustive coverage of the passage of the Civil Rights Act of 1964, which was held up by a filibuster. In 1979, Mudd hosted a memorable *CBS Reports* special on Edward M. Kennedy, during which he asked the senator why he wanted to be president. Kennedy hesitated, and his bid for the Democratic Party nomination never materialized. When Cronkite retired in 1980, CBC executives considered Mudd for the anchor spot, but chose Dan Rather instead, so Mudd left CBS and joined rival NBC.

At NBC, he was paired with Tom Brokaw as co-anchors of the *NBC Nightly News*. But poor ratings led NBC to drop Mudd as co-anchor in 1983, and he assumed the title of senior political correspondent. While at NBC, he conducted another noteworthy interview with presidential candidate Gary Hart, asking him questions concerning the credibility of national political figures. Debate over Mudd's aggressive interviewing ensued. In 1987, Mudd left NBC and began contributing regular essays to *The MacNeil-Lehrer NewsHour* on PBS. He has hosted several PBS specials, including *Learning in America: Schools That Work*. Mudd returned to teaching in 1992, serving as a visiting professor at Princeton University and later at his alma mater, Washington and Lee University. In 1995, he began hosting the program, *History Alive*, on A&E's History Channel.

Mudd has won numerous television journalism awards. He also served on the board of the PEN/Faulkner Awards. *Ford Risley*

Further Reading

Gates, Gary Paul. *Air Time:The Inside Story of CBS News*. New York: Harper & Row, 1978.
Matusow, Barbara. *The Evening Stars: The Making of the Network News Anchor*. Boston: Houghton Mifflin, 1983.

Rupert Murdoch

One of the most successful and controversial figures in the business of modern television news, Rupert Murdoch is the chairman and chief executive officer of the Sydney, Australia-based News Corporation and owner of the Fox Network. A talented, shrewd, and highly successful entrepreneur, Murdoch's worldwide media enterprises include newspapers, interactive online services, books, magazines, films, videocassettes, and television (broadcast, cable, and satellite). A hallmark of his career has been the acquisition and linking of communication systems.

The son of Australian newspaper executive Sir Keith Murdoch and Dame Elisabeth Murdoch, Rupert Murdoch was born in Australia in 1930 and studied at Oxford's Worcester College. After graduating, he served a brief apprenticeship on Lord Beaverbrook's *Daily Express* in London, where he is said to have acquired his fascination with news—the business, content, and delivery of news—that would inspire his astounding and provocative rise to the position of a worldwide media magnate.

Murdoch's empire had its roots in the 1950s, when he acquired newspapers in Britain and Australia, where he purchased his father's newspaper, the tiny *Adelaide News*. Since then, he has left "footprints" of media ownership over two-thirds of the globe, today serving all continents but Africa. During the current era of concentrated ownership of media news outlets, News Corporation enjoys the greatest geographic reach of giant media firms. In 1997, Murdoch's media empire was valued at an estimated $12 billion.

In 1986, Murdoch succeeded, when no one thought it possible, in building a successful fourth American television network, the Fox Network. In 1995, Murdoch announced that Fox would be the first to offer presidential candidates free air time during prime time for the 1996 election, a significant contribution to the democratic process. In addition to helping Fox affiliates position themselves as strong competitors in the business of local television news, Murdoch introduced Fox National News, a 24-hour cable news venture, to rival CNN. In coming years, Fox is expected to lead the networks in transitioning to the new high-definition, digital transmission of signals. Murdoch has also made pioneering accomplishments in direct broadcast satellite (DBS) technology.

Some critics have warned that Murdoch's global imprint in television news thus far lacks depth in journalistic coverage. Previously, various Murdoch-owned news enterprises have been accused of sensationalism. Additional regulatory and ethical questions have focused on antitrust and conflict-of-interest issues because of the expanse of his holdings and his ownership of *TV Guide*. Murdoch intends to be a nonexclusive chairman of News Corporation, at least to age 80. His children manage succesful media enterprises, the two eldest running Murdoch-owned subsidiaries. No matter how many chapters of his life are written, Rupert Murdoch will retain his position as one of the most dynamic influences on the worldwide business of television news.   *Jeanne Marie Garon*

Further Reading

La Franco, Robert. "Rupert's on a Roll." *Forbes,* 6 July 1998, 182–188.
Shawcross, William. *Murdoch.* New York: Touchstone, 1994.

Edward R. Murrow

CBS Photo Archive

Edward R. Murrow was among the first reporters to broadcast news on an international basis and to demonstrate journalistic ethics in radio and television. His name is synonymous with courage and ethical behavior at a time when professional ethical practices and codes of conduct were first being discussed and developed in broadcasting.

Born Egbert Murrow in Polecat Creek, North Carolina, in 1908, Murrow spent most of his young life in the northwest corner of Washington state. It was during his teen years that he changed his name to Edward. He worked at logging camps and attended Washington State College (now Washington State University), now the home of the Edward R. Murrow School of Communication. There, he learned philosophy and something about character from a young speech instructor, Ida Lou Anderson, who taught him about good books and good music and gave him a deep sense of values. Murrow described her influence as appealing to his desire to achieve.

At Washington State, Murrow was active in drama and ROTC and was in the first class in broadcasting, a course in "radio speaking." He was also active in student politics and was elected to student body president during his senior year. Such political activity helped launch him into his professional path when he graduated in 1930. In his first job out of school, he served as the president of the National Student Federation Association (NSFA), with an office in New York City. From there, he went to the International Institute of Education, encouraging student exchange among the countries of the world.

In 1935, Murrow was hired by the Columbia Broadcasting System (CBS) as the network's director of Talks. This gave him the opportunity to use the medium of radio to bring information from different parts of the world about various cultural events. He was in this role when, in 1938, he found himself in Europe at the onset of events that lead to World War II. He reported from Vienna on Hitler's German-Austrian *Anschluss*. These events were critically important in the world scene, and Murrow's reports were compelling. With intriguing detail, he described the people and the mood in the air. His reports immediately captured the attention of those at CBS and listeners throughout the country.

As Hitler was moving his Third Reich to the west coast of Europe, Murrow based himself in London and reported on the war, usually from the basement of the BBC's Broadcast House. Each day his reports came across the Atlantic by shortwave radio, then were relayed across the United States on *CBS News*. They soon became America's link with the volatile situation in Europe. Murrow's dramatic introduction to his reports seemed to match the events themselves; he would begin by intoning, "This is London." Reports were not only of the war, but of the determination of the British people, the damage from German aircraft, and the horrors of war. When U.S. planes began bombing German sites, Murrow rode in a British bomber during a night raid, recording his experience. His words became ever more dramatic and full of images. on December 3, 1943, he described the incendiary bombs dropping from the bombers, for example, like white rice thrown on black velvet.

Near the end of the war, Murrow described the horrific sight of the Nazi concentration camps as the Allied troops first entered them. Although his descriptions were vivid and awful, they did not come close to the deep emotions he felt in covering the holocaust: "If I have offended you by this rather mild account of Buchenwald, I'm not the least bit sorry." After the war, he was named vice president in charge of news and public affairs of

CBS News, and with producer Fred Friendly, created a radio series entitled *Hear It Now*.

A short time later, television came along, and Murrow was among the first newsmen in the new medium. His radio program converted to television as *See It Now*. In 1952, he hosted a coast-to-coast live television program, where he noted how remarkable it was to see—live—first the Brooklyn Bridge on the east coast, then within the blink of an eye, the Golden Gate Bridge in San Francisco. *See It Now* earned historical fame for two programs. One followed the discharge from the Air Force of a young lieutenant, Milo Radulovich. He was regarded as a security risk because some of his family members were allegedly sympathetic to communist causes. These charges were either not true or so oblique as to be ridiculous. But this was the time of the Cold War and fears that communists were hiding everywhere. An episode of Murrow's *See It Now* discussed that fear and the unfair accusations against Radulovich, resulting in the restoration of his commission and reputation.

This all set the stage for what was to be perhaps Murrow's most famous program, an investigation of the tactics of the junior senator from Wisconsin, Joseph R. McCarthy. The program used mostly the senator's own words from his hearings and from his speeches. The results were that his tactics and demagoguery were apparent. Murrow concluded the program by appealing to patriotic reasons why Americans needed to defend freedom—both abroad—and at home.

The public reaction to the program was enthusiastic. McCarthy was allowed to reply on CBS, but the only things to refute were McCarthy's own words. McCarthy's rebuttal only deepened public perception of the truths that Murrow had put forth. Murrow's work took on new dimensions with his project *Person to Person*. This was an interview program focusing on the personalities of the rich and famous, such persons as the U.S. senator John F. Kennedy and his wife, Jacqueline; artist Grandma Moses; Marilyn Monroe; and even Harpo Marx.

At the 1958 convention of the Radio-Television News Directors' Association, Murrow condemned the growing practice of broadcast news becoming decadent, escapist, and insular from the realities of the world in which they live. While not all news practitioners appreciated his candor, others saw it as another mark of courage for a figure who had established new definitions of what courage meant.

Murrow continued with CBS through 1960. Toward the end of his career, Murrow, with Fred Friendly, produced other powerful documentaries in the *CBS Reports* series, the most noteworthy being "Harvest of Shame." This documentary revealed the plight of the migrant farm workers, their squalid living conditions, travel conditions, and pitiful wages. The program's on-site producer, David Lowe, also showed how the children of migrant farm workers were cared for and educated. In one segment, southern blacks were shown jumping onto a flatbed truck, after being hired to go pick cotton for a meager day's wage. "We used to own our slaves," Murrow narrated. "Now we just rent them." He concluded the program by reminding viewers that while the workers themselves could not effect legislation, those viewing the documentary could. Protective legislation for migrant farm workers was enacted soon after.

In 1961, newly elected President John F. Kennedy asked Murrow to serve in his administration as director of the U.S. Information Agency. Murrow obliged, often finding himself on the opposite side of the reporting process. He stayed in that position until cancer forced his resignation in 1963, shortly after Kennedy's assassination.

During his life, Murrow achieved both professional and patriotic awards, including the Medal of Freedom, the country's highest civilian honor. For his contributions to England, Queen Elizabeth knighted him. Murrow died on April 17, 1965, two days after his 57th birthday, and perhaps not coincidentally, about the same time that the "golden age of television" had begun to fade. Murrow is remembered as the first broadcast journalist to have a U.S. postage stamp issued in his memory. The first day of issue ceremony for the stamp took place at the Edward R. Murrow School of Communication at his alma mater, Washington State University. *See also* Fred W. Friendly.

Val E. Limburg

Further Reading

Bliss, Edward, Jr. *In Search of Light: The Broadcasts of Edward R. Murrow.* New York: Alfred Knopf, 1967.

Cloud, Stanley, and Lynne Olson. *The Murrow Boys.* Boston: Houghton Mifflin, 1996.

Kendrick, Alexander. *Prime Time: The Life of Edward R. Murrow.* Boston: Little, Brown, 1969.

Persico, Joseph. *Edward R. Murrow: An American Original.* New York: McGraw Hill, 1988.

Sperber, Anne M. *Murrow: His Life and Times.* New York: Freundlich, 1986.

Lisa Myers

Born in Joplin, Missouri, Lisa Myers graduated from the University of Missouri School of Journalism and attended the Georgetown University Institute on Comparative Political and Economic Systems. In the spring of 1973, she joined the staff of the Bureau of National Affairs (BNA), which compiles specialized political issue newsletters for select clientele. The work led her to investigate congressional travel activities. She sold articles resulting from these investigations to the *Chicago Tribune,* the *Washington Post*, and the *Washington Herald.*

In 1976, she left the BNA for Chicago, where she continued writing newspaper stories on politics and economics before accepting a position in 1979 at the *Washington Star* where she became a White House correspondent. In August of 1981, the *Washington Star* folded, and Myers was hired as general assignment reporter for NBC. Since then, she has covered political campaigns, becoming the chief congressional correspondent while also appearing as a panelist on *Meet the Press.*

Myers received a 1990 Headliner Award, a 1988 Clarion Award from the Women in Communications, and a 1985 Humanitas Award for her work on the *NBC News Special Report* "Women, Work and Babies: Can America Cope?" She has been honored on two different occasions with an annual award from American Women in Radio and Television.

Pamela K. Doyle

Further Reading

Ginsberg, Gary."The Torch's Past." *George,* October 1997, 52.

"Highlighting the Year's Worst Reporting." *Indianapolis Business Journal,* 2 January 1995, 6B.

Stein, Harry."Introducing the Harry's for TV Class Acts of '93." *TV Guide,* 1 January 1994, 39.

N

National Academy of Television Arts and Sciences (NATAS)

The National Academy of Television Arts and Sciences (NATAS) is more than Emmy Awards. Seventeen different chapters across the United States and an international council administer awards and organize a multitude of events. The 17 chapters cover 97 percent of the United States. Each chapter conducts its own regional awards program. The Emmy statue, recognized as the worldwide standard in television excellence, may be the most sought-after award among industry professionals. NATAS serves the international arena through its headquarters in New York. The International Council presents awards for achievement in television around the world.

NATAS is unique among professional organizations because of its breadth of associate groups in the industry—members include writers, directors, actors, engineers, craftspeople, and executives. Professionals from a variety of backgrounds intermingle to share views that serve to strengthen the industry. The primary focus of the organization is to raise standards. To that end, the awarding of Emmys, the coveted golden statue, is served by all members. Each person casting a vote for a selected award has seen and compared every nominee for that honor. The national Emmys are presented in five categories: Daytime, Sports, Scientific and Technical Achievement, Community Service, and

News and Documentary. To be eligible, an entry must be able to be seen by 51 percent or more of the nation.

The Emmy is a golden statue that stands 15 inches tall and weighs four-and-a-half pounds. The name is a variation of "Immy," a term used for early image orthocon camera tubes. The statue was originally nicknamed the "Ike," but that name was never used publicly in deference to President Dwight "Ike" Eisenhower. The statue depicts a winged woman holding up the universal emblem of the electron above a globe circled with the words: National Academy of Television Arts and Sciences. NATAS was born in 1955, at a luncheon arranged by Ed Sullivan and attended by 50 leaders in television. The organizers were concerned about television's future. One of the missions of the organization was to ensure the highest standards as television evolved. Within two weeks of the initial meeting on November 15, 1955, the organization doubled in size to become the "Committee of 100." This group committed itself to establishing a National Television Academy.

Today, NATAS sponsors programs for people in the industry, presents the annual Emmy Awards to recognize individual achievements in television, and publishes *Emmy* magazine. Affiliate chapters recognize excellence by awarding regional Emmys. The Television Academy Foundation was established as a companion organization. It is responsible for the College Television Awards, internship programs, a faculty seminar, and maintenance of both the Television Archives at the University of California at Los Angeles and the Foundation Library at the University of Southern California.   *Elizabeth J. Leebron*

Further Reading

Averson, R. *Electronic Drama: Television Plays of the Sixties.* Boston: Beacon Press, 1971.
National Academy of Television Arts and Sciences. *Emmy's Twentieth Anniversary Album.* New York: NATAS, 1968.
Orlik, Peter B. *The Electronic Media.* Boston: Allyn and Bacon, 1992.

National Association of Broadcasters

The National Association of Broadcasters (NAB) focuses on the governmental, legal, and technological issues in broadcasting in order to help members of the industry operate more successfully. It has been a central resource for the broadcasting business since its inception in 1923. In 1997, NAB had approximately 7,500 members.

NAB represents the interests of broadcasters to Congress and federal regulators. It provides practical support for members of the industry, including seminars and expositions, as well as publications that inform members of up-to-date issues and business strategies. NAB also sponsors its own industry research and development programs.

The specific services of NAB extend to all areas of the broadcast industry. For example, NAB has confronted programming issues faced by broadcasters by developing a set of voluntary principles to address children's television, indecency, violence, and drug and substance abuse depicted in broadcast programming. It aids the operation of television and radio stations by instructing station managers in the latest research techniques. For example, NAB has assisted managers in developing in-house audience research departments and has initiated development of related computer programs. The NAB reference library offers books, periodicals, clippings, monographs, and archival material about broadcasting. NAB sponsors awards to promote excellence in all facets of the industry and maintains the Broadcasting Hall of

Fame. NAB also offers employment services, including minority placement.

The National Association of Broadcasters is divided into three departments. The Television Department and the Radio Department concentrate on the concerns of their own segment of the broadcast industry. The Science and Technology Department deals with the concerns of broadcast engineers, particularly in terms of the future development of broadcast technology.

The NAB Television Department represents 85 percent of all network-owned and affiliated television stations, as well as 40 percent of all independent and public stations in the United States. The department aids television broadcasters by organizing task forces and expert committees to help examine and advise on challenging issues such as children's programming and adapting electronic technologies. It also conducts specialized programs and seminars, including the Annual NAB Television Management Conference, and informs members of the latest issues in the industry through *TV Today*, a weekly newsletter, and *Telejournal*, a monthly closed-circuit, satellite-fed program.

The Science and Technology Department produces several NAB publications, including *TechCheck*, a weekly faxed newsletter, and the *NAB Engineering Handbook*, a comprehensive reference book. Both publications deal with technical issues of interest to broadcast engineers. In addition, the NAB Science and Technology Department is involved in various efforts aimed at developing future broadcast systems, including the National Radio Systems Committee (NRSC), Digital Audio Broadcasting (DAB) Subcommittee, High-Speed FM Subcarrier Subcommittee, Radio Broadcast Data System (RBDS) Subcommittee, and National Data Broadcasting Committee (NDBC).   *Elizabeth J. Leebron*

Further Reading

Dominick, Joseph R. *The Dynamics of Communication.* New York: McGraw-Hill, 1996.
National Association of Broadcasters Home Page. <http://www.nab.org>.
Sherman, Barry L. *Telecommunications Management: Broadcasting, Cable and New Technologies.* New York: McGraw-Hill, 1995.

National News Council

The National News Council began during the Nixon-era attacks on the media and gave the public a way to complain about press performance without having to resort to lawsuits. The News Council sought to increase the credibility of journalism and reduce libel suits. Upon receiving a complaint, the council's staff decided whether it fell within the council's authority and warranted a hearing. Before a scheduled hearing, the council's staff tried to get the contesting parties together to resolve their differences. If that process failed, the council met to hear the charge and the news organization's response, and after deliberation, a ruling was issued. The council depended on publicity to satisfy complainants. The parties signed waivers of subsequent libel actions and agreed not use information generated by the News Council in lawsuits.

The News Council was founded in 1973 with grants from the Twentieth Century Fund, the Markle Foundation, and other major foundations. Unfortunately for the News Council, many major news outlets, including networks, failed to cooperate. They refused the necessary publicity and support. The first chairs were former judges Roger Traynor and Stanley Fuld. Within two years, the council had the support of 30 news organizations and began publishing decisions in journalism publications. Former newspaper editor Norman Isaacs became the first news professional to serve as chairman in 1977. When Isaacs retired in December 1982, he was succeeded by Lucy Wilson Benson, former president of the League of Women Voters, and Edward Barrett, former *Newsweek* editor and founder of *Columbia Journalism Review*. In May 1983, former CBS president Richard Salant took over.

About a quarter of the 242 complaints the council heard in formal actions involved television or other broadcast reports. The council heard, for example, a complaint against "An Unauthorized History of the NFL," a 1983 *Frontline* documentary questioning whether the National Football League adequately protected the game against gamblers' influence. The council often ruled in favor of broadcasters. A national gay rights group charged that an ABC *20/20* report exaggerated the dangers to gay men of contracting AIDS. The council issued an opinion on December 1, 1983, finding the complaint unwarranted, given the uncertainty about AIDS at that time. The News Council also published pamphlets, including *An Open Press,* about accountability. The News Council decided to dissolve itself in February 1984, because of lack of funds and lack of media support.   *William E. Huntzicker*

Further Reading

Brogan, Patrick. *Spiked: The Short Life and Death of the National News Council.* New York: Priority Press Publications, 1985.
Dooley, Patricia L., David Klaassen, and Richard Chapman. *A Guide to the Archives of the National News Council.* Minneapolis: University of Minnesota Silha Center for the Study of Media Ethics and Law, 1986.
In the Public Interest—1973–75, In the Public Interest—II 1975–1978, and *In the Public Interest—III 1979–1983,* Reports from the National News Council. New York: National News Council, 1975, 1979 and 1984; *Supplement to In the Public Interest III.* Minneapolis: University of Minnesota Silha Center for the Study of Media Ethics and Law, 1983.

NBC News

The first big news out of NBC was its own epochal premiere on radio, beamed from New York's Waldorf Astoria Hotel on November 15, 1926. But not until compelling events like Charles Lindbergh's 1927 transatlantic flight did the network begin making wide journalistic impact. The network in 1928 gave major coverage to the presidential race and took credit for bringing millions of voters to the polls. That year, what was to become New York's WNBC-TV was set up experimentally by RCA. Television was developing; few Americans had home sets even a decade later, when NBC pioneered regular TV broadcasting. It won the first television license in time to cover the 1940 Republican National Convention. Before World War II, NBC controlled two radio networks, nicknamed the Red and the Blue. The government in 1941 ordered the company to divest one, so it sold the Blue. The war permitted unprecedented news effort. Covering the 1944 D-Day invasion, NBC pre-empted entertainment for many hours, and its correspondents claimed the first eyewitness interview from Normandy beaches.

Political coverage, along with the "space race," brought the network prominence throughout broadcasting's mid-century period. Reuven Frank, groundbreaking producer and twice NBC News president, identifies the political conventions of 1948 as the starting place of television news. Chet Huntley and David Brinkley made their debut as co-anchors at the 1956 Democratic convention. NBC broadcast post-Sputnik rocket launches from Cape Canaveral, and the assassination of President Kennedy spurred all three networks into marathon specials in 1963.

As at all networks, the archetypal reporter at NBC evolved over time. Most early broadcast journalists had newspaper or wire-service experience and were prized for their accuracy, thoroughness, and insight. Some who performed solidly in radio did not survive the move to television; in 1965, NBC President Robert Kintner suggested appearance and visual acceptability were criteria for success. Kintner exemplified the wide range of corporate leaders under whom NBC's journalists would serve. Later bosses might pinch pennies, dilute standards, and sneer at tradition, but not Kintner: A demanding and cantankerous news hound, he spent big money on stories and fostered specials that squeezed out prime-time programs—a concept which would become anathema to later executives. His news-division head, Bill McAndrews, inspired the division's troops.

Major events, including the tumultuous 1968 Democratic convention in Chicago and Neil Armstrong's 1969 walk on the moon, as well as a war in Asia that seemed to be worsening nightly, ratcheted up an appetite for television news. Vietnam brought tension and complexity to TV news decision making. Distinguished author and critic Edwin Diamond credited NBC for its singularly fine performance when the network gave major play to The Pentagon Papers, documents revealing secret war plans.

As broadcasting expanded in the 1960s and early 1970s, networks sharpened their images. CBS, nurturing the Edward R. Murrow legacy and showcasing Walter Cronkite, was seen as hard hitting, generally dominating national ratings. Late-comer ABC remained in the rear, wagering its future on hungry correspondents and a mix of talent. NBC had no Murrow-lit past but did have strong producers effectively using film; the network was spending heavily on foreign news and giving correspondents time to develop stories.

Marketplace and management changes began shaking NBC in the post-Vietnam 1970s. Chet Huntley was gone; the son of founder David Sarnoff was ousted as RCA board chairman; ABC news emerged as a contender. The "Peacock Network" envied the success of *60 Minutes* and had begun to launch magazine programs, most of them doomed—because of failure to give them time to find an audience. A lively and unique NBC News program, *Weekend,* stood out but lasted less than four years. Meanwhile, parent corporation RCA diversified, and its managers focused new financial scrutiny on news. Winning now seemed more important than playing nobly; old ways were pushed out. Network television journalism's days as a public-spirited loss leader were waning.

NBC leadership kept changing hands as profit demands grew, and patience with slow-growing programs diminished. For example, *NBC News Overnight* arrived in 1982; it was a wee-hours concoction of offbeat reporting, skillful writing, and sassy anchoring by Lloyd Dobyns and Linda Ellerbee. Its audience was ferociously loyal but too small to please accountants, and the show expired. The 1980s and 1990s brought massive change. NBC's David Brinkley jumped ship, reportedly alienated by transitional management, and other veterans were terminated or marginalized. Corporations with limited journalistic traditions started acquiring major broadcasters. Radio news began losing audiences to "talk radio" and diminished in importance.

Generally, NBC did make lots of money—one reason that in late 1985, General Electric was moved to buy RCA, and with it, the network. Budget cuts and downsizing followed; technicians went on strike but lost more than they gained. Overseas bureaus were closed, and fewer news crews ranged across America; local affiliates' videotape filled gaps. Journalistic judgment appeared to weaken during this period.

In 1992, *Dateline NBC* used small, hidden rockets to enhance a demonstration of fire hazards in General Motors pickup trucks, but neglected to tell viewers. GM exposed these tactics, NBC News was disgraced, and its president left. In the mid-1990s, ratings for *NBC Nightly News* edged past those of now-strong ABC; *Dateline NBC* flourished; and the *Today* show, always a strong news vehicle, was riding high through its fifth decade. Network news audiences shrank as alternative information sources proliferated, but NBC effectively scrambled for a future niche. In the mid-1990s, it joined with Microsoft to establish MSNBC, which delivered news to an embryonic audience on the Internet. *See also* David Brinkley, Tom Brokaw, Chet Huntley.   *James Upshaw*

Further Reading

Campbell, Robert. *The Golden Years of Broadcasting: A Celebration of the First 50 Years of Radio and TV on NBC.* New York: Scribner, 1976.

Kintner, Robert. *Broadcasting and the News.* New York: Harper & Row, 1965.

National Broadcasting Company, Inc. *32 Hours a Day! Every Day in the Year, Each of Two Great Coast-to-Coast Networks—NBC Blue and NBC Red—Fill 17 ½ Hours.* New York: NBC, 1937.

New Technology

By its very nature, television news is intertwined with technology. From the earliest development of the medium, to the switch from film to videotape, and electronic news gathering, television news has always relied upon innovation, thus symbolizing technological advancements in the 20th century.

The development of satellite technology, miniaturized news-gathering equipment, and portable microwave transmission systems have provided television with perhaps its greatest competitive advantage—stations and networks can broadcast from the scene of a story almost instantaneously. The executive director of NBC News, David Verdi, says advanced communication technologies provide the capability to air live pictures within five minutes of an event happening anywhere in the nation. The same technology also expands the potential for immediate coverage of news occurring around the globe. When a large group of hostages was taken captive at an embassy in Peru, technol-

ogy enabled NBC to go live, with a reporter at the scene, within hours.

Communication technology has also added to the portability of television news. News crews go aloft to cover traffic and to show viewers pictures of special events or breaking stories such as fires, police chases, and flooding. The use of helicopters by television stations has become commonplace in the top-50 markets, even at a lease cost of up to $200,000 per year for an aircraft outfitted with state-of-the-art equipment. The price will continue to escalate as stations use increasingly sophisticated technology. A new helicopter that KNBC in Los Angeles leased includes a nose-mounted, remote-controlled, gyrostabilized camera system; internal cameras to photograph on-air reporters; a mini-control room with M2 and Beta tape decks; a microwave transmission system; and a computerized system that uses aviation, forest, and street maps with Global Positioning Satellites to pinpoint the location of stories to within 10 feet.

Technology plays a central role in the daily operations of television newsrooms. Software applications like Newstar, Basys, and AP Newscenter allow newsroom personnel to write, edit, and file stories, facilitate production of newscasts with show rundowns, and link scripts with character generators and teleprompters—all in a single, integrated computer system. Beyond computerization, wireless technology, including voice and pager systems, allows for communication between newsroom and field crews. Many news operations now also use e-mail to keep personnel and satellite offices coordinated. The vice president of the MSNBC cable network, Mark Harrington, says they use developing computer networks to maintain open communications between NBC News bureaus around the globe and affiliate stations around the nation. Harrington believes the editorial process is enhanced because of this unique interaction between groups of journalists.

Increasingly, reporters are relying on the developing computer-mediated communication technology as a resource for gathering background information, statistics, government documents, and other data. The Internet provides a bountiful array of information sources that reporters often access directly from their desks or from a designated "net" station located in the newsroom. To assist in using the Internet as a tool, the *Columbia Journalism Review* has a Web page with resource tools that are of special interest to reporters <http://www.cjr. columbia.edu/sources.html>.

Developing technologies also create more outlets for news and more opportunities to air coverage. Satellite technology, the subsequent advance of cable television, and increased channel capacity cleared the way for the creation of 24-hour news channels, including both CNN and CNN Headline, other information providers like C-SPAN and CNBC, and news operations like Fox and MSNBC.

The irony is that as technology provides the opportunity for more television news outlets, it appears that fewer individuals are watching. In the early 1980s, the evening newscasts of the major networks were watched in a total of more than 40 percent of all American homes. By the middle 1990s, that number had fallen to about 25 percent, with the additional cable news channels not making up the difference. The result was a smaller news audience divided into more pieces.

The fragmentation of the audience facilitated by developing technology is further exacerbated by the changing nature of some of the newer outlets catering to specialized interests. For example, CNBC particularly targets those interested in financial news, while Washington watchers keep closely tuned to C-SPAN. Given the fragmentation of the audience and the increasing abundance of available options, it is no surprise that competition is fiercer than ever, with networks and stations spending heavily on technology and promotion to boost viewership.

The future promises more innovation for newsrooms and perhaps new forms of interaction with viewers. Some researchers and news organizations are experimenting with 360-degree digital panorama cameras and interactive networking technology that would give viewers the ability to select the angle and field of vision from which they want to observe an event or breaking news story. Developing interactive technology also provides the potential for immediate polling of viewers and prompt feedback on content.

The rapidly expanding digital information environment, however, also means television news organizations could be competing directly with traditional print news outlets. Already, the World Wide Web is the home to a multitude of news sites that are operated not only by television networks and stations but also by magazines, newspapers, radio stations, and wire services. Many of the sites operated by traditional print journalism organizations include audio and video, blurring the traditional boundaries between the media.

While developing computer network technology removes the time limits that television journalists must face on a daily basis, the competitive ramifications for all news-gathering organizations are daunting. While technology helps to create a more mobile, immediate, interactive television news product, it also fosters more competition and audience fragmentation. This could result in the elimination of some print and electronic news-gathering organizations. *Stuart L. Esrock*

Further Reading

Dickson, G. "KNBC Cruises L.A. Skies with New Bird." *Broadcasting & Cable,* 3 February 1997, 79–80.

Fulton, K. "A Tour of Our Uncertain Future." *The Columbia Journalism Review* On-Line, Available: <http://www.cjr.columbia.edu/kfulton/contents.html>.

Edwin Newman

A journalist and cultural critic best known for his wit and sardonic humor, Edwin Newman has spent his career in a variety of roles in Europe and the United States. He was born on January 25, 1919 in New York City. He received a bachelor of arts degree in political science from the University of Wisconsin–Madison and also studied for one semester at Louisiana State University in Baton Rouge. He began his journalism career in 1941 with the Washington Bureau International News Service and in a short time moved to United Press (UP). He worked as an assistant to Eric Sevareid in the Washington bureau of CBS from 1947 to 1949. For a while, his career was centered in Europe. From 1949 to 1951 he worked as a free-lance writer and broadcaster in London. In 1951, Newman worked for the European Recovery Plan (the Marshall Plan).

In 1952, Newman joined NBC and served as a bureau chief in London in 1956, Rome in 1957, and Paris from 1958 until 1961. He returned briefly to the United States to cover the 1960 political conventions and then moved back permanently in 1961 and took over as the summer replacement for Chet Huntley on the weekly *This Is NBC News.* He served as an NBC News commentator until 1983. His numerous assignments included moderating the 1976 Ford-Carter presidential debate and narrating numerous television specials including "Pensions—The Broken Promise" in 1972 and "Violence in America" in 1977. He was also the narrator and interviewer on an NBC special about Nikita Khrushchev.

Newman served as the drama critic for WNBC-TV from 1965 to 1971, giving capsule reviews of Broadway plays. In a rather well-known feud, producer David Merrick barred Newman from all of his productions after he panned a Merrick play. NBC gave Newman its support, and he eventually was named critic-at-large for NBC and reviewed musical performances and films, as well as performers.

Newman's work has earned him seven Emmys, a Peabody Award (in 1966), an Overseas Press Club Award (in 1961), and a Headliner's Award (in 1967), and he is a decorated chevalier of the French Foreign Legion. In 1966, he served as president of the Association of Radio-Television News Artists (ARTNA). The School of Journalism of the University of Wisconsin presented him with a special honor in 1967.

Newman became well known as a writer who advocated precise English to promote organized thought, but who also could be humorous about the misuse of language. He is author of several books, including *Strictly Speaking: Will America Be the Death of English* (1974), *A Civil Tongue* (1976), *Sunday Punch* (1979), and *I Must Say: On English, the New and Other Matters* (1988). His articles have been published in *Esquire, Atlantic Monthly, Harper's, New York Times Magazine, Opera News,* and several British publications. In addition to his journalism assignments, he has also

appeared as himself on entertainment programs such as *Murphy Brown* and *Saturday Night Live*. He also anchors USA Cable's Saturday evening series *Weekly World News*, emphasizing many fictitious, humorous, tabloid-style events.

Mary E. Beadle

Further Reading

King, Susan. "Have Aliens Taken over Edwin Newman's Brain?" *St. Louis Post Dispatch*, 23 March 1996, D6.

Newman, Ewin. "Some Thoughts about the News Business. *Television Quarterly*, Summer 1983, 33–36.

"Newman-at-Large." *Newsweek*, 26 June 1967, 79.

News Directors

In the early days of television, a news director often doubled as an anchorperson and staff supervisor while programming a half hour of news per day. Today, only in the smallest markets might anchoring be part of the director's job. The staff may number 50 or more in a medium-sized market and be responsible for four to seven hours of news programming per day. Even medium-market news departments have multi-million dollar budgets. Through the 1960s and even the 1970s, the news director may not have been expected to run a profitable department. Since the 1980s, a profitable news operation has been normal. In the 1960s, most markets had three network affiliates competing for audience. Today there may be six more players in the race for dominance.

And the challenges listed above do not address the information-gathering decisions that news directors must make today. Satellite technology means the local news team can present reports from around the world. Local news departments routinely send a reporter or anchor to provide live coverage of a disaster hundreds of miles away. Or, if they do not send their own representative, they often will have a live report from an affiliate's reporter.

One of the toughest challenges news directors face is the struggle to attract and maintain viewers, especially young ones. A Pew Center poll in 1996 stated that 59 percent of the people surveyed had watched a newscast the day before; a few years earlier that figure had been 74 percent. Surveys also showed that viewers were increasingly uninterested in news about public affairs. Coverage of school board meetings and city hall meetings was not routine in the 1980s and 1990s. Instead, many news directors filled expanded program hours with increased coverage of crime and features of the "news-you-can-use" vein. And many minutes of today's newscasts are filled with teasers of upcoming stories.

With today's large staffs and competitive pressures, news directors spend far more time with management duties than in editorial work. Assistant news directors and executive producers generally run the news department, though many news directors like to take part in planning meetings if time allows. The news director, working with the general manager and often with news consultants, sets the long-term plan for the news operation and hires key people. News directors have historically been appointed by and report to a station's general manager. Some groups of stations have news executives who have some authority over the local news directors. A news director's career path often includes several years as a news producer, then promotion to an executive producer or assistant news director. Like others in broadcasting, news executives often move to larger markets as they get more experience.

A good relationship between the news director and general manager is vital to the news director's success and tenure. The average tenure of a news director in 1990 was two-and-a-half years, according to a Radio-Television News Director Association (RTNDA) survey. If a news employee works for the same station for many years, he or she is likely to have worked for perhaps a half dozen news directors. There are few news directors who have long tenures (spending 20 or more years with one station or group). News directors since the late 1970s have increasingly relied on news consultants for advice on how to improve their positions with the viewing audience. When news consultants first became active, they were greeted with disdain in many newsrooms, but today's news director probably has spent his or her entire career in a consultant-influenced newsroom

and is better able to decide when to use the advice and when to reject it. Nowadays many former news directors become news consultants, and it is not unusual for individuals to go back and forth between the two roles.

Before the late 1960s, news directors generally hired and supervised entirely white male professional staffs. Women entered the profession in force throughout the 1970s, and by the 1980s, several became news directors. By the mid-1990s, according to research by the RTNDA, 17 percent of the nation's news bosses were women. Minorities were being hired in American newsrooms in the late 1960s as well, but by 1995, their ranks among news directors had grown to only 9 percent. Minorities held 19 percent of all television news jobs.

Since women make up more than one-third of the television news work force and outnumber men two-to-one in production roles, the question arises why more of them have not become news directors. Women hold almost half of local television's executive producer positions, but they are behind men as assistant news directors. Some argue that women choose not to aspire to top management due in large part to family responsibilities. Others argue that general managers still like to hire people who look like themselves.

A successful news director in a large market can command an excellent salary. In the top five markets, news directors can make a quarter of a million dollars a year, including bonuses and incentives. Many news director salaries are now tied to profit-margin incentives. According to a 1996 RTNDA survey, the median salary for a news director in a top-25 market was $107,500; in markets 26 through 50, the median salary was $80,000 in 1996. In recent years, many news directors have capped their careers with a position in general management. This results not only from the managerial and accounting skills news directors develop, but from the news department's increasing importance to the station's image and bottom-line, and from the increasing emphasis on marketing and promotion.
Marjorie Fox

Further Reading
Frankola, Karen. "Who Uses Consultants and Why?" *RTNDA Communicator,* August 1990, 12.

Papper, Bob, Michael Gerhard, and Andrew Sharma. "More Women and Minorities in Broadcast News." *RTNDA Communicator,* August 1996, 8.

Prato, Lou. "The Business of Broadcasting: Not So Merry-Go-Round of TV News Directors." *Washington Journalism Review,* October 1990, 21.

Newseum

The Newseum is the first of its kind—a $50 million, 72,000-square-foot, state-of-the-art news museum located in Arlington, Virginia. The Newseum, developed by The Freedom Forum and open to the public, is the world's only interactive museum of news. It contains a one-block long video news wall, two stories high, displaying newscasts of 170 video news sources from around the world. It provides visitors with images of prominent reporters such as Edward R. Murrow and Helen Thomas. Also on display are the first studio color cameras used to broadcast the *CBS Evening News* with Walter Cronkite and Peter Arnett's CNN microphone from his coverage of the Persian Gulf War. Archival audio reports on CD-ROM are also available.

The Newseum provides an interactive approach that allows visitors to create their own newscasts and even perform in anchor roles. Budding anchors can work in a co-anchor format, and after a single rehearsal, more ambitious participants are allowed to go on camera (complete with TelePrompTer) for a 45-second news report from a location of their choice. Another feature permits visitors to broadcast radio commentary (from a glassed-enclosed, sound-proof broadcast booth) as a supplement to a sporting event. Tapes of these events are available for purchase from the Newseum store.

Visitors may participate in video games that simulate coverage of real-life events with reporters and editors calling the shots and testing visitors' decisions in a variety of different circumstances. An Ethics Center demonstrates the choices editors must make regarding ethical issues, such as confidentiality of sources or alteration of news material for effect. The goal in each case is to have visitors gain a better understanding of the process and importance of information gathering in a free society. The facility is, therefore, regarded by its founders

as an ongoing educational project which will provide a better and more realistic perspective of our First Amendment freedoms, as well as opportunities for free expression.

One exhibit allows visitors to use video touch-screen technology to hear major television news figures, such as Roger Mudd and Mike Wallace, discuss their work. An indoor attraction with an outdoor exhibit entitled Freedom Park contains a glass and steel memorial dedicated to journalists who lost their lives while reporting. Created by the design firm of Ralph Appelbaum Associates, the Newseum has galleries devoted to the history of news, a domed theater, and the "News Byte Cafe"—complete with computer terminals and access to online news services. In the future, national and local programs will emanate from the location, with participants available to discuss their work.   *Michael D. Murray*

Further Reading
Flander, Judy. "Spotlight on Media at Newseum." *Communicator*, April 1997,12.

Streitmatter, Rodger. "Journalism History Goes Interactive at the Newseum." *American Jounalism,* Winter 1997, 92–96.

Newsmagazines

In the early 1960s, *David Brinkley's Journal* broadcast news stories in a combination magazine/documentary format. But the development of the current television newsmagazine can be directly traced to the September 1968 arrival of CBS's *60 Minutes,* devoted to covering three or more subjects. Before that, *See It Now*, *The 20th Century,* and *NBC Reports* tended to investigate one significant issue at length, sometimes extending beyond a one-hour block.

60 Minutes established the newsmagazine style and tone in its very first episode by opening with the image of a moving stopwatch. By 1975, the series moved into prime time on Sunday, and by 1979, it took the number one spot in the television ratings. The show became a consistent top 10 Nielsen performer. Before its domination, *60 Minutes* faced competition from both ABC and NBC, as these networks developed their own newsmagazines. Four months into *60 Minutes*, NBC unveiled *First Tuesday*. The show aired from 1969 to 1973 and was hosted by Sander Vanocur. Each program normally ran for two hours and carried up to eight story segments. *First Tuesday* stories varied widely. It was not unusual to see stories ranging from the occult to baton twirling.

Shortly after the demise of *First Tuesday*, NBC News executive Reuven Frank unveiled another news program that emphasized what he termed "movement" and little talk. The show was *Weekend*, which started as a 90-minute program in the late evening and had news segments mixed with lighter fare. In 1978, NBC moved *Weekend* to prime time and brought in Linda Ellerbee. It was canceled the following year, and in 1978, ABC finally entered the fray. On June 6, Harold Hayes and Robert Hughes opened *20/20*, a show designed to capture some of the successful elements of the competition—investigative reports, personality pieces, and lighter fare. Scathing reviews prompted the departure of Hayes and Hughes, and Hugh Downs quickly arrived as host. Barbara Walters became a co-host in 1984. *20/20* continued to use "pop pieces" on celebrities, fads, and fashions in order to keep viewers tuned in for more hard-hitting segments on subjects like children's heroin use. *20/20* is consistently in the top 20 Nielsen shows.

Undaunted with the failure of *First Tuesday* and *Weekend*, in 1979, NBC premiered *Prime Time Sunday*. Hosted by Tom Snyder, it veered sharply from *Weekend*'s irreverent tone, sticking with hard news and human interest stories. Jack Perkins contributed the human interest pieces, and Chris Wallace provided investigative reports. By the summer of 1980, however, *Prime Time Sunday* was gone, and NBC tried yet again, unveiling *NBC Magazine with David Brinkley*, a program featuring stories ranging from Titan Missile defects to profiles of James Cagney and Rudolph Nureyev. In a reversal of protocol, *NBC Magazine* put correspondents Garrick Utley, Jack Perkins, and Betsy Aaron in charge of the story direction, bringing in a producer to work out related details.

After two years, Reuven Frank canceled *NBC Magazine* and created *Monitor,* hosted by Lloyd Dobyns, but the show suffered abysmal ratings. The program was slightly retooled and appeared in 1984 as *First Camera*. However, it too performed poorly in the ratings, almost always the lowest-rated network show, and it was canceled. NBC had tried, and failed, with nine different newsmagazine formats. NBC then took a hiatus from any serious attempt at a newsmagazine.

In 1988, the new Fox Network premiered *The Reporters*, its first newsmagazine. It had some distinctions—it ran in prime time on Saturdays, had no host, and featured reporters who had some kind of involvement with the tabloid show *A Current Affair*. However, by 1990, the show was canceled, and Fox has not pursued this format.

Throughout these events, CBS had not been passive, as competitors attempted, with little success, to mimic the *60 Minutes* format. In January 1977, the network unveiled *Who's Who*, exclusively devoted to in-depth personality pieces: Jack Nicklaus, Andrew Young, and Rosalynn Carter, with Charles Kuralt's "On the Road" segments featuring lesser-known persons, including the inventor of the supermarket shopping cart. In 1985, CBS offered *West 57th*. Featuring young correspondents such as Meredith Vieira and Jane Wallace, it was designed for younger audiences. Many of the segments focused on youth-oriented items like teenage arsonists, drug use, and the attraction of cosmetic surgery. By 1987, the show was broadcast year round, but by September 1989, it was canceled.

CBS's current newsmagazine success, other than *60 Minutes*, is *48 Hours*, which first broadcast in January 1988. The original concept was to follow a story as it developed over a two-day period. This approach had not been done on a regular weekly basis since the *CBS News Hour* left the air in 1971. Dan Rather was the studio host for shows featuring correspondents reporting on such topics as the devastation of Hurricane Andrew and the abduction of Polly Klaas. By 1996, however, the show began doing some multiple story segments, completely abandoning the original premise.

48 Hours is also known for the reporters' longevity. Some correspondents such as Bernard Goldberg, Phil Jones, Harold Dow, Erin Moriarty, and Richard Schlesinger have been with the show since its opening season.

In recent years, ABC and NBC have found success. Heartened by high ratings of *Prime Time Live* and the continuing success of *20/20*, in 1994, ABC, unveiled two occasional series, *Day One* and *Turning Point*. NBC premiered *Expose* in 1991, hosted by Tom Brokaw and in 1992, retooled the program into the currently high-rated *Dateline*, with Stone Phillips and Jane Pauley as co-anchors. *Dateline* has received considerable attention over the years—its 1992 staging of a GM truck "explosion" earned the emnity of critics. However, in recent years it has dominated ratings through strategically placed multi-day programs and a mix of hard news and tabloid-like material (often connected with Court TV). In 1996, *Dateline* added a Sunday broadcast, going head-to-head with *60 Minutes*. By 1998, CBS was planning another evening newsmagazine with a strong *60 Minutes'* influence, ABC was expanding *20/20* to twice a week, and *Dateline* added yet another evening, Wednesday, to its regular weekly schedule. ***See also*** *Dateline NBC, 60 Minutes.*

Burton St. John

Further Reading

Bluem, William A. *Documentary in American Television.* New York: Hastings House, 1965.
Madsen, Axel. *60 Minutes: The Power and the Politics.* New York: Dodd, Mead,1984.
Murray, Michael. *The Political Perfomers.* Westport, Conn. Praeger, 1994.

Newsreels

As the predecessor of television news, the newsreel pioneered many of the conventions of contemporary television journalism, such as the voice-over, and the mixing of drama and human interest with major news events. The golden age of newsreels was during the decades before the rise of television news in the 1950s. During the height of its popularity in the 1930s and 1940s, the typical American newsreel ran for about 10 minutes between showings of a feature film in movie houses. Some theaters, such as New York's Embassy Newsreel Theater, showed only newsreels. Newsreel production companies released new versions twice weekly. Most newsreels covered major news events, sports, society news, and occasionally crime and disaster.

Charles Pathe developed the first newsreel, the *Pathe Journal*, in France during 1907, and in 1911 he produced, in a New Jersey studio, the first newsreel for American audiences, titled *Pathe's Weekly*. Pathe was greatly influenced by documentary-film experiments prevalent in France during the period. By 1914, Pathe, who now employed 37 people in his North American newsreel operation, had to compete with two other newsreel producers, Vitagraph and the Hearst film interests.

During World War I, newsreels became very popular because they showed actual footage from the war, and in the 1920s, each of the major movie studios began producing newsreels. In 1927, Fox Movietone News released the first sound newsreels, and the company amazed audiences in May when it released a sound newsreel of Charles Lindberg's takeoff for Paris. In 1929, *Hearst Metrotone News,* later renamed *News of the Day*, began to release sound footage. Other major players came to include Paramount News and Universal News. In 1937, Castle's *News Parade* added a twist to newsreel marketing when it began selling 16 mm and 8 mm newsreels of events such as the Hindenburg disaster to those having home film projectors.

In 1935, *Time* magazine founder Henry Luce's *The March of Time* began to compete with the established newsreels. Its format was different in that social issues were explored in some depth through a documentary form that sometimes eschewed standards of objectivity. *The March of Time* did not hesitate to use reconstructions and impersonators as it attacked such figures as Huey Long, Father Coughlin, Hitler, and Mussolini. Louis de Rochemont, a journalist and filmmaker, produced more than 300 episodes of *The March of Time* for *Time*. An estimated 20 million people in 9,000 theaters viewed the monthly *Time* productions during the newsreel's 16-year run.

During World War II, newsreels devoted much coverage to the war. During the height of the war in 1943 and 1944, half of newsreel coverage was of the war, with the rest split among sports, film stars, society news, disasters, and crime. During the war, people often attended theaters as much to see the newsreels as the feature motion pictures. The end of newsreels began when television became a social force. By the early 1950s, newsreel companies were beginning to sell their film libraries to television networks. Soon the newsreel operations were closing. *The March of Time* ended its movie-house productions in 1951. *Pathe News*, which had become a Warner Brothers subsidiary, closed in 1956. Paramount ended its newsreel operations in 1957, and Fox, in 1963. Hearst and Universal held out until 1967.

Charles Lewis

Further Reading

Barnouw, Erik. *Documentary: A History of the Non-Fiction Film.* New York: Oxford University Press, 1982.
Fielding, Raymond. *The March of Time, 1935–1951.* New York: Oxford University Press, 1978.
Jowett, Garth. *Film: The Democratic Art.* Boston: Little, Brown, 1976.

A.C. Nielsen

To most Americans, "Nielsen" is a fancy word for television ratings. Few, if any, outside the industry associate the name with a business empire or a person. The person, Arthur Charles Nielsen, was a brilliant engineering student who loved tennis and numbers. He graduated valedictorian in 1918 from the University of Wisconsin, with a degree in electrical engineering. That university would later award him an honorary doctorate of science in 1974. By the time he died on June 1, 1980, advertising and marketing industry groups recognized him as one of the developers of modern market research. Manufacturers sought his consumer research on spending and consumption. The broadcast and advertising industries relied on his numbers as authoritative measurements. Even though the majority of his life's work was in consumer research, he thoroughly eclipsed all competition when it came to figuring out which radio and television programs were most popular. "Nielsen" came to mean television ratings in American popular culture. His company's numbers now decide what the American public sees.

Arthur Charles Nielsen was born on September 5, 1897, in Chicago, Illinois. He grew up in the Chicago suburbs and attained academic and athletic success at the University of Wisconsin. While earning record high grades, Nielsen captained the university's tennis team from 1916 to 1918. Tennis would remain a life-long interest. He won the Michigan doubles championship in 1923 and the national father-and-son as well as father-and-daughter hard-court championships in 1946. He was named to the National Lawn Tennis Hall of Fame in 1971.

Arthur C. Nielsen headed his growing empire until his death in 1980. In a tribute after his death, the *New York Times* described him as an unpretentious man who did not seek the power his ratings generated, but became famous when his Nielsen "families" determined broadcast rating success. After raising start-up funds from his old fraternity brothers, A.C. Nielsen started a company to rate the effectiveness of heavy machinery. As the Depression approached, some of Nielsen's major clients lost up to 90 percent of their business. Nielsen almost went bankrupt himself. He credited a suggestion from an associate, William B. Murphy, and a 1933 trip to New York City with helping him change his focus from heavy machinery to consumer goods.

Nielsen chose sample stores and visited them to learn what brands sold best. He then convinced skeptical retailers that his results were sound by estimating retail sales. Often, his estimates were within 1 percent of actual sales. By the late 1930s, Nielsen's expanding consumer market research firm was successful, but he was always looking for new ways to survey markets. In 1936, he visited the Massachusetts Institute of Technology to see a demonstration of the "audimeter," a device developed by Robert Elder and Louis Woodruff to keep a minute-by-minute record of when the radio was on and what station was tuned in. Nielsen bought the device—for a reported $7,000,000—and spent the next six years refining and testing it. In 1942, using an 800-home sample, he began the Nielsen Radio Index. It provided the most precise record of radio listening available. Nielsen's reputation as a preeminent consumer marketing researcher assured advertisers his sample was valid. He reported what people did (recorded by the audimeter) rather than what they remembered or said.

Applying the same techniques to television, in 1950, Nielsen bought out his major competitor, Hooper, for $600,000. He continued to develop ratings systems, using diaries to gain demographic information valuable to advertisers. In these diaries, viewers recorded their age, gender, race, education, and income. In 1953, the company introduced "recordimeters" to verify the accuracy of diaries in Nielsen Television Index homes. The first meters were placed in 1,170 households selected after studying U.S. Census data. "Nielsen families" agreed to serve in the sample for up to five years. There was a 33 percent sample turnover each year, and Nielsen employees visited households to verify demographic information. Nielsen Media Research placed devices on televisions and recorded the number of households tuned to each network during every minute of broadcast. By 1973, national daily ratings were possible through new technology called Storage Instantaneous Audimeter.

The growing use of video tape players and the emergence of cable television concerned advertisers who had relied on daily television to deliver their messages. In 1980, the Nielsen Homevideo Index provided a measurement service for cable and home video. Two years later, daily cable ratings became available. In 1984, Automated Measurement of Lineup (AMOL) allowed the Nielsen Company to document exactly what program was shown on what channel at any time using an identification code within locally transmitted television signals for network and nationally syndicated programs.

The company next measured syndicated programming and formed Nielsen Syndication Service in 1985. By 1987, Nielsen was calling its improved metered device the People Meter and using it exclusively for national ratings. The sample size was approximately 5,000 households. People Meters measure television viewing by using a separate button for each household member, as well as visitors. In the 1990s, field testing started on passive people meters. The company joined with Univision and Telemundo to work on measuring Hispanic audiences, the fastest growing population segment. The company also moved into cyberspace, measuring the use of nontraditional media and the Internet.

Nielsen's business was acquired by Dun & Bradstreet in 1984. In 1996, Dun & Bradstreet split into three new, publicly traded companies—Cognizant, ACNielsen, and Dun & Bradstreet. ACNielsen focuses on consumer research. Nielsen Media Research measures broadcast, cable, and Internet ratings and is part of Cognizant.

There are industry criticisms of Nielsen ratings. Not all of the nation is metered, and some argue that samples are too small or are biased. Whether by meter or diary, Nielsen measures only households—not hospitals, prisons, sports bars, or college dormitories. Yet, as the unassuming Arthur Nielsen once observed, "You might say, Nielsen is everywhere." *Elizabeth Ryan*

Further Reading

Basler, B., A.C. Nielsen. "Who Devised System That Rates TV Programs, Dead." *New York Times,* 4 June 1980, A26.
"A.C. Nielsen, Ratings Firm Founder, Dies." *The Chicago Tribune,* 3 June 1980, 3–7.

Nightline

ABC's News *Nightline*, provides late-night viewers with timely and in-depth coverage of the day's key issues. *Nightline* debuted in March 1980 and quickly proved that there was both viewer and advertiser support for a late-night news program. The program not only identified this important niche, but displayed such quality in content and format that it has been a favorite of media critics ever since.

Much of *Nightline*'s success has been hinged to the professionalism and credibility of its host, Ted Koppel. An experienced diplomatic correspondent and expert interviewer, Koppel is known for treating guests with balance and fairness, yet he challenges them when he detects inconsistencies or unsubstantiated claims. *Nightline* evolved from ABC News's coverage of the 1979 American hostage crisis in Iran. ABC News president Roone Arledge aggressively programmed late-night updates, taking advantage of this event to demonstrate that ABC could best cover breaking stories. The late night updates entitled, *The Iran Crisis:*

America Held Hostage, were initially hosted by news anchor Frank Reynolds.

When the dual duties became a strain on Reynolds, Koppel was assigned to fill in. He had already received major exposure during the hostage broadcasts because of his role as ABC's chief diplomatic correspondent. When the specials evolved into *Nightline,* Koppel was the obvious choice to be host. *Nightline* continued to cover the hostage crisis as developments warranted, but also began to treat other relevant news of the day. The program is scheduled for a half-hour each night, but runs past the allocated 30 minutes when breaking news necessitates. *Nightline* was expanded to a full hour on a nightly basis in spring, 1983. But the ratings lagged in the second half hour, and local affiliates wanted to return to the original half-hour version. *Nightline* returned to the 30-minute format in January 1984 and has remained that way since.

The *Nightline* format usually consists of a program introduction by Koppel, followed by a setup piece in mini-documentary style. The setup can be reported by a number of ABC's correspondents, but regular *Nightline* correspondents Chris Bury and Dave Marash generally handle those duties. The program frequently involves interviewees, with opposing views on the particular subject, in joint discussion with Koppel. It is in these situations that Koppel shines. He allows the guests appropriate opportunities to air their views and even argue with each other at times. But he maintains an opportunity for each guest and demands that they not only remain civil, but on topic.

A key strength of *Nightline* is its ability to cover timely events and topics. When there is no particular breaking news, *Nightline* provides in-depth analysis and interpretation on a current issue. The program occasionally delves into feature coverage. With virtually no news competition in the late-night venue, *Nightline* can take risks to challenge the medium and its own format. *Nightline* has expanded its vision from time to time with a series of programs on a particular topic, or even with programs that allow for audience participation. Topics such as prison life, political struggle in South Africa, and race relations in America have been treated in series form.

America in Black and White began as a five-part series in May 1996 and has continued on a periodic basis by providing new perspectives as needed.

Broadcast "town meetings" feature Koppel interacting with members of a live audience to get the public's perspective on current issues. These programs run much longer than *Nightline*'s normally allotted 30 minutes. Topics have included AIDS, the legalization of drugs, health care, and the Oklahoma City bombing. Another late-night offering occasionally programmed during *Nightline*'s time slot is called *Viewpoint*. This program takes a critical look at whether members of the media are doing their jobs responsibly. Koppel coordinates a panel of media practitioners and various newsmakers affected by the press. Members of a studio audience may ask questions of the panelists.

Over the years, *Nightline* has been an outlet for virtually every major newsmaker of both the domestic and international import. Significant guests on *Nightline* have included South Africa's Desmond Tutu, Libyan colonel Muammar Qaddafi, Israeli prime minister Shimon Peres, Vietnamese negotiator Le Duc Tho, and former Presidents Nixon, Carter, Ford, Reagan, and Bush. Since its founding in 1980, *Nightline* has been at the scene of every major historical worldwide event. *Nightline* provided in-depth coverage of the fall of the Iron Curtain, the unrest in Moscow, student demonstrations in Tiananmen Square, and the Middle East peace process.

On the national scene, *Nightline* tracks political campaigns, the economy, and social issues. The show has promptly covered late-breaking stories such as the explosion of TWA Flight 800 off the coast of Long Island. *Nightline* closely followed the Whitewater investigations, the O.J. Simpson trials, and the Unabomber case. *Nightline* has been praised consistently by media critics for its news judgment, fairness, and balance. The program has received numerous awards from the broadcast industry. *Nightline* has been recognized in the Peabody, Overseas Press Club, Emmy, and duPont-Columbia Awards competitions.

In spite of its critical acclaim for balanced coverage, *Nightline* was once criticized by the liberal watchdog group Fairness and Accuracy in Reporting (FAIR) for reporting with a conservative bias. FAIR tracked 865 *Nightline* broadcasts over a more than three-year period in the late 1980s. FAIR concluded that *Nightline* too often featured conservative guests with connections to the Republican administrations of the time. Although the image of *Nightline* is closely associated with that of its host, Tod Koppel, the show has featured guest hosts when Koppel is away. ABC correspondents Forrest Sawyer, Chris Wallace, and Cokie Roberts have all substituted for Koppel in recent years. **See also** Ted Koppel.   *Jeffrey M. McCall*

Further Reading

Bliss, Edward Jr. *Now the News: The Story of Broadcast Journalism.* New York: Columbia University Press, 1991.
Koppel, Ted, and Kyle Gibson. *Nightline: History in the Making and the Making of Television.* Westminister, Md. Times Books, 1996.
Matusow, Barbara. *The Evening Stars: The Making of the Network News Anchor.* New York: Ballantine Books, 1983.

Robert Northshield

Robert "Shad" Northshield has produced news, public affairs programs, and documentaries for CBS, ABC, and NBC. His greatest broadcast achievement to many was the highly regarded *CBS Sunday Morning,* for which Northshield served as senior executive producer. Born in Oak Park, Illinois, in 1922, he received his bachelor's degree from Knox College. Before becoming a broadcaster, he worked at the *Chicago Sun-Times.*

In 1953, Northshield began his association with CBS's *Adventure* series and was the producer of *Seven Lively Arts* in 1957, before ABC lured him away. Between 1960 and 1977, he was producer of NBC News special events and *Today.* He served as executive producer of the *Huntley-Brinkley Report* and oversaw election coverage. He earned an Emmy as writer for the *NBC White Paper* "Suffer the Little Children" and received a Writers Guild of America Award for "Guilty by Reason of Race."

He returned to CBS in 1977 as an executive producer, quickly moving to the documentary area.

He was given the task of revamping the weekday morning news after having great success in developing *CBS Sunday Morning.* He continued with that program until 1987, earning numerous awards, then left to work as executive producer on pilot programs and CBS specials.

Doug Underwood

Further Reading

Gates, Gary Paul. *Air Time.* New York: Harper & Row, 1978.
Hammond, Jr., Charles Montgomery. *The Image Decade: Television Documentary: 1965–1975.* New York: Hastings House, 1981.
Joyce, Ed. *Prime Times, Bad Times.* New York: Doubleday, 1981.

Deborah Norville

© 1996, KingWorld/*Inside Edition*

Deborah Norville is the anchor for King World's *Inside Edition.* As a television news personality, Norville has received many awards for broadcast journalism, including two Emmy Awards—one for her reporting of the democratic uprising in Romania in 1989 and another for her examination of the 1993 Mississippi floods and subsequent southeast drought.

Born in Dalton, Georgia, on August 8, 1959, Norville started her career at WQMT-FM in Chatsworth, Georgia. Her first television work was for Georgia Public Television. While a student at the University of Georgia, she reported for

WAGA-TV, Atlanta's CBS affiliate. In 1982, she joined WMAQ-TV, the NBC affiliate in Chicago, and held that position until joining NBC News in 1986. In 1989, she replaced Jane Pauley as co-host of the *Today* show. While on maternity leave, she was dropped from the show in the spring of 1991 in a highly publicized incident. That fall, she began an evening talk show on ABC Radio, and in 1992, she joined CBS News.

At CBS, Norville handled a mix of investigative reports, breaking stories, and features for *CBS Evening News* and the network's newsmagazines. She regularly anchored the Sunday edition of *CBS Evening News*. In 1995, Norville became host of *Inside Edition*. Outside the newsroom, Norville is a contributing editor for *McCall's* magazine, serves on the Board of Directors for the New York City Council of Girl Scouts, and is on the Steering Committee for the Rita Hayworth Gala benefiting Alzheimer's research.   *Lawrence J. Mullen*

Further Reading

Littleton, Cynthia. "Programers Take Aim at V-chip." *Broadcasting & Cable,* 15 July 1996, 24.

Norville, Deborah. *Back on Track: How to Straighten Out Your Life When It Throws You a Curve.* New York: Simon & Schuster, 1998.

Shister, Gail. "*Inside Edition's* Deborah Norville Upset about V-chip Ratings Threat." *News-Times,* 4 June 1996, 1–2.

Thigpen, David E. "Seen & Heard." *Time,* 31 October 1994, 91.

O

Off-Camera Personnel

Viewers of television newscasts know their favorite anchors and reporters by sight and by name. They might be surprised to find out how many professionals, whose names they do not know, are working behind the scenes making programming happen. Key among them, the news director is the member of a station's management team supervising the entire newsroom operation. The news director is responsible for defining the station's news philosophy and communicating it to the news staff, as well as to other station departments such as sales and promotions, which must understand the news product successfully to sell it to advertisers and promote it to the audience.

The news director sets operating policies, such as how to cover natural disasters or whether to accept amateur videotape for airing; allocates the news department budget; and handles all news personnel matters—hiring, firing, scheduling, and salary negotiations. The news director reports to the station manager, directly in some stations, and in others, through another level of management such as a program director or operations director. In some stations, even in contemporary times, one person takes on both station manager and news director duties. Where the news director fits into the station management hierarchy is often a good measure of how important providing local news is to the station's owners and managers. The larger the station, the more likely a news director is to have an assistant news director to handle the de-

tails of such projects as coordinating special event coverage, evaluating new equipment for purchase, or providing regular critiques to on-air personnel.

Day-to-day coverage of the news starts with the assignment editor or assignment manager. The assignment editor begins the workday by reviewing files of scheduled events and deciding which teams of reporters and videographers should cover which stories. The assignment desk is an area of the newsroom equipped with telephones and phone books; maps; television, radio, and wire service monitors; newspapers; and scanners. Throughout the day, the staff at the assignment desk keep track of events happening in the coverage area and maintain contact with the reporters in the field, getting progress reports, answering questions, and often reassigning reporters to cover unexpected "breaking" news.

Most news departments have several producers. The term "producer" is a flexible title covering many areas. A program producer is responsible for shaping all the individual items of information generated by the news staff—packages, weather forecasts, sports scores, feature items—into a single, coherent program. Program producers decide what is important enough to be the lead story, which items can be dropped if time runs short, and how to fill up the program on a slow news day. Program producers edit scripts for style and accuracy and screen them for potential legal or ethical problems. Some stations have an executive producer. At larger stations, a field producer may join the reporter and videographer team to help cover individual stories. The story producer is usually the station-bound team member, working on the telephone to find background information and schedule interviews. At smaller stations, reporters handle these duties.

Larger stations may have writers whose only job is to write scripts, but at most stations this is a collaborative effort, with nearly every member of the news team staff contributing some of the program copy. Very large news operations, such as those at the national networks, may also have researchers to assist the staff. The work of videographers is indispensable to television news. A good videographer is as much a journalist as a reporter, using news judgment, curiosity, and sensitivity to tell stories visually. Ideally, reporters and videographers covering a story together make decisions about where and what to shoot. At many stations, the videographer is also the videotape editor, while at larger stations, the tape may be turned over   to be edited by another person. As more departments adopt digital disk camera and recorders, and desktop nonlinear video editing, the need for journalists who can communicate visually will not diminish, but job functions may be assigned in different ways. The graphic artist combines computer art and communication skills to create charts, maps, diagrams, drawings, and sometimes even animations to help tell the day's stories.

Several other areas help the news department get its programs on the air. The engineering staff installs and maintains electronic equipment. Most businesses today depend on many different pieces of computer hardware and software, and news operations are no exception. A station may have a separate management information systems department to handle computer equipment.

Putting a live program on the air requires several members of the production or technical staff. The job titles given to members of the production crew can seem confusing because they vary widely from station to station. The newscast director, not to be confused with the news director, calls the commands directing the work of the rest of the crew during the broadcast. The program producer usually sits near the newscast director during the program to advise him or her about last-minute changes in the show's content. The technical director operates the video switcher to put the appropriate pictures on the air, while the audio operator does the same for sound. Camera, character generator, graphics, and videotape operators take responsibility for their respective pieces of equipment, while a floor director supervises communication between the director in the control room and the anchors in the studio. After a newscast, the scripts and videotape may end up in the office of an archivist, who logs and files the material for future reference. Often these duties are given to secretarial staff or student interns, who also deal with mail, telephone, and e-mail messages to and from the newsroom.   *LuEtt Hanson*

Further Reading
Mayeux, Peter E. *Broadcast News: Writing and Reporting.* Dubuque, IA: W. C. Brown Publishers, 1991, 206–14.
Stephens, Mitchell. *Broadcast News.* Fort Worth, TX: Harcourt Brace Jovanovich, 1993, 404–18.

Office of Telecommunication Policy

Established in 1970 by President Richard Nixon, the Office of Telecommunication Policy (OTP) was established to serve as presidential adviser on matters dealing with the electronic media. As stated in the president's reorganization plan submitted to Congress, the agency was to "enable the executive branch to speak with a clearer voice and to act as a more effective partner in the discussions of communications policy with both the Congress and the Federal Communications Commission." OTP was reorganized out of existence with the creation of the National Telecommunications and Information Administration under President Jimmy Carter.

Most broadcasters in the 1970s saw OTP as an attempt to gain greater control over electronic communications. The agency's first director, Clay Whitehead, spoke out against network domination, stating that stations were responsible for programming despite who produced it. The implication was that stations needed to be certain that what they received from their networks was not biased.

The Nixon administration was already vocal in criticizing networks for news bias and reruns that resulted in unemployment in the entertainment industry. Although no regulation or action resulted, networks were attentive to the OTP, which negotiated a compromise between the National Association of Broadcasters and the National Cable Television Association, leading to a 1972 cable television FCC rule.   *Dom Caristi*

Further Reading:

Foote, Joe. *Television Access and Political Power.* New York: Praeger, 1990.

National Telecommunications and Information Administration. *Telecom 2000.* Washington, D.C.: USGPO, 1988.

U.S. President. Executive Order No. 11556, Reorganization Plan No. 1. (1970).

Roger O'Neil

Roger O'Neil has been an NBC News Denver bureau chief and correspondent since 1983. For nearly 15 years, O'Neil has been the voice of the American West, espousing in his own work the independence and ruggedness of opinion, characterizing a life not too removed from the frontier. From the Mississippi River to the Pacific Ocean, O'Neil's booming bass voice has been a constant presence on environmental issues and other countless stories.

He joined NBC in 1979 as a Chicago-based correspondent. Before coming to NBC News, he worked for NBC affiliates in West Virginia, Kentucky, and Texas. Born on April 17, 1946, O'Neil is a 1969 graduate of the department of Radio-Television at Southern Illinois University at Carbondale. He was the lead reporter for NBC during the Oklahoma City bombing and the trial of Timothy McVeigh. He has reported on a variety of domestic stories, including the dramatic Yellowstone fires, the battle between a cleaning lady and a store owner over the possession of a $30 million lottery ticket, and the last passage of the trans-Canadian train. O'Neil's creative writing, along with his unique ability to match pictures to words and his knack for finding stories that matter to all Americans, make him a valuable part of NBC News.   *Cindy Price*

Further Reading

O'Neil, Roger. "Bottom Feeders." In *Live from the Trenches: The Changing Role of Television Correspondents,* edited by Joe S. Foote. Carbondale, IL. Southern Illinois University Press, 1998.

Smyth, Jeff. "As Network News Cuts Back, Technology Offers Other Opportunities." *St. Louis Journalism Review,* May 1996, 13.

On the Road

On the Road, a series of television essays on America and Americans, ran on the *CBS Evening News* starting in the middle 1960s. The segment lasted more than 20 years, interrupted briefly in 1980–1981, while its correspondent, Charles Kuralt, anchored *CBS Morning Show.* The series became distinguished for the genius of CBS correspondent Charles Kuralt, who formed the unhurried and colorful language on the topics on America's grassroots. This, together with the photography and ideas of his crew, generated unique stories. Kuralt has been called America's television poet, and his style had been compared to that of Walt Whitman, Mark Twain, and Will Rogers. The program brought to light stories of the back roads of America, the rural byways, small towns, and the lives of the common person.

The *On the Road* crew traveled in a motor home and made it a point to stay off the freeway and on the forgotten roads that once defined the nation. The genius of the program was the combination of topics and the vividly colorful storytelling of Kuralt, blended with striking photography. Kuralt studied and learned the narrative style by listening and watching Edward R. Murrow, one of his mentors. He became the youngest correspondent at that news organization. And although his appearance and style were perhaps not consistent with the formal image of CBS News, his talent with language was unmistakable. He could form words to fascinate those yearning to hear real stories, including an appreciation of down-home wit and an irreverence for the clamor of hard news and the glamor of celebrities.

From his adventures *On the Road*, Kuralt won three George Foster Peabody Awards and 12 Emmy Awards. The *On the Road* series of well-told stories are best explained by looking at examples. One story was of North Carolinian George Black who made bricks from mud. His work was still in demand where handmade bricks were at a premium. Kuralt recounted that Black's town of Winston-Salem gave him a birthday party in the middle of the main street on his 100th birthday.

Another story involved Americans who solve problems, including Gordon Bushmill who always thought there ought to be a straight highway from Duluth to Fargo. Since the state would not built it, Bushmill decided to construct it himself. Kuralt explained how, about 30 years ago, Bushmill single-handedly set out to do so. When Kuralt met him, Bushmill was 78 years old. He finished 11 miles of his road but had about 180 miles to go.

According to Kuralt, the *On the Road* series also revealed a sense of national conscience, one touched by people outside of government, demonstrating that one man or one woman can make a difference. After the series finished its run on CBS with Kuralt's retirement in May, 1994, some of its timeless reruns were aired, perhaps with the nostalgia of what some news features could accomplish. More recently, the series was run on cable television's Travel Channel. Kuralt died on July 4, 1997. His works are also found in six books and in his memoirs, *A Life on the Road*, the number one nonfiction best-seller of 1990. *See also* Charles Kuralt.

Val E. Limburg

Further Reading

Kuralt, Charles. *Charles Kuralt's America.* New York: G.P. Putnam's Sons, 1995.

Kuralt, Charles. *Dateline America.* New York: Harcourt Brace Jovanovich, 1979.

Kuralt, Charles, Creason Lecture, University of Kentucky Honors Day, 28 April 1989, Lexington, KY. Also: Kuralt, Charles, "On the Road and Beyond: Observation about the USA and How It Has Changed for the Better," The Freedom Forum, 6 November 1996.

Charles Osgood

Charles Osgood has been a familiar voice in radio news for the past 30 years and is best known for his creativity in turning offbeat stories into witty, sometimes touching verse. Wearing his trademark bow ties, he also has been a regular contributor to CBS television where he now serves as the anchor for the critically acclaimed program *CBS Sunday Morning*.

Osgood was born in Baltimore, Maryland, in 1933, and he graduated from Fordham University with a degree in economics. As a student, he worked at the college radio station with, among others, actor Alan Alda. After a stint in the U.S. Army, where he served as an announcer for the army band, he went to work for ABC Radio. While at ABC, he was asked to drop his real last name, Wood, for his middle name, Osgood, because there already was a Charles Wood at the network.

After four year at ABC, Osgood was hired by CBS in 1967 to be the morning anchor at CBS News Radio in New York City. He eventually moved on to the CBS Radio news network as a New York–based correspondent. There he first incorporated a short rhyme into his broadcast. Network executives did not like it, but after a short interval, he tried it again. Listeners said they enjoyed the little poems, and Osgood began incorporating them into his commentaries which became known as *The Osgood Files*. The verse usually addresses an offbeat subject that he has read on the news wires.

Osgood soon moved over to the television side of CBS News, filling in at the anchor desk for Walter Cronkite and Roger Mudd. In 1981, he became an anchor of the *CBS Sunday Night News* where he continued doing his verse. The show aired until 1987. Osgood later became co-anchor of the *CBS Morning News* while continuing his weekday radio commentaries. In 1994, he replaced Charles Kuralt as the anchor of the popular and long-running magazine show *CBS Sunday Morning*. Despite a hectic schedule, he also continues writing and delivering *The Osgood Files* weekdays on CBS Radio. In fact, his insistence on continuing to do commercials on his radio broadcasts almost prevented him from getting the *CBS Sunday Morning* anchor spot. The ethical guidelines of CBS News prohibit employees from endorsing a product, but CBS executives granted Osgood an exemption, despite some criticism.

Osgood was selected as "Radio Reporter of the Year" five times by readers of *Washington Journalism Review* (now *American Journalism Review*). He received the George Foster Peabody Award in 1985 and 1988. In 1990, he was inducted into the National Association of Broadcasters Hall of Fame.

Ford Risley

Further Reading

Flander, Judy. "The Best in the Business for 1991." *Washington Journalism Review,* March 1991, 50.
Osgood, Charles. *There's Nothing That I Wouldn't Do If You Would Be My POSSLQ.* New York: Holt, Rinehart and Winston, 1981.

P

William S. Paley

The founder and chairman of CBS, William S. "Bill" Paley was born in Chicago on September 28, 1901. He attended the University of Pennsylvania. Paley saw the great potential of radio and radio advertising firsthand while working in the family's cigar business. When cigar sales for his La Palina brand more than doubled after the company began buying radio time, Paley became convinced that the infant medium would become very successful.

United Independent Broadcasters (UIB) network was formed in 1927 and fell on hard financial times almost immediately. Later that year, UIB merged with Columbia Phonograph to form the Columbia Phonograph Broadcasting System. "Phonograph" was dropped from the name, and while it was still facing financial difficulties, Paley purchased a controlling interest in the Columbia Broadcasting System in 1928, two days before his 27th birthday. In less than five years, the network owned five stations, had more than 90 affiliates, and grossed more than $11 million annually.

Paley was responsible for building CBS News. In 1928, the network covered the Republican and Democratic National Conventions and provided election returns. In 1929, the network began its first daily newscast and inaugurated a 15-minute weekly news commentary featuring H.V. Kaltenborn. In the early 1930s, radio news was seen as a threat by newspaper publishers. Publishers succeeded in blocking radio from receiving any news from wire services. Paley responded by creating the Columbia News Service to provide radio news and commentary. In less than a year, representatives of publishing, broadcasting, and the wire services created the "Biltmore Agreement," named for the New York hotel where the meeting was held. Wire services would provide news for radio if their broadcasts were limited to specified times. Paley agreed to discontinue his own news service. The terms of the agreement were quickly forgotten as radio increased its news coverage throughout the 1930s.

Bill Paley is also well-remembered for the top professionals he recruited to CBS. Dr. Frank Stanton started in the promotions department but became Paley's chief researcher, then network president in 1946—although Paley maintained control as chairman.

Paley directed much of his attention to the entertainment aspect of the business. His early radio "talent raids" on the entertainment side were legendary, stealing away Amos 'n Andy, Jack Benny, Edgar Bergen, Bing Crosby, Red Skelton, and others from rival networks. Unlike David Sarnoff at NBC, Paley was very outgoing and enjoyed interacting with many of the performers in his programs. Paley also helped create a talent pool for early news development at his network. During the 1930s, CBS hired little-known figures who were credited for their specialized knowledge and went on to become some of the most famous in broadcast journalism history including Charles Collingwood, Elmer Davis, Howard Smith, Eric

Sevareid, and the best known of all, Edward R. Murrow.

Murrow was hired in 1935 and became famous at first for his firsthand reports from Europe during World War II. Paley developed a strong friendship with Murrow in 1943, while he served as deputy chief of the Office of Psychological Warfare in London. By the time CBS began its television news operation, the network had already established its strength as a news organization. Many of the CBS News radio staff, including Murrow and his documentary partner, Fred W. Friendly, made the transition most effectively to television.

Paley was always a friend to news development at CBS, but not always a champion of news coverage that cost the company. In 1956, when the U.S. State Department took a hard line against China, Paley agreed to a State Department request that no news reports come from China. He once even prevented a commentary on the subject by Eric Sevareid. It was Paley who decided, in 1958, that Murrow's popular *See It Now,* would be canceled, for financial reasons, as well as for the controversy it generated. In 1972, when Walter Cronkite devoted 14 minutes of his nightly newscast to the Watergate scandal, Paley told CBS News president Richard Salant that part two of the report should not be aired the following week. Part two did air, but in a radically shortened version. Paley contended in his autobiography that his concern with that broadcast was not that he had been contacted by Nixon's staff and offered some possible repercussions, but that Cronkite had sacrificed objectivity by including a report in a newscast which would have been better presented in another format. Paley died in New York on October 26, 1990. ***See also*** CBS News.   *Dom Caristi*

Further Reading

Paley, William S. *As it Happened: A Memoir.* Garden City, NY: Doubleday, 1979.

Paper, Lewis J. *Empire: William S. Paley and the Making of CBS.* New York: St. Martin's Press, 1987.

Smith, Sally Bedell. *In All His Glory: The Life of William S. Paley, the Legendary Tycoon and His Brilliant Circle.* New York: Simon & Schuster, 1990.

Ike Pappas

Ike Pappas was born on April 16, 1933, in New York City. He attended Long Island University and, while studying there, began working as a reporter for United Press International. He was a reporter for WNEW Radio News in New York City for five years, from the late 1950s to the mid-1960s. While in that position, he provided an eyewitness report of the murder of Lee Harvey Oswald.

In 1964, he joined CBS Radio News as a writer and reporter. His duties expanded to producing and general assignment reporting for both radio and television in 1965. By 1967, he had become a television correspondent for CBS News. During his almost quarter-century with CBS, Pappas covered important domestic and international stories. As a correspondent based in the CBS Chicago bureau, he was the only national television network reporter at the scene of the Kent State University shootings on May 4, 1970. He reported for the *CBS Evening News* from more than 30 countries, including war zones in Vietnam and Lebanon. In the United States, he covered such stories as the Civil Rights movement, presidential campaigns, the space program, and major defense issues.

Pappas lost his job with CBS in March 1987, in a massive layoff of over 200 members of the network's news division. Known to some as the "slaughter on 57th Street" (the location of the CBS News Manhattan headquarters), the cost-cutting action was attributed to the bottom-line sensitivities of new ownership. This followed several other instances of corporate downsizing and divestiture, as well as falling ratings for the *CBS Evening News.* Pappas was one of 14 correspondents let go, along with other personnel from support staff to producers. At the same time, the network also closed bureaus in Warsaw, Bangkok, and Seattle.

Speaking at a Writers Guild picket line outside the CBS headquarters several days later, Pappas commented on what he viewed as the decline of quality. Because of Pappas's visibility and outspokenness, he became something of a symbol for what many journalists felt was a sacrifice of news standards to profit-making concerns.

Pappas later founded the television production company Ike Pappas Network Productions, specializing in the development and production of programs for broadcast and corporate use. Clients of the company include Digital Equipment Corporation, the state of Kuwait, and Special Olympics International. Ike Pappas Network Productions has won several industry awards, including the Cindy Award of the Association of Visual Communicators and the Silver Inkwell Award of the International Association of Business Communicators. Pappas also lectures, writes scripts, and narrates documentaries including *Dreams of Flight: To the Moon and Beyond* for PBS. He has played himself in several theatrical movies, including *Moon over Parador.*   *LuEtt Hanson*

Further Reading
Alter, J. "Rethinking TV News in the Age of Limits." *Newsweek,* 16 March 1987, 7.
"Hill Concerned over CBS News Cuts." *Broadcasting,* 16 March 1987, 39–40.
Zoglin, R. "Hard Times at a 'Can-Do' Network." *Time,* 23 March 1987, 75.

Jane Pauley

Jane Pauley achieved almost instant recognition at the young age of 25, when she began her 13 years as co-host for the popular early morning NBC television show, *Today*. For millions of Americans, she was as much a part of each morning as waking up with a cup of coffee. People identified with her and followed her every career move as they watched her grow up on television.

Born in Indianapolis in 1950, Pauley was raised in a middle-class home with traditional Midwestern values. She battled shyness to become a skilled public speaker and debater in high school. After graduating from Indiana University, she worked for the presidential campaign of Democratic, New York City mayor John V. Lindsay in 1972. Changing directions, she started as a news reporter for WISH-TV in Indianapolis and, in 1975, departed to become a co-anchor at WMAQ-TV in Chicago. When Barbara Walters left *Today* in 1976, Pauley landed the coveted seat, launching her national broadcasting career.

In 1990, when Deborah Norville joined the program the public became outraged, believing that Pauley was being replaced by a younger person. Pauley left the show and its ratings dropped, much to the delight of other early morning network shows. Pauley struggled initially to find a new niche. Breaking into prime-time was not easy. She switched from being a substitute anchor for NBC News to being a news show host for the show, *Real Life with Jane Pauley* before settling in at *Dateline*.

Pauley's staying power in broadcasting is often attributed to her determination as a professional to hold her competitive side in check while striving to be a team player. Her interviewing style is less confrontational or aggressive than other broadcasting figures. She deliberately avoids going after the shock value in stories and instead, works to create a natural conversation. Over the years, the public has responded to her personality, while watching her interviewing skills sharpen. Pauley recently personally funded a detailed study of broadcast journalism education.

Married to *Doonesbury* cartoonist Garry Trudeau, she balances a high profile broadcasting career with family life. *See also Dateline NBC.*
Julia A. Spiker

Further Reading
Dowd, Maureen. "Jane Pauley's Real Life." *Redbook,* September 1991, 89–91.
Hoban, Phoebe. "The Loved One: Back from the Brink, Jane Pauley Has Become America's Favorite Newswoman." *New York,* 23 July 1990, 24–31.
Jerome, Jim. "Saint Jane." *TV Guide,* 10–16 December 1994, 14–20.
Pauley, Jane. "Defending *Dateline*." *The Quill,* November/December 1994, 63–64, 69.

Peabody Awards

The George Foster Peabody Awards are among the most distinguished and competitive of the many broadcasting honors. As "prestige awards" of the industry, they are similar to the Pulitzer Prizes in print media. Administered by the Henry W. Grady College of Journalism and Mass Communication at the University of Georgia, the Peabody Awards recognize significant investigative journalism and exceptional entertainment domestically and globally.

In an attempt to signify excellence and highest achievement in radio, the National Association of Broadcasters (NAB) established a committee in 1939 to formulate a prize. They hoped to get a foundation or other group outside the industry to develop an award for broadcasting, similar to prizes for print awarded by the Pulitzer Foundation at Columbia University. They were convinced that such an award would be more meaningful if it could be administered independently. The chairman of the committee, Lambdin Kay, a pioneer broadcaster and manager of WSB Radio in Atlanta, found John E. Drewry, director (and later dean) of the Journalism School at the University of Georgia, enthusiastic and willing to sponsor the program. This was quickly endorsed by both the NAB and the Board of Regents of the University of Georgia.

Consequently, the Peabody Awards were established in 1940, as annual awards to perpetuate the memory of George Foster Peabody, a distinguished patron and life trustee of the University of Georgia. Born in Columbus, Georgia, in 1852, Peabody was successful in business and had been a partner in Spencer Trask and Company, an investment firm that, among other accomplishments, provided money to help Thomas Edison develop his incandescent electric lamp. He became interested in helping the university in his native state after he met Dr. Andrew H. Patterson, a physics professor at the University of Georgia. Peabody contributed $250,000 to the institution for a new library, a forestry school, and in recognition of its agriculture school and other projects. He was named the first non-resident trustee in the university's history. His contribution to higher education in the South was highly regarded at the time.

The first Peabody Awards were presented in 1941, for radio programs aired in 1940. The first awards for television were presented in 1948; and for cable television, in 1981. The awards have been presented to major media networks, as well as to small independent stations. The first year, only four awards were presented, one to CBS Ra-

dio; and one each to a large, medium, and small radio station—WLW, Cincinnati; WGAR, Cleveland; and KFRU, Columbia, Missouri. Since then, approximately 900 awards have been given, from about 30,000 program entries. With growth, Peabody Award categories have been revised several times. At present, entry categories include news, entertainment, children's programs, education, documentary, and public service, as well as personal and organizational achievement. From among approximately 1,000 entries each year, 25 to 30 entries are honored.

The National Advisory Board (composed of broadcasters, critics, educators, and other leaders in the field) select the entry programs. Frances Preston, president of Broadcast Music; James Sidney, former vice president of Time; former presidents of the Federal Communications Commission Newton Minow, and Paul Porter; and Henry Pringle, Pulitzer prize-winning author, have all served on the Peabody Board. Under a rotation system adopted in the 1970s, all board members may serve two consecutive three-year terms and must have a year off before being considered for reappointment.

The Peabody Awards have been a symbol of excellence in broadcasting for distinguished achievement and meritorious services. Award winning programs include *Hear It Now* and *See It Now*, by CBS; *Mister Rogers' Neighborhood*, by National Educational Television; *All Things Considered*, by National Public Radio; *CBS's M*A*S*H**; *The National Geographic Specials*, by National Geographic Society and WQED-TV; *The Jewel In the Crown*, by Granada Television; *L. A. Law*, by NBC; *The Making of a Legend: Gone with the Wind*, by Turner Network Television; and *Sesame Street*, by Children's Television Workshop.

Most of the Peabody Awards recognize achievement by distinguished broadcasters, such as Edward R. Murrow, for his contribution to broadcast journalism. Other honored individuals include Walter Cronkite, Orson Welles, Mary Tyler Moore, Oprah Winfrey, and Barbra Streisand. Peabody Awards are also presented to distinguished media agencies and organizations such as BBC Television, for overall achievement. BBC programs have been awarded many times for their promotion of international understanding. The first international Peabody Award was given in 1941 to shortwave broadcasters' innovative reports about World War II. In the past five decades, entries have come from all over the world including Japan and France. In the 1990s, international entries for Peabodys have increased to 129 entries.

The Peabody Awards committee has developed an extensive collection of the best programming that broadcasters have produced. For many years, the Peabody collection was maintained in the College of Journalism and Mass Communication and was inaccessible to the public. But, in the 1970s, it was moved to the main library of the university and opened to historians and other interested parties. At the same time, efforts were made to catalog all materials and to re-record older programs.

Peabody Awards have won great respect from the industry they serve because they are selective and administered by a highly regarded educational institution and because the board is composed of individuals knowledgeable in the field, yet not directly associated with it. Through the effort of many people, especially the three directors—John Drewry, Worth McDougald, and Barry Sherman—the Peabody Awards have become an outstanding program for recognition of excellence.

Lena Liqing Zhang

Further Reading

Peabody Awards Program. *Peabody: The Annual of the Georgia Foster Peabody Awards 1991*. Athens, GA: College of Journalism and Mass Communication, University of Georgia, 1991.

Peabody Awards Program. *Peabody: The Annual of the Georgia Foster Peabody Awards 1990*. Athens, GA: College of Journalism and Mass Communication, University of Georgia, 1990.

Potter, B. A. *The George Foster Peabody Radio and Television Awards: Highlights of a Forty-Year History*. Master's thesis, University of Georgia, 1980.

Persian Gulf War

Rarely have Americans followed a conflict that television appeared to bring so near, and of which critics claim the TV broadcasts were so carefully controlled by the White House and the American military. The Persian Gulf War erupted on prime-time television on January 16, 1991. ABC's Gary Shephard interrupted a live telephone interview from Baghdad four minutes into *World News Tonight* to report, "Something is definitely underway here, something is definitely going on . . . obviously an attack is underway of some sort." Before the evening was up, millions of Americans, including President George Bush, would sit enthralled during 12 consecutive hours of Cable News Network (CNN) coverage of the allied bombing raid over Baghdad. The world would tune in as Peter Arnett, Bernard Shaw, and John Holliman broadcast the battle over a four-wire phone from the al-Rashid Hotel in the heart of Baghdad.

In the 42 days that followed, there was no escaping network coverage of the air campaign or of the five-day land war that led to the expulsion of Iraqi soldiers from Kuwait by a multinational United Nations force led by the United States, Great Britain, France, and Gulf and Arab states. More than 120,000 Iraqis and several hundred coalition troops were killed in a conflict that was precipitated by the Iraqi invasion of Kuwait on August 2, 1991. Robert Lichter notes that in the five-and-a-half months that followed, the three major networks broadcast 4,383 Gulf War–related stories on the evening news, with a total air time of 126½ hours. But this was only a fraction of the networks' saturation coverage. Expanded news reports pushed into prime time and broke into programming as events warranted. Economic sanctions, international public opinion, as well as a highly publicized allied military buildup in the Gulf attempted to force Iraqi president Saddam Hussein into withdrawing troops. This high drama CBS billed as "Countdown to Confrontation." News anchor Dan Rather flew to Baghdad for an interview with Hussein on the eve of the war and dutifully told viewers what it "felt like." Instant analysis on the networks often followed this pattern, with some experts interpreting the mind and motives of Saddam Hussein, with PBS's *Frontline* finding him a "malignant narcissist."

Two hours after the outbreak of the air war, Bush delivered an address from the Oval Office, to the largest television audience in history. Administration officials and the military dominated live coverage of the conflict. Rigid pool protocols which called for sharing resources, facilities, and security clearances restricted network activity and irritated reporters. The Pentagon claimed network pool coverage was the only way to protect the safety of 1,400 reporters gathered in the Gulf. News organizations claimed the Pentagon's purpose with these restrictions, was to control information. Problems arose. When Bob Simon, a veteran CBS Middle East correspondent, and his camera crew were captured by Iraq forces, on January 21, 1991, near the Iraq-Kuwaiti border, it seemed to support the Pentagon's claim that the media needed military protection. However, reporters continued to take their chances. Bob McKeown of CBS beat American forces to Kuwait City and reported the Saudi and Egyptian liberation of the capital on February 23, 1991. Two day later, military censors insisted that a missile attack, which killed 28 American soldiers in Dhahran, be covered from the city of Riyadh, 150 miles away, and not by reporters stationed only a few miles from the scene.

The public was on the Pentagon's side. Three-quarters of all Americans knew Gulf War news coverage had to be approved by the military, and 8 in 10 thought that this was a good idea. The crippling of Iraq's television transmission facilities meant the first signs of civilian casualties in the war were not Iraqis but Israelis, who American network news anchors erroneously identified as victims of an Iraqi poison gas attack. The Iraqis had not used chemical weapons in their SCUD missile attacks on Israel, but that did not stop NBC from charging Iraqi leader Saddam Hussein with "doing the unthinkable" when a network cameraman became faint after covering a missile attack in Tel Aviv. During the six-week, or 1,000-hour war, Israeli casualties were one-quarter of all shown by the networks' evening newscasts, even though Israel, for political purposes, remained a non-combatant. Iraqi dead and wounded were less than half of all casualties shown, despite their staggering death toll. The allies were five times more likely to show an Iraqi prisoner to American viewers than Iraqi dead.

Miniature cameras in the nose cones of American "smart bombs" seemed to substantiate Pentagon claims that the air war was being won with a minimum of civilian casualties. Later, however, military officials admitted that barely 7 percent of all bombs dropped on Kuwait and Iraq were smart bombs and that three out of four of all other types of bombs missed their targets. President Bush's popularity soared to an unprecedented 91 percent when American troops began coming home on March 9, 1991, five days after Iraq unconditionally accepted allied terms. Flag waving ceremonies at airports seemed to purge the demons of the nation's ambivalent support of Vietnam War veterans two decades earlier. It seemed a just, clean war. Even televised images of hundreds of Iraqis incinerated on February 26, 1991, when they were hit by cluster bombs as they tried to flee across the Iraqi border, did little to dampen the euphoria about the job the Joint Chiefs of Staff chairman Colin Powell and field commander Norman Schwarzkopf had done in vanquishing the Iraqi. Schwarzkopf's military briefings at the close of the fighting, which depicted his use of military tactics and the media, made the general a sensation. Powell's deft handling of the media and his trustworthy image made him presidential timber.

News shots celebrating the prowess of American military technology were second only to anchors and experts in television coverage of the Gulf War. Such images outnumbered staged interviews with military personnel nearly two to one. Ninety-five percent of the more than 300 sources the networks used praised the American military. Sports metaphors predominated. Early in the air war, Dan Rather told viewers, "so far, it's a blow-out." Television's insistence on pictures extended to reporters stationed in Saudi Arabia. One-third of all reports from there came at sunrise or sunset. Critics saw in the canvas an affirming image of destructive powers. Home front news celebrated the victory by focusing on small-town heroes and community support of the war effort. Some local anchors donned yellow ribbons to show a similar sentiment. Viewership soared. The nation became absorbed. CNN's audience increased 10-fold. Six in ten Americans thought Ted Turner's network was doing the best job of covering the war. Two-thirds of all of those surveyed reported that they were following war news "very closely." One in five said they couldn't concentrate on their work or sleep nights because of it.

The Gulf War demonstrated how fundamental television news had become to modern warfare. Five of President Bush's eight closest advisers on the war had worked on media relations during presidential campaigns. The rosy war coverage did not buy Bush another term, but did signal a public willingness to trust its military commanders over its press. War was again seen as a patriotic celebration and technological triumph. Its coverage resembled a video game. The Pentagon liked to call it "a controlled information environment." When CNN reported the allied bombing of an Iraqi milk factory Peter Arnett was denounced on Capitol Hill as an Iraqi stooge. Civilian casualties were euphemistically called "collateral damage" by war planners. But Americans were described as "human shields" 2,600 times when put in harm's way.

Survey research found that most learning about Desert Shield and Desert Storm was "image-oriented" information offered by television news. It was here that Saddam Hussein, a pariah in the Middle East, was successfully demonized by the White House. Coverage of antiwar protests was muted and public opposition to protestors was considerable. Nine in ten Americans had more respect for the military as a result of the war. Six in ten felt that way about the media. The Pentagon spokesman, Pete Williams, thought that the American public got "the best war coverage they ever had." Many in the press argued there was little that was instant in the government's "instant replay" war. Veteran CBS news anchor Walter Cronkite said he had never seen such a tightly controlled press and argued that such censorship gutted the public's right to know. Lieutenant General Bernard Trainor, a career Marine officer who became an ABC military analyst, recognized two wars in the Gulf. The first pitted coalition forces against the Iraqis and was easily won. The second battle saw the American military take on the press. In the eyes of many, it was again victorious.

Bruce J. Evensen

Further Reading

"The Gulf War." *Frontline*, Public Broadcasting System (January and February, 1997), available on video, contains extensive interviews with officials responsible for planning the American action and press coverage of the conflict. Also, the Spring, 1994 edition of *Journalism Quarterly*, volume 71, No.1, contains articles profiling media coverage of the Persian Gulf War.

Greenberg, Bradley S., and Walter Gantz, eds. *Desert Storm and the Mass Media.* Cresskill, NJ: Hampton Press, 1993.

Jeffords, Susan, and Lauren Rabinovitz, eds. *Seeing Through the Media: The Persian Gulf War.* New Brunswick: Rutgers University, 1994.

Stone Phillips

Co-anchor, with Jane Pauley, on *Dateline NBC*, Stone Phillips has contributed a wide variety of important reports, including an investigation into the disappearance of a Vietnam veteran, later discovered living in New Zealand under an assumed name. Phillips interviewed the wife and adult children abandoned by the former soldier, and then tracked him down to discover the motivation for his actions. More recently, Phillips interviewed his own father and, in a moving segment, traced his roots, coming to grips with his father's disability and Phillips's own role as a national broadcaster.

Phillips was born in Texas City, Texas in 1954, and was raised in St. Louis, Missouri. He graduated with honors from Yale University, where he was quarterback of the football team. He spent 12 years at ABC News then switched to NBC. He started out as reporter and producer for WXIA-TV in Atlanta, then joined the ABC News *Close-Up* documentary unit. He became a general assignment editor for ABC in the nation's capital, serving as substitute host for *Good Morning, America* and *World News Sunday*, before joining *20/20* in 1986. In addition to anchoring for *Dateline*, he has been a substitute anchor for both the *NBC Nightly News* and *Meet the Press*. He has also hosted *Today* and contributes to MSNBC.

Phillips went home to Waxahachie, Texas, just south of Dallas, with plans to do a story on the changing economy of the diverse community of close to 20,000 people. In this "Going Home" segment, which aired in January of 1997, Phillips focused instead on his father's World War II experience and the effects this had on his life. When NBC broadcast the story they also offered viewers a chance to investigate city home pages and tourist information from the reporter's hometown. *See also* Dateline NBC. *Michael D. Murray*

Further Reading
Rice, Lynette. "Network News Magazines: Competition Is King." *Broadcasting & Cable,* 4 November 1996, 29–30.
Zurawik, David, and Christina Stoehr. "Eclipsing the Nightly News." *American Journalism Review,* November 1994, 32–38.

Deborah Potter

Photo courtesy The Poynter Institute

A broadcaster and an educator in broadcast journalism, Deborah Potter spent 13 years working for CBS News as White House, State Department, and Congressional correspondent. While at CBS she also reported for the newsmagazine, *48 Hours*, and hosted the interview program, *Nightwatch*. In 1991, Potter joined CNN as a Washington correspondent, reporting on environmental and political issues. She was newsanchor for CNN and hosted the media criticism program, *Reliable Sources*. Since 1993, Potter also has co-hosted programs for the Radio-Television News Directors' Foundation.

Potter took a hiatus from broadcast news in 1994 to teach at American University where she had earned her masters degree in broadcast journalism. The next year she co-authored *The Poynter*

Election Handbook: New Ways to Cover Campaigns. She has published articles in the *Christian Science Monitor*, the *St. Petersburg Times*, the *National Civic Review*, *Nieman Reports*, and *News Photographer*. She is currently on the faculty of The Poynter Institute in St. Petersburg, Florida and her research interests include media coverage of political elections, civic journalism, and reporting from an environmental perspective. In addition to her teaching responsibilities, she hosts the PBS series, *In the Prime*, focusing on issues faced by baby boomers, including career change, retirement planning, aging parents, and use of leisure time. *Kathryn J. Sasina*

Further Reading
Potter, Deborah. "Wanted: Less Spin, More Substance." *Christian Science Monitor,* 9 October 1996, 19.
Potter, Deborah. "Not Even One Line?" *Nieman Reports,* Winter 1996, 23.
Potter, Deborah. "Making a Difference: Covering Campaign '96." *Poynts of Interest*, May 1997, 4.

Mark Potter

Mark Potter has been a correspondent for ABC News in Miami since 1983. In that role he covers most of Florida, Cuba, Central America, South America, and the Caribbean. Potter was one of the first American Agenda correspondents, where he focused on drug trade and related problems. During his tenure at ABC, he has also covered such major stories as the Manuel Noriega arrest and trial, the Grenada invasion, violence in Haiti, and numerous stories about Cuba and its economy.

Potter was born on July 7, 1953, in Sedalia, Missouri. He graduated from the University of Missouri School of Journalism in 1975 and began as a reporter for WTVH-TV in Evansville, Indiana. He moved to WCKT-TV in Miami, Florida, now WSVN, and spent four-and-a-half years covering law enforcement and the federal courts. In January of 1981, he went across town to the ABC affiliate, WPLG and became a full-time investigative reporter. Potter attracted national attention with his series *Human Cargo*, which won duPont-Columbia, Robert F. Kennedy, and Investigative Reporters and Editors awards. He was the first reporter to discover the lucrative and violent business of smuggling Haitians into South Florida, and the first local reporter to have a story run on *20/20*.

He covered the drug wars of Medellin and established a link between drug-related violence in Miami and the Colombian drug lords. His work on these stories led to his move to the network. Potter has covered most major stories of the past 20 years in Florida, the Caribbean, and Latin America. He has covered the murder of Gianni Versace, the Andrew Cunanan suicide, the Atlanta Olympic bombing, the Peru hostage crisis, and the Pope's visit to Cuba. Potter is married to Judith Rodriguez, a former ABC Bureau administrator.

Max Utsler

Further Reading

Koppel, Ted, and Kyle Gibson. *Nightline: History in the Making and the Making of Television.* New York: Random House, 1996.

Presidential Press Conferences

The presidential press conference is an established, yet still evolving, institution of American politics. A much used, but often maligned, method of communication between the president and the press, and the president and the public, the press conference has been molded by the presidents of the twentieth century. It developed with modern technology—most notably the advent of television—and changing expectations for the roles of the president and the press. It is a dialogue in which the president is expected to think and speak spontaneously, to account for actions, and to present his policies for questioning.

Throughout the twentieth century, customs for press conferences have changed. Control of the time, place, setting, and agenda rarely passes from the hands of the White House staff and the president. Although there is no law requiring the president of the United States to meet with the press, the symbiotic relationship of the White House and press corps necessitates the occasion. Theodore Roosevelt was, perhaps, the first president to recognize this relationship in shaping opin-

ion. He first invited small groups of reporters into the White House in 1902. These meetings were informal, often occurring while Roosevelt shaved. Taft did not continue the practice, but press meetings were reintroduced by Wilson in 1913—the first president to hold regular press conferences open to all accredited reporters.

The administrations of Harding, Coolidge, and Hoover continued regular meetings with the press. All three—even Harding, a former publisher—required questions in advance. Although Coolidge met with members of the press 520 times, he would never allow the press to quote him. Franklin D. Roosevelt introduced the presidential press conference as it's known today. Meeting with the press 998 times in over 12 years as president, Roosevelt allowed spontaneous questions. He also required some answers be kept "off the record."

In 1950, to make the conference more formal than the Oval Office talks hosted by Roosevelt, and to accommodate increasing numbers of reporters following World War II, Truman moved the meetings to the Indian Treaty Room in the Old Executive Office Building. The physical appearance of those assemblies resemble today's conferences. Reporters were seated prior to the president's arrival and they identified themselves before questioning. Truman's conferences were the first to be recorded for radio, making the "off the record" custom more difficult.

Eisenhower held the first televised press conference in 1955. Eisenhower's conferences also were the first to be professionally transcribed for reporters. During his eight years in office, Eisenhower met with the press 193 times. During his administration, White House officials at the cabinet level began to hold their own press conferences. After his participation in the 1960 presidential debates, Kennedy agreed to hold live, televised press conferences. The first one was held at 6:00 P.M. (EST) on January 25, 1961. This press conference was attended by 418 reporters—over 100 more than usual. Kennedy's conferences were moved to the State Department Building to accommodate the larger numbers and cameras.

Presidents since Kennedy have continued to adapt the conferences to suit their needs, but the basic elements remain relatively unchanged since the 1960s. During the administrations of Johnson and Nixon, the number of press conferences declined. This may be due to the adversarial relationships these presidents had with members of the press. While his use of prime-time speeches increased, Nixon held only 30 conferences in his first term in office and 9 in his last 20 months.

Ford, trying to repair the president's relationship with the press, held 39 conferences. Carter attempted to hold regular meetings twice monthly; he held a total of 70, with only 6 during the Iran hostage crisis in 1980. This is a pattern that has become more evident in recent administrations. The president attempts to meet with the press regularly in the beginning of his term. As the term continues or during times of crisis or turmoil, the number of presidential press conferences decreases. Reagan met with the press rarely. He introduced a new method of reporter and question selection; the "jelly bean" press conference attempted to restore order and decorum to the conference by eliminating the shouting and hand raising of reporters. Instead, questioners were chosen by lot from Reagan's jelly bean jar. The practice was condemned by reporters and later abandoned for the previous, more competitive method.

In the Bush and Clinton administrations, the declining use of presidential conferences has continued while spokespeople and surrogates increasingly meet with the press. Over the past 20 years, the overall frequency of press conferences has declined. Today's conferences usually include a prepared statement followed by an opportunity for questions from reporters. The agenda is often predetermined. The *ad hoc* character of the press conference is more an illusion than reality. Broadcast coverage of conferences have been diminished to clips and sound bites. This necessary and traditional occasion has become stale. Journalists and political analysts posit that the contemporary presidential press conference has outgrown itself and the needs of the press, public, and president. While custom guarantees that the president will formally meet with the press and that reporter Helen Thomas will ask the first question, the tenor of the meetings has changed since the days of Teddy Roosevelt and Franklin D. Roosevelt.

Several recommendations to mend presidential press relations have been made including holding regular monthly press conferences and holding weekly informal meetings, like those of Teddy Roosevelt or Franklin D. Roosevelt. The contemporary adversarial relationship between the press and the White House, however, may preclude the latter from ever occurring again. The presidential press conference is truly a phenomenon of twentieth-century politics and media. Its role in presidential news coverage in the twenty-first century is yet to be determined.   *Karen Lane DeRosa*

Further Reading
Kennedy School of Government, Shorenstein Center on the Press, Politics and Public Policy. *A Report on the Presidential News Conference: Reviving the Presidential News Conference.* Cambridge, MA: Harvard University, 1988.
French, Blaire Anderson. *The Presidential Press Conference: Its History and Role in the American Political System.* Washington, D.C. : University Press of America, 1982.
Smith, Carolyn. *Presidential Press Conferences: A Critical Approach.* New York: Praeger, 1990.

Press Secretaries

Just as television has profoundly, and irrevocably, altered the American presidency, it has also redefined the role of the White House press secretary. Never an easy job—at one time there were more living ex-presidents than living ex-presidential press secretaries—the press secretary has, since the dawn of the television politics in the early 1950s, evolved from a media liaison, who worked mainly behind the scenes, to a high-profile television personality with celebrity status. To an ever-increasing extent, the presidential news conference has been replaced by a daily briefing conducted by the White House press secretary.

The last pre-television president, Harry S. Truman, held one or two news conferences each week. These were informal meetings with a White House press corps still small enough to fit inside the Oval Office. Television cameras were not allowed at the news conferences, but Truman's press secretary, Charles G. Ross, would sometimes arrange limited opportunities for television reporters to film important questions and answers afterward. Dwight Eisenhower, elected in 1952, became the first president to hold news conferences on live television—this at the urging of his press secretary, James C. Haggerty. But while Eisenhower proved persuasive and ingratiating on television, he also dreaded the intense preparation and memorization of facts required for a successful performance on live television. As a result, he rationed his question-and-answer sessions with journalists, sometimes going for months without holding a news conference or having any formal contact with the press. Daily briefings by "a White House spokesman"—usually the press secretary—were employed in an attempt to satisfy the needs of an expanding, and increasingly competitive, Washington press corps.

Succeeding administrations followed much the same pattern, and White House press secretaries attained increasinging stature, if not always admiration, through their televised news briefings. Some of the more illustrious presidential press secretaries of the television era include Pierre Salinger (who served during the presidency of John F. Kennedy), Bill Moyers (Lyndon B. Johnson), Ron Ziegler (Richard M. Nixon), J. F. terHorst and Ron Nessen (Gerald Ford), Jody Powell (Jimmy Carter), James Brady (Ronald Reagan), Marlin Fitzwater (George Bush), and Dee Dee Myers—the only woman ever to be a presidential press secretary—and Mike McCurry (Bill Clinton).

Every press secretary has had to deal at times with a press corps that was not only massively inquisitive, but sometimes openly hostile. Ziegler, as an example, endured harsh questioning throughout the Watergate scandals, which involved high level, illegal campaign activity, and which ultimately forced the resignation of Richard M. Nixon. Bill Moyers's years as press secretary found him facing deep cynicism from both the press and the public regarding the war in Vietnam. Jody Powell's tour of duty at the White House coincided with rough economic times, and Ronald Reagan's presidency was faced with some open opposition on grounds that Reagan was able to control many elements of the mass media, especially television, by virtue of his personal appeal

and experience as a former actor. An ability to instill some form of "spin control" on events was often cited. Similar charges were made in the George Bush era when the press became resentful of limited access during the Persian Gulf War.

Press secretaries continue to deal with a society that seems far less trusting and respectful of presidential leadership. Another disturbing trend, at least in the view of many observers, is the intensified interest in the private lives of U.S. presidents—a topic that, in a milder era, would have been considered strictly off-limits. In addition, as all-news television cable networks came upon the scene in the 1980s, the White House press office was obliged to deal with a nonstop news cycle and demands for information from the press and public that seemed insatiable. Talk radio, tabloid newspapers, tell-all television talk programs, and the Internet have added considerably to the work of the president's press secretary. Douglass Cater, who served on the White House staff of Lyndon Johnson, once pointed out that the attention paid to presidents is unique, even by the standards of today. No movie star, ax murderer, or foreign head of state has ever had to endure the constant press attention and, to a large extent, intrusion, as that of the U.S. president, since all activity (work or play), is considered fair game for press corps' scrutiny. Relatively minor matters, including all variety of medical concerns or even dietary questions can create major questions and evolve into central issues involving the nation's press. In 1997, Mike McCurry pointed out that the flow of information is almost constant and the effort to maintain current in many areas presents a challenge even to the most efficient presidential press office.

Even so, White House press secretaries have not been helpless and, indeed, often have skillfully presented the news with a "spin" that showed their boss, the president of the United States, in the most favorable light possible. In spite of their mandate to "sell" the president, most press secretaries have survived their White House years with credibility intact. Lyndon Johnson's press secretary, Bill Moyers, achieved considerable status in his post-White House life, as both a major newspaper editor and premier producer of documentary television programs for both CBS and the Public

Broadcasting Service. On the other end of the spectrum, even the most beleaguered press secretary of the television age, Ron Ziegler, was not personally blamed for the cover-up surrounding the Watergate scandal. Indeed, though every presidential press secretary has endured stormy sessions from time to time, with the Washington press corps, most have been given generally high marks from the correspondents, when their arduous press secretary duties at the White House were ended.

Ronald T. Farrar

Further Reading

Cater, Douglass. *The Fourth Branch of Government.* Boston: Houghton Mifflin, 1959.

Farrar, Ronald T. *Reluctant Servant: The Story of Charles G. Ross.* Columbia: University of Missouri Press, 1968.

Rivers, William L. *The Opinionmakers.* Boston: Beacon Press, 1965.

Prime Time Access Rule (PTAR)

Passed by the FCC in 1970, the Prime Time Access Rule (PTAR) limited the number of hours that television stations could use for network programs during prime time. In 1995, the FCC voted to rescind the rule after a one-year transition period. As part of deregulation efforts, the FCC argued that the rule was no longer needed given the growth in video outlets during the 25 years it had been in effect. The FCC passed PTAR as a means of providing outlets for new productions. In the 1960s, television producers had a limited number of outlets. The three commercial television networks programmed nearly all prime time. A great deal of network-produced material was being used in other time slots—original programming and reruns of older material. Independent syndicators had few opportunities to sell programming to stations.

Because the FCC's jurisdiction is over licensed stations rather than networks, the PTAR governed station operations, not networks. The rule stated that network-affiliated stations in the 50 largest markets had to limit the amount of network product used during prime time (defined as 7–11 P.M. eastern time) to no more than three hours. The restriction applied both to programs currently airing on networks, as well as to any that had previously aired—the reruns. In 1975, the FCC revised the rule to allow more than three hours of network programming for live sporting events, feature films, news and public affairs, and children's programs.

The PTAR did result in a number of new syndicated programs, some of which even served the FCC's purpose, but in many cases, production companies simply began producing "night-time versions" of popular game shows airing on networks at other times. Technically, the shows were not network products since they were produced by other companies and independently syndicated. They did not serve the FCC's goal of diversifying the program landscape. The average viewer saw no difference in daytime or nighttime versions of *Wheel of Fortune*.

One unique offering which resulted from the rule was *PM Magazine*. Westinghouse was able to syndicate a 30-minute weeknight newsmagazine program by pooling feature stories produced first by its own stations, then expanded to other stations. Each station syndicating the program was expected to provide stories to the pool, which were then redistributed. Local stations also provided hosts who introduced the segments while standing near prominent landmarks, giving the show a local look in each market. The development of newsmagazine programs was undoubtedly stimulated while the PTAR was in effect. With 150 stations needing syndicated programming, a market was created for programs such as *Entertainment Tonight, Inside Edition,* and *Current Affair.* While these programs and others may have been launched without the PTAR, their prospects were brighter because the rule existed.

Dom Caristi

Further Reading

Federal Communications Commission. *Competition and Responsibility in Network Television Broadcasting.* 23 F.C.C. 2d 1835 (1970).

Federal Communications Commission, 50 F.C.C. 2d 829 (1975).

Krattenmaker, T. "Prime Time Access Rule: Six Commandments for Inept Regulation." *Communication-Entertainment Journal,* 1984.

Prime Time Live

ABC created the newsmagazine, *Prime Time Live*, in 1989 to capitalize on its coverage of breaking news events and the star power of co-anchors Diane Sawyer and Sam Donaldson. ABC News President Roone Arledge recruited Sawyer from CBS's *60 Minutes* for a salary estimated at $1.7 million. Donaldson was well known to viewers as ABC's White House correspondent. Chris Wallace, formerly with NBC News, and Judd Rose of ABC News, joined the team as chief correspondents, while Richard Kaplan moved over from *Nightline* to be the executive producer.

Arledge conceived of the program with associates Phyllis McGrady and Dorrance Smith. It would cover the world in a style similar to ABC's *Wide World of Sports* with commentary on events as they unfolded. As is typical of such experiments, mistakes abounded in the beginning, and television critics were swift to respond. *Prime Time* appealed to the audience's playful instincts, with mixed results. Sawyer reproved Donaldson at the end of one program for kicking Barbara Bush's dog during a White House tour. While the studio audience laughed and applauded, television critics asked whether this was serious or just for laughs. The tension seemed to grow hotter when Donaldson's live interrogation of Louisiana's David Duke engendered sympathy for the Klansman-turned-legislator, and Sawyer's softball exchange with Roseanne Barr was viewed as network public relations. The *New York Times* doubted if the pair had a sufficient amount of "on-air chemistry." *Prime Time* moved one anchor to New York City and the other to Washington, D.C.; abandoned the studio audience; and reduced the repartee between anchors to salutations. This strategy seemed to work very well.

Prime Time Live began breaking new ground in investigative journalism. Diane Sawyer's report on the misdeeds of televangelists cost some religious broadcasters their church and audience. Sam Donaldson's interview with Supreme Court Justice Thurgood Marshall revealed the judge's opinions of President Bush's record on civil rights and of his nomination of Supreme Court Justice David Souter. Donaldson's coverage of the Tailhook scandal and his exposé of a military base in Ber-

muda, which substituted as a resort for the top brass, won recognition from the press and viewers as well. A *Prime Time* feature about mammography in February 1992 produced a dramatic rise in calls to the American Cancer Society. The program was credited for generating a public discussion about the safety and necessity of mammography procedures.

Prime Time's trademark use of hidden cameras revealed inadequate day-care facilities, patient neglect in veterans' hospitals, and the effect of racism in America. It was long thought that capturing racism on camera was nearly impossible, but the producers of *Prime Time* proved it could be done in one report on the "little outrages" black Americans are forced to endure daily. The program created a case study when it sent two young men, one white and the other black, into the field to report on their experiences in otherwise identical situations. The American Library Association began showing this segment, "True Colors," to its staffers as a way to sensitize them to the roadblocks African Americans face in securing employment, locating housing, buying a car, or just shopping at the mall. *Prime Time's* hidden cameras also showed a series of emotional encounters between delinquent fathers and their children to whom they owed support; this reporting technique also raised questions about privacy and fairness.

The increasing attention the program received and its ambitious investigations, however, sometimes backfired. *Prime Time's* investigation of Food Lion stores in 1992 resulted in a $5.5 million punitive damage award against the network. The jury saw outtakes of the footage taken by concealed cameras. The 27-minute piece, aired November 5, 1992, presented one Food Lion employee complaining about out-of-date marinated chicken, but failed to show that the employee went to dispose of it at the manager's request. After *Prime Time* aired this segment, Food Lion's stocks fell drastically; 84 stores were shut down; and 3,500 workers were laid off. A North Carolina jury held that the producers committed civil fraud by concealing their identities and falsely claiming experience, and that the producers were trespassing in nonpublic areas of the stores when they took video of the meat-wrapping facilities, and they violated the duty of loyalty that employees lawfully owe their employers.

The personality interviews of Diane Sawyer contributed to some of the program's highest ratings. Her televised meeting with Patricia Bowman, the female plaintiff who accused William Kennedy Smith of rape, was one of *Prime Time's* top-rated programs. Sawyer also spoke to pop star Michael Jackson's first wife, Lisa Marie Presley. Elvis's daughter confided to her and millions of other viewers that Jackson had indeed consummated their marriage. Sawyer's interview with Nicole Brown Simpson's family was more poignant. The Browns talked about the last time they had seen Nicole alive at her daughter's dance recital. Ironically, media obsession with the O.J. Simpson case was one reason newsmagazines began to lose ratings in 1994, but *Prime Time Live* maintained popularity, occasionally rising to be among the top-ten-rated programs of the week. Entering its ninth season, *Prime Time Live* continued to earn profits for ABC News. In fall 1998, *20/20* took over *Prime Time Live;* co-anchors Sam Donaldson and Diane Sawyer are now with *20/20*. **See also** Sam Donaldson, Diane Sawyer.

William R. Davie

Further Reading

Auletta, Ken. *Three Blind Mice: How the TV Networks Lost Their Way.* New York: Random House, 1991.

Gunther, Marc. *The House that Roone Built.* New York: Little, Brown, 1994.

Al Primo

A local news director, network executive, and pioneer consultant, Al Primo was an innovator in television news, spearheading a movement by local television stations in the 1960s and 1970s to humanize newscasts and appeal to the mass audience. As principal architect of local television's *Eyewitness News*, Primo established techniques that became the standard at both local and national levels.

Born in 1937 and raised in Pittsburgh, Primo received his bachelor of arts degree in 1958 from the University of Pittsburgh. He did graduate work at Carnegie Mellon University in 1959-1960. He began his broadcasting career at KDKA in 1954 and was transferred to Cleveland's KYW, KDKA's Westinghouse sister station, in 1963. It was as news director in Cleveland that Primo introduced the *Eyewitness News* concept by promoting heavy emphasis on film, on-scene reports, and visualization. Each of these techniques marked a departure from what was then known as the "man-on-camera" format. The overnight popularity of Primo's newscast compelled rival Cleveland station, WJW, to emulate the techniques, leading to television's first "news war," as well as the further emulation of the technique by hundreds of stations. In 1965, the FCC transferred the KYW license to Philadelphia. There Primo implemented television's first on-camera reporting team and encouraged "reporter involvement" in stories. Prior to 1965, mainly because of cosmetic considerations, only anchors were permitted to be seen on camera during newscasts.

The highlight of Primo's career, and watershed in the broader development of nightly newscasts, began in 1968, when he became news director at WABC, ABC's flagship station in New York. Again initiating *Eyewitness News*, Primo refined concepts further by hiring women and minorities, developing sophisticated visuals and graphics, and adding a wide range of aesthetic devices, including music and elaborate studio sets. Several figures hired and or trained by Primo in these "Eyewitness News" contexts gained additional recognition, including Howard Cosell, Geraldo Rivera, Roger Grimsby, Bill Beutel, Rose Ann Scamardella, and Tom Snyder. Meanwhile, however, Primo and ABC were criticized for encouraging informal interactions between anchors and reporters. This component of *Eyewitness News* was known as "happy talk." Nevertheless, Primo's newscasts were so popular with viewers that they almost instantly became the dominant news source in New York. By the time Primo left ABC in 1976, then as the producer of ABC's evening news, *Eyewitness News* could be seen on local television stations coast-to-coast. Two years later, ABC's revamped network news, *World News Tonight,* adopted several of the original *Eyewitness News* principles.

Primo's additional contribution was in helping legitimize the first two news consulting firms,

McHugh & Hoffman and Frank N. Magid Associates. In the 1970s, these firms were instrumental in the nationwide expansion of *Eyewitness News.* Primo left ABC in 1976 to form a third national consulting firm, Primo Newservice. The company thrived through the 1980s and by the 1990s had a worldwide clientele. ***See also*** Eyewitness News.

Craig Allen

Further Reading

Allen, Craig. "Tackling TV Titans in Their Own Backyard: WABC-TV in New York." In *Television in America: Local Station History,* edited by Michael D. Murray, and Donald Godfrey. Ames: Iowa State University Press, 1997.

Klein, Paul. "Happy Talk, Happy Profits." *New York,* 28 June 1971, 60–61.

Powers, Ron. *The Newscasters.* New York: St Martins, 1977.

Public Journalism

Public journalism, or civic journalism, as it is also called, is a movement that began in the 1990s as an effort to change the nature of news so that it is more relevant to citizens and thus, more likely to prompt citizens to take active roles in the democratic process. Journalistic reformers leading this movement contend that fewer Americans are reading or watching the news because the news media exploit problems while neglecting to offer any solutions.

According to the advocates of this new movement, public journalism promises to reenergize a flagging democracy. It promises to end the alienation of its citizens, and promises to bring new respect and purpose to journalism. Public journalism, according to its proponents, is a new way to present the news that addresses and corrects a number of news media failings. Among these failings are—an orientation toward conflict, emphasis on negatives, and the goal of impartiality and detachment. The news value of "conflict" has for years been taught in journalism textbooks as a primary criterion for deciding what makes an event newsworthy. When two aldermen square off over how to get drug dealers off the street, that is considered news. When two state legislators dispute passage of a concealed weapons bill, that is con-

sidered news. When two presidential candidates debate federal funding for abortion, that is also considered news. Public journalism eschews this conflict-oriented coverage. Advocates for the conflict approach argue that providing balance, when it gives voice to opposing positions on important issues, leads to public confusion and cynicism. Public journalists would end this conflict reporting and begin encouraging hopefulness about public life, as well as solutions to community problems.

Traditional journalists have often subscribed to a watchdog role, sniffing out government malfeasance and political corruption. As a result, failures and shortcomings are favored as good copy. Negative stories often dominate. Public journalists contend there has been too much emphasis on the negative. They believe it encourages a feeling of helplessness among members of the general public or what the Pew Center's Ed Fouhy describes as the feeling that problems are so vast and complex that they are beyond the capacity of ordinary men and women.

Traditional journalists subscribe to an elusive ideal of objectivity, or at least, fairness. They believe that important stories at the top of a newscast should be reported in an impartial manner and that opinions and agendas belong in another venue, with the presentation clearly labeled as opinion or commentary. To ensure fairness, they contend journalists should be detached and should refrain from joining organizations and actively championing the causes they write about.

Public journalists scoff at the idea of objectivity, and believe journalists should become stakeholders in their communities. This means joining with citizen groups, public officials, and other constituencies in determining and acting to achieve a common good or public agenda. From its inception, public journalism has been accompanied by controversy. Many practitioners reject the movement's easy dismissal of traditional ideals of objectivity and detachment.

Most experiments in public journalism are traced to a series published by the *Columbus Ledger-Enquirer* in which the newspaper surveyed households and initiated a task force on community improvement. Since this introduction into public journalism, hundreds of projects have been conducted around the country. Many of these projects have been funded by foundation money. A number of these reporting endeavors have been collaborative projects involving television, radio stations, and newspapers in the same market.

An example of a collaborative public journalism project is the "We the People, Wisconsin" initiative that was jointly conducted by a CBS affiliate, Wisconsin Public Radio, and the *Wisconsin State Journal* in Madison. This project included town hall meetings, focus groups on issues, and a so-called "people's state budget program," which was aired by local stations. The state budget program involved two-and three-hour sessions at three Wisconsin sites where citizen participants drafted their own state budgets. The work session was followed by live broadcasts in which participants addressed issues raised during the sessions. The program ended with state legislators reacting to participants' ideas. The broadcasts were also followed by call-in opportunities on the subject of the state budget. Presumably, the state budget project was meant to educate citizens about the hard choices to be made in arriving at a state budget and to provide state politicians with a citizen perspective on what budget priorities should be.

Most of the criticism of public journalism has come from those within the profession of journalism. They argue that the projects smack of public relations and "civic boosterism" and that the news media cannot impartially cover events that they themselves have put together. Public journalist Davis "Buzz" Merritt admits that he is not entirely comfortable with all of the experiments. He argues that misguided projects are the product of journalists who do not fully understand public journalism and have not made the "intellectual journey" to come to grips with its concepts. Public journalism spokesperson Jay Rosen argues that the phenomenon is a work in progress and cannot be realistically assessed for several years.

The future of public journalism as a movement remains unclear. Proponents say it will result in fundamental shifts in thinking about ways to perform journalism and will transform the practice of writing and reporting news. Others say some of the successful projects will be absorbed into the regular practice of journalism, while much of its philosophy will fall by the wayside. Opponents of the movement contend that it is a fad that will disappear if foundation money supporting public journalism reporting projects disappears.

Don H. Corrigan

Further Reading

Black, Jay. *Mixed News: The Public/Civic/Communitarian Journalism Debate.* Hilldale, N.J.: Lawrence Erlbaum Associates, 1997.

Charity, Arthur. *Doing Public Journalism.* New York: The Guilford Press, 1995.

Merritt, Davis. *Public Journalism and Public Life: Why Telling the News Isn't Enough.* Hilldale, N.J.: Lawrence Erlbaum Associates, 1995.

Q

Sally Quinn

While her early reputation was cemented during a four-year stint as a reporter for the *Washington Post*, Sally Quinn spent a brief but event-filled interlude in the broadcasting field as the anchor of the CBS *Morning News* in 1973 and 1974. Born in Savannah, Georgia, on July 1, 1941, she earned her bachelor of arts degree from Smith College in 1963, spending most of her time working in the theater. Despite her educational preparation, her career began rather inauspiciously, working as a translator, librarian, secretary, public relations agent, summer stock actress, and dancer. Quinn also worked for one of her father's friends, Barry Goldwater, then switched parties to work for Robert Kennedy and Eugene McCarthy. She finally landed a reporting position as a profile writer at the *Washington Post* in 1969, covering many Washington insiders. Those stories gained her the reputation as one of the best-read writers on the *Post*, and transformed her into something of a Washington insider herself.

She left the newspaper in late 1973 to serve as the anchor at the *Morning News* after some friends at a party introduced her to CBS President, Richard Salant. Her friends insisted he hire a woman anchor for the show; and he did. But the arrangement was not suitable to her or CBS, and she returned to the *Post* in 1974. Although she was reportedly fired from the anchor position, she asserted that she had in fact resigned because of the incessant backbiting and bitterness that enveloped the staff. Her days as anchor with co-host Hughes Rudd are documented in her book, *We're Going to Make You a Star,* in which she offered comparisons of two of the nation's leading communications companies: CBS, the traditional leader in broadcast news and the *Washington Post*, a nationally known daily newspaper, where she gained her initial exposure.

Quinn resigned from the newspaper in 1980 and is a prolific free-lancer, working from her home in Maryland. She has published two novels: *Regrets Only* in 1986 and *Happy Endings* in 1991 and recently published a book about Washington. She has covered three presidential campaigns and celebrations of Iran's 2,500th anniversary. Her work has appeared in *Architectural Digest, Esquire, Redbook, Family Circle, Cosmopolitan, New York, Vogue, Harper's Bazaar,* and other national publications. Quinn is married to former *Washington Post* executive editor Ben Bradlee.

Carol A. Atkinson

Further Reading
Bradlee, Ben. "The Bradlee Files." *Newsweek*, 25 September 1995, 63.
Quinn, Sally. *We're Going to Make You a Star.* New York: Simon and Schuster, 1975.

Quiz Show Scandals

The quiz show scandals of the late 1950s involved human greed, ethical dilemmas, and differing perceptions of truth and entertainment in a still-developing medium of communication in which parameters for program performance were yet to be defined and fully understood. The first quiz show, CBS's *$64,000 Question*, premiered on June 7, 1955. Sponsored by Revlon cosmetics, the show was loosely based on an old radio quiz program, *Take It or Leave It*. On the *$64,000* Question, contestants could win vast sums of money over successive weeks by correctly answering questions. Contestants were chosen on the basis of their unique television appeal and a combination of personal qualities: a grandmother who specialized in baseball statistics; a shoemaker whose passion was the opera; a 10-year-old mathematics wizard; an attractive, female psychologist who was also an expert on boxing. During the show, contestants were locked in soundproof "isolation" booths and answered questions that had been developed by a team of academic researchers and guarded until show time by a local bank manager.

Within a month, the *$64,000 Question* was at the top of the ratings and Revlon cosmetics were selling out all over the country. The program demonstrated the extent to which television viewers identified with program contestants and their prospects for monetary reward—at a then unheard of level. It also reinforced how viewing patterns enhanced sales of a sponsor's product. The success of the *$64,000 Question* led to the development of a number of other quiz shows including the *$64,000 Challenge*, *Treasure Hunt*, *Lotto*, and *Twenty-One*. At the height of their success, the *$64,000 Question* and the *$64,000 Challenge* were first and second in the ratings, and five new quiz shows debuted on the air in a single day. Many of these programs were produced by advertising sponsors for the networks. The prize money won on these shows made headlines in many locales and established some of the contestants as overnight celebrities. For some participants, the fame was fleeting, but others seemed to catch on with the public. Charles Van Doren, a Columbia University instructor, and a relative of authors Carl and Mark Van Doren, became the best known quiz show contestant. Audiences loved watching Van Doren, a personable and scholarly young man from a famous family, who appeared on the NBC quiz show *Twenty-One*.

In 1959, a New York grand jury and a House of Representatives subcommittee on legislative oversight conducted hearings on the quiz shows. Van Doren appeared before the House subcommittee and described how he had been convinced, for the sake of entertainment, to accept help with his answers. He explained that at the time he signed on with *Twenty-One*, the current champion, Herbert Stempel, was unbeatable, but had become unpopular with the viewers. In addition to receiving answers to the quiz show questions in advance, Van Doren was taught dramatic methods to build suspense and increase his popularity with audience members. Although he became a national celebrity and boosted the ratings considerably, after 15 weeks on *Twenty-One* and earning $129,000, Van Doren asked to be released and was finally allowed to lose. He was then hired by NBC as a cultural affairs critic for the *Today* show. Van Doren said that he did not want to betray all the people who believed and supported him. Other witnesses testified that on all of the quiz shows contestants were coached and rehearsed and that ultimately, to some degree, all of the shows were fixed.

The public was shocked by Van Doren's and other witnesses' admissions, and they demanded changes. In response, Congress amended the Communications Act of 1934, making it unlawful to give help to game show contestants. The networks canceled the quiz shows and reinstated a higher percent of public service programming. Some of the most highly regarded documentary programs came from this period. The networks also began to take back programming control from advertisers. They decided that programming content would be decided, scheduled, and controlled by the networks who would then negotiate sales time with advertisers. Van Doren and other contestants who had been indicted by the grand jury received suspended sentences. Yet Van Doren probably suffered most from the scandals. He was fired from Columbia and from NBC. He eventually became an editor for *The Encyclopaedia Britannica*.

The quiz show scandals illustrate the differing perspectives on the role of broadcasting in U.S. society at that time. Producers and contestants viewed the programs as entertainment, and evaluated performances on the basis of ratings, excitement, and audience suspense; home viewers believed that they were watching real competitions of intelligence and knowledge. Ultimately, the negative effect the quiz show scandals had on the credibility of television was quite limited. By the 1960s, most program suppliers no longer contracted with advertising agencies and instead worked directly with the networks. The networks began to create celebrity-based game shows such as *What's My Line* and *I've Got a Secret* in which the competitive and financial aspects were downplayed and the audience began to see these shows purely as entertainment.

In the 1990s, motion picture actor and director, Robert Redford, produced a film docudrama based on these events, and a new generation of Americans became educated to the pitfalls of television programming that enlists real people with prospects for winning major prizes. The introduction of the film also re-opened the debate in some quarters about the use of deceptive practices and the influence of television on American society. Within the broadcast industry itself, the episode further reinforced the importance of having program producers and the networks responsible for the content of the medium.   *Bonnie Brennen*

Further Reading

Anderson, Kent. *Television Fraud: The History and Implications of the Quiz Show Scandals.* Westport, CT: Greenwood, 1976.

"Dress Rehearsals Complete with Answers?" *U.S. News,* 19 October 1959, 60–62.

"Out of the Backwash of the TV Scandals." *Newsweek,* 16 November 1959, 66–68.

United States Congress. House. Subcommittee on Legislative Oversight. *Investigation of Television Quiz Shows.* 86th Cong., 1st sess. 1960.

R

Race-Relations Coverage

The issue of race and racism has been an ongoing topic in television news as people of various races and cultures have struggled to find benchmarks for the medium. Few can argue that race and racism became prominent news during the Civil Rights movement of the 1950s and 1960s, when African Americans were fighting for their equal rights as citizens in America. The late Supreme Court Justice Thurgood Marshall's victory in the landmark 1954 U.S. Supreme Court decision, *Brown v. Board of Education,* brought race and racism to the spotlight as the integration of public schools became news and the struggle for civil rights took center stage. Television news was clearly the medium providing images to home viewers depicting societal problems.

The Civil Rights movement was a significant event in the history of television news as it changed many existing situations for African Americans. As a news medium, network television brought into homes highly dramatic images of the racial struggle going on in the South. Viewers saw buses being burned and stoned, Martin Luther King Jr., leading marches and being arrested, and dramatic pictures of George Wallace, governor of Alabama, standing defiantly at the schoolhouse door as the first African American students entered. Viewers saw the March on Washington, the bombed-out Birmingham church where four little girls were killed, as well as reports of the violent deaths of Medgar Evers and Martin Luther King Jr.

The decades of the 1950s and 1960s were turbulent times for race relations and television news was the dominant medium. It showed the audience what it meant to be separate and unequal. While African Americans were newsmakers in the 1950s, African American reporters on television were virtually unheard of during the era, except for Louis E. Lomax who joined WNTA-TV in New York City in 1958. In 1962, Mal Goode was hired by ABC News, Bob Teague and Bill Matney joined NBC in 1963, and Hal Walker appeared on CBS the same year. They opened doors for more African American reporters to be hired as the Civil Rights movement continued to cause changes in media practices. Many African American reporters were hired initially to cover riots of the 1960s.

Racial disturbances continued during that decade and television news provided coverage. Television news received some criticism for its attention to civil rights and in 1964, the United Church of Christ launched the first television license challenge against WBLT-TV in Jackson, Mississippi, based on discrimination in programming and the inability to serve the entire community's public interest. This landmark case, *Office of Communication of the United Church of Christ v. Federal Communications Commission,* set the stage for many precedents affecting station licenses.

One of the most significant studies in the portrayal of race and racism in mass media was commissioned in 1967 by President Lyndon Johnson. A seminal study, the Kerner Commission Report was issued in 1968 and is still cited today.

The Kerner Commission Report held that the news media failed to accurately portray the scale and character of the race riots and the black experience in general. The commission further stated that television had been guilty of flaunting the affluence of white society, called the American media "shockingly backward" in hiring practices, and urged immediate policy change. The commission believed that until management and ownership opened up, ethnic groups would continue to perceive the mass media as a tool of the status quo. The recommendations of the Kerner Commission Report opened doors in the mass media for African Americans and other people of color. By the 1970s, many African Americans and other people of color were hired as reporters. Schools and foundations also established scholarships for minority students. Under the leadership of Fred Friendly, Columbia University set up a special program to assist minority students in journalism.

While the Kerner Commission Report was a significant landmark study creating opportunity for people of color, African Americans, Latinos, Asians, and Native Americans did not find their numbers multiplying significantly or chances for advancement expanding in the television news at the end of the 1970s and into the 1980s. The portrayal of people of color did not improve significantly. African Americans were still, more often than not, depicted as poor, violent, and unintelligent. The decade of the 1990s brought race relations to the forefront of television news once again.

The beating of Rodney King by members of the Los Angeles Police Department, the 1992 Los Angeles riots, the Million Man March, and the O.J. Simpson trial all directed attention toward the medium and race relations. These stories reported and dramatically displayed to the world a society still divided by race. Coverage of these events generated the same criticisms as those of the 1960s. Almost 30 years after the Kerner Commission Report, the struggle for people of color continues for diversity and an opportunity to gain a place of significance in television news. With a few very prominent exceptions—such as Oprah Winfrey, Bryant Gumbel, Carole Simpson, and Ed Bradley—in terms of numbers, promotions, and man-

agement, people of color still trail white colleagues. From the audience standpoint, many people of color are still concerned that television does not accurately report their story.

Besides the ability to inform, persuade, educate, and entertain the public, television news has the responsibility to serve the public interest. This includes balanced reporting and fairness. Television news has, on occasion, contributed to the portrayal of negative stereotypes in depicting people of color and cultural differences, and this has a profound effect on race relations as the Kerner Commission eloquently stated. In the future, television news faces a challenge to deliver news reflecting a balanced view of all races and cultures. *See also* Civil Rights Coverage, Minority Groups.

Dhyana Ziegler

Further Reading

Entman, Robert M. "Modern Racism and the Images of Blacks in Local Television News." *Critical Studies in Mass Communication,* Fall 1990, 332–45.

Hernandez, G. H. "The Race Quotient." *Editor & Publisher*, August 1994, 11–12.

Ziegler, Dhyana. "Significant Events in the History of Blacks in Network Television News." *Master's thesis*, Southern Illinois University, 1982.

Radio-Television News Directors Association (RTNDA)

The Radio-Television News Directors Association (RTNDA) is the only professional association devoted exclusively to electronic journalism. RTNDA members come from local and network news organizations—radio, broadcast television, cable, and other electronic media—from more than 30 countries.

The RTNDA constitution contained in the annual membership directory issue of *The Communicator,* states the organization's goals: "the achievement of high professional standards of electronic journalism, the exchange of professional knowledge among members, the promotion of public understanding of electronic journalism, and the fostering of principles of journalistic freedom to gather and disseminate information to the public." The RTNDA, in partnership with its affiliated charitable institution, the Radio-Television News Directors Foundation (RTNDF), works toward these goals through a variety of projects, including the annual International Conference and Exhibition, awards, scholarships, fellowships, professional development programs, research, and publications.

The RTNDA International Conference is held in a different major U.S. city every fall. Activities include panel discussions on topics of interest to electronic news professionals, sessions for students and entry-level professionals, speeches by prominent reporters and executives, and an exhibition of news-related equipment and services. At the conference, RTNDA presents several awards. The Edward R. Murrow Awards honor excellence at all levels. The Paul White Award, RTNDA's highest award, recognizes an industry leader's lifetime contribution. Some of the people who have received this award are Walter Cronkite, Eric Sevareid, Paul Harvey, Barbara Walters, and Ted Turner.

RTNDA traces its roots to March 1946, when John Hogan of Portland, Maine, issued a call for the formation of a national association to set standards for radio news gathering and reporting and to support radio reporters' claim that they were legitimate journalists. The organization emerged from its first convention in Cleveland later that year as the National Association of Radio News Directors. The name was changed to RTNDA in 1952 to include television journalists. The organization adopted its first code of ethics in 1946 and presented its first awards in 1948. Canadian members organized RTNDA Canada in 1962.

Through the years, RTNDA conventions have been addressed by such notables as Senator John F. Kennedy, FCC Chairman Newton Minow, and California Governor Ronald Reagan. Perhaps the most famous speech convention attendees ever heard was the one by Edward R. Murrow in 1958. He castigated the broadcast industry, from local station owners to the FCC, for allowing television to become escapist and profit-oriented. In what has become one of the most quoted lines regarding the medium, he warned that television without a sincere effort to enlighten viewers "is merely wires and lights in a box."

RTNDA is governed by officers and a board of directors elected by voting members. The board of directors hires a chief operating officer to conduct its business. National offices for both RTNDA and RTNDF are located in Washington, D.C. *See also* Barbara Cochran.

LuEtt Hanson

Further Reading

Murrow, Edward R. Speech to the National Convention of the Radio Television News Directors Association, October 15, 1958. Reprinted in Edward Bliss, Jr., editor, *In Search of Light: The Broadcasts of Edward R. Murrow, 1938-1961.* New York: Avon Books, 1967, 374–84.

Radio-Television News Directors Association Constitution and Bylaws, as Amended June 13, 1994. *The Communicator.* Vol. III, No. 1, January 1998, 37–47.

Sperber, A. M. *Murrow: His Life and Times.* New York: Freundlich Books, 1986.

Dan Rather

© 1996 CBS News

Dan Rather was born in Wharton, Texas, in 1931, but moved with his family to Houston when he was less than a year old. Son of an oil pipe layer and a mother who sacrificed to help him get to college, Rather, brags about both his parents and his home state of Texas. While attending Sam Houston State Teachers College in Huntsville, he worked at KSAM radio and two wire services. He graduated in 1953. After a hitch in the Marines, Rather went to work for the *Houston Chronicle,* followed by a move to KTRH radio where he became news director.

Rather's first year in television was 1959 as reporter for Houston's KTRK-TV, later moving to the news director position at the CBS affiliate, KHOU-TV. He joined CBS News in 1961, serving as the network's London bureau chief and later as White House correspondent, covering many historic events. He was in Dallas in 1963 reporting around the clock on the assassination of President John F. Kennedy, and in Chicago for the volatile Democratic National Convention in 1968. He covered the wars in Vietnam, Afghanistan and the Persian Gulf, along with the civil rights movement in the South, and Watergate. Rather has covered each of the Democratic and Republic national conventions since 1964, as well as most of the major news stories of his time, both nationally and internationally. His confrontation with President Richard Nixon in 1974 helped to mark him as a hard hitting reporter who would not back down, even for a president. Rather's style of reporting has alienated some, including some of those on the politically conservative right, but has garnered praise from others, especially in his profession.

Reaching a milestone in a CBS News career sparkled with many accomplishments, Rather was named to the coveted *CBS Evening News* anchor position in 1981. When he was selected to replace Walter Cronkite, it came after network consideration of Roger Mudd, who appeared to some to be heir apparent to the coveted anchor seat. The struggle in the news division had been intense, and within a few months Mudd moved to NBC.

Dan Rather has anchored all or part of the network's television programs *CBS Reports*, *60 Minutes,* and *48 Hours*, along with the *CBS Evening News*. He has received recognition many times for this work, including numerous Emmy Awards. The distinguished journalist has authored or co-authored four books: *I Remember, The Palace Guard, The Camera Never Blinks,* and *The Camera Never Blinks Twice*. On September 17, 1997 Dan Rather was recognized for "his lifetime contribution to electronic journalism" with the

Paul White Award, the highest honor bestowed by the Radio-Television News Directors Association.

David M. Guerra

Further Reading
Gates, Gary Paul. *Air Time: The Inside Story of CBS News.* New York: Harper & Row, 1978.
Rather, Dan, and Mickey Hersowitz. *The Camera Never Blinks.* New York: William Morrow, 1977.
Rather, Dan, and Mickey Hersowitz. *The Camera Never Blinks Twice.* New York: William Morrow, 1994.
Stoehr, Chris, and David Zurawik. "Rather Remarkable." *American Journalism Review,* May 1998, 36–39.

Robert Read

Photo courtesy *Inside Edition*

Under the leadership of producer Robert Read, the investigative unit at *Inside Edition* has won awards from Sigma Delta Chi, the National Press Club, the Deadline Club, the Investigative Reporters and Editors, and the National Headliners Club. In addition, one report earned the program the George Polk Award for Best National Reporting. This was the first instance of the award being given to a syndicated newsmagazine.

Robert Read was born December 10, 1960, in Oceanside, New York. He earned a bachelor of fine arts degree from the C.W. Post College of Long Island University in 1982. Six months later he began working for the ABC News television series *20/20*. During his eight years at *20/20,* he produced news, feature, and investigative reports. He spent three years as a producer of investigative reports for the television series *Inside Edition* and *Dateline NBC*. Read became senior producer for the investigative reporting units of both *Inside Edition* and *American Journal* in 1994. Both are television newsmagazines syndicated by King World. Read had headed the unit at *Inside Edition* from 1993 to 1994. He has also served as panelist for the Poynter Institute for Media Studies, the National Institute for Computer-Assisted Reporting, and Investigative Reporters and Editors. He also testified before a Congressional subcommittee on health fraud, about an undercover investigation of a Nevada medical clinic.   *Steven Phipps*

Further Reading

Mink, Eric. "'Inside' Look at School Busing—25 Years Later." *New York Daily News,* 20 December 1996, 97.
Paterno, Susan. "The Lying Game." *American Journalism Review,* May 1997, 40–45.

Ronald Reagan

As 40th president of the United States, Ronald Wilson Reagan at the age of 69 was the oldest individual and first movie actor ever sworn into the nation's highest office. His mastery of television produced two electoral landslide victories in the 1980 and 1984 presidential campaigns and helped him maintain an image that made him a popular president.

Born on February 6, 1911, in Tampico, Illinois, Reagan had roots in small town, middle America. He worked his way through Eureka College receiving a bachelor of arts degree in 1932. Reagan married actress Jane Wyman in 1940, divorced in 1948, and in 1952, wed Nancy Davis. He had success as a radio sportscaster in Iowa, then began movie acting with Warner Brothers in 1937and appeared in 53 films. His television work started in 1954, as host of the weekly dramatic anthology series, *General Electric Theater*. In 1964, he hosted and sometimes acted in a the popular television western anthology series, *Death Valley Days*.

On October 27, 1964, Reagan's political career on television began with a speech he taped for Barry Goldwater's bid for the presidency. "A Time for Choosing" was the title of the 30-minute nationally televised address. After the speech, Reagan was no longer seen as a fading Hollywood actor. Instead, he was considered, by many, as one of the foremost conservative politicians in America. He was elected governor of California in 1966. After stepping down from the governorship in 1975, Reagan announced his intention to seek the Republican presidential nomination of 1976. After losing the first three primaries he entered, Reagan made the decision to use most of his campaign funds for a television ad to be used for the North Carolina primary. The risk paid off and paved the way for other successes, enabling him to stay in the campaign. The political potential of television was clear; he fell just 60 votes short of the nomination. In the 1980 election his use of television would help him unseat incumbent president, Jimmy Carter.

Reagan is considered by many to be the first true television president. His style of presentation and behavior in front of the camera fit the medium in terms of form, content, and professional standards. He made television his instrument of governing. Despite blatant gaffes, poor grasp of some issues, and questionable policy decisions, Reagan used television to maintain personal popularity, and due to this, became known as "the Great Communicator." His vocal delivery and photogenic persona, groomed during his days as a Hollywood actor, helped to create this image. His success on television however, cannot be attributed to his acting ability alone. Reagan had a skillful team of advisers who helped shape his image. Three officials in his administration were primarily charged with this responsibility. They included James Baker, White House chief of staff during Reagan's first term and secretary of the treasury in the second; David Gergen, White House director of communications; and Michael Deaver, Reagan's deputy chief of staff during the first term. Baker presided over the entire communication apparatus of the Reagan administration and was adept at running national campaigns. Gergen and Deaver were responsible for generating positive press coverage.

Deaver was especially good at providing visually attractive, prepackaged news stories and photo opportunities for television.

Reagan and his advisers were brilliant manipulators of his image. For example, as the country's first divorced president and a father reportedly not close to his children, Reagan was portrayed as a defender of family values and able to create the impression of a committed family man. This sort of image control testifies to his effectiveness as a communicator. He also played a role in some memorable television images during his presidency, most of which were staged by his advisers. Examples include images of him on the shore of Normandy in remembrance of D day, congratulating U.S. Olympians, conversing with troops in Korea, saluting the Tomb of the Unknown Soldier, comforting the widow of a slain American soldier after a Lebanon terrorist bombing, and at the Statue of Liberty celebration.

The relationship between television journalism and the White House was in the midst of change during his time in office. For Reagan these changes were favorable. During his presidency, it was common to see images of the president on the evening news. Before this, network newscast coverage of the presidency featured stories from Capitol Hill, the State Department, or elsewhere in government. Though it began during Nixon's presidency, the practice of using the White House as a prism through which American politics are seen was greatly enhanced by the Reagan administration.

Reagan's amiability and sincere manner played an important part in molding his on-camera appearance. Self-disclosure, the ability to tell a story, and a comedic sense of timing were among the unique qualities Reagan possessed that appealed to the television audience. The Iran-Contra guns-for-hostages deal was the exception in which his style of presentation failed him. Though saving himself politically, Reagan's self-disclosure of this incident showed the American public, through a televised speech, his ineffectiveness and lack of control over his staff. Otherwise, the characteristic enhancing his popularity was the consistency of his on-camera and off-camera personality. Whether functioning as public speaker, inter-

viewee, question answerer, greeter of foreign diplomats, or part of the crowd at a baseball, game he presented the same personality. He employed what scholar Kathleen Hall Jamieson has called a consistent conversational style, which was effective and endearing. Instead of being tense in front of the television camera, like some previous presidents, Reagan's on-camera appearance was natural and believable.   *Lawrence J. Mullen*

Further Reading

Denton, Robert E., Jr. *The Primetime Presidency of Ronald Reagan: The Era of the Television Presidency.* New York: Praeger Publishers, 1988.

Hertsgaard, Mark. *On Bended Knee: The Press and the Reagan Presidency.* New York: Schocken Books, 1989.

Jamieson, Kathleen Hall. *Eloquence in an Electronic Age: The Transformation of Political Speechmaking.* New York: Oxford University Press, 1988.

Harry Reasoner

CBS Photo Archive

Harry Reasoner, the son of educators, was born in Dakota City, Iowa, on August 17, 1923. He started his career as a reporter for the *Minneapolis Times* in September 1946. However, it was not long before he left the print medium for broadcast journalism. Reasoner began his broadcasting career with a Minneapolis radio station in 1950, as a news writer and kept on writing in every subsequent assignment he held. Prior to joining CBS in New York in 1956, he had published a novel, been in the Army, been an information officer for the U.S. Information Agency in the Far East, and completed some basic training in radio and television news at WCCO and KEYD in Minneapolis. In 1957, Reasoner became the first full-time CBS television correspondent. By 1960, however, he seemed to have faded because, while continuing to write, he was passed over for various anchoring assignments and was assigned to do two hourly newscasts a day on CBS Radio.

While doing the newscasts on radio, Reasoner began to make a conscious attempt to inject more color into his writing than was customary during that period. Once, after a Portuguese ocean liner was hijacked and the story continued for days, he started writing the coverage like a soap opera. When Ernest Hemingway died, Reasoner gave his obituary written in Hemingway's style. He also began to mock the use of journalistic clichés in his writing which won additional attention, especially among colleagues who valued good writing. While doing these things, Jack Gould, the distinguished radio-television reviewer of the *New York Times,* "discovered" Reasoner and devoted an entire column to praising him, particularly his writing ability and sense of humor. Reasoner's career seemed to skyrocket after Gould's positive comments. CBS, recognizing Reasoner's talents, suddenly rewarded him with a number of prime assignments. One assignment was hosting *Calendar,* the forerunner of *CBS Morning News.* He also was a requent substitute for Walter Cronkite on the *CBS Evening News.*

In 1964, Reasoner replaced Dan Rather as the CBS White House correspondent. Reasoner was one of the recognizable star reporters for CBS who flanked Walter Cronkite on the *CBS Evening News.* However, as early as 1966, Reasoner started to encounter some challenges at CBS. During that year, in the view of some critics, he muffed his election assignment by seeming unprepared. By 1968, when choice assignments were given for CBS News's election coverage, Reasoner came up empty-handed. Bill Leonard, then vice president in charge of special events and documentaries, perceived that Reasoner was lacking in aggressiveness at that time. Nonetheless, he was on the air as

co-host of *60 Minutes* when it made its debut. But he soon departed.

In 1970, Reasoner left CBS for ABC, when an anchor position was created for him on Sunday evenings. For ABC, the acquisition of Reasoner was a spectacular gain. They lacked tradition and Reasoner added instant credibility. The personable Reasoner, who had a middle-class Midwestern charm, and always very calm while on camera, was also a hit with advertisers. During that period, ABC salespeople reportedly sold advertising time on Reasoner's program with tremendous enthusiasm and sales in turn, for the *ABC Evening News,* markedly increased. While the audience and the advertisers seemed to like Reasoner, affiliates were slower to respond. In 1971, more than one-third of ABC's 168 affiliates did not carry the program, while others aired it in off-hours. But within a year-and-a-half of a speech Reasoner gave to ABC affiliates in Century City, California, assuring them of his resolve to compete, almost 100 percent of the stations bought and aired his program.

Reasoner did not forget the people who helped make his program successful. Reasoner got to know his writers and producers and occasionally found time to have lunch with them. An excellent writer himself, he was quick to show his appreciation for those skills. In the mid-1970s, Reasoner was paired with Howard K. Smith on the *ABC Evening News*, later known as *World News Tonight.* At first this was a ratings success, but by 1975, the Reasoner-Smith team had peaked and the program ratings started to decline. Reasoner then anchored alone, and Smith was relegated to a nightly commentary role. But Reasoner's ratings never matched Cronkite's, his nightly competitor. Soon after Roone Arledge took over ABC's news operation in 1977, Reasoner returned to CBS. Arledge and Fred Silverman both noted that there was a relationship between a popular evening news program and strong prime-time ratings. They were inclined to believe that Reasoner's falling ratings were affecting the rest of the schedule. Disagreements over the role of Barbara Walters, who had assumed the co-anchor chair after much fanfare about her large salary and lack of "hard news" credentials, would give ABC further impetus to remove Reasoner.

Upon returning to CBS News in 1978, Reasoner came back to friendly confines with former colleagues who appreciated his talent and on-air personality. Reasoner was assigned to the firmly established, secure, and highly successful *60 Minutes*, which was now offered on Sunday evenings. The most successful newsmagazine in history, *60 Minutes*, on the air since 1968, reached approximately 32.6 million viewers per week. After a long and successful role as co-investigator and anchor of the series with Mike Wallace, Morley Safer, and Dan Rather, Reasoner was eventually relegated to a supporting role on *60 Minutes* due to health problems. Reasoner stepped down from his correspondent role on *60 Minutes* at the end of the 1990–1991 season. Reasoner, who was 67 at the time, became an editor emeritus and appeared occasionally on the show until shortly before his death on August 6, 1991. He died of cardiopulmonary arrest in Norwalk, Connecticut. *See also 60 Minutes.*   *Tommy V. Smith*

Further Reading

Bedell, Sally. "What Made ABC's Harry Reasoner Switch Back to CBS?" *TV Guide,* 27 January 1979, 25–28.

Matusow, Barbara. *The Evening Stars: The Making of the Network News Anchor.* Boston: Houghton Mifflin, 1983.

Reasoner, Harry. *Before the Colors Fade.* New York: Alfred A. Knopf, 1981.

Religion Coverage

News coverage of religion is as old as the nation itself and has evolved in the modern electronic age. Popular revivalists such as Aimee Semple McPherson used radio extensively. Television coverage began on a grand scale when Bishop Fulton Sheen's weekly discussion of moral and ethical issues was watched by families from the whole spectrum of religious faiths. While he discussed issues covering a range of topics, Sheen wore clerical robes and referred to an "angel" who erased the chalkboard between segments.

Coverage of the presidential campaign of John F. Kennedy focused on issues such as whether a Roman Catholic president would owe allegiance to the pope. Kennedy engaged in question-and-answer sessions with many groups, including a well-known appearance addressing this issue with the Houston (Texas) Ministerial Association. More recently, issues have focused on televangelists and corruption. Jim and Tammy Faye Bakker became archetypes and few of the televangelists escaped the eye of the press, including Billy Graham, who served as adviser to every president since Dwight Eisenhower.

Additional coverage has focused on forms of religious extremism. Cults, such as Jim Jones in Guyana, and the Branch Davidians in Waco, Texas, were the focus of major television news scrutiny. Schisms, such as that in the Southern Baptist Convention, also received widespread attention, including several programs by Bill Moyers for the Public Broadcasting Service. Visits by Pope John Paul II and the death of Mother Teresa were covered extensively by television. Regular coverage of the abortion debate has been evident for years. Also, there was extensive coverage on the anniversary of the founding of the Church of Jesus Christ of the Latter Day Saints, with news reports, as well as noncommercial documentaries and made-for-television movies.

While most prime-time television is secular in nature, there have been network and local programs focusing on religious issues. Some change is seen with the addition of reporters covering religion such as *ABC World News Tonight*'s Peggy Wehmeyer, a born-again Christian who studied at the Dallas Theological Seminary. Pat Robertson's Christian Broadcasting Network (CBN) and *The 700 Club*, represent yet another facet of religion coverage. There are now many local religious broadcast stations. Religions other than Protestant, Catholic, and Jewish receive much less coverage, except for occasional stories concerning religious factions in the Middle East. Some speculate, that with the changing makeup of the U.S. population, attention to Islam, Buddhism, and other religions will increase. *See also* Peggy Wehmeyer.

Edward H. Sewell Jr.

Further Reading

"The Faith of Journalists: Does Their Religion Help or Hinder Them Professionally?" *Nieman Reports,* Fall 1997, 4–49.

Neff, David. "On the Faith Beat: Peggy Wehmeyer Pioneers Religion on ABC's World News Tonight." *Christianity Today*, 15 August 1994, 15–16.

Stout, Daniel A., and Judith Buddenbaum. *Religion and Mass Media: Audiences and Adaptations.* Thousand Oaks, CA: Sage Publications, 1996.

Ralph Renick

The premier news anchor for WTVJ-TV in Miami, Florida, Ralph Apperson Renick achieved a national reputation while serving as a south Florida newsman for 35 years with affiliations that included both CBS and NBC News networks. He was born in New York City, on August 9, 1928. He moved with his family to Miami at the age of 11 and graduated from the University of Miami in 1949, having received a fellowship in the name of noted newsman H. V. Kaltenborn.

Renick became associated with important early stories at the Sunshine State's first television station, WTVJ, and he was often in the middle of key events at the start of his career. The 10-minute program which bore his name, *The Ralph Renick Report,* went on the air on July 16, 1950. Renick handled all aspects of the production including the film and technical work, ending each program with, "Good night, and may the good news be yours." In 1952, Renick was on the scene with one of the first remote television news reports in Miami, covering the return of a just-extradited child kidnapper from Cuba. The story, focusing on the kidnap of a child of a wealthy Miami family, made headlines across the region. When the assailant emerged from the airplane he ignored newspaper reporters, heading instead for Renick, calling out for legal representation.

Renick also gained attention when he mediated a three-day dispute in 1955 revolving around race relations and the integration of an area north of Miami, Delray Beach. When national conventions emanated from Miami, Renick became a frequent network contributor. In 1957, WTVJ became the first television station to begin daily editorials, with Renick advocating construction of a firehouse on the island of Key Biscayne. In the close to 30 years which followed, Renick delivered more then 5,000 editorials. He served as anchor, news direc-tor, and editorial voice for an extended period of time and was often at the center of news stories involving developments in Cuba. Renick was one of the first news reporters to interview Fidel Castro. He also produced a documentary on the "Cuban Revolution" and organized a reporter's tour of the Soviet Union, emphasizing ties between Cuba and the former Soviet Union at that time.

Renick resigned as vice president of WTVJ News in 1985 and ran for governor of Florida. Unsuccessful in his gubernatorial bid, he joined WCIX-TV in 1988, retiring from that station in 1990. He died on July 11, 1991 and the following year WTVJ renamed the street just outside of the station Ralph Renick Way. *Fran R. Matera*

Further Reading

Alexander, S. L. "May the Good News Be Yours: Ralph Renick and Florida's First TV News." *Mass Communication Review,* 19, Winter-Spring 1992, 57-61.

"He Had Sand in His Shoes." *Miami Herald,* 13 July 1991, 25A.

Matera, Fran. "WTVJ, Miami: Wolfson, Renick, and 'May the Good News Be Yours.'" In Michael D. Murray and Donald Godfrey. *Television in America.* Ames, IA: Iowa State University Press, 1997, 106-127.

Frank Reynolds

Leading political reporter and ABC anchor Frank Reynolds was born on November 29, 1923, in East Chicago, Indiana. He attended Wabash College for one year and then enlisted in the U.S. Army. He received the Purple Heart and was promoted to the rank of sergeant. After completion of military duty in 1947, he found his first broadcasting position at WJOB in Hammond, Indiana, where he worked in news and sports. He joined WBBM, the Chicago CBS-owned station in 1950, and worked as a news reporter there until 1963, when he joined rival ABC affiliate, WLS, then known as KBKB.

Reynolds left to join ABC News as a correspondent in Washington, D.C., in 1965, and was network news co-anchor, with Howard K. Smith, from May 1968 until December 1970. Reynolds was replaced by Harry Reasoner, then spent the next eight years covering the space race and major political stories, including the Senate Watergate hearings. He returned to anchor the ABC Evening News in 1978 from his base in Washington, D.C., as part of a three-anchor format, along with Max Robinson and Peter Jennings. He held that position until just four months before his death from cancer on July 20, 1983, at the age of 60. At the time of his death, one of his five sons, Dean Reynolds, was the Washington correspondent for CNN. *Michael D. Murray*

Further Reading
Goldberg, Robert, and Gerald Jay Goldberg. *Anchors*. New York: Birch Lane Press, 1990.
Small, William. *To Kill a Messenger: TV News and the Real World*. New York: Hastings House, 1970.
Westin, Av. *Newswatch*. New York: Simon and Schuster, 1982.

Geraldo Rivera

Geraldo Rivera, an investigative reporter, news producer, author, and talk show host has been in broadcast journalism for nearly 30 years. Born in New York City, in 1943, he was educated at the University of Arizona; Brooklyn Law School; University of Pennsylvania, where he did post doctoral work; and the Columbia University Graduate School of Journalism.

Rivera's news instincts, interviewing skills, and emotional delivery made him a star almost as soon as he began his career. He worked as an investigative reporter for *Eyewitness News* on WABC-TV in New York City (1970-1974), for *Good Night America* (1972-1977), *Good Morning America* (1974-1977), and ABC News *20/20* (1978-1985). He left ABC to form the Investigative News Group for the purpose of producing a series of live specials. Also, from 1987 to 1996 he had his own talk program, *Geraldo*. In 1994, he joined CNBC to host an issues-oriented nightly news hour, *Rivera Live*.

One of Rivera's career highlights, for which he won an Emmy, was the 1972 presentation of 10 reports exposing the deplorable condition of the Willowbrook State School for the mentally retarded. In 1975, when the school was closed down, a federal court ordered that institutional care for the mentally disabled be phased out in favor of community-based group homes. Other career highlights include a report of migrant workers in California, an investigation into the death of Elvis Presley, and the securing and airing of the Zapruder film of the assassination of President Kennedy. Since 1970, Rivera has covered seven wars and interviewed such figures as Fidel Castro and Charles Manson. Some of his documentaries and news specials include "The Littlest Junkie: A Children's Story" (1973), "Innocence Lost: The Erosion of American Childhood" (1986), "American Vice: The Doping of a Nation" (1986), "Sons of Scarface" (1987), and "Murder: Live from Death Row" (1988).

Rivera has contributed much to the format of television talk shows. For *Geraldo*, Rivera added taped reports from reporters in the field. He also broadened the range of topics. In 1988, during a program about skinheads, a fight broke out on stage. When Rivera tried to break it up, his nose was broken. Due to this incident, and increased talk show competition which made sensationalism the norm, in 1996, *Geraldo* was replaced with *The Geraldo Rivera Show*. Rivera abandoned the old format, returning to the role of investigative reporter and advocate for ordinary people, attempting to be thought-provoking instead of just plain provoking. In addition to the many honors he has won, including a Peabody Award, a duPont-Columbia Award, and ten Emmys, Rivera has written five books and been involved in many philanthropic endeavors. Rivera lives in New Jersey.
Joan O'Mara

Further Reading
Rivera, Geraldo (with Paisner, D.). *Exposing Myself.* New York: Bantam, 1991.
Rivera, Geraldo. *A Special Kind of Courage*. New York: Simon & Schuster, 1976.
Rivera, Geraldo. *Willowbrook: A Report on How It Is and Why It Doesn't Have to Be That Way.* New York: Random House, 1972.

Cokie Roberts

Mary Martha Corinne Morrison Claiborne Boggs Roberts, "Cokie"—from her brother's inability to pronounce "Corinne"—was born in New Orleans on December 27, 1943, into a southern family big

© 1997 Steve Fenn/ABC, Inc.

on tradition. Traditions in her Louisiana Catholic family included more than a passing interest in the press and a passion for politics.

Cokie Roberts's great-grandfather was a newspaper publisher and a judge, and her mother Lindy Boggs, who served nearly 18 years in the U.S. Congress, flirted with journalism in college, while her father Hale Boggs, Speaker of the House, was a college journalist. But as Roberts suggested in 1990, "Politics is our family business." Her relatives have included U.S. congressional representatives, governors, and a popular mayor of New Orleans. After a childhood shuttling between her New Orleans hometown and Washington, D.C., Roberts earned a bachelor of arts degree from Wellesley College in 1964, and while working in television, married *New York Times* writer Steve Roberts.

Roberts worked in Los Angeles and Greece before returning to Washington, in 1977, where she went to work for National Public Radio's *All Things Considered* and later *Morning Edition*. One of her first assignments was covering the 1978 installation of Pope John Paul II. Roberts anchored and reported for the PBS series about Congress, *The Lawmakers*, then joined the *MacNeil-Lehrer NewsHour*. She began working for ABC-TV News in 1987.

Cokie Roberts suffered two publicized family tragedies. In 1972, her father, Congressman Hale Boggs, disappeared on a campaign flight to Alaska; in 1990 her sister Barbara Sigmund,

mayor of Princeton, New Jersey, died of cancer, leaving Roberts and one brother, Thomas Boggs, a Washington lawyer and lobbyist.

Roberts maintains her NPR position as a senior news analyst and functions as a special correspondent at ABC. She was one of many ABC staffers involved in a public debate about broadcasters accepting speakers' fees. In addition to news reports, her duties include substituting for Ted Koppel on *Nightline*. In 1994, she and husband Steve Roberts began a weekly syndicated column. Cokie Roberts and Sam Donaldson were named as co-moderators to replace David Brinkley on *This Week* in 1996.

Roberts has received many awards, including an honorary doctorate from Loyola University, which had awarded similar honors to Hale Boggs and Lindy Boggs. In 1997, she followed notables such as Walter Cronkite and Charles Kuralt in receiving the Allen Neuharth Award for Excellence in Journalism. Asked how she would like to be remembered, Roberts says people tell her they are grateful to have a "middle-aged commonsensical woman" on the air. But in her view, it is sad that in the last half of the last decade of the century, being female is still an issue.   *Sherry L. Alexander*

Further Reading

Hendrickson, Paul. "Roberts Rules." *Washington Post Magazine,* 20 June 1993.
Roberts, Cokie. *We Are Our Mother's Daughters.* New York: William Morrow, 1998.

Deborah Roberts

A Georgia native, Roberts graduated from the University of Georgia and received a Distinguished Alumnus Award from that institution in 1992. She began her television work at local affiliates in the south including WTVM-TV in Columbus, Georgia, and WBIR-TV in Knoxville, Tennessee, where she gained special recognition for reports on state government. She served as bureau chief at WFTV in Orlando, Florida covering NASA as a field anchor and was eventually named top local female anchor by the *Orlando Sentinel*.

Roberts joined NBC News as a general assignment reporter in 1990 and earned a slot on

Dateline. She covered stories in Atlanta and Miami before being sent overseas to Saudi Arabia and Kuwait to report on the aftermath of the war in the Persian Gulf. She also reported on the Summer Olympics from Barcelona, Spain, and subsequently was honored with an Emmy Award. Currently, a correspondent for the ABC newsmagazine *20/20*, Roberts has profiled civil rights pioneer Rosa Parks and has done stories on children of divorce who preferred going to jail over meeting with their fathers. She has also reported on allegations of animal abuse in circuses and conducted the first American television interview with the convicted murderer of popular Tejana music performer, Selena. Roberts lives in Manhattan with her husband, NBC weathercaster Al Roker. *See also 20/20.*   *Michael D. Murray*

Further Reading

Heyboer, Kelly. "Two for *20/20.*" *American Journalism Review*, June 1995, 9.
Rice, Lynette. "Network News Magazines: Competition Is King." *Broadcasting & Cable*, 4 November 1996, 29.

Max Robinson

Max Robinson Jr. is credited with having been the first African American to anchor a prime-time network newscast. From 1978 to 1983, Robinson was one of three anchors on ABC's *World News Tonight.* Born in Richmond, Virginia in 1939, he attended Oberlin College on a scholarship in 1957, but interrupted his studies to work in television news in Portsmouth, Virginia. He reportedly responded to a "for whites only" position advertisement, but to the surprise of many, Robinson got the job. While he was not seen on the air, at age 19, Max Robinson was one of the first African American newsmen in the country to at least to be heard on television. Later that same year, Robinson joined the Air Force. Color blindness prevented him from becoming a pilot, so he was sent to the Air Force Language Institute at Indiana University to study Russian and become a language specialist.

After leaving the military, Robinson continued his television quest. While working several odd jobs, he landed a position as a cameraman-reporter for WTOP-TV in Washington, D.C., in 1965. Robinson was instantly admired for his resonant voice and on-air camera presence. In 1966, he joined WRC-TV as a news correspondent covering Capitol Hill and the White House. He anchored *Today in Washington* and won a national Emmy Award and journalist of the year recognition from the Capitol Press Club. He returned to WTOP-TV in 1969, and became a midday anchor for *Eyewitness News,* thus becoming the first African American to anchor a newscast in Washington, D.C. Two years later, he became co-anchor with Gordon Peterson, of the 6:00 P.M. and 11:00 P.M. news. Robinson remained at WTOP-TV until 1978. He also taught broadcasting at Federal City College in Washington, D.C.

In 1978, Robinson was selected to head the national desk in Chicago for *World News Tonight* along with Peter Jennings and Frank Reynolds, who headed the Washington and foreign news desks. Although Robinson's arrival was not well received by some colleagues in the local news area, his presence on *World News Tonight* enhanced his career as a network correspondent. His reporting skills, strong camera presence, and resonant voice earned him respect. Robinson won a Capitol Press Club Award and another Emmy Award in 1981. He helped found the National Association of Black Journalists.

Robinson was outspoken about his views on the media and racism, and openly criticized the networks for what he perceived as racist practices at ABC. He lost his network anchor job in 1983, after the death of Frank Reynolds. ABC selected Peter Jennings as the sole anchor for *World News Tonight.* In 1984, Robinson joined WMAQ-TV as a co-anchor of the evening news until 1985, when his career declined while he was battling alcoholism and Acquired Immune Deficiency Syndrome (AIDS). Max Robinson died in 1988. *See also ABC News.*   *Dhyana Ziegler*

Further Reading

Matusow, Barbara. *The Evening Stars.* Boston: Houghton Mifflin, 1983.
Ziegler, Dhyana. "Max Robinson, Jr.: Turbulent Life of a Media Prophet." *Journal of Black Studies,* September 1989, 97–112.

Walter Rodgers

Walter Rodgers is a 1962 bachelor's and 1964 master's graduate of the department of history at Southern Illinois University at Carbondale.

During his journalism career, Rodgers has covered stories that had worldwide impact, including the U.S.–Soviet presidential summits, the assassinations of Israeli Prime Minister Yitzak Rabin and Martin Luther King Jr., the war in Sarajevo, the Chernobyl nuclear disaster, and the Iranian hostage story. He was one of the first correspondents to break the story about the attempted assassination of President Reagan. In addition to his work in broadcast journalism, Rodgers has written for the Associated Press, the *Washington Post,* the *Christian Science Monitor,* and the *Washingtonian Magazine.*

Rodgers worked for ABC News for 12 years, including time as a Washington and London correspondent and Moscow bureau chief. He was in Moscow during the collapse of communism and subsequent coup attempts.

Rodgers joined CNN in 1993, as the Berlin correspondent. He serves as Jerusalem bureau chief and correspondent in one of the toughest and most challenging assignments in the world. In Jerusalem, Rodgers has covered numerous high profile bombings, retaliations, and peace discussions in the Middle East.　*Cindy Price*

Further Reading

Rodgers, Walter. "The Network Correspondent as Historian, Diplomat, Student and Vampire." In *Live from the Trenches: The Changing Role of Television Correspondents,* edited by Joe S. Foote. Carbondale, IL: Southern Illinois University Press, 1998.

Smyth, Jeff. "As Network News Cuts Back, Technology Offers Other Opportunities." *St. Louis Journalism Review,* May 1996, 13.

Al Roker

Veteran weather specialist for the NBC *Today* program, Al Roker also hosts the popular Public Broadcast System series, *Going Places*, produced by WNET-TV. Born on August 20, 1954, in Queens, New York, he majored in communications in college and enrolled in some meteorology courses, while working at the campus radio station at the State University of New York at Oswego. In his sophomore year, he started doing the weekend weather at WTVH-TV in Syracuse and evolved to a full-time staff member by the time he graduated from SUNY.

After graduation, he moved to WTTG-TV in the nation's capital, where he established professional ties with Willard Scott, who served as his mentor and for whom Roker would eventually substitute on the *Today* program. Roker next joined WKYC in Cleveland, and was there from 1978 to 1983. By 1983, he was at WNBC in New York, learning still more from another weather veteran, Frank Fields. When Fields moved to WCBS, Roker replaced him at the NBC station. Roker eventually assumed duties at *Weekend Today*, then in 1996, took over as full-time weathercaster and as feature reporter for *Today*. He also hosted his own talk program. His hour-long PBS travel series, *Going Places*, has taken him to Australia, England, and Louisiana. Roker is married to Deborah Roberts, a correspondent for ABC News. ***See also** Today*.　*Michael D. Murray*

Further Reading

Brady, James. "In Step with Al Roker." *Parade Magazine*, 5 January 1997, 18.

Andy Rooney

Andy Rooney is a reluctant television performer, having earned his fame relatively late in life. Known to the public as the curmudgeonly essayist on the CBS newsmagazine *60 Minutes*, Rooney has also had a distinguished career as an author, columnist, and broadcast writer. His half-century of journalistic experience runs the gamut from reporting for the military publication *Stars and Stripes* during World War II to interviewing Dr. Jack Kevorkian on the subject of doctor-assisted suicide.

Rooney was born in Albany, New York, in 1919. Rooney began his career as a writer for the college newspaper while a student at Colgate University. He did not complete his degree, however, as World War II intervened. Rooney earned three years of additional journalistic experience in England for *Stars and Stripes*. This eventually led to the writing of one of his 11 books, *Air Gunner: The Story of The Stars and Stripes*. Returning home from the war, Rooney served as a writer for radio personalities including Arthur Godfrey, Garry Moore, and Victor Borge. He began writing video essays with CBS correspondent Harry Reasoner in 1964, with their first collaboration titled "An Essay on Doors." Rooney's 1971 essay on war was broadcast on *The Great American Dream Machine* after CBS refused to air it. Rooney stayed with the educational program until its demise in 1972.

After a short period working with Reasoner at ABC, Rooney returned to CBS. In 1978, *60 Minutes* broadcast segments titled "Three Minutes or So with Andy Rooney" as a summer replacement for James J. Kilpatrick's and Shana Alexander's political "Point/Counterpoint." Rooney's musings on everyday life, now known as "A Few Minutes with Andy Rooney," resulted in 1979, 1981, and 1982 Emmy Awards. Other awards include an Emmy for "Black History: Lost, Stolen or Strayed," six Best Script of the Year honors from the Writer's Guild, and a Peabody Award for the CBS special, *Mr. Rooney Goes to Washington*.

Despite numerous awards, Rooney has not been immune to criticism. In a 1989, CBS special, *A Year with Andy Rooney*, he commented that there had been recognition during the year that homosexual unions were among a number of actions which could lead to premature death. After much criticism from the homosexual community, Rooney's comments led to his being suspended by CBS in February 1990. Rooney felt his comments about gays were misunderstood. His three-month suspension was shortened considerably by CBS, and Rooney returned to his position at *60 Minutes*. *See also 60 Minutes*. *James E. Reppert*

Further Reading

Coffey, Frank. *60 Minutes: 25 Years of Television's Finest Hour.* New York: General Publishing Group, 1993.

Head, Sydney W., Christopher H. Sterling, and Lemuel B. Schofield. *Broadcasting in America: A Survey of Electronic Media.* New York: Houghton Mifflin, 1996.

Slater, Robert. *This ...Is CBS.* Englewood Cliffs, N.J.: Prentice-Hall, 1988.

Charlie Rose

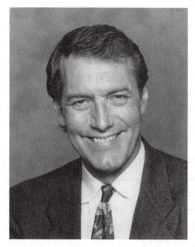

Courtesy Rose Communication/PBS

Regarded as one of television's most skilled and sensitive interviewers, Charles Peete Rose Jr. is executive producer and host of the talk program bearing his name, *The Charlie Rose Show*, originating from New York. Born on January 5, 1942, in Henderson, North Carolina, Rose is known for his ability to get his guests to talk candidly. Rose did undergraduate work and attended law school at Duke University, graduating in 1968. Rose took a bank position in New York and his wife Mary joined CBS's *60 Minutes*. Rose landed a part-time reporting position at WPIX-TV and was recommended to Bill Moyers. Moyers hired him as assistant, and Rose later became an executive producer of *Bill Moyers' Journal*.

Rose served as host of WLS's *AM Chicago*, then joined KXAS-TV in Dallas-Fort Worth as program manager and host of *The Charlie Rose Show*. In 1980, he moved his program to Washington, D.C., with the goal of gaining a wider syndication. He accepted a position as host of the CBS *Nightwatch* program, a position he held until 1990. Rose also briefly hosted the Fox network's *Personalities* program, then returned to PBS and his popular talk program in 1993. *The Charlie Rose Show* is presented by New York City's PBS station WNET and funded mostly by USA Network's cable channel as their means of supporting quality television in a different context. Underwriting support for the endeavor, raised by Rose himself, comes from The Robert Wood Johnson Jr. Charitable Trust, The Vincent Astor Foundation, Rosalind P. Walter, and the Union Pacific Corporation. The program is seen on over 200 public broadcast affiliate stations around the nation.

The program currently broadcasts from Bloomberg Television studios on Park Avenue in New York City. Rose maintains a residence in Manhattan, but he often commutes on weekends to a farm in North Carolina. He is known to viewers for his sincerity, and his goal is to conduct lengthy interviews with guests who have contributed to American society or shaped American culture. The program comes close to being unedited and attracts artists, writers, scholars, scientists, and major figures in the news. Rose regards the interviews he has conducted with Arthur Ashe, Newt Gingrich, and George Mitchell as among the best he has done. He dislikes guests with established agendas, such as actors promoting a recently released film or someone on a national book tour. These are guests who fail to distinguish between the unique qualities of this extended conversation program and many commercial programs.

Michael D. Murray

Further Reading

Rose, Van. "Rose Blooms on PBS." *The Times Leader,* 4 June 1997, C1.

Mills, James F. "Exciting Conversation." *The Herald-Sun,* 7 January 1993, 1A.

Ungar, Arthur. "Charlie Rose: PBS' 'Nightly Window on the Culture.'" *Television Quarterly,* 1997, 2–15.

William, Scott. "Charles de Rose." *New York Daily News,* 9 June 1997, 3.

Brian Ross

Brian Ross has played a major role in investigative reporting on both the nightly news and newsmagazines. His career, now spanning over 25 years, has featured several cutting-edge investigations and earned him numerous journalism awards.

Ross was born in Chicago in 1948 and raised in Highland Park, a Chicago suburb. He earned a bachelor's degree from the University of Iowa in 1971, and began his broadcasting career as a news reporter at KWWL-TV in Waterloo, Iowa. From 1972 to 1976, he reported from affiliates in Miami, Cleveland, and New York City. In 1976, he joined NBC News as a correspondent. That same year, he won the Sigma Delta Chi Award and a National Headliner Award for a series about the Teamsters Union. In 1977, he received another National Headliner Award for a five-part investigation of organized crime in the United States.

Ross continued breaking investigative ground in the 1980s and 1990s. He received yet another Headliner Award for the 1980 ABSCAM story. In 1982 Ross escaped terrorists from a hijacked Honduran airplane. He and colleague, Ira Silverman, were given unusual autonomy and time to develop stories at NBC and were rewarded with a staff consisting of a second producer and a full-time researcher. Working as a team, their stories frequently resulted in extended reports for *NBC Nightly News,* and in 1982, were recognized by duPont-Columbia for many years of investigative teamwork.

His 1989 stories on the Colombian drug cartel, including the revelation that Israeli mercenaries were training Colombian assassins, earned Ross still further recognition. In March 1990, only months before the Iraqi invasion of Kuwait, Ross exclusively reported that Iraq was trying to buy nuclear weapon trigger mechanisms. Other reports included the big business of garbage disposal, drug-smuggling and corruption in the U.S. Coast Guard, and the BCCI scandal.

In 1992, Ross became the investigative reporter for NBC's most-successful newsmagazine to date, *Dateline.* His two-part report on Wal-Mart's "Buy American" campaign revealed that a sizable amount of the store's private label clothes were being produced by children in warehouses in Bangladesh. Ross received a George A. Polk Award, to go along with other awards he had won in 1992—the Peabody Award, the National Emmy Award, and the Overseas Press Club Award.

In July 1994, Ross became chief investigative correspondent for ABC News. He subsequently appeared on several ABC news programs, including *20/20, Day One, Nightline, World News Tonight,* and *Prime Time Live.* His reports have included the Valujet plane crash, the Unabomber investigation, and the Oklahoma City bombing investigation. Early in his career, Ross broke the ABSCAM story and also discovered the whereabouts of financier Robert Vesco, after a three-week stakeout in Cuba. Ross is regarded by some critics as the highest-profile and most well-respected national investigative reporter on national television. *Burton St. John*

Further Reading

Madsen, Axel. *60 Minutes: The Power and the Politics of America's Most Popular TV News Show.* New York: Dodd, Mead, 1984.

Matusow, Barbara. "NBC's Intrepid Investigators: Brian Ross and Ira Silverman." *Washington Journalism Review,* June 1986, 19–22.

Louis Rukeyser

Photo by Susan Noonan/Maryland Public Television

Louis Rukeyser is host of the Public Broadcasting Service's *Wall $treet Week With Louis Rukeyser,* which is consistently one of the top-rated and most highly respected programs on that network. The half-hour financial and economics affairs program, which celebrated its 25th anniversary in 1995, appears each Friday and attracts more than 10 million viewers. Both the program and Rukeyser have received a great deal of recognition and have won

dozens of national awards. Rukeyser is also a well-known lecturer, writer, and editor. His books include *What's Ahead for the Economy: The Challenge and the Change, How to Make Money in Wall Street,* and *Louis Rukeyser's Book of Lists.* Since 1992 he has been editor of a monthly newsletter *Louis Rukeyser's Wall Street,* and in 1994 he launched another monthly newsletter, *Louis Rukeyser's Mutual Funds.*

Rukeyser was born on January 30, 1933, in New York City. He began his journalism career after he graduated from the Woodrow Wilson School of Public and International Affairs at Princeton University in 1954 and joined the *Baltimore Sun* newspapers. He stayed for 11 years as a political and foreign correspondent, including chief political correspondent, chief of the London bureau, and chief Asian correspondent. While working for the *Sun,* he received a number of international honors, including two Overseas Press Club Awards. Rukeyser entered broadcasting in 1965, when he became a Paris correspondent for ABC News, followed by a stint as chief of the network's London bureau. Three years later he became the network and television's first economic editor, and he also served as a commentator for ABC radio and television. His radio commentary entitled, *Rukeyser's World,* won the George Washington Medal of the Freedoms Foundation. He won a second Freedoms Foundation Award in 1978 for his widely read weekly syndicated newspaper column, which he began writing in 1976. The column has been published for nearly two decades.

His *Wall $treet Week With Louis Rukeyser* program features a panel of ecomonic experts and a guest who is an expert in a particular financial area. The program, with Rukeyser in charge, has received dozens of national awards, including the G.M. Loeb Award in financial journalism—the first time the award had ever been bestowed on a broadcaster. In 1990, he became the first male recipient of the Women's Economic Round Table Award "for outstanding service in educating the public about business, financial, and economic policy." He has been called "everyone's favorite economic commentator" by the *Washington Post* and "the economic guru of the industry" by *New York Daily News* columnist Kay Gandella. In

1996, he also began offering a twice a week commentary on personal finance and investment information on the CNNfn cable network.

Roy L. Moore

Further Reading

Natalie Davis. "Louis Rukeyser Celebrates a Silver Anniversary: 25 Years of Financial Forecasts; Host of Television Program 'Wall $treet Week With Louis Rukeyser.'" *Business Credit,* March 1996, 18.

"Wall $treet Wise Guy Marks 20 Years on the Air; Media against the Gray Flannel of the Financial World, Louis Rukeyser Is Practically Psychedelic." *Los Angeles Times,* 12 November 1990, D2.

Tim Russert

Photo courtesy of Tim Russert

Since 1991, Tim Russert has been moderating NBC's *Meet the Press*. He first appeared as a panelist on that program in 1990. He is also a political analyst for *NBC's Nightly News* and *Today,* and anchors *The Tim Russert Show* weekly on CNBC. Russert joined NBC News in 1984 as a vice president. He supervised live *Today* program broadcasts from Rome; served as a vice president for NBC News projects from South America, Australia, and China; reported from six U.S.–Soviet Summits; and produced the special, *A Day in the Life of the White House*.

Born on May 7, 1950, in Buffalo, New York, Russert is a graduate of John Carroll University in Cleveland. He served as president of the Student Union at John Carroll and received the Centennial Medal, which was awarded to 100 distinguished alumni. A graduate of Cleveland-Marshall Law School, he was admitted to the bar in New York State and Washington D.C.

Prior to working at NBC, he served as a counselor to New York Governor Mario Cuomo and was chief of staff for New York Senator Patrick Moynihan. In 1994, Russert was nominated for Cable Television's Ace Award as "Best Interviewer." Other awards include the John Peter Zenger Award from the New York Bar Association and honorary degrees from Canisius College and Marist College. Russert is married to Mauren Orth, a writer for *Vanity Fair*. ***See also*** *Meet the Press*.

Mary E. Beadle

Further Reading

Aucoin, Don. "Meet the Host: Tim Russert is the Big Reason 'Meet the Press' is Riding High." *Boston Globe,* 12 October 1997, N1.

Boyer, Peter J. *Who Killed CBS?* New York: Random House, 1988.

Murphy, Mary. "Talk Scoop." *TV Guide,* 2 November 1996, 48–52.

Randolph, Eleanor. "Host of 'Meet the Press' A Self-Made Player on '96 Election Scene." *Los Angeles Times,* 19 June 1996, A5.

S

Morley Safer

In 20 years as a war correspondent, Morley Safer covered nine wars. He made his reputation in Vietnam. His coverage there earned numerous awards including three Overseas Press Club Awards, a George Polk Memorial Award from the Radio-Television News Directors Association, and a Paul White Memorial Award. Safer's Vietnam war coverage also won him one of his two George Peabody Awards. His 1965 film report showing a marine at Cam Ne setting a hut on fire with a cigarette lighter almost singlehandedly ushered in the era known as "the living room war."

President Lyndon Johnson was irate over the negative publicity Safer created concerning the Vietnam War and unsuccessfully pressured CBS to censor him. Fred Friendly, then head of CBS News, protected Safer from most of the government's pressure but, as Safer put it, he got the "big freeze" from American officials in Vietnam.

Safer was born on November, 8, 1931, in Toronto, Canada. He attended the University of Western Ontario, graduating in 1953. Safer began his career as a reporter for newspapers and wire services in Canada and England. Prior to joining CBS News as a correspondent based in the London Bureau in 1964, he was a correspondent and producer with the Canadian Broadcasting Corporation. Safer immigrated to the United States in 1964. In that same year, he teamed with veteran correspondent Charles Collingwood to cover the British elections and the death of Churchill.

In 1965, he opened CBS News's Saigon bureau and served two tours in Vietnam. Instead of relying on the censored reports handed out by the U.S. public information offices, Safer and his Vietnamese cameraman, who doubled as an interpreter, would go "jungle-bashing" with the troops. In 1967, he was named CBS's London bureau chief covering Europe, Africa, and the Middle East. In December 1970, Safer left London to join *60 Minutes* in New York as the replacement for Harry Reasoner. Within months Safer was turning out his own share of investigative pieces and revealing profiles. Known for his gentlemanly reserve yet tenacious pursuit of stories, Safer played a prominent role in establishing the tone of *60 Minutes*. Perhaps one of broadcasting's most gifted writers, he infuses reports with a personal point of view while maintaining high professional standards.

At least four of his programs at *60 Minutes* have won Emmys. These include "Pops"(1979); "Teddy Kolleck's Jerusalem" (1979); Investigative Journalism "Air Force Surgeon" (1982); and Correspondent "It Didn't Have To Happen" (1982). In May 1994, Safer hosted "One for the Road: A Conversation with Charles Kuralt and Morley Safer," a CBS News Special, marking his colleague's retirement. *See also 60 Minutes.*

Dan B. Curtis

Futher Reading

Hewitt, Don. *Minute by Minute.* New York: Random House, 1985.

Madsen, Axel. *60 Minutes: The Power and Politics of America's Most Popular TV News Show.* New York: Dodd House, 1984.

Safer, Morley. *Flashbacks: On Returning to Vietnam.* New York: Random House, 1990.

Richard Salant

President of CBS News from 1961 to 1964, and again from 1966 to 1979, Richard Salant expanded the evening newscast from 15 to 30 minutes and was responsible for the development of *60 Minutes,* the first and most successful television newsmagazine. His decision to broadcast the controversial documentary "The Selling of the Pentagon" in 1971 incurred the wrath of the White House and some members of Congress. A passionate defender of the First Amendment, he later criticized broadcasters who seemed more interested in ratings than news quality.

Salant's rise to the top news position at CBS was unique because he was not a journalist, but an attorney. Born in New York City, on April 14, 1914, he graduated from Harvard College in 1935, and its law school in 1938. The only writing experience he had was as editor of his prepatory school paper and on *The Harvard Law Review.* After graduating from law school, Salant worked for the National Labor Relations Board (NLRB) in Washington and then for the U.S. solicitor general from 1941 to 1943. After a stint in the Navy as a lieutenant commander, he went into private law practice after the war, for the law firm of Rosenman, Goldmark, Colin, and Kaye, which represented CBS. In 1952, he joined that network as a vice president.

Salant represented CBS in matters before the Federal Communications Commission and in litigation against NBC over which network would develop color television. Despite his network's loss in the case, Salant impressed CBS president Frank Stanton, who appointed him to lead CBS News in 1961. During his two tenures with CBS News (interrupted in 1964 when he was named as special assistant to the network's president), he was credited with raising news standards, not only with expanded news coverage, but also with a strong sense of integrity. He once said that his competitive pressure was driven not so much for ratings but for recognition and respect of peers.

In addition to lengthening evening newscasts and starting *60 Minutes,* he was in charge during some of most seminal events of the time, such as the assassinations of President John F. Kennedy and Martin Luther King Jr., the Vietnam War, the Apollo 11 moon landing, and the Watergate scandal. CBS devoted more airtime to Watergate than the other networks, sometimes to the consternation of CBS chairman William S. Paley who questioned Salant about the need for so much coverage.

In 1971, "The Selling of the Pentagon" examined the military's manipulation of public opinion and the media. It brought criticism, with White House officials attempting to pressure CBS to replace reporters. Some members of Congress wanted to cite the network and Frank Stanton for contempt. CBS did not waiver. Although Salant was a staunch defender of the First Amendment, he did not hesitate to question when he felt broadcasters acted improperly or unethically. He criticized the use of fictionalized versions of news events and was especially critical of the staging of a car explosion by NBC News to illustrate a design defect.

Salant retired from CBS in 1979, upon reaching the mandatory retirement age of 65. He became a vice president at NBC News and served from 1979 to 1982. Salant died on February 16, 1993, at age 78 in Southport, Connecticut. *See also* CBS News. *Mark Conrad*

Further Reading

Paper, Lewis. *Empire: William S. Paley and the Making of CBS.* New York: St. Martin's Press, 1987.

"Richard Salant, 78, Who Headed CBS News in Expansion, Is Dead." *New York Times,* 17 February 1993, B8.

"Richard Salant, 78, Ex-Chief of CBS News." *Newsday*, 17 February 1993, 86.

Marlene Sanders

Marlene Sanders is notable for a number of accomplishments including her historic visit to prime time television in 1964—the first appearance of a female newsanchor on the evening network news. She subsequently has become among the most venerated of woman broadcasters. She spent nearly 20 years in radio and television, 14 years at ABC and 10 at CBS. She also worked in independent syndicated programming. She has written much, served in countless organizations, won innumerable awards, and is currently a faculty member at New York University.

Born on January 10, 1931, in Cleveland, she attended Ohio State University from 1948 to 1949. Sanders accepted a writer and producer position at WNEW-TV in New York City in 1955. Serving at WNEW until 1960, Sanders moved to Westinghouse Broadcasting Corporation as producer and writer for *P.M.* for a year, and in 1962, she moved to WNEW-Radio as an assistant director for news and public affairs. In 1964, Sanders moved back into television as a correspondent for ABC News.

While at ABC News she covered President Kennedy's funeral, the March on Washington in 1963, the inauguration of President Johnson in 1965, and did a tour of Vietnam in 1966. She also covered Lynda Bird Robb's White House wedding in 1967, and the visit of Prime Minister Golda Meier to the United States in 1969. Sanders left her correspondent duties to become a documentary producer from 1972 to 1976, and then in 1976, became vice president and director of ABC television documentaries, a position she held until 1978.

Sanders returned to daily news work as a correspondent for CBS in 1978 and stayed there until 1987, when she became the host of *Currents* at WNET-TV in New York, and from 1988 to 1990, she served as the host of *Metropolitan Week in Review*. Since 1991, she has been a professor at New York University in the Department of Journalism. She plays an active role in many programs sponsored by The Freedom Forum, Media Studies Center, and Columbia University. In 1995 she joined the new Prime Life Network (aimed at viewers over 50 years old), as a newsanchor. Since her debut as the first female evening anchor, Sanders has won several Emmy Awards, was named Woman of the Year by the American Women in Radio and TV in 1975, and earned the Silver Satellite Award in 1977. She is also a past president of Women in Communications.   *Carol A. Atkinson*

Further Reading
"Bylines: Prime Time." *American Journalism Review*, December 1995, 8.
Sanders, M., and M. Rock. *Waiting for Prime Time: The Women of Television News.* New York: Harper and Row, 1988.

Mark Sauter

Courtesy *Inside Edition*

Mark Sauter was born on January 29, 1960 in New Bedford, Massachusetts. He began his broadcast journalism career as an investigative reporter for KIRO-TV in Seattle. After working as an investigative reporter for three years for the television series *American Journal,* Sauter joined newsmagazine, *Inside Edition,* as investigative reporter in August 1996. He received a bachelor of arts degree from Harvard University in 1982 and a master of science degree from the Columbia University Graduate School of Journalism in 1987. Sauter completed military service from 1982 to 1986 as an Army officer in the light infantry and special forces units.

One of his most noteworthy reports while at *Inside Edition* investigated the frequenting of KOA campgrounds by people accused of violent crimes. Sauter, however, regards his 1989 investigation into the transferral of American POWs from Korea to the Soviet Union as perhaps his most significant story. He is the co-author of two books concerning the POW/MIA issue.

Sauter's reports have earned him a number of distinctions and awards including two Emmys, the Radio-Television News Director's (RTNDA) Edward R. Murrow Award, and also the RTNDA's Oldfield Fellowship. He left *Inside Edition* in August, 1998 to co-found APB Multimedia, the first brand for police and crime news with an immediate goal to launch a Web site called "APB Online." The organization provides material to a variety of media outlets. his current title is Director of Content. *Steven Phipps*

Further Reading

Sanders, James D., Mark A. Sauter, and R. Cort Kirkwood. *Soldiers of Misfortune: Washington's Secret Betrayal of American POWs in the Soviet Union.* Washington, DC: National Press Books, 1992.

Sauter, Mark, and Jim Saunders. *The Men We Left Behind: Henry Kissinger, the Politics of Deceit and the Tragic Fate of POWs After the Vietnam War.* Washington, DC: National Press Books, 1993.

Van Gordon Sauter

Van Gordon Sauter, a former president of CBS News and Fox News, became famous for adding emotional "moments" to network news program. Sauter was born September 14, 1935, and grew up in Dayton Ohio. After graduating from Ohio University in 1957, Sauter joined the executive training program at McCann-Erickson advertising agency in New York City. He resigned to pursue a master's degree in journalism at the University of Missouri.

After working for the New Bedford, Massachusetts, *Standard-Times*, he was hired by the Detroit *Free Press*. As a correspondent for the *Free Press* and the Knight Newspapers, he went to Vietnam twice. When he joined the *Chicago Daily News,* he covered urban riots. In 1968, the CBS-owned WBBM-AM in Chicago adopted an all-news format and Sauter became a correspondent. He rose to news director at WBBM before heading to New York to handle special events for CBS Radio. Sauter returned to Chicago in 1972 for his first television assignment as news director of WBBM-TV. He decided to try anchoring but after

eight months, it proved to be a disaster. He returned to CBS News to work as a correspondent in Paris, but by 1976, Sauter returned to the states, this time as CBS vice president of program practices, examining thousands of programs and commercials for anything "disgusting or dirty."

Sauter gained a reprieve from his role as censor when the network-owned KNXT in Los Angeles hired him to become station manager. Sauter took control of the troubled CBS Sports. In less than 16 months, CBS Sports began to show a surge in momentum and morale. When CBS News President William Leonard announced his retirement in 1981, Sauter took over. He presided during a turbulent period. General William Westmoreland sued the network, alleging a conspiracy to distort reports of enemy troop strength in Vietnam. It was also on Sauter's watch that personnel cutbacks began. In 1986, he left CBS and began teaching and writing in California.

In 1992, News Corporation Chairman Rupert Murdoch asked Sauter to take charge of Fox News. At the time, only 34 of 140 Fox affiliates carried local news and Sauter set a goal of attracting between 70 to 80 percent of the stations. He wanted to produce a national newscast at Fox. Sauter left Fox in May 1995, to become general manager of KVIE-TV, Sacramento, California. He left KVIE in 1998 and moved to Los Angeles. *William R. Davie*

Further Reading

Friend, Tad. "Not Necessarily the News." *Vanity Fair,* October 1992.

Sobran, Joseph. "Whodunit?" *National Review,* 22 July 1988, 43–44.

Jessica Savitch

Jessica Savitch was one of the nation's best-known television news personalities until her premature death in 1983. In life, she was seen as a pioneer and role model for aspiring women journalists. In death, however, she has been seen by many as a symbol and victim of television's excesses.

Savitch was born in Pennsylvania in 1947. She began her broadcasting career at the age of 14 at an Atlantic City radio station. She attended

Ithaca College while working as a disc jockey in Rochester. After graduation, she briefly worked at WCBS-AM in New York. In 1971, KHOU-TV in Houston hired Savitch and soon made her the first woman television anchor in the South. She then moved to KYW-TV in Philadelphia, where she won awards for series on topics ranging from rape to natural childbirth. Long determined to become a network correspondent by age 30, Savitch got her wish in 1977. NBC gave her a contract to anchor its Saturday newscasts and cover the U.S. Senate.

As an anchor, Savitch was a great success, noted for having an extraordinary rapport on camera. She did occasional stints on *Meet the Press* and *Today* in addition to NBC *News Digest*, a brief headline update that ran during prime-time programming. Soon, she was routinely listed as one of the most popular anchors in the country. In 1982, PBS hired her to host its new documentary series *Frontline*, hoping to use her celebrity status to entice people to watch.

But if Savitch was a celebrity as an anchor, she often struggled as a reporter. She was not adequately prepared to cover the Senate beat and was soon pulled from it. Many at NBC scorned her as being symptomatic of television news' increasing preoccupation with image rather than substance. Many also disliked Savitch for her sometimes difficult off-camera behavior. Widespread rumors of drug abuse arose after she stumbled badly on the air during an October 1983 broadcast. Shortly after that incident, she was killed in a rather unusual car accident.

Savitch's death came as a shock to many who saw her as an inspiration. She had helped break ground for women in broadcast news virtually everywhere she had worked, and she had targeted her popular 1982 autobiography particularly at young women. But two tell-all biographies published after Savitch's death focused more on her tumultuous personal life: her long, abusive relationship with a newsman; her failed marriages, the second of which ended when her husband hanged himself; and her exploitation by the television industry. In 1995, Lifetime aired a made-for-television motion picture, *Almost Golden: The Jessica Savitch Story*, based on one of those books. The following year, Disney released *Up Close and Per-*

sonal. Ostensibly based on Savitch's life, the movie omitted most of the personal details in favor of a conventional Hollywood romance.

Matthew C. Ehrlich

Further Reading
Blair, Gwenda. *Almost Golden.* New York: Simon & Schuster, 1988.

Nash, Alanna. *Golden Girl.* New York: E. P. Dutton, 1988.

Savitch, Jessica. *Anchorwoman.* New York: G. P. Putnam's Sons, 1982.

Diane Sawyer

© 1992 ABC, Inc. Photo by Timothy White

Diane Sawyer is one of the best-known newswomen in America. Winner of eight Emmy Awards, she has been a mainstay in news programming for more than 15 years. Sawyer's career was launched in the early 1980s, when CBS named her anchor of the *CBS Morning News* and subsequently selected her as the first woman correspondent for *60 Minutes*. Respected as one of the most thoughtful, articulate, and balanced analysts of politics, economics, and culture on American television, Sawyer now co-anchors an edition of *20/20* with Sam Donaldson on ABC, and along with Barbara Walters and Forrest Sawyer, is one of the network's first choices for other magazine news shows. She is also a substitute anchor for *World News Tonight* and *Nightline*.

Born in Glasgow, Kentucky, on December 22, 1945, Sawyer received her bachelor of arts degree from Wellesley College in 1967. Her first reporting position was with WLKY-TV in Louisville from 1967 to 1970. From 1970 to 1974, she worked in the White House press office and in the mid-1970s helped to research information for the memoirs of former president Richard M. Nixon. Moving back into journalism as a general assignment reporter for CBS from 1978 to 1981, Sawyer was named co-anchor for *CBS Morning News* in 1981. Other positions she has held include co-anchor of the *Early Morning News* at CBS from 1982 to 1984, correspondent and editor for *CBS's 60 Minutes* from 1984 to 1989, co-anchor at *Prime Time Live* on ABC from 1989 to 1998, co-anchor of *Turning Point* in 1994, and co-anchor of *ABC's Day One* in 1995. Recently, Sawyer has reported on public school bureaucracies, toxic waste, incorrect drugstore prescriptions, Robert McNamara and the Vietnam War, actor Carroll O'Connor and the death of his son, and the wife of a convicted CIA spy. She also reported on fraud in the diamond industry, on age discrimination, and on the leadership of Russian President Boris Yeltsin.

During the 1991–1992 season, Sawyer received several national journalism awards. Her investigation of racial discrimination, comparing how white and black applicants for employment were treated, won the grand prize in the Robert F. Kennedy Journalism Awards. Her story about daycare centers and their unsanitary conditions and inattentive workers won the National Headliner Award, the Ohio State Award and the Sigma Delta Chi Award. Sawyer has won several public service accolades in addition to her Emmy Awards. She also has been inducted into the Broadcast Magazine Hall of Fame and has received the University of Southern California Distinguished Achievement in Journalism Award. She was selected as a participant at Washington State University's Edward R. Murrow School of Communication to commemorate Murrow's contributions and discuss the qualities needed for today's professional broadcasters. ***See also** Prime Time Live.*

Jan Whitt

Further Reading

Flander, Judy. "Women in Network News." *Washington Journalism Review,* March 1985, 39–43.

Gates, Gary Paul. *Air Time: The Inside Story of CBS News.* New York: Harper and Row, 1978.

Winfield, Betty Honchin. *The Edward R. Murrow Heritage: Challenge for the Future.* Ames, IA: Iowa State University Press, 1986.

Forrest Sawyer

Forrest Sawyer is co-anchor of the ABC newsmagazine *Turning Point*. He is also a frequent guest host on *Nightline* and *World News Tonight*. Born in Lakeland, Florida, in 1949, Sawyer graduated from the University of Florida at Gainesville in 1971, majoring in Eastern philosophy and world religion. He earned a master's degree in education in 1976.

Sawyer began his career working at numerous radio stations including WGST Newsradio in Atlanta, WDVH-AM in Gainesville, Florida, and WVBF-FM in Boston. He was newsanchor at WAGA-TV in Atlanta from 1985 to 1987. He joined ABC News in July 1988, as co-anchor of *World News This Morning* and the news segments on *Good Morning, America*. He later was the sole anchor of *Day One*.

Sawyer's career has taken him around the world. He always carries his passport in his pocket so he can leave on a moment's notice, describing himself as a "utility infielder." But the Persian Gulf War took him from pinch-hitter to powerslugger. Sawyer filed the first footage of Iraqi deserters and the first live report from the front. He has received numerous honors including a Peabody Award, three Emmy Awards, two Sigma Delta Chi Awards, and an Associated Press Award.

Jack Hodgson

Further Reading

Diamond, Edwin. "Who Won the Media War" *New York,* 18 March 1991, 26–29.

Gerston, Jill. "Forrest Sawyer: Gathering the Spoils of War." *New York Times,* 12 April 1992, sec. 2, 27.

Hall, Jane. "Day Premiere." *Los Angeles Times,* 6 March 1993, sec. F3.

Chuck Scarborough

Charles Bishop "Chuck" Scarborough III was born in Pittsburgh, Pennsylvania on November 4, 1943. A veteran of the United States Air Force, he is a 1969 alumnus of the University of Southern Mississippi in Hattiesburg. Before entering college as a radio-television major, Scarborough had already gotten his start in newscasting at WLOX-TV in Biloxi, Mississippi. He eventually advanced to anchoring the ABC affiliate's daily newscasts.

While in his last year at the University of Southern Mississippi, Scarborough started his association with the NBC network. He anchored and reported the news at WDAM-TV in Hattiesburg. He was noted for his coverage of Hurricane Camille, which struck the Mississippi Gulf Coast full-force, in August 1969. After graduating, Scarborough served in the dual role of anchorman and assistant news director at WAGA-TV in Atlanta, a CBS affiliate at that time. During his two-and-a-half year tenure there, he coordinated and supervised the station's production of all special reports and news programming.

In 1972, Scarborough moved from Atlanta to Boston. While in Boston, he worked as an anchor and reporter at another CBS affiliate, WNAC-TV. Scarborough was responsible for coverage of both local and national news during the WNAC's 6 P.M. and 11 P.M. newscasts. In 1974, Scarborough took over the co-anchor position with Jim Hartz during the station's two-hour early evening news at WNBC-TV, in New York City. The program was later expanded and he was given a position at the NBC network. Scarborough's new network duties included serving as co-anchor on the NBC News *Update*, consisting of news shorts along with Edwin Newman and Tom Snyder. In 1989, Scarborough was offered a co-anchor position with Maria Shriver and Mary Alice Williams for a new show on NBC entitled, *Yesterday, Today, and Tomorrow*. The program was presented to the viewing public as a prime-time news program.

Scarborough, known in New York for his investigative reporting skills, has garnered six Associated Press Awards and an Emmy. Currently, he is anchoring and reporting on the *News 4 New York* program at 6 P.M. on weeknights. Scarborough fre-

quently serves as a master-of-ceremonies, a presenter of awards during events in and around New York City, and a ambassador of goodwill for the metropolitan area. He is often identified as the prototype of the involved newsanchor, with a strong stake in the community, who is able to stay detached and objective on critically important stories. In November 1995, Scarborough participated in the National Urban League's Community Heroes Award at its Equal Opportunity Day dinner. There he presented an award to Oseola McCarty, the 87-year old laundry woman who gave $150,000 of her life savings to Scarborough's alma mater, the University of Southern Mississippi.

Tommy V. Smith

Further Reading

Matusow, Barbara. *The Evening Stars, The Making of the Network News Anchor.* Boston: Houghton Mifflin, 1983.
Powers, Ron. *The Newscasters: The News Business as Show Business.* New York: St. Martin's Press, 1978.

Bob Schieffer

Bob Schieffer holds the record for the longest run as an anchor on a regularly scheduled network newscast, the Saturday edition of the *CBS Evening News,* for 20 years, from 1976 to 1996. Bob Lloyd Schieffer was born in Austin, Texas, on February 25, 1937. He grew up in Fort Worth and began reading newspapers, mostly the comic pages, in the first grade. He had wanted to be a reporter, (but a print reporter) since he was in the eighth grade before television even came to Fort Worth. Schieffer attended Texas Christian University. During his second year, he got his first reporter's job, driving the mobile unit for KXOL. Schieffer did on-the-scene broadcasts taken from monitoring the police radio. He was also a member of the Air Force ROTC, and after graduating with a bachelor of arts degree in 1959, he went to Travis Air Force Base in California where he was in charge of base publications and handled the duties of an Air Force Information Officer.

After three years in the Air Force, Schieffer joined the *Fort Worth Star-Telegram.* He was working on Friday, November 22, 1963, and covered the events surrounding the Kennedy assassination for the *Star-Telegram*. He was one of three major figures, along with Dan Rather and Robert MacNeil, who covered those events first-hand. Toward the end of 1965, the paper sent him to Vietnam. He regarded that five-month assignment as one of his most personally satisfying, because he wrote about soldiers from the Fort Worth area. The paper prominently ran these stories which were well received. In fact, when Schieffer returned he discovered that he had become something of a media celebrity. He was interviewed over the local NBC affiliate WBAP-TV (now KXAS-TV) and was offered a job as evening anchor.

In 1969, Schieffer joined the CBS News bureau in Washington, D.C. He covered all four major beats in the nation's capital: the White House, the Pentagon, the State Department, and Capitol Hill. He has been chief Washington correspondent since 1982, host of *Face the Nation*, and occasional substitute for Dan Rather on the *CBS Evening News*. In 1989, he co-authored *The Acting President* about the Reagan years. Schieffer has won numerous awards including some of the most prestigious from Sigma Delta Chi and the Associated Press Managing Editors Association. He says the trust of the audience is the greatest honor he can receive. His calm, measured, on-camera presence has made him a trusted figure.

Suzanne Huffman

Further Reading

DeParle, Jason. "Dressing Down the Bureau." *Washington Journalism Review,* January/February 1983.
Goldberg, Robert, and Gerald Jay Goldberg. *Anchors.* New York: Birch Lane Press, 1990.
Townley, Roderick. "Serious Artist? Manic Golfer? Good-Ol'-Boy Texan? Bob Schieffer?" *TV Guide,* 8 November 1986.

David Schoenbrun

David Schoenbrun was one of the group of foreign correspondents hired by Edward R. Murrow, referred to as "Murrow's Boys," whose reporting elevated CBS News to a premier position in broadcast journalism in the 1950s and 1960s. Schoenbrun, especially during his tenure as the head of the CBS Paris bureau from 1947 through 1961, became renowned for knowing everyone in French politics from President Charles De Gaulle to the head of the Communist Party.

Schoenbrun was born in New York City in 1915. After graduating from City College of New York with a bachelor of arts degree in 1934, he taught languages in the New York City Public School system. In 1939, he became a freelance writer and translator. When World War II started he worked at the Office of War Information, then in 1943 enlisted as a private in the U.S. Army. While serving in Algiers in 1943 with military intelligence, Schoenbrun met Murrow, who was impressed that Schoenbrun had taught school and promised him that after the war, "I could give you the largest classroom in the world" (David Schoenbrun, *America Inside Out,* New York: McGraw-Hill, 1984, p. 165).

After the war, Schoenbrun worked in Paris for the Overseas News Agency and as a stringer for CBS. In 1947, he was hired as chief of the CBS Paris bureau. Schoenbrun became legendary for his knowledge of France and the French people. Indeed, it was said that after a journalist presented credentials at the Elysee Palace their next stop was a visit to Schoenbrun's CBS office. With innumerable contacts in the French government, and access to General Dwight D. Eisenhower, whom he had met in North Africa, Schoenbrun scored many firsts. He was the first to report that General Matthew Ridgeway would replace Eisenhower as head of the NATO forces, that France would pull its navy out of NATO, and that John Foster Dulles would resign as secretary of state.

Even while stationed abroad, Schoenbrun made frequent trips to the United States. One of the most important trips was for his coverage of the Eisenhower presidential campaign in 1952. Before Eisenhower had decided to campaign for the presidency, Schoenbrun gave him tips on how to effectively use television. In 1962, Schoenbrun returned home to head the CBS Washington bureau. However, his stay there was short-lived and he was replaced in 1963. Shortly thereafter, in 1964, he resigned from CBS. Following this,

Schoenbrun wrote a number of books, including *The Three Lives of Charles De Gaulle* and *Soldiers of the Night*. In 1981, he became an analyst for Independent Network News. Schoenbrun was a recipient of both the croix de guerre and the French Legion d'Honor. He died in New York City on May 23, 1988.   *Albert Auster*

Further Reading

Cloud, Stanley, and Lynne Olson. *The Murrow Boys: Pioneers on the Front Lines of Broadcast Journalism.* Boston: Houghton Mifflin, 1996.
Schoenbrun, David. *On and Off the Air: An Informal History of CBS News.* New York: Dutton, 1989.
Sperber, A.M. *Murrow: His Life and Times.* New York: Bantam, 1986.

Reese Schonfeld

When Ted Turner asked Reese Schonfeld his astrological sign, Reese knew he might be in trouble. In 1978, the outspoken Turner had decided to create a 24-hour news channel and had selected Schonfeld from New York to make a go of it as president of the new Cable News Network (CNN). When Turner asked Schonfeld how much it was going to cost him to have him come on board for the new venture, Schonfeld reportedly said that he had to make enough so that when Turner fired him, he would not have to work again. Turner's response was to compare their astrological signs and declare it a perfect match.

Schonfeld was not new to the news arena. His career began with United Press International (UPI), where he moved up to become vice president of the television division, United Press International Television Network. Schonfeld's experience with UPI challenged him to consider the most efficient newsfeeds and the benefits such feeds provided individual television stations. In 1975, he left UPI and created a partnership with 25 independent television stations that he called the Independent Television News Association (ITNA). ITNA provided a nightly national newscast for its affiliates. On several occasions, Schonfeld approached Turner at various national cable conferences regarding the possibility of signing him up for the service. Turner insisted he was not interested in news.

In 1978, Turner called unexpectedly, declaring that television could do four things: movies, sports, sitcoms, and news. From Turner's perspective, the only area that he had not tapped was news. He sold the all news network idea to Schonfeld, who had already pitched it unsuccessfully within his own organization. Schonfeld flew to Atlanta the next week, and while on the plane, used the back of an envelope to sketch out a budget and programming clock for a 24-hour news channel.

He envisioned a news network that, in its coverage of the story, was part of the story. He believed CNN was his opportunity to create such a network. During the 1980s and under Schonfeld's leadership, CNN began as "chicken noodle news" and finished the decade as a valid news competitor. CNN's noted coverage of national and international disasters secured its reputation as being able to bring viewers timely reports.

Schonfeld's experience with CNN not only taught him about news, but provided the inside track on what makes a cable channel successful. In the early 1990s, Schonfeld founded the Television Food Network, TVFN. Even though he is no longer acting president of TVFN, he does serve as vice chairman and retains equity in the cable network. Occasionally, Schonfeld can be seen and heard giving commentary on current broadcast and cable news issues. *See also* CNN.   *Connie Book*

Further Reading

Goldberg, Robert, and Jay Goldberg. *Citizen Turner.* New York: Harcourt Brace, 1995.
Scholosser, Joe. "No Couch, but Lots of Potatoes." *Broadcasting & Cable*, 10 March 1997.
"Sweeps Get National Attention." *Television Digest*, 20 January 1997.

Daniel Schorr

Daniel Schorr, currently senior news analyst for National Public Radio and contributor to the *New Leader*, is the last member of the legendary Edward R. Murrow team still active in daily journalism. Born in 1916, his career spans nearly six decades. From 1941 to 1953, he freelanced for the *Christian Science Monitor* and the *New York Times*. In 1953, his radio reports from Holland attracted Murrow's attention, and Schorr was invited to join CBS News in Washington. In 1955, he opened the CBS Moscow bureau, and arranged the first television interview with a Soviet leader. He then served as bureau chief in Germany and Central Europe.

In 1966, he returned to the United States. While covering the congressional investigation of the CIA, he risked a contempt citation for refusing to reveal the source of a copy of the House intelligence committee's secret Pike Report, which he had given to *The Village Voice*. Schorr later resigned from CBS. He wrote *Clearing the Air*, and then in 1979 helped create CNN, functioning as the senior Washington correspondent until 1985. Schorr has won numerous awards, including Overseas Press Club citations, Emmy Awards, a lifetime Peabody Award, and the 1996 duPont-Columbia Golden Baton.   *Joan O'Mara*

Further Reading

Hilliard, Robert L., and Michael C. Keith. *The Broadcast Century*. Boston: Focal Press, 1992.

Schorr, Daniel. *Clearing the Air*. Boston: Houghton Mifflin, 1977.

Schorr, Daniel. "Richard Nixon: The Best of Enemies." *New York Times Magazine,* 1 January 1995, 32.

Willard Scott

Willard Scott has been described as "America's best known weatherman," "offbeat," "zany," and "folksy." His replacement on the *Today* show, Al Roker, calls Scott his "second dad." Scott is probably best known for his *Today* show feature, begun in 1983, wishing Happy Birthday to centenarians.

Born on March 7, 1934, in Alexandria, Virginia, Scott began his career with NBC at age 16 as a page at WRC in Washington, D.C., in 1950. He also was a weekend disc jockey, and with Eddie Walker, formed the Joy Boys, a broadcast team which stayed together until 1974. In 1953, NBC hired Scott as a summer relief announcer and two months later he became the second youngest regular staff announcer ever to work at NBC. He received a bachelor of arts degree in philosophy and religion from American University in 1955. His weather reports were heard on WRC-AM from

1956 to 1972. During Navy service, Scott produced a five-minute radio program for NATO which was broadcast on Armed Forces Radio.

His television career began in the early 1950s as host of a children's show, *Barn Party*. In 1959, he became Bozo the Clown. Bozo was so popular that when McDonald's opened in the Washington area, Scott was asked to make personal appearances at every new store opening. Bozo went off the air in 1962, and Scott created Ronald McDonald. When the rights to the character were bought out by McDonald's, Willard lost his role to a circus clown.

In 1967, he became a weathercaster on WRC-TV. From the beginning, his presentations were folksy and often filled with clown antics. On Groundhog Day, Scott dressed like a groundhog and emerged from a manhole cover; on April 15 (tax day), he dressed in a barrel. He became the weathercaster on the *Today* show in 1980. Although there was a negative response at first, by the summer of 1980, he was accepted as something of a "national folk hero." In 1989, he was the center of a public dispute with *Today* host Bryant Gumbel, when the contents of a memo written by Gumbel revealed complaints about Scott's style.

He has played himself on a number of television shows and currently hosts *Willard Scott's Home and Garden Almanac* on HGTV. With comedian Jonathan Winters, he made a video based on the Old Farmers Almanac, which included both offbeat advice and practical tips. During the bicentennial of the American Consitution, Scott broadcast radio spots about constitutional history over NBC radio. He has written four books including an autobiography, a cook book, and a mystery novel. He is also well known for his commitment to a wide variety of public service organizations. For this work, he has received many awards including the Private Sector Award for Public Service (1985). *See also Today.*   *Mary E. Beadle*

Further Reading

Davis, Gerry. *The Today Show: An Anecdotal History.* New York: Quill, 1987.

Scott, Willard. *Willard Scott's The Joy of Living.* New York: Putnam, 1982.

Mertz, R. *The Today Show.* Chicago: A Playboy Press Book, 1977.

See It Now

On November 18, 1951, *See It Now* began as an early public affairs experiment and became the ultimate "sight-and-sound development" in television for seven years. Broadcaster Edward R. Murrow explained on the inaugural program that it was an old team in a new trade, adding "we only hope that we are up to it—as reporters we only hope that we never abuse it." Murrow, Fred Friendly, and an innovative team of reporters and cameramen were the new team during that golden decade of early television. *See It Now* became the exemplar of nonfiction television and helped to establish the CBS television network as a leader in documentary news programming and as a responsible media organization. As the most honored program of its time, from 1951 to 1958, *See It Now* won four Emmys; three Peabodys; and assorted awards from the Overseas Press Club, *Look Magazine's* Best Public Affairs Series, the New York Newspaper Guild, and *Saturday Review*. *See It Now* also received the Robert Flaherty Award for Creative Achievement and the Alfred I. duPont–Columbia University Award.

See It Now had critics praising the program's honesty, pace, informativeness, and innovation. Having a sponsor was necessary; the Aluminum Company of America, Alcoa, had just emerged from losing an antitrust lawsuit and wanted an image brightener—association with the well-known Edward R. Murrow would help. Originating from radio's previous, *Hear It Now*, the new program had the same producers, Murrow and Friendly, and set the standard for documentary innovations. For example, rather than the usual built-up artificial set as an entertainment program, *See It Now* kept the image of a realistic news set, doing the show from the control room of Studio 41.

During the first program, Murrow showed the switches from different monitors at the same time. Unprecedented in 1951, viewers could see both the Atlantic Ocean and the Pacific Ocean—live. With combinations of film, audiotape and live material, *See It Now* reported on the year's major figures, issues, and events each week for half an hour. In addition, the writing differed from that of writing for radio, as Murrow and Friendly recounted, employing fewer words and letting the visual elements and indigenous sounds tell the story.

See It Now did not rely on directors, but rather on great reporters, such as Ed Scott and Joseph Wershba, who criss-crossed the country in search of stories. Journalists and camera crews frequently traveled internationally. In 1952, the series moved 15 reporters and cameramen to Korea for a single week to record "The Face of the War." On September 15, 1953, the program crew traveled to Berlin to show that city during the Cold War. They had also covered the Missouri River floods, in April, 1952; the eye of Hurricane Carol; the brass bands in Canon City, Colorado; and the atomic laboratories with Robert Oppenheimer in 1954. *See It Now* targeted critical issues such as the question of statehood for Alaska and Hawaii, the loss of American civil liberties, and the rise of McCarthyism.

The series and its producers achieved legendary status with a series of programs on American civil liberties, especially for two particular programs on McCarthyism. The "Report on Senator Joseph R. McCarthy," aired on March 9, 1954, and used the senator's own words and film of his public talks and actions to demonstrate his techniques. It became television's boldest and "finest hour." "The Case of Lieutenant Milo Radulovich," shown on October 20, 1953, gave an example of McCarthyism at its worst. A University of Michigan graduate student lost his Air Force Reserve status because of his family ties. The issue in this case was freedom of association. Such coverage was so controversial that Murrow and Friendly paid for the newspaper advertisements themselves in order to call attention to the upcoming programs, programs which CBS and Alcoa had ignored.

Yet, with such courage, *See It Now* became CBS's prototype of responsible television, and it lasted as the centerpiece of CBS's news effort until network business managers began questioning costs, and the executives began to worry about the weekly controversies. From 1955 until CBS canceled it three years later, there were sponsorship problems, reduced air time, and fewer programs. The business of broadcasting changed. The series died on July 9, 1958, a victim of both commercialism and McCarthyism.

The well-known Murrow and Friendly became established as the original "odd couple" of television news. The program offered future generations prominent examples of Murrow's ideas about television. This reputation lasted beyond Murrow's death on April 27, 1965. A series of books and documentaries focusing on Murrow's life and work centered on *See It Now* as the key to his success. A number of prominent journalists started in television on *See It Now*. Those directly involved in the *See It Now* program went on to establish their own reputations and reinforce many of the principles and techniques they developed as Murrow protégés.

Fred Friendly kept an unerring sense of energy, innovation, and showmanship going as president of CBS News and as a documentarian and broadcast educator for three more decades. Don Hewitt, later a top executive producer and creator of *60 Minutes*, introduced America to a new form of magazine which, like *See It Now* in its heyday, often made national headlines with investigative reports. Of *See It Now*'s reporters, especially noted is Wershba, who started with the program and remained a CBS producer for close to a quarter century. Cameraman Charles ("Charlie") Mack and European producer Bill McClure also continued on with other CBS News programs. *See also* Fred W. Friendly, Edward R. Murrow.

Betty Houchin Winfield

Further Reading

Murray, Michael D. *The Political Performers, CBS Broadcasts in the Public Interests.* Westport, CT: Praeger, 1994.

Murrow, Edward R., and Fred W. Friendly. eds. *See It Now.* New York: Simon and Schuster, 1955.

Sperber, A.M. *Murrow: His Life and Times.* New York: Freundlich Books, 1986.

Barry Serafin

Recipient of an Emmy Award for contributions to the *CBS Special Report* "Watergate: The White House Transcripts," Barry Serafin has specialized in political reporting at CBS and more recently, at ABC News. Serafin started out in radio in the western United States. He was born in Coquille,

Oregon, on June 22, 1941 and graduated in 1964, from Washington State University in Pullman.

Serafin worked first at KOAP-TV, then KOIN-TV, both in Portland, Oregon. He moved to St. Louis, Missouri and became a reporter and anchor at CBS affiliate, KMOX-TV, before moving to the network's Washington bureau for a decade of service. In 1976, he reported on Ronald Reagan's presidential campaign and the vice presidential race of Robert Dole. Serafin joined ABC News as a national correspondent in 1981, reporting on politics for *World News Tonight* and adding environmental reports for the *America Agenda* segment.

He covered the Iran hostage situation, and during the U.S. invasion of Grenada, he reported from Cuba. He also reported on the Falkland Islands dispute between Great Britain and Argentina. In 1992, he was honored by Washington State University with the Regents Distinguished Alumnus Award.

Michael D. Murray

Further Reading

"Barry Serafin Receives Award and Meets with Students." *Murrow Communicator*, Fall 1992, 1.

Gates, Gary Paul. *Air Time: The Inside Story of CBS News.* New York: Harper & Row, 1978.

Matusow, Barbara. *The Evening Stars: The Making of the Network News Anchor.* Boston: Houghton Mifflin, 1983.

Eric Sevareid

CBS Photo Archive

Growing up in the 1960s or 1970s meant watching Eric Sevareid on CBS News to understand the many meanings of one of the century's most perilous periods. For eloquent commentary, the North Dakota native had no peer. His 38 years on the air helped define broadcast journalism. For his quality writing and deep ideas, which set an unparalleled standard of excellence, he won three Peabody Awards, two Emmys, and generations of admirers inside and outside the field of journalism.

He regarded his position as one of privilege because of the status conferred on national news figures during his lifetime. Reality threatened twentieth-century living and required reporters to record and interpret it. CBS colleague Charles Kuralt often identified Sevareid as the best broadcast writer of his era. Veteran CBS news producer Don Hewitt said Sevareid "had a better fix on America . . ." explaining "us to us about as well as anyone could." When Sevareid retired from CBS News in 1977, Dan Rather noted that there was no thought of replacing him as commentator.

NBC news anchor and analyst John Chancellor suggested that Sevareid was "made of Nordic granite." Sevareid was a man of the Great Plains who observed the reconstruction of the world following World War II, and who thought America had a unique role in leading the world that was coming into being. Crucial to this role was an informed electorate. This was why Sevareid turned down the opportunity to anchor the *CBS Evening News* in exchange for writing and presenting what he liked to call his essays. Those commentaries expressed Sevareid's vision of an ideal democracy—one in which the vitality of the American people worked to establish social justice at home while helping to uplift other societies. Chancellor saw in Sevareid's "gloomy brilliance" the pre–Vietnam War certainty of America's greatness in the world, a greatness that originated in Sevareid's unflagging respect for the intelligence of his television audience.

Sevareid was born Arnold Eric Sevareid on November 26, 1912, in Vewa, North Dakota. He graduated from the University of Minnesota and also attended the London School of Economics in 1938. He came to CBS in 1939 when Edward R. Murrow hired him to report on the war in Europe.

At the time, Sevareid was a wire service reporter in Paris who had chronicled the approach of war in the pages of the *International Herald Tribune*. Sevareid's international reputation followed his reporting on the fall of France in 1940, the Battle of Britain later that year, the war in Italy, and the liberation of France. He covered the founding of the United Nations in 1945 and for 13 years was the chief correspondent of CBS News, based in Washington, D.C. Sevareid thought Washington "the greatest news center since ancient Rome," and from there, he reported and analyzed the great postwar stories: the Marshall Plan, the cold war, and the "red scare." Between 1959 and 1964, Sevareid became a correspondent-at-large, reporting political news from London and New York. His award-winning commentaries looked at America and, as he admitted, with America.

When Sevareid spurned the opportunity to anchor the *CBS Evening News*, it was given to Walter Cronkite. He likened the job of relaying hard news to "shoveling gravel" and preferred the finely crafted word to "a thousand pictures." In the 13 years he gave his almost nightly commentaries on the *CBS Evening News*, Sevareid never warmed to performing on television. The lights and cameras were, in his view, too distracting. Viewers may have disagreed with his early opposition to the war in Vietnam, the "shame and sadness" he felt for Richard Nixon following the president's resignation in August of 1974, and his crusty complaint that ethnic groups were becoming economic demand groups. Nearly all, however, saw in Sevareid's modesty and diffidence, an attractive antidote to the civil unrest and political failures of the 1960s and 1970s. They also liked his tendency to balance observations with humor. In a 1974 commentary for CBS News, he likened "happy news" to a revival of vaudeville, suggesting a local newsanchor turned "actor" might do "a buck-and-wing stark naked" in search of ratings.

CBS's mandatory retirement policy forced Sevareid from the nightly news in 1977, but not before a memorable series of reminiscences affirmed his vision for America. Sevareid's reluctant optimism could be seen in year-end summaries of world events broadcast by CBS and through occasional interviews and articles. While some of his commentary decried changes in the broadcasting business, he also noted that journalists had become more educated than they had been when he began his newspaper career in the middle 1930s. He held to his view that the American people had a tough, undiminished instinct for fairness. That gave him reason to hope that the country's greatest days might yet be before it. His final work on the 50-year remembrance of Pearl Harbor affirmed this sentiment. That was why, when Sevareid succumbed to stomach cancer in July 1992, Charles Kuralt celebrated Sevareid's undying devotion to Thomas Jefferson's view of America's greatness. Andy Rooney of *60 Minutes* said, "If you had to pick the single greatest broadcast journalist there ever was, you'd pick Eric Sevareid. I feel sorry for all the people too young to know how great he was." *See also* CBS News.   *Bruce J. Evensen*

Further Reading

Schroth, Raymond A., *The American Journey of Eric Sevareid.* New York: Steerforth Press, 1995.
"A Conversation with Eric Sevareid," a recording produced by Grolier Education Corporation, Vital History Project (1977), and "Eric Sevareid Remembered," *CBS News Special Report,* 9 July 1992.
Sevareid, Eric. *CBS Evening News,* 22 April 1974.
Sevareid, Eric. *Small Sounds in the Night.* New York: Knopf, 1956.
Sevareid, Eric. *Not So Wild a Dream.* New York: Antheneum, 1946.

Bernard Shaw

Bernard Shaw's coverage of world events and his exclusive interviews with a variety of international leaders have earned him the respect of his peers and the public. His accomplishments as CNN's principal anchor and his status as a leading black newsperson, and an anchor sensitive to important national and international events, have given him and his network worldwide acclaim. His reputation is built on solid reporting of political and international affairs. Shaw has covered a large number of political events, and he served as moderator for the second U.S. presidential debate in 1988 and for the third Democratic presidential candidates' debate in 1992.

Courtesy Cable News Network, Inc.
© 1996   Photo by Andrew Eccles

Over the years, Shaw has also covered a number of key national events of historic importance. In 1968, he reported first-hand on the assassination of Martin Luther King Jr., in Memphis, Tennessee and King's funeral in Atlanta, Georgia. He also conducted an exclusive interview with Attorney General John Mitchell during the Watergate scandal. He covered the 1979 hostage crisis at the American Embassy in Tehran, Iran, and ten years later, reported from Beijing, China, on the Tiananmen Square protests. Shaw, along with his CNN colleagues, set the standard for international coverage, when they provided first-hand reports on the Persian Gulf War in 1991. On January 17, 1994, he was the first correspondent to break the news of the earthquake in Los Angeles, California.

Born in Chicago on May 22, 1940, Shaw joined the U.S. Marine Corps after graduating from high school. He later attended the University of Illinois, majoring in history and started his journalism career while he was still in college, working as a news reporter for WNUS-Radio, Chicago. In 1969, he became the White House correspondent for Westinghouse Group W. His first television reporter's position was with CBS News in 1971, which he left in 1977 to become ABC News Latin American correspondent and also that network's bureau chief. He is credited with providing leadership for the CNN network in its formative period on the air, and he has been in charge of anchor duties for its most demanding, live network assignments.

Shaw has been honored with many distin-
guished accolades for his work as a reporter and
network anchor. His awards included a Peabody
Award, Golden ACE Cable Award, Dr. Martin
Luther King Jr. Award, an Emmy Award for In-
stant Coverage of a Breaking News Story for
"Coverage of the Olympic Park Bombing" in
1996, and also in 1996, the Paul White Lifetime
Achievement Award from the Radio-Television
News Directors Association (RTNDA). He was
also once named the Journalist of the Year by the
National Association of Black Journalists. *See also*
CNN (Cable News Network).   *Lovette Chinwah*

Further Reading
Dates, Jannette L., and William Barlow. *Split Image:
    African Americans in the Mass Media.* Washing-
    ton, DC: Howard University Press, 1990.
Head, Sydney, Christopher Sterling, and Lemuel
    Schofield. *Broadcasting in America.* Boston:
    Houghton Mifflin, 1994.
Sloan, William David, and James Startt. *The Media
    in America: A History.* Northport, AL: Vision
    Press, 1996.

Lynn Sherr

A correspondent for *20/20*, Sherr was born March
4, 1942, in Philadelphia and is a graduate of
Wellesley College, where she received the Alum-
nae Achievement Award. She gained recognition
as correspondent at WNET in New York and
WETA in Washington. She held assignments with
WCBS-TV and the Associated Press, and was editor for Conde Nast Publications. She hosted the
MacNeil-Lehrer NewsHour on PBS and became
an ABC News correspondent in 1977.

Sherr reported major political stories and covered NASA space shuttle missions. She was substitute anchor for *Nightline* and handled "Special
Assignment" coverage of the CBS-General
Westmoreland case and reported on the Claus von
Bulow trial. She has been recognized on many
occasions for her work,which included an hour-
long report during the 1994–1995 season on an
alternative treatment for eating disorders, a subject
revisited in 1997 in the aftermath of the death of
Diana, princess of Wales, when it was learned that

she sought assistance as the result of Sherr's report.

Sherr has also reported on differences in the
way men and women communicate in the workplace and instances in which husbands have been
battered by their wives. Among her many awards,
Sherr received two Women in Radio and Television Commendations, one for the special, "Susan
B. Anthony Slept Here," the subject of one of her
books. *See also 20/20.*   *Michael D. Murray*

Further Reading
Bauer, Douglas. "Typecast for Television News." *TV
    Guide,* 2 August 1980, 26–28.
Flander, Judy. "Women in Network News." *Washing-
    ton Journalism Review,* March 1985, 39–43.
Sherr, Lynn. *Tall Blondes: A Book about Giraffes.*
    New York: Andrews McMeel, 1997.

Maria Shriver

News correspondent Maria Shriver has a reputation for getting and conducting tough interviews
with major political and entertainment figures. As
anchor of *First Person with Maria Shriver*, a series of prime-time specials beginning in 1990,
Shriver has talked with Sarah Ferguson, the duch-
ess of York; Raisa Gorbachev, wife of the Russian
president; media mogul Ted Turner; actor Billy
Crystal; singer Sinead O'Connor; Russian gym-
nast Olga Korbut; and rap musician M. C. Ham-
mer. She has been honored on many occasions for
her work. For example, Shriver's interview with
former Miss America and incest survivor Marilyn
Van Derbur on November 12, 1991, won an award
from the American Women in Radio and Television.

During her career, Shriver has served as an
anchor for numerous NBC News programs and
has been a contributing anchor for *Dateline*, reporting and addressing subjects concerning such
controversial issues as child custody disputes,
male infertility, advocacy for battered women, and
other controversial topics. Her stories on Cuban
leader Fidel Castro, Jordanian ruler King Hussein,
and former Philippine president Corazon Aquino
illustrate her proximity to breaking news. She won
the exceptional merit media award from the Na-

tional Women's Political Caucus for the Aquino interview. Shriver's NBC news specials include "Fatal Addictions," "The Baby Business," "Men, Women, Sex, and AIDS," "Wall Street: Money, Greed, and Power," "God Is Not Elected," and "Women Behind Bars."

Shriver was born in Chicago, on November 6, 1955, to Robert Sargent and Eunice Mary Kennedy Shriver. She received a bachelor of arts degree in American studies from Georgetown University in Washington, D.C., in 1977. Shriver became a news producer for KYW-TV in Philadelphia, from 1977 to 1978. Then for two years, she was producer for WJZ-TV's *Evening Magazine* in Baltimore, reporting on public affairs, sports, and local news. Broadcast positions since then include roles as a national reporter for *P.M. Magazine* in 1981; a news reporter in Los Angeles for CBS News from 1983 to 1985; and a news correspondent and co-anchor for *CBS Morning News* in New York in 1985. In 1986, she joined NBC News as correspondent for the prime-time news hour *1986*. Working for NBC News, Shriver then became co-host of *Sunday Today* in 1987 to 1990; an anchor for *Main Street*, a newsmagazine for young people; a co-anchor of *Yesterday, Today and Tomorrow;* an anchor for *NBC Nightly News Weekend Edition*; *Cutting Edge with Maria Shriver*; and *First Person with Maria Shriver* starting in 1990.

In addition, she was co-anchor for the 1988 summer Olympics in Seoul, Korea and has been a guest anchor on *NBC News at Sunrise*, *Today,* and *NBC Nightly News.* Shriver also has co-anchored two special projects for WTBS Atlanta on the Olympics and on the 104th Kentucky Derby. Shriver, niece of the late President John F. Kennedy and the late Senator Robert F. Kennedy, is married to actor Arnold Schwarzenegger. *See also Dateline NBC.*   *Jan Whitt*

Further Reading

Boyer, Peter J. *Who Killed CBS?* New York: Random House, 1988.

Jackson-Han, Sarah. "Making Inroads." *Communicator,* August 1994, 24–26.

McCabe, Peter. *Bad News at Black Rock.* New York: Arbor House, 1987.

Bob Simon

Since he joined CBS News over 30 years ago, Bob Simon has reported from 67 countries, including every major nation in the Middle East. He has covered, from the front lines, just about every major crisis in the last 26 years, including those in Biafra, Beirut, Saigon, the Sinai Peninsula, Cyprus, El Salvador, the Falklands, Northern Ireland, the Philippines, Romania, South Africa, Poland, Beijing, Iraq, Somalia, and Sarajevo. He is among the most respected broadcast journalists of his day and is considered a throwback to the era in which the foreign correspondent, often appearing impervious to danger, reported directly from the scene of violence and chaos across the globe.

Bob Simon joined CBS as reporter/assignment editor based in New York in 1967. In 1969 he was assigned to the London bureau and in 1971 and in 1975 worked in the Saigon bureau. He covered the withdrawal of American troops and returned to Saigon to report on the end of the war in Vietnam. In 1981 Simon was assigned to Washington as a State Department correspondent. The next year he was named national correspondent in New York. He became chief Middle Eastern correspondent in 1987.

During the opening days of the Persian Gulf War in 1991, Simon and three other members of the CBS news team stepped across a deserted border post between Saudi Arabia and Iraqi-occupied Kuwait. The news team was captured, and spent 40 days in Iraqi prisons. Simon describes these experiences in his book, *Forty Days.* Later Simon revisited Iraq to make the hour-long documentary, *Bob Simon: Back to Baghdad.* Simon is known as someone who has excellent sources and can get his stories on the air in an era in which international news is in general decline.

Simon was born in the Fort Apache section of the Bronx. He has been recognized for his work with such honors as ten Emmy Awards, four Overseas Press Club Awards, and a Peabody. He was honored for reporting on the journey to Jerusalem by Egyptian President Anwar Sadat and also received the David Kaplan Award from the Overseas Press Club for coverage of the assassination of Israeli Prime Minister Yitzhak Rabin. Rabin had been a frequent source of information for Simon, and an occasional tennis partner. In 1996 Simon won an Edward R. Murrow Award from the Radio-Television News Directors Association for Overall Excellence in Television. He has a multi-year contract with CBS which stipulates that he remain headquartered in Israel. Simon speaks fluent French. His daughter Tanya is an associate producer for CBS News's *48 Hours*.

Joan O'Mara

Further Reading

Erndst, James. "Gonzo Journalist with Patrician Polish." *St. Louis Post-Dispatch,* 8 April 1997, 3D.

Hubbell, Stephen. "Iraq around the Clock (A review of *Forty Days*)." *Nation,* 23 March 1992, 382–85.

Simon, Bob. *Forty Days.* New York: G.P. Putnam's Sons, 1992.

Schwarzkopf, Brenda, and Ron Arias. "Heroes of the War." *People Weekly,* Spring 1991, 45–47.

Carole Simpson

Carole Simpson has devoted three decades to broadcasting. Beginning at a small radio station in Chicago, Simpson is now a well-known anchor for ABC's *World News Sunday* and an Emmy-award-winning senior correspondent. Simpson's reports have appeared on *20/20* and *Nightline*, and she was a contributor to *This Week with David Brinkley* and a substitute anchor for *World News Tonight*.

Married and the mother of two, Simpson identifies with women juggling professional responsibilities and family. Remaining an advocate for women and minority rights, she reports frequently for the *America Agenda*. She can also boast of numerous awards, several from groups working to end gender, racial, and ethnic discrimination, including the National Commission of Working Women, American Women in Radio and Television, and the National Association of Black Journalists. Simpson is featured in *Waiting for Prime Time: The Women of Television News* by Marlene Sanders and Marcia Rock for helping end gender discrimination by the networks. According to that book, in 1983, there were nearly 100 correspondents at ABC News, but only 15 of them were women. Also, they were not getting on the air as

often as male counterparts and were not assigned the best beats or stories.

They requested meetings with management, but it was not until 1985 that the women confronted ABC News president Roone Arledge with the results of a two-year survey. That confrontation took place at a luncheon honoring Barbara Walters for an American Women in Radio and Television Award. Simpson, scheduled to speak, let Arledge know that, although the correspondents regarded Walters very highly, they believed a pattern of institutionalized gender discrimination existed. The women passed out their findings while Simpson reviewed them for the audience. Because of the women's courage, formal meetings and network concessions followed.

Simpson was born in Chicago, on December 7, 1940. She received her bachelor's degree from the University of Michigan in 1962 and did graduate work at the University of Iowa. She began her career in radio and became a reporter and anchorwoman at WBBM in Chicago. Twice she served as a faculty member, first at the Tuskegee Institute (Alabama) and later in the Medill School of Journalism at Northwestern University (Evanston, Illinois). Moving to television in 1970, Simpson was news reporter at WMAQ-TV in Chicago. Hired by NBC News as a Midwest bureau correspondent in 1974, she transferred to Washington, D.C. That assignment led to her role as the anchor for *World News Saturday* and *World News Sunday*.

Other opportunities have put Simpson in the spotlight. In 1989, she and two of her colleagues anchored the documentary, "Black in White America," and in 1992, she moderated the second U.S. presidential debate from Richmond, Virginia. Over the years, viewers have also seen Simpson cover such stories as the release of Nelson Mandela, the Persian Gulf War, the fall of Philippine president Ferdinand Marcos, and the Clarence Thomas–Anita Hill hearings.

Simpson's commitments are obvious in her choice of organizations. Chair of the ABC News Women's Advisory Board, Simpson is also vice-chair of the International Women's Media Foundation, a member of the board of directors of the National Commission on Working Women, on the board of trustees for the Radio-Television News Directors Association (RTNDA), a member of the National Academy of Sciences forum on the future of children and families, and a member of the board of the National Press Foundation. ***See also*** ABC News.   *Jan Whitt*

Further Reading

Flander, Judy. "Advocate for Change." *Communicator,* August 1994, 14.

Flander, Judy. "Women in Network News." *Washington Journalism Review,* March 1985, 39–43.

O'Reilly, Stefanie, and David Lee. "Peers to Simpson: Can't You Hold a Job?" *Iowa Journalist,* Fall 1995, 31.

60 Minutes

60 Minutes is the most successful news documentary program in the history of television and one of its more controversial ones. The program is heralded for its innovation and influence at the same time that it is lambasted for sensationalism and revenue-producing popularity. *60 Minutes* has been accused of "checkbook journalism" and of catering to celebrities and paying for interviews. Ultimately, though, *60 Minutes* has reigned as the longest running, regularly scheduled prime-time broadcast; as a top-10 finisher in the Nielsen ratings for 16 consecutive seasons; and as the only regularly scheduled broadcast to finish in first place in each of three decades.

The series has won 42 Emmys, six George Foster Peabody Awards, two George Polk Memorial Awards, 10 Alfred I. duPont–Columbia University Awards, and one Christopher Award. In sum, *60 Minutes* proved that the mass audience could be drawn to documentary news, if it were packaged well. *60 Minutes* was created by Don Hewitt, now its executive producer. It features Mike Wallace, the only reporter who has been with the show since its beginning in 1968. Harry Reasoner, who left to join ABC in 1970, returned to *60 Minutes* from 1978 to 1991. Dan Rather joined in 1975 and left in 1981 to replace Walter Cronkite on *The CBS Evening News.* Diane Sawyer signed on in 1984 and left to host ABC's *Prime Time Live* in 1989. Morley Safer, Ed Brad-

ley, Steve Kroft, and Lesley Stahl are the current correspondents for the program.

Others were also included in the *60 Minutes* cast. In 1972, Hewitt initiated a "Point/Counterpoint" format, featuring conservative columnist James Kilpatrick of the *Washington Star* and liberal columnist Nicholas von Hoffman of the *Washington Post.* In 1977, Shana Alexander of *Newsweek* replaced von Hoffman. The audience responded enthusiastically, and the two were parodied on *Saturday Night Live* by Dan Aykroyd and Jane Curtin. When Alexander left, Hewitt replaced the segment with *A Few Minutes with Andy Rooney* in 1978.

Rapidly becoming television's darling, *60 Minutes* was the first news show to make the top 10 in ratings. To a large extent, *60 Minutes* caught on because of Hewitt's insistence that the reporters "talk like folks." Quoted in *60 Minutes: 25 Years of Television's Finest Hour,* Hewitt said he encouraged Mike Wallace to write an introduction for one of his stories by thinking about what he would tell his wife when he got home, emphasizing candor and dialogue.

In 1967, Hewitt wrote an internal CBS memo proposing a different kind of news program, "Somewhere in all the minutes of make-believe . . . couldn't we make room for 60 minutes of reality?" *60 Minutes* began on Tuesday, September 24, 1968, at 10 P.M. with stories on relations between police and citizens in urban areas, Richard Nixon and Hubert Humphrey, and a film, "Why Man Creates." Put up against ABC's popular drama *Marcus Welby,* the show fell to the bottom of the ratings. During its first six seasons, it was in danger of being dropped.

By 1975, however, *60 Minutes* began a steady ratings ascent, moving from 101 to 52 in the ratings. By the end of spring 1977, *60 Minutes* was tied with *Hawaii Five-O* for number 18. By the end of the 1978 season, it was number 6. And in 1980, it was number 1 out of 106 programs. By the following year, Hewitt had 10 Emmys and *60 Minutes* was still at the top. In *Securing the Middle Ground: Reporter Formulas in '60 Minutes,'* television critic Richard Campbell explains the show's phenomenal success, focusing on what he calls the "mythic narrative pattern of *60 Min-*

utes and other news programs." According to Campbell, reporters function in various roles in the series. Often they are featured as detectives, even wearing trench coats, as they confront villains and solve crimes. They also serve as analysts, offering solutions for societal conflicts and conducting profile interviews with everyone from the Shah of Iran to 1980 presidential candidate John Anderson to entertainer Lena Horne. Finally, the reporters appear to the viewing audience as tourists, providing trips through small-town America, the trucking industry, or a foreign country.

Whatever the formula, *60 Minutes* is a relatively low-cost, spectacularly revenue-producing success. In in 1991–1992 season, the one-hour show was listed as the one that was the least expensive to produce. It cost CBS about $600,000 per episode, compared to one episode of *Knots Landing*, which cost Lorimar $1,375,000 per episode. Considered a "premium program" as were entertainment programs such as *Hill Street Blues*, *Northern Exposure*, and *Seinfeld*, *60 Minutes* appeals to a broad audience, but especially to upscale viewers whom advertisers want to reach.

60 Minutes has wielded a great deal of power, even with advertisers. For example, *60 Minutes* learned that the Ford Pinto had a design flaw—if the car were rear-ended, it could explode. *60 Minutes* revealed this to American car buyers in 1978 in a show called "Is Your Car Safe?" Ford pulled its advertising, but not surprisingly, returned the following week. Those featured on the show over years include show business celebrities, literary giants, prominent media personnel, and political figures Elizabeth Taylor, Moshe Dayan, Maria Callas, G. Gordon Liddy, Betty Ford, Jesse Jackson, Katharine Hepburn, Arthur Fiedler, Johnny Carson, Bette Davis, Anne Morrow Lindbergh, Lena Horne, Gary Hart, Manuel Noriega, Ray Charles, Barbra Streisand, Woody Allen, and Boris Yeltsin.

60 Minutes will expand to a second edition in 1999. *60 Minutes II* will include many elements of the original, including some appearances by its veteran correspondents and the familiar opening of a ticking stopwatch. *See also* Don Hewitt.

Jan Whitt

Further Reading

Campbell, Richard. *'60 Minutes' and the News: A Mythology for Middle America.* Urbana: University of Illinois Press, 1991.

Flander, Judy. "Hewitt's Humongous Hour." *Washington Journalism Review,* April 1991, 26–30.

Henly, William A. "Don Hewitt: Man of the Hour." *Washington Journalism Review,* May 1986, 25–29.

Hewitt, Don. *Minute by Minute.* New York: Random House, 1985.

Madsen, Axel. *'60 Minutes': The Power and the Politics of America's Most Popular TV News Show.* New York: Dodd, Mead, 1984.

O'Connor Jr., John. "Sometimes Crow Can Be Tasty." *New York Times,* 18 February 1973.

William Small

© 1988 Maria R. Bastone for Fordham University

A distinguished manager, William J. Small served as senior vice president of CBS News in New York, president of NBC News, and president of United Press International. Upon leaving broadcasting, he became the Felix J. Larkin Professor of Communications, director of the Center for Communications, and the dean of the Graduate School of Business at Fordham University.

Small was born on September 20, 1926, in Chicago, Illinois and was a graduate of the University of Chicago, where he also received his master's degree. Small served as a news director at two key CBS stations, WLS in Chicago and

WHAS, Louisville, before being named CBS News Washington bureau chief in 1962. He acquired a reputation for being a strong administrator and became senior vice president of CBS News in New York a decade later, and served as corporate vice president back in Washington, D.C., during his last year at CBS. Small also held leadership posts in a variety of professional organizations. He was national president of two leading journalism groups: the Radio-Television News Directors Association and the Society of Professional Journalists, Sigma Delta Chi. He also served on the executive board of both the Washington Journalism Center and the National Association of Broadcasters.

Over the years, Small authored a number of articles for *The Quill* and in 1970, wrote *To Kill A Messenger: Television News and the Real World*, which included an in-depth account of television coverage of the 1960s from the perspective of one who had held the key broadcast management post in Washington, D.C., during that era. Small oversaw the development of a strong Washington bureau including the recruitment of Fred Graham from the *New York Times*, the transfer of Marvin Kalb from Moscow in 1963, and Eric Sevareid's move from New York. He also recruited Daniel Schorr and John Hart from other CBS bureaus and gained additional attention with some new hires such as Bruce Morton and Bob Schieffer. During Small's tenure, Dan Rather and Roger Mudd developed a significant following for their Washington reporting from the White House and Capitol Hill.

Small authored another major book, *Political Power and the Press,* at a time when the television networks were under fire from the Nixon administration for having a liberal, left-leaning bias. This book and Small's earlier work on the events of the 1960s served as a counterpoint to allegations of political favoritism. Small has received every major professional journalism recognition including two of the most distinguished: the Paul White Award from the Radio-Television News Directors Association and the Wells Key Award, from the Society of Professional Journalists. Small retired from his teaching and administrative post at

Fordham University in 1996. *See also* CBS News, NBC News.　　　　　*Michael D. Murray*

Further Reading
Gates, Gary Paul. *Air Time: The Inside Story of CBS News.* New York: Harper & Row, 1978.
Small, William. *To Kill A Messenger: Television News and the Real World.* New York: Hastings House, 1970.
Small, William. *Politcal Power and the Press.* New York: W. W. Norton, 1972.

Harry Smith

CBS News correspondent and anchor Harry Smith was born on August 21, 1951, in Hammond, Indiana. Smith attended Central College in Pella, Iowa on a football scholarship, majoring in communications and theater. He started in radio, working as host and disc jockey at WLW in Cincinnati, and then at KHOW and KIMN in Denver, between 1973 and 1981. Smith was a reporter and anchor at KMGH-TV in Denver from 1982 to 1985, was a Dallas-based CBS News correspondent from 1986 to 1987, and served as co-anchor of *CBS This Morning* from 1987 to 1996.

Smith met his wife Andrea Joyce when she co-anchored news in Denver. She later shifted to sports at the CBS affiliate in Detroit and now is with CBS Sports network.　　　*Jack Hodgson*

Further Reading
Brady, James. "In Step with Harry Smith." *Parade Magazine,* 2 February 1989, 18.
Sanz, Cynthia, and Alan Carter. "Anchors in Love." *People Weekly,* 5 May 1991, 67–69.
Sherman, Ellen. "Wild about Harry." *Family Circle,* 11 August 1992, 38.

Howard K. Smith

Howard K. Smith counted it as the best of good fortune to have been one of Edward R. Murrow's "boys." That group, among them Eric Sevareid, Charles Collingwood, and William L. Shirer, rose to prominence in broadcast news through their CBS Radio assignments, under Murrow's direction, during World War II.

Born in Ferriday, Louisiana, in 1914, Smith grew up in New Orleans. He entered Tulane University in 1932 on a scholarship. Because his family had no resources to help with his education, Smith chose journalism as his major on discovering that this made him eligible for $100 awards offered by the *New Orleans Times-Picayune*. He won these awards, and another $100 for a story about World War I veterans. Smith graduated in 1936 with highest honors.

His ultimate ambition was to become a foreign correspondent, a goal brought closer following graduation, when he won a summer grant to study at Heidelberg University. On his return, he became a reporter for the *New Orleans Item* earning $15 a week. He longed to go back to Europe and did so in 1937, spending two years as a Rhodes scholar. In 1939, he was hired as a United Press (UP) correspondent in Germany, where he gained the friendship of Shirer of CBS and moved to the network when the opportunity opened up (as did several others from UP who became top reporters for the network). At the age of 26, Smith was the CBS correspondent in Berlin, working under Murrow, and based in London. He was also hired to write for the Berlin bureau of the *New York Times*. This provided his first chance to write longer reports than UP or CBS allowed. His biggest challenge proved to be revising broadcast copy into coherence after it was received from the German censors.

Smith had a strongly independent side despite his courteous demeanor. He did nothing to endear himself to Nazi officials while in Berlin and would have been interned with other correspondents in Germany had he not taken the advice to get out hours before the Japanese attack on Pearl Harbor on December 7, 1941. He was on the last train to leave Berlin on the eve of the U.S. entry into the war.

Smith went to neutral Switzerland, and during his first three months there, wrote a book about his time in Germany, *Last Train from Berlin*, which became a bestseller in the United States. He reported from Switzerland into 1943, at first by cable, then erratically by radio. Allen Dulles, who later became head of the Central Intelligence Agency, was one of Smith's main sources.

In 1944, along with Richard C. Hottelet, Smith covered the Battle of the Bulge, one of the most difficult sieges of the war. He was back in Berlin for the German surrender to the Russians in May 1945. After the war, Smith covered the trials of Nazi war criminals at Nuremberg and then was named by Murrow to succeed him as chief European correspondent for CBS in London. In that post, he was able to express himself freely and often criticized U.S. foreign policy. He also began appearing on television. In one *See It Now* program, he rebuked the practice of apartheid in South Africa.

Smith's independent ways came under closer scrutiny when he returned to the United States in 1957, after 20 years in Europe. He angered CBS superiors when he compared Ku Klux Klansmen to Nazi thugs in his coverage of racial violence in Birmingham, Alabama. He was so outspoken in commentaries for the Douglas Edwards news program that CBS chairman William S. Paley ordered Smith's television commentaries be reviewed in advance of broadcast and altered if necessary. Smith moderated the first Nixon-Kennedy debate in 1960 and anchored several successful *CBS Reports*, one of which won him a George Polk Award and an Emmy. In 1961, he was named Washington bureau chief, but said he would stop doing news analysis for the Douglas Edwards program unless he was allowed more freedom. Neither Smith nor Paley would budge, so Smith resigned.

He got his own program, *Howard K. Smith— News and Comment*, on ABC in 1962. Smith was allowed the freedom of opinion he desired, and the program became popular, mainly because Smith spoke his mind. This soon got him in trouble again, however, and after a major sponsor deserted the program, ABC canceled the show. Although he was discontent for the next six years, he stayed at ABC and in 1969, became a co-anchor with Frank Reynolds on ABC's evening news program. In 1974, he was teamed with former CBS colleague Harry Reasoner. Their egos clashed and Smith was dropped as co-anchor, to be replaced by Barbara Walters from the NBC *Today* show. The program remained in third place among the three network evening news shows. Smith's commentaries were dropped. On April 20, 1979, he posted his resignation on the bulletin board at ABC's Washington bureau. In retirement, Smith wrote his memoir, published in 1996, and lectured occasionally on politics and the media. He felt shunned by both CBS and ABC, because neither network, his wife said, ever invited them to take part in their gatherings. *See also* ABC News, CBS News.

Daniel W. Pfaff

Further Reading
Cloud, Stanley, and Lynne Olsen. *The Murrow Boys.* Boston: Houghton Mifflin, 1996.
Schroth, Raymond. "The Old Glamor Boys of Broadcast News." *Nieman Reports,* Fall 1996, 84–85.
Smith, Howard K. *Events Leading Up To My Death.* New York: St. Martin's Press, 1996.

Tom Snyder

Tom Snyder is one of television's most flamboyant personalities. His ability as a broadcaster is so diverse that, in the 1970s, he was considered a top candidate to replace either John Chancellor on *NBC Nightly News* or Johnny Carson on *The Tonight Show*. Neither event took place. Snyder's legacy will be that of host of the thoughtful, provocative late-night talk show which aired after Carson on NBC in the 1970s, and after David Letterman on CBS in the 1990s.

Snyder was born in Milwaukee, Wisconsin, in 1936. At Marquette University, he had planned on studying to become a doctor, but found he became squeamish during animal dissections. Instead, he developed a love for broadcasting and landed a job at WRIT-AM in Milwaukee. Snyder pursued a television career in Savannah, Atlanta, Los Angeles, and Philadelphia. He worked as a reporter in Los Angeles in the 1960s, then moved to Philadelphia. In August 1970, he returned to Los Angeles to serve as an anchor of KNBC-TV newscasts, which quickly resulted in increased ratings.

In 1973, NBC selected the popular anchorman to serve as the host of *Tomorrow*, a 60-minute program following *The Tonight Show*. Snyder's freewheeling interviewing style and dominating personality made both him and *Tomorrow* cultural icons of the 1970s. Snyder's guests included John Lennon and Alfred Hitchcock. The Emmy Award-winning *Tomorrow* also featured controversial topics, including a visit to a nudist colony. His booming laugh and billowing cigarette smoke made him a target for satire by *Saturday Night Live*. In addition to his duties as host of *Tomorrow*, Snyder served as anchor of the short-lived *Prime Time Sunday* newsmagazine, hosted *Celebrity Spotlight* interviews, and anchored weekday WNBC-TV and weekend *NBC Nightly News* newscasts.

When Johnny Carson switched *The Tonight Show* to a 60-minute format in 1980, *Tomorrow* received a face-lift. It was expanded to 90 minutes, renamed *Tomorrow Coast to Coast*, and added Rona Barrett. The move backfired, as Snyder, accustomed to quiet sets, now was confronted with a studio audience and rock bands to attract younger viewers. Barrett was dropped as co-host, and Snyder was eased out to make way for David Letterman's *Late Show*. The nine-year run of *Tomorrow* officially ended in January 1982. But Snyder regained a national audience on radio, hosting a late-night show on ABC from 1987 to 1992. In 1993, the self-titled program *Tom Snyder* began a two-year run on the CNBC cable television network. It had the look and feel of the old *Tomorrow* show. Snyder's trenchant "colorcast" included viewer call-ins, a staple of his ABC radio show.

In 1994, David Letterman asked Snyder to host a 60-minute television program which would follow *The Late Show* on CBS. *The Late Late Show* premiered in January 1995 and Snyder received widespread critical acclaim. It is simulcast on many CBS Radio stations as *The Late Late Radio Show*.

James E. Reppert

Further Reading
Edelstein, Andrew J., and Kevin McDonough. *The Seventies.* New York: Dutton, 1990.
Matusow, Barbara. *The Evening Stars.* Boston: Houghton Mifflin, 1983.

Space Coverage

When Americans think of the six space flights of Project Mercury, America's first manned space missions, they do not remember pictures in *Life* magazine or newspaper headlines, they recall seeing it on television. Anyone who was four years old or older on February 22, 1962, probably has some memory of watching John Glenn's orbital flight. Ask for the name of a reporter who covered space, and the one that comes immediately to mind is Walter Cronkite, or perhaps Jules Bergman or Hugh Downs.

Like the Atlas rocket fired from the launch pad, television rose into the stratosphere with one of its biggest stories during the early 1960s. By the end of Project Mercury in 1963, television had become the dominant medium in America, and newspapers were unable to regain their dominance. At the beginning of the NASA years in late 1958, television news had been a hybrid of newsreels and radio news. By the time the astronauts walked on the moon on June 20, 1969, cameras were riding along, giving the world a firsthand look. Television continues to be the medium of choice for space coverage, showing us dramatic views of the planets, comets, and space stations under construction. Even Mars is being scrutinized by television cameras following the July 4, 1997 landing of Pathfinder.

Television's coverage of the space program is as old as the space program itself. Representatives of the then established national networks (ABC, NBC, CBS, and Mutual) and wire services (Associated Press, United Press, Reuters) covered Cape Canaveral on a regular basis after *Sputnik*, the Russian space satellite, was launched in October of 1957. The press fought restrictions and barriers, and many were regulars on Bird Watch Hill, a site just outside Cocoa Beach, Florida, where they waited for nighttime missile launches. (Before computerized missile tracking, rockets were launched at night to allow visual tracking.) While there were lights on the launch pad, camera operators stood with eyes glued to viewfinders of their cameras.

The job of early television reporters was significantly effected by NASA's strict rules concerning the filming of the early Mercury flights. With America in the midst of the cold war, officials were concerned about leaks, so they limited access. But, the television outlets needed footage to make newscasts of the flights. NASA would not

permit cameras close to rockets, and since most flights were short, there was no time to get from Cape Canaveral to Grand Bahama Island to cover both the liftoff and recovery. NBC's Roy Neal, a veteran producer who had covered space since the days of Bird Watch Hill devised a solution. Working with Project Mercury, Neal supervised the 1960 development of an elaborate pool system that brought outstanding results.

According to Erik Barnouw, a one-network feed had been used before, during the Kennedy-Nixon debate and 1960 election. But this was different, as four broadcast organizations pooled all their footage from a variety of sites on launch day, and shared equally in the rewards. The role of pool producer rotated and each network assigned reporters and camera operators to different jobs. Everyone who was assigned prepared an elaborate notebook of information for his or her network.

Within the year, this pool system became standard practice. In fact, NASA television and radio transmission today continues to be based on this system. NASA adapted pool transmissions to the broadcast standards after the Apollo missions ended in 1972. In a memo dated April 13, 1961, just a few weeks before the flight of Alan Shepard, CBS outlined the pool policy. Coverage was coordinated by a complex of remote outlets, both on the Cape and down-range, from two large vans. All video and audio were fed through this point. From there, the video portion was sent to New York for distribution. The audio was distributed at the switching center to all pool members for the purpose of mixing with the anchor's voice. Composite audio was sent to network headquarters. The pool site was equipped with projectors, processors, and editors.

There were strict rules at that first flight, and these are still in operation—no cameras are permitted in the blockhouse or at Mission Control. Any glimpse would be offered by NASA's cameras. There was, and is, voice relay from this area, however, including the familiar sound of the countdown on launches. Gradually technology changed, and broadcasters adapted. By July 1962, the *Telstar I* communication satellite was launched, relaying all forms of communication to earth. By February 1963, Communications Satellite Corporation (COMSAT), a private corporation now in change of international satellite communication, was formed to regulate the industry.

By the end of Project Mercury, satellite technology allowed NASA to receive videotaped shots on board the space craft and feed it to networks. This was the first time Americans saw astronauts moving in space. Transmissions during Project Gemini showed the first manned space walks, on July 20, 1969. As reflected in the video "Walter Cronkite Remembers," the broadcaster showed his enthusiasm after as astronaut Neal Armstrong made "One small step for man, one giant leap for mankind." Cronkite was among those selected as candidates to be first journalist in space. That mission was scrapped with the explosion of the space shuttle *Challenger*. Ironically, only the NASA pool cameras and those from CNN were rolling in January of 1986 when *Challenger* exploded after liftoff, killing its seven occupants.

In the 1990s, Americans saw a renewed interest in space coverage and reporters such as CNN's John Holliman covered the linkups of U.S. space shuttles with the Russian space station *Mir*. A crowd of reporters was on hand for the first footage from *Pathfinder* when it landed on Mars on July 4, 1997. Space is an important story for broadcasters, one that evolved in only 40 years. In his memoir, *A Reporter Remembers*, Walter Cronkite pointed out, "Any reporter who didn't want to cover space was missing something." *See also* Jules Bergman, Walter Cronkite.

Ginger Rudeseal Carter

Further Reading

Barnouw, Erik. *Tube of Plenty*. New York: Oxford University Press, 1990.

Cronkite, Walter. *A Reporter Remembers*. New York: Simon & Schuster, 1997.

Frank, Reuven. *Out of Thin Air*. New York: Simon & Schuster, 1991.

Susan Spencer

Susan Spencer was born in Memphis, Tennessee, and received her undergraduate education at Michigan State University. She completed her master's degree in journalism at Columbia Univer-

Courtesy CBS News/*48 Hours*

sity in 1969 and was awarded the Sevellon Brown Writing Award. She found a position in film production, became a news producer at WKPC-TV in Louisville, Kentucky, and then worked in research at WCBS-TV, New York. From 1971 to 1977, she held several positions, including reporter and co-anchor, at WCCO-TV in Minneapolis.

Spencer joined CBS News in 1977, as a reporter in the Washington bureau and became a correspondent the following year. She covered politics and served the network in a variety of positions including science and health correspondent, and also handled duties as a primary correspondent for the *Eye on America* series. In 1989, she reported *The Dawn of a New Era* from Japan, consisting of eight consecutive telecasts over a ten-day period, and included reports on the Japanese culture and education, the rise of urban Japan, and new militarism.

Spencer has been a White House correspondent and also anchored the Sunday edition of the *CBS Evening News*. She took a major role in coverage of the Persian Gulf War, reporting from Riyadh, Saudi Arabia. In 1993, Spencer joined the staff of *48 Hours*. *Michael D. Murray*

Further Reading

Biagi, Shirley. *NewsTalk II*. Belmont, CA: Wadsworth Publishing, 1987.

Rather, Dan, with Mickey Herskowitz. *The Camera Never Blinks Twice: The Further Adventures of a Television Journalist*. New York: William Morrow and Company, 1994.

Zurawik, David, and Christina Stoehr. "Saving CBS News." *American Journalism Review,* April 1997, 16–23.

Lawrence Spivak

Lawrence Edmund Spivak was born in Brooklyn, New York, on June 11, 1900. He attended Harvard University, where he graduated cum laude and wrote his thesis on the topic of "Democracy and the News." He joined the staff of *Antiques* magazine and contributed stories to other magazines including *Hunting & Fishing*, before landing a position at the *American Mercury*, H. L. Mencken's former publication. Spivak subsequently started a radio program based on *American Mercury* stories, which was critiqued by a contributor with some radio experience, Martha Rountree. She had hosted a number of panel programs which consisted almost exclusively of women guests addressing topics of special interest to female listeners.

In 1945 Spivak and Rountree decided to collaborate on an alternative public affairs series, *Meet the Press,* over the Mutual Radio System. The program consisted of the moderator, a panel of reporters, and various national and international news sources, usually political figures, but also economists, and even poets such as Robert Frost. Spivak moved to television and the NBC network three years later. In spite of a calm outward demeanor, he developed the reputation for being a very tough interrogator when directly questioning guests. He broke a number of important stories in the early era of television news, including mention by the former Ambassador to Moscow, General Walter Bedell Smith, that the Soviets may have had atomic weapons in 1949. Whittaker Chambers charged that Alger Hiss was a communist on *Meet the Press,* and Thomas E. Dewey threw his support to GOP candidate Dwight Eisenhower on that program.

As *Meet the Press* developed, Spivak became increasingly regarded as a very demanding, independent, and highly conservative provocateur who relished opportunities to discuss the anti-communist theme of the day. When senator Joseph R. McCarthy, for example, appeared, McCarthy enjoyed referring to the *Washington Post* as the "Washington Daily Worker." Spivak also enjoyed pointing to the increasing attention made to the program by daily newspapers whenever a presidential candidate or head of state would visit, which happened regularly. The program was imitated by the other networks but the qualities Spivak brought to it made it very difficult to emulate successfully. In many ways, he and his program set the stage for current political policies and procedures, such as the presidential press conferences, which are now taken for granted.

Spivak retired from *Meet the Press* in 1975. He died of heart failure on March 9, 1994, at Sibley Memorial Hospital in Washington, D.C., at the age of 93. *See also Meet the Press.*

Michael D. Murray

Further Reading

Monroe, Bill. "The Passing of a Pioneer." *The Communicator,* May 1994, 30–31.
"Lawrence Spivak Dies; Began 'Meet the Press.'" *St. Louis Post-Dispatch,* 10 March 1994, 7A.
Rudolph, Ileane. "Bless This Press." *TV Guide,* 8 November 1997, 37–39.
Widmer, Ted. "50 Years of '*Meet the Press.*'" *George,* November 1997, 132–38.

Sports Coverage

Within the hierarchy of television news, sports occupies a unique status. The relationship that developed between news and sports programming on television offers insight into the complex ties between entertainment and information. With roots in newspaper journalism and the once-dominant print culture, sports was viewed as a significant news area constituting a special section in most daily newspapers, even those publications with a national readership. In contrast to network news, it may seem unusual that a key specialty—one which constitutes a major segment of program content in local level newscasts—is regarded as separate, and sometimes ignored altogether, by the national television news organizations. This can be attributed in part to the tremendous record of success achieved by sports as an entertainment vehicle, first on radio, and then as a significant draw for corporate sponsorship on television.

The entertainment value of sports programming and the nature of sports information itself, distinguishes it from hard news in important ways, although the two have crossed paths in television coverage on many occasions, most notably during Olympic games. Within a society in which the importance of sports has grown considerably in stature, stories and issues from the news coverage of the personal lives of individual athletes inevitably contribute to the public fascination with televised athletic competition.

From the earliest telecasts, sports programs demonstrated the potential to attract large numbers of viewers with the promise of commercial sponsorship, initially at minimal expense to advertisers. The tradition in radio was to establish close ties between announcers, team owners, and products, with owners generally calling the shots. In some cases, early televised sports programs were offered by professional teams in exchange for the price of a ticket to the sporting event or the cost of a seat on which a camera could be set during a game. An awareness and understanding of television's potential role in boosting interest in products was apparent at the outset. Some commercial sponsors quickly jockeyed for limited billboard space in the baseball outfield, for example, with the knowledge that television viewers would be observing those ads at no additional cost. Early experiments in sports programming included baseball, football, boxing, and professional wrestling. These offered the prospect of transporting sports fans to the scene of live events, thus giving them the thrill of rooting for the home team from their living room. News held the same promise for television, of course, but breaking events seldom stood still for coverage in the early days of heavy cameras. The few exceptions, televised crime hearings, for example, were of limited duration.

The first televised baseball game, between prominent university teams, Princeton and Columbia, was a single-camera experiment from an NBC mobile unit, and took place on May 17, 1939. It occurred nearly a decade before television became popular nationally, and well before most Americans had televisions in their home. Shortly thereafter, the same mobile unit, this time equipped with a pair of cameras, provided coverage of a contest between two professional teams, the Brooklyn Dodgers and Cincinnati Reds, live from Ebbets Field. Amateur athletic contests and exhibitions such as figure skating from Rockefeller Center during wartime provided additional entertainment for home viewers at minimal cost, while network chiefs focused on improvements in equipment. By 1946, the champion prizefight pitting Joe Louis against Billy Conn produced rave reviews for picture quality. Shortly after that, another baseball contest between the Dodgers and Reds was televised again, when CBS initiated use of the Zoomar lens.

Network news developed and struggled with technology to cover events from the 1950s, with the likes of John Cameron Swayze "hop-scotching the globe" from his New York studio set. Network chiefs came to understand that news would likely attain the dubious standing of financial loss leader in contrast to entertainment fare. At the same time, they were also discovering that certain televised sporting events could attract very large and fairly predictable numbers of viewers, plus increased advertising revenue. The potential was underscored when CBS purchased the New York Yankees in 1964, and was willing to pay nearly $30 million to telecast National Football League games. When two New York baseball teams, the Giants and Dodgers, were transplanted to the west coast, San Francisco and Los Angeles respectively, prospects for subscription television were part of the equation.

Broadcast technology kept pace and complemented program development. Viewer interest followed. The male-dominated sports audience grew on weekends and led to the expansion of sports in the prime-time schedule, to the extent that ABC-TV's *Monday Night Football*, with Howard Cosell behind the microphone, achieved unprecedented national interest. Cosell's close association and coverage of Muhammad Ali—a Black Muslim who protested American military involvement in Vietnam on religious grounds, also expanded horizons for reporting controversy involving prominent sports figures.

ABC's Wide World of Sports established the network as a leader in the field, which helped its chief executive, Roone Arledge, achieve status as a visionary, especially when sporting events intersected with hard news events. ABC television was involved with all but four Olympic games beginning in the mid-1960s. During the televised games of the 20th Olympiad from Munich, Germany in 1972, sports announcer Jim McKay's coverage of a terrorist kidnapping and murder of 11 Israeli offered a very vivid news story. Coverage of a bomb explosion outside the Olympics in the late 1990s in Atlanta, also followed hard news interests.

Television coverage of sports was also credited with creating interest in special issues such as equal opportunity for women, encouraging participation by female athletes, as well as contributing to a growing interest in physical fitness in general. A generation of gymnasts was encouraged by televised appearances by Olga Korbut and Nadia Comaneci in the 1970s and two decades later, a widely reported dispute involving Olympic ice skating competitors, Nancy Kerrigan and Tonya Harding, again carried interest in women's sports into the news area. Also, the issue of race in sports management has been raised and a national furor was created when Los Angeles Dodger vice president, Al Campanis, remarked about "necessities" for managers in baseball, when a guest on ABC's *Nightline*. A wide-ranging discussion beginning with the accomplishments of Jackie Robinson became a highly charged indictment of white attitudes among those in baseball leadership positions. This ultimately resulted in establishing a pool of minority managerial candidates in baseball.

As television sports programs grew in stature, the issue of the extent of news coverage and intrusion into the private lives of sports figures became an issue. Barbara Walter's *20/20* interview of boxer Mike Tyson introduced controversy regarding his treatment of women, including his wife. Former baseball star Pete Rose was also scrutinized in news reports, when allegations of gambling were first presented, and again when there were attempts to have Rose elected to Baseball's Hall of Fame. Tennis standout Arthur Ashe Jr., held a widely covered televised press conference to explain his struggle with AIDS, which he presented as part of a broader educational effort concerning that disease. A former college football

coach led a national movement, The Promise Keepers, urging men to take personal responsibility for their actions.

Social issues were often tied to coverage of some of America's most talented athletes. Race became an aspect of reporting the aftermath of the murder trial of former football great O. J. Simpson. Race also emerged as part of the televised coverage of the story of black golfer, Tiger Woods, one of America's premier athletes in a white-dominated sport.

Some popular television sports broadcasters, such as Bryant Gumbel and Bob Costas, extended their influence and made the transition to popular, non-sports programs. Meanwhile, networks struggle to achieve balance in reporting stories of accomplishment and controversy involving athletics.
Michael D. Murray

Further Reading

Barnouw, Erik. *Tube of Plenty.* New York: Oxford University Press, 1990.
Koppel, Ted, and Kyle Gibson. *Nightline: History in the Making and the Making of Television.* New York: Times Books, 1996.
McKay, Jim. *My Wide World.* New York: Macmillan, 1973.

Lesley Stahl

CBS News correspondent Lesley Stahl did not seriously consider journalism as a profession until she was 30. After deciding to pursue it, she was turned down for jobs at both the *New York Times* and the *Boston Globe*. Now one of the most experienced and well-known journalists in American television, Stahl has covered stories ranging from Watergate to the 1981 attempt on President Ronald Reagan's life. As a Washington correspondent and news analyst, until she joined *60 Minutes* in 1991, she covered every U.S.–Soviet summit since 1978, every economic summit since 1979, and every national political convention and election night since 1974. She has also covered three American presidents for CBS News: Jimmy Carter, Ronald Reagan, and George Bush.

Stahl was born in Swampscott, Massachusetts, on December 16, 1941. She received her bachelor of arts degree cum laude from Wheaton

College in Norton, Massachusetts, in 1963. After graduation, she worked as a speechwriter for the mayor's office in New York City from 1966 to 1967. Her first media position was in 1967 as a research specialist for the *Huntley-Brinkley Report*. From 1970 to 1972, Stahl was a producer and reporter for Boston's WHDH-TV, a position she regarded as a turning point in her career and love of broadcasting.

Stahl joined CBS News in 1972 as a Washington-based reporter, just in time to cover a seemingly unimportant burglary at the Watergate Hotel. The "routine" police story catapulted Stahl into national attention. By 1977, she had been named anchor of *CBS Morning News*, the second female anchor in the history of the network. A year later, CBS made her White House correspondent, and she served as moderator for *Face the Nation* from 1983 until 1991.

Recently, Stahl is perhaps best known for her role as co-editor and correspondent for *60 Minutes*, a position she has held since 1991. Her report on the selling of babies in Romania, in April 1991, was followed by a piece on the plight of Kurdish refugees in Iraq, in May of 1991. She also has contributed to CBS News *48 Hours* and has been a substitute anchor on *CBS Evening News with Dan Rather*. Stahl won an Emmy Award for her report entitled "Lambs of Christ," which aired in February 1992. The program dealt with a radical pro-life group that uses scare tactics to prevent doctors from performing abortions.

She was named "Best White House Correspondent" by the *Washington Journalism Review* in 1991. Stahl also has been honored, in 1990, with the Dennis Kauff Journalism Award for lifetime achievement in the news profession and the Matrix Award for broadcasting given by New York Women in Communications, in 1993. *See also 60 Minutes.*   *Jan Whitt*

Further Reading

Battiata, Mary. "Lesley Stahl." *Washington Journalism Review,* October 1982, 43.
Gates, Gary Paul. *Air Time.* New York: Harper and Row, 1978.
Hewitt, Don. *Minute by Minute.* New York: Random House, 1985.

Frank Stanton

Longtime president of CBS Frank Stanton's central interest was CBS News. In 1960, with his influence, the U.S. Congress was persuaded to lift the equal time requirements of the Communications Act of 1934, thereby permitting the broadcast of the Kennedy-Nixon debates. A decade later, Stanton risked a congressional contempt citation by steadfastly, on First Amendment grounds, refusing to yield to the House Committee on Communication non-broadcast materials, which were used in preparation of the CBS documentary, "The Selling of the Pentagon." After three committees voted to cite Stanton for contempt, the full membership of the House voted 226 to 181 not to go forward with the action.

Stanton was born on March 20, 1908, in Muskegon, Michigan, and grew up in Dayton, Ohio. He graduated from Ohio Wesleyan University, and at Ohio State University, developed a recording device for measuring radio audiences. Immediately after receiving his doctorate in 1935, he joined CBS, working principally on studies of the radio audience. Ten years later, William S. Paley, then president of CBS, asked Stanton to become president and chief operating officer of the company. In his new role, Stanton moved CBS into television and organized the company into distinct operating divisions: CBS News, CBS Radio, CBS Television, and CBS Records.

During almost 30 years as president, Stanton worked with Chairman Paley in building the company. Paley concerned himself chiefly with the entertainment schedules. Stanton ran the company. Along the way, however, it was Stanton who spotted Arthur Godfrey and brought him to New York from WJSV, Washington, D.C. *Playhouse 90* was also a Stanton creation, and he played a critical role in bringing Lucille Ball and Jackie Gleason to CBS. It was during his tenure that upcoming programs were first prescreened for press review.

CBS buildings on both coasts carry Stanton's mark: Television City in Hollywood and Black Rock in New York. His deep interest in design, graphics, and architecture encouraged special attention and led to world-class work. He was involved directly in developing the CBS Eye graphic, and the CBS Laboratories Division was a distinct interest to him. From this division, the long-playing record revitalized the music market and the color television timetable worldwide was advanced by the seminal work of CBS scientists. Stanton did the first network editorial and introduced *CBS Reports*. As a result of frequent testimony at congressional and FCC hearings, Stanton became the preeminent spokesperson for broadcasting. Throughout his congressional appearances, the First Amendment was his guide. President Johnson and later, President Nixon named Stanton chairman of the U.S. Advisory Commission on Information.

Stanton also had broad interests beyond the walls of Black Rock. He served on the boards of PanAm, ARCO, and American Electric Power, and was the founding chairman of the Center for Advanced Study in the Behavioral Sciences. He worked closely with Paley in the planning and manning of the Museum of Television and Radio.

Following mandatory retirement, he was appointed chairman of the American Red Cross by Presidents Nixon and Ford. He served as a director of the *Observer (London)* and the *International (Paris) Herald Tribune*. In 1979, Stanton was elected an overseer of Harvard College, the first non-Harvard person so elected in this century. A chair was created in honor of Stanton at Harvard University, John F. Kennedy School of Government—the Frank Stanton Chair of the First Amendment. *See also* CBS News.

Michael D. Murray

Further Reading

Dunham, Gordon B. *Fighting for the First Amendment: Stanton of CBS vs. Congress and the Nixon White House.* Westport, CT: Praeger Publishers, 1997.
Stone, Emerson. "Talking with Stanton." *Communicator,* October 1994, 37–38.
West, Don. "Broadcastings Finest First Amendment Hour." *Broadcasting & Cable* 2 February 1996, 20.

Carl Stern

Carl Stern was the law correspondent for NBC News, reporting court trials for 26 years. A li-censed attorney, he used his skills to successfully sue the government, forcing the release of FBI documents about bureau harassment. Stern was born on August 7, 1937, in New York, and graduated from Columbia University, with a bachelor's and a master's degree. In 1959, after military service, he became a radio host with KYW in Cleveland. Two years later, he became a reporter for WKYC-TV. He received his law degree from Cleveland State University in 1966.

Stern became the law correspondent for NBC in 1967 and covered the U.S. Supreme Court and the Justice Department. He also covered a number of celebrated trials, including those of Jimmy Hoffa, Muhammad Ali, Patricia Hearst, and Oliver North. In 1973, he reported extensively on Watergate, focusing on the trials of Watergate burglars and the congressional hearings under Senator Sam Ervin. As an attorney admitted to the District of Columbia and Ohio bars, he sought disclosure under the Freedom of Information Act of an FBI program, begun in the late 1960s, which secretly targeted individuals and groups opposed to the Vietnam War. After the FBI refused to release the documents, Stern sued and received the documents. A subsequent lawsuit forced the FBI to identify top officials disciplined for misleading superiors and Congress about the harassment of left-wing radicals. In 1993, Stern left NBC to join the Justice Department, where he has served as spokesperson.

Mark Conrad

Further Reading

Powers, Richard Gid. *Secrecy and Powers— The Life of J. Edgar Hoover.* New York, 1987.
"A Sampler of Legal Journalists." *National Law Journal,* 6 June 1988, 35.
"NBC Demotes High Court Beat: Reporter Carl Stern Taken Off the Air as Coverage Shifts." *Washington Post,* 25 October 1991, B1.

John Stossel

John Stossel is a consumer affairs specialist and regular contributor to ABC's *20/20*. Born in 1947, in Chicago, Illinois, he graduated in 1969 with a degree in psychology from Princeton University. Stossel began his career at KGW-TV, Portland,

Oregon, as a producer and reporter, then became a consumer editor for WCBS-TV, New York.

Stossel has contributed consumer reports on the ABC Radio Information Network and was consumer editor for *Good Morning, America,* before joining *20/20* in 1981. Within 10 years of joining *20/20* Stossel had won 19 Emmy Awards. Stossel's contributions to *20/20* include reports on the workplace, the courts, and life—how false sexual abuse charges have forced teachers to distance themselves from children; and the distortion of statistics to serve special-interest agendas. His first prime-time special, in April 1994, attacked government waste and preoccupation with minor issues of employment or what Stossel viewed as "trivial risks." His February 1995 special contributing to the nature-versus-nurture debate on gender identity also drew attention for its personalized approach.

The author of *Shopping Smart,* Stossel was honored on a number of occasions by the National Press Club and many other organizations. He has been recognized by the National Environmental Development Association for balance and fairness in journalism and by the Retirement Research Foundation for a report on greedy guardians of the elderly. *See also 20/20.*   *Linda M. Perry*

Further Reading

Johnson, Rebecca. "The Gotcha Guy." *George,* May 1997, 84–102.
Stossel, John. "Hysterical About Everything." *Communicator,* May 1995, 45.
Spencer, Miranda. "Desperately Seeking Difference: ABC Finds Biology In Destiny." *Extra,* 6 May 1996.

Howard Stringer

An award-winning writer, producer, and director, Howard Stringer is one of the most highly respected programmers in American television. He spent 30 years at the CBS network in news and management. Stringer was born in Cardiff, Wales, in 1942. His association with a group of Rhodes scholars at Oxford University stimulated his interest in the United States. After receiving a master's degree in history, Stringer drove a long-distance truck for six months in order to finance his voyage across the Atlantic. In 1965, he was hired as a log clerk at a CBS affiliate in New York but was soon drafted into the U.S. Army and sent to Vietnam. Stringer considers this experience a valuable lesson in that he became acquainted with America and Americans while serving in the army. Returning from Vietnam two years later, he found a job as a news writer at a local CBS Radio, WCBS, and thus began his career in the news field.

Stringer moved to CBS television when a well-known documentary producer, Perry Wolff, hired him for *CBS Reports.* During his tenure in the news division, Stringer distinguished himself as an executive producer of *CBS Reports,* as well as *CBS Evening News With Dan Rather*, as a creator of *48 Hours* and *CBS This Morning*, and eventually as a vice president. His exceptional abilities as a broadcast journalist are verified by the 31 Emmy Awards given to his documentary team between 1976 and 1981, including 9 awards for his own work.

In 1985, CBS was acquired by Laurence Tisch who made Stringer the president of CBS News and three years later, the president of the CBS Broadcasting Group. Under the directive from Tisch concerning strict financial control, Stringer was able to, not only maintain high-quality programming, but accomplish the unprecedented feat of turning around and leading the network from third to first place in a single season. Award-winning programs, including *Northern Exposure*, were produced during Stringer's presidency. Stringer is also often referred to as charming. He is well-liked and respected by those who have worked with him, including David Letterman, whose move from NBC contributed to CBS's financial improvement in the early 1990s.

Although he was a strong advocate of free television amidst the rising popularity of cable television and direct broadcast satellite (DBS) technology, Stringer resigned the presidency of the CBS Broadcast Group in February 1995, in order to head up Tele-TV, a joint venture of Pacific Telesis, Nynex, and Bell Atlantic, for the development of interactive digital television and in April 1997, Stringer joined Sony as president of Sony Corporation of America. Some people attributed his departure from CBS to a belief in the value and virtue of broadcast journalism which was different from a focus on profits. **See also** CBS News.

Yasue Kuwahara

Further Reading

Unger, Arthur. "CBS's Howard Stringer: The Man Who Repolished the Tiffany Network." *Television Quarterly,* 1993, 18–32.

Rothenberg, Randall. "Brave Old World." *Esquire,* August 1995, 722–79.

Gunther, Marc. "The Man the Phone Companies Forgot." *Fortune,* 27 May 1996, 107–12.

David Susskind

Moderator of a popular and often controversial syndicated talk show from the 1960s, David Susskind also was a talent agent and produced a wide-ranging series of television programs and Broadway shows. He was born in New York City, December 19, 1920. He was raised in Brookline, Massachusetts and attended the University of Wisconsin for two years, before transfering to Harvard. He graduated with honors, in 1942, from Harvard College and served in the U.S. Navy, seeing action in Iwo Jima and Okinawa.

When he was discharged from military service, he entered the entertainment business as an agent and producer in Manhattan. He started his extended format, highly combative talk program, *Open End* in 1958, at WNEW-TV, New York. The program addressed serious topics and had no set time limit. It often hosted major political figures. Susskind also became well-known as a critic of television arguing for better quality and live programming. He adopted a two-hour format and the program became *The David Susskind Show* in 1967. It lasted until September 1986. Six months later, in 1987, Susskind died at the age of 66.

Michael D. Murray

Further Reading

Barnouw, Erik. *Tube of Plenty: The Evolution of American Television.* New York: Oxford University Press, 1990.

McFadden, Robert D. "David Susskind, Dies at 66, Talk Show Host." *New York Times*, 23 February 1987, A1.

Watson, Mary Ann. "Open End: Mirror of the 1960s." *Film & History,* May/September, 1991.

John Cameron Swayze

John Cameron Swayze was a well-known news figure to those adventurous late-1940s Americans determined to be one of the first to buy into the new television technology. In 1949, Swayze began appearing on NBC for 15 minutes, five nights a week, "hop scotching the world for headlines," on the *Camel News Caravan.*

As one of the very first network evening news anchors, he sat at a desk prominently displaying the sponsoring tobacco company's logo, and read the news from a script that was produced with the help of one writer. He wore a trademark carnation and it was not until the show went to color in 1954, that viewers were aware the carnation was red. The program, which replaced NBC's straight newsreel format, had few visuals—only occasional wire photos or grainy film clips. Swayze filled his "live" 15-minute broadcast each night with news, interviews, and roundups by commentators from different cities.

Occasionally criticized for his emphasis on pictures and personalities, Swayze countered that he never intended to do hard-hitting news. He often said in interviews that his goal was to leave people feeling good. He was replaced on the evening news in 1956, by two young upstart reporters who had become overnight sensations covering political conventions that year—Chet Huntley and David Brinkley. Despite his role in early television news, Swayze is remembered today for Timex watch commercials, in which he repeated the line, "It takes a licking and keeps on ticking." The phrase was adopted in sports, politics, and business to suggest toughness. The commercials, which ran until the mid-1970s, featured Timex watches being subjected to abuse, but running flawlessly.

Swayze was born in Wichita, Kansas, in 1906. He had always intended to be an actor, but instead began a news career at *The Kansas City Journal-Post.* He worked in radio during the 1930s and 1940s, before getting his start with NBC. His first television effort was covering the 1948 presidential nominating conventions in Philadelphia. NBC executives were sufficiently impressed with Swayze's performance to persuade him to move to television full-time. At first he turned them down because the real money, he believed, was in radio. In addition to his news program, Swayze served as a panel member on NBC's quiz show *Who Said That?* He impressed the audience with an encyclopedic memory of events. He later invented a board game called *Swayze* in which players tested their knowledge of current events. Swayze also was the master of ceremonies of a children's educational show, *Watch the World*, and he hosted the television program *Sightseeing with the Swayzes* in which his wife, son, and daughter appeared with him.

Swayze died in August 1995, at the age of 89. After Swayze's death, his son, John Cameron Swayze Jr., noted that his father had always managed to project feelings of innocence, promise, and genuine friendliness. His favorite sign-off line was, "That's the story, glad we could get together." *See also* Camel News Caravan, NBC News.

Patsy G. Watkins

Further Reading

Kennedy, Randy. "John Cameron Swayze, 89, Journalist and Pitchman, Dies." *New York Times,* 16 August 1995, D20.

Kennedy, Randy. "John Cameron Swayze, 89, Journalist and TV Pitchman." *New York Times,* 17 August 1995, B12.

Snyder, Tom. "John Cameron Swayze: The Original Tom, Dan and Peter." *New York Times Magazine,* 31 December 1995, 39.

T

Tabloid Television

The 1973 CBS broadcast of a *60 Minutes* segment entitled "Tabloid News in San Francisco," marked the beginning of widespread public awareness of a variety of criticisms directed toward local television news. Mike Wallace tried to shame San Francisco's KGO-TV and a competing station KRON-TV for airing high proportions of fire, crime, and sex stories based on an analysis by graduate students at the University of California at Berkeley. Wallace's segment served to document the first of numerous techniques local television stations were using to effectively boost sensational stories, bizarre situations, graphic visuals, sex, and crime reports.

Over the next two decades, news consultants replaced standards established by Murrow, Severeid, Stanton, and Friendly, with a formula for boosting ratings and making local news broadcasting's most important source of advertising revenue. Happy talk, pretty faces, and news promos became more commonplace. Critics, especially newspapers, claimed that electronic journalism is nothing more than "show business," infotainment, junk-food journalism, or worse. Entertainment values replaced good, sound judgment in broadcast journalism and a number of major newsanchors spoke out publicly about the quality and course of television news. Walter Cronkite and Eric Severeid both castigated efforts by news directors to jazz-up their news product or employ special reporting methods or promotional measures to attract a bigger audience.

Perhaps the most grisly example of tabloid television occurred on Thursday, January 22, 1987. Pennsylvania State Treasurer R. Budd Dwyer, at a news conference in Harrisburg, pulled out a handgun, put it in his mouth, and fired. None of the several cameras that recorded the incident was on the air live, but four television stations decided to broadcast the scene as part of their newscast. Other local stations, and the networks, stopped the video before the trigger was pulled and let the audio run, so that the viewer heard, but did not see the suicide.

A 1993 survey showed crime coverage on the network evening news programs doubled over the previous year, even as the actual crime rate was going down. In 1993, for example, the networks aired almost 2,000 stories concerning crime, an average of five stories each evening—a jump from the previous year when there were less than half that number of crime stories reported. Local television news coverage of crime was even higher. In a study of 50 station newscasts, in 29 cities, videotaped on the night of January 11, 1995, the percentage of news was heavily weighted towards mayhem. Stories about crime, disaster, and war made up 53 percent of the news, and well in excess of 70 percent on some big-city stations.

Spokespersons for professional organizations, such the National Association of Broadcasters (NAB) and the Radio-Television News Directors

Association (RTNDA), fiercely defended television news's right to cover crime fully. They pointed out that there is an obvious public appetite for Hollywood-style crime stories, such as those involving the Bobbitts, the Menendez brothers, Tonya Harding, and O. J. Simpson. The O. J. Simpson story, in particular, created what was often described as an inevitable media feeding frenzy with court proceedings, including elements of celebrity, sex, murder, and even racial issues. This was followed by extensive coverage of the Diana, Princess of Wales, and accusations that photojournalists contributed to this catastrophe. While questioning motives in covering crime news, there was no denying public interest. Many news directors believe there is a public backlash against the "if it bleeds, it leads" news philosophy used by some local stations. Their promise to refrain from showing violent video during early evening news shows was labeled "family-sensitive news." The early evening newscast differs from the newscast an hour later in that graphic video and offensive words are usually omitted. Wide shots of crime scenes are used and viewers are verbally warned of a "troubling story."

AR&D, a Dallas consulting firm, recommended to their clients that they offer family-sensitive newscasts and eliminate gratuitous violence in response to the public's growing frustration and skepticism. Some skeptics have concluded that broadcast news directors have invented something of a formula for coverage, generally ignoring public concerns. (If news directors are sincere, the critics contend, this type of attention would be paid to every newscast.) Twenty-five years of tabloid news appears to have changed television newsroom policies and news-gathering procedures in a way that is unlikely to be reversed.

Television's other entry into the tabloid market started with national talk shows hosted by Morton Downey Jr., and Geraldo Rivera leading up to Jerry Springer. This genre of programs was also referred to as "trash TV." The talk shows often focused on interpersonal or family relationships, infidelity, or lewd behavior, but some also represented an undercurrent of violence that sometimes was displayed on the air, as happened when Geraldo Rivera had his face smashed with a chair

and his nose broken during a show about race relations. In another particularly alarming nationally televised example, a participant in the Jenny Jones talk program was embarrassed when his sexual orientation was called into question, and a homicide later occurred. This resulted in a lawsuit and a series of critical questions regarding deceptive practices and how program participants are screened and consulted prior to taping. Talk shows also spawned "reality-based" programs that sometimes featured bizarre tragedies, confrontation, reenactments, sensationalism, or titillation. Programs often identified with this trend include: *A Current Affair*, *Special Edition*, *America's Most Wanted*, *Hardcopy*, and *Inside Edition*.

Audience popularity, ratings, and advertiser support for "reality-based" programming, in turn, affected news and public affairs programming. Coverage of the scandal involving President Clinton and Monica Lewinsky became a sounding board for public criticism of press performance. Since many of the tabloid talk programs and reality shows were lead-ins to the local newscast or a bridge between the evening newscast and network prime time, ratings and content led some local news departments to use the same type of sensationalism and hype. Some news departments claimed that legitimate news could not compete with a hyped-up version of reality, thus compounding the pressures to produce tabloid news. Although some of the trash TV shows were canceled, when viewers and advertisers shied away or got fed up with them, the phenomenon has yet to fade completely. A new appeal to morbid curiosity is available through direct video sales. Credit card holders can now purchase personal VHS copies of *Caught on Camera*—a video portfolio of actual accidents, crashes, and disasters showing death and dismemberment as it occurred. ***See also*** Consultants, Happy News.   *Roger Hadley*

Further Reading

Levy, Steven. "New Media's Dark Star," *Newsweek*, 16 February 1998, 78.

Morrow, Lance. "Journalism after Diana," *Columbia Journalism Review*, November/December 1997, 38–41.

"The White House and the Media," *Columbia Journalism Review*, May/June 1998, 34–35.

Viles, Peter. "News Execs Grumble about Tabloid TV." *Broadcasting & Cable*, 27 September 1993, 42–43.

Cal Thomas

Photo courtesy of Cal Thomas

As a journalist, author, and broadcaster, Cal Thomas has had many incarnations. While he was gaining attention for his twice-weekly column in more than 440 daily newspapers (distributed by the Los Angeles Times Syndicate since 1984), he began his career in broadcast journalism in suburban Washington, D.C., and continues to work there in both radio and television.

Cal Thomas was born in Washington, D.C., on December 2, 1942. He began his broadcasting career at WINX in Rockville, Maryland, in 1959, as a radio announcer and news reader. Thomas served in the U.S. Army from 1965 to 1966. Following his discharge, he found a position with the Armed Forces Radio and Television in New York City and Washington, D.C., and worked as a civilian employee until 1967.

In 1968, Thomas graduated from American University with a major in English literature. He worked at KPRC-radio and television, an NBC affiliate in Houston, in 1968 and again in 1973. By the time he left in 1977, he had advanced to anchor status. In 1977, Thomas helped organized International Media Service (IMS), a national radio news service, and in 1980, he left IMS and joined the Moral Majority, a conservative, political

organization, where he was vice president of communications. The next year, he began a syndicated daily radio commentary, now heard on more than 200 stations. In 1984, he started his column and then left the Moral Majority in 1985. He began hosting his own show on CNBC in 1994, as part of its Talk All-Star lineup, and earned a Cable Ace Award nomination in 1995, for best interview program. The series ended in 1996. He has also worked for the Public Broadcasting Service.

Among his books are *Public Persons and Private Lives, Liberals for Lunch* with political cartoonist Wayne Stayskal, *Occupied Territory, The Death of Ethics in America, Uncommon Sense,* and *The Things That Matter Most.* Fox News hired Thomas as a commentator and analyst, with duties including guest-hosting *Hannity and Colmes.* Whether broadcasting or writing, Thomas has gained a reputation for his quick wit, his conservative politics, and his evangelical faith.

His columns on biblical truths, published in secular newspapers, have won him many honors including an Amy Writing Award. In addition, his work has received a Texas Headliner Award, a George Foster Peabody Team Reporting Award for a special series on crime victims, and numerous other journalism honors, including recognition from both the Associated Press and United Press International. He was honored by Regent University's College of Communication for status as an outstanding communicator.

Michael R. Smith

Further Reading
Ferguson, Tim W. with Jospehine Lee. "Spiritual Reality." *Forbes,* 27 January 1997, 70–76.
Guetschow, Elizabeth J. "Life Outside the Catacombs." *Religious Broadcasting*, June 1994, 16–19.
Lamb, Chris. "Conservative Has a Growing Readership." *Editor and Publisher*, 27 February 1993, 32–33.
Zipperer, John. "Don't Blame Washington." *Christianity Today*, 25 April 1994, 12–13.

Lowell Thomas

Lowell Jackson Thomas, adventurer, author, and broadcaster, wanted to be seen as a mix of author and adventurer. He was born on April 6, 1892, in

Woodington, Ohio. His father, a great lover of learning, changed his career to medicine and moved the family to Colorado. It was in the gold mining boom town of Cripple Creek that Lowell Thomas heard and saw people live lives of adventure. He wrote down their stories, and, at his father's request, practiced his elocution by retelling of their struggles in the West.

From 1909 to 1916, Lowell Thomas graduated from four different universities and attained six degrees while working as a newspaper reporter, teaching public speaking, and giving extended talks based on his travels. He arranged for free passages in exchange for his travelogue talks which became quite popular. For a trip to Alaska, he picked up a movie camera, and from then on his talks were illustrated shows, not lectures. The U.S. Secretary of the Interior hired him to promote *See America First*, but in 1919, the job was converted into reporting on World War I, with photographer Harry Chase. He covered U.S. troops in Europe, then went to the Middle East, to cover the British war effort. There he discovered Colonel T. E. Lawrence. After the war, while making Lawrence of Arabia famous, Thomas gained international fame as he filled the great halls of New York and London with his exciting tales of military excursions from his bestselling book, *With Lawrence in Arabia*. His presentations, prepared with the assistance of Dale Carnegie, were major shows replete with sets, dances, music, and film, and were enthusiastically received.

Thomas continued his adventures all over the world, presenting shows and writing about the places he encountered. In the mid-1920s, he hired writer Prosper Buranelli, and later others, to write many books reflecting these interests and adventures. He also purchased Quaker Hill, a large homestead in Dutchess County, New York, where he would entertain many distinguished guests, including U.S. presidents, famous sports figures, explorers, and the Dalai Lama. It was here where he brought his friends, including Reverend Norman Vincent Peale and Edward R. Murrow, to participate in live program broadcasts.

In 1930, CBS asked Thomas to replace Floyd Gibbons as their daily news commentator. The first broadcast included comments about Adolf Hitler, a reference to Napoleon, and an admonition

to the German leader about his international goals and ambitions—particularly as they applied to Russia. Thus, began his career as the longest continuing daily broadcaster, first on CBS and then NBC, for a time heard over both, then, eventually back to CBS. The popular H. V. Kaltenborn began his newscasts that same year, but Thomas more than held his own. In fact, he was often chosen as the nation's favorite news commentator during that era. He set the stage for informed perspective and raised listener expectations to receive information from a source who had visited first-hand the far corners of the globe and had met with international authorities. Thomas reached his height of popularity in 1936, with an audience estimated at 20 million. For the most part, his newscasts relayed not only the major world events of that day, but also the tales of human conquest and adventure. He always closed his broadcasts with the phrase ". . . and so long until tomorrow." In 1934, he started his 17-year stint as the narrator for Fox Movietone newsreels.

In 1939, Thomas anchored the first television newscast, a simulcast of his radio program. Although, later, Thomas would be involved in television as an investor and host and producer of adventure films, he preferred radio for news broadcasting and continued to place a great deal of emphasis in that area. In 1945, Thomas arranged for Frank Smith, an experienced financial advisor, to be his business manager. Smith helped him negotiate his move from NBC back to CBS, and introduced Thomas to Hollywood filmmaker Mike Todd. This meeting led to his eventual involvement in the Cinerama project, starting with seed money and resulting in three groundbreaking films including *This is Cinerama* in 1952. Smith also encouraged Thomas to become one of the founding investors of Hudson Valley Broadcasting, later to become Capital Cities Communications.

In 1949, Thomas and his son, Lowell Jr., were the seventh and eighth westerners to travel in Tibet and the film of this life-threatening expedition became part of a television series. From 1957 to 1959, as president of Odyssey Productions, Thomas produced and hosted *High Adventure with Lowell Thomas,* a series of 11 television specials, films of expeditions he made all over the world, from Nepal to Madagascar, New Guinea to the Arctic. They aired on the CBS network and later went into worldwide syndication. Odyssey Productions also gained the sole film and distribution rights to the Eichmann trial in Israel in 1961. In 1965, Thomas produced another popular series, *The World of Lowell Thomas*, with the BBC. Later, he produced a 39-week series, *Lowell Thomas Remembers*, for the Public Broadcasting Service, which was broadcast across the nation. Lowell Thomas died in his sleep on August 29, 1981.

Margot Hardenbergh

Further Reading

Mazzaco, Dennis W. *Networks of Power: Corporate TV's Threat to Democracy.* Boston, MA: South End Press, 1940.

Thomas, Lowell. *Good Evening Everybody: From Cripple Creek to Samarkand.* New York: Morrow, 1976.

Thomas, Lowell. *So Long Until Tomorrow: From Quaker Hill to Kathmandu.* New York, Morrow, 1977.

Today

Today made its debut on NBC in New York City on January 14, 1952. Sylvester "Pat" Weaver developed the concept of *Today*. He came from advertising in 1949, and became a television vice president. Weaver's goal was to create a two-hour breakfast show that would draw radio listeners to television by providing a variety of news, music, weather, time reports, and features. He aimed for programming that offered both quality and a sense of culture. He pursued his goal and convinced advertisers to invest.

Today was first broadcast from a storefront facility located in the RCA Exhibit Hall on 49th Street, which also served as promotional window to display RCA television sets. Weaver hired Dick Pinkham as the show's first executive producer and Mort Werner as producer. Dave Garroway, an easy-going on-air personality, served as the first host of *Today* with Jim Fleming as the newscaster. Jack Lescoulie appeared as a panelist to provide some comic relief. Although *Today* got off to a shaky start with the telephones, teletype, teleprinters, wire, and facilities for trans-Atlantic communication it needed for broadcast coverage, Weaver's enthusiasm continued. He revised his strategy, his dream became a reality, and a new era in television programming began. Weaver's vision and tenacity brought *Today* to prominence and success. Weaver became NBC's president in 1953.

During Garroway's tenure as host on *Today* from 1952 to 1961, several women made regular appearances as "*Today* Girls." Estelle Parsons was the first *Today* Girl to appear as a regular. Helen O'Connell became a *Today* Girl in 1956. Actresses Betsy Palmer and Florence Henderson, and former Miss America Lee Ann Meriwether were also *Today* Girls. Estelle Parson introduced *Today* chimp, J. Fred Muggs, who became a co-star with Garroway, Jack Lecoulie, and Frank Blair (who joined the show in 1953).

Dave Garroway's intelligence, magnetism, and easy-going style contributed greatly to the early success of *Today*. Garroway left the program in 1961 and was replaced by John Chancellor. Chancellor was joined by Edwin Newman, with Blair remaining to deliver the news. But Chancellor was considered to be too bland, Newman's humor was dry, and Blair projected great dignity. The team did not excite viewers. The audience began to slip and major sponsors removed advertising.

In 1962, Hugh Downs replaced Chancellor. Downs, who was previously the announcer for the *Jack Paar Show*, infused life into the show. He was intelligent, and well-informed, with an "all American" image viewers liked. The Hugh Downs period, 1962–1971, was considered the highlight for *Today* as it related to quality with a touch of class. Barbara Walters entered the *Today* lineup in 1961. Walters was hired as a writer who also appeared on camera. Producer Robert "Shad" Northshield and Hugh Downs were impressed with Walters and gave her regular assignments. She gained a reputation for her ability to ask deep questions and was selected to replace Maureen O'Sullivan as the *Today* Girl in 1964.

After Hugh Downs left *Today* in 1971, Frank McGee came aboard as the new host from 1971 to 1974. McGee, a tough interviewer, had little appreciation for Walters's talent even though she had a proven track record including interviews with Richard Nixon, Henry Kissinger, and Anwar

Sadat. Nonetheless, they meshed well on the air as a team. After McGee's death in 1974, Jim Hartz co-anchored the program with Barbara Walters, until she left NBC to join ABC in 1976. Hartz failed to bring the ratings up and was replaced.

The next wave of *Today* personnel arrived in 1976, with Tom Brokaw and Jane Pauley. Brokaw demonstrated intense curiosity. Pauley, who did not join the show originally as co-host but appeared as part of the team, was affectionate and bright. In the beginning of the Brokaw era, ratings slipped, but began to rise again after a change in approach and a format calling for fewer scripts and a more informal style. Additionally, the team of Brokaw, Pauley, *Today* critic Gene Shalit, newscaster Floyd Kalber, and weather and sportscaster Lew Woods brought a more animated quality to the news delivery. *Today's* ratings soared and became the top morning program. Weatherman Willard Scott joined *Today* in 1980.

Tom Brokaw left *Today* to anchor the network evening news and Bryant Gumbel became host in 1981, with Jane Pauley serving as co-host. Gumbel, the first African American host of *Today*, was a tough interviewer who knew how to get to the heart of the matter. He interviewed everyone from Richard Nixon to Miss Piggy. However, the lack of chemistry between Pauley and Gumbel was evident and Pauley was replaced by Deborah Norville in 1990. Norville's tenure lasted only one year, and Katie Couric joined *Today* as a national correspondent and substitute co-anchor in 1990. She became the permanent co-anchor in 1991. Couric's bubbly personality blended well with the serious Gumbel style. The co-hosts broadcast *Today* from Rome, Vietnam, Cuba, China, Africa, and the Kremlin.

Today returned to its storefront studio look in 1994 and moved to a three-story, 18,000 square-foot space that formerly housed a bank. Gumbel left *Today* on January 3, 1997. He is credited with being the longest reigning *Today* host to date, marking a 15-year tenure. Matt Lauer, who served as the news correspondent on *Today* from 1994 to 1996, became a co-anchor with Couric in January 1997. *Today* is still the top-rated morning news program.   *Dhyana Ziegler*

Further Reading

Goodman, M., and T. Kahn, "Yesterday and *Today.*" *People,* January 1992, 83–85.
Gliatto, T., and A. Longley. "Kiss *Today* Goodbye." *People,* January 1997, 62–65.
Mertz, R. *The Today Show.* Chicago: A Playboy Press Book, 1977.

Liz Trotta

Liz Trotta was one of the first female reporters on network television. Trotta's career started when news organizations only hired the token woman here and there and were more concerned about women's appearances than their abilities. She persevered however, and was noted for her Vietnam War coverage for NBC in the late 1960s and early 1970s. That experience and tales of resistance she encountered from men who did the hiring and promoting in network news are told in her 1991 autobiography.

Trotta grew up in New Haven, Connecticut. She graduated from Boston University and in 1961, earned a master's degree in journalism from Columbia University. Her first job after school was on the *Chicago Tribune.* When she tried to get promoted at the *Tribune* she was told she was after a man's job. After getting similar messages from other potential employers, she joined the Associated Press in Miami. That experience led to a job in 1963 with *Newsday,* in Garden City, New York.

Her work soon caught the attention of WNBC, the network-owned station in New York. In 1965, the boss was looking for "a girl reporter" and Trotta got the job. The ambitious young reporter was soon angling for a position with the network. She always wanted to be a foreign correspondent. Trotta got her network break in 1968 and was assigned to cover the Democratic primary campaign.

Trotta was assigned to Vietnam in the summer of 1968. There she faced the hazards of combat reporting, in addition to an often hostile and patronizing male press corps. But Trotta quickly proved she could do the job and her work won the Overseas Press Club Award. She reported from Vietnam from 1968 to 1970, and returned for a tour in 1971. She worked as NBC's Southeast Asia bureau chief in Singapore and was in Vietnam for the departure of American troops. NBC then assigned Trotta to the London bureau.

By 1975, a new regime was in command at NBC and there was no place for Liz Trotta. She was sent back to WNBC in New York. When she inquired about another network assignment, she was told she would have to audition. Trotta was hired by CBS News in 1979. She covered the revolution in Iran and the 10th anniversary of America's withdrawal from Vietnam. All told, her experience at CBS was not happy. She was not on the team of preferred correspondents for the *CBS Evening News with Dan Rather* and she along with others, was laid off, in 1985. Trotta joined the *Washington Times* as New York bureau chief and authored the top-selling book, *Fighting for Air,* about her experiences in the field.

Marjorie Fox

Further Reading

Trotta, Liz. *Fighting for Air: In the Trenches with Television News.* New York: Simon & Schuster, 1991.

Sanders, Marlene, and Marcia Rock. *Waiting for Prime Time: The Women of Television News.* Urbana: University of Illinois Press, 1988.

Elwood-Akers, Virginia. *Women War Correspondents in the Vietnam War, 1961–75.* Metuchen, NJ: Scarecrow Press, 1988.

Robert Trout

Robert Trout was one of CBS's best-known and most highly regarded radio correspondents. He was considered to be one of the three or four best extemporaneous broadcasters in the news business. Trout was born October 15, 1908, in Wake County, North Carolina, and graduated from Central High School in Washington, D.C., in 1931. Trout became well-known in the 1930s for announcing conventions, covering by visits heads of state, and presidential news conferences for CBS. He was a traditional network newsleader from CBS Radio. Often, Trout talked without notes. At times, he could successfully ad lib for as much as two hours. He was known for doing careful research for his broadcasts, something not usually done for broadcasts. He also had the distinction of

"anchoring" *European Roundup* featuring Edward R. Murrow, William L. Shirer, Frank Gervasi, and U.S. Senator Lewis B. Schwellenbach.

CBS gave news high priority. Network news director Paul White built a staff of stellar correspondents headed by Edward R. Murrow. The organization came into its own during World War II and made the daily *CBS World News Roundup* one of radio's most credible offerings. Even as CBS continued to trail NBC in terms of total listeners and advertising revenue, its news made it the more respected network. Three young CBS staffers, Murrow, Charles Collingwood, and Trout began to build their reputations in blacked-out London. Murrow became the network's best-known figure and was especially recognized for his *This is London* series. However, when the Allies received a message from the Japanese accepting surrender, Trout was there to announce it over the CBS airwaves.

By 1964, Trout was one of broadcasting's respected elders. He joined Roger Mudd on CBS television for a key assignment, replacing Walter Cronkite at the Democratic National Convention. Mudd had held a correspondent assignment in the Washington bureau and came to CBS's attention as a result of marathon coverage of a Senate filibuster on civil rights. The pairing of Mudd and Trout was done in the wake of the trouncing NBC gave CBS in ratings of coverage of the Republican National Convention. Considered an attempt to outdo NBC's Huntley-Brinkley combination, the experiment failed miserably. The 1964 Democratic National Convention was the only national political gathering Cronkite did not anchor from 1952 through 1980. Trout and Cronkite co-anchored *Election Night: 1964,* when Lyndon Johnson won a landslide victory over Barry Goldwater. Trout continued anchoring the Channel 2 News in New York but left that position in 1965 to become a roving correspondent based in Madrid, first for CBS News, then for ABC. In 1980, Trout accepted a Peabody Award for his nearly 50 years as a broadcast commentator.

Tommy V. Smith

Further Reading

Barnouw, Erik. *The Image Empire: A History of Broadcasting in the United States from 1953.* New York: Oxford University Press, 1970.

Matusow, Barbara. *The Evening Stars, the Making of the Network News Anchor.* Boston: Houghton Mifflin, 1983.

Paley, William S. *As It Happened.* New York: Doubleday, 1979.

Edward Turner

Edward "Ed" Turner is often confused with Ted Turner's father, another Ed Turner. The confusion is due to Ed Turner's prominent position at the Cable News Network. When Reese Schonfeld became president of CNN in 1980, he used a hand-picked staff to sell his vision of what a 24-hour news channel could be for the American people and the field of journalism. Ed Turner, no relation to Ted, was one of those hand-picked employees and he has churned and remolded Schonfeld's original dream for CNN. As CNN's executive vice president of news-gathering, Ed Turner was responsible for the rhythm of its news coverage and answered to CNN President Tom Johnson.

Insight regarding CNN's direction is especially interesting when it originates from Ed Turner, because he served on the board since the early days and the bulk of his news experience is with 24-hour news. Not one to shy away from controversy regarding CNN's news policies, Ed Turner's remarks regarding how CNN covers the news can be found often in newsmagazines and the trade press. Turner has also described the phenomenon of CNN, in combination with the First Amendment, as an active voice for freedom. He describes modern technologies as the roads on which freedom travels.

In 1994, Ed Turner described CNN as not "any one thing . . . not a wire service, not a newscast, not a newspaper, not a magazine." He goes on to describe CNN as a combination of journalism tools, unlike any other. Turner argues that, since 1980, CNN has paid its dues and deserves legitimate respect from other news media. He and others in charge of the news operation have acknowledged that CNN is more of a "go to" network, tuned to most often when a crisis erupts. Making CNN more attractive to viewers on a daily basis is one of Ed Turner's missions, and hurdles. As Ed Turner puts it, "What to do when the earth isn't on fire is of great concern to me."

In 1994, Johnson appointed Ed Turner to a panel to investigate the news network's loss of viewers, which had declined by 10 percent the year after the Cable Act of 1992 passed. The three-man panel met and determined that CNN needed to keep its focus on domestic news and move the international news to a separate, specialized news network. Ed Turner has supported this trend, evidenced in the appearance of specialized networks for sports and financial news. ***See also*** CNN (Cable News Network). *Connie Book*

Further Reading

Turner, Ed. "Reflections on the Sixtieth Anniversary of the Communications Act." *Federal Communications Law Journal* 47 (2), 1989: 391–93.

Turner, Ed. "Networking." *The New Republic,* 5 September 1994.

Bauder, David. "CNN Trying to Move Beyond Crises for Its Future." *Chicago Tribune*, 12 March 1997, 6.

Ted Turner

Courtesy Cable News Network, Inc.
© 1996   Photo by Mark Hill

Ted Turner, an outspoken and aggressive entrepreneur, built his father's ailing billboard business into a multibillion-dollar media empire, including the first 24-hour television news channel. In 1995, he merged Turner Broadcasting Company with Time Warner, reportedly for more than $7 billion and became corporate vice president in charge of cable operations. By 1997, Turner remained Time

Warner's largest stockholder with 11 percent of the company's stock.

Robert Edward Turner III was born on November 19, 1938, in Cincinnati, Ohio. Ted's demanding father, Ed Turner, founded a billboard company to compete with a former employer and expected Ted to work his way up from menial jobs to an entry-level sales position, to management. Ed Turner expanded his operations into Georgia and Tennessee, became overextended, and committed suicide on March 5, 1963. The event had a profound impact on the 24-year-old Ted, who shocked family and friends by stopping his father's nearly completed sale of the failing business and vowing to turn the business around.

When Ted was not in boarding schools, he spent his childhood as his father's errand boy. He attended Brown University but did not graduate.

In the early 1970s, Turner purchased WTCG, Channel 17, a struggling UHF channel Atlanta television station. The station was losing more than $600,000 a year. He also purchased a failing Charlotte UHF station, Channel 36, dubbing it WRET, his initials. He convinced the Atlanta Braves that he could improve their visibility by increasing the number of televised games and by offering those to regional stations. Both he and the Braves gained exposure, and Turner eventually bought the team. He also acquired professional wrestling venues and the Atlanta Hawks of the NBA.

Turner changed his major station to WTBS (Turner Broadcasting System) and began transmitting to local cable companies by satellite, in 1976. Within a year, its signal was reaching Alaska and Hawaii. Identifying with underdogs, Turner said he represented people in small towns with no local stations. Turner often criticized the major networks for corrupting American morals, but his alternative station provided baseball, wrestling, recycled network shows, and old movies. Some critics charged that these programs contained more violence than network television. With his own station, he seemed indifferent, some thought almost hostile, to news, until he hit on the idea of a 24-hour news station, which he introduced with Cable News Network (CNN) in 1980.

With CNN in the planning stage, executives thought their plan might be scuttled when they heard news reports that Turner was missing while yacht racing. But he survived to purchase financially troubled MGM studios in 1986, and although he reportedly did not realize how financially troubled the studio was, he acquired an incredible archive that provided the content for several cable channels, including WTBS, Turner Network Television (TNT), Turner Classic Movies, and after the purchase of Hanna-Barbera, the Cartoon Network. He recycled material through colorizing black-and-white movies, television syndication, and home videos. The average cost per title was roughly equal to the contemporary cost of producing a weekly situation comedy, and given the decline in network audience, the purchase turned out better than analysts predicted.

Turner then began investing in land and tried unsuccessfully to buy CBS Television. The 1995 merger of his operations with Time Warner, the world's largest media empire and owner of cable companies, provided distribution for movies.

In late 1996, Turner clashed with media mogul Rupert Murdoch. They fought over access to New York City's cable for their news networks and competed directly with Turner's Cartoon Network and Murdoch's Fox Children's Television Network. Turner's Time Warner and Murdoch's News Corporation were among contenders for access to wires that eventually would control access to American homes for telephones, computers, television, and movies. At the time, Turner and Time Warner controlled 16 of New York City's 75 channels, including HBO, CNN, and several pay-for-view venues for movies and sporting events. By 1997, Turner and Time Warner controlled Castle Rock Entertainment, New Line Cinema, the Atlanta Braves, the Atlanta Hawks, the Omni Coliseum in Atlanta, a ticket sales agency, and World Championship Wrestling, and Turner became vice president of cable operations, including Time Warner's HBO. He is married to actress Jane Fonda.   *William E. Huntzicker*

Further Reading

Bibb, Porter. *It Ain't as Easy as It Looks: Ted Turner's Amazing Story.* New York: Crown Publishers, 1993.

Goldberg, Robert, and Gerald Jay Goldberg. *Citizen Turner: The Wild Rise of an American Tycoon.* New York: Harcourt Brace, 1995.

Williams, Christian. *Lead, Follow or Get Out of the Way: The Story of Ted Turner.* New York: Times Books, 1981.

20/20

One of the most respected television news programs in America, ABC's *20/20,* with Hugh Downs and Barbara Walters as co-anchors, has delivered impressive ratings since its inception. *20/20* premiered on Tuesday, June 6, 1978. As the first prime-time newsmagazine for ABC News, *20/20* was the innovative leader in this area of programming. *20/20's* success has lead to many similar programs, such as *Prime Time Live.* Newsmagazine programs, including *60 Minutes* at CBS and NBC's *Dateline* magazine, continue to pull high ratings for the major networks, but few national programs have enjoyed the lasting success of *20/20.*

The original *20/20* co-hosts were Harold Hayes and Robert Hughes. The first program featured Sam Donaldson and Senator Edward Kennedy in a grave-side interview marking the 10-year anniversary of Robert Kennedy's assassination, and a conversation between the hosts and California Governor Jerry Brown. These two political stories, although expected to attract a large audience, paled in comparison to the segment in which entertainer Flip Wilson cried over his regret about lashing his daughter with his belt. Wilson's tears were followed by a graphic and bizarre report by Geraldo Rivera about greyhounds killing jack-rabbits. The trial run of Hayes and Hughes did not impress Roone Arledge or other ABC executives, and one week later Hugh Downs replaced them as the single anchor for the series.

20/20 was positioned on Thursday evenings from 1979 until 1987, when it was moved to Friday nights. It then expanded to twice a week in 1997. The first year of programming was tenuous. With a formula for giving the audience what it wanted, a mix of investigative and entertainment fare, often featuring interviews with national celebrities, *20/20* survived the first year and has not looked back. Holding true to its concluding tag, "We're in touch so you be in touch," *20/20* has kept its word. Although the feature reports have included sports figures and rock-n-roll stars, terrorists and political leaders, one thing that has remained constant is the program's entertainment value. Throughout its early years, *20/20* was given a boost from the investigative reporter, Geraldo Rivera. Rivera built a reputation as a savvy, street-smart proponent for the defenseless. With his background in law, and a history of important, award-winning investigative reports, Rivera brought high ratings to *20/20* and the program made him a bona-fide television star.

Barbara Walters's distinction as premier interviewer brought additional attention to the popular program. In September 1984, she was formally appointed as co-host of *20/20.* Walters was an enormous success and is the most visible woman in television news. ABC hired her from NBC in 1976 as the first female evening news anchor. Walters' high-profile career move drew a great deal of media attention, both to ABC and *20/20.* The matching was not new, however, since Downs and Walters had worked together previously, when Walters was the *Today* Girl and Downs was the show's host. Their partnership has endured with great success.

Under the direction of executive producer Victor Neufeld since February 1987, *20/20* has appealed to a wide audience through its exemplary personality profiles, medical reports and investigations, and special features coverage that often has held cultural significance or political intrigue. In addition to Downs and Walters, the current staff features associates Bob Brown, Tom Jarriel, Lynn Sherr, and John Stossel, all award-winning ABC News correspondents. In 1995, Arnold Diaz and Deborah Roberts were additions to the cast of contributors. Sam Donaldson and Diane Sawyer joined as co-anchors in the fall of 1998, when *Prime Time Live* became part of *20/20.*

20/20 has held its ground among a tightly fought battle for prime-time entertainment success and finished the 1995–1996 season in 11th place out of 166 prime-time programs, making it the leading weekday newsmagazine program on the air. This positioning is more impressive considering *20/20's* near 20-year existence. The 1995–1996 season marked the shows' highest-rated year so far. The recipe for this success includes wide-ranging and sometimes groundbreaking personal profiles such as the 1995–1996 interviews with Republican presidential prospect General Colin Powell; First Lady Hillary Rodham Clinton; Los Angeles Deputy District Attorney Christopher Darden, right after the O. J. Simpson trial; and Senator Bob Packwood, immediately following his resignation from the Senate.

Recent features also have included reports on allegations that Islamic extremists were attempting to persuade young black Americans into terrorism, accusations of sexual misconduct in the U.S. Navy involving a female sailor and 30 male sailors and officers, and implications of the wide recommendations by teachers for the use of the drug Ritalin among their students. In addition, controversial and sometimes emotional, heart-warming medical reports continue to comprise a large part of *20/20's* programming. Of particular note is the special chronicle of Downs's double-replacement knee surgery. The *20/20* cameras were with Downs throughout his operation and recovery. Downs had the doctors administer local anesthetic so that he could remain respondent to the cameras.

Walters's interviewing skills have enabled her to consistently procure more notable guests than those of any of her competitors. One recent example is her September 1995 interview with actor Christopher Reeve shortly after his paralyzing horseback-riding accident. Her interview regimen not only produced one of the highest rated *20/20* programs ever, but also earned a prestigious George Foster Peabody Award. The Peabody Award is among the nearly 300 awards received by the show to date. The impressive list of distinctions includes 46 Emmy Awards, two Alfred I. duPont–Columbia University Awards, 16 National Headliner Awards, 8 American Women in Radio and Television Awards, 4 Clarion Awards, and 4 CINE Golden Eagle Awards. *See also* Hugh Downs, Barbara Walters. *John C. Tedesco*

Further Reading

Downs, Hugh. *On Camera: My 10,000 Hours on Television.* New York: G. P. Putnam's Sons, 1986.

Oppenheimer, Jerry. *Barbara Walters: An Unauthorized Biography.* New York: St. Martin's Press, 1990.

Young, Josh. "What Makes Barbara Cry? *George,* November 1997, 108–44.

U

Dr. Art Ulene

Born in 1936, Dr. Art Ulene is best known as the health correspondent for NBC's *Today* show. He has authored several books on nutrition and weight loss, including *The Nutribase Nutrition Facts Desk Reference, Dr. Art Ulene's Low-Fat Cookbook,* and *Count Out Cholesterol.* He has also appeared in several health-related videos, including *Dr. Art Ulene's Stress Reduction Program* and *How to Lower Your Blood Pressure.* Ulene's reports are aimed more at providing simple, practical advice rather than describing research.

In the 1970s, Ulene was a faculty member at the University of Southern California Medical School, specializing in gynecologic oncology. He worked behind the scenes on two television news series on breast cancer and weight management before joining *Today* as a correspondent in 1976. In 1991, Ulene left the *Today* show for a short period to become a correspondent for ABC's *Home* program. He later rejoined *Today* and has appeared in several health segments, including advice on dealing with cancer and on smoking cessation. A series on weight loss on *Today* was so popular that it was rebroadcast and provided the basis for Ulene's book, *Lose Weight with Dr. Art Ulene.* Ulene also has worked for KABC-TV in Los Angeles and was involved in his own syndicated series, *Feeling Fine,* which was broadcast in more than 100 cities. *See also Today.*

Derek Moore

Further Reading

Hall, Jane. "Dr. Art Ulene Leaves NBC to Join ABC's Home." *Los Angeles Times,* 13 July 1991, F4.
Kelly, Dennis. "The Networks' Doctors on Call." *USA Today,* 5 January 1989, D4.
Wark, John T. "*Today* Doctor Brings His Popular Health Tips to Book Stores." *Detroit News,* 8 January 1996, B3.

Univision

Since 87 percent of Hispanic Americans speak Spanish at home, they generally do not turn to CNN or the more established networks when news breaks. Instead they rely on the Miami-based Univision Television Network, the fifth-largest broadcast television network in the country. Founded in 1961 as the Spanish International Network (SIN), this top Spanish-language network currently reaches 92.3 percent of U.S. Hispanic households, far surpassing its only rival, Grupo Telemundo. The main source of news and information for the nation's 29.3 million Hispanics, Univision has 12 full-power stations covering 12 of the top 15 Hispanic viewer-designated media market areas.

Former Housing and Urban Development (HUD) secretary Henry Cisneros, who was named president and chief operating officer of Univision Communications in January 1997, believes the network has an obligation to provide, through newscasts, newsmagazines, and public affairs programs, information people need to integrate into the American mainstream. Univision's national newscasts, including *Noticiero Univision* (Univision News) and *Noticiero Univision Edicion Nocturna* (Univision News Evening Edition), rival leading English-language affiliates and network newscasts in some major markets.

The network also produces newsmagazine programs, *Primer Impacto* (First Impact) and *Primer Impacto Extra* (First Impact Extra) and *Aqui y Ahora con Teresa Rodriguez* (Here and Now with Teresa Rodriguez), a *20/20*–like program that airs about six times a year. A weekly national public affairs program, *Temas y Debates* (Themes and Debates), is produced in Washington, D.C.

Noticiero Univision, the network's highly-rated, award-winning news program, premiered as *Noticiero Sin* in June 1981, and was the nation's first Spanish-language newscast from Washington, D.C. In 1984, *Noticiero Sin* provided, for the first time, extensive coverage of the Democratic and Republican National Conventions. Joaquin Blaya, president of Univision from 1988 to 1992, was the driving force behind *Noticiero Univision*'s success. Former UPI chief, Luis Nogales, also played a big role in improving and expanding the network's news programming. Beginning in 1987, the year SIN became Univision, Nogales tripled Univision's news coverage. He launched the first late-evening network newscast, *Noticiero Univision Edicion Nocturna*, and half-hour Saturday and Sunday reports.

In 1986 SIN had a newsmagazine, *America*, which first originated out of Washington, D.C. *Noticias y Mas* (News and More), was introduced in 1991, followed by newsmagazine *Primer Impacto* which premiered on February 14, 1994. *Aqui y Ahora* premiered on December 8, 1994. The programming is produced in the network's 6,800-square-meter studios and production facilities in Miami. The network also has six news bureaus (Los Angeles, Miami, New York, San Francisco, Washington, D.C., and San Francisco). Although Univision news personnel all speak Spanish, they typically are multilingual and multinational. The Washington bureau of the Univision news service, for instance, has a staff of 19, in-cluding reporters and videographers from Argentina, Bolivia, Chile, Cuba, Colombia, El Salvador, Mexico, Peru, Puerto Rico, and Venezuela.

All full-power, owned-and-operated stations produce local newscasts that reflect the community served. Early and late local newscasts are produced by all but one of the network's owned-and-operated stations. Univision's Miami affiliate, WLTV, has had a higher-rated newscast than either CBS, NBC, or Fox. In Los Angeles, the nation's number two market, Univision's flagship station, KMEX-TV, regularly beats its Big Three competitors among young adult viewers.

Univision has also been an innovator in Spanish-language news. In 1968, for example, the network broadcast the presidential election results for the first time in Spanish; in 1972, it was the first network to use electronic newsgathering (ENG) cameras and AKAI 1/4-inch tape in its news operations and the first network to produce an all-news television program in the United States. In 1976, it became the first commercial broadcaster to distribute programming directly to its station affiliates by domestic satellite. In addition, Univision's reporters are frequently the first on the scene of a breaking story, especially in Latin America. Monica Seone, Univision's widely lauded Central American correspondent, got an exclusive interview from Panamanian General Manuel Noriega before any other major network reporter did. Other Univision reporters were first with stories about the Colombian drug cartel and the elections in Chile and Argentina.

For 36 years, Univision, as well as its predecessor, SIN, tried to aim its news programming at its disparate Hispanic viewers, no matter what their nationality, race, or accent. However, there has been some recent criticism that Univision's news programming does not adequately cover three major U.S. Hispanic groups—Mexicans, Puerto Ricans, and Cubans—and focuses too much on issues of importance to Latin Americans rather than to U.S. Hispanics.

Univision Communication also owns Galavision, the nation's leading Spanish-language cable network, with its roughly 1.5 million Hispanic subscribers, representing approximately 45 percent of all Hispanic households that subscribe to cable television. The Mexico-based international news service, ECO, airs part-time on Galavision's schedule. ECO is owned by Televisa, Mexico's media giant, which is also part owner of Univision and provides much of its programming. This news service has twice as many news bureaus around the world as CNN, Fox News, or any other cable news network. Galavision also claims that ECO gives its audience more news than any Hispanic broadcast network and more in-depth coverage of news relevent to the Hispanic-American community. In an attempt to test audience demand for ECO news, Galavision became the first Hispanic cable network to sign a deal with Nielsen's Hispanic Television Index.

The Univision Television Network also contracted with Nielsen. Beginning in 1992, it asked Nielsen to develop ratings measuring Hispanic viewership, both at the network and local market levels. Using these Nielsen ratings, Univision is now able to demonstrate to advertisers its ability to reach the Hispanic audience through its news programming.

Lately the television industry itself has begun recognizing Univision's efforts in the field of television news at the highest levels. *Noticiero Univision* and KMEX-TV, Los Angeles, recently received Edward R. Murrow Awards from the Radio-Television News Directors Association for overall excellence in television. KMEX has been a leader in local news for decades—receiving a Peabody Award in 1970, and recently "America's Best Newscast" Award, the first such award to be presented to a Spanish-language news broadcast.

Victoria Goff

Further Reading:
Dolan, Kerry A. "Muchas Gracias, Congress." *Forbes,* 7 October 1996, 46–47.
Goldblatt, Henry. "Univision: The Real Fifth Network." *Fortune,* 8 August 1997, 42.

LaBrecque, Ron, and others. "Cisneros Goes to Broadcast." *Columbia Journalism Review,* May–June 1997 19.

Garrick Utley

Born in Chicago, Illinois in 1939, Utley is the son of two distinguished NBC reporters, Clifton and Frayn Utley. He grew up in Pennsylvania and received a bachelor of arts degree from Carleton College in Minnesota. He served in the U.S. Army and studied Eastern European affairs at the Free University in Berlin. He joined the NBC News bureau in Brussels on the recommendation of family friend, John Chancellor, in 1963, and was assigned as that network's first full-time correspondent in Vietnam. His coverage from Saigon coincided with NBC News's expansion to a half-hour.

Returning to the United States, Utley anchored *Vietnam Weekly Review* and received a Peabody Award for his retrospective, "Vietnam: Ten Years After." He reported on the Russian invasion of Czechoslovakia, and received the Overseas Press Club Award for coverage of Soviet-American relations. He spent three years moderating *Meet the Press* from Washington, D.C., and also anchored NBC's weekend news from New York. Utley left NBC in 1993 and joined the ABC network where he was chief foreign correspondent based in London. He returned to the United States in 1996, to contribute to CNN and participate in special projects, among them as hosting the PBS television series from the Metropolitan Opera. *See also Meet the Press.*   *Michael D. Murray*

Further Reading:
Frank, Reuven. *Out of Thin Air.* New York: Simon & Schuster, 1991.
Matusow, Barbara. *The Evening Stars.* Boston: Houghton Mifflin, 1983.

V

Richard Valeriani

Photo courtesy of Richard Valeriani

After nearly four decades in broadcasting, Richard Valeriani spends his days helping corporate executives fine-tune their images and assists them in creating messages appropriate to address the press. His broadcasting assignments are rare these days, consisting primarily of retrospective pieces; nonetheless, Valeriani is well known for his extensive career with NBC News. His career highlights include covering the civil rights marches in Selma and Birmingham, Alabama, the social revolution in the South, and three years with Secretary of State, Henry Kissinger.

Valeriani covered the Civil Rights movement between 1962 and 1965. He published *Travels with Henry* in 1979, based on his time spent cover-

ing the globe-trotting state department chief, Henry Kissinger, from 1973 to 1976. Other career highlights include his coverage of the Bay of Pigs invasion in 1961 and the presidential campaigns of the 1960s and 1972. In 1979, Valeriani scored a major story when he was able to determine that Ramsey Clark of the U. S. Department of State would be interceding on behalf of the American hostages in Iran. His insight came from enterprise reporting, in this case calling the air transportation support staff and asking if any state department officials were planning a trip to Tehran.

Richard Gerard Valeriani was born on August 29, 1932, in Camden, New Jersey. He earned a bachelor's degree from Yale University in 1953 and, from 1953 to 1954, studied at the University of Pavia in Italy. He began his career as a news reporter for the Trenton (N.J.) *Trentonian*, in 1957. He gained additional experience as a news writer for the Associated Press (AP) in New York. From 1959 to 1961, he covered Havana, Cuba, for the Associated Press. In 1961, Valeriani became a television reporter for NBC News, covering domestic and international politics, including the civil war in the Dominican Republic in 1965. He received critical praise and a Peabody Award for a television special on civil rights, and then progressed to top-level assignments at the State Department and the White House, where he served with distinction in the early 1970s, opposite CBS News's correspondent Dan Rather.

In addition to his extensive work in television news, he has published articles in popular periodicals, including *TV Guide,* and has written news and documentary scripts for television. He currently divides his time between Sherman, Connecticut, and New York City.   *Michael R. Smith*

Further Reading
Goldberg, Robert, and Gerald Jay Goldberg. *Anchors: Brokaw, Jennings, Rather and the Evening News.* New York: Birch Lane Press, 1990.
Matusow, Barbara. *The Evening Stars: The Making of a Network News Anchor.* Boston: Houghton Mifflin, 1983.

Vanderbilt Television News Archive

The Vanderbilt Television News Archive contains videotapes of television news programs dating back to 1968. The nonprofit archive videotapes and archival evening news programs aired on the television networks (ABC, NBC, CBS) and cable's CNN, as well as selected public affairs programs. Housed and financially supported by Vanderbilt University and private sources, the archive is located in Nashville, Tennessee. Created in 1968 by a Vanderbilt University alumnus, Paul C. Simpson, in conjunction with Vanderbilt University, the Vanderbilt Television News Archive has survived several legal battles to become a unique library resource.

The idea for the archive originated in the 1960s, when Simpson discovered that the television networks did not retain permanent copies of their evening news broadcasts. Simpson's actions in helping to create the archive were based upon the belief that a public record should be kept of this valuable information source. Videotaping of television newscasts began on August 5, 1968, and the Vanderbilt Television News Archive became a comprehensive source of television news programming. It has proved to be an invaluable resource for classroom instruction and for researchers studying the content and influence of television news upon public opinion.

The creation and continued existence of the Vanderbilt Television News Archive has been challenged by the television networks. The Columbia Broadcasting System (CBS) filed a lawsuit against Vanderbilt University, in 1973, under copyright law. CBS argued that the Vanderbilt Television News Archive infringed on CBS's copyright because the television evening news program was a product it created and owned. The lawsuit charged that Vanderbilt was misusing a CBS product by selling edited portions of the television evening news programs and depriving CBS of potential sales. Vanderbilt University argued television news was an important resource that should be preserved and available for free public access. Vanderbilt University further argued that it charged compilation fees, but did not sell the videotaped programs. CBS wanted the courts to close down the archive and force it to give all videotapes of CBS news programs to CBS.

The case was fought in a lengthy battle all the way up to the Supreme Court. The process was slow, in part because the laws had not kept up with society's technological advances and so the existing laws were not applicable to the uniqueness of the case. The copyright laws, at that time, did not provide clear guidance on television network news rights in relation to public interest and free access. So in 1978, Congress created a clause in the copyright law which permitted Vanderbilt to continue videotaping news programs as long as the programs were not resold. The CBS lawsuit was settled and the Vanderbilt Television News Archive was legally cleared to continue its collecting and circulating practices.

In addition to housing the videotape collection, the archive also compiles and publishes abstracts which index and describe segments within the news and public affairs programming. The abstracts were first published in March 1972, and paper copies can be found in libraries. Although the abstracts are sometimes used as a sole data source for researchers, independent of viewing requested tapes, typically, patrons will review the Vanderbilt abstracts in order to request loans of videotapes from the archive. Events, topics, persons, places, dates of broadcast, reporters, and commercials broadcast within the news program are all categories included within the abstract. Videotapes can be compiled according to the requests of the patrons. Fees are charged for this compilation and mailing service. The loan agreement requires users to return the videotapes and users are not allowed to duplicate the videotapes.

In 1994, the abstracts became available on the Internet <http://tvnews.vanderbilt.edu/>. This electronic access made the abstracts available to more people and helped save money for the financially strapped archive. Between 1985 and 1992, the Vanderbilt Television News Archive accumulated a debt of $1.5 million. By 1993, the mounting debt threatened the continuation of the archive. Through financial restructuring, including staff reductions, revising the fee framework, and publishing the abstracts on the Internet, the archive was able to continue collecting television news.

The Web site of the Vanderbilt Television News Archive is simply designed. It provides links to the *Evening News Abstracts*, *Special Reports and Periodic News Broadcasts*, *Specialized News Collections*, and *Vanderbilt University*. The *Evening News Abstracts* provides story summaries and time lengths for each of the three television networks and CNN. The *Special Reports and Periodic News Broadcasts* provides summaries of special news events, such as party conventions. The *Specialized News Collections* summarizes news coverage of major world events.

Web site users may browse the abstracts by selecting month, day, and year; or by keyword searching. Users may also add their names to the Vanderbilt Television News Archive newsletter or send feedback through e-mail. Distributing the abstracts by the Internet has drawn the attention of the television networks to the Vanderbilt Television News Archive, but the abstracts are created by the archive, which also controls its distribution, so the networks cannot legally challenge it.

At this time, only the abstracts are available on the Internet, even though technological capabilities could enable the distribution of the actual video footage through the Internet. While the archive has no plans for electronic video distribution at this time, the television networks have already expressed concern that Internet distribution and accessibility would be the next step. *See also* Archives for Television News.   *Julia A. Spiker*

Further Reading
Kies, C. "Copyright Versus Free Access: CBS and Vanderbilt University Square Off." *Wilson Library Bulletin,* November 1975, Vol. 50. No. 3, 242-46.

Rawley-Saldich, Anne. "Access to Television's Past." *Columbia Journalism Review,* November/December 1976, Vol. 15, No.4, 46–48, 50.
Wilson, D. L. "Vanderbilt Archive Puts Abstracts of TV Broadcasts on the Internet." *The Chronicle of Higher Education,* 8 June 1994, Vol.40, No.40, A16.

Sander Vanocur

Sander Vanocur, host *Movies in Time,* the History Channel. Photo by Tess Steinkolk

A veteran of more than 40 years of broadcast and print journalism, Sander Vanocur is best known for his work with NBC and ABC News. Born in Cleveland, Ohio, on January 8, 1928, Vanocur graduated from Northwestern University with a bachelor of arts degree. He spent a year in graduate study at the London School of Economics and began his journalism career in London, writing for the *Manchester Guardian* while simultaneously providing commentary for the North American Service of the BBC and working for CBS News. After leaving England, Vanocur worked as a general assignment reporter for the *New York Times* in New York City, beginning in 1955.

He joined NBC News and worked for the network from 1957 to 1971, gaining national prominence while serving as a White House correspondent for three years. During his 14-year stint, Vanocur was the Washington correspondent for *Today,* contributing editor of *The Huntley-Brinkley Report,* and gained attention for a long, spontaneous interview he conducted with Lyndon Johnson after Johnson's presidential acceptance speech. Vanocur also hosted *First Tuesday*, a monthly two-hour magazine program. In 1971, he became the senior correspondent for PBS's National Public Affairs Center for Television. In 1973, he became a consultant to the Center for the Study of Democratic Institutions, and professor of communications at Duke University.

From 1975 to 1977, Vanocur was the television editor and critic for the *Washington Post*. He joined ABC News in 1977, and in 1980 and 1984 covered the national political elections as the ABC News chief "overview" correspondent. He worked as a floor reporter for both the Republican and Democratic National Convenions in 1980, and covered the podium at the 1984 national conventions in San Francisco and Dallas. He was chief diplomatic correspondent assigned to the Department of State in 1981, and the next year, he became senior correspondent in Buenos Aires covering the Falkland Islands War between Great Britain and Argentina.

In 1986, Vanocur became the anchor of ABC News's *Business World*, a program featuring live interviews with such figures as Alan Greenspan and Paul Volcker. Vanocur also interviewed the presidential candidates, Vice President George Bush and Governor Michael Dukakis, on their economic agendas, distinguishing *Business World* for questioning both the candidates exclusively on those issues. Vanocur has been covering international news since 1958 and handled reporting duties for both the Tokyo and Venice economic forums in 1987. He also covered the economic summits in Toronto in 1988, and Paris in 1989. In 1991, Vanocur left ABC News to form his own company, Old Owl Communications, primarily a consulting corporation. In addition to his regular reporting and consulting assignments, Vanocur functioned as a professional in residence at The Freedom Forum and hosted a popular cable series for the History Channel.   *Michael R. Smith*

Further Reading
Frank, Reuven. *Out of Thin Air.* New York: Simon & Schuster, 1991.

Matusow, Barbara. *The Evening Stars.* Boston: Houghton Mifflin, 1983.
Shanley, John P. "White House Man for NBC." *New York Times*, 17 December 1961, X25.

Elizabeth Vargas

Elizabeth Vargas was born on September 6, 1962, in Paterson, New Jersey. She graduated with a bachelor's degree in Journalism from the University of Missouri—Columbia, where she began her career as a reporter and anchor for KOMU-TV. She then worked as a reporter and anchor for KTVN-TV, the CBS affiliate in Reno, Nevada, and then, from 1986 to 1989, she was the lead reporter for KTVK-TV, the ABC affiliate in Phoenix, Arizona.

Vargas moved to Chicago and spent four years as a reporter and anchor for WBBM-TV, the CBS affiliate. She then took a position at NBC News, spending three years as a correspondent, working on *Dateline*. Vargas also served as a substitute co-anchor and newsanchor for NBC News's *Today,* and as substitute anchor for the weekend editions of *NBC Nightly News*.

In June 1997, Vargas joined ABC News and was named correspondent for *20/20* and *Prime Time Live*. In addition to daily reporting duties, she has profiled many people, including the Tony Award winning choreographer, Savion Glover; the embattled lieutenant governor of New York, Betsy McCaughey; and the CEO of Valujet, Lewis Jordan. Vargas also serves as a substitute co-host. Vargas made her debut on *Turning Point* in November 1996, with an hour-long report on same-sex marriages, following four couples and reviewing the related legal and political issues.

Joye C. Gordon

Further Reading
Lipton, Michael A. "Making News." *People Weekly,* 9 September 1996, 113.
Max, J. "Showdown at Sunrise?" *TV Guide,* 13 July 1996, 26.
Rose, David James. "Making News." *Hispanic,* July 1994, 52.

Videographer

A videographer is a video photographer generally identified with the television newsroom. The terms videography and videographer came into existence during the late 1960s and early 1970s, when the electronic newsgathering (ENG) camera replaced the film camera in television newsrooms. The term videographer came to be synonymous with a field camera operator or film photographer also known as a "shooter." These terms describe the photographic elements associated with their work. The only differentiation is electronic versus film technology.

The videographer is the primary figure in visual information gathering. Like the photographer, he or she gathers the visual elements of a news scene or event. A key to effective news gathering, videographers often accompany the reporters in the field and thus work as a team. The videographer is responsible for gathering the sights and sounds of the story. Videographers are also associated with electronic news-gathering equipment, satellite news-gathering setups, microwave reports, and all of the mobile units associated with processing a news event.

The responsibility of a videographer requires technical knowledge, solid news judgment, and a command of visual grammar. The technical requirements are related to the operation of the electronic gear—the camera and editing capabilities of differing equipment configurations. The news judgment required is the same as for the reporter who is gathering the facts and researching the information. Understanding visual grammar is using the camera to tell the story. The videographer or editor has the responsibility of gathering visual information and breaking it into its component parts in order to tell the story.

It is most often the reporter who is given the credit for today's news-gathering. As a result, the videographer is often the unsung hero of many news departments. Ironically, visual credits acknowledging their work such as "produced by . . ." and "videographer . . ." have only recently been appearing in the increasing number of newsmagazines even though videographers, just like reporters, may lay their life on the line to gather information for important news stories. David Brown, for example, gave his life covering the Jonestown massacre. His camera kept rolling, even though he was mortally wounded. Another videographer, David Crockett, threw a camera over his shoulder while running away from Mount St. Helens and captured some of the most dramatic footage seen of the mountain's eruption.

Classic documentary producers have long used the camera and photographic or videographic arts to tell stories. Investigative reporter, Jay McMullen, was using hidden camera techniques in his 1961 documentary, "Biography of a Bookie Joint" before they were used in today's ambush journalism. Frederick Wiseman, a documentary producer, has used the camera on many historic occasions, without narrative, to tell a story in his documentaries, such as *High School* and *Meat*. *National Geographic* video documentary specialists and other naturalist photographers have also let the camera tell their story—through the science and art of the videographer. *Donald G. Godfrey*

Futher Reading

Altheide, David. *Creating Reality: How TV News Distorts Events.* Beverly Hills, CA: Sage, 1976.
Koppel, Ted. "Going Live." *Communicator,* June 1994, 16-18.
Shook, Fred. *The Process of Electronic News Gathering.* Mayfield, CA: Mayfield Press, 1990.

Meredith Vieira

Vieira was born on December 30, 1953. She is a native of Providence, Rhode Island, and a graduate of Tufts University. She began her broadcasting career in 1975, at WORC Radio in Worcester, Massachusetts, and was a reporter and anchor at WJAR-TV in Providence. For three years she reported and substitute-anchored for WCBS-TV in New York, where she received the Front Page Award for reports on child molestation.

Meredith Vieira gained recognition as correspondent for magazine programs at CBS before joining ABC News's *Turning Point* as a chief correspondent in 1993. She had also contributed to the *CBS Evening News with Dan Rather* and spent a year as co-anchor of the *CBS Morning News*. While at *60 Minutes*, she received Emmy Awards for reports on an AIDS ward, which she dubbed one of the most emotional of her career, and a report on the Holocaust, focusing on Christians who rescued Jews. After joining *Turning Point*, Veira received acclaim for a story about conservationists and effects of fighting poachers in Zambia, and a story about the rise of children's drug use. She joined *The View*, a daytime talk program created by Barbara Walters, in August 1997.

Vieira lives in New York and is married to television producer Richard Cohen.

Michael D. Murray

Further Reading

Brady, James. "In Step with Meredith Vieira." *Parade Magazine*, 30 November 1997, 20.
Collins, Monica. "60 Minutes Won't Tinker with Success." *USA Today*, 11 August 1989, 3D.
Galloway, Stephen. "The Toughest Stories We Ever Covered—and How We Got 'Em." *TV Guide*, 19 January 1991, 5–6.
Rouch, Matt. "Critic's Corner." *USA Today*, 29 March 1996, 12D.

Vietnam War Coverage

Called the "living room war," the Vietnam conflict raged through broadcast programming for nearly 15 years. At the inception of the National Front for the Liberation of South Vietnam in 1960, the American press documented the horrors of war, the failures of the American military battling foes they were conceptually unprepared for, and the tragedy of the demise of American strength at the withdrawal of western troops on April 30, 1975. Reseacher George Bailey called the coverage of the conflagration "television's longest running story."

Despite recollections of dramatic images, however, broadcast coverage was largely headline news provided by news anchors, such as Walter Cronkite, and occasionally, Harry Reasoner. At NBC, the American public heard from Chet Huntley and David Brinkley with Garrick Utley reporting from the scene. At ABC, the anchors were Peter Jennings, Bob Young, Frank Reynolds, and Howard K. Smith. But, in fact, many of the daily news stories originated with military public relations. The American Military Command provided

daily information with primary attention to such things as ground and air action, official statements, instruments of war, and body counts.

The anchors augmented their reports with film coverage provided by correspondents in Vietnam. One of the best-known war correspondents was the CBS London bureau chief Morley Safer. In 1965, Safer opened CBS News's Saigon bureau and served two tours there. Instead of relying on the censored reports handed out and "sanitized" by the U.S. government's public information offices, Safer and his Vietnamese cameraman, who doubled as an interpreter, went "jungle-bashing" with the troops. Safer's 1965 film report showing a marine at Cam Ne setting a hut on fire with a cigarette lighter almost single-handedly ushered in the era of the "living room war."

Other sensational stories provided by on-site correspondents included the "Loan Story" documented by NBC correspondent Howard Tucker, who had Vietnamese brothers working for him as cameramen. The filming took place on February 2, 1968, in the Cholon, or Chinese, quarter of Saigon. Tucker's crew filmed a close-up of Brigadier General Nguyen Ngor Loan shooting a prisoner in the head at point-blank range. The prisoner was a Viet Cong commander. After overcoming some logistical problems in getting the unprocessed footage out of the country, NBC broadcast, 46 hours later, a brief, edited portion of the film. Concurrently, AP photographer Eddie Adams, who shared a car ride with the NBC crew, photographed the same event. His still photographs of the shooting were reproduced all over the world. In 1969, Adams won a Pulitzer Prize for the photographs.

In addition to broadcast coverage, military and civilian photographers provided extensive coverage of the war in Vietnam, making it not only America's longest war but the most photographed. Many photographs are indelible images. Among those who compiled the photographic record were the more than 1,500 military photographers, representing all branches of service, who were assigned as combat photographers. Vietnam was a new experience for photojournalists because they were given considerable freedom and the broad mandate to document activities of the U.S. military in

Southeast Asia. Also, they were often uncensored and were generally transported by military helicopters to wherever they desired. These men, according to Nick Mills, worked in the same manner as civilian counterparts, but did so in a way the civilians could not; they wore the same uniforms, ate the same food, and drew the same pay as the soldiers. They also took the same risks and suffered the same casualties. While a member of the 221st Signal Company (Pictorial), this author was informed that the highest loss of life in the 1st Signal Brigade from 1969 to 1970 was the loss of combat photographers.

The 221st Signal Company (Pictorial) served as the U.S. Army's photographic unit in the war. It provided the manpower for the Southeast Asia Pictorial Center (SEAPC). SEAPC had motion picture and still photograph capability, its own lab complex for still-photo processing and printing, and six permanent military detachments located throughout South Vietnam. The equipment and air-conditioned labs were valued at approximately $5,000,000. This author was the commander of the lab complex, which provided support for the six remote detachments.

In spite of the general belief that most Americans watched the fighting and dying in Vietnam on television on a regular basis, Northwestern University Professor Lawrence Lichty and USC Journalism School director Murray Fromson suggest a few images are remembered by the American public as symbolic of the Vietnam War. Those few images would likely include the Buddhist monk taking his own life by dousing his body with gasoline and setting himself on fire, General Loan and the Viet Cong, the little girl accidentally hit by napalm, and the marine with the cigarette lighter. Perhaps, selective perception and retention by the American public of dramatic events, such as these four examples, may have led to the thinking that these events were characteristic of television and photo coverage of the Vietnam War. This was not true.

As Oscar Patterson notes, these were not the stuff that daily broadcast coverage was about. These were the highly dramatic exceptions. Certainly the vivid, the novel, the grotesque, and the unusual attract and maintain our attention and retention of certain events. Patterson concluded that "a few graphic, highly dramatic events" impinged on the national consciousness, so as to dramatically alter recall of daily Vietnam War coverage. Certainly, the first televised and most extensively photographed war in American history, it brought vivid images into the home.   *Dan B. Curtis*

Further Reading

Bailey, George. "Interpretive Reporting of the Vietnam War by Anchormen." *Journalism Quarterly,* Summer 1976, 319–23.

Bailey, George. "Television War: Trends in Network Coverage of Vietnam 1965–1970." *Journal of Broadcasting,* Spring 1976, 147–58.

Bailey, George, and Lawrence Lichty, "Rough Justice on a Saigon Street." *Journalism Quarterly,* 49 (1972), 221–29, 238.

Mills, Nick. *Combat Photographer.* Boston, MA: Boston Publishing, 1983.

Patterson, Oscar. "An Analysis of Television Coverage of the Vietnam War." *Journal of Broadcasting,* Fall 1984, 397–404.

W

Chris Wallace

Chris Wallace was born on October 12, 1947, in Chicago, Illinois. Harvard educated, Wallace, served as a reporter for *The Boston Globe* and a commentator for WGBH-TV, Boston, before joining WNBC as an investigative reporter in New York. His unit received both Associated Press and Peabody Awards in 1977. He covered Congress, handled the national convention coverage in 1980, and was the first to report Ronald Reagan's selection of George Bush as his running mate. Wallace became a Washington correspondent for *NBC Nightly News* the following year.

Wallace was named Washington anchor of the NBC *Today* program and anchored the Sunday *NBC Nightly News*. He accompanied Reagan on his European trip and reported meetings with French president Francois Mitterrand. Wallace reported on Reagan's speech to British Parliament and Reagan's meetings with Queen Elizabeth II. He also served as the moderator of *Meet the Press*. Shortly after Michael Gartner took over as president of NBC News, Wallace left the network and joined ABC News, becoming a senior correspondent for *Prime Time Live* and a substitute host of *Nightline*. Wallace interviewed members of the Polish Solidarity Underground and reported from South Africa on secret assassination squads. Chris Wallace is the son of *60 Minutes* correspondent Mike Wallace and was a stepson of the late Bill Leonard, former CBS News President.

Michael D. Murray

Further Reading:
Auletta, Ken. *Three Blind Mice: How the TV Networks Lost Their Way.* New York: Random House, 1991.
Davis, Gerry. *The Today Show: An Anecdotal History.* New York: William Morrow, 1987.
Donlon, Brian. "*Meet the Press,* at 40, Presses On." *USA Today,* 5 November 1987, 3D.

Mike Wallace

Since CBS's *60 Minutes* premiered in 1968, millions of viewers have tuned in to watch Mike Wallace apply his no-holds-barred interviewing techniques to a wide variety of the famous and the infamous, among them Richard Nixon, Deng Xiaoping, General Manuel Ortega, the Ayatollah Khomeini, Mikhail Baryshnikov, Nancy Reagan, and Johnny Carson.

Wallace was born on May 9, 1918, in Brookline, Massachusetts, and attended the University of Michigan. His experience as a reporter dates back to the 1940s, when he worked for the *Chicago Sun*. After service in the U.S. Navy during World War II, he became a reporter for WMAQ radio in Chicago, where he and his wife, Buff Cobb, began doing a midnight radio show from a nightclub. In 1951, CBS hired the Wallaces to do a daytime talk show called *Mike* and *Buff*, which ended in 1955 when they divorced. Wallace then tried his hand at acting in the Broadway play, *Reclining Figure;* hosting a NBC quiz program, *The Big Surprise;* and leading an interview program called *Night Beat,* from 1956 to 1957, which was aired locally in New York.

It was on *Night Beat* that Wallace first gained notoriety for his interviewing style, with critics referring to him as "Mike Malice" and "the Grand Inquisitor." Based on the tremendous ratings success of *Night Beat*, ABC hired Wallace to host *The Mike Wallace Interview,* from 1956 to 1958. On *The Mike Wallace Interview*, he continued his sledgehammer interviewing style that differed considerably from the vapid pleasantries then exchanged on talk shows. Poor ratings caused ABC to cancel the program in 1958. Over the next four years, Wallace appeared as an anchor of a local New York newscast, hosted a local talk show called *PM,* and occasionally appeared as a celebrity guest on game shows. By the early 1960s, the bulk of his income was derived from the commercials he did for Parliament cigarettes. Not satisfied with his career, Wallace wrote to the presidents of all three network news divisions, asking for a position as a correspondent.

Perceived by some as a light-weight celebrity interviewer and something of a huckster for cigarettes, none of the three networks was interested in hiring him as a serious news correspondent. But the management of NBC News became impressed when Wallace offered to buy up the remaining Parliament commercials to keep them off the air. In 1963, Wallace debuted as the anchor of the *CBS Morning News*, which, in its 10 A.M. time slot, quickly became popular with viewers. Departing from NBC's *Today* format, the *CBS Morning News* put heavy emphasis on topics of interest to women, foraying into such taboo subjects as birth control, menopause, and venereal disease. The program's ratings declined when it was shifted to 7 A.M. in 1965.

Wallace anchored the *CBS Morning News* for another year, then became a correspondent for the *CBS Evening News.* From 1966 to 1968, Wallace's reputation as a reporter grew as he covered the Nixon presidential campaign in 1968 and the war in Vietnam. Ironically, he was offered the position of press secretary for Richard Nixon but he turned it down. He has often speculated on what his career might have been had he accepted that position. When *60 Minutes* went on the air in Septem-

ber 1968, Wallace was selected by Don Hewitt initially to co-host and co-edit the program. Wallace later served as a senior correspondent. He set the standard for investigative reporting on the program—the only series to rank number one in three different decades—through his use of confrontational interview techniques.

Wallace's early interviews concerning the My Lai massacre in Vietnam, and reports on Eldridge Cleaver and the Black Panthers, brought him attention. In spite of his tough reputation, many of his stories have been favorable to his subjects. His work ethic and demanding travel schedule earned him key stories, additional respect, and the admiration of colleagues in the field. Over the years, he has uncovered a large number of deceptive practices in a variety of professions and national contexts, and in the process has won many awards, among them 15 Emmy Awards, 2 Alfred I. du Pont–Columbia University Awards, and 3 George Foster Peabody Awards.

Wallace was the talent for the controversial *CBS Reports* documentary program in 1982, "The Uncounted Enemy: A Vietnam Deception," which resulted in an exhaustive internal investigation, by Burton Benjamin, of network decision making and methods. This program and the study that followed (which was published) was a public ordeal for Wallace and broadcast news because it resulted in a libel trial that revealed, in great detail, the extent to which producers, rather than reporters, construct and control television documentary programs.

In 1995, Wallace received the Robert F. Kennedy Journalism Award Grand Prize for *CBS Reports,* "In the Killing Fields of America," a three-hour report on violence in America. The Mike and Mary Wallace House, at the University of Michigan in Ann Arbor, was established as a gift from the CBS News veteran and his wife, a former producer for CBS. It is the current headquarters for the Michigan Journalism Fellows, which includes the Mike Wallace Fellowship in Investigative Reporting, a program to enable professionals to study in comfortable surroundings. In 1991, Wallace was inducted into the Television Academy Hall of Fame. He continues with *60 Minutes.* Mike Wallace is the father of ABC news correspondent, Chris Wallace. *See also 60 Minutes.*

Kim A. Smith

Further Reading:
Gates, Gary Paul. *Air Time: The Inside Story of CBS News.* New York: Harper and Row, 1978.
Boyer, Peter J. *Who Killed CBS? The Undoing of America's Number One News Network.* New York: Random House, 1988.
Wallace, Mike, and Gary Paul Gates. *Close Encounter.* New York: Harper and Row, 1984.

Barbara Walters

© 1993, ABC, Inc.

Twenty-one years ago, Barbara Walters was caricatured in a *New Yorker* cartoon as a member of a chorus line, holding a microphone while in mid-kick telling viewers of events in Beirut. It was an ignominious time for Walters and for women in television. She had just signed a $1 million-a-year contract with ABC to become the first woman co-anchor, sharing prime time with Harry Reasoner. More recently, in April 1997, the National Association of Broadcasters (NAB) bestowed upon her the NAB Distinguished Service Award, an honor recognizing significant and lasting contributions. Walters, indeed, has come a long way and is now recognized as one of television's most distinguished figures.

Walters was born in Boston, September 25, 1929. Her father was famed New York and Miami nightclub owner Lou Walters. A graduate of Sarah Lawrence College, Walters trained in television production. She began her career as a producer for WNBC, then moved to CBS as a newswriter. In 1961, she took a writing position with *Today* and

within a year was a reporter. In 1974, she was promoted to co-host—the first female co-host of *Today*. Walters also hosted her own syndicated series, *Not For Women Only*, which lasted five years. Broadcasting with distinction at NBC for 15 years, Walters was coaxed away, in 1976, to serve as co-anchor of the nightly news on ABC with Reasoner. When news of her $1 million-a-year contract hit the press, many in broadcasting lamented her lack of traditional print journalism credentials.

The criticism began and it lasted throughout her short tenure in that assignment. The mainstream press labeled some interviews "theatrical," Reasoner was sometimes curt, and the *ABC Evening News* continued to languish in third place. After two years with Reasoner, Walters left. The next year, she became the co-host of *20/20* with Hugh Downs, where she remains. Walters, now in her mid-60s, is considered television's premiere interviewer; she has garnered numerous awards as one of the few women broadcast pioneers to stay in prime time. In fact, Walters's interviews, aired under the title *The Barbara Walters Specials* continue to be among the top-rated programs. She started the interview series, *The View*, in August 1997.

In 1988, Walters received the Overseas Press Club's highest award—the President's Award. She was honored in 1996 by the Museum of Television and Radio for contributions to broadcast journalism; in 1993, she received a Lifetime Achievement Award from the Women's Project and Productions; in 1992, she was honored by the American Museum of the Moving Image; in 1991, she received the Lifetime Achievement Award from the International Women's Media Foundation; and in 1990, she received the Lowell Thomas Award and was inducted into the Academy of Television Arts and Sciences Hall of Fame.

These awards recognize some of her most notable achievements, but the respect she has earned has come, almost exclusively, from her talent for interviewing. Early in her *Today* career, she tried to be assigned political stories or stories on international issues. Realizing those topics went to men, Walters did what she knew best—interviewing. She has interviewed some of the most notable people of the twentieth century. Walters has interviewed every American president since Richard Nixon, and received international attention when, in 1977, she arranged a joint interview with Egypt's president Anwar Sadat and Israel's prime minister Menachem Begin. Another pathbreaking interview, translated into numerous languages, airing all over the world, was an hour-long discussion with Cuba's Fidel Castro. She was part of the news team sent to the People's Republic of China to cover the visits of Richard Nixon and later Gerald Ford. Walters was also the first to interview General Colin Powell after his retirement from the Joint Chiefs of Staff, and she also interviewed Hillary Rodham Clinton at the peak of the Whitewater controversy. She broke the news of swimmer Greg Louganis being HIV-positive.

In September, 1995, Walters conducted an interview with actor Christopher Reeve after a horse-riding accident which left him paralyzed from the neck down. That one-hour interview was watched by nearly 30 million viewers making it the highest rated *20/20* program in recent years, and also earned the series a George Foster Peabody Award in April 1996.

In 1991, Walters began negotiations with CBS News, talking with its news hieracrchy about a $4 million-a-year contract, more than any other newsperson was earning at that time. She fnally agreed to sign a five-year contract with ABC, the terms of which were kept secret. Walter's current salary is estimated at nearly $3 million a year. In addition she signed for the rights to her library of celebrity specials; those rights are reportedly worth millions of dollars.

Walters recently marked her 20th anniversary at ABC, airing a 90-minute career retrospective, which included some of her most memorable interviews—Bing Crosby, John Wayne, Bette Davis, Laurence Olivier, and the Shah of Iran. The announcement of Walters's National Association of Broadcasters Distinguished Service Award was accompanied by a statement from NAB president, Edward Fritts, noting her undisputed recognition as one of the world's most respected interviewers and journalists. With nearly four successful decades in front of the camera, those words serve to punctuate the talent and depth Walters has brought to broadcasting. *See also* ABC News, *20/20*.

Carol A. Atkinson

Further Reading

"DSA Winner Walters: 'I Feel Blessed.'" *Broadcasting & Cable*, 9 April 1997, 11.

Heinemann, Sue. *Timelines of American Women.* New York: Perigee Books, 1996.

Power, Ron. *The Newcasters.* New York: St. Martin's Press, 1977.

Weathercasters

Television weather reporting has alternated between serious and silly during the past 50 years. In the 1940s, weather was taken seriously, with most weathercaster positions held by military veterans. The tone of weathercasting changed during the mid-1950s, an era when television tried attracting a large audience. On the silly side, Tex Antoine at WABC in New York, employed a puppet, Uncle Wethbee, whose mustache would droop or curl depending on the forecast. WBBM-TV Chicago had two-dimensional paper creations representing weather forces and KTUL in Tulsa had "Gusty," a cartoon character, drawn by weathercaster Don Woods to illustrate the weather.

At this time, women began to provide weathercasts, but the focus was often on clothing, hairstyle, or demeanor. The best known of the early female forecasters was Carol Reed, who debuted in 1952, at WCBS in New York. By 1955, women represented the majority of weathercasters. Among those especially well-regarded at the time were: Cindy Dahl at WTTG in Washington, D.C. Kay Field at WISH in Indianapolis, Eugenia Burke at WARM in Scranton, and Judy Marks at WOKY in Milwaukee.

The trend in the 1960s, consistent with societal conflicts of the time, was more serious, followed by the era of "happy news" in the 1970s. This produced another mixture of serious and silly weather reporting, including instances in which animals were displayed during weathercasts. KABC's George Fischbeck had a lion and a lamb in the Los Angeles studio on the first of March, while WLS's John Coleman once read a Thanksgiving Day forecast to a turkey. By 1978, the Public Broadcasting Service unveiled *A.M. Weather*. This 15-minute program, anchored by meteorologists from the National Oceanic and Atmospheric Administration, stayed on the air for 15 years, without flashy graphics, proving viewers wanted substantial weather information.

Morning programs on ABC, CBS, and NBC have had weather segments since their beginnings. On ABC's *Good Morning, America*, the news anchor originally read the weather before John Coleman arrived. Coleman continued until 1983. He was replaced by Dave Murray and in 1986, Spencer Christian took over the position. CBS employed "weathergirls" through the mid-1960s on their morning program. News anchors took over and continued until 1980, when CBS hired the first female meteorologist, Valerie Voss. Gordon Barnes followed in 1980, then Steve Deshler, Steve Baskerville, and finally Mark McEwen. Frank Blair was the NBC's *Today* weathercaster from the late 1950s until 1974. After using anchors to read the weather, NBC hired Bob Ryan, in 1978, and he continued until Willard Scott took over. Al Roker followed Scott on *Today*.

Most television stations today have three or four weathercasters on staff. While competing with cross-town stations, they now must also compete with The Weather Channel (TWC). Since its beginnings in 1982, under the direction of John Coleman, TWC has continued to grow in popularity. This network provides the viewer with specific weather information on a national level. In order to compete, TWC also provides local weather forecasts six times each hour. Very few individuals, however, actually watch The Weather Channel for the local forecast. Instead, live reports by meteorologists and special features keep the viewers watching. The Weather Channel is carried by over 6,000 cable systems in the United States and reaches almost 70 million subscribers in the United States and another 26 million worldwide. The network's expansion recently has increased the staff to 400 people, with 85 full-time meteorologists.

Today, most television weathercasters have the Seal of Approval from either the American Meteorological Society (AMS) or the National Weather Association (NWA). The AMS Seal of Approval started in 1959. The requirements for earning the seal have changed several times since its inception. At present, a weathercaster must pass an educational standard (based on college tran-

scripts) and a broadcasting standard (based on the candidate's on-air weathercasting abilities). The NWA Seal of Approval began in 1976 and has also changed over time. At present, the NWA requires that the candidate pass a written test in meteorology and submit on-air weathercasts for evaluation. In addition, the NWA requires that a weathercaster be recertified every three years in order to retain the seal.

In television today, weather coverage is the number one draw in most markets. According to a 1997 survey by Frank N. Magid Associates, 92 percent of news viewers say weather is something they "really want to see covered" in local news. This percentage was higher than those for local news and live coverage of breaking news (both at 89 percent).

Salaries for weathercasters averaged $54,000 in 1997, according to the National Association of Broadcasters (NAB). There was a tremendous range in salaries however, from $25,000 in smaller markets to $180,000 in the top-ten markets. Starting salaries showed a similar range, from $20,000 in the smaller markets to $75,000 for the largest markets.

While the salaries for television weathercasters continue to rise, so do the equipment costs associated with the weathercasts. Today, there are several companies involved in producing state-of-the-art weather graphic systems. A television station must have a stream of weather data for the weathercaster to examine and turn into slick eye-catching graphics. Weather Services International is one company doing this work. They bill their weather producer as an integrated data-to-graphics workstation with a price tag of around $90,000. Viewers not only want the slick graphics, but they want accurate information. Nothing has become more sophisticated in the last decade than the presentation of radar data. Baron Services is one company selling Doppler radar systems. A radar system that the television station can control easily costs $500,000. The benefit is enormous—a radar system from Baron Services can, for example, pinpoint the street where the rain is falling, something unheard of 10 years ago.

Mark Binkley

Further Reading

Henson, Robert. *Television Weathercasting: A History.* Jefferson, NC: McFarland and Company, 1990.

Maher, Edwin. *Now to the Weather: Confessions of a TV Weatherman.* Burnwood, Victoria, Australia: Eagle Eye Publishing, 1996.

"Seal of Approval Program for Radio and Television." *Bulletin of the American Meteorological Society,* Vol. 77, No. 8, August 1996, 1821–34.

Weathercasting

Weather information first appeared in the mass media during the 1870s in the *New York Times.* Weather forecasting and weather news advanced dramatically during World War I and most newspapers were publishing weather maps by the 1920s. In the late 1930s, weather information was being heard on radio stations. The first television weathercast is thought to have been in Cincinnati, Ohio, by Jim Fidler, during the late 1930s on an experimental television station. In 1941, WNBT, now WNBC, was the first New York City station to introduce weather.

Approximately 70 television stations were on the air in the late 1940s. The weather at this time had a serious tone. With the end of World War II, most weathercasters were men just out of the military, and not polished announcers. With most cities having only one station, there was no competition to spur new approaches. The tone of weathercasting changed during the mid-1950s with the expansion of television. The number of television stations increased dramatically, most larger cities had at least two stations competing for viewers, and nationwide programs started drawing huge audiences. To attract viewers, polish, appearance, and gimmicks became important tools. Weather evolved into a primary role for making news more palatable. This was television weather's uninhibited period, with puppets, costumes, and "weathergirls."

1950s weather graphics were drawn each day, to full-dimension, around 5 by 10 feet, on a fixed background containing geographic boundaries. There were challenges associated with going from one large map to another with only two cameras. To solve this problem, stations used techniques such as plexiglas boards and magnetic symbols. The weathercaster would stand in front of the plexiglas and write all of the information on the map. More dynamic weathercasters could stand behind the plexiglas and write backwards to always face the camera. A more elaborate setup was to use magnetic symbols to depict weather features with symbols picked up and moved during weathercasts to explain changes underway.

While comical weathercasts were at their peak in the mid-1950s, a few stations started using radar—the first scientific instrument available, providing visual appeal as well as weather information. Radar became valuable for several reasons. It could be updated every few minutes and, since the radar was local, the graphic matched, local viewing areas. More importantly, it allowed television stations to use visual information to warn viewers of approaching storms.

The 1960s were a more serious time for television weather. The American Meteorological Society created the AMS Seal of Approval in 1959, based on guidelines for completeness, clarity, and professionalism. The Seal of Approval did not have a great impact until the mid-1960s.

The mid-1960s saw the addition of the most useful meteorological item to weathercasts to date. With the launch of America's first weather satellite in 1960, snapshots from space were used by weathercasters to pinpoint storms, such as hurricanes, that were still days away. This provided viewers with a chance to see what was approaching. Modern television weathercasting started in the 1970s. Until this time, there was very little interaction among anchors. News, sports, and weather segments were often listed separately. In the mid-1970s, the "happy news" format began. A unified news team approach was formed with conversation between the anchors. Joking weathercasters fit this mold and a more humorous tone for the weather became the norm.

The decade of the 1970s saw an explosion in weather graphics, primarily due to computers. A major problem in television weathercasting had always been how to present text on-screen. By the late 1970s, companies were producing character generators that allowed displays of the forecasts and current conditions. A new generation of weather satellites was launched in the mid-1970s—stationary satellites. More images could now be shown and more frequently. Stations could loop video to show storm motion. Radar systems also improved. A computer technique, known as analog-to-digital conversion, allowed data to be shown in discrete levels. When color was added, viewers could instantly see where intense storms were located.

The recent decades saw the happy news format remaining as a dominant force in weathercasting. With stations having similar styles, weather graphics became key to attracting viewers. Computerized graphics systems became standard. These systems could analyze data, build maps, and create a program with minimal input. One final piece to the puzzle was needed. The weathercasters were knowledgeable of the science, they had radar and satellite information, and they had computers to analyze data and create superb graphics. The trick was how to display both the weathercaster and the graphics on screen at once. The answer was a device known as a chromakey. The chromakey allowed the weathercaster to stand in front of a blank, blue or green, wall with the computer-produced graphics projected on to the wall. The weathercaster could move and point to particular items on the graphics. With a push of a button, the graphic would change and the weathercaster could continue.

Television weathercasting today is a high-tech business. With so much emphasis on weather graphics, the weathercaster must be a scientist and a graphic artist. Stations have their own radar systems, use "3-D" graphics, move icons on the weather maps with "magic wands" and are constantly finding new tools to attract attention. New graphic devices are adding visual qualities. With viewers becoming more interested about the weather in local areas and nationwide, high-tech graphics allow weathercasters to better explain the forecast. *Mark Binkley*

Further Reading

Henson, Robert. *Television Weathercasting: A History.* Jefferson, NC: McFarland and Company, 1990.

"Seal of Approval Program for Radio and Television." *Bulletin of the American Meteorological Society,* Vol. 77, No. 8, August 1996, 1821–34.

"National Weather Association Broadcast Committee and Seal of Approval Qualifications and Procedures." *National Weather Digest,* Vol. 21, No. 1, September 1996, 49–52.

Pat Weaver

Sylvester "Pat" Weaver was the president of the NBC TV network between 1949 and 1953. He is regarded as one of the most innovative network executives in the history of American television who, with his creative mind and fresh vision, not only laid the groundwork for programming, but made television an indispensable part of the American household.

Born in Los Angeles, California, in 1908, Weaver began his career as the editor of the *Advertising Club* magazine. After working for local CBS Radio stations in Los Angeles and San Francisco, as a writer and producer, in 1935, Weaver moved to New York to produce the *Fred Allen* radio show at Young & Rubicam advertising agency. He then became their broadcasting chief. He also worked for American Tobacco Company as an advertising manager before he joined NBC as the president of the television network in 1949.

During his brief tenure at NBC, Weaver built the framework for the future of American television. Weaver communicated his ideas in long memoranda for which he was known among his staff. Reflecting his slogan, "Let us dare to think and let us think with daring," which he wrote, Weaver's "grand design" resulted in segmented sponsorship enabling several advertisers to buy time during a single program; spectaculars, one-time 90-minute special programs, designed to break viewing habits; the magazine format that combined features within a single program; and a 3-hour variety program on Saturday nights, *Your Show of Shows,* which set the first example of block programming. Through these innovations Weaver helped the network gain programming control from advertising agencies for the first time since the 1920s.

Weaver's idea for an 18-hour program service was translated into the *Today* show and *The Tonight Show*, both of which remain staples of the NBC network. Weaver believed television could not only entertain, but elevate the taste and standards of the audience, and he often articulated this view through his memos. Under the policy called "enlightenment through exposure," he added commentary to television news and created *Wisdom*, and *Wide, Wide World*, a distinguished, hour-long documentary and interview series, which he jokingly referred to as "Operation Frontal Lobes."

In 1953, Weaver became the president of the parent company, NBC, to vacate his position for Robert Sarnoff, the son of the RCA owner. His new role was not exciting enough and he resigned from NBC in 1956. A true visionary, Weaver knew and wrote about the videocassette recorder, cable, and satellites years before most others did. He was involved in pay-TV ventures, including Subscription TV, during the 1960s and 1970s. Weaver, the father of actress Sigourney Weaver, lives in Santa Barbara, California.   *Yasue Kuwahara*

Further Reading:

Weaver, Pat, and Thomas M. Coffey. *The Best Seat in the House: The Golden Years of Radio and Television.* New York: Knopf, 1994.
"Pat Weaver." In *The Golden Age of Television: Notes from the Survivors,* edited by Max Wilk. New York: Delacorte Press, 1976. 236–45.
Kisseloff, Jeff. *The Box: An Oral History of Television,* 1920-1961. New York: Viking, 1995.

Peggy Wehmeyer

Peggy Wehmeyer was the first network correspondent to report full-time on religion, beginning in 1994. She studied and worked at the Dallas Theological Seminary and graduated, with honors, in journalism from the University of Texas at Austin. She was recruited from the network's Dallas affiliate, WFAA, for the special assignment to report on religious issues by ABC News's Peter Jennings. Wehmeyer began as a weekend assignment editor at the Texas station in 1980 and quickly advanced to reporting duties. She serves as a correspondent for *World News Tonight with Peter Jennings* and the *America Agenda* series for that nightly news program.

Wehmeyer has received numerous awards from broadcasting groups and religious organizations including two Cine Golden Eagle Awards, an International Film & Video Festival Award, and a Covenant Award from the Southern Baptist Radio and Television Commission. She is also among a select group requested to serve as spokesperson on coverage of notoriously under-reported stories having to do with religion and spiritual issues. She has commented on the nature of that beat—the seemingly sudden recognition of its importance—and her personal goal to address a wide range of religious and spiritual issues with viewers.

Michael D. Murray

Further Reading

Govier, Gordon. "Religion Reporter at ABC." *Communicator*, May 1994, 23.
Shepard, Alicia C. "Questions About Faith." *American Journalism Review,* December 1995, 23.
Shepard, Alicia C. "The Media Get Religion." *American Journalism Review,* December 1995, 19–25.

Joe Wershba

Joseph "Joe" Wershba's career spanned the growth of television's history. Associated with award winning CBS programs, Wershba began as a writer-reporter and co-editor on *CBS Views the Press* in 1947 and 1948, before moving over to *See It Now*. He ended up as a producer of *60 Minutes* from 1964 to 1988. During 40 years, Wershba did over 100 television reports.

Wershba received many awards including two Emmys for the CBS documentaries: "What Happened in Tonkin Gulf, August 1964?" in 1971, and "What About Jerusalem?" in 1975. For outstanding journalism, Wershba received the American Bar Association Gold Gavel in 1964 for the documentary "Civil Liberties" and two Sidney Hillman Awards, one for "Clarence Gideon: Poor Man and the Law" for *CBS Reports* in 1965 and another for "The Case of Milo Radulovich" with Edward R. Murrow for *See It Now* in 1953. In 1988, the Silurian Society gave him a 25-year medal for outstanding lifetime reporting work.

Wershba learned from the best—Edward R. Murrow and Fred Friendly on *See It Now,* and Don Hewitt with *60 Minutes.* Murrow biographer A. M. Sperber called Wershba "one of the almost fanatically devoted reporters." Born on August 19, 1920, in New York City, Wershba graduated from Abraham Lincoln High School and attended Brooklyn College from 1937 to 1940, before being drafted into the Army during World War II in 1942. In 1948, he married Shirley Lubowitz, a CBS news writer and later producer with news programs: *MacNeil-Lehrer NewsHour,* ABC's *World News Tonight,* and *60 Minutes.*

Wershba started his broadcast career as a news writer with Wells "Ted" Church, the director of CBS Radio, before moving over to *CBS Views the Press.* In 1948, he became an on-air Washington correspondent and then reporter on Edward R. Murrow and Fred Friendly's *I Can Hear It Now* from 1949 to 1951. When Murrow and Friendly began *See It Now*, Wershba was a key reporter and producer, connected with a large number of outstanding programs including those addressing civil liberties cases. He did the background reporting for the much-heralded "Report on Senator Joseph R. McCarthy" and the subsequent "Annie Lee Moss," a film interrogation by McCarthy. Wershba also did the reporting on the "Supreme Court Desegregation of Publc Schools," as the Civil Rights movement began in earnest.

Wershba left CBS to become an independent producer and a reporter, feature writer, and columnist for the *New York Post.* In 1964, Wershba returned to produce *CBS Reports* with Fred Friendly until 1968, when he became one of the early producers of *60 Minutes*, where he remained until retirement in 1988. Since then, Joe and his wife co-produce videos, and films for Disney, and have served as researchers and consultants for Walker Cronkite's book, *A Reporter's Life* (1996), and the 1997 Discovery channel series, *Cronkite Remembers. See also See It Now, 60 Minutes.*

Betty Houchin Winfield

Further Reading:

Kendrick, Alexander. *Prime Time: The Life of Edward R. Murrow.* Boston: Little Brown, 1969.
Persico, Joseph E. *Edward R. Murrow, An American Original.* New York: McGraw Hill, 1988.
Sperber, Anne M. *Murrow: His Life and Times.* New York: Freundlich, 1986.

Av Westin

Av Westin served as executive producer of *ABC Evening News* and was responsible for *Close-Up* and *20/20.* Westin accomplished many firsts in television news. He was the first newsman to become a director, the first recipient of an overseas assignment as a network field producer, and the first producer to work on the first satellite broadcast. Westin introduced *CBS Morning News with Mike Wallace*, collaborated with Fred Friendly on *CBS Reports*, and developed the first experimental public television network program.

Westin was born in New York City on July 29, 1929. In 1946, he enrolled in New York University, receiving his degree in 1949. A few years later, Westin was named recipient of the first CBS Foundation Fellowship to Columbia University, where he earned a master's degree in 1958.

During his undergraduate years, Westin worked for CBS Radio, becoming a newswriter after graduation. For 20 years, Westin held a variety of positions, serving as the news editor of the *CBS Morning News*, director of the *Good Morning Show*, the *CBS Six o'Clock Report*, and the *CBS Morning News.* In 1959, he was named producer of the documentary series, *CBS Reports.* A $10 million grant from the Ford Foundation in 1967, and congressional passage of the Public Broadcast Act enabled Westin to initiate production activities at the Public Broadcast Laboratory (PBL). He was named executive director of a magazine designed to show the quality of public affairs programming television could produce. After a groundbreaking first show, PBL floundered through its inaugural season, but began to realize its vision in the second season. Just before Martin Luther King Jr., was assassinated, a PBL camera crew documented King's tour around the country. That footage provided a eulogy and earned "Television Documentary of the Year" honors from the Venice Film Festival.

After just two years, Westin moved to ABC News and joined forces with Roone Arledge. They redesigned *World News Tonight* and created *20/20.* In an 18-page memo, "Days of Penury, Days of Affluence," he criticized the influence money had on television news. The manner in which he distributed his ideas was given as cause for his release from ABC News in 1987. Predicting that network news would one day be replaced by local news, Westin left network news altogether in 1989 and joined King World Productions as senior vice president. He also became co-executive producer of *Inside Edition*. In 1992, Time Warner signed Westin to head a production unit that would translate some magazine properties into reality-based series or specials for television. *See also* ABC News, CBS News.   *William R. Davie*

Further Reading
Freeman, Mike. "Time Warner Leaps into Reality." *Broadcasting & Cable,* 20 July 1992, 16–17.
"Leaked Document Has Av Westin's Head on Platter." *Variety,* 4 March 1987, 86–103.
Westin, Avram R. *Newswatch: How TV Decides the News.* New York: Simon & Schuster, 1982.

David Westin

The current president of ABC News, David Westin was born July 29, 1952 in Flint, Michigan. He is a summa cum laude graduate of the University of Michigan and also received his law degree from that same institution. He was law clerk for U.S. Supreme Court Justice Lewis F. Potter in 1977-1978 and joined the law firm of Wilmer, Cutler & Pickering in 1979. In 1982-1983 he served that firm in their London offices, becoming a partner in 1985. He was also adjunct law professor at Harvard and Georgetown universities.

Westin joined the ABC network as vice president and general counsel in February, 1991. He became president of the ABC Television Network Group on September 20, 1994 and was named president of ABC News on March 6, 1997, taking over the very highly regarded position held by Roone Arledge since 1977. Arledge remained as chairman of ABC News, but relinquished control as president on June 1, 1998. Westin's goal was to work particularly to help reclaim the leading position of ABC's *World News Tonight* from newsleader NBC News. *See also* Roone Arledge.
          Michael D. Murray

Further Reading
Carter, Bill. "Shift at ABC News Prepares for Successor to Arledge," *New York Times,* 7 March 1997, 2-D.
Lafayette, Jon. "ABC News Shuffles Top Brass: Westin, Arledge Swap Places," *Electronic Media,* 10 March 1997, 3.
McClellan, Steve. "Arledge Hands News Reins to Westin," *Broadcasting & Cable,* 1 June 1998, 14.

George F. Will

In 1978, syndicated columnist George F. Will explained his role. He noted the long history of commentary that was popular in eighteenth-century English journalism and wrote in his *The Pursuit of Happiness and Other Sobering Thoughts* that he wanted his columns to address the issue of the character of those in politics. His columns are meant to present what he refers to as meditations from conservative philosophy to reveal the soulcraft in statecraft. Will's television identity tends to return to the theme.

Philosopher-pundit and former political philosophy professor at Michigan State University and Toronto, Will was one of the most vocal voices of *Agronsky and Company* television panel through 1981. In 1983, he penned *Statecraft As Soulcraft* which he termed a footnote to Christian apologist C. S. Lewis's *The Abolition of Man,* recognizing that the state must be concerned about character among citizens.

He appeared on public television as a correspondent for *Assignment America* in 1975. He interviewed Alf Landon, the 1936 Republican nominee for president, and *Playboy* founder Hugh Hefner. Although Will has spent three decades in television, he views himself as a writer. He is best known as a conservative who shares hard-to-predict political ideas as analyst for Capital Cities ABC News Television Network Group. In 1981, he became a participant on *This Week with David Brinkley,* and has been part of ABC's reporting team for both the Democratic and Republican National Conventions.

Will was born on May 4, 1941, in Champaign, Illinois. He graduated from Trinity College, Hartford, Connecticut in 1962, then spent two years at Oxford. He earned his doctorate at Princeton with a dissertation on the tension between the rights of the individual and community rights. From 1970 to 1972, he served as a congressional aide, worked as a Washington editor for *National Review* (from 1972 to 1976), and became a contributing editor at *Newsweek*.

He received a Pulitzer Prize in 1977 for commentary. His columns have appeared in five books and he has written on political ideology. Will is a baseball lover, serving on the board of the Baltimore Orioles, the San Diego Padres, and commissioner of the Texas-Louisiana Baseball League, a minor league organization. He wrote the bestseller, *Men at Work: The Craft of Baseball.*

Michael R. Smith

Further Reading

Clapp, Rodney, and Beth Spring. "The Convictions of America's Most Respected Newspaper Columnist." *Christianity Today,* 13 July 1984, 22–26.
Ferguson, Tim W. "Good Will." *The American Spectator,* February 1994, 64.
Will, George F. *Men at Work: The Craft of Baseball.* NY: Macmillan, 1990.
Will, George F. *Statecraft As Soulcraft.* New York: Simon & Schuster, 1983.

Brian Williams

Brian Williams was a White House correspondent who, in quick succession, became a substitute for Tom Brokaw on the *NBC Nightly News*, and a Saturday evening anchor, and in July of 1996, prime-time anchor and managing editor of *The News with Brian Williams* on MSNBC, the joint all-news cable channel of Mircrosft and NBC. Williams also hosted *Meet the Press* and received an Emmy Award for his coverage of the 1993 Iowa flooding.

Williams was born May 5, 1959. A native of Elmira, New York, and Middleton, New Jersey, he attended both Catholic University and George Washington University. He completed an internship in the Carter White House and worked briefly for the National Association of Broadcasters. He held reporting positions at KOAM in Pittsburg, Kansas, WTTG-TV in Washington, D.C., WCAU-TV in Philadelphia, and WCBS in New York.

Williams joined NBC in March 1993, and accepted the position as White House correspondent the next year. He welcomed anchoring the Saturday *NBC Evening News* and the MSNBC position. Williams is credited for his versatility and a personality permitting him to adapt to change. The MSNBC assignment provides an opportunity to conduct extended live interviews and to do more in-depth reports in areas such as international issues. He has traveled extensively with President Clinton and led NBC News's coverage of elections in South Africa. ***See also*** NBC News.

Michael D. Murray

Further Reading

Gunther, Marc. "The Cable Guy." *American Journalism Review,* January/February, 1997, 41–44.
"Network News Retreats on Diversity." *St. Louis Journalism Review,* April 1996, 3.

Palmer Williams

Palmer Williams is best known for his long career handling technical and managerial matters for documentaries at CBS. His behind-the-scenes efforts were instrumental in the production of some of the network's most renowned documentary series, including *See It Now*, *CBS Reports*, and *60 Minutes*. But it was Williams's variety of experiences before he was hired by CBS News that made him uniquely qualified to serve as an operations manager and producer for the network's most prestigious documentary programs.

Born in Tenafly, New Jersey, on October 7, 1916, Williams grew up in the New York City area. As a boy, he spent many summers traveling around the United States and Europe, developing an interest in far-away places that served him well throughout his career in broadcasting. After high school, he spent the next 16 years moving between a wide assortment of jobs in theater, feature film, radio, and documentary production before hiring on with *See It Now* in September 1951.

During this developmental period, Williams worked with many of the most successful professionals in the entertainment and documentary fields. In 1933, he spent a season acting with

Isadora Reed's Red School House Group. At 19, he briefly worked in Hollywood as a film extra before joining the research staff of *Newsweek* magazine's stage and screen department. After that, Williams supported himself as a set designer, actor, and cashier. He also did stints with American Radio News and the American Film Center before joining Film Associates and concentrating primarily in the documentary area.

During World War II, he worked under Frank Capra, gathering stock footage for the Army's famed *Why We Fight* documentary series, which helped educate American servicemen and gave them perspective on the war effort. He was also an associate producer for the Office of War Information's overseas film series. After being drafted in 1943, Williams worked on *Screen Magazine*. Anatole Litvak ordered him to assist and compile footage for Gar Kanin and Carol Reed's *The True Glory*, which won an Academy Award. He did freelance work with Gilbert Seldes at CBS before being discharged in 1946. After another acting stint, Williams served as production supervisor for Pare Lorentz, who had a contract to produce pacification documentaries for Japanese and German audiences. Williams continued doing documentary work around the world for Film Associates, and later, for New World Films (which became Media Productions).

Once when he was between projects, a friend told Williams to meet Fred Friendly at CBS because Friendly needed someone with Williams's skills. Friendly hired Williams as *See It Now's* production and operations manager for $200 a week. Williams handled all of the logistics, technical problems, and production decisions that needed to be made prior to filming in the studio. Williams referred to those early years in 1950s television journalism, as inventing the wheel. Ironically, he noted, many of *See It Now* innovations were actually the products of mistakes made when filming under very difficult conditions. Friendly described Williams as one of his teachers in the art of film.

Williams worked with Friendly and Murrow to establish the premier documentary television series, offering viewers a variety of serious and sometimes controversial fare. He was among a small group of CBS staff members directly involved in the preparation of the critically acclaimed documentaries on civil liberties issues and McCarthyism. Williams worked on *See It Now* until the program was taken off the air in 1958. He continued working closely with Friendly on CBS News documentaries, including the network's new *CBS Reports* series.

For the 1961 documentary, "Biography of a Bookie Joint," Williams helped equip producer Jay McMullen with one of the earliest hidden cameras. The powerful images evoked by the exposé drew public attention to the issue of illegal gambling. After Friendly became head of CBS News in 1964, Williams succeeded Arthur Morse as executive producer of *CBS Reports*, a position Williams held until the spring of 1966. The first *CBS Reports* under his leadership were multi-subject programs covering two stories in a single hour. In 1966, he moved from executive producer back into production.

While Williams experimented with a multi-subject format for *CBS Reports*, he also began lobbying CBS for a weekly multi-subject program. Don Hewitt, who had worked with Williams on several CBS programs, eventually sold the idea to management. Williams joined the *60 Minutes* staff when the program was launched in 1968. He remained with *60 Minutes* and worked under a variety of titles until he officially retired in 1982. He consulted for CBS News until 1986.

In 1948, Williams summarized his career aspirations in a letter to Burgess Meredith, "I would rather work on pictures that reach a larger audience, but which are still documentary in style, honest in content, and adult in execution." At CBS he realized those ambitions. Palmer Williams died on January 1, 1996. *See also CBS Reports.*

Richard J. Schaefer

Further Reading

Bliss, Edward Jr. *Now the News: The Story of Broadcast Journalism.* New York: Columbia University Press, 1991.

Friendly, Fred W. *Due to Circumstances Beyond Our Control...* New York: Vintage Books, 1967.

Walter Winchell

America's fascination with celebrity journalism is evidenced in the extraordinary career of Walter Winchell, a Harlem boy, who went from a second-rate vaudevillian with a sixth-grade education to one of the best-known journalists of his generation. Across three decades, from the 1930s to the 1950s, 60 million Americans, more than a third of the population, by some estimates, followed Winchell's newspaper column and his 15-minute program on the NBC Blue Network, one of two radio networks operated by that company during the early era. Winchell failed in his bid to master television, but still succeeded with inventive journalism on a grand scale.

Winchell attracted attention, whether dishing dirt or heaping praise, with what critics admitted was "a billion dollar voice" of the quintessential man-in-the-know. Movies were made and songs sung praising and sometimes scorning the wise-cracking Winchell, who over-eagerly pounded a telegrapher's key and launched into each newscast with the breathless "Good evening, Mr. and Mrs. North America, and all the ships at sea! Let's go to press! Flash!" Intimations of Winchell's journalism could be found in back-stage gossip when he took his Broadway column to the *New York Graphic* in 1924. He moved to the *New York Mirror* in 1929. Doormen, headwaiters, cab drivers, and press agents sought to get him news. His radio debut coincided with the 1932 Lindbergh baby kidnapping case. Nattily tailored, he loved visibility. His nocturnal wanderings at news scenes made him a hero to listeners and a nuisance to the working press who envied his $800,000 annual earnings.

Winchell was an early supporter of Roosevelt's New Deal, an intimate of J. Edgar Hoover, and foe of fascism. Hitler's Germany and Stalin's Soviet Union fingered Winchell as a fear monger. His war of words with African-American entertainer Josephine Baker combined with his backing of Joe McCarthy, making him anathema to liberals. Jergens, his longtime radio sponsor, dropped him, sensing he was out of touch with female audiences. When he took his radio program to television in 1952, he gradually slipped to 111th in the ratings. Winchell struck younger viewers as being out of touch. ABC dropped the program in 1954. *The Walter Winchell File*, a 1956 television series, starring Winchell, and profiling the seamier side of New York life, lasted five months.

It was as narrator for *The Untouchables*, a popular ABC television series, premiering in 1958, that Winchell is best remembered. ABC president Ollie Treyz is certain Winchell's distinctive and memorable voice gave the Depression-era tale of crime and vice in Chicago instant authenticity. A strike at the *Mirror* in 1962 ended Winchell's column. A brief reprise in the *World Journal Tribune* ended when the paper folded. At its height, his column had been carried in nearly a thousand newspapers. He simulated his broadcasts on stage in Las Vegas. Reclusive in retirement, he died in 1972, at the age of 74, having outlived a time in American cultural history when audiences were shocked by private secrets of the rich and famous. The cultivation of celebrity, so characteristic of late twentieth century mass-mediated living, is a stepchild of Walter Winchell.

Bruce J. Evensen

Further Reading

Gabler, Neal. *Winchell.* New York: Knopf, 1994.
Klurfeld, Herman. *Winchell: His Life and Times.* New York: Praeger, 1976.
Thomas, Bob. *Winchell.* New York: Doubleday, 1971.
"Walter Winchell: The Voice of America." *Biography*, Arts and Entertainment Network (March 28, 1996).
Winchell, Walter. *Winchell Exclusive.* Englewood Cliffs: Prentice-Hall, 1975.

Oprah Winfrey

Oprah Winfrey has been described as the "queen" of television talk shows. *The Oprah Winfrey Show* is the highest-rated talk show in television history and scores as number one overall program in daytime television. Winfrey was born in Kosciuske, Mississippi, in 1954. The daughter of Vernita and Vernon Winfrey, she experienced a turbulent childhood.

Despite the challenges of her childhood and well-publicized, admitted drug use in her 20s, Winfrey beat the odds and found an incredible niche. After earning a degree from Tennessee State

University and winning the title of Miss Black Tennessee, she started her career at WVOL Radio as a reporter. She quickly moved into television. Winfrey is credited with being the youngest woman and the first African American to anchor the news at WTVF-TV in Nashville from 1973 to 1976. She later joined WJZ-TV as news anchor from 1976 to 1978 and then became a host for the morning talk show, *People Are Talking*.

In 1984, Oprah moved to Chicago to host *AM Chicago* at WLS-TV. Within a year, she became the host of *The Oprah Winfrey Show* and sealed a deal with King World to put the program into national syndication. Winfrey took center stage and became one of the most powerful women in the industry. The success of *The Oprah Winfrey Show* can be attributed to her ability to generate topics that affect real people and a willingness to inject herself intimately into her programs. She interacts with her guests on the show and shares personal problems and dilemmas. Her personal approach, coupled with her ability to generate content from guests and audiences, has proven highly effective, earning her a place of distinction in television history.

Besides her success as a television talk show host, Oprah Winfrey has a notable career as an actress in film and as a business entrepreneur. She was supporting actress in *The Color Purple*, earning her an Academy Award, as well as a Golden Globe nomination. In addition, she was the principal actress and the producer for the television mini-series, *The Women of Brewster Place*, and had the starring role in Richard Wright's *Native Son*. Oprah Winfrey owns HARPO, her own production company and a multimillion dollar studio. She has received every major broadcasting award and distinction.   *Dhyana Ziegler*

Further Reading

Beasley, Maurine H., and S. Gibbons. *Taking Their Place.* Washington, DC: University Press of America, 1993.

Hosley, David, and Gayle Yamada. *Women in Broadcast News.* New York: Greenwood Press, 1987.

David Wolper

Much of American history has been seen by the American people through the eyes of David Wolper. He was born on January 11, 1928, in New York City. His company, Wolper Productions, has produced some of the most notable moments that can be recalled by television viewers. The nationwide celebration of the 100th anniversary of the Statue of Liberty, the closing ceremonies of the 1984 Olympics in Los Angeles, the mini-series "Roots" and a host of other presentations have captivated the eyes and ears of the nation. The entertainment industry has also acknowledged Wolper's productions with 2 Academy Awards, 40 Emmys, 7 Golden Globes, 5 Peabody Awards, and the French National Legion of Honor.

Wolper's passion for video was ignited at the 1939 World's Fair, when, at the age of 11, he saw television demonstrated for the first time. He described that moment as life-changing in that he could envision a future in television at a very young age. When the time came for Wolper to go to college, an education in television production was not yet available, so in 1947 he enrolled at the University of Southern California and began studying cinema and journalism. Between studies, Wolper worked as the campus magazine's business manager. After two years, Wolper was ready to put his media management skills and education to use and left school to open a film distribution company.

For several years, he and a partner sold films to television stations across the country, but his desire was to be more involved in the medium and soon Wolper began to produce television programs. His first documentary, *Race for Space* (1958) won him recognition, and since then Wolper Productions has continued to create successful documentaries.

During the 1970s, when television moved away from airing documentaries and focused on entertainment programming, Wolper switched fields and began producing situational comedies. Along with another television producer, James Komack, Wolper brought audiences popular series such as *Welcome Back, Kotter* and *Chico and the Man*. Perhaps one of Wolper's greatest contributions is his ability to combine entertainment and history into captivating television. His shows *This Is Elvis* (1981), and *Imagine: John Lennon* (1988), along with his Jacques Cousteau specials and National Geographic series, have educated and stimulated millions.

David Wolper continues his humanitarian efforts by serving on the boards of several associations and was recently awarded an honorary doctorate for his work as a public servant and entertainment professional from his alma mater, the University of Southern California (USC). The dean of the USC School of Cinema-Television commented that Wolper contributions embody the medium as catalyst for cultural awareness, political commentary, and social change.

Connie Book

Further Reading

Benecke, Larry. "The Sky's the Limit." *Sales and Marketing*, October 1991, 90, 92.
Martz, Larry. "A Part for the Lady." *Newsweek*, 7 July 1986, 14–17.
Wynne, Robert. *Chronicle*. University of Southern California, May 1996.

Women in Television News

In 1992, M.J. Bridge's *Women, Men and Media* revealed that men reported over 85 percent of broadcast news stories and were news sources almost 80 percent of the time. The number of women correspondents reporting news overall dropped from 16 percent in 1991 to 14 percent in 1992. By 1994, females on the three major nightly news programs (ABC, CBS, and NBC) constituted just over 20 percent of the correspondents. By 1995, the percentage dropped. While some improvement had been made during those three years, the figures indicate women in the field are still far behind.

Indeed, the broadcast news field has been dominated by men from its inception. At times it was because women were regarded as incapable of providing credibility to news, now perhaps its because of tight budgets for news programming. There are few women broadcasters who became as

well known as did Edward R. Murrow or Walter Cronkite. In fact, if radio is considered as well, early twentieth century had only a few pioneers who cut a path for the Barbara Walters and the Diane Sawyers of the 1990s.

One of the earliest female broadcasting personalities was Ruth Crane on WJR in Detroit from 1929 to 1944. Crane was later joined by Mary Margaret McBride at New York's WOR in 1934. In 1933, CBS created the first radio news team, Paul White and Florence Conley, a *New York Journal- American* reporter. Conley had the good fortune to do the feature news segment. Kathryn Craven was the first woman news commentator and launched a five-minute program, *News Through a Woman's Eyes* in 1936. CBS dropped the program in 1938. By 1946, women comprised 28 percent of the broadcasting ranks, but by 1983, for example, CBS was the only radio network to employ women as general managers.

Women in television have fared about as well, although their names are a bit more memorable. One woman who made the conversion from radio into television was Shirley Lubowitz Wershba who served as radio news writer in the 1940s and moved into television news as a director. Ruth Ashton had also become a news broadcaster and, in 1953, Pauline Frederick became the first woman to work full-time for a television network and do her own stories. She was followed by Marlene Sanders. The originator of *Meet the Press*, developed in the 1950s, was a woman, Martha Rountree. Alice Weel Bigart, one of the first women news producers, worked on *Douglas Edwards with the News*; Joan Snyder joined her in those pioneer ranks when Snyder became one of the first female field producers in the 1960s. The first local news affiliate anchorwoman was Dorothy Fuldheim in Cleveland, Ohio.

In 1976, Barbara Walters became the first female network news anchor on network television. That same year, Catherine Mackin and Linda Ellerbee became the first women to co-anchor a network news program. The 1970s brought numerous women's names and faces to television news. Jessica Savitch was the principal anchor of the Saturday edition of *NBC Nightly News*; Charlayne Hunter-Gault became the first black woman to be a correspondent on a daily network news program, *The MacNeil-Lehrer Report*; Renee Poussaint became the Washington, D.C. anchor. Leslie Stahl emerged as a Washington reporter for CBS News, and became a White House reporter as well as a mainstay of *Face the Nation,* and now a correspondent and host at *60 Minutes*. Judy Woodruff became a network White House correspondent in 1977, then moved to the *MacNeil-Lehrer NewsHour* in 1983 as the chief Washington correspondent.

In the 1980s Cheryl Gould became a senior producer of *NBC Nightly News*; Jane Pauley became a co-host of *Today* in 1976, then an anchor of *NBC Nightly News* in the 1980s, before signing on as co-host on *Dateline*. Diane Sawyer left CBS News and *60 Minutes* for ABC to co-anchor *Prime Time Live* in 1989. In the 1990s, many of these women are coming into their own, bringing the same credibility to the news as do many of their male counterparts. Connie Chung won a spot as co-anchor of the *CBS Evening News with Dan Rather*, but that relationship soured shortly after its inception. In 1994, Diane Sawyer earned a contract from ABC to co-anchor a weekly newsmagazine, *Turning Point*. Paula Zahn co-anchored the *World News Now* from 1987 to 1990, and co-anchored *CBS This Morning* from 1990 to 1996. Katie Couric served as correspondent for the *NBC Network News* from 1989 and became the co-anchor of *Today* in 1991.

On the international front, several women have blazed trails—two of the most notable are Hilary Brown, a foreign correspondent for ABC in the 1970s, and Christiane Amanpour, who covered the Persian Gulf War for CNN in 1991. Amanpour has become one of the most credible foreign correspondents of the 1990s. One important footnote to these women's accomplishments was a listing of top ten reporters in 1993, that included three female correspondents: NBC's Andrea Mitchell and Lisa Myers, and Rita Braver of CBS.

There is much to be said for accomplishments by women who fought battles on this front. Consider Christine Craft's court fight. There are also two bright spots for women journalists revealed in the *Women, Men and Media* 1995 report: CNN's *World Today* and PBS's *NewsHour*. While the three broadcast networks assigned women to present just 20 percent of news in 1995, when the *NewsHour* was included, as well as CNN's coverage, the percentage of stories provided by women increased to 30 percent of all aired. Those outlets serve as a boon to women journalists. The report's conclusion was short and simple: the term "newsworthy" was infrequently applied to female accomplishments. The horizon for women remains narrow but is broadening. ***See also*** Barbara Walters. *Carol A. Atkinson*

Further Reading

Hosley, David, and Gayle Yamada. *Women in Broadcast News*. New York: Greenwood Press, 1987.

Marzolf, Marion. *Up From the Footnote: A History of Women Journalists*. New York: Hastings House, 1977.

Judy Woodruff

Courtesy Cable News Network, Inc.
© 1996   Photo by Andrew Eccles

One of the first female network news Washington correspondents, Judy Woodruff covered Presidents Jimmy Carter and Ronald Reagan. She called that beat an "extension of the people's right to know how their government works." A veteran of more than 20 years in broadcast journalism, Woodruff joined CNN in 1993. She is a prime anchor and senior correspondent, and also co-anchors *Inside Politics* and *World Today*.

Prior to joining CNN, she was a Washington correspondent for PBS and *The MacNeil-Lehrer NewsHour*. During her tenure at PBS, she moderated the 1988 Vice President Debate and covered the 1984, 1988, and 1992 national political conventions and presidential campaigns. From 1984 through June 1990, Woodruff anchored public television's award-winning documentary series, *Frontline*. In 1975, Woodruff received an Emmy Award from the National Academy of Television Arts and Sciences, and in 1976, she was honored as Outstanding Communicator by Atlanta Women in Communications. She was also honored by the Washington Radio-Television Correspondents for her series on national defense.

Woodruff is founding co-chair of the International Women's Media Foundation, an organization dedicated to promoting and encouraging women in communications industries worldwide. Born on November 20, 1946, in Tulsa, Oklahoma, Woodruff is a graduate of Duke University, where she serves on the Board of Trustees. Woodruff is married to Al Hunt, executive Washington editor of *The Wall Street Journal*.

Gloria G. Horning

Further Reading

Sanders, Marlene, and Marcia Rock. *Waiting for Prime Time: The Women of Television News*. Urbana, IL: University of Illinois Press, 1994.
Maxa, Kathleen, and Judy Woodruff. *This is Judy Woodruff at the White House*. Reading, MA: Addison-Wesley, 1982.
Woodruff, Judy. "Women Covering Politics." *Media Studies Journal*, Spring 1997, 155–58.

Jim Wooten

Since 1965, Jim Wooten has reported on politics, wars, revolutions, floods, and famines from 25 countries on 5 continents. As political correspondent, he covered candidates for eight presidential campaigns. During his more than 30-year career, Wooten has written for both print and broadcast news. This experience also qualifies him as a well-informed critic of the news profession, who is disappointed in television's influence on newspapers. He decries beginners whose motive for entering the television news business is celebrity.

Wooten was born in Detroit, Michigan, on July 13, 1937. He wrote for *Esquire*, the *Philadelphia Inquirer*, and the *New York Times* before making the move to ABC in 1979. It was while he was working as a political correspondent for the *New York Times* that Wooten wrote a biography of President Jimmy Carter, opening with an icy inaugural day in 1977, before tracing Carter's path from Georgia to Washington, D.C. Wooten continued covering politics from 1992 to 1994, and was ABC's chief reporter on the Whitewater investigations story.

Events in Africa sent him overseas reporting for *Nightline*. Wooten told a powerful story of Rwandan refugees in the summer of 1994. The extent of devastation created by warring factions in Rwanda was eloquently expressed in Wooten's painful reports of starvation and death among thousands of exhausted refugees. He received an award for the Rwandan coverage at the Overseas Press Club's 55th annual awards ceremony in April 1995. Following his reporting on the Dole presidential campaign in 1996, Wooten signed a new four-year contract with ABC and moved his base of operations to the network's London bureau.

Sandra L. Ellis

Further Reading

Buckman, R. "TV Newsman Zaps TV News." *Editor & Publisher*, 25 April 1995, 14.
Wooten, J. "Another Day at the Border." *New York Times Magazine*, 18 September 1994, 60.
Wooten, J. "Parachuting into Madness." *Columbia Journalism Review*, November/December 1994, 46–47.

World News Tonight

As the evening newscast of ABC, *World News Tonight* established the network as an innovator and leader in television journalism. Under the leadership of Roone Arledge, the program became the most widely-watched evening newscast, known for its serious and thoughtful coverage, particularly of breaking and foreign news. For the early part of its history ABC News was a distant third to CBS and NBC. The news budget was limited, and the network did not have a half-hour newscast until 1967, four years after CBS and NBC had expanded. The news division was one of the main reasons ABC earned the nickname in the industry as the "Almost Broadcasting Company."

The outlook changed in 1977, when Arledge, then head of ABC Sports, was named the president of ABC News. Although initially viewed skeptically for the glitz he brought to sports broadcasts, Arledge moved quickly to reshape ABC News. He scrapped the *ABC Evening News* and renamed the newscast *World News Tonight*. Recognizing that he had no anchor to rival Walter Cronkite of CBS or John Chancellor of NBC, Arledge employed three anchors—Frank Reynolds in Washington, D.C., Max Robinson in Chicago, and Peter Jennings in London. The idea was to make the presentation of the news the essence of the broadcast, instead of building it around personalities, as the other networks had done.

Gradually, *World News Tonight* improved. As its name implied, the program gave attention to foreign news, more than the competitors did. The newscast also was visually arresting, as directors took advantage of new video technology. Maps, charts, and illustrations were used extensively. The journalism of *World News Tonight* also got better. Arledge raided rival networks for correspondents, adding them to the already established ABC correspondents Ted Koppel, Barbara Walters, and Sam Donaldson. Some of his hiring moves proved to be mistakes, such as making famed Watergate reporter Carl Bernstein the Washington, D.C. bureau chief. Arledge also was unsuccessful in attracting other top talent to ABC, such as Dan Rather and Tom Brokaw. But he lured such names as Sylvia Chase and Richard Threlkeld from CBS, and David Brinkley and Carole Simpson from NBC.

Eventually, the three-anchor format proved to be unworkable. Reynolds, Robinson, and Jennings each regularly complained that they were not getting enough airtime. When Reynolds died of cancer in 1983, the opportunity arose to change the format. Jennings was named as the sole anchor, while Robinson was assigned to handle the Sunday night news. Jennings grew skilled in his anchor role and was backed by an outstanding group of on-air and off-air talent. In the late 1980s, *World News Tonight* changed the organization of the newscast, breaking it into segments, and emphasizing a long centerpiece story that came to be known as *America Agenda*.

Although ABC News was forced by its new owner, Capital Cities Communications, to make a series of budget cuts, *World News Tonight* could boast, by the end of 1989, that it had won the Nielsen ratings for an entire year for the first time. In the early 1990s, a now mature *World News Tonight* had solidified its position as a top-rated evening newscast. Viewers consistently turn to ABC News and *World News Tonight* for breaking events such as the Persian Gulf War. *See also* Peter Jennings.   *Ford Risley*

Further Reading

Goldenson, Leonard H., and Marvin J. Wolf. *Beating the Odds: The Untold Story Behind the Rise of ABC*. New York: Charles Scribner's Sons, 1991.

Gunther, Marc. *The House that Roone Built: The Inside Story of ABC News*. Boston: Little, Brown, 1994.

Kaye, Elizabeth. "Peter Jennings Gets No Self-Respect." *Esquire,* September 1989.

INDEX

by Linda Webster

Boldfaced page numbers refer to the principle entry on the topic. Italicized page numbers refer to photographs.